MW01044576

The St. Louis Cardinals Encyclopedia

Bob Broeg
and Jerry Vickery

NTC/Contemporary Publishing Group

A Masters Press book
Published by Contemporary Books
A division of NTC/Contemporary Publishing Group, Inc.
4255 West Touhy Avenue, Lincolnwood (Chicago), Illinois 60646-1975 U.S.A.

Printed and bound in the United States of America
International Standard Book Number: 1-57028-171-8
10 9 8 7 6 5 4 3 2 1

Library of Congress Cataloging-in-Publication Data
Broeg, Bob, 1918-
The St. Louis Cardinals encyclopedia / Bob Broeg and Jerry Vickery.
p. cm.
Includes bibliographical references.
ISBN 1-57028-171-8
1. St. Louis Cardials (Baseball team) -- History. I. Vickery, Jerry. II. Title.
GV875.S74B76 98-15508
796.357'64'0977866--dc21 CIP

Credits:
Imaging and Graphics Assistance: Christina M. Smith, Terry Varvel, Nathan Bekianes and Jason Higgley
Editor: Ken Samelson
Editorial Assistance: Holly Kondras, Heather Lowhorn, Chad Woolums and Kim Heusel
Proofreader: Pat Brady

Table of Contents

This book is dedicated to those who, like the authors, have bled Redbird red – even St. Louis brown, lower and upper case – with the delightful, confusing, colorful history of this boys' game played by men for love and, obviously, money. Especially to those most patient and helpful: Lynne Broeg, the real-estate lady, and Jerry's Patti Vickery and Jerry No. 2 "Charley" Vickery.

ACKNOWLEDGEMENTS

The authors would like to thank the following organizations and individuals for their help in bringing this project to fruition:

The St. Louis Cardinals, L.P.
Bill DeWitt III, Marty Hendin, Brian Bartow, Paula Homan, Erv Fischer

The *St. Louis Cardinals* Magazine
Steve Zesch

Fowl Ball Magazine
Jim Mense

The National Baseball Library
Pat Kelly

The Mercantile Library
Charlie Brown

Masters Press
Tom Bast, Tom Doherty and Ken Samelson

The Missouri Historical Society

The Sporting News
Steve Gietschier

The St. Louis *Post-Dispatch*

Superior Sportcard Auctions Inc.

Amadee

Richard Leach

Jerry McNeal

Mark Okkonen

Todd Reigle

Randy Reitz

Rick Salamon

Barry Sloate

Mark Stang

Mark Stangl

Butch Yatkeman

They would also like to acknowledge the kind assistance of the following:

Scott Allen
Diane Becker
Megan Barr
Blanche Bolweg
Ed Brock
Lou Brock
Chicago White Sox, Jeff Sznal
Columbus Clippers, Joe Santry
Ann Conlisk
Bing Devine
Danny Danielson
Rich Egan
Paul Fauks
Alfred Fleishman
Bill Greenblatt
Don Gutteridge
Jack Jarvis
Bud Kane
Jim Kreuz
David Lipman
Lew Lipset
Bill and Betty Maasarand
Marty Marion
Stan Musial
New Jersey Cardinals, Herm Sorcher
Herb Pape
Jason and Jennifer Phelps
Randy Pierce
Marty Prather
Steve Prozorowski
John Schoon
David Smith
Mark Stallard
Brendan Stevens
Tom Sullivan
Tim Sweeney
Robert Tiemann
David Vincent
Lee Wall
Cynthia Wilber
Maddie and Ali Wojcik
Lenny Yochim
Dick Zitsman
St. Louis Cardinals Team Photographers
Dan Donovan, Steve Goldstein, Jim Herren, Scott Rovak, Bill Stover

---

As this is my first book, I asked that I be given the opportunity to express a few of my own thank-yous. To Bob Broeg, who I roped into this project by telling him that his part would be "small." His time and efforts were anticipated, but his friendship and understanding are among the greatest gifts I have ever received. To Grandpa Lewis, Grandpa Huffhine, Uncle Calvin, Mom and Dad, because without their support and encouragement I would have never become the fan, the collector and the historian that I am. To my sisters, who let me have a turn at bat, and the best brothers I never had, Mark Stangl and Terry Stevens. And finally a heart-felt "thank you " to my wife and son who allow me to be nine years old every day, I love you all. – *J.V.*

PHOTO CREDITS

The photography for this project came from a variety of sources. Every reasonable effort to properly credit the photographers whose work is represented within has been made. If there has been an error, please notify the publisher. We will gladly correct any inadvertant errors or omissions in subsequent editions.

The following organization photographers were of inestimable help in compiling this unique collection of Cardinals' photography. Alongside each of their names is listed the chapter in which their work appears.

The St. Louis Cardinals Photographers
Dan Donovan, The Franchise History
Jim Herren, The Franchise History and The All-Time Roster
Scott Rovak, The Franchise History
Bill Stover, The Franchise History
Steve Goldstein, The Franchise History

The St. Louis Cardinals Magazine
Steve Zesch, The Franchise History

Fowl Ball Magazine
Jim Mense, The Franchise History and The All-Time Roster

New Jersey Cardinals
Herm Sorcher

The Sporting News
Steve Gietschier, The Franchise History and The Ballparks

The National Baseball Library
Pat Kelly, The Franchise History and The All-Time Roster

The St. Louis Post Dispatch
The Franchise History and The All-Time Roster

Missouri Historical Society
The Franchise History, The All-Time Roster and The Ballparks

Mercantile Library
Charlie Brown, The Franchise History and The All-Time Roster

The following photographers, artists, historians and clerical associates also contributed their work, time and memories for use in this book:

PHOTOGRAPHY:
David Smith, The Numbers Through the Years
Jerry McNeal, World Series rings for use in color inserts
Butch Yatkeman, The Franchise History
Stan Musial, The Franchise History
Bing Devine, The Franchise History
Rick Salamon, The Franchise History
Randy Reitz, The Franchise History
Richard Leech, The Franchise History
Rich Egan, The Franchise History
David Lipman, The Franchise History
Herb Pape, The Franchise History
Ann Conlisk, The Franchise History
Bill and Betty Maasarand, The Franchise History
Jack Jarvis, The All-Time Roster
Diane Becker, The Owners
Lenny Yochim, The All-Time Roster
Superior Sportcard Auctions Inc., The All-Time Roster
Lee Wall, The Franchise History
Alfred Fleishman, The Franchise History
Jim Mense, The Franchise History
Marty Prather, The Franchise History
Barry Sloate, The All-Time Roster
Jim Kreuz, The All-Time Roster
Randy Pierce, The Franchise History
Bud Kane, The All-Time Roster
Tom Sullivan, The All-Time Roster
John Schoon, The All-Time Roster
Tim Sweeney, The All-Time Roster
Jeff Sznal of The Chicago White Sox, AA Champion Trophy in color insert
Lew Lipset, The All-Time Roster and Coaches and Managers
Joe Santry of the Columbus Clippers, The All-Time Roster and Coaches and Managers
Blanche Bollweg, The All-Time Roster
Ed Brock, The All-Time Roster
Bill Greenblatt, The Franchise History
Don Gutteridge, The Franchise History
Lou Brock, The Franchise History
Cathy Wilbury, The Franchise History
Marty Marion, The Franchise History
Dan Danielson, The Franchise History
Steve Prozorowski, The Franchise History

SOURCE MATERIALS (used with permission)
Baseball by the Numbers: A Guide to the Numbers of Major League Teams, by Mark Stang and Linda Harkness. Published by Scarecrow Press, 1996.
The Baseball Encyclopedia, Jeanine Bucek, Editorial Director. Published by Macmillan, 1996.
Total Baseball, edited by John Thorn, Pete Palmer and Michael Gershman. Published by Viking Press, 1997.

OTHER CONTRIBUTORS:
Amadee, original cartoon art in The Franchise History
Marc Okkonen, original artwork of uniforms in color inserts and of parks in The Ballparks
Todd Reigle, original artwork of uniforms and characitures in The All-Time Roster, Coaches and Managers, The Owners and color inserts
Dave Smith, *Retrosheet*, research, All-Time Records and Achievements
Mark Stangl, research, editing and photography, The Franchise History
Robert L. Tiemann, research, The Numbers Through the Years
David Vincent, research, The Numbers Through the Years
Paul Fauks, statistics and research
Jason Phelps, research and editing
Patti Vickery, data-entry
Megan Barr, data-entry

The Franchise History

By Bob Broeg

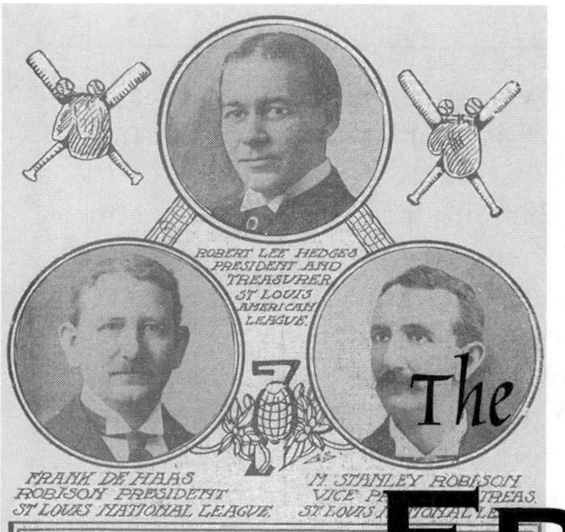

ONE OF ST LOUIS' TWO BASE BALL PARKS

SPORTSMANS PARK & CLUB.. OFFICE
Vandeventer Ave. & Natural Bridge Road.
CHRIS VON DER AHE, Prest. & Treas.
B.S. MUCKENFUSS, Secy.
ST. LOUIS, May 26, 1896.

Mr . Dominic Delebar,

City.

Dear Sir---

This will introduce the bearer Mr. F. J. Merwin, who wishes to see you in regard to some business matters, and if you can favorably consider any proposition he may make you, you will confer a favor which will be appreciated.

Mr. Merwin is perfectly reliable and you can talk to him in full confidence.

With best regards I am,

Very truly yours,

B S Muckenfuss

want guarantee for 5 to 600 in case they need it.

PIECES OF HISTORY: Top left, turn-of-century club executives and Cardinals' first park. Below, Pitcher Johnny Lush models the new 1907 uniform. Upper right, fancy letterhead of a distant day (1896). Secretary Ben Muckenfuss' signature is pretty fancy, too, Bottom, the "1" of a kind before the other "1" of a kind: Ozzie Smith's predecessor with a famed number – Pepper Martin.

Jeremiah Fruin: Jere came from back East to show St. Louis kids a better way to catch a ball. His construction company helped build Busch Stadium years later.

If the man who brought big-league baseball to St. Louis hadn't been offended a year later, the old French fur-trading post might never have been out of the majors and might have missed two colorful front-office characters from the beer business, Chris Von der Ahe and Gussie Busch. But then if you have to wonder what might have been then, how about Gen. George Armstrong Custer?

The same year the National League was formed, 1876, St. Louis and Chicago could have been playing ball on the west banks of the Mississippi, the same warm, windy June afternoon Custer divided his Seventh U.S. Cavalry into three units on the bank of Montana Territory's Little Big Horn River and lost his command and his life. Grumpily, West Point's "biggest loser," Custer could be second-guessed, but then so could the man who brought big-league ball to his home town, real estate heir John B.C. Lucas, Jr. whose family gave many things, including the site for the main public library downtown. The adjacent pocket park bears his name. Cincinnati formed the first professional team, unbeaten in 1869, but St. Louis wasn't far behind.

Fact is, St. Louis benefited from the presence from the East of an engineer named Jeremiah Fruin, who came out in the Civil War era with a better concept of the new game, including a better way to catch the ball rather than just palm it. Oddly, the Fruin name still stands significant in St. Louis, a result of the Fruin-Colnon's company participating in the building of Busch Stadium downtown.

Next to Fruin the stepping stone of Alexander Cartwright's diamond-shaped game were the brothers McNeary—Thomas, John and Frank—who followed behind A.W. Williams. He organized the St. Louis Reds in 1871, building seats and stands at Compton and Missouri Pacific railway, later the home of the brilliant black-league Stars, adjacent to Harris-Stowe State College.

Actually, Mr. Williams came up short and turned to the McNearys, largely to Tom, an early "fanatic", as baseball fans were called, when they weren't listed as "kranks." When Williams couldn't make it, the eldest McNeary, stuck with the mortgage, finished Reds' park, i.e., Stars' Park.

By 1875, with a home-town Christmas baby, 19-year-old Jimmy (Pud) Galvin as pitcher, the Reds were officially members of the National Association, immediate precursors of the National League. Ailing Tom stepped down and brothers John and Frank kept up the Compton Avenue grounds as a semi-pro park and at their summer garden cooling Uhrig's Cave, Washington and Jefferson, they also built the Coliseum, a magnificent indoor facility for years.

So for the National League, formed at New York's Park Central Hotel in 1876, the nation's centennial year and General Custer's last, St. Louis owed its presence to John B.C. Lucas, like the McNearys a real-estate whiz. John B.C. Lucas and his associates fielded an imported team and called them the Brown Stockings.

Of the eight cities, called to order by Chicago's William Hulbert early in '76 for National League organization in New York, Philadelphia, Boston, Brooklyn, Louisville, Hartford, Chicago and St. Louis—only Hulbert's own Chicago franchise never missed a season. Louisville and Hartford long since lost major-league status before the Boston-to-Milwaukee move in 1953 precipitated musical chairs and expansion.

St. Louis just might have shared the proud continuity role with Chicago because the city, then one of the nation's largest in population, had early interest in baseball. A St. Louis lawyer, C. Orrick Bishop, wrote the league's constitution and the long-time reserve clause that might have been favored by his father, a former Virginia slave owner. Judge Bishop, the old boyhood right fielder, lived long enough to see the later NL franchise, the Cardinals, win pennants in 1926 and 1928. Lucas set up shop for the well-recruited Browns downtown at 406 North Fourth Street, close by manager S. Masson Graffen's cigar-and-sporting goods store at 619.

The captain, a position of authority in those days, Harmon Dehlman, played first base. In that beanbag era when hitting was rare and home run virtually a dodo of the

Charles Comiskey: The famed first baseman and ball-club owner managed St. Louis' first champions in the 1880s.

diamond, St. Louis's early hero was pitcher George Washington (Grin) Bradley, who pitched the NL's first no-hitter against Hartford and had an excellent 45-19 record for a ball club that went—surprise—45-19. Trouble was, Chicago's player-manager, Al Spalding, a name to remember as sporting goods' A.G. Spalding, had an even better record for the White Stockings, as the future Cubs then were called. He was 47-13, then was smart enough to wave $2000 in the dancing eyes of Bradley. "Grin" grinned, took it and fled to Chicago.

Lucas's team fell back to fourth in 1877, ahead of retreating Chicago in a race won by Boston, but JBC prepared to try again in '78 by acquiring six players from second-place Louisville. When four of the six were exposed as having thrown games, drawing career suspensions, suggestions that Lucas knew about it offended the sensitive sportsman.

•••

Lucas quit the league and game, though a younger brother would try later, so St. Louis had no big-league team until 1881 when two of the game's colorful figures entered the picture. Charley Comiskey came to town and a local affluent grocer and saloon keeper, Chris Von der Ahe, stuck his big red nose, his money and his opinionated Dutch accent into baseball. Von der Ahe was a character, amusing largely in his use of the language, but he wasn't funny funny. First, Chris was wise enough to recognize that better use of nearby Grand and Dodier ball park, Sportsman's, meant better business for his beer taps a couple blocks away at Spring and St. Louis. He was smart enough also, to listen to Al Spink, founder of a famous publications family, The Sporting News. The first of four Spinks was fascinated by Comiskey, a rangy first baseman-outfielder of Dubuque's semi-professional Rabbits. He wanted Comiskey for a new major league, the American Association, that would return professional baseball to St. Louis. Von der Ahe looked, listened and acted. He brought the franchise and Comiskey to town.

"Commy," they called the Irishman before the appellation became a dirty designation, later, the "Old Roman," Comiskey, generally regarded as the first first baseman to play off the bag, knew talent, too, putting together for Von der Ahe and St. Louis four pennant winners, 1885-88, including what amounted to an early-day world champion in '86. The honor roll included Comiskey, first base-manager; Yank Robinson, second base; Bill Gleason, shortstop Arlie Latham, third base; outfielders Tommy McCarthy, Hugh Nicol, Curt Welch, James (Tip) O'Neill; catchers Albert (Doc) Bushong, Jack Boyle and Jack Milligan and pitchers Parisian Bob Caruthers, Dave Foutz, Nat Hudson and Charley (Silver) King, who anglicized his Germanic surname, Koenig.

DER POSS: A seldom-seen young sketch of Chris Von der Ahe when the operator of the Browns was No. 1 in the public image, even making this early version of a modern-day collector's card.

Von der Ahe's own use of a low Deutsche accent in a community heavily populated by Germans led to frequent direct quotes of the club president. This was a journalistic vogue. So Von der Ahe was fair game to the press of his day when he proudly referred to himself as "der poss bresident." Der Poss Bresident was foil for his frolicking third baseman, Arlie Latham. Arlie liked to tease the clubowner, i.e., setting up a party and sticking the clubowner with the bill. Latham soon would live up to his self-styled description as "The Freshest Man on Earth." Latham, a peppery base burglar, had his major moment just after Comiskey's Browns won their second Association pennant in 1886. They faced the favored National League White Stockings in a best-of-seven series that began in Chicago.

It's a wonder they ever met, a result of more nonsense than sense in an 1885 Series when the teams were fit to be tied, which, by the way, they really were if you accept the verdict of most observers, press and public.

The Series actually began with a tie game at Chicago, 5-5. The umpire, a National League arbiter named Dave Sullivan, was good enough for Comiskey to approve his working the second game, but the arbiter, handicapped in part by working solo in the style of the times, had his troubles.

The worst offense came in the sixth when Chicago fashioned a 5-4 lead. Sullivan, wheeling from the infield to call a potential play at the plate, didn't keep his eye on the ball long enough to give an "out" call on a play at first base. This led to a stormy session in which Commy threatened to leave the field with the Browns.

Arlie Latham: Arlie was almost as good as he thought he was as third baseman for the old championship Browns, and funny, too.

Sullivan stopped that threat by pulling his watch. An instant later, Ned Williamson hit a slow foul-fair-foul grounder finally ruled fair. Comiskey insisted the play was foul by American Association standards, but when Cap Anson asked to see the rule book, Commy had none. When he stormed off with his ball club, Sullivan, escorted off the field, ruled the inevitable—a 9-0 forfeit victory for Chicago.

With the Series tied through six games (2-2-1), the seventh was ruled decisive. St. Louis won the game, 13-4, and the Browns claimed World Championship but Pop Anson's whining—they labeled his team "Anson's Crybabies" and the general attitude officially and unofficially was that the Series was what it really seemed to be—fit to be tied. Ergo, a deadlock.

Still, they agreed to have it again in 1886 with A.G. Spalding offering a winner-take-all threat, one that caused Comiskey to gulp and accept, fearful how Von der Ahe might take the verdict, but, Chris was eating high on the head cheese now. So ultimately with total receipts $13,900, Der Poss Bresident kept half and split the rest among his players, $590 apiece.

The reason the Brownies prevailed was a dramatic finale. With Parisian Bob Caruthers down to workhorse John Clarkson, 3-0, Anson's meal ticket weakened. In the eighth, Comiskey singled, Curt Welch bunted and reached on a two-base error, Comiskey scoring. With one out, Welch moved to third on a passed ball.

A popup and a base on balls to Doc Bushong brought up chatterbox Arlie Latham, who had been silent all day, the third baseman's bat and his mouth. Still, the crowd roared in anticipation.

Latham doffed his cap. "Never fear, Arlie's here," he proclaimed and when Clarkson got two quick strikes, he was upbeat. "Don't worry, I've got another one left."

Indeed, in a situation that might remind more recent fans of Ozzie Smith's surprise homer that beat Los Angeles in the 1985 National League playoffs, Walter Arlington Latham slugged a two-run triple.

And when the mighty Michael (King) Kelly couldn't handle one of battery mate Clarkson's pitches, Latham waltzed home with the tying run. In the Browns' tenth, Welch singled, moved to second on a sacrifice and to third on an infield out. Here, Clarkson committed what was perpetrated the "$15,000 slide" by Welch, a result of a wild-high pitch, permitting Welch to swish home with the winning run of the series.

In disgust, Kelly threw his mask into the grandstand. Multi-talented Kelly, fast-running and fast-drinking, hit a league-leading .388 for Spalding that seventh season as the Cubs' most popular player. The entrepreneur startled the sport by selling the King to Boston for $10,000,a staggering sum and one that caught Von der Ahe's attention, too.

After a third straight pennant in 1887, without consulting Comiskey, Der Poss Bresident sold Caruthers for $8,000 to Brooklyn alone, plus Foutz and Bushong.

He also dispatched Gleason and Welch to Philadelphia. This might have been Commy's finest hour until he helped Ban Johnson organize the American League, then owned the Chicago pennant winner in 1901, and soon after built the ball park that bears his name. The Brownies of 1888 won it again, aided by local favorite King's league-leading 45-21 record and the hitting of O'Neill. Tip led with .335 after an incredible .492 in '87, a year when his 50 walks were counted as hits. He led everything except in taking tickets—hits, runs, doubles, triples and homers at a time RBIs were not recorded.

A year later, aided by Von der Ahe's largesse of Caruthers' pitching, Bushong's catching and Welch's outfielding, Brooklyn beat out the Browns. When players of both the National League and the Association revolted, forming the Players League in 1890, Comiskey went to the Chicago club as player-manager of the outlaw league. Although both leagues were hurt, the Players actually drew more than the National, but spokesman Spalding bluffed the employees, apparently with phony attendance figures. When the Players League folded after one season, Comiskey, like many others, went back to his old job, hat in hand, but Comiskey's relationship with Von der Ahe was as cold as Chris's beer and, unfortunately, his ball club. Geographically, baseball wasn't the same, either. The experience with the "Brotherhood" as the Players League was called, created back-biting, contract-jumping and double shuffles which the weakened Association lost in 1891. In December the National bought out Association franchises in Chicago, Boston, Columbus, Philadelphia and Milwaukee for $135,000. Washington, Baltimore, Louisville and Von der Ahe's St. Louis team, were welcomed to the new 12-team league. Poor Chris! Treated like a country cousin, shortchanged with other Association members by the National in a distribution of talent from folded clubs, he first lost Comiskey to Cincinnati as player-manager. Next, he stuck his prominent cherry-red proboscis in the dugout. He went through five field foreman alone in the year of the City's return to the NL, 1892, as the Browns finished eleventh. Chris would attempt to change his luck with the help of the Lindell Street Car Company.

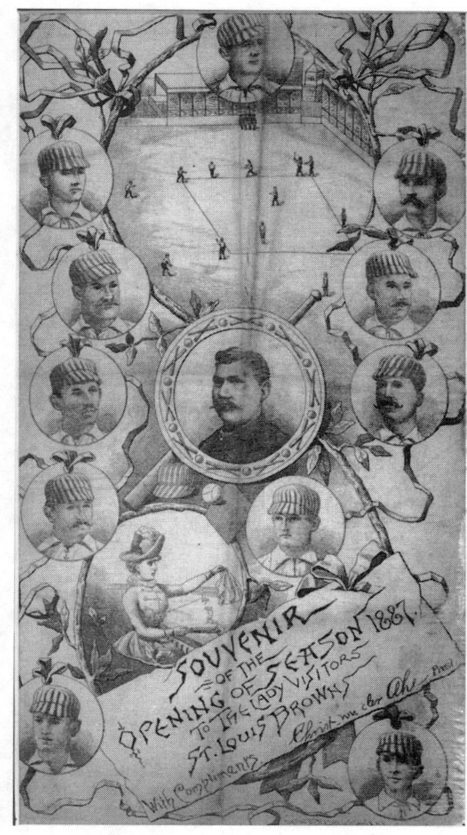

Lovely Thought: This is a copy of a silk souvenir given by Chris Von der Ahe to women patrons at the opening game of his world champion Browns in 1887. The attempt to lure feminine fans was a wise one, leading to a regular Ladies Day. In the sketch, Von der Ahe is centered and manager Charley Comiskey at the top.

At the conclusion of the 1892 season Chris accepted a proposition from the company that would help him construct a park at the end of their line at Vandeventer Avenue and Natural Bridge Road. A turn-around loop would empty Browns' fans right at the new park's door step. The most beautiful baseball and athletic park in America, as noted by the St. Louis press, would be christened NEW SPORTSMANS PARK. It seems baseball's early innovator had trouble coming up with new and original names at least where the ball club is concerned, first with his pilfering of the Browns nickname and then to spite the Old Sportsmans Park owner's naming his park New Sportsmans Park.

The spacious park, especially deep in left field, created room for Von der Ahe to continue as baseball's early day Bill Veeck, Ray Dumont and Larry McPhail as baseball's innovator promoter. Chris put a "chute the chutes" carnival ride, an early-day water slide in which patrons boarded boats atop a large tower for a wet trip down the slide into a man made lake below. Just beyond the left field fence a beer garden, night horse racing, boating, boxing, a wild west show and an all-girls Silver Coronet Band rounded out the amusements. Unfortunately for Chris on the field the picture was far from amusing. In their first seven National League seasons, the Browns finished 11th-10th-9th-11th-11th-12th-12th under 21 managerial changes that include 3 stints by Der Poss himself in which he managed only three victories to 13 defeats.

Off the field Von der Ahe's personal life, went from bad to verse... oops, worse, cli-

CAPITAL STOCK $50,000.

No 26 — 1 Shares

SPORTSMANS PARK AND CLUB

ST. LOUIS, MO.

This Certifies that L. J. Holthaus is entitled One Shares of Twenty Five Dollars, each in the Capital Stock of the SPORTSMANS PARK AND CLUB. transferable only on the Books of this Company in person or by Attorney on the surrender of this Certificate.

ST. LOUIS, MO. Febry 7 1891

Witness the hand of the President of said Company and its corporate seal hereto affixed attested by the Secretary.

Geo. Munson, Secretary — Chris Von der Ahe, President.

FREY STATIONERY CO ST. LOUIS

FULL PAID AND NON ASSESSABLE.

Look Out Below: At the time the Browns were beginning to tilt like the Titanic in 1891, Chris Von der Ahe sold that share of stock to a gentleman who must have liked lost causes. Notice that Sportsman's Park had no apostrophe in the place of title at the time.

maxed by his "kidnapping" in February of 1898 at a time he was mustache-high in a divorce suit with dear Della, untold debts and a rumored sale of his first love , the ball club. An old problem reared its ugly head and thrust Chris into a downward spiral that would prove his undoing. Thanks to the work of SABR researchers J. Thomas Hetrick and Mark Stangl, this story can be told.

Back in 1890, a wild year in a feud between the National League, the American Association in a fight over leftovers from the short-lived Players League, Von der Ahe had arrested a Pittsburgh interloper trying to steal his old Brownie pride-and-joy, Silver King, and a catcher. After interloper Mark Baldwin was arrested, he sued Chris for $10,000 for false arrest.

The case lasted until 1898—sounds like modern times—and the only means to collect was to get Chris in Pittsburgh, which wasn't easy since every effort was made to avoid the golden triangle. So they kidnapped him, screaming and kicking, by carriage to East St. Louis for train passage in which a Pullman conductor conveniently looked the other way. Even Von der Ahe's attempts to draw attention by eating expensive meals couldn't unfrock the scheme. He was jailed on arrival in Pittsburgh and after a series of hearings in which his attorney was able to post bail for a day or so of respite from confinement, the judge would hear Von der Ahe's final plea.

Finally when the Pittsburgh court ruled, it didn't. Von der Ahe's plea, that his abduction and transport to Pennsylvania was unconstitutional, was taken under advisement by the court. Unfortunately State Law provided that when a judgment for torts was unpaid, in which there was false imprisonment, the defendant could be placed in jail until the judgment is satisfied. The defendant could be released after 60 days only by swearing the debtors oath. He was soon to be re-arrested on the grounds the judgment was never satisfied. Created was a never ending chain of 60 day sentences coupled with the bi-monthly embarrassment of the debtor's oath, and with club president Muckenfuss unable to raise the monies to satisfy the judgment (or so he said), Chris was locked up.

Von der Ahe's 60 days included meals of bread and coffee, bacon and bread, and potatoes on tin dishes. However most of his time was spent wiring club president Muckenfuss for money. As Hetrick put it "Those bread and water days must have been miserable for a man who once hosted lavish banquets for his glorious ball players..."

The St. Louis newspapers twitted Von der Ahe with cartoons, and The Sporting News, Al Spink's legacy that once had supported the grand saloonkeeper, wrote of poor Chris:

"He could grow rich on an ash pile, but would go broke on a plantation". 'Der bublic be tammed was original with him, not with Mr. Vanderbilt..."

The embarrassed National League helped bail out Von der Ahe, but they wanted him out, not St. Louis, then one of the nation's largest cities, just Chris. And so the Browns began the 1898 season with its ownership in jeopardy, and nearly broke. Only Muckenfuss's sandbagging of Von der Ahe's pleas for cash allowed them to field a team. Von der Ahe's last manager, Tim Hurst, would survive a season that would include the horror of a blazing grandstand and the craziest play yet to come along in the game of baseball. First the crazy, the Browns would be victims of a double play in which not a single fielder touched the ball with his hands. Not possible, you say, not by today's rules, but back in '98 this is what happened, according to Al Spink. The Browns were playing the Athletics of Philadelphia. Clements, the St. Louis catcher, was on third base, and Monte Cross, the St. Louis short–fielder on second.

The pitcher had the batsman three and two, and both the runners moved with the pitch. Cross, faster than Clements, was sprinting at full speed for third when the batsman drove a vicious liner down the third base line.

Big, clumsy Clements tried to dodge the flying sphere, but it hit him on the leg and then caromed off, hitting the oncharging Cross. Both were called out for being hit by a batted ball.

You could imagine Hurst saying aloud, "What else could possibly go wrong"? Well, the park burned down, the grandstand and the office, a place Chris spent many an evening while avoiding his latest divorce in the making, all a total loss. Gone were mementos and championship trophies from the glory years of the Association, but these paled in comparison to Chris's greatest loss, that of his beloved greyhound, Fly. Chris would attempt a valiant rescue charging into the blazing building in search of possibly his only friend, only having to be rescued himself by firefighters on the scene. Unfortunately, Fly was not the only loss of life on that day as the stands were near capacity when the fire broke out. One fan, William Duncan, lost his life. Scores of others were injured creating more lawsuits than the destitute Von der Ahe already faced. The team would work late into the night constructing bleachers for the following day's game, a loss in which many of the players were too exhausted to compete. But judging by the 12th place finish in '98 the whole lot might have made better carpenters. It was so bad that at the close of the season manager Hurst would switch back to umpiring, stating, "You can't beat them hours."

Von der Ahe left many goodies of which the authors' favorite could have been the time he complained at a league meeting of so many of his games having been prevented by rain. Huffed old Chris, "I don't vant to be greedy, but next year let it rain in Zinzinnati or on that dumpkopf (Von der Horst) in Baltimore!"

With the 1898 season less than a success, Von der Ahe's creditors began to line up. No longer could he be bailed out by his long - time angel, Edward C. Becker. When the bonds of the club's secured creditors came due, Chris was unable to obtain the funds to satisfy them. The club was placed in receivership and slated for auction on the courthouse steps. Several groups came to town in hopes of securing the franchise in addition to the entire group of creditors who banded together under their attorney G.A. Gruner. All the creditors, that is, except for Edward C. Becker, Chris's Angel, right? Wrong.

At the auction Mr. Gruner placed the winning bid of $33,000. However, it was contested by Becker on the grounds that he was not part of the group, and that the group headed by Gruner would have difficulty securing National League approval for the sale. Becker's answer to this was a counter offer that would satisfy all of the existing creditors, with the exception of Von der Ahe's claims against the company. This would allow Becker the opportunity to finally profit from his years of support of Von der Ahe.

Poor Chris was now really Poor Chris. For a personal finale, with only a handsome burial statue put up when he was in the chips, Christian Frederick Von der Ahe died destitute in 1913 at age 62, but Der Poss Bresident stands tall in the graveyard and in St. Louis baseball memories. The only possession of value from the glory days of the four-time winners was a trophy willed to his old manager, Charles Comiskey.

THE MONUMENT: Even if Der Poss Bresident couldn't rub one buffalo nickel together with another, Chris Von der Ahe had ready a bigger-than-life statue at Bellefontaine Cemetery when he died in 1913 at age 63.

So with Poor Chris out of the way, Mr. Becker set about the business at hand, and within three days of a judge and other creditors accepting his offer, the club was incorporated under the name of The American Base Ball and Athletic Exhibition Company of St. Louis.

In addition to the incorporation of the ball club the National League took an additional step to prevent any legal action on behalf of Von der Ahe. The NL voided the old agreement and issued a new franchise.

All of this maneuvering led one to believe Edward C. Becker to be nothing more than a straw purchaser who would within weeks turn over the operations to the brothers Robison, who owned Cleveland's capable Spiders. They were Ft. Wayne traction men who also controlled Cleveland's Streetcar system. In a syndicate ownership that long since would have been a no-no under Judge Landis and subsequent commissioners, the Robisons practically switched ball clubs, in fact only Sudhoff would remain from the '98 Browns. Cross would be sent back from Cleveland midway through the season. The Robisons sent their talented Spiders to St. Louis, which had supported good ball clubs, and the Browns' coffee dregs to Cleveland.

Taking the names of their third-place predecessors as the Exiles, Wanderers, Tramps and Tourists, they seldom played a home game due to the Robisons' displeasure with Cleveland's fan support. Cleveland's National League denouement included a miserable 20-134 record, the lousiest last-place percentage ever.

Cy Young left Lake Erie for the Mississippi. Others joining him on the club managed by Patsy Tebeau, late of St. Louis's Goose Hill, included .400 hitting outfielder Jesse Burkett, outfielder Emmet Heidrick and shortstop talent Rhoderick (Bobby) Wallace, who became a St. Louis legend.

The 1899 opener was a milestone date. Despite a streetcar strike, when few could putt-putt in a horseless carriage, an overflow 18,000 crammed into the newly renovated Natural Bridge park, renamed League Park. Cy Young pitched the first of his 26 victories, drubbing the Cleveland team of former Brownies.

Though many in town were still calling them the Browns, Frank Robison's earliest intention was to have no nickname at all for his new team. Having the team known for the city it represented was good enough for him. Uniforms both home and road would have ST. LOUIS emblazoned in red across the front of the jersey, in an attempt to bury the past and spruce up the present.

The thought of no nickname for a ball team bothered the fans and it horrified the sports writers. What could they call this team, the Reds? Too confusing. They tried Tebeau's Terrors, too scary, Tebeau's Braves, Tebeau's Tigers, Tebeau's Charges, and finally a name that stuck, Perfectos. Well, almost.

One day, Willie McHale, a sports reporter for the St. Louis *Republic* heard a female fan praise the color as "a lovely shade of cardinal." So McHale called them "Cardinals." It stuck. In 1900 the Robisons made it official, but it would be more than two decades before Branch Rickey, attending a luncheon as a speaker, saw that a woman had transferred the color to a bird. Her bird-on-a-bat table placement became perhaps baseball's most famous insignia.

Back in 1899 Tebeau's team broke out with seven consecutive victories, still a franchise best, but the team waffled and fell to fifth, an impressive 84-67 and good enough at the gate to draw 373,909, more than double the 151,700 in Von der Ahe's farewell season.

No wonder Frank Robison, a man about town, could draw $100 every morning when the C-note at the turn of the century seemed larger than a thousand dollars as the next century neared. Yeah, especially when Robison tried to spend it all that day—every day.

Before the first season of the Twentieth Century, the National League lopped off four clubs—Cleveland, Louisville, Washington, and Baltimore—where the remnants of the championship Orioles had helped Brooklyn to the 1899 pennant. Baltimore's player-manager, third baseman John McGraw, and star catcher Wilbert Robinson refused to give up their café and bowling alley. They held out.

So did a good young second baseman, Billy Kiester. Boldly, Frank Robison bid for the talented trio and got them for $15,000 several weeks into the season, then met them at Union Station with a band and a champagne party. They signed, but, chillingly, McGraw, for whom Robison had managerial designs, wouldn't sign a contract and agreed only to play for $100 a game.

He wouldn't sign because he knew Ban Johnson and the American League were only a rumored season away from dear Baltimore. McGraw playing sparingly for a handsome $9900, hitting .344. Even when Tebeau resigned as manager in August of the disappointing season, McGraw wouldn't take the job.

With the season over, Muggsy and Robinson quickly hopped a train for Baltimore and ceremoniously dropped their red-trimmed uniforms into the Mississippi.

McGraw, who not only had loftier ambitions, also had the notion that a ball club in St. Louis had to be 25 percent better because of the heat. Big Cy Young didn't like the heat, either, after a 20-win season, but he liked it when the Boston Red Sox of the new American League offered more money to Cy and batterymate Lou Criger. Among others lured away by more money from the "other" league was Lave Cross, who became captain and third baseman of Connie Mack's winning Philadelphia team.

Robison tried to salvage as many players as possible after finishing fourth under new manager Patsy Donovan in a weakened, talent-draining season, but the damage done was compounded when president

1899 BUTTON, ST. LOUIS BUTTON CO.: Frank Robison's decision to go with no team name left local button-makers with only one option: the home team.

John Joseph McGraw: Pugnacious, pennant-winning player at Baltimore and .333 career hitter for 16 seasons, the third baseman hit .344 in one season with the Cardinals, 1900, then became a 30-year legend as manager of the New York Giants, winning nine pennants. Elected to the Hall of Fame in its second year, 1937.

Ban Johnson of the American League moved his season-old Milwaukee franchise to St. Louis in 1902. There they were rechristened the popular name of the championship 1880s – the Browns – and also moved into the original Sportsman's Park, the one that lasted through 1966.

Johnson put Robison's former Cleveland center fielder, Jimmy McAleer, in charge with enough money to lure away from the Cardinals their remaining top talent, including future Hall of Famers Wallace and Burkett. Seven shed for Brown, another orange for Baltimore, managed briefly by McGraw before his 30-year, 9-pennant stint with the New York Giants.

The Cardinals wouldn't see the first division until 1914. Meanwhile, it didn't help when Robison gave the Chicago Cubs a kid who became a Hall of Fame pitcher — Mordecai "Three Finger" Brown. Brown mortified the Cardinals the next 15 years, helping the Chicago Cubs to four pennants and himself into the Hall of Fame. The Cardinals' only achievement in the period was a fifth-place finish under Hall of Fame pitching great Charles (Kid) Nichols in the Worlds' Fair year, 1904, a season in which they drew a record 386,750.

By 1906, hurting financially and heart - broken from the loss of good players to the American League, especially the rival Browns, Frank Robison stepped down as president and returned to Cleveland, where he died two years later at only 54. Brother Matthew Stanley, blinking in the spotlight, had little income to help Honest John McCloskey as manager, though Mac's contributions included two colorful characters, a candy-maker called the Big Bohemian Chocolate Dropper, hard-hitting first baseman Ed (Koney) Konetchy and a brilliant pitching boozer, Arthur (Bugs) Raymond. One more, too, but McCloskey didn't see in pitcher Babe Adams a future pitching ace who would win three games for Pittsburgh in the 1909 World Series.

McCloskey and Robison, cutting corners, slept a couple of winters in the clubhouse above the Natural Bridge playing field, rechristened League Park. Following two last-place seasons – it was nice that the last now was only eighth, not twelfth – the club president asked the league for relief in helping him acquire a meaningful pennant. John J. McGraw had just the man, capable catcher Roger Bresnahan, for whom Muggsy's asking price was pretty stiff – outfielder Jack (Red) Murray and the satiated screwball, Bugs Raymond, who led the League in excuses if not victories.

Challenged by McGraw with a private detective's report card of his nocturnal prowling, having included, "seven ryes, seven beer-chasers, cheese, eight onions," Bugs interrupted, "That's a lie, Mac! I didn't have but two onions all evening."

It wasn't funny when Bresnahan wanted $10,000, a sizable sum then. Wasn't funny, either, when the brainy catcher, fast enough at times to lead off for McGraw, dropped back from catching nearly all the Giants games to fewer than half for the Cardinals. "The Duke" as he was know (short for the Duke of Tralee) wasn't born in Ireland but he came from Toledo, Ohio, where he died as a prison turnkey in 1945, just after he had been elected into the Hall of Fame. Elected as a player, largely, not as a manager.

They said the Duke fought the umpires too often rather than work with his young pitching staff, one of whom was a delightful version of another Rube Waddell. Slender southpaw Harry "Slim" Sallee had a sidearmed serve that bailed out many a lefthanded hitter, and he pitched creditably for inferior clubs for nine St. Louis seasons even when he wasn't staying up late, helping milkmen deposit their bottles or riding downtown to Produce Row with area farmers.

Before his second straight seventh-place season, 1910, Bresnahan acquired a slumping 31-year-old Cincinnati native from the Reds. Little Miller Huggins at 5'6" and 140 pounds was a pasty-faced pint and a quiet man, but also a leader, a walk-wheeling leadoff man who stood up against the best of them at second base. He would have an effect on Bresnahan's life, his own, the Cardinals and baseball's. Huggins was a leader in 1911, a memorable season for a ball club that really hadn't had one since the year the Robisons moved from Cleveland, 1899.

The 1911 team got off to a handsome start, close up in a five-way race until late July even after a harrowing train wreck in which the Duke of Tralee emerged a hero. Bresnahan grumped about the noisy location of his team's traveling Pullman up front near the engine, so a railroad, placating ball clubs at the time, moved the Cards' car far back. The New York, New Haven and Hartford's Federal Express – President Howard Taft's train – hit a viaduct and hurdled down an embankment near Bridgeport, Connecticut. Fourteen persons were killed, three times that many hurt.

A day coach, moved up to where the Cardinals' Pullman had been located, jacknifed and crashed. The ball players, jolted but not hurt, worked 15 hours from the wee hours of the morning to help. They were honored and manager Bresnahan, in turn were hailed by many for having saved their lives.

The Duke couldn't save his own athletic future because, as the saying goes, he didn't know how to treat a lady, especially when he already was sour because he headed a group that had been turned down with a $500,000 bid for the ball club. Pretty good bid but—.

That 1911 season produced the first season over .500—one game over—and drew a handsome 444,768 that research writer Fred Lieb said produced a profit of $165,000, good enough to wipe out old debts.

Happiest was Helene Hathaway Robison Britton, daughter of Frank and niece of Stanley. When her uncle died in spring training, 1911, at older brother's deceased age, 54, she inherited the club. Helene, that is, and her mother Sarah. Young Mrs. Britton, an attractive woman, got 75 percent. She soon thrust herself into the business, bringing "petticoat rule to baseball," as the fussbudgets put it.

Lady Bee temporarily opened the role of president for husband Schyler, a roving rascal, but she soon divorced him. She lived on Lindell Boulevard, across from Forest Park, still fashionable. The gracious hostess had two children, daughter Marie and a son DeHass.

Always a fan, happy with the finish in the standings and at the boxoffice, she got carried away. She extended Bresnahan's contract for five years and 10 percent of the profits, but—oops—the great expectations exploded early in 1912.

Bresnahan, hurt, couldn't help and the ball club floundered at a time the clubowner faced expensive lawsuits over her uncle's estate, plus an ugly charge, finally ruled unfounded, that Bresnahan had favored the Giants' friend McGraw over Philadelphia in the pennant race. The Cardinals, floundering early, finished a sad sixth and saw their attendance nearly cut in half.

Worse, called in on Lady Bee's royal carpet for an accounting, Bresnahan blustered over the second guess and suggested in the most vulgar language of the dugout that the blankety-blank woman didn't know her blankety-blank derriere from her blankety-blank elbow about the game and his job or hers.

Mrs. Britton ruled him out of bounds and out of the house. Even if the Cardinals couldn't afford it, she wanted the club's attorney, James C. Jones, to pay Bresnahan off. Jones worked a deal by which the Cubs would claim the Duke on waivers and the Cardinals would pay him half of the $40,000 as a compromise. He later managed Chicago part of his final playing season, 1915.

When Mrs. Britton tapped second baseman Huggins to manage, Bresnahan accused the Mighty Mite of having carried tales about the Duke, even hinting of a romance between the club owner and the bachelor. A seventh-place finish didn't help, either. The gossip didn't help, but a questionable deal perpetrated by Huggins with Pittsburgh before the 1914 season helped, even though two pretty good outfielders, Rebel Oakes and Steve Evans, jumped to the "third" major, the Federal League. The Feds, co-owned by Phil Ball, were managed by the great pitcher who got away from the Redbirds, Three Finger Brown. They played

MAMA'S BOY: Lady Bee's son, DeHaas Britton, in training to play for the ball club his dear mother never kept.

Big Ed and Buddy: Rangy, powerful Ed Konetchy, first baseman for the Cardinals from 1907 through 1913, covers the bag in drab attire. Koney, as they called him, had been a teammate with the runner, Jack (Red) Murray, until Murray went to the New York Giants in the 1909 deal for catcher-manager Roger Bresnahan.

at Handlan's Park, located at the site of St. Louis University's Busch Center on Grand and Laclede.

When Pittsburgh's Barney Dreyfuss panted for first baseman Ed Konetchy, third baseman Mike Mowrey and pitcher Bob Harmon, dreaming pennant, Huggins got five for three—second baseman Jack (Dots) Miller, right fielder Owen (Chief) Wilson, shortstop Art Butler, left-handed pitcher Hank Robinson and utility infielder-outfielder Al (Cozy) Dolan.

The criticized deal, supplemented by other deals, spurred Huggins' guys to the finest season since Chris Von der Ahe's old Association Browns of the 1880's. St. Louis was so thrilled that, as noted by Fred Lieb in his book about the Cardinals, a whopping 27,000 crowded in for a late August doubleheader. The foe was McGraw's Giants at Robison Field, as Helene lovingly had renamed the park in honor of her father and uncle. The rickety wooden place held only 17,000 so 10,000 crammed the outfield behind ropes. Romantically, manager Huggins walked, stole second and scored on a squeeze play to give Bill Doak a 1-0 victory over Rube Marquard.

A second-game win would mean first place. Trouble was, Christy Mathewson, always a spoilsport against the Cardinals and many others, won the second game, 4-0 and with "miracle" Boston Braves following, winning three out of four and then catching New York in a Labor Day doubleheader, Boston won the pennant. The Cardinals' third-place finish, 81-72, produced a 140,000 attendance hike, but the season-long 346,025 reflects the fact that St. Louis then had three big-league ball clubs.

More players jumped to the Federal League—outfielder Lee Magee even went to the Brooklyn Feds as player-manager—and poor Mrs. Britton couldn't keep up the economic fight. Still, for only $500 she got a skinny Texan kid, finishing his second professional season, who got into a big-league boxscore in early September, 1915. The name, as one writer cracked, sounded like an orchestra leader: Rogers Hornsby!

The peppy kid hit .247 in 18 games with the sixth-place ball club. At season's end, Huggins explained he would have to farm him out. Oh, that wouldn't be necessary, naively explained Hornsby, then a shortstop. He could go to his father's farm. He did and after a winter of hard work, many steaks and more milk, the 155-pound infielder, aged 20, reported at an impressive 180. At camp the scout who had signed him, Bob Connery, suggested he back off the plate and take a full swing at the ball. He did. Hornsby's stance proved as unusual as his hitting through nearly a quarter century, .358. It began with .316 that first full season, 1916, sixth place for the ball club—and the last for Lady Bee. Sapped by the Federal League that just had folded, Mrs. Britton was beset by losing—her family life and a ball club that lost too many games with too many seats—so she told lawyer Jones and manager Huggins about selling out, giving them first option. Excitedly, Huggins, a graduate lawyer, wanted the right to go back to Cincinnati to persuade his friends, the prominent Fleischmann yeast people, to bankroll him for the $375,000 project.

Just about the time Hug would announce the rights to purchase the ball club, Jones disclosed in St. Louis a similar intention. At the time franchise movement was not in the air, Jones' gut feeling about home ownership had to be applauded then, like Fred Saigh's beau geste 35 years later and, finally, Anheuser-Busch's seek-and-find efforts for St. Louis money when they wanted out. Ultimately, the sale of the Cardinals and the Robison real estate property, which became St. Louis's Beaumont High School, made the deal seem a steal, but not then. Ultimately, Jones and his legal associates agreed to scrub their $25,000 for putting through the deal.

Shares sold from $50 up to a maximum of $10,000. You know, civic duty, step right up, fellas. One, insurance man W. E. Bilheimer, suggested a Knot Hole Gang, an offer to a stockholder of a free bleacher seat for a needy kid with a purchase of a $50 share. If, as indicated, they were seeking to curb juvenile delinquency, the plan proved one of the most inspiring in baseball history. Soon, the notion was to let any kid in any day, except weekends or holiday, and to put them in the grandstand. Soon, all a kid needed, 10 to 16, was a couple of durable legs or streetcar fare. And the Cardinals had a built-in rooting system that was young and rewarded with a good show—a winning show.

To put it all together, lawyer Jones wanted the advice of the city's newspaper sports editors and baseball reporters on a ball club operator. At an informal meeting, the barrister asked seven to write down their suggestion. Branch Rickey went 7 for 7! Rickey, 36, then was business manager and former field manager of the Browns. He had been most responsible for having recruited the Brownies' great pitcher-first baseman, George Sisler, whom he had coached at the University of Michigan. To retain Sisler in a bitter contract dispute with Pittsburgh, Rickey demonstrated many gifts to observing writers—shrewdness, an English teacher's polysyllabics, religious reverence and, to use his pet substitute for profanity, Judas Priest, baseball know-how.

Wesley Branch Rickey had come a long way from a poor Ohio farm kid who worshipped sports with a stocky, competitive body and the education he pursued doggedly. With the first $35-a-month job, he bought a bike to go 18 miles a day to teach school and earn money for college. After attending Ohio Wesleyan, he used summers to play baseball professionally and fall football, too, until he suffered a broken leg. By 1905, Branch was good enough to win a big-league spot with the Browns as a catcher and, playing sore-armed, had a record 13 bases stolen against him in one game. Two years later he quit the New York Highland-

LADY BEE: Although Helene Hathaway Robison Britton wondered, as did others, how the Cardinals would compete, the Redbirds did all right. With Miller Huggins finishing with the century's first team in the first division – third – the 81-72 Cardinals drew 346,025.

The Rajah:
Aptly nicknamed as he averaged .400 for five seasons through 1925, Rogers Hornsby player-managed the Cardinals to their first National League pennant and world championship in 1926.

ers, as the Yankees then were known, and crammed a three-year law course into two at Michigan, coaching baseball and assisting in football to pay his way. The task brought a nervous breakdown and a trip west to Boise City, Idaho, where the broad-beamed man with the western hat hung up his law shingle. Considering his revolutionary farm-system concept early and his breaking the color barrier later, considerable baseball history might have been rewritten, most certainly the Cardinals' history, if Branch Rickey had not returned to baseball. He came back in 1913 at the persuasive invitation of the Browns' Robert Lee Hedges, who only recently had rebuilt Sportsman's Park.

Serving as Hedges' right-hand man in the office and then—the job he liked best—as manager of the Browns in 1914-15, Rickey finished fifth and sixth, but he ran into an obstacle and almost out of one job when Phil Ball, who owned the St. Louis Federals franchise, was awarded the right to buy the Browns. Ball, an ice-and-fuel magnate and curmudgeon, didn't like Rickey, who some found sanctimonious, and preferred his own Federal League manager, Fielder Jones. However, The Fielder couldn't come close to bringing back the success of his famed "Hitless Wonders" Chicago White Sox of 1906. Except for American League president, Ban Johnson, Ball would have canned "business manager" Rickey then, but when lawyer Jones called on behalf of the Cardinals, Ball fought Rickey in court to block the move, but lost. Good thing, too, because Phillip DeCatesby Ball didn't like Wesley Branch Rickey's idea of developing your own players.

With beginner's luck and a little wheeling and dealing, Rickey helped the Cardinals to a robust third-place finish in 1917 with their finest record to date, 82-70, but the bows deservedly went mainly to Huggins, bench manager for the first time. Hug, in time, was helped by Hornsby, who hit .327. The Mighty Mite manager's two third-place finishes in five seasons with a rag-tag team impressed many, including the American League's Johnson, eager to improve the New York franchise and to repay the Cardinals for the Browns' loss of Rickey.

With the assistance of J. G. Taylor Spink, Ban convinced Huggins to accompany *The Sporting News* publisher to New York. Like the pot calling the kettle copper, sawed-off Spink admonished little Huggins, "Don't wear that damned (street) cap. He'll think you're a jockey!" The "he" was brewer Jacob Ruppert, whose partner, Col. T. L. Huston was in France with American troops. Huston preferred Wilbert Robinson. Ruppert hired Huggins, who gave the Yankees six pennants and three world championships before he died of erysipelas late in the 1929 season at the age of 50.

Rickey himself was overseas as a major in chemical warfare. Under Jack Hendricks in the abbreviated 1918 season, the Cardinals finished last. The Cardinals not only were so poor in 1918 that they trained at Washington University, but they were having a hard time paying off Mrs. Britton. At this point, Sam Breadon stepped aggressively into the picture. "S. Breadon", as he always signed himself, had come as far himself as Rickey did from that poor Ohio farm. Breadon, pronounced Bray-don, was a poor kid who skinnydipped off Manhattan's docks into the Hudson River. He gave up a $125-a-month bank clerk's job to follow a dream that the "horseless carriage" might have a better future than a buggy whip.

Breadon learned the automobile game as a grease monkey, impressing others as too proud to accept a tip—his pride was evident throughout his life—and soon became a good salesman and a partner of Marion Lambert of St. Louis airport family fame. They early on handled Fords. Breadon had the prestigious Pierce Arrow before he stepped out of the business wealthy in 1936. Sam, a baseball fan who didn't go to many games, was persuaded by close auto friend Fuzzy Anderson to contribute $200 in 1917 for four shares of stock.

Later, Fuzzy twisted his wrist to go to a stockholders meeting and a chance to meet Huggins' players. Carried away, Breadon pledged $1800 more. Soon, at the emergency meeting to try to meet the note to Lady Bee, Breadon offered a $5000 loan if others would. They contributed $15,000 more. Another loan of $18,000, as the club owner reminisced for Fred Lieb, put him far ahead of the $2,000 stock.

Now, he had a serious investment and a need to express himself. He was named to the unwieldy 25-man board of directors. Lawyer Jones wondered if he'd become president. "Only if you cut the board to five", Breadon said, accepting seven as a compromise. When Samuel Breadon became president in December, 1919, the ball club's history changed even more than the life of the man.

Ultimately buying stock to the point he had 78 percent after 21 years of nine pennants and six world championships, Breadon succeeded by putting his money where Rickey's mouth was. Sam got there by convincing Phil Ball to let the Cardinals become tenants at Sportman's Park, enabling him to sell Cardinal Field, as that sagging field on Natural Bridge had been renamed again. The $275,000 sale of the site for a high school and for a streetcar turnaround paid off clinging Cardinal debts and enabled Breadon to tell Rickey to put it to use.

Thus began the incredible quarter-century relationship between baseball's Odd Couple. They were utterly unalike. Breadon, neat and trim, a New Yorker who never lost his accent. Secretary Mary Murphy was "Miss Moiphy" and the ball club was the "Cawd-nals." He was "Lucky Sam," a man for whom it never rained in opportunistic situations. He also was "Singing Sam," a Scotch-sipping Democrat who lifted his voice and elbow in the convivial-ity of barbershop harmony. Rickey, two years younger, was a bible-quoting, psalm-singing Republican, a teetotaler, a tousel-haired, cigar-chewing orator of emotional elocution, as rumpled as an unmade bed, but a brilliant mind tuned to making money, yet spending the club's excessively if Breadon weren't there to nix the most expensive or unpredictable.

Anchored to the big bat of Hornsby, who blazed into the lively ball era of the 1920's, Rickey and the Redbirds prevailed despite the death of a good catcher, Bill (Pickles) Dillhoefer at the outset of the 1922 season, a victim of pneumonia, and then after that second third-place season the shocking loss of outfielder Austin McHenry, Rickey's pride and joy. McHenry hit .350 the year before he suffered a fatal brain tumor. At a time ball clubs sought 500,000 home attendance as a break-even point, the '22 Cardi-

MIGHTY MITE: Miller Huggins, a good player in St. Louis, better as a manager with the Cardinals and great with the New York Yankees.

Death on the Diamond: Austin McHenry, rangy right-handed hitter and manager Branch Rickey's pride and joy, misjudged two fly balls in a 1922 game at New York's Polo Grounds. The outfielder was diagnosed with a brain tumor and died that November at 27 after having hit .350 in 1921 and .303 before he was sidelined.

nals got there with 536,343, but it was a special period in which the two great St. Louis hitters, the Cardinals' Hornsby and the Browns' Sisler, created a hometown rivalry, The Rajah versus The Sizzler. That year, as the Browns narrowly missed a pennant won by the Yankees, Sisler hit .420. Hornsby hit .401 with 42 homers, aided by the more accommodating measurements of Sportsman's Park compared with the old former National League park.

In the last full season at the old park—called the second Sportsman's Park, League Park, Robison Field and Cardinal Field, take your pick—Hornsby had been the only batter to lift one over the distant left-field fence. Even before Breadon took over as president, the New York Giants offered $250,000 for the superstar converted to second base. By 1923, the offer was twice that much. In 1924, the year Rog hit the century's highest average, .424, William Wrigley of Chicago offered a price-is-no-object. "You name your price on Hornsby and we will meet it."

Breadon, gulping because acquisition of farm clubs had cost money, still said no, particularly interesting because Hornsby and manager Rickey had come to blows. Breadon, inspired by Rickey's two third-place finishes and early arrival of young talented farm players, did the most unlikely for him. He signed Rickey to a five-year contract as manager, then saw the club sag to fifth and his box-office attraction clash with the field foreman. By the time Cardinals dipped to sixth in 1924 and attendance to 272,884, Sam had a change of heart.

In spring training, 1925 at Stockton, Calif., he asked Rickey to step down. B. R. refused. Just ahead of Memorial Day, Breadon asked the ticket office about sales for the last-place club's holiday doubleheader. Mighty few. Breadon entrained to Pittsburgh, saw Rickey and said he'd make the change. Unhappily, Rickey recommended his coach and "Sunday manager," Burt Shotton. Breaden wanted Hornsby at a time player-managers were the rage—Sisler, Ty Cobb, Tris Speaker, Eddie Collins, Bucky Harris. The club owner thought kicking Rickey upstairs would be a great favor. B. R. disagreed. If he couldn't manage, he didn't want to hold stock. Breadon shrugged and arranged for a note to permit Hornsby to get Rickey's $30,000 par value stock for $50,000. Within two years, Hornsby got $118,000 for it.

Rickey's grand plan hadn't quite manifested itself, though he brought up little lefty Bill Sherdel in 1919. A year later when the club still had the financial shorts, he talked Kansas City out of another durable player, right-hander Jesse Haines, for $10,000 B. R. didn't have. And then they had begun to come up—outfielder Ray Blades, first baseman Jim Bottomley, outfielders Chick Hafey and Taylor Douthit, handyman Roscoe (Watty) Holm, infielder Jake Flowers and pitchers Bill Hallahan and Charles (Flint) Rhem.

The enterprising Rickey took chances. He introduced a pitcher who wore glasses, Lee Meadows, and an infielder, George (Specs) Toporcer, but maybe he was a better teacher than manager, or, putting it another way, maybe the academician taught more than he led. At least Hornsby thought he did. Rog, handsome and dimpled, actually was a tough-talking Texan. Replacing Rickey, he ordered Rickey's clubhouse blackboard discarded. "This ain't football," he snapped.

Hornsby, taking over with the ball club last on Memorial Day at 14-25, went 63-51 the rest of the way. The Cards finished fifth, a game over .500, inspired largely by Hornsby's third .400 season, including 39 homers to go with his .403 average. Sunny Jim Bottomley at first base hit .367, and a catcher Rickey obtained just before he stepped down, Bob O'Farrell, hit .278. When Rickey directed early that young shortstop Tommy Thevenow be farmed out to Syracuse for experience, Hornsby bided his time. He went to Breadon and asked for the slick-fielding kid. "Experience, hell, he'll learn here quickly," he said. Thevenow came back and a year later would play every game and, though a light hitter, led the World Series in batting.

At spring training, 1926, Hornsby began his preaching. If-you-don't-think-we-can-win-get a rail ticket home. For a sly guy who never roused foes, he privately preached pennant for a city that hadn't won one since Grover Cleveland sat in the White House. Grover Cleveland, that is, not Alexander. Old Pete played a pivotal part in Hornsby's story book season.

Shortly before the June 15 trading deadline, with Hornsby's alleged contenders still atop only the second division, John McGraw paid them an unexpected favor. He offered veteran right fielder Billy Southworth to get younger, more fleet Clarence (Heinie) Mueller for center field. Alexander's availability came unexpectedly with Rickey out of town inspecting a farm club. One of the pitching greats, Alex the Great, was making it tough on rookie Cub manager Joe McCarthy, smarting off at clubhouse meetings when under the influence, which was often.

The Cubs asked waivers on Alexander, but four lower clubs had priority on St. Louis. They passed. Breadon thought a bid made sense. Hornsby was even more positive. Rog could hit Alex, but most others still couldn't because the crafty veteran had added a screwball to augment his pinpointed control of his fast ball and dinky curve.

Alcoholic, epileptic, and his own worst enemy, Alexander paid off immediately. His first start was against the Cubs. He won in 10 innings, 3-2, before a record 37,718. Quite conveniently for Lucky Sam Breadon, the Browns' Phil Ball, expecting his team to make a run for it under George Sisler, had expanded Sportsman's Park seating capacity from 18,000 to 34,000.

The good fortune continued. Southworth, playing right field, hit .320. Bottomley leveled off to .299, but Sunny Jim led the league with 120 RBI's. Hornsby, himself injured, hit a disappointing .317, but the young third baseman he boosted, Les Bell, hit .325 with 100 RBI's. Douthit batted .308. Blades hit .305 before he was hurt, Chick Hafey showed fierce line-drive ability, and O'Farrell, as mentioned, catching virtually every game, was perfect for old Chicago teammate Alexander and the other pitchers. He batted .293 and won MVP honors.

Among the pitchers, young Flint Rhem was the leader with 20-7, Wee Willie Sherdel went 16-12, occasionally hurt Jesse Haines 13-4, lefty Art Reinhart 10-5, Vic Keen 10-9

THE CHAMPIONS: Manager Bill McKechnie's 1928 champions for whom Jesse Haines was a 20-and-8 winner.

and Alexander 9-7 with the team's lowest earned-run average, 2.91. A key contest was won by a seldom-seen veteran, Allen Sothoron. Sothoron, also serving as pitching coach, picked up a 3-1 victory on the last day of August, sending the Cardinals into first place and into the month in which they had folded in the past—and with every game on the road!

With exhibitions scheduled for his weary ball club, Hornsby asked Breadon to cancel one at New Haven, Connecticut. The club owner picked the moment after a losing game to walk in and say it couldn't be done. Mr. Blunt, as Hornsby was called both affectionately and accurately, made what the *Post-Dispatch*'s gifted J. Roy Stockton recommended as "an utterly impossible disposition" of the game. A blushing Breadon walked off, never to set foot in the clubhouse until he sold 20 years later, but with his pride deeply offended. So deeply that after the Cardinals won the World Series and trained back in triumph to St. Louis, sports editor Sid Keener of old St. Louis *Times* told his young neophyte, Sam Muchnick, that he expected hero Hornsby to be traded.

Ol' Pete: Legendary Grover Cleveland Alexander, who won two games and saved one in the World Series, was knock-kneed with a crooked grin – and possessed one of the greatest pitching careers in baseball.

To win with those gray flannels that grew more grimy than the race, the Cardinals, twice knocked out of the lead by Cincinnati, found help in unusual places. The Giants did their part as Frankie Frisch, a name to be remembered, emerged from John McGraw's doghouse with a tenth-inning homer over the Reds that put the Redbirds in front to stay. On September 25, the Cardinals clinched the pennant at the Polo Grounds. With Sherdel relieving Rhem, Southworth hit a pennant-winning homer, 6-4.

The Cards finished 98-65, two games better than Cincinnati. Back home they celebrated second only to the World War armistice in 1918. However, they would have to wait more than a week to honor Hornsby's heroes, who faced old boss Miller Huggins' Yankees in the first two World Series games at Yankee Stadium.

Before the World Series Cinderella finish, the highlight was the third game, immediately after the long-awaited ticker-tape parade of the returning pennant winners. Jesse Haines won it, 4-0, and also hit a home run, but they really had seen nothing yet. The next day Babe Ruth hit three home runs in a Yankee rout. When crafty Herb Pennock decisioned fellow southpaw Sherdel in the fifth game 3-2, after having also won the opener from Wee Willie, 2-1, the Yankees went home only one game away from the championship.

First, backed by a robust attack, Alexander beat them, 12-2, an eight-hit effort compared with a four-hitter in which he struck out 10 in the second Series game. Hornsby congratulated Old Pete and asked him to take it easy just in case. By the seventh inning of the seventh game, played on a raw, rainy day, Alex sat cross-legged in the visitors' bullpen, wearing a thick red woolen sweater and with his cap pulled down over his eyes. Asleep? Maybe.

Suddenly, rallying from a three-run deficit, the Yankees found Haines wild and ineffective. Hornsby trudged in from second base. Gutty-guy Jess had enough. In the bullpen, Hornsby had two pitchers warming up, Reinhart, a left-hander, and the right-handed Rhem. He wanted neither. He wanted the old man. Alexander got up, stretched, slowly took off his sweater and, aware rookie right-handed-hitting second baseman Tony Lazzeri awaited him, the old-timer ambled slowly to the mound in a great circle route. At shortstop, Hornsby met him, noting the sleepy gray eyes. "We're up 3-2, Pete, three on, two out and Lazzeri up," said the manager, certain Alexander at least was reasonably sober.

Old Pete grunted. "Guess there's no place to put him, eh Rog?" The four-pitch strike out of Lazzeri, commemorated on

Alexander's Hall of Fame plaque, represents just about the most tense moment in the history of the World Series. The 3-2 lead held up for the championship when Ruth, walking on a questionable borderline pitch with two out in the ninth, was thrown out trying a surprise steal, O'Farrell to Hornsby.

For Hornsby, tagging the Babe ranked as the greatest moment of his career. And Rogers then hurried to catch a train back to Hornsby Bend, Texas., where his mother had died a few days earlier with the wish that her tough-talking son put his job first. For a new contract, Hornsby wanted to go from $30,000 to $50,000, second only to Babe Ruth's salary, and for three years. Breadon countered with one year. Things came to a head in late December.

Suddenly, red-faced and angry, Hornsby stormed out of Breadon's office. Breadon picked up the telephone to New York. Moments later he told Rickey the news; Hornsby was sent to the Giants for Frank Frisch and pitcher Jimmy Ring! To stunned Cardinal fans, Santa Claus threw a shovel of coal into their Christmas stockings. The Chamber of Commerce denounced Breadon by resolution. Bitter fans draped Sam's auto agency with black crepe. They adorned his fashionable Washington Terrace home with funeral paper.

Of the players acquired, the veteran Ring said he doubted whether he would move to St. Louis. Too bad, parenthetically, that he came, because he went 0-and-4 before the Cards released him and they lost the 1927 pennant by only a game and a half! Frisch, stunned to be removed from his handsome home on New Rochelle's Fenimore Road, 45 minutes from Broadway, was miffed, too, but too smart to quit. With the competitive fire that made him an odd mixture of fun-and-fury in his career, Frisch took wife Ada upstate to Lake Placid, where the former Fordham baseball, basketball and football captain skied, skated and romped in the snow with his dogs.

Rickey, wanting to see for himself, used a winter trip to Syracuse to beckon Frisch with a better contract and a pep talk. Breadon's offer was $27,500 each for two years. Frisch, whose $25,000 had been more than even John McGraw paid Christy Mathewson, was satisfied. He didn't need the pep talk. "Tell Mr. Breadon I'm in the best shape ever."

Indeed, with an opening day triple and homer off the Cubs' Pat Malone for a 4-3 victory, Frisch was a whirling dervish. He hit .337 even though his average suffered in September when he had a swollen wrist. He struck out only 10 times, stole a league-leading 48 bases and, in effect, played both sides of second base.

A broken leg suffered by brilliant-fielding Tommy Thevenow in early June left a gaping hole at shortstop. Frisch, great at going to his right, urged inexperienced rookie Heinie Schuble to protect the hole toward third. As a result, the Fordham Flash gathered in a record 641 assists, and became the only infielder other than a first baseman to be involved in more than 1000 plays (1037). The 1927 record in eight fewer games still stood 70 years later.

Jesse Haines had a career season, 24 wins. Old Pete Alexander won 21 and Sherdel 17. Bottomley drove in 124 runs and Hafey, emerging as a power hitter whose only trouble was that his line drives didn't go high enough, hit .329 with 18 homers.

Hornsby almost created an unhappy, impossible disposition because neither the league nor commissioner would permit a St. Louis stockholder to play second base for New York. Rog boldly wanted three times what he had paid for Rickey's stock, not just double, the amount Breadon offered. Finally, uniquely, each National League club had to pony up $5,000 to make up the difference. Hornsby, signing with the Giants for $40,000 as McGraw's captain, made a difference, but not big enough as the Giants finished third behind Pittsburgh and

SUPER STARS: Babe Ruth, then 31, and Rogers Hornsby, 30, two of the greatest players ever, posed at Yankee Stadium before the opening of the 1926 World Series. The Babe hit three homers in one Series game, a record, but Hornsby tagged him out stealing on the final play of the Series for, as he put it, Rog's biggest career thrill.

the Cardinals. His .361 with 26 homers and 125 RBIs, didn't keep a disgruntled front office from trading him—shockingly again—to the Boston Braves.

Frisch finished ahead of Hornsby and narrowly behind Pittsburgh's Paul Waner in the MVP voting. Breadon assessed the situation when he was dying of cancer in 1949. He remembered that the Cardinals had won three more games in 1927 and drew nearly 100,000 more fans, 763,615. Said Breadon, "The greatest player I had for one season was Frank Frisch in 1927. He took me off the spot. Him, too. I never again was afraid to trade a player." Mr. Breadon certainly wasn't afraid to fire managers, either. Bill McKechnie replaced Bob O'Farrell for 1928.

The 1928 season was an especially good one for Rickey and, of course, boss Breadon. The first of May, shoring up right field, Rickey dealt O'Farrell to the Giants for a veteran left-handed-hitting outfielder, George Washington Harper. Next, with Breadon agreeing to pay for once, rather than receiving, Rickey gave young catcher Virgil (Spud) Davis, outfielder Homer Peel and $25,000 for the poverty-stricken Philadelphia Phillies' great defensive catcher, Jimmy (Ace) Wilson.

Earlier, at spring training camp, Rickey and Breadon hoped to unload Les Bell, who just hadn't been the same since Hornsby left. They wanted handy Andy High, a St. Louisan, as a utility infielder, but Hornsby wasn't speaking to either man. Cutely, they used young baseball writer Ray Gillespie of the *Star-Times* to serve as intermediary. The deal was done and the pennant won, clinched just after a late-season game at the Polo Grounds, where George Harper hit three home runs against his mentor, McGraw, and then thumbed his nose at the famed manager when he circled the bases.

The team won 95 games to finish two games in front of the Giants. They were led offensively by Jim Bottomley, who won the Most Valuable Player award with a .325 average in which 93 of his 187 hits were for extra bases—42 doubles and league-leading 20 triples, 31 homers and 136 RBIs. The Yankees avenged their Series loss of two years earlier as the Cardinals were creamed four straight—4-1,9-3, 7-3 and 7-3—but the results seemed worse, since the Bombers were supposed to be "hurt". Truth was, Herb Pennock was out, Earle Combs only pinch-hit, Leo Durocher caddied in late innings for Tony Lazzeri and even the Babe limped. Uh-huh, limped to and onto the plate scoring nine times in the four games with 10 hits, including three doubles, three homers, driving in four runs, batting .625. Gehrig, cleaning up behind the Babe, hit .545 with six hits, including a double and four homers, for nine RBIs. Breadon was hurt and angry. McKechnie, a pitcher's manager, maybe didn't try often enough to pitch around Ruth and Gehrig. Boldly, Breadon asked McKechnie to take a demotion to Rochester in a job swap for 1929.

Here, Breadon showed his honest approach as well as his obvious interest as a fan masquerading as a club owner. By midsummer, 1929, convinced that Southworth could win at Rochester, but that he didn't have temperament to handle men, some of whom had played for him, Breadon sent Billy back to Rochester and asked

The Old Flash: As Fordham Flash Frankie Frisch appropriately labeled himself late in his career, shown here hitting left-handed in spring training 1935, his last reasonably successful season. The glove-in-the-pocket habit of players then showed how much smaller fielding mitts were. Yeah, the Old Flash was getting heavy, wasn't he?

McKechnie to return. Deacon Will did and did well enough with his fourth-place finish that the boss wanted him back, but spurned once and aware that Breadon ruled by heart as well as head, McKechnie took a five-year contract from Boston.

At Boston, McKechnie was reunited with the 1928 Cardinal championship shortstop, Rabbit Maranville. The Redbirds might have had better shortstops, not many much better than the little Hall of Famer, and none more colorful. For years, Rabbit was a pie-eyed pixie, a Peter Pan who helped the Braves win their "miracle" last-to-first pennant in 1914. At 36, Rabbit came back to the Cardinals, where he had been sent as a reformed alcoholic. Frank Frisch would recall, "If they had brought up Rabbit earlier than the last couple of weeks in '27, we'd have won that one, too"

Walter James Vincent Maranville, famous for his belt-high basket catches Willie Mays later copied, hit .308 in the 1928 Series debacle against the Yankees, exactly what he had hit in the Braves' World Series upset of Connie Mack's Philadelphia powerhouse 14 years earlier. If not a chance to retain, Rabbit thought he had a commitment from Rickey, his sobriety mentor, for a playing pilot's job at Rochester. Instead, Rickey sold him back to the Braves.

When Breadon looked for a successor to McKechnie, who would achieve championship success at Cincinnati, Sam already had dismissed one candidate. When ex-outfielder and coach Earle (Greasy) Neale talked too much football to suit the boss, Breadon eliminated him. Neale later coached the Philadelphia Eagles to the 1950 National Football League championship. Breadon's choice , Charles (Gabby) Street, was surprising if only because he had failed in one of his biggest tasks, playing nursemaid as coach to Alexander, who slipped more often with John Barleycorn as his batterymate. A good-field, no-hit catcher in his playing days, Gabby was best known for having caught a ball Walter Johnson dropped off the Washington Monument.

The 1930 Cardinals weren't expected to do much and, in fact, didn't for the first four and a half months of the season. By mid-August, they were fourth only one game over .500, 53-52, and were 12 games behind first place Brooklyn with Chicago and New York in the way, too. They'd have to play musical chairs up front or the Cardinals had to win consistently. Both happened. They were still fourth, seven and a half games out, as they went into September and on the road. By late that month, Brooklyn had regained the lead, but the red-hot Redbirds had moved up to a game out for a series at Ebbets Field. Then "it" happened.

"It" was Flint Rhem's story when, the morning of the first game, he told how he had been picked up at gunpoint outside his New York hotel the night before, whisked by car into New Jersey and forced to drink "cups" of raw whiskey. At a twenty-fifth reunion Fred Saigh threw for the 1926 Cardinals, Rhem blabbered and spoiled a good story about his famed "kidnapping." Street asked Bill Hallahan to move up a day, setting up a low-scoring pitching thriller in a season in which, for instance, the Cardinals averaged 6.5 runs, scoring a record 1004 and still had a team average no higher than fifth with .314. Philadelphia hit .319 and finished last!

So this one was a classic between short, stocky southpaw Hallahan and big, ruddy Dazzy Vance, the league's most prominent pitcher whose fast ball was faster and his jagged curve even better than Hallahan's. Wild Bill and The Dazzler dueled into the

LADIES DAY FAVORITE: A bachelor most of his playing career, cap perched cockily on one side of his head and with a swaggering walk, Sunny Jim Bottomley most certainly was the ladies' day choice in the Depression era when the free gate was as attractive to women fans as the sexy-looking first baseman.

tenth inning scoreless. In St. Louis's ninth, Dodger infielder Mickey Finn roughed up Charley Gelbert at shortstop. When Charley limped up to hit in the tenth, manager Street sent up left-handed-hitting Andy High as a pinch-hitter. Vance blazed two fast balls past High. Andy remembered Dazzy's great curve, too, but his eyes would squint in a merry grin, "He made a mistake of hanging one."

High's double off the right-field fence, followed by Taylor Douthit's single, scored a precious run. With High moving to third base and Sparky Adams shifting to shortstop, Brooklyn filled the bases with one out in the bottom of the inning. Dodger catcher Al Lopez grounded sharply to short, where the ball bad-hopped. Adams juggled the ball and still not in control, shoveled the ball to money man Frisch, whose whirlwind pivot nipped Lopez at first. Hallahan's 1-0 masterpiece tied the race. The next day, Handy Andy, as they called High, delivered a pinch double, and the Cardinals rallied to win over a tough-nut Cuban curveballer, Dolph Luque. They were in first place.

Spitballer Burleight Grimes, a key mid-season pickup from Boston, won the next day, 4-3 for his 13th victory since joining the team. Sweeping the showdown series, the Cardinals were in front to stay. They won 39 of their last 49, clinching it on the final Friday with Grimes' road roommate, Jesse Haines, beating Pittsburgh, 10-5. The torrid .786 pace put them two games up over Chicago. Angrily, the Cubs' William Wrigley fired Joe McCarthy for Rogers Hornsby, kicking McCarthy upstairs into Yankee history.

With 55 National League players hitting .300 or better — .303 for the league average — Redbird averages, regular or part-time, were spectacular: Ray Blades, 396; George (Showboat) Fisher, .374; Watty Watkins, .373; Frank Frisch, .346; Chick Hafey, .336; .Ernie Orsatti, .321; Jimmy Wilson, .318; Sparky Adams, .314; Charley Gelbert, .304; Jim Bottomley, .304; and Taylor Douthit, .303 and — more about this later, George Puccinelli, .563, with 9 for 16, including a double and three homers.

Despite the September surge of 21 out of 25 for total victories, no pitcher had extraordinary figures. Hallahan led with 15 wins, but Grimes, Haines, Rhem and Syl Johnson all were in double figures. When they clinched with two games to go, manager Street used the last day to introduce a lanky,

Storybook Stars: Fourth in early August, only one game over .500, the 1930 Cardinals won 39 of their last 49 games and the pennant.
Back Row: Lindsey, Bell, Johnson, Haines, Grimes, Bottomley, Hafey, Fisher, Wilson, Puccinelli.
Middle Row: Grabowski, Hallahan, Mancuso, Orsatti, Frisch, Gelbert, Blades.
Front Row: Watkins, Coach Wares, Batboy Motts Conlisk, Mgr. Street, High, Adams, Douthit, Smith.

lean, high-cheekboned right-hander, up from Houston with a record and an unusual nickname.

That final day, St. Louis mayor Victor Miller, calling over Street to a private box for congratulations, wondered about the pitcher warming up in front of the dugout, nicknamed Dizzy—Jay Hanna or Jerome Herman Dean .What about him, Sarge? "Mr. Mayor," said Street slowly, "I think he's going to be a great pitcher, but I'm afraid we'll never know from one minute to the next what he's going to do." That day Dizzy three-hit the Pirates, 3-1, and drove in a run with a base hit and, no, podnuh, nobody ever knew what to expect from the pitcher, who in all modesty—as he put it—wasn't the best pitcher, but he was "amongst 'em."

MOMENT OF TRUTH: Before the first game of a pivotal September series at Brooklyn in 1930, Cardinals' left-hander Wild Bill Hallahan posed with pitching rival, and future Hall of Famer Dazzy Vance. In the highest-scoring era, they pitched a masterpiece won by Hallahan in 10 innings, 1-0. The Cards tied for first and never looked back.

Despite lively hitting, pitching in the 1930 World Series was prime. That is, pitching over hitting if not over power. For instance, in the opener at Philadelphia, Grimes allowed only five hits, but two were homers, by Mickey Cochrane and Al Simmons. Behind the great Lefty Grove, 28-and-5, the A's won, 5-2. The second game went to big George (Moose) Earnshaw, 6-1, with Cochrane homering off Rhem. But with the Series back in St. Louis, Hallahan shut out another left-hander, Rube Walberg, 5-0, and the dean of the St. Louis staff, Haines, injured earlier in the season, topped the mighty Grove, 3-1.

The fifth game was pivotal. It went into the ninth scoreless. Mack, pulling out all stops, pinch-hit for Earnshaw in the eighth and then turned to Grove. For the Cardinals, "Old Stubblebeard," – Grimes' nickname because he didn't shave on days he pitched because of chafing caused by the resin he chewed for his spitter—worked into the ninth, cupping his hands to his lips every pitch, spitter or not.

Earlier, he had struck out Jimmy Foxx with a slow curve. With one on in the ninth, "Double X"guessed curve. "X" marked the spot high in the bleachers where he hit it for a 2-0 victory. So back in Philadelphia, with Earnshaw hot again and Hallahan not, Philadelphia won going away, 7-1.

The Cardinals bussed from their hotel to the railroad. In the back of the bus, young slugger Puccinelli's sing-song was, "It's all over now, it's all over now" Up front, Grimes, sitting with a new friend and old foe, Frank Frisch, whom he had knocked down often in the past, looked at Frisch with a scowl. Frisch cursed. Burleigh leaped up, strode to the back and, standing over the towering Puccinelli, growled, "Listen, you big S.O.B., we know it's over, but, dammit, we don't want to hear about it."

Puccinelli wasn't with the 1931 Cardinals. Neither was Showboat Fisher, despite his .374 average as a part-time outfielder. Showboat fielded erratically as if first bounces were out. Dizzy Dean didn't make it, either. In spring training the colorful carefree character was so obnoxious that Breadon, Rickey and Street decided to farm him out. "That," said big reliever Jim Lindsey, aware of the kid's boasts, "is the first time a ball club ever lost 30 games in one day!"

Still, the '31 Cardinals won from here to there. They were aided by a rookie they kept, big Paul Derringer, who won 18 of their 101 victories, a wire-to-wire pennant 13 games ahead of the Giants. Many baseball men regard this ball club as the best in team history with the possible exception of the 1942 club. They had speed, defense, pitching and experience. They had the National League's Most Valuable Player,

Commanders in chief: Manager Gabby Street (left) and second baseman-captain Frankie Frisch lead the downtown parade along Washington Avenue the next-to-last day of the 1930 season, 24 hours after clinching the pennant.

Frisch, and two of the top three hitters in a batting race won by Hafey over Bottomley and New York's Bill Terry by less than a decimal point at .349. Injuries limited Sunny Jim's games, giving a chance to first-base newcomer, Rip Collins.

Another rookie, Johnny Leonard Roosevelt (Pepper) Martin, stormed into Rickey's office one day and, simulating his idol's use of a substitute for profanity, he wailed: "John Brown, Mr. Rickey, either play me or trade me." Mr. Rickey liked Pepper Martin. Just about everybody did, except an opposing infielder or catcher who felt the viciousness of his slide. Pepper, as B. R. put it, played with a "spirit of adventure." Back at Rochester, where he had spent enough time, they already called him the "Wild Horse of the Osage". So Pepper touched Rickey's heart and Breadon's pocketbook. With perhaps as good an eye as any about tell-tale lapses in talent, Mr. Rickey had noticed that ballhawk Douthit in center field had become a tad late when pulling the ball. Besides — and important to Rickey who got 20 per cent of the profits and a handsome salary — Douthit made a nice salary for the time, $14,500 compared to Martin's $4500. So even though a suspicious Douthit pounded out eight hits in a Sunday doubleheader after the deed had been done — for Monday announcement — Douthit went to Cincinnati and Martin to center field. In the regular season he batted .300 and impressed the *Post-Dispatch*'s astute baseball writer, J. Roy Stockton, who suggested that the 27-year-old Pepper just might be a Series hero.

A Series hero and then some when it began against the powerful Athletics, seeking a third straight world championship. In the opener, semi-crouching with his bat slung over his back arm, Pepper prayed, "Please, God, let me do well." He smoked a double and two other hits in a 6-2 loss to Grove, a 31-and-4 pitcher. The next day, facing Moose Earnshaw, who had allowed only two runs in 25 innings the previous October, Martin doubled, stole third and scored on a fly ball. Later, he singled, stole second, moved to third on an infield out and eluded catcher Cochrane's tag on Gelbert's squeeze bunt. So it was Martin 2, Philadelphia 0 into the ninth when Hallahan, seeking a shutout with two out and two runners moving up on a full-count pitch, broke off a sharp overhanded curve that pinch-hitter Jimmy Moore missed for a third strike. A third strike, but not an out because Jimmy Wilson, catching, scooped it out of the dirt. If things hadn't worked out, they would have sung the "Rock of Ages" in memory of Wilson, a dunce cap in defeat.

Jimmy could have tagged the transfixed Moore or fired quickly to Bottomley at first base, but instead, he lobbed toward third where Jake Flowers stood several feet off the bag. The throw was high, Flowers reached up for it and in a split instant looked for a nephew in a nearby box. Jake had promised the kid a ball and this one was in play. A toss into the stands would have been a two-run boo-boo bigger than Wilson's!

Coaching third, as fans poured from the stands and hesitating Cardinals trotted off the field, wise old Eddie Collins ran down toward the third-base dugout, to which Moore retreated, urging him to run to first base. American League umpire Dick Nallin, working home plate, stayed nearby. Suddenly, out of crazy confusion, the crowd was shooed back into the stands and the

Cardinals onto the field.

Hallahan now had to face Max Bishop, the A's left-handed-hitting leadoff man. Hallahan, who had walked eight in his three-hitter, got the ball over and Bishop fouled behind first and the nearby low-slung temporary seats. Bottomley, bumping hard into the barrier, reached in and back-handed the ball.

With a travel day and a rainout, Mack had a rested Grove for the third game, but Martin had two hits and Grimes, finally getting his first chance, pitched a one-hit shutout into the ninth. Al Simmon's two-run homer merely made the final score 5-2. Pepper tried hard in the fourth game, getting two hits off Earnshaw, but those were the club's only hits in a 3-2 loss for Syl Johnson. In the fifth game at Shibe Park, Hallahan topped Waite Hoyt, 5-1, aided by three hits by Martin, including a homer.

Back at St. Louis, Derringer and associates were bombed by the A's and Grove, 6-1, and an embarrassing thing happened. World Series tickets were sold only in three-game blocks. The seventh game, the fourth for Sportsman's Park, was not covered. Too many home-town fans didn't think the Cards could do it. So when games there had drawn nearly 40,000, with no playing-field standees, just 20,805 saw the showdown. For the second straight game, Martin was silenced, but the Cardinals were good and lucky against Earnshaw, who was good and unlucky. The Moose, again brilliant with a 1.88 ERA, allowed only five hits, but they were clustered at the top of the batting order. Andy High, leading off, got two and George Watkins three. The A's fell victim to hard luck, to Redbird speed, to the gallant heart of Grimes and the invincibility of Hallahan.

In the home first, High blooped a single to short left. Watkins lofted another just between shortstop and left field. Frisch promptly sacrificed. With Martin moved up to clean-up, Earnshaw, bearing down, uncorked a run-scoring wild pitch and Watkins took third. Martin was walked intentionally and immediately stole second. Earnshaw struck out Ernie Orsatti, but the ball squirted away from Cochrane, who threw out the fleet Orsatti. Meanwhile, alertly, Watkins broke for the plate and when Jimmy Foxx's return throw was high—ruled an error—Watty was safe.

PEPPER'S PET: Tenderly, Pepper Martin (left) and Rip Collins (right) took care of a young man with Down's Syndrome known only as "Yoyo" during the championship springs of the early 1930s at Bradenton, Florida. Yoyo was a happy voyager on this simulated fishing trip.

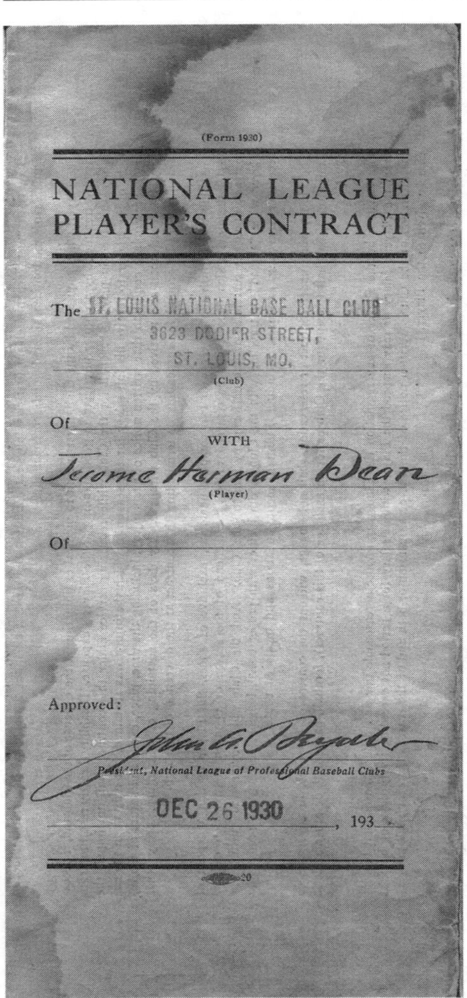
(Form 1930)

NATIONAL LEAGUE
PLAYER'S CONTRACT

The ST. LOUIS NATIONAL BASE BALL CLUB
3623 DODIER STREET,
ST. LOUIS, MO.
(Club)

Of

WITH

Jerome Herman Dean
(Player)

Of

Approved:

President, National League of Professional Baseball Clubs

DEC 26 1930, 193

In the Money: Dizzy Dean's contract jacket for 1930 when Jay Hanna thought he was Jerome Herman.

Two innings later, High again goosed a little hit into left field. When Watkins batted, High would recall, he believed the A's thought Street was having Watty sacrifice. Instead, he hit the first pitch onto the pavilion roof. Earnshaw didn't allow another base runner, but it was too late. Grimes carried a five-hit shutout into the ninth.

Beforehand, bullpen coach Mike Gonzalez moseyed up the home dugout, ostensibly for a drink of water, but he recalled, he wanted to see the eyes of the 38-year-old pitcher. They were weak and glassy and, in fact, Lord Burleigh was headed for an early appendectomy. In Gonzalez's fractured English, Mike told "Moong"—his pronunciation for the "Moon" that was the round-faced Hallahan's nickname—to get ready. "There's no tomorrow, Moong," said Gonzalez, who had Hallahan limbering when Grimes weakened. He walked one nemesis, Simmons, but got another, Foxx, to pop out and dangerous Bing Miller forced Simmons. Only one to go, but Jimmy Dykes walked and Dib Williams bounced a single over High's head, filling the bases. Rookie pinch-hitter Roger (Doc) Cramer followed with a two-run single. Gabby came out slowly, removed Grimes and brought in Hallahan to face Bishop, who he'd retired for the last out in the second game. "Moong" got a pitch fat into the strike zone. Bishop hit it sharply to center field in the October dusk to fast-charging Martin, who juggled the ball and then held it aloft to secure the 4-2 championship victory.

Martin was the biggest hero of the Series, even though he hadn't hit the last two games. He batted .500 on 12 hits, including four doubles and a walk, and scored five runs, stole five bases and drove in five runs. In the Cardinal clubhouse, commissioner Landis came in and threw his arms around the grinning Wild Horse. "Young man," he said, "I'd rather trade places with you than anybody else."

Pepper laughed. "That's fine, Judge," he said, "'long as we can change salaries," aware it was $60,000 against $4500. Still, with more than $4000 Series money, Pepper had a chance on the dying vaudeville circuit, signing for a traveling $1500-a-week personal appearances for nine weeks. But he tossed away $7500, explaining in Louisville: "Hell, I ain't no actor. I'm a ball player cheatin' the public and the guy who's paying me. 'Sides, the huntin' season is on in Oklahoma—and that's more important."

More important was 1932, the season of a world champion's greatest flop, and Pepper was part of it, going from his high to career low, a .238 average marred by injuries, but in the dip from first to a tie for sixth—a drop of 26 games—it was, beg the sarcasm, a team effort. The front office was involved. The manager, too. The fatheaded leftover talent and the pivotal player, captain Frank Frisch.

Frisch played the 1931 World Series with grit, a result of painful lumbago that doubled him up in the rainout before game three at Philadelphia. As Pulitzer Prize winner Red Smith noted, trainer Doc Weaver taped the second baseman like a mummy. Handicapped, Frisch had seven hits, including two doubles, a stolen base and 42 fielding chances that helped turn five double plays.

After the Series victory at a private victory party, architect Rickey sat silently, wondering what the Cardinals would do with a replacement for Frisch. Frisch, meanwhile, hurried to San Francisco with three other future Hall of Famers of the A's, Lefty Grove, Al Simmons and Mickey Cochrane. A Japenese liner awaited them with their wives and other All-Stars like Lou Gehrig, Lefty O'Doul and Rabbit Maranville for a trip to Japan, where they creamed college-age competition.

When the rest returned to the States,

Frankie took advantage of diminishing prices for a six-week round-the-world ship trip with dear wife Ada. His only exercise was playing catch with the crew. And as both a gourmand and gourmet, he didn't miss many of the liner's favorite distraction and attraction—food. So Frisch was as fat physically and as soft in the legs as teammates were in their heads at Bradenton, Fla., where they partied at the beaches.

Manager Street, to whom and for whom they had pulled hard, suddenly believed his press clippings. Now, he would call the shots. The shots weren't too easy to call, however, because Breadon and Rickey had lost Chick Hafey and Burleigh Grimes. Always tough to sign, Burleigh was vying for top salary with Frisch, who hadn't been too happy, either, at a cut to $20,000. So Rickey dealt Grimes to the Cubs for left-hander Bud Teachout and one of baseball's biggest names, Hack Wilson. Just two seasons previously the stocky slugger had hit the most National League home runs, 56, and an RBI record, 190, that offensively still impressed players more than any other record. He had slumped in 1931, but the right-handed-hitting outfielder always had hit well with Sportsman's Park short right-center. Chances are, Mr. Rickey didn't expect to keep Wilson as king of the busthead alcoholics, but the deal curbed discontent with dismissal of Grimes. The truth came out when Rickey sent Wilson a belated contract offer, a cut from $31,000 to $7500. Responded Hack, "Hell, Mr. Rickey, that ain't a cut, it's an amputation."

So, with Rickey's hand quicker than the eye, like the old pea-under-the-pod game, Wilson was gone to Brooklyn and the Cardinals were $45,000 richer. Besides, maybe they could sign Hafey. Not when the batting champion wanted not only the $15,000 they had denied him the previous year, but also return of the $2100 they had trimmed off the top. For an instant when they invited him to Florida, the Calistoga chicken-farmer thought he had deal. When he didn't, he drove his handsome 1929 Auburn across Arizona's ribbon roads at 90 miles an hour, back to California. Opening day, 1932, they traded Hafey to Cincinnati, the Siberia of National League, for a couple of warm bodies and undetermined cold cash.

With John McGraw reported ready to end 20 years as Giants' manager and rumors persisting that McGraw wanted back favorite son Frisch with whom he'd kissed and made up, the Flash couldn't have been too happy when boss Breadon squelched the rumors. Forty games into the 1932 season, Mr. McGraw had seen enough—with good reason. At St. Louis, that magnificent Redbird rookie Dizzy Dean, who would win 18 games for a losing team, popped a bunt over a charging New York third baseman's head. Dizzy legged it out for second and when the left fielder's return throw was high, he hurried to third and, taking advantage of the right fielder's errant peg to third, he hurried across the plate. In effect, a "home run" on a bunt!

Back in New York, McGraw resigned. The job went to his great first baseman, Bill Terry, who brought the last-place team home sixth, tied with the Cardinals. In the off-season, Terry sat down as Rickey's counterpart and worked for a four-for-two deal with the Cardinals, seeking catcher Gus Mancuso. Recalled Terry, "I always delighted in talking with Mr. Rickey, a genius, and proved I beat him a couple of times. I wanted Mancuso to catch my low-ball pitchers (Carl Hubbell's screwball, Hal Schumacher's sinker and Fred Fitzsimmons' knuckler.)

The 1933 Giants won the world championship, the Cardinals improved only to fifth so Terry did outpoint Rickey. One of B.R.'s acquisitions, fashionable East St. Louis left-hander, Bill Walker, would help. Another, Ethan Allen, figured in an incident amusing to all except Joe Medwick.

TWO SMART DUMMIES: "Smart dummy" was the highest accolade of Mike Gonzalez (right) in the Cuban's cracked-ice English compliment. His pal, Clyde (Buzzy) Wares coached even longer than Gonzalez for the Cardinals, 1930-1952. Wares, first-base coach, made sure that few balls were apprehended by the players.

Money Man:
Fast-firing Bill Hallahan, with a jagged overhand curve, was a lefthander troubled too often by wildness, but he harnessed himself in big games, including three World Series in which he won three of four games and allowed only four earned runs in 39 innings. Wild Bill, a gentle man, had one other honor. He was the favorite player of long-time clubhouse equipment manager Morris (Butch) Yatkeman.

Muscles Medwick—Ducky Wucky—waddled up from Houston late in the 1932 season, proving that Rickey's farm system did deliver, just as did Dean. Jersey Joe hit .349, launching a 17-year career as a hit-hungry player, one who didn't appreciate a gaffe by Allen. At the Polo Grounds in the single season in which he batted .300 for the Cardinals, handsome Allen hit a home run, but he batted out of turn. So the proper hitter was out, meaning Medwick, and Allen, batting over, popped out and hit no other homer that '33 season. Truth is, if Medwick hadn't been restrained, Allen would have gone earlier to inventing a popular scientific baseball board game and coaching Yale University.

Maybe Street would have liked to choke Frisch, too, after the .292 season of 1932 in which the captain didn't play up to his performance. Fact is, Sid Keener wrote a column accusing the Flash of "laying down" on Gabby. When Roy Stockton mentioned the story to Frisch on the road, Frank took the sports writer up to his room and exposed two taped thighs. "I'm not in the shape I should have been, but I'm hurt now," he said, "so I can't run out every play, but, dammit, Roy, on one leg I'm better than Jimmy Reese on two. I don't want the old buzzard's job, but if I ever manage, you can bet I'll keep the press involved when I used a player under par." He did.

Street angrily had wanted Breadon and Rickey to fine the player $5000 but they refused. Instead, with Bottomley aging and Rip Collins hitting hard, they dealt Sunny Jim to Rickey's favorite pawnshop, Cincinnati. The 1933 Cardinals didn't parallel their second-division kissing cousins of '32, meaning the pennant-bound Giants. Breadon didn't like that. He didn't think Street could control the club any longer. Others thought Gabby was trying too hard to impress his expertise on resentful veterans who had helped him.

Shortly after the first All-Star game in July at Chicago's Comiskey Park, the owner picked up the manager's modest tab, $7500. For the first All-Star game, national vote of fans picked four Redbirds—Frisch, Martin, Wilson and Hallahan. Wild Bill got the start from John McGraw, acting manager for the Nationals because the Giants' Terry had asked the old boss not to start Carl Hubbell. Just a couple of days earlier as part of a historic doubleheader, Hubbell had shut out the Cardinals for 18 innings, 1-0. The Giants won the second game by the same score, Roy Parmelee beating Dizzy Dean. In the All-Star game, won by the American League, 4-2, Hallahan was touched for a decisive two-run homer by Babe Ruth. For the Nationals—to Breadon's joy—Frisch singled and also homered left-handed off Washington's Alvin Crowder.

Player-managers were the vogue. Fact is, a year later when Charley Dressen replaced Bob O'Farrell, all field foreman were players. The Cardinals' was Frisch, who was 10 games over .500 the last third of the '33 season, but still only fifth. Taking over, presumably avoiding a further cut in a salary that had dwindled from $28,000 to $18,500 with the depths of the Depression, Frisch had a message. "I'm not going to worry too much what the players do off the field, but I want nine Pepper Martins on the field—all to play with Pepper's all-out hustle!"

With Martin himself having emulated the way he'd seen Frisch play, this was the rough, aggressive attitude that turned the Cardinals into the Gas House Gang, a state of mind as well as a colorful ball club of whom Frisch later would say, "They managed themselves—if you know what I mean!"

Frisch's hiring created a sticky-wicket, as the British would say. One of the men Frank handled just so briefly was his old rival and the man for whom he had been traded, Rogers Hornsby. The Rajah had been rehired as an out-of-work aging superstar, cut loose by the Cubs as manager in late 1932 because he'd borrowed from his players to pay off race track bets. When the Cubs rallied to win the pennant for Charley Grimm, they didn't give a World Series share to the man who had managed them two-thirds of the season.

With the Cardinals having lost young shortstop Charley Gelbert to an accidental gunshot wound to a leg suffered when hunting, management briefly toyed with the idea of Frisch moving to shortstop, Hornsby playing second base. That was a horrible experiment. Frisch didn't have a shortstop's sure hands and wasn't as effective moving to his left as to the right. Hornsby always did play tight to second so that he could cut directly to the bag in a double-play situation and fire abruptly across his uniform letters. Frisch, with his rare humor, would reflect, "So with my shading to my left and Rog to his right, we looked like a couple of conventioneers camping around second base."

So Hornsby had become a pinch-hitter par excellence as Rickey gave up promising Paul Derringer for famed good-field, no-hit Cincinnati shortstop, Leo Durocher, brassy but brilliant. Unflappable, Durocher stormed into Rickey's office — Leo called him "Branch" when even lovely Jane Rickey called him "Mr. Rickey" in public — but The Lip wasn't about to shake more than his $6000 out of his contract. Rickey, adroitly, then took advantage of the recent death of Browns' owner Phil Ball to convince Brownie front-office stewardship that Hornsby was just the big-name choice as their player-manager, in July 1933. So the awkward Frisch-over-Hornsby situation was avoided.

Durocher added more bluster to the luster of the Gas House Gang he helped create with a comment to a New York writer. Leo, a slick Springfield (Mass.) pool shark, became the mentor of the swaggering young left fielder, Joe Medwick. Medwick was almost as mean as his big black bat, a great bad ball hitter. The first baseman, grinning, banjo-eyed James (Rip) Collins was a pixy who set the scene for many of the acts of mischief perpetrated by Dizzy Dean and Pepper Martin. The Ripper, one of three switch-hitters at a time few turned around at bat, had his career season in 1934 when he hit .333, led the league with 35 homers and drove in 122 runs. The only thing he lost was a clubhouse scuffle to Medwick when Frisch, weary of his Joey's skirmishes, let Collins and Medwick have at it until they tired.

Movie-struck Ernie Orsatti, whose brother was a Hollywood agent, was fast-on-his-feet center field. He liked to circumvent Frisch's occasional bed checks, tipping a hotel operator to direct calls to Orsatti in the supper club at midnight. The right

FEROCIOUS GENTLEMEN: To use Branch Rickey's substitute expression for the Gas House Gang, of which Leo Durocher (right) and Joe Medwick were chief proponents. Shortstop Durocher led the league in arguments, Medwick in hitting and fights, sometimes with teammates. Clotheshorse Lippy Leo also was Medwick's haberdashery mentor.

Happy Hunting: Pepper Martin receives two new shotguns as part of a day in his honor in 1939. The Wild Horse of the Osage, Irish with a little Indian thrown in, loved to hunt in Oklahoma and wherever the deer cavorted and the bobwhite flew.

fielder, Jack Rothrock, a switcher capable of hitting behind the runner, was Frisch's notion of a professional. The first-string catcher originally was Virgil (Spud) Davis, reacquired from Philadelphia when the Phillies wanted Jimmy Wilson as player-manager. Rickey had a notion Spud, better offensively than defensively, might need a replacement. At spring training, thinking aloud to Cardinal publicist Gene Karst, B. R. thought he'd like to deal an over-the-hill Frisch to Boston for catcher Al Spohrer. "But Frank is Sam's boy," said Rickey, meaning Breadon's. The deal wasn't made and Spohrer lasted only another year in the majors, while Frisch, the old money player, led his ball club into his eighth World Series.

A deal for Spohrer well might have muddied once of the most delightful developments of 1934. Brought up from Columbus with Dizzy Dean's younger brother, Paul, was a knock-kneed left-handed-hitting catcher, Bill DeLancey. Although tuberculosis after his second season would ruin DeLancey's career, the 22-year-old catcher became so good at the plate and behind it that he won high honors. In Rickey's lifetime summary in a book brought out just behind his death, the old master had Frisch among the best players he had seen, as well as DeLancey.

Frisch, showing early appreciation in DeLancey, constantly admonished the kid about laying off change-up pitches. Frank later would recall that when DeLancey timed a let-up at Cincinnati and hit a home run, he returned to the bench and, taking a swig of water, mumbled, "I wonder how the old Dutch buzzard liked that one." Enough, of course, to catch DeLancey more often and every game of the World Series. Dizzy Dean liked the fresh young kid even though DeLancey would stalk to the mound and thunder, "Listen, Big Shot, when I'm catching, don't horse around on me."

DeLancey would hit .315 with 15 homers in just 93 games, and the other rookie, Columbus batterymate Paul Dean, 21 was highly effective, too. Frisch stayed with him one early knockout after another, needing another starting pitcher and aware of the box office potential in which, of course, Mrs. Breadon and Rickey were interested. Finally, with Frisch helping at bat, P. Dean beat Hubbell in 10 innings, 3-2. He was off and running to 19 victories.

The biggest character, of course, teaming with Pepper Martin, was the lean, lanky guy who, at only 23, called himself "Old Diz". Dizzy Dean, aptly nicknamed by an Army Sergeant when he briefly did peacetime duty in the military, lived up to Gabby Street's evaluation of him. He cut up hitters on the mound and cut up off it. Dizzy's ability to throw a baseball exceptionally hard, with vastly improved control, was helped by a good curve and great letup.

Before the 1934 season for which his pay was $7500, the third-year man predicted that if they would give the Deans the ball often enough "Me 'n Paul will win 45 games." When Dizzy won 30 in a Most Valuable Player performance, plus two each with brother Paul in the World Series, the total was 49. "After all," he said, "when you're good enough to do what you're saying you're going to do—and then some—heck, that ain't bragging."

With Pepper, Dizzy would do the darndest things. The summer of 1934 was second only to '36 for summer-long heat in St. Louis, but especially with Ladies Day encouragement, Ol' Diz and the Wild Horse would pitch a small fire outside the dugout and, sitting like Indians on their haunches, drape a blanket over their shoulders. Lamented former opposing catcher Al Lopez, "You'd come in there cool from Boston and they'd psyche you out!" They would put on quite a show.

Great, yes, but not too many people saw what would be a team of destiny. Why? Chances are the Depression and the fact that they still had two teams in what was obviously big enough for only one. In addition, Sam Breadon permitted himself to accept the consensus that providing ball games on radio was like giving away the product. New York, for instance, had a four-year blackout until Larry MacPhail, the man who got the night-ball recognition that might have been Breadon's, broke down the barrier at Brooklyn in 1938. When Breadon and the Browns agreed to no radio reporting of games in '34, one of Sam's Scotch-sipping partners, Thomas Patrick Convey of KWK, decided to pirate the games. He would post a ladder atop the North Side "Y" across the street in center field and use binoculars. Breadon threatened a lawsuit. "Thomas Patrick," as Convey shortened it for radio, didn't live to see the results. He died of emergency surgery that summer.

Strangely, the Cardinals came together without the brothers Dean. At a time Dizzy was grouching that Paul was getting only $3000, same as catcher DeLancey, the Deans conveniently skipped an August exhibition at Detroit. Once before Dizzy had pulled that one on Gabby Street, but escaped a $100 fine only by pitching a shutout. "Nobody is bigger than this game, nobody," insisted Frisch in a clubhouse meeting.

Back in St. Louis, Dizzy tore up his uniform and, obliging a photographer who had missed it, he tore up another. Young treasurer Bill DeWitt presented him a bill for twice $18.75, the cost of the flannels then.

At a time player limits had been reduced from 25 to 23 for economy purposes, the Cardinals had only 21 players and two of them were pitching greybeards, old Brooklyn star Dazzy Vance at 43 and redoubtable Redbird Jesse (Pop) Haines, 41. They were members of a pitching staff that numbered eight with the Deans, but lefty Bill Walker just had returned from a broken wrist. Walker helped. Bill Hallahan came out of a slump. Tex Carleton pitched well. With Pepper hurt, Frisch moved to third base and played Burgess Whitehead at second. They won eight out of nine before the Deans were reinstated, only after the commissioner, Judge Landis, came to St. Louis to make certain the athletes hadn't been mistreated.

The characters had character. Even though they lost a Labor Day doubleheader at Pittsburgh and trailed New York's world champions by seven games, they were coming. At the Polo Grounds, five and a half down with 14 to play, they won two before 50,000 in a doubleheader. Frisch singled home the winning runs in the first game, 5-3, and Pepper Martin's eleventh-inning homer gave Paul Dean, in relief, his second extra-inning victory of the series, 3-1.

Given permission to play a make-up doubleheader at Brooklyn, the Cardinals were great and the Deans even better. Dizzy pitched the opener, held the Dodgers hitless until the eighth, then won a three-hit 11-0 laugher. Paul followed with a 3-0 no-hitter. Ol' Diz was apologetic. "Gee whiz, if I'd-a known Paul was goin' do it, I'd a throwed one, too" With Me 'n Paul working in and out of turn, the Cardinals got into the final week trailing the Giants by two games.

With four games left to play, Terry's Gi-

DEE-LIGHTFUL: Bill DeLancey, "Dee" to his teammates, was so great in a career cut short to two years by tuberculosis that Branch Rickey listed the Gas House Gang rookie as one of the three best catchers, all-around, in his written memoirs.

ants lost twice to the Phils. Their showdown was with the Dodgers of whom Bill facetiously had wondered the previous winter if they "still were in the National League." From Flatbush to Greenpoint, toting appropriate nasty signboards or catcalls to Terry, they crossed the Brooklyn Bridge.

In the Saturday semi-windup big Van Lingle Mungo beat the great Carl Hubbell, 5-1. In St. Louis, putting the Cardinals in first place, Paul Dean beat Cincinnati, 5-1.

The final day, the eastern time zone final score of Brooklyn 8, New York 5 prompted whistles to whistle, and horns to honk even before Dizzy Dean shut out the Reds, 9-0. Afterward, Ripper Collins led an appropriate hit song of the day—"We're in the Money"—and while many more of the approximate 100,000 that had seen the last week wished more than 334,866 had seen the Gas House Gang's season, the Redbirds made merry downtown at Jim Mertikas's old Grecian Gardens, an area that now houses Busch Stadium.

Heck, who could fear the G-men managed by catcher Mickey Cochrane, Detroit's Charley Gehringer, Hank Greenberg, Goose Goslin and Gee Walker? At an open date workout at Detroit's Navin Field, Dizzy stepped up to the plate in street clothes, borrowed Greenberg's bat and hit one into the towering left field seats.

With the Ford Motor Company having bought the first World Series radio rights, Diz's friend, Will Rogers, the cowboy actor-humorist-columnist, took him out to elderly Henry Ford's for breakfast, urging the pitcher to address the pioneer master as "Mr. Ford." When the old man greeted him, Dizzy breezed, "Put 'er there, Henry. I'm sure glad to be here 'cause I heard so much about you, but I'm sorry, podnuh, I'm a-gonna have to make pussycats out of your Tigers."

He did in the opener, 8-3. Next day Frisch was raving mad as misplays behind Bill Walker in relief lost, 3-2, a game Hallahan had won. The Flash cautiously had saved rookie Paul Dean for a home crowd and Paul won 4-1. So the Series was tied when the Tigers teed off on Tex Carleton and associates, 10-4. That game was famous for Dizzy's injury as a pinch-runner.

Trying to break up a double-play ball, he went in straight up. Shortstop Bill Rogell, undaunted, low-bridged Dean by conking him in the forehead. Dizzy was carried off, to a hushed crowd, but Paul was sure he was all right. Dizzy had been talking. Saying what? The press wondered. "Nuthin', just talkin'." Hospitalized overnight, Dizzy crawled out from under the bed sheets to pitch well in the fifth game, but he lost a 3-1 duel to curve ball king Tommy Bridges. So now they went back into the other court, down three games to two, in a series that had been rough and ready.

Before the Series opener, they had heard Schoolboy Rowe, winner of a record-tying 16 straight, ask his fiancee in Arkansas, "How 'em I doin', Edna." The Redbird bench jockeys never let Schoolie hear the end of it. Or catcher Cochrane, who had gone to the hospital for repairs after a collision with Martin. A photograph that listed Black Mike as "Our Stricken Leader" brought out the beast and best in the jockeys. And there was a tit for tatter when aggressive Detroit leadoff man JoJo White bowled over the aging Frisch at second

High Hopes: The brothers Dean, Paul and Dizzy, were under fire even before Paul won his first game in his rookie season, 1934.

base. Durocher suggested that next time he ought to cover second. "No, no, next time" said Frisch brightly, "we'll both cover." They did. Frisch plopped heavily on White's head and Lippy Leo sat on JoJo's chest. Durocher rose to the occasion for the sixth game.

Leo, that is, and Paul Dean. Durocher got three hits and P. Dean pitched well and drove in the deciding run in a Series-evening 4-3 victory. Frisch, collared by the press, said his seventh-game pitcher would be Hallahan, a big-game warrior.

Privately, Durocher protested. When Frisch went into the shower, Dizzy followed him, protesting, too. Finally, the manager told him, "You're starting, Jerome, but I just wanted to see how much you wanted it, enough not to sit up all night with Will Rogers, telling or listening to stories. Win this one and it could be worth $50,000 or more in commercials and other things to you and Paul."

Before the seventh game, jacket over his shoulder, Dizzy passed behind the dugout area where Elden Auker, fourth-game winner, was warming up with his unique underhanded delivery. Until Cochrane angrily shooed him away, Dizzy said sarcastically, "You don't expect to get anyone out with that (bleep), do you?"

With one out in the scoreless third, Dizzy drilled a base hit to left and, legging hard and surprising Goslin, he stretched the single into a double. So when Martin bounced far to Greenberg's right at first base, Hank had no chance for an easy force-out at second and peppery Pepper beat Greenberg's throw to Auker at first. So it was first and third, one out, rather than first only with two down. Surprisingly, Martin stole second. With Rothrock hitting better than the aging Frisch, Auker walked the right fielder to fill the bases. Now, the weary 38-year-old manager came up, determined not to be punched out on strikes or to hit into the middle of the infield for a double play that would keep Medwick from having a chance.

Behind him, Frisch had 57 Series hits, still a record for National League players. Now he wanted his biggest hit and, repeatedly fouling off full-count pitches, he hit one over Greenberg's head into the right-field corner. Galloping with his triumphant prance, he watched Dean score along with Martin and Rothrock. When he paused at second, as Cochrane changed pitchers, he sat down on trembling old legs. It led to a "7" on the scoreboard that inning, the blow that broke up an 11-0 game, featured only thereafter by Detroit fans angrily throwing lunches and other debris at Medwick after Joe had a seventh-inning kick-in with Marv Owen when sliding into third base.

Seeking a release, they bombarded Medwick, hands on hips, warily out of reach. Joining him in left field, Durocher urged him to stand fast. Snapped Joe, "If you're so brave, you play left field and I'll play shortstop." Aware of the Cardinals'

SONS OF THE SOUTHWEST: Dizzy Dean sought out Will Rogers before the 1934 World Series opener. Rogers, former cowboy with the same twang of the Oklahoma territory, was a humorist, actor, columnist and No. 1 in movie box office at his death in '35.

Duck Diz: Dizzy Dean dropping, skulled by Tiger shortstop Bill Rogell's throw when breaking up a double play in the 1934 World Series. Rogell and second baseman Charley Gehringer watch the impact of the beanball episode.

lead, reluctant and unwilling to declare a Series forfeit, Judge Landis ordered Medwick removed, to the player's displeasure and Frisch's.

Afterward, the brothers Dean headed in one direction of barnstorming and other goodies lined up for them by Bill DeWitt as temporary agent. The happy Cardinals, meanwhile, caught a midnight train to St. Louis with Medwick given special attention by a couple of Detroit detectives who ate dinner with him in his hotel room.

Jersey Joe was hot in 1935, too, hitting .353 with 23 homers and 122 RBIs. With a rapid-running, rookie fly-chaser Terry Moore having a strong season at bat and center field, the '35 Cardinals were, yes, a game better than in '34—a better team. The brothers Dean won 47—Dizzy 28, Paul 19 again—and Hallahan was better and Walker good enough. They were a bit short because Tex Carleton had been dealt to the Cubs (Tex didn't like Diz and maybe the vice was versa.) Replacement "Fidgety Phil" Collins, obtained from the Phillies, wasn't more fidgety than helpful. Still, it looked as if the Cardinals might overcome their Russian roulette stockpiling of strong-contending Chicago. Presumably with too much talent, Rickey had sold the Cubs big Bill Lee and batterymate Ken O'Dea. O'Dea caddied Gabby Hartnett, and Lee matched Lon Warneke's 20-game season.

On the Fourth of July at Wrigley Field, the Cardinals lived up to their glamorous nickname. The won a 12-inning opener when Martin knocked over O'Dea in a collision at the plate and when the ball rolled free, Orsatti, following Pepper, knocked over Warneke, covering home on a throw from O'Dea. The Cards won the second game, too. Remarkably, Jolly Cholly Grimm's guys lost only five of 48 remaining home games—fact is, just 54 all season—and the last loss came in the second game of a Labor Day doubleheader, the same day Frisch's Cards won two from Pittsburgh at Sportsman's Park. They were two up over Terry's Giants, whom they had caught earlier this time, and two and a half in front of Chicago—five on the defeat side. And the rest on the month with home cooking. If a leading ball club wins 19 of its last 30, that should be good enough, but not if the club behind them wins 21 games in a row. That's what the Cubs did, led by Hall of Fame catcher Hartnett's .344 and Billy Herman's .341.

Herman was the league's best second baseman, replacing Frisch, for whom he'd filled in at the 1934 All-Star game in New York after Frisch bowed out that day with a homer, a single and that convenient aching back. The back didn't ache in 1935, but a jagged spike wound on a tag kept Frisch and barking dogs out of the lineup. Whitehead filled in much of the time as the Redbirds used the franchise's longest winning streak, 14 games, to take the lead.

Frisch, decidedly a better hitter than Whitey, was in the lineup in September, a month in which as the oldest player, 38, he and the youngest Moore, 23, were the hottest. Moore, a .500 hitter down the stretch, suffered a blow to himself and the ball club when he suffered a broken leg. Replacing him, Orsatti misjudged a fly that cost a precious game.

By the time the Cubs came to town for the season's last five games, they had won 18 in a row and owned the lead. The Cards, who had won 11 of 16 from Chicago, needed four of five. In the first game, 18-year-old-rookie Cubs' first baseman Phil Cavarretta, broke up a scoreless duel between Paul Dean and Warneke, hitting a late-inning homer, 1-0. Next day old pro Frisch, a .400 hitter the final month, gave Dizzy

Dean an early lead over Bill Lee, but, led by Fred Lindstrom's four hits, the Cubs won the game 6-2, and the pennant.

Second place like second base was a pain in the posterior and a problem. With the pennant decided with three games to go, Frisch played a Class "C" whiz in his place. Lyle Judy had stolen more than 100 bases at Springfield, Mo. They never would learn whether Judy could steal first base. He was severely injured in an off-season accident. Meanwhile, Rickey traded the graceful Whitehead to the Giants for a pitcher, Roy Parmelee and, of course, cash. Whitehead, playing virtually every game for the Giants for two years, shored up a weakness when helping to win two pennants before he collapsed in a nervous breakdown.

With the Cardinals, a fleet 1936 replacement, pencil-thin Stuart Martin, handicapped by an early indiscretionary ailment, played more than a fading Frisch. Stu was an answer, but not necessarily the right one. Frisch, hitting his final career homer after a damaging error, won the second game of the season for Paul Dean, 3-2. The younger Dean—never "Daffy" as the pressbox poets liked to put it—won five straight games before something popped. He never was the same.

Years later, reminiscing, P. Dean noted that he had held out all spring for a $1000 raise to $8500. Signing late, heavy-legged despite a slender build, he suffered shin splints and tried for proper conditioning despite one-day exhibition railroad stops. "I wasn't really ready," he said, "but I don't blame Dutch (Frisch)." At only 23 when it really should have been beginning for Paul Dean, it was over. For brilliant batterymate Bill DeLancey, too, sidelined by tuberculosis that took his life several years later.

Surprisingly, the old Gang hung in the title fight a long time even though pitching was short, skimpy except for workhorse Dizzy Dean, who led the league in games pitched (51) and innings (315) and second only to New York's amazing Carl (26-6) Hubbell with his 24 victories. At bat, Medwick, .351 with 18 homers and league-leading 138 RBIs, had a new partner, Johnny Mize, who took over at first base as Rip Collins faltered. Mize wore the birds-and-bat uniform only because Cincinnati had turned him back as damaged goods, i.e., a painful groin spur, but the skill of Dr. Robert F. Hyland brought him around. The ponderous left-handed hitter hit .329 with 19 homers, 93 RBIs and happier cleanup days ahead.

After leading most of the way from early May to late August, the 1936 Cardinals, their victory total reduced from 95 to 87, backed down embarrassingly into a second-place tie the final two games of the season at home. They lost Saturday and then Dizzy Dean was beaten by Lon Warneke in the finale 6-3. The game had an interesting postscript. With Collins hurt and Mize thrown out of the game, late-inning first base was filled by Walter Alston. He had one time at bat and struck out. And he fielded .500 the hard way, muffing one of two chances. The future Hall of Fame manager of the Dodgers never played in another big-league game.

Even though the Cardinals had the top two hitters in the league—Triple Crown Joe Medwick with .374-31-154 and Mize close by with .364-25-113—they could finish no higher than fourth in 1937. Rickey had tried to shore up pitching, acquiring Warneke from the Cubs for Rip Collins, and the Arkansas Hummingbird won 18 games. Lefty Bob Weiland won 15, and Silas Johnson – not Syl – struggled with 12. But, podnuh, when you ain't got a Dizzy Dean "a-

SOUR GRAPES: Down 10-0 in the seventh game of the 1934 World Series, fans in the towering single-deck bleachers of Detroit's Navin Field showered left fielder Joe Medwick with debris after a baseline brush. Ultimately, Medwick (7) retreated before commissioner K.M. Landis ordered him removed for safety's sake. Others (from the left) are Pepper Martin, 1; Leo Durocher, 2, playfully throwing back leftover lunches; Dizzy Dean, semi-obscured; Rip Collins, 12, and player-manager Frank Frisch, 3. The Cards won 11-0.

Artist's View: Talented New York cartoonist Willard Mullin, who later labeled the 1942 Cardinals as the St. Louis Swifties, put gifted art crayon in hand in the mid-1930s to assist Dizzy Dean in a "strike" against Sam Breadon. The Yankees' Lou Gehrig just had been given a $750 bonus.

woofin'" you ain't got nuthin'.

Dizzy wouldn't sign "nuthin'" either, after umpire George Barr called a balk on him and Dizzy popped off that the ump and National League president Ford Frick were the "two biggest crooks in baseball." Frick suspended him, pending an apology that didn't come. So Dizzy was an overworked 12-and-7 at the All-Star break when he decided to skip the game at Washington. Even wife Pat, who could be hardnosed, too, told him he was wrong. At a time few used planes, Cardinals' president Sam Breadon flew the six hours with him to D.C.

Showing off, following three perfect innings the year before, he was one strike away from another scoreless stint. Lou Gehrig, hitting a home run he regarded as one of the most significant of his career, kept Ol' Diz on the mound one batter too long. Cleveland's Earl Averill, who had a reputation for hot shots through the box, lined a single off the big toe of Dean's planted left foot.

Painfully hurt, Dizzy was put into a splint by Dr. Hyland, who cautioned him not to pitch too soon. But for a guy who ducked an exhibition at the drop a railroad schedule—he preferred trains to planes—Dean was a professional highly competitive and a team man. His field foreman, Frisch, needed his meal ticket. Warming up with a limp at Boston, where Braves' manager Bill McKechnie saw him favoring the injured foot, McKechnie warned Dizzy that he would hurt his arm. Late in a tight game, he felt something pop in his shoulder. So Dizzy won only one more game in four decisions the rest of the season and he won only 25 more, roughly one season's work, in six calendar years.

Just before the Saturday spring city series opener with the Browns in 1938, Rickey dropped the bombshell. He had dealt Dizzy Dean to the Cubs for pitchers Curt Davis and Clyde Shoun, outfielder Tuck Stainback and $185,000 of the sportsman Wrigley's gum profits. With honesty, Rickey had let the Cubs know that Dizzy was damaged goods, caveat emptor. So Phil Wrigley didn't get much except seven critical victories against one defeat by a softserving cunning Dean in a pennant-winning season. And as Wrigley would ruminate later, "No regrets because having Dizzy Dean around was like traveling with a circus."

At the Chamber of Commerce's leadoff luncheon the day before the season opened, Rickey intoned that "except for pitching, this is probably the best ball club the Cardinals ever had." The comment prompted Terry Moore to lean over to the player next to him and comment, "Oh, oh, I don't think the Flash is going to last long."

Frisch ended up lasting until late in the sixth-place 71-80 season in which Mize and Medwick again starred, a frisky kid named Mickey Owen became the regular catcher and a career right fielder, Enos Slaughter broke in. Near tears with a couple of weeks to go, the club owner called in Frisch for an official good-bye to his favorite player and former manager. Frisch, misty-eyed, said, "Don't feel bad, Mr. Breadon."

For a successor, Rickey prevailed over Breadon. Sam opted for Branch's old "Sunday manager," Burt Shotton, who had a later date with destiny in Brooklyn. B. R. wanted and got Francis Raymond Blades—Ray Blades, a home area kid who had impressed him as far back as 1913. Rickey umpired a championship Post-Dispatch grade school game. Blades, a fiery little guy, caught B.R.'s attention and held it. Blades, who might have been a star if he hadn't damaged a knee in a collision with the left field wall, underwent helpful surgery from Dr. Hyland, but became a part-time player with a .301 career average. He was smart, observant, Rickey's kind of guy, and had been successful at Rochester and Columbus.

At 43, Blades would have only a short-lived managerial career in the majors, but as noted by oldsters still alive close to the Twenty-First Century, he brought to the game the first emphasis on heavy use of the bullpen, a stepping stone to the era of the "closer" and the "save" statistic. For instance, willowy, pale-faced Curt (Coonskin) Davis, who won 22 games, finished only 13, yet wound up as the last pitcher in 19 games, officially saving seven. Davis, 2-and-5 in relief, also hit .381. If Davis wasn't Most Valuable, he most certainly was close to it.

So was fast-firing Clyde (Hard Rock) Shoun, also obtained by Rickey in the Dean deal. The heavy-duty southpaw appeared in a record 53 games. Other young pitchers, right-handers Bob Bowman and Mort Cooper, helped in Blades' medley relay of pitchers, but the Cardinals didn't have the book-end-anchored staff of old friend Bill McKechnie at Cincinnati. Deacon Will's aces were 20-game winners Bucky Walters and former Redbird Paul Derringer.

To stave off the Cardinals, the Reds had to be good because the Cardinals hit a robust .294 as a team, including batting champion Mize at .349 with Medwick at .331, cranky that Breadon had cut his salary by $2000 and unhappy that Blades now and then would replace him in the late innings with defensive outfielder Lynn King. Don Padgett, an outfielder trying to catch, hit .399 in 92 games. Others who hit .300 or close to it included Pepper Martin, Jimmy Brown and Terry Moore.

And there was one more, the second-season outfielder Shotton had nicknamed "Country" at Columbus—Enos Slaughter. At 22, Slaughter had a robust .320 season—and the Cardinals didn't have to worry about right field for a long time.

Despite the climb from sixth place to close contention—second place—the 1939 Cardinals drew only 410,778, considerably more than 295,229 in Frisch's last year, but less than they did in 1937. The strong surge to 92 victories made the Cardinals preseason favorites for 1940. They got off poorly. Blades' unorthodox multiple use of pitchers boomeranged. By Memorial Day, a memorable day in Breadon's handling of managers, Rickey came out and gave Blades a vote of confidence. Trouble was, the long-awaited first night game came for Breadon, who had fought to be first, and followed the rival Browns' prior rights as property owners. The lowly Browns played a grand game, lost to Bob Feller on Feller's home run 3-2. The Cardinals, playing Brooklyn, where old friend Leo Durocher had become a rival, gave up five runs in the first inning, en route to a 10-1 rout.

The fans booed that one even more than the deal Rickey had rigged with the Dodgers, sending Medwick and Davis for culls and cash. The $100,000 came with three

MEAL TICKET: Frisco honored '34 Cards with private rail menu.

KERPLOP: Stanley (Frenchy) Bordagaray (center) gives it the Pepper Martin bellyflop in spring training, 1938, with jacketed Joe Medwick sliding at the left and Enos Slaughter at the right.

players, one of whom, former football star Ernie Koy, actually out-hit Medwick that year. Jersey Joe had lost favor with personal petulance, and Blades had lost patience with the man who counted most—Breadon. Without telling Rickey, Breadon flew to Rochester after the night-game nightmare and the boss talked with and hired Southworth, the man he had hired and fired at mid-season 11 years earlier.

John Robert Mize: Big, slugging home-run hitter who was a contact batter, striking out fewer times (42) than he hit homers (51) in peak power season (1947). Batted over .300 nine straight years, a so-so first baseman whose defense delayed Hall of Fame induction until 1981.

Oddly, the "new" Southworth was a reclamation project of Rickey. Billy the Kid, too often tilting the flowing bowl, had lost his last big-league chance as a coach with the Giants. He took a swing at manager Bill Terry in 1933, a year New York won the world championship. Mr. Rickey hired Southworth first as a minor-league instructor, giving Billy a chance to help a rumpy kid named Slaughter with his base-running technique. In the interim, Southworth had impressed Rickey, and obviously Breadon with his revival at Rochester.

Even without Medwick and an injured Padgett slumping, the Cardinals hit well enough, led by Mize's .314 that included 137 RBIs and the club's single-season home run record, 43, that still stood in 1998. Why, the 1940 Cardinals even had pretty good offense from a couple of new names around second base, Joe Orengo, who would have only a cup of coffee with the Cards, and Marty Marion, a long-standing start as Mr. Shortstop. Marty hit .278 that year, pretty good for a 'glove' man.

Others included a left-hander with a future, Max Lanier, and a flashy handy first base-outfielder, Johnny (Hippity) Hopp. Under Blades in 1940, the Cardinals were 14-24. Under interim manager Mike Gonzalez, they were 1-5. Under Southworth, they were a lusty 69-40, good for 84 victories, third place and a promising future, but only 331,889 paid for the inevitable testimony. The land of milk and honey was just ahead.

Just about the time Sam Breadon decided to end the Odd Couple relationship with Branch Rickey, declining to renew B.R.'s seven-year contract a season in advance, the grand master of grow-your-own talent, whose farm system of clubs owned or working agreements had reached 30, reached his peak. In 1941, the Cardinals won both ends or half of split seasons in the top minor leagues—Sacramento in the Pacific Coast League, Rochester in the International, Columbus in the International and Houston in Texas League—and the high-flying Redbirds engaged Brooklyn in one of the most amazing races ever.

Even though the crippled Cards had numerous injuries, they were as close to the Dodgers throughout as one second to another on a clock and, grudgingly, finally finished second. The Brooks and the Birds were so far ahead of the field that defending champion Cincinnati, third, was 10 games behind St. Louis.

The situation probably was best expressed by a minor-league player and former national table tennis champion, Bud Blattner, who would become a fair infielder and a great play-by-play broadcaster. Said Blattner, surviving his last years in the minors at Sacramento under Pepper Martin as an unorthodox manager, "If you had taken an All-Star team of our top farm clubs, I honestly think we could have finished third in the National League to Brooklyn and St. Louis."

Could be in the most amazing fairy-tale season ever. A Class "D" pitcher who had listened with scorecard to the 1940 major-league All-Star game, won by the National at St. Louis, began the 1941 season as a dead-armed outfielder in Class "C". Then, bless Branch Rickey's arched eyebrows, that tanned apple-cheeked kid, in effect, led the Western Association in hitting, the International League and the National. Of course, Stanley Frank Musial officially led no league because he spent insufficient time to qualify, but the 20-year-old was spectacular from Springfield, MO., to Rochester, N.Y., and to the final day of the Cardinals' home season. Called up after the Red Wings lost in the International League playoffs, he stepped into the crippled St. Louis outfield and hit .426 in 12 games.

That final home Sunday, shortly before the Cardinals finished two and a half out, Musial had an amazing doubleheader against the Cubs. In the first game, playing left field, he made two good catches, threw out a runner at the plate, hit two doubles, two singles, stole a base and scored the winning run from second on a squibbed single just about 15 feet in front of home plate! Second game, playing right field, he dived to his right for one catch, somersaulted for another and, capping victory, he bunted safely and also singled. Manager Jimmy Wilson of the Cubs said, "Nobody can be that good, nobody!"

Nobody, yet close enough to Musial was a player who made the difference in that pennant race, Brooklyn's rookie center fielder, Harold Patrick (Pete) Reiser, a hometown boy of whom Rickey and chief scout Charley Barrett were most fond and most hopeful. Trouble is, when Judge Landis freed 101 St. Louis farm hands in the celebrated 1938 "Cedar Rapids case," Reiser was among them.

The Judge's scrupulous search in Rickey's closet for players covered up included the commissioner's distaste for a big-league club having interest in two clubs in the same league. Heck, St. Louis, "owned" the six-club Nebraska State League. Breadon, a proud man, recoiled at the Judge's decision, his resentment aimed more at Rickey.

For B.R., accustomed to some getting away in mass-method tryout camps, Reiser was a jewel. Rickey's old Columbus sidekick, Larry MacPhail, was asked to sign the kid at Brooklyn and play him minimally in the minors so that he wouldn't attract attention. In return, the Cardinals would turn over talent to the Dodgers. MacPhail promised, but, recklessly, he let Reiser into the big-league camp, where switch-hitting, rapid-running Pistol Pete got several hits in a row, impressing Durocher, a noisy observer, and enthusiastic New York baseball writers.

So Reiser, hitting .343, leading the league in runs, doubles, triples and beginning a rare ability to steal home, also was a super player afield. With MacPhail having bought Mickey Owen from the Cardinals to shore up his catching and acquiring Billy Herman as an eleventh-hour second-base acquisition, dangerous Dolph Camilli and Dixie Walker, the Dodgers had enough to back up 20-game winners Whitlow Wyatt and Kirby Higbe.

Early, the Cardinals displayed such pitching depth that in what seemed like a contest to pick one, Hank Gornicki pitched a one-hitter and was sent down the next day, but an incredible injury jinx hit pitching along with other phases for the "St. Louis Swifties," as New York cartoonist Willard Mullin labeled the run-sheep-run Redbirds. Big Mort Cooper needed elbow surgery and was limited to 13 victories, four fewer than aging Warneke and dapper left-hander Ernie White. Mort's younger brother, Walker, broke a collarbone and a shoulder blade. Hustling Jimmy Brown caved in his nose with a hot smash, then broke a finger. A new nimble second baseman, Frank Crespi, the best Marty Marion said he ever saw for one season, was sidelined briefly. The biggest blow came when Enos Slaughter, the club's hottest hitter, diving over Terry Moore in right center, ripped his collarbone against the pavilion wall. The climax came one day at Boston when left-hander Art Johnson beaned and hospitalized Terry Moore. At the scene, mumbling to himself, was big Mize, whose absence with a thumb injury rankled Southworth and some players. Said the Big Cat in a stage whisper: "This is the final straw."

It was, too, even though greybeard gaffer Estel Crabtree continued to help, playing or pinch-hitting,

MAN AS BOY:
Stan Musial, climaxing an incredible 1941 season as dead-armed Class "D" pitcher who hit hard at Springfield, Mo., and Rochester, NY, joins the Cards in September, 1941 after the International League playoffs – and hit .426 in 12 games. Brooklyn fans named him "The Man" five years later.

GOOD SCOUT: Charley Barrett might have been *the* best purveyor of player talent for the Cardinals until his death in 1939. Barrett teamed with Branch Rickey with the Browns, then joined B.R. with the Cardinals in time to assess and sign raw talent, the last of whom was Brooklyn's young superstar, Pete Reiser.

batting .341. Brown batted over .300, as did handyman Hopp. And young Howard Pollet, called up in August, won five of seven decisions. Just too late, as mentioned, came Musial, the man who would become known as The Man. A decisive moment in the final series with the Dodgers, with whom they split 22 games, came in the important two-game swing in a series of three.

A scoreless overtime duel between Wyatt and Cooper reached an extra inning with Dixie Walker perched on second base. Alertly, Dixie picked up catcher Walker Cooper's breaking-ball sign and relayed it to Herman, a great curve ball hitter. Herman's double decided the game and, in a sense, the Redbirds' finest hour in defeat.

Because of the thrilling race, limited night ball and maybe a few more folks in defense work, the attendance of 642,496 was the most since the record 1928. For Breadon and the Cardinals, if not for lame-duck G.M. Rickey, the outlook was fair and warmer. With the Cardinals having played so well and gallantly taped up like the Spirit of '76, they were strong favorites in 1942, but someone forgot to tell the Dodgers.

For Leo Durocher, Larry MacPhail had acquired Arky Vaughan, hard-hitting shortstop to play third base. The Cardinals, meanwhile, doing what seemed so naturally, sold Johnny Mize to the Giants for $50,000 and three players. One thing the Redbirds had was pitching, which would reflect itself in subsequent seasons.

Manager Southworth could play eenie-meenie with Mort Cooper, Max Lanier, Howard Krist, Howard Pollet, Ernie White, Harry Gumbert and Lon Warneke, but they had minor leaguers like Harry Brecheen, Murry Dickson and George Munger, names to remember, and a handsome dude up from New Orleans, Johnny Beazley.

With all that pitching, kept or sent out, a ball club can't win without scoring. The Cardinals, shut out five times in the first 24 games, struggled long to get over .500, salvaged only by an ability to beat the Dodgers or, if you will, that well-dressed hair shirt, Durocher. Even when those St. Louis Swifties righted themselves with a new look, they were discouragingly far behind Brooklyn.

Frank (Creepy) Crespi, the gutty, fleet second baseman, handicapped by a spring training hold out, played poorly enough for Southworth to move Brown from third base to second. At third, Billy put in a rookie from Rochester, George (Whitey) Kurowski. The stocky Kurowski, who could run despite his girth, played with his right arm a few inches shorter than his left, a result of osteomyelitis at 10 that required removal of bone. Tightened muscles helped physically, Kurowski's heart did the rest because he hung in competitively over the plate. At first base, the versatile speedy Hopp filled in for rookie Ray Sanders, a former hometown softball star who had developed into a hard-hitting minor leaguer.

When Breadon waived Warneke back to the Cubs for the waiver price, the media suggested hotly that the owner merely was removing his highest-salaried player, $15,000. The colorful Arkansas Hummingbird, cheek stuffed with tobacco that made him look like cartoon character Popeye, had begun to develop a home-run ball, so ...

Warneke went to Chicago and would play a part in the dramatic windup of the season. The Hummer's disappearance proved an addition by subtraction, as Beazley was promoted to the starting rotation and became their second best winner. Pitching and defense did it for a ball club that was 10 games out early in August.

Casey Stengel, managing the Boston Braves, had the ticket on the Redbirds and Musial, the kind of sagacity that put the craggy clown into the Hall of Fame. About Stan, Ol' Case said, "You're going to be hearin' from this fella for 12-15-20 years." About the Redbirds, Stengel would make his point shortly after it looked as if the Dodgers, overly aggressive under Durocher, appeared to have withstood St. Louis's surge.

At mid-season Southworth's Swifties were 47-30, but in early August they still trailed by 10 games. Big Mort Cooper, who chewed aspirin to kill the elbow pain even after helpful surgery, winced at never having won more games than his uniform number "13". After a couple of failures, Coop squeezed into the "14" Gus Mancuso had worn. Next, up the numerical lineup with great success.

Brooklyn suffered a severe blow this time. Reiser, perhaps destined to be one of the best ever, crashed into the center field concrete at Sportsman's Park in St. Louis, his home town and, unconscious, dropped the ball that gave Slaughter an inside-the-park-homer and the Cardinals a 1-0 victory. Reiser returned to the lineup too soon, and his average dipped to .310. He never was the same.

The Brooks were a solid seven up when they made their last visit to St. Louis in late August. A year before they had prevailed. This time, before a record night-game crowd of 25,840, Lanier won, 7-1. Next night, Mort Cooper, squeezing into Ken O'Dea's "16," duelled with rival Whit Wyatt until the 13th when the Dodgers scored. Delightfully 33,527 saw the Cardinals tie in their half and win in the 14th, 2-1. Beazley's 16th victory in extra innings in the third series game, 2-1, made the fourth game obviously the biggest, but the Dodgers' 4-1 win seemed to ease the pressure except that by now, the Redbirds rarely lost, as Stengel noted.

Casey's Braves, Brooklyn cousins, just had won a game that became a knockdown, drag-out affair so severe that the National League president Ford Frisch took action. Durocher and Wyatt started it by throwing at a hitter. Manny Salvo of the Braves, ducking a ball thrown at him in reprisal by Wyatt, flung his bat and then won the game with a base hit. Steaming over a cold beer afterward, Casey said, "If I had a ball club as good as (Durocher's), I wouldn't have thrown at a ball club as bad as mine. I've talked to other managers who feel the same"—and he mentioned Jimmy Wilson at Chicago and Frank Frisch at Pittsburgh.

"Ya know, those jack-rabbits from St. Louis are comin'. Why, I've never seen anything like 'em. Every sonofagun can run like a stripe-tailed ape. They make my infield and outfield jittery trying to hurry and handle the ball." And Stengel punctuated his comments by imitating players handling the ball as if it were a hot potato.

The club that couldn't lose for winning kept coming. By the time they made the far turn in the last eastern trip in September, they had won 26 of 31, but even with injuries, they were only two behind, eyeball to eyeball, when they played for the last time at Ebbets Field. Suddenly, they were quiet, reserved, no longer playing a kid's game. The p-r-e-s-s-u-r-e manifested itself when Jimmy Brown backed up with trembling legs for a pop fly, but on the mound, Cooper was magnificent as he beat Brooklyn a fifth time. Mort even singled home a run in a 3-0 win over the wonderful Wyatt. The showdown next day was between two southpaws, Lanier of the Cardinals and ex-Redbird Max Macon for the Dodgers. Macon was good, Lanier better, winning 2-1 on a home run by Kurowski. With 29 out of 34, the Cardinals had collared Durocher.

Next day at Philadelphia, the best the Swifties could get was an even split in a doubleheader, but the Dodgers dropped a

BROWNS BLAST GROVE, 11-9

Story on Page 34

Narragansett Mutuels
1-2-1 $153.80
1-2-3-5-7 $234.80
1 $292.00
Three $165.40
Five $235.60
Seven $292.00

DAILY RECORD

THE RECORD-AMERICAN HAS THE GREATEST CIRCULATION IN NEW ENGLAND

Vol. 260, No. 185 Editorial Office Liberty 4000 Business and Advertising Offices Liberty 4000 2 CENTS (BEYOND 15 MILES 3 CENTS)

AUGUST 21

CARDS' MOORE BEANED

BRAVES LOSE 2

Story on Page 31

TERRY MOORE PROSTRATE AFTER BEANING

Terry Moore, St. Louis Cards' star center fielder, prone on ground in batter's box after being beaned in third inning by Art Johnson, Braves' Winchester rookie, in National League Field, Allston. Moore, rushed to St. Elizabeth's Hospital, Brighton, in police ambulance, was found to have cerebral concussion, slight laceration below left ear. Dr. Edward J. O'Brien believes he will recover. X-rays will be taken. He was unconscious a half-half and was rational when he regained consciousness. (Daily Record Photo)

NATIONAL LEAGUE

At Boston: First Game

		R	H	E
Cards	011000000—	2	6	2
Braves	000000000—	0	6	0

White and Cooper; Johnson and Masi.

Second Game

		R	H	E
Cards	110010000—	3	10	3
Braves	010000001—	2	4	2

Pollet and Mancuso; Javery and Berres.

At Philadelphia: First Game

		R	H	E
Reds	002000000—	2	5	0
Phillies	000000000—	0	3	1

Vandermeer and Lombardi; Hoerst, I. Pearson and Warren.

Second Game

		R	H	E
Reds	010000002—	3	6	0
Phillies	000000000—	0	6	1

Riddle and West; Melton and Livingston.

At Brooklyn:

		R	H	E
Pirates	006000000—	6	6	5
Dodgers	401000101—	7	7	1

Sewell and Lopez; Higbe, Casey, Allen and Owen, Franks.

At New York:

		R	H	E
Cubs	211301001—	9	16	0
Giants	000200011—	4	8	3

Eaves and McCullough; Hubbell, Carpenter, Adams, Wittig and Danning.

FINAL STRAW: As Johnny Mize mumbled when Terry Moore was skulled with a late-August pitch in Boston, as caught by Hearst's morning tabloid. Tee Moore's loss was the latest in an incredible list of injuries for the valiant 1941 Cardinals.

pair to Cincinnati, giving the Cardinals a lead they never lost even though Brooklyn won its last eight games. No wonder Durocher and other Dodgers would react profanely when suggested they had "choked". After all, they won 104 of 154 games.

Rallying remarkably time and again, the Cardinals even squeaked out a 1-0 win over old foe and friend Warneke at Wrigley Field, a result of a double steal that scored Hopp. So down to the last day, playing a doubleheader, the fairy-tale fellas needed only one game. Once more, they faced Warneke, who reminded many of many things, especially Moore about the 21-game Cubs' winning streak in 1935 that ruined Tee's rookie season. The Hummer beat Paul Dean that pivotal game the final series in 1935 and he topped Dizzy Dean for a second-place day the final game in '36.

Now, the lean, lanky guy was an early victim and, taking the short cut through the third-base home dugout, looking neither left nor right, Warneke said, "All right, you buzzards, there's your lead, let's see you hold it." He soon became a National League umpire, then a municipal judge back home in Hot Springs, Arkansas.

The pennant was won behind Ernie White, 9-2, as Musial gathered in a fly ball in left field, and, putting frosting on the cake, they won the final game behind Beazley, too, 4-1. So they finished with 43 of the last 52 for remarkable 106 victories.

Arkansas Hummingbird: Lon Warneke, jaw packed with a Popeye-sized chew of tobacco, tried to keep hopes high with his lighthearted philosophy and, if possible, the ball down. Those sinkers that don't sink spell "home runs" even for a top pitcher.

They won with limited offense in a season of limited hitting with Slaughter's .318 and rookie Musial's .315 close behind the league-leader, Boston catcher Ernie Lombardi, but they still led in scoring, 755 to 742 for Brooklyn in runs, .268 to .265 in batting average. The difference was in pitching with the 1942 Cardinals permitting only 482 runs, an average of only 3.06 a game, compared with runner-up Brooklyn's 5.10. Cooper was the National League's Most Valuable Player, 22-7 with a 1.78 earned-run average. Unofficial rookie of the year, Beazley, was 21-6, 2.13 ERA; Howard Krist, 13-5, 2.52; White, 7-5, 2.52; Howard Pollet, 7-5, 2.58; Murry Dickson, 6-3, 2.91; Max Lanier, 13-8, 2.93, and Harry Gumbert, only one over three-a-game, 9-5, 3.52.

The 1942 World Series has to stand out as the most satisfying in the history of the Cardinals. Most satisfying because 1942 was a war year only on the calendar, not in the competition between baseball's foul lines. Few players had gone into service, most certainly limited stars and none of the competing clubs. That meant, therefore, that the Yankees sought their ninth world championship without a loss during a period in which they had won 32 of 36 Series games since Bob O'Farrell gunned out Babe Ruth for the last out in 1926.

And the 1942 Series opened just like the others in between. Charley (Red) Ruffing, the veteran husky from nearby Nokomis, Ill., toyed with the Cardinals and Mort Cooper. Led by Joe DiMaggio with three hits, the Yanks not only breezed into the ninth, up 7-0 but Ruffing hadn't allowed a hit until Moore singled in the eighth. Suddenly, with Musial out to open the home ninth, the Redbirds rallied for four runs, forcing Ruffing's removal for Spurgeon (Spud) Chandler. Truth is, Musial, batting again, hit a hot game-ending shot to Buddy Hassett at first base.

That uplifting finish to the 7-4 game was manifest the next day when Beazley and the Birds got off to a 3-0 lead against Ernie (Tiny) Bonham, but New York came alive in the eighth. "Five O'Clock Lightning," is the way they described belting by the Bombers and when Charley (King Kong) Keller lined a shot to the right-field roof with one on, the score was tied, 3-3. This was gulp time for historians even more than the Cardinals, but off Bonham in the eighth, Slaughter doubled and Musial, then hitting behind Enos, drove in the lead run. Could it be?

Opening the Yankees ninth, Bill Dickey singled and Tuck Stainback ran for the

Indian-Given: This rare American Association championship trophy was awarded to the Browns' Chris Von der Ahe in 1885 and is now housed in the Chicago White Sox's trophy room. It was willed by Von der Ahe to manager-first baseman Charley Comiskey, late founder of the Sox. Four straight pennants won permanent possession of the 32-inch silver tribute.

WORLD SERIES ORIGINAL: Although the modern Series didn't begin until 1903, St. Louis earned the first inter-league honor, presented to Chris Von der Ahe's Browns after they beat Cap Anson's Chicago team in an 1886 post-season playoff. Happy home-town fans presented one each to manager Comiskey, the first baseman, and his other regulars. From top center clockwise: Robinson, O'Neill, Latham, Gleason, Foutz, Comiskey, Caruthers, Bushong and Welch.

Rings for Their Fingers: And, if not bells for their toes, a polished anthracite 1926 trophy awarded the Cardinals for their first championship. The rings are the first of thirteen sets of rings collected and photographed by Jerry McNeal, senior reptile keeper at the prestigious St. Louis Zoo, a great Redbirds fan... Notre Dame, too.

ANOTHER ST. LOUIS FIRST: The Commissioner's trophy, awarded by William D. Eckert in 1967, now a standard, coveted baseball bauble. Title rings are shown in these views – left side, top and right side. Toughest ring for McNeal to locate? The 1931 Burleigh Grimes ring pictured in the upper left-hand corner. (Trophy photo by Dan Donovan)

ENCORE: The last Commissioner's trophy won by the Cardinals in 1982, with hopes of more to come. (Trophy photo by Dan Donovan)

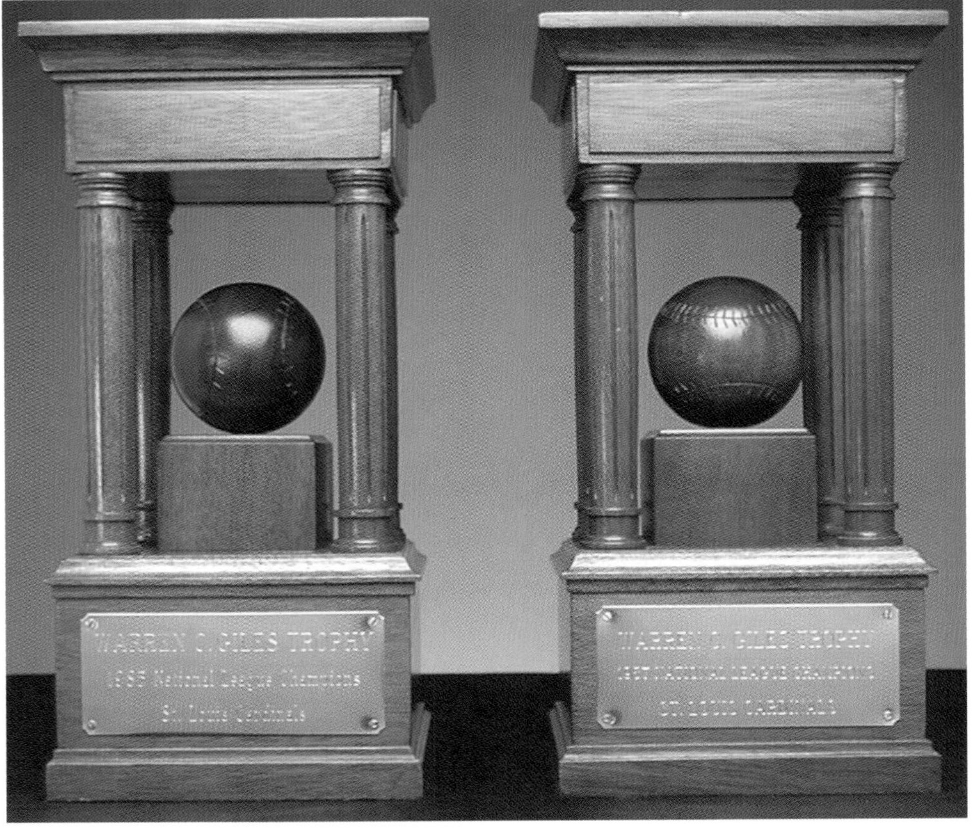

Cheerful Cherrywood: Symbolic of National League pennants, awarded the Cardinals by the NL in 1985 and '87. Rings on this page of Butch Yatkeman and Ozzie Smith are also courtesy of Jerry McNeal.

ONCE UPON A TIME: Home-town rivals were saluted by *The Sporting News* in a trophy presented by J.G. Taylor Spirk in 1939, long after the Cards played the Browns. Researcher Mark Stangl located 267 games played spring and fall, 1903-1953. Although the Cards became predominant, Brownies won 137 to 117 with 113 ties. (Trophy adorns Busch Stadium office of Bill DeWitt III, grandson of Cards' and Browns' executive.

THE HALL OF FAME:
In 1997, the St. Louis Cardinals Hall of Fame Museum joined with the International Bowling Museum and Hall of Fame to form a unique partnership dedicated to "exhibit, educate and preserve" two great St. Louis sports. Providing an excellent pre-game family activity, as well as year-round operations, the two museums can be toured for a single admission. Visitors can enjoy extensive displays on the history of both sports, videos on both sports in the Busch Theater (seating 125) and bowling on modern lanes. For an additional fee, visitors can take a Busch Stadium Tour. The International Bowling Museum, home of the St. Louis Cardinals Hall of Fame, is located on the northwest side of Busch Stadium, directly across the street from the Cardinals administrative offices. For information call (314) 231-6340. (Photographs by Dan Donovan)

slow-moving catcher. Next up, Hassett hit a line drive to right between Slaughter and the foul-line. Enos dashed to his right, gloved the ball, pivoted and made a perfect throw on which Stainback tagged himself out when sliding into Kurowski. So Ruffing, pinch-hitting, lifted a fly that merely was a second out when it would have tied the score. And when Beazley got Phil Rizzuto, the Cardinals had won one, 4-3—heading into Yankee Stadium!

The crowd there was a whopping 69,123, an intimidating sight for many kids from the Carolina cotton country, and other whistle stops, but one of those millhands himself a cottontop, blond Ernie White, pitched masterfully. Aided by a circus defense, one the pitcher who had battled a sore arm could appreciate, White walked none and scattered six hits. The 2-0 victory over Chandler and a shaky bullpen was achieved because the Cardinals' great outfield defense rose to the occasion.

In the sixth, a man on base, DiMaggio hit a savage liner to left-center, where Moore, with Musial slipping, dived for a backhanded catch of what could have been a triple or maybe inside-the-park homer. An inning later Musial backed to the low-sweeping left-field stands for a good catch. In the ninth with DiMaggio on base, Keller flied deep to right, where Slaughter leaped at the wall for a game-ending catch, just as an orange whizzed across his face. Moore, hurrying over from right field, challenged first-base umpire Cal Hubbard, hurrying out to watch the play at a time only four umpires were used. Hubbard insisted that if Slaughter had dropped the ball, he would have called out Keller for interference.

Years later in a gravelly laugh, Slaughter would comment, "That would have been something, an American League umpire calling out an American League hitter on a technicality in an American League park."

The shutout defeat was the first suffered by the Yankees in the Series since Jesse Haines of the Cardinals did it back in 1926, and the low-run jewel was followed by a slugfest in which the Cardinals overpowered—and outran the Yankees—even running rapidly first to third on the great

TOP TRIO:
One of the best outfields ever, shortened by World War II, was one that won championships in 1942 and 1946. From the left, Enos Slaughter, Terry Moore and Stan Musial.

DiMaggio. With the Yankees' Hank Borowy leading Cooper 1-0, Musial began the fourth with a safe bunt and as the Cardinals lowered the boom at bat and on the bases, Stan batted a second time and drove in the sixth run of the inning. Briefly, the Yankees tied with a big sixth against Cooper , but Pollet and particularly Lanier held the Bombers the rest of the way. The Redbirds roughed up Atley Donald and Bonham to win 9-6.

When the Redbirds were challenging Yankee arms—outfield and pitching—there was usual hijinks in the Cards' dugout. Trainer Weaver was leading the funny frenzy. He had a toy railroad tower car in which he would plug in the green light for the Redbirds to move, a red to stop the Yankees psychologically as well as hopefully physically. The Cardinals' bantam equipment manager, Morris (Butch) Yatkeman hovered close around.

Before the fifth game at home plate, Moore as captain exchanged lineup cards with jut-jawed Yankee coach Art Fletcher. Beefy, red-faced plate umpire Bill Summers told Moore that manager Joe McCarthy objected to the presence of "that little guy" in the dugout. Incredulous, Moore wondered. Butch? Fletcher nodded. One Irishman quickly saw more red than the others. "Listen, Chisel Chin," Terry snapped, "tell Mac there ain't going to be no tomorrow in this

Series."

There wasn't, either, as Beazley won again. In a 2-2 game of home runs—Rizzuto and Slaughter had homered into the ninth—Kurowski homered off Ruffing in the ninth to break the tie 4-2. The dramatics weren't over. The Yankees' Joe Gordon, like Cooper an MVP bust in the Series, singled and when Brown committed his second error of the game on Dickey's grounder, the Yankees had tying runs aboard. As Jerry Priddy batted, Crespi suggested in hopefully high spirits that it was time for Dr. Harrison J. Weaver to exercise his "double whammy". Gravely, the good massage-and-morale man agreed.

Ceremoniously, Doc crossed his wrists, hand back to back, then closed the second and third fingers of each hand so that the first and third fingers protruded in upside down Hook-'em Horns. Then with a threatening grimace, he pointed the twin hexes toward second and at .095 Series hitter Gordon. When Rizzuto missed a bunt attempt, Marty Marion, gliding right, slipped in behind Gordon, and Walker Cooper rung him up with a perfect throw. Priddy then popped to Brown and when pinch-hitter George Selkirk grounded to Jimmy, the Yankees had lost four straight in one World Series compared with only four in the previous 36 games.

DOUBLE-WHAMMY DOC: Harrison J. Weaver, osteopathic trainer of the Cardinals from 1927 until his death in 1955, was quaint and ingenious, a creator of gizmos. One was Doc's double-whammy jinx, shown here, that with double-layered hook-'em horns flummoxed the foe.

In the Cardinals' clubhouse, obviously with Kurowski and Beazley the center of attention, Southworth's young champions ripped up league president Ford Frick's hat and hoisted up happy general manager Branch Rickey, who would leave the ball club with a whopping season of $88,000 of salary and 20 per cent profits. And, of course, with pride about his farm system's finest hour.

With "Pass the Biscuits, Mirandy" clang-clanging one last time, the Cardinal hurried to Penn Station, not for the expected continuance of the Series, but in victory celebration, leaving Musial standing in the station, awaiting a train to Pittsburgh and crying. When you've made $4250 all season and $6192.50 in one week—with things to do for wife Lil, young son Dick, Mom and Pop and something left over for war bonds—it was time to cry for joy.

For the National League, it was time to cry in frustration because as more and more ball players turned in their flannels for khaki, the Cardinals obviously had more talent to lose. As a result, they won two more pennants even more handily, though losing great talent. For instance, Series hero Beazley, Capt. Moore and roomie sidekick Slaughter and the versatile Creepy Crespi before the 1943 season and Brown, Murry Dickson and Pollet early in the race.

Pollet, the stylish southpaw Eddie Dyer had scouted as a junior American Legion star in New Orleans, was so good when he was called —after three successive shutouts and 28 straight scoreless innings—it seemed as they still were using the "balata" ball.

For players fortunate enough not to be called into service, it was one thing to train at times with ear muffs or gloves—the Cardinals' site was Cairo, Ill., a river pinpoint where the Ohio flowed into the Mississippi—but the balata was a disaster. The ball was as hard as a rock and sounded like one—clunk!—and it looked as if a batter were swinging a banana stalk. A gummy substance from a tree of the same name, the balata was a Spalding company device to use re-processed rubber rather than the precious war priority item itself. If they had stayed with it, the deadball president Franklin D. Roosevelt might have wondered why he ever gave baseball a war-time "green light" or Judge Landis might have wondered why they bothered.

As world champions, the Cardinals were shut out 1-0 opening day in 11 innings—only 11 runs were scored in four games that day—and next day they again lost, 1-0, even though Musial died on third with a triple. Third game, Musial stole home for one run and raced from first to third on a wild pitch after a second single, then scored on a passed ball. With just four runs in four games, the switfies split their first series. Eleven games into the season, the Yankees' Joe Gordon hit the first homer. Angry clubs with leftover 1942 balls were permitted to use them. Under pressure, Spalding agreed to replace the balata, acknowledging it was at least 25 per cent less resilient. First day the bing came back into the bang, the American League, which had hit only nine homers in 72 games, hit six that afternoon.

Fairy Tale Finish: George (Whitey) Kurowski, one of numerous rookies on the Cardinals' fabulous 1942 champions, gets a hero's hoist after his ninth-inning, two-run homer finished a five-game upset over the New York Yankees in the World Series. Holding Kurowski at the the left, bareheaded, another rookie, Harry Walker. At the right, cap askew, relief pitcher Howard Krist. Clockwise from the left, traveling secretary Leo Ward, Enos Slaughter and Marty Marion at the top left. Behind Krist are two other first full-season players, Howie Pollet and Stan Musial. Manager Billy Southworth shakes Kurowski's hand. The winning pitcher, not shown, was a two-game Series star, Johnny Beazley.

Musial responded with his first batting championship and first Most Valuable Player award, hitting .357 with 220 hits of which 73 were for extra bases, though only 13 homers. He hadn't become a home-run hitter as yet. Whitey Kurowski also hit 13, Ray Sanders 11 at first base as a clutch hitter. Marion, .280, had a new second baseman, Lou Klein, who batted .287. Harry Walker, Tee Moore's stand-in, was close to .300. Danny Litwhiler, obtained from the Phillies to play left field as Musial moved to right, helped. Most certainly did Walker with .318, nine homers and a club-leading 81 RBIs. Rangy, square-jawed Walker Cooper, catching brother Mort, a 22-game winner, saw little Harry (The Cat) Brecheen come in belatedly from the minors to work well with other winners, including Lanier, Krist, Gumbert, Red Munger and service-bound Dickson. Brecheen, hunched over, as quick as a feline from whom he got his nickname, would prove a big pitcher as a little man. He was 9-6 in '43.

Even though the Redbirds romped—nearly 20 games ahead of Cincinnati, 24 in front of Brooklyn—the Dodgers were co-pennant favorites, as oddsmakers and other remembered the two previous races. The Brooks dogged the Birds into July in a series at St. Louis. Knockdown artist Les Webber again low-bridged a better-controlled Musial four times. Menacing W. Cooper, up next, blasted the pitcher, grounded out and, in obvious anger, stepped on Augie Galan's foot at first base. Trailing the play as a hustling player, little catcher Mickey Owen saw the incident at first base, deemed it no accident and leaped in full equipment on Cooper just as big Walker turned. Cooper slammed Owen to the ground, precipitating a fight that led to 11 straight Redbird victories, a Brooklyn slump—and see you later, alligator!

Even though the Cardinals won 105 games, defending against the Yankees they had dispatched in five games, St. Louis was not favored in the travel-saving, one-trip 1943 World Series. The Yankees had seen

Handsome Does: Terry Moore did, beginning with his rookie season, 1935, after only one full season in the minors. Tee Moore, one of the greatest defensive centerfielders ever, had a 6-for-6 game and a good first year that failed only because the Chicago Cubs won 21 straight in September. Moore used that near-miss to inspire younger teammates in the 1942 and '46 pennant races.

the great DiMaggio and Rizzuto follow Johnny Sturm and Buddy Hassett into service. They had a new first baseman, Nick Etten; new third baseman, Billy Johnson, and a big hulking center fielder, Johnny Lindell.

They also had a remarkable pitcher, Spud Chander, who had a 20-4 record and outstanding 1.64. The sturdy Georgia bulldog won the opener over Lanier as Southworth delayed use of Mort Cooper, who had been hit hard by the American League in the previous Series and All-Star games. Lanier's error and wild pitch helped unfrock him 4-1. That night, planning to go to St. Louis for the weekend games, Robert Cooper died. He was the Cooper's father, a 58-year-old a mailcarrier at Independence, MO. Southworth gave the brothers the option of going or staying. They said they knew what their father would want. Big Mort, his heart as heavy as his forkball, used home runs by Marion and Sanders for a lead that held up 4-3, when brother Walker gloved a game-ending foul.

The same 69,000-plus crowd—bless that nickel subway to Yankee Stadium in gas rationing!—saw the decisive third game in which sidearmed southpaw Alpha Brazle, like Brecheen an over-ripened rookie, led Hank Borowy into the eighth inning, 2-1. Now, the faultless defense betrayed the Cardinals. Lindell singled to center and when Walker juggled the ball, the big guy legged it to second. Batting for Borowy, Snuffy Stirnweiss bunted toward first, too hard, but Sanders, gambling on a play at third, had trouble getting the ball away. So the ball and big Lindell barreled into Kurowski. Whitey couldn't handle the throw. Undeservedly, he got the error. When Tuck Stainback flied out, Stirnweiss alertly took second on the throw to the plate that momentarily checked Lindell, Southworth opted for an intentional walk to veteran Frank Crosetti, loading the bases. The manager forced righthander Krist to face righthanded newcomer Johnson. Billy drilled a back-breaking triple, the big blow of a five-run inning and a 6-2 Yankee win.

Here, gambling on lefty Maruis Russo, a 5-10 regular-season pitcher, McCarthy was rewarded in St. Louis, where Russo helped bat and pitch himself to victory, 2-1, contributing two doubles off Lanier and giving up only six hits, two each to Musial and to Marion, the Redbird Series leader at .357. The deciding run in the fifth game was driven in by Bill Dickey. The Hall of Fame catcher, a Little Rock fan of the Cardinals except when they faced the Yankee pinstripes, came up in the fifth inning of the fifth game and drilled a two-run homer off Mort Cooper. Meanwhile, Chandler, tiptoeing on the Perils of Pauline, gave up 10 hits, walked two and was victimized by an error, but with only one double play behind him, the Series hero pitcher worked a close-out shutout, 2-0. Spud's ERA was 0.50 for 18 innings.

Rubbing it in, Yankee coach Fletcher led the offkey musical clubhouse version of a novelty number of the war—"Pistol-Packin' Mama, Lay that Pistol Down!"—and a slightly worse-for-celebrity, Dickey, wove his way back to the Chase Hotel. On the elevator he met a soldier, little White Sox infielder Dario Lodigiani, who bet Bill didn't know his name. If he had, he might not have been able to pronounce it, but, smiling faintly, Dickey confessed, "No, I don't, pal, but I know how we pitched you."

The 1944 National League pennant race wasn't funny. Nor was the American except if the guy or gal was a long-suffering Browns fan, of whom there had to be many even though not enough put their affection into attending. Suddenly from the time they won their first nine games until they took the last four straight from the Yankees—of all people!—the lowly St. Louis Americans were the talk of a pastime international because of so many men overseas. Among them were Brazle and Walker, headed for combat, and others were absent from the 1943 pennant-winners, including Klein.

A feisty fella from Lincoln, Ill., Emil Verban, replaced him as part of a keystone combination with the incomparable Marion. By now, they called him "Slats", "The Octopus" or, this sounded best, "Mr. Shortstop". Even though he had better seasons at bat, the self-made former "out" man won the Most Valuable Player award with his glove, largely the first tribute of its kind until Brooks Robinson. With M. Cooper, Lanier, Brecheen and Munger leading the way—until Red was called into service—wide-shouldered Ted Wilks waddled in from the inexhaustible minors and won 11 games. Cooper had 22 again, Lanier 17, Wilks 17 and Brecheen 16.

Musial led the attack with .347, but lost the batting title to Dixie Walker when he was hurt in an outfield collision just about the time the Cardinals experienced an odd slump that perhaps kept them from beating the 1906 Chicago Cubs' 116 victories. They reached victory No. 100 earlier than any club ever, but to the proud Breadon's dismay they lost nine straight to Frankie Frisch's second-place Pitsburgh. Still, they finished 14 games ahead of the Pirates with—again!—105 victories that gave them a three-season total of 316. Small wonder they were a decisive favorites over the Brownies, whose efforts had prompted Musial's wife, Lil, to proclaim, "Why, this is a Browns' town!"

That year, yes, with a slight box office edge over the Cardinals' 486,751. Obviously the home-side NL fans were bored, but not the Brownies, not after a hectic finish that was even more remarkable than the start. They had to win four in a row from the Yankees and they did, thanks largely to the two-run homers off the bat of a sawed-off, in-again, out-again war plant worker, Chet Laabs. Previously Laabs had been best known negatively for having struck out five times the last day of the 1938 season with Detroit when Cleveland's Bob Feller fanned a record 18, but as Chet would note with a grin, facing Feller's flame-thrower the final day of the season, he was hoping more not to be hit by the ball than to hit it. Laabs' homers and one by Vern (Junior) Stephens gave Sigmund (Jack) Jakucki a 5-2 victory. Good thing the Browns owned Sportsman's Park. The delirious 37,000 might have taken it home as souvenirs.

Shrewdly, general manager Bill DeWitt had sifted through castoffs, cuthroats and 4-F's to give smart former catcher Luke Sewell a menagerie he could handle. Of his players, gifted first baseman George McQuinn hadn't been good enough for the Yankees when Lou Gehrig was around. Stubby center field veteran Mike Kreevich could hit and field. Hustler, holler guy Don Gutteridge was an ex-Gas House Gang player at second base. Top winner on a team that won with only 89 games was handsome young Jack Kramer, plus established professionals Nelson Potter, Bob Muncrief and Denny Galehouse.

Sewell had only two problems—whom to pitch and where to stay. Conveniently, he and Redbird field foreman Southworth took turns with the same suite at the Fairgrounds Hotel, close by Sportsman's Park. Galehouse had been only 9-10 among pitchers with winning records, but Sewell went with him in the Series opener. That decision helped almost to achieve an upset as surprising as the one by which the Chicago White Sox's Hitless Wonders knocked off the 116-win Cubs in 1906 and the "miracle" Boston Braves swept Connie Mack's great Philadephia A's in 1914. That decision and "that" play, to be described in due time.

For the first and only all-St. Louis shootout — the Streetcar Series — the weather was a lot better than Sportsman's Park, its grass weary from two clubs' constant use and a shortage of groundskeepers. The Browns fielded as if the park were at fault, but not in the opener.

BROTHERS VALIANT: Walker Cooper, catcher, and older brother, Mort, a standout pitcher, were standouts with the 1942 Cardinals.

THEY CALLED HIM "GABE": Rangy Ray Sanders, a home-town player nicknamed Gabe, is shown with Mr. Shortstop, Marty Marion, in World War II when a heart condition kept Sanders out of service and a boyhood leg injury kept Marion 4-F. Sanders, a good RBI man and loosey-goosey guy in the clubhouse, replaced Johnny Mize at first base, then was sold to the Boston Braves in 1946. There, he suffered a broken arm that shortened a career.

Hard-luck Mort Cooper allowed only two hits, but Gene Moore singled in the fourth and McQuinn homered. Galehouse won, 2-1. Only fielding flaws by Nellie Potter in the second game kept the Cardinals in a 2-2 game in which the Browns threatened in the eighth until stocky Sylvester (Blix) Donnelly came out of the bullpen to stop that one. Three innings later, Blix was in trouble when McQuinn doubled to open the tenth and Mark Christman bunted perfectly toward third base. Check signals, maybe not "perfectly", but so good that Kurowski had to stick to the bag, and Donnelly, falling off the mound to his right, one-handed the ball, spun, and pegged perfectly to Kurowski's spikes, tagging out McQuinn. Failure there could have meant a big inning and in view of the Browns'í third-game victory, a 0-and-3 deficit never overcome in the World Series play. Repreived, the Redbirds won in the home eleventh, 3-2, on a pinch-hit by Ken O'Dea.

Behind Kramer, the Browns bombed out Wilks in the third game, 6-2, and, as mentioned, could have had a formidable lead, but in the fourth game they ran into a big-game pitcher, Brecheen, and a big-name player, Musial. Stan (I-Ain't-The-Man-Yet) homered with one on against Jakucki in the first inning. Stan had two other hits and Brecheen breezed, 5-1. The Sunday game was sun-splashed. It was a hard-to-believe-we're-at-war-day. Shirt-sleeved fans helped pitchers and hurt batting backgrounds, as reflected in a magnificent reprise between Cooper and Galehouse. Together they struck out a Series record 22 batters—10 by Galehouse, 12 by Cooper—and this time the only runs came off the bat of Gabe Sanders and Danny Litwhiler. Each homered in a 2-0 shutout for Coop.

So Potter faced Lanier again in the sixth game with the smallest crowd, 31,630. In the Redbird third, the bottom of the batting order—Verban and Lanier with five of the Cards' 10 hits—drove in two of the three runs. They led by two into the sixth when Lanier, wild even though having allowed just three hits, was replaced by Wilks, who faced and retired the final 11 batters. Hardly had the final out been made when the skinny National League second baseman, Verban, a .412 Series hitter second only to McQuinn's more vigorous .438, detoured by way of a box next to the visiting Browns' first-base box. To startled Browns' owner Don Barnes, he snipped, "Now you're sitting behind the box," a reference to the fact that Redbird wives and families had been seated poorly for games hosted by the American Leaguers.

The sum-up of the Trolley Series was that the Browns made 10 errors, the Cards just one. Three of the Brownies were committed by Junior Stephens, the slugging shortstop. The third was damaging on what might have been a double-play ball in the climactic three-run third in the 3-1 windup. By contrast, Marion, sparkling afield, once more underlined not only the continued emphasis on defense, but his significance to it. And because the good-natured, grinning and gangly guy was a super-salesman as well as a super shortstop, he created inadvertently a breach that possibly kept the Cardinals from winning again—not necessarily next year, but in the future.

Wages—presumably—had been frozen at an amount of the ball club's highest salaried player. With Warneke having gone to the Cubs, the Cardinals' top was Terry Moore's $13,500. So Breadon relied on that unwritten regulation in rebuffs to Marion and the Cooper brothers until Marty, who could sell a bikini to an eskimo, convinced the dear boss that he could pay more.

Breadon made it $15,000 and was prepared to do the same for the Coopers, but there was a delay during which they spoke unkindly of him. Now Mr. Breadon could be quite nice—in Mort Cooper's alcoholic decline Sam helped constantly—but remember what happened to Rogers Hornsby?

So with the mighty Musial gone to the Navy along with Walker Cooper, the tank was pretty empty despite the center field contributions of Buster Adams, who hit .292 with 20 homers, 102 RBIs and deceived some that he could break into the post-war outfield. Whitey Kurowski thrived again with 20 homers and 102 RBIs. And when floods at Cairo forced the Cardinals back to Sportsman's Park to train, a skinny, freckled kid shagging fly balls for coach Mike Gonzalez startled the Cuban coach. "Hey, Beel," Mike warbled excitedly to manager Southworth. "That Rad , she can do."

Indeed, "Rad" or, rather Red Schoendienst, originally a shortstop, played a brilliant left field that season and led the National League with a modest 28 stolen bases. But too much talent was gone, and Schoendienst was too young. The worst part of Breadon's dealing Mort Cooper to Boston early in the season was that he didn't want Walker Cooper back, either. In big Coop's pitching place, Charley (Red) Barrett came over, a garrulous guy with a big mouth and well-controlled soft pitches. He won 21 games for St. Louis, raving about Marion and Verban turning base hits into double plays. Another pitcher with an odd shotput delivery, Ken Burkhart, won 19. Brecheen was 15-and-4.

But general manager Jim Gallagher of the Chicago Cubs pirated away Hank Borowy from the Yankees in mid-season, sweetening waivers with a $100,000 commitment. Borowy's 11-2 record was the difference, along with Phil Cavarretta's .355 batting championship and Stan Hack's .323 leadoff excellence. So even though the Cardinals won 95 games and beat the Cubs 16 of 22 times head to head, Chicago won 98 for a three-length victory. Astonishingly, in view of Cubbies' success over previous years, 1945 was the last time a World Series was played at Wrigley Field.

For the Redbirds, with Japan having signed surrender aboard the U.S.S. Missouri in mid-August, the question of how many more pennants St. Louis could win was offset by how many more players they could keep, not sell. They didn't have Branch Rickey measuring weights and measures. Soon they wouldn't have his farm surplus, either. Breadon was shortchanged even before he boldly began to cut players, entirely necessary with so many returning from service.

First, manager Southworth, obviously tampered with by Boston, asked out of the second year of a contract to take a longer, more meaningful job with the Braves. Financially threadbare for years, Boston had the money. With Southworth as field foreman, they soon became the Cape Cod Cardinals—and pennant-winners. Breadon, proudly declining to negotiate, immediately hired as manager a virtual unknown to the average St. Louisan. He was 45-year-old Eddie Dyer, briefly a sorearmed lefthanded pitcher with the Cardinals, on and off from 1922 to '27. A star football and baseball player at Rice, Dyer had an insurance agency in Houston, his adopted home town. There, he assisted Rice in football coaching and worked Southwest Conference football games when not managing, scouting or serving as St. Louis farm director.

The boss immediately hit the new manager in the solar plexus. He sold Walker Cooper to the New York Giants for $175,000 using as part excuse that Cooper didn't like Dyer from an episode in the minors. Dyer, though a hot-tempered Irish-Cajun, was a graceful, persuasive man. His lament was that he didn't have a chance to patch differences. Sale of big Cooper, the most prominent departure of first-base slugger Johnny Mize and pitcher Murry Dickson in the 1940s, proved an immediate and long-range blow.

Veteran replacement Ken O'Dea, expected to move up, suffered back spasms and played seldom. Trigger-quick fire sales of players seemed to be the biggest problem with

TROLLEY SERIES SOUVENIR: A Cardinals' scorecard from the 1944 World Series in which the rival Browns' King of St. Louis shield is mentioned minutely. Below: a billing of a mid-summer '45, fund-raising exhibition in which, using a different pitcher for nine innings, Luke Sewell's Browns shut out the Cards.

Tuesday NIGHT - JULY 10
GIGANTIC WAR RELIEF
BENEFIT GAME
St. Louis Cardinals vs. St. Louis Browns

Beau Geste: In what really amounted to Sam Breadon's last official act the long-time owner of the Cardinals (seated right) enables smiling Eddie Dyer to put away a new signed contract for 1948. Shortly, Breadon ended his 27 years as club president by selling to Robert E. Hannegan and Fred Saigh. Watching the signings (from the left) Harry Brecheen, George Kurowski, Enos Slaughter, Terry Moore, Ron Northey and Howard Pollet.

Breadon rummaging out his Redbirds. The sale of Jimmy Brown to Pittsburgh and Danny Litwhiler to Boston was understandable enough and maybe it wasn't so silly as to wait and see whether Johnny Beazley's arm was all right after pilot service in the Air Corps or whether Ernie White's perennially tender arm would be all right. Maybe they really wouldn't need the firepower of baseball's best pre-war minor league pitcher, John Grodzicki, who suffered a career-crippling injury. A bullet in the buttocks area severed a nerve and produced a dropped left foot, the pushoff anchor foot for a righthanded pitcher.

Worse, without waiting to see whether Dick Sisler, son of the Browns' famed George Sisler, could make it at first base, Breadon sold both Johnny Hopp and Ray Sanders to the Braves. Sanders would suffer a career-shattering broken arm in mid-season, 1946, but Hopp hit .333 that year and in a career that extended seven more years he helped the Yankees, too. Meanwhile, the Cardinals were vulnerable at first base as well as behind the plate. Sisler, a big lefthanded hitter, had come out of the service and, playing for coach Mike Gonzalez's winter-league franchise, had impressed the canny Cuban. "If he play every day," said Gonzalez, "he hit 30 home run—ceench!" That would be more than half Dick's career total of 55 in eight seasons of assorted use, including the 13th of his best season, 1950, when he hit it on the last day to win a pennant for Philadelphia.

Behind the plate with lefthanded-hitting O'Dea unable to function, the job fell immediately to a rangy second-season man, Del Rice, a capable catcher, but a light hitter and slow-footed. Awaiting Breadon was a 20-year-old hometown player, belatedly to be discharged from the Army in the Philippines, where he had hit a tape-measure home run. The name would be recognizable over the years for many things other than the ability to hit a baseball or catch it—Joe Garagiola! Another more prominent thing occurred at spring training. Until Musial belatedly came out of the Navy, startling everyone with a handshake that left a false thumb in a startled grasp, the left fielder was Red Schoendienst. With Kurowski a holdout through the length of spring camp, Schoendienst moved to third base.

Opening day, with Dyer sentimentally starting Beazley for his heavily favored Cardinals, neither Two-Game Johnny was ready nor Kurowski, playing with abbreviated training. They lost the opener, but with Schoendienst moved to third base and Kurowski benched for more conditioning, they won seven in a row. Briefly, with Marion hurt, Red then moved to shortstop. What comes after third base and shortstop? Second base, minus any Abbott or Costello gibberish. Early, the skinny Schoendienst, though profanely suggesting he wasn't going to be "Dyer's utility boy," had said he didn't want to play second. Now, with Emil Verban dealt in a three-club deal for catcher Clyde Kluttz, second base was in Lou Klein's hands—and Klein had seen the writing on the outfield wall.

In mid-May as the Cardinals met their bitter old Brooklyn rivals, Durocher's Dodgers had come back to pre-war brilliance, holding a game and a half lead. Max Lanier won the opener for the Cardinals in 11 innings. Next day the outfield circus of Musial-Moore-and-Slaughter manifested itself, with emphasis on the Slaughter. That day behind Howard Pollet, the outfield trio made a great catch each and Slaughter's came just after old friend Les Webber had thrown repeatedly at him. Enos drag-bunted down first base and ran up the pitcher's back, prompting a brief skirmish and loud Flatbush boos as the Redbird right fielder raced to his position. After Carl Furillo singled, Slaughter dashed in and made a typical seat-of-the-pants slide for a low line drive off Augie Galan's bat. When Ferrell Anderson belted an apparent run-scoring double to the base of the right-center field wall, Slaughter raced over to make a brilliant backhanded catch, followed by a bulls-eye throw that doubled Furillo off first.

The 1-0 result put the Cardinals in first place, temporarily, but mainly it shushed the crowd. With Lanier having won his first six straight games, all compete, the Cardinals moved over to the Polo Grounds, where the veteran lefthander left town and left behind an informative message to young road roommate, Schoendienst. Max, reliever Fred Martin and Klein were jumping to Mexico. In the note, Lanier concluded, "And keep hitting those line drives, Red."

Lanier, making only $10,000 after eight seasons of 64 and 48, including big-game victories over Brooklyn, was among the many unhappy players wooed by Jorge Pasquel, proprietor of the Mexican League and enjoying the sweet smell of success in luring disgruntled U.S. players. First, Pasquel had lured catcher Mickey Owen from the Dodgers and then moved on.

Lanier's loss as the leader of the staff highlighted one of the most remarkable days in the history of the Cardinals. Beazley, making a rare, temporary recovery, beat the Giants at the Polo Grounds, 4-1. Meanwhile, a national rail strike paralyzed travel at a time planes were few and autos still hard to get in the slow plant comeback from war-time tanks, etc. Faced with a forfeit and $5000 fine if the Cardinals did not show up in Cincinnati for a Friday night game after the triple-dip Thursday disaster, traveling secretary Leo Ward wangled a DC-3 that would take part of the ball club's roster. For 1946, rosters had been expanded to 30 players if they included at least five ex-servicemen.

The plane trip for Dyer, Ward, coach Gonzalez, equipment manager Butch Yatkeman and 17 players was almost as funny as the belated arrival by private bus of the rest of the squad and press, originally dumped in Washington in a two-day trip to Cincinnati. The Reds' players had to get home from Buffalo, N.Y., by hiring a fleet of taxicabs. The Cards' late Friday plane flight hit an ominous black wall at Dayton, Ohio, prompting a virtual emergency landing.

With a police escort to Cincinnati about 50 miles distant, wheezing, over-aged taxis had a hard time keeping up, especially one with an ancient hood that popped up. The cabbie suggested that one of the players drape himself across the hood. Passenger Musial suggested that, no, the driver should provide the human ornament and that Stan would be happy to drive. With Musial peering out a side window, they arrived late at the Crosley Field parking lot, where a capacity crowd awaited the game in which the Reds' dimpled darling of the diamond, Ewell (The Whip) Blackwell,

THE WHIZ KID: Billy (The Kid) Southworthy was cover boy for the *Baseball Register* in 1945 after the Cards' third straight pennant.

FIRST-RATE FOURSOME: The Cardinals' championship infield of 1946 – third baseman Whitey Kurowski, shortstop Marty Marion, second baseman Red Schoendienst and first baseman Stan Musial.

IN GOOD HANDS: His own and the trainer's. Senior citizen Marty Marion, famed "Mr. Shortstop" throughout the flourishing '40s, displays a bookend given him with the bronzed hands of trainer Harrison (Doc) Weaver, with whom he roomed. (Note the World Series ring.) Doc not only cared for Marty's chronic aching back, but also acted as his associate in outlining the 1946 Marion pension plan, the basis for baseball's great retirement fund.

sidearmed Harry Brecheen and mates into 3-1 submission.

The rest of the team arrived just before dinner by second bus Monday, minus Marty Marion and roommate trainer Doc Weaver, who had declined to fly or to risk the shortstop's aching back. When President Harry S. Truman stepped in and ordered rail hands back to work, Marion and Weaver leisurely took a train to Chicago, next stop on the trip. So Marion didn't see the debut of Garagiola in Cincinnati. Yogi's pal Joey had joined the ball club back east, timidly walking the corridors rather than risk awakening Marion, to whom he had been assigned. Joe's debut at Cincinnati included dropping the first pop foul hit above him. He spent the next nine years proving he wasn't as good as Breadon hoped, but as better than he said he was, ultimately a standout in baseball's first playoff ever and in the World Series.

The Cardinals faced two problems, and Musial solved them both, en route to his second Most Valuable Player award, a .365 average and the league lead, too, in hits (228), doubles (50), triples (20), and runs scored(124). He drove in 103. Stan solved the first by moving to first base in Sisler's place in early June, shortly after he had solved the other by turning back five $10,000 Pasquel bonus checks on a hotel bed and an offer of $125,000 for five years when he was making only $13,500. Capt. Moore and Slaughter turned back lesser amounts, too.

Breadon, as a result, in defiance to new commissioner A.B. (Happy) Chandler's decree, flew to Mexico City to meet, blue eyeballs to brown, the man "who was good enough to take my players." Pasquel, impressed at the clubowner's approach, said he would try no more with St. Louis players. An angry Chandler fined Breadon $5000 and suspended the Cardinals from 30 days of front-office activity, but he couldn't make the edict stick. Breadon was an honorable man, respected by fellow clubowners. Chandler was no Landis.

At the time of unhappy troops, club officials urged players to make their requests. National League president Ford Frick disclosed that 50 major leaguers were making less than $5000. Players clamored for a bigger basic salary, more meal money, club baggage handling of individual bags and buses from trains to hotels and ball parks. Penny-ante requests compared with the Cardinals.

One rainy day at the Hotel New Yorker, trainer Weaver, nearing retirement, sat with roomie Marion—"the smartest player I ever had," said Breadon—and they crafted what temporarily was called the Marion pension plan. Through $2 daily player deductions, matched by management, and with All-Star game receipts, World Series radio money and, if necessary, a mid-summer exhibition between natural rivals, they sought a $100-a-month pension for 10-year men at age 50. A laughable amount in view of galloping inflation later, but sensible enough for owners like Breadon, Boston's Tom Yawkey, Chicago's Phil Wrigley and the Yankees' Larry MacPhail to encourage pension pursuit. Before the reserve clause brought free agency and average salaries of more than one million dollars, the Cardinal-proposed pension plan had reached the federal limit of $100,000-plus.

Back there in 1946, though, they still were chasing the precious "buckerino," Doc Weaver's good-humored bastardization of American slang and Gonzalez's use of the Spanish "dinero" for money. They even dusted off their biscuit-making Mirandy, the good-luck charm of 1942. Harry Walker suggested it as he had when they switched from another novelty number, "Jingle, Jangle, Jingle." Trouble was, when mother-hen Weaver looked, his record cupboard was bare. Good ol' Doc explored music and second-hand stores without success, but Dr. Robert F. Hyland, a dignified man, yet also a helluva fan, persuaded a radio station to cut a record of the dilly disc. And, bless their superstitious hearts, that very night Goodtime Charley (Red) Barrett pitched a one-hitter against the Phillies. And Barrett, the hit of 1945 and the miss of '46, won only three games that season.

The Cardinals still trailed the Dodgers by seven and a half games on the Fourth of July. What they needed was a confrontation against Durocher and the babbling Brooks. That happened in mid-July and by the time the Cardinals swept four at Sportsman's Park, they had a dog race and the genesis of Stan Musial's nickname. He hit so hard in that one, that when the Cardinals soon reached Ebbets Field, mumbling Flatbush fans shrilled, "Here comes the Man." And you didn't have to be a brain surgeon as a baseball writer to explain the story and arrange it as Stan (The Man) Musial.

The Cardinals might have won one game if Musial, tagging up at third base, hadn't heard Gonzalez warble, "Go, go" when the coach later insisted he had said "no, no." Strong-armed Carl Furillo, even madder at the Cardinals than at Mr. Rickey for paying him only $3750, gunned out the fleet runner from here to there. Little things add up in a race that ends even like in Steven. The Cardinals won one game when giant good-natured Walt Sessi, who got to bat only 14 times all season, pickled an 0-2 pitch off the Giants' Bill (Ninety-Six) Voiselle for a game-winning, two-run homer. So angry that Voiselle hadn't wasted a pitch, manager Mel Ott fined Bill more than the uniform number that qualified for his oddly named South Carolina home town. Then there was the Cardinals' Erv Dusak, considered by many or some even better than Musial when they came up together in the fall of 1941. Erv, good defensively and a versatile outfielder who could even pitch, learned everything except how to hit the curve ball. So he had a short career, but long enough for a couple of game-winning homers that made "Four-Sack" Dusak a logical nickname.

In a race reminiscent of 1941 and '42, '46 went down to the last day when disappointingly, both teams lost, particularly embarrassing for the Cardinals. First, because their old teammate, ailing-armed Mort Cooper, jerked up a 4-0 shut out for Boston over Brooklyn, giving the Cardinals a chance to repay the Braves by beating Chicago. Otherwise, the Braves and the Cubs would share third place. For the Cardinals' windup at Sportsman's Park, Musial got the Cardinals out in front with a third-inning homer off southpaw Johnny Schmitz, but George (Red) Munger couldn't face responsibility. He was knocked out in a five-run sixth. Final: Chicago 8, St. Louis 3.

Result: First pennant playoff ever because the famous Merkle boner post-season game in 1908 had been a replay of a tied game. The historic event required a telephonic flip of the coin conducted in New York by commissioner Ford Frick with Breadon and the Dodgers' manager, Durocher. Leo the Lip, the consummate gambler, won and gave the Cardinals the first game in the best-of-three playoff, though he confided to New York writers en route to St. Louis by train that he wished it would be winner-take-all. "I'm confident," said Durocher, "that we can win two straight."

For one thing, he had confidence because newcomer Ralph Branca had pitched a critical late-season shutout against the Cardinals, but he didn't consider that his side would have to make two clickety-click trips by rail. He didn't remember, either, that the best thing that could happen to Dyer's Redbirds was a game against Durocher's Dodgers. St. Louis had won the season series, 14 games to eight.

For the Cardinals, a ranking candidate for the Cy Young award if it had been established was pitching with a bad back, taped, but the handsome young associate in Dyer's insurance business rose to the occasion. In a season in which he won 21 games, saved five and had a league-lead-

PLUMB GOOD: Martin Leo Ward, a young lefthanded plumber who could get lots of work, yet not get paid for it in the depths of the Depression, joined the Cardinals and became traveling secretary in 1937. Soft-spoken and sartorial, Leo was the front man for the Cardinals from Breadon-through-the-brewery for more than 30 years.

ing 2.10 earned-run average, Howie Pollet was good, gritty and great. Pollet labored, winning, 4-2, in a game in which the youngest and oldest were best. The lefthander's young batterymate, Garagiola, a struggling .237 hitter, had three hits and two RBIs. Old folks Moore, struggling with legs hurt on sandy St. Petersburg soil in spring training, also had three hits.

At Brooklyn, bantam Murry Dickson, a 15-6 pitcher with a 2.88 ERA, toyed with the Dodgers. The Merry Magician, who winked about the "woofle dust" he sprinkled on his pitches, helped himself in a 13-hit attack that included triples by Dickson, Slaughter and Dusak and doubles by Musial and Moore. Dickson led 8-1 into the ninth, with the Ebbets Field faithful, of which there were none richer, stony silent until the beloved Bums rallied. An angry Dyer finally lifted Dickson for his roommate and hunting partner, Harry Brecheen.

The Cat, a deceptive 15-15 regular-season pitcher, had a tell-tale 2.49 ERA and a deceptive screwball. Not immediately successful, Brecheen suddenly faced an 8-4 lead with the bases loaded, clutch-hitting Eddie Stanky and big Howie Schultz coming up with a beckoning bleachers only a grand-slam away. The Cat fanned walking-man Stanky, who seldom struck out, and dipped a pennant-winning third strike past Schultz.

With a final 16-to-8 ratio over the Dodgers, the Cardinals deserved a pennant, notably Musial and Pollet, Kurowski with a .301 season after his holdout and Slaughter, whose .300 even average included a league-leading 130 RBIs. Opening day on the road that season, with Schoendienst and Musial on base, the stocky right fielder slashed a ground ball to second base, an apparent double play, yet legged it out for a run-scoring forceout. In the pressbox Cubs' general manager Jim Gallagher snarled around his cigar, "That big-butted baboon goes into the Army (Air Corps) for three years, drinks beer and comes out running harder than ever."

For the Series, though, the Boston Red Sox, who had won 105 games and lost only 49, were strong (7-to-20) favorites. Joe Cronin's club included a 25-game winner, young Dave (Boo) Ferriss and 20-game Tex Hughson, the staff leader, and a pesky southpaw, who figured to be troublesome, Mickey Harris. And speaking of pesky, Johnny Pesky hit .335 at shortstop, defensive genius Dom DiMaggio .315 in center field and, then of course, wonder man Ted Williams.

Teddy Ballgame had come back from three years in the Marines and hit .342 with 38 homers and 123 RBIs. Williams figured to love the close-up screened right-field pavilion, second only to Detroit's short right-field porch in his fabulous career. If it wasn't a case of playing far enough away, but high enough. Dyer borrowed the "Williams shift," used by Cleveland's Lou Boudreau in desperation to stop those blue-darter sharp grounders and line drives that whizzed through and over the infield. Dyer, who remembered in his playing day when National League clubs put on a similar shirt for dead right-field pull-hitter Cy Williams of the Phillies, made a slight change, suggested by Kurowski. Because lanky Marion covered so much ground, third baseman Kurowski moved over to the second base side, permitting Schoendienst to move into the hole next to deep-playing Musial at first base.

The Cardinals got a break and the Red Sox a bad one in a brief tune-up series the Sox played against American League All-Stars during the week-long delay caused by

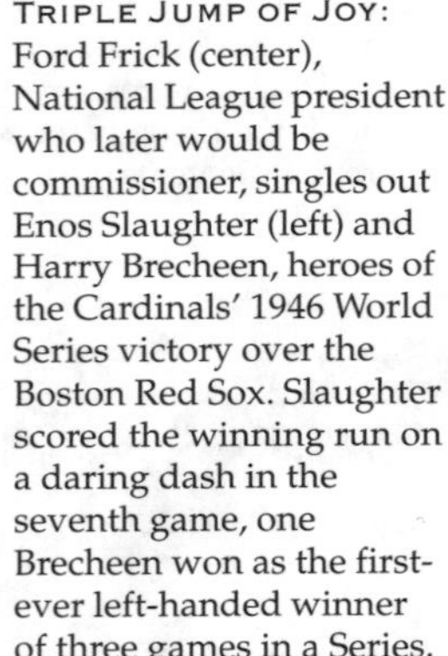

Triple Jump of Joy: Ford Frick (center), National League president who later would be commissioner, singles out Enos Slaughter (left) and Harry Brecheen, heroes of the Cardinals' 1946 World Series victory over the Boston Red Sox. Slaughter scored the winning run on a daring dash in the seventh game, one Brecheen won as the first-ever left-handed winner of three games in a Series.

the NL playoff. Washington southpaw knuckleballer Mickey Haefner hit Williams on the right elbow, and the funny bone wasn't funny, a decided handicap. So, too, was St. Louis lefthanded pitching, especially Brecheen.

Pollet's loss in the first game of the Series was a double-edged blow. For one thing, the ailing lefthander couldn't come back. For another, with a 2-1 lead in the ninth, the great pitcher lost a likely out when Mike Higgins' one-out grounder skidded freakishly through Marion's leg for a hit. Rip Russell pinch-singled the tying run to third, but Roy Partee, batting for Hughson, struck out. One out away, Dyer, calling signals from the bench, wig-wagged for a fast ball sign to righthanded-hitting Tommy O'Brien. Garagiola relayed to Pollet. Howard shook him off. The same sign came, bench to plate to mound. Again, Pollet shook off the sign. Dyer relented and the pitcher served up a slow curve O'Brien bounced past Kurowski for a seeing-eye, game tying basehit to left. In the Boston tenth, big Rudy York hit the hot dog stand for home run that won for the Sox, 3-2. When Dyer lamented the loss as "the worst I ever suffered" neither press nor public knew the sign-defiant dispute.

Brecheen four-hit the Sox in the second game, driving in one of his own runs in 3-0 win over lefty Mickey Harris, but at Boston, facing shutout winner Ferriss, the Cardinals had no chance after York unloaded a three-run homer off Dickson in the first inning of a 4-0 game. For the fourth game Cronin came back with Hughson, Dyer led with Munger and St. Louis pressbox cynics wondered if his teammates could score enough for the big, squeaky-voiced guy who wasn't nearly as tough as that king-sized tobacco chaw made him look. They certainly didn't let George do it.

The Cardinals crammed out a record 20 hits off Hughson and associates—four each by the 4-5-6 men in the batting order, Slaughter, Kurowski and Garagiola. They won handily, 12-3. Frustrated by Williams' failure to hit even more than by the unorthodox defense, Ted bunted safely once toward third base. Late-afternoon Boston tabloids proclaimed the feat in large type:

"TED BUNTS"

Pollet tried to suck it up for the fifth game, but Dyer gave his prize pupil the managerial coup d' grace after a tortuous one-third on an inning in which he allowed three hits, and the first of six runs by which Joe Dobson coasted, 6-3. Dobson's four-hitter was highlighted by a pitch that crushed against Slaughter's right elbow, apparently sidelining him for the rest of the Series. Dr. Hyland, normally aggressive as an early practitioner of what became athletic medicine, urged Slaughter not to play, noting that movement or flaking off the huge blood clot could be fatal. Enos' answer was that he would play and that the life was his.

En route on the 24-hour train trip to St. Louis, Doc Weaver alternated hot and cold packs day and night. Slaughter played, contributed a hit, an RBI and a good catch as aging teammate Moore also rose to the occasion defensively, especially against Williams, who fouled off repeated pitches as long strikes or couldn't pull pitches down and away. Brecheen beat Harris again, 4-1 in the sixth game, and then teamed up with Slaughter to make the '46 Series one of the most memorable in Cardinals' famed World

THE CAT'S MEOW: Harry (The Cat) Brecheen, nicknamed for his quick fielding skill, was one of the Cardinals' best pitchers ever in a career shortened in part by a late major-league start at 28. A lefthander with an effective screwball, shown here with a reverse twist of the wrist, was a little man, but a big-game pitcher. Bandy-legged battler from Broken Bow, Oklahoma, had a peak season in 1948 with 20 victories and a league-low 2.24 ERA. Won 133 games, lost only 92, 4-1 in World Series.

Series history.

Dickson, starting slowly against Ferriss, gave up a first-inning run, knocked in by DiMaggio, but the Cardinals forced out Ferriss in the fourth, a result of runs driven in by Walker, Dickson and Schoendienst. The tinkerer of the toeplate, Thomas Edison Dickson was perfect into the eighth, bouncing gingerly on the mound. Then pinch-hitters Russell and George (Catfish) Metkovich delivered a single and double that imperiled the 3-1 lead. Dyer, annoyed at Dickson's apparent nonchalance in stressful moments and aware lefthanded hitters were next up, moved quickly to southpaw Brecheen. The Cat fanned tough Wally Moses, but Pesky lined to Slaughter, too short and too shallow to risk trying the magnificent cripple's throwing arm. When DiMaggio followed with a two-run double off the right-center field wall, tying the score, Dominic sprained an ankle. Leon Culberson ran for him. Tension mounted. A foul tip split Garagiola's finger creating a delay. Rice went in to catch, and Williams, only one-for-11 against Brecheen, popped out.

Leading off in the home eighth, Slaughter batted with a mission and a notion. The mission was to get on base and the notion, if at all possible, was to run. Enos had been brought up that way, fast and aggressive on the bases. Fact is, he had grumped to Dyer earlier in the Series when Gonzalez held him up on an overthrow at third base. Slaughter knew he could have scored and complained about it. Dyer pacified him with a smile."Kid," he said, "when I first had you back at Columbus, Ga., in '36, you wouldn't say boo. Now boo is just about the only word you don't say. Okay, okay if it happens again and you think you can score, go ahead. I'll take the rap."

Truthfully, Dyer had lost some faith in Mike himself. Gonzalez had seemed preoccupied, understandabley, because commissioner Chandler declared any organized player, coach or manager ineligible if they competed against players who jumped contracts to Mexico. And for good obvious, financial reasons the Cuban Winter League, in which Mike made a heckuva lot more money as owner-manager of the Havana Reds, were going to use box office Lanier, Owen and others. The bursting Mexican bubble had put them in need. So unless Gonzalez gave up his winter job, good ol' Mike would not be back as a coach in 1947.

One thing more, Gonzalez never had achieved with Dyer the friendship he had with Frankie Frisch, who butchered the senor's first name as Mig-u-el. As a freshman manager, Eddie wanted to lean heavily on the experience of the coach, but Mike had been stung when Billy Southworth passed the buck to boss Breadon one time.

Panama Pals: Terry Moore, centerfielder, and captain of the world champion Cardinals, went into service and was stationed in Panama with friend Sam Muchnick, former St. Louis sportswriter and future wrestling promoter. Muchnick, past 90 with this book was published, quipped, "Terry defending the Canal with his bat and me with my typewriter!"

Why, it had been Mike's idea, Mr. Breadon. So when Dyer asked for advice in a particularly sensitive situation that would include the front office, Gonzalez frankly told him of his bitter experience. He didn't want to be twice burned, so he gave Dyer advice that Eddie would pass along from time to time, one that lingers with the authors more than a half-century later. Said Gonzalez to Dyer in his flavored English, "Skeep, nobody die for you, but you." Verily.

Aware that this third-base traffic cop was a virtual lame duck, Dyer didn't know what to expect when Slaughter opened the home eighth in the seventh game of the '46 Series with a single to center off a veteran former Pittsburgh reliever, Bob Klinger. Playing for a run, the manager put down the bunt sign, but Kurowski botched it with a pop foul caught by the pitcher. Batting in place of injured Garagiola, a more dangerous out, Rice was retired. Two outs and still 270 feet from home plate and baseball history, Slaughter was off and running on a pitch to lefthanded hitter Harry Walker, a hitting hero, a .412 average and six RBIs. Even before broad-beamed number "9" hit second base and saw Walker's arching fly fall safely into medium-deep left field, he knew he would try to score. "That Culberson ain't no DiMaggio" he told himself. When Culberson fielded the ball DiMaggio might have caught, he threw accurately, but not powerfully to Pesky, the shortstop relay man. Whether second baseman Bobby Doerr or third baseman Higgins thought he'd score, Pesky never heard from them as Slaughter wheeled past Gonzalez, whose arms flapped in what might have been frustration or alarm. As Pesky would repeat wearily to an old friend years later, the pivoting shortstop turned to face the late autumn sun forming a haze through grandstand louvres behind home plate and even before he threw off-balance, the blurred runner seemed out of reach. True. Photos show catcher Partee charging forth and flopping to his knees to smother his throw as Slaughter slid grandly across the plate. Safe—easily!

That proved to be the winning run, just barely, 4-3, in a game in which Brecheen became the first lefthanded pitcher ever to win three games in a World Series. His closest friend didn't share it with him in the clubhouse. An angry Dickson had dressed hurriedly, jumped into a car and heard the outcome on radio.

The ninth was tense. York opened with a single and Doerr, a .409 Series hitter, also singled. Here, Kurowski at third base made a smart play and a good one. When Higgins bunted for a sacrifice, Kurowski threw to Marion at second base, forcing Doerr, rather than to Schoendienst covering first. So when Partee failed to score the tying run with the second out, the leading run still was on first base when Tom McBride grounded to second, where the ball bad-hopped against Schoendienst's chest. Red trapped the ball near his right armpit, carefully working to extract it as captain Moore, racing in from center field, hollered, "Throw the damn ball, throw it." Red did with a relaxed Series-ending, force-out flip to Marion at second base.

A young reporter hurrying to the clubhouse couldn't resist criticizing older, more respected men sitting like Three Wise Men as official scorers. They had scored Walker's hit as a double, one that would muddy the dash and daring Slaughter. "Gentlemen," the kid said, "you've taken the romance out of a great play."

Defeat was so devastating and Williams so pathetically whipped, weary and downcast that rules were established thereafter preventing photos in the losing side's clubhouse in a World Series. Teddy Ballgame, limited to five singles and one RBI, batted .200 and turned over his modest Series check to Boston's equipment manager and good friend, Johnny Orlando. There's a tendency to bracket Musial because he batted only .222, but his six hits included four doubles, a triple and four runs batted in. For Stan the Man, now official, this marked four World Series and three championships in his first four full seasons in the majors, but, alas, to his surprise and probably to boss Breadon's, too, it would be the last for number "6".

For Breadon, 1946 had been a financial bonanza as the Cardinals, like many other clubs, passed the million-mark in atten-

S-A-F-E: Yeah, safe by what seems like a mile even though this might be regarded as one of the most audacious World Series runs ever. Enos Slaughter, show sliding across home plate in the seventh game of the 1946 World Series at St. Louis, scored from first on what was recorded as a short double by Harry Walker to left center. Slaughter, running through third-base coach Mike Gonzalez's stop sign, caught the Red Sox defense unaware. Shortstop Johnny Pesky's off-balance throw sagged, prompting catcher Roy Partee to slide out and smother the throw. The umpire is Al Barlick, the lanky on-deck hitter is Marty Marion.

dance for the first time, 1,062,563, nearly 300,000 more than the previous best in 1928. And, mind you, at the limited salaries that drove players to Mexico. To enhance his promotional product, Breadon was persuaded to sell radio rights to one organization that would set up a network. When the boss and radio sponsor, Griesedieck, a St. Louis-based beer, preferred Harry Caray and former home-town manager Gabby Street, competitive stations were thrown out, including long-time KMOX announcer France Laux and commentator Cy Casper and KWK's Johnny O'Hara and colorful Dizzy Dean.

Ol' Diz, forced over to the Browns and ultimately to national television celebrity status with rival beer Falstaff, took the decision as an affront. Initially, the talented Caray, who made every game and play even better than they were, and the homespun Street were on KXOK, but soon, retuning from CBS in Chicago as an advertising executive, the son of the team surgeon, Robert Hyland, jettisoned soap operas and brought baseball back to the first station that had aired the first games by Garnet Marks in 1926. KMOX was—and is—the flagship of the far-flung network of stations.

Breadon wouldn't enjoy that association, but, first, he was faced with strong demands by players for more money. Symbolizing the increases, though by far the largest, was holdout Musial's leap from $13,500 to $31,000, the most Breadon ever paid a player. Well aware that slow starts kill off summer advance sales, the ailing 70-year-old businessman panicked after a stumbling start.

After dividing their first four games, the Cardinals lost nine in a row. Casting about for reasons, Breadon wondered if the distraction of baseball's first black player of the century, Brooklyn's Jackie Robinson, was affecting the Redbirds. Would they even refuse to play against the talented young man given a chance by Branch Rickey? Over a toddy or two, Breadon expressed his concern to Dr. Hyland. Doc Hyland liked liquid bull-sessions with writers, too, among them Rud Rennie of the New York *Herald-Tribune*. Rennie, like most other New

York writers, liked Breadon as one of their own. When Rennie came to town and wondered how dear Sam was holding up, the surgeon told the writer of the clubowner's boycott fears.

Unwilling to break a confidential note, Rennie phoned his boss, Stanley Woodward, sports editor of the *Herald-Tribune.* Meanwhile, Breadon had flown to New York, seeking out the opinion of his two trusted senior players about Dyer as a manager. Both Terry Moore and Marty Marion supported the field foreman. Even though they indicated no concern about a threatened strike against Robinson, Breadon mentioned his concern in a visit to president Ford Frick in New York. Hell's bells, Sam, said Frick, they couldn't do that.

Breadon flew back to St. Louis after agreeing with Dyer on a swap of Harry Walker for a hard-hitting, less-talented Philadelphia outfielder, Ron Northey. First day aboard, Round Ron hit a home run at Boston to break the losing streak and, as always, the Cardinals went into Brooklyn and won two out of three from the Dodgers. Robinson played first base without incident. The May morning after the series windup victory over the leading Brooks, a bit of boomeranging history hit the newstand, coupled with a shock that Musial, who had missed the victory the night before, was quite ill. Equally disturbing was Woodward's story that only Breadon's persuasion and especially Frick's threat of career suspensions had kept the Cardinals from striking against Brooklyn's use of a black player.

The canard still hangs heavy over the Cardinals, some of whom didn't want to play against Robinson, but wise enough to know, as captain Moore said, "We're not dumb enough to think we could do anything so heavyhanded. We'd forfeit ball games and lose our pay." Breadon, asked for comment in St. Louis, said he had investigated and found it "only a tempest in a teapot." In Frick's autobiography as commissioner, published in 1973, he remembered Breadon's comments. Frick wrote:

"Because of that ill-timed publicity, the Cardinals were unfortunately marked publicly as the great dissenters when, in reality, their players adjusted more quickly than many of the other players who were vocally vehement in their clubhouse condemnations."

One good reason for the Redbirds' restraint was the leadership of manager Dyer, who as an all-around athlete respected Robinson even more for his talented versatility and competitive drive. Eddie also had played with Frank Frisch when the former three-sport Fordham captain won over St. Louis in 1927. Dyer explained the courtesy of his "hiya, Jackie" winning a smile and a nod from Robinson. "I told my fellows to let him alone. He's like Frisch. Get him mad and he'll beat you by himself."

Yet more than a half-century later, the canard about a strike against the Cardinals lingers. It's as unfair as a situation that occurred that same gray May day when Musial, hitting only .140, was sidelined in his hotel room, unable to accompany the ball club on a day trip to Pittsburgh. The Hotel New Yorker's doctor diagnosed the illness as acute appendicitis, indicating a need for surgery. Musial, naked on his hotel bed, vetoed surgery in New York. Dyer suggested a flight back to St. Louis for examination by Dr. Hyland.

With catcher Del Wilber accompanying him, Musial was met at his plane in St. Louis with an ambulance to St. John's Hospital. There, the doctor confirmed inflammation, but, with an eye to incapacitation, suggested he could freeze the infected appendix and remove it after the season

FRIENDLY FOE: Jackie Robinson, grinning at the jibes of Cardinals, takes a shortcut through the home dugout in September 1949, a key pennant series won by Brooklyn. Robinson was ejected by plate umpire Bill Stewart in a game promptly won by the Cardinals on a base hit off his second-base replacement, Eddie Miksis. Laughing at the left, jacketed in his 1-0 duel with Don Newcombe, is left-hander Max Lanier. Coach Terry Moore leans back against the post, catcher Del Rice has his right hand on the upright.

Weak, Wan and Wilber: Stan Musial, though his face seems more slender because of the hat style in May, 1947, was weak and wan after an attack of appendicitis in New York. For examination in St. Louis, manager Eddie Dyer sent him with catcher Del Wilber as an escort. Dr. Robert F. Hyland met the flight with a hospital ambulance and determined he could freeze the appendix.

ended. Musial approved and gradually improved from .140 to .300 in August, just about the time a national magazine appeared in which *Collier's* Kyle Crichton suggested that the over-rated player had been hospitalized because of a physical beating from teammate Enos Slaughter.

Trouble was, three St. Louis newspapermen had been in Musial's hotel room when Stan didn't have a mark on him or a bedsheet, either. Ordinarily accessible, Musial had been unable to honor Crichton's request for an interview.

Slaughter knows about those things, too. In August he cut Robinson in a play at first base, accidental in Slaughter's judgment, but one which has grown over the years from a slight ankle wound to one described in Ken Burns' baseball television series as one in which "he leaped and slashed Robinson in the thigh." Ask-no-quarter ex-Gas Houser Slaughter twice put Eddie Stanky out of the lineup with rough slides in 1946. A couple of years later he almost stepped on Monte Irvin's foot at first base in a game against the Giants. Irvin confirms what Enos told him:

"Watch your damned foot, Monte. They're still on my back about Robinson."

Robinson, playing magnificently under the pressure of the first of his race, was Rookie-of-the-Year in 1947, a season in which, recovering, the Cardinals made a race of it after sweeping a four-game series in St. Louis at a crippling time of the U.S. Open golf tournament and a streetcar strike!

Hurting even more than the subpar season of Musial—.312 with 19 homers and 95 RBIs—was the virtual loss of big-game winner Pollet, suffering an ugly aftermath of his physical difficulties down the stretch in 1946. Munger was the big winner, 16-5. The only big hitter in a general downside was Kurowski, .310 with 27 homers and 104 runs batted in.

Dramatically, with a need for a righthanded bat to complement lefthanded Northy, the Cardinals made a surprising May Sunday pickup of a well-traveled player recently released by the Yankees. When he waddled up to pinch-hit in the first game and the field announder intoned,"For the Cardinals, pinch-hitting JOE MEDWICK, " a stunned crowd applauded return of a fallen hero. And when Muscles hit the first pitch off the wall in right-center for a double, Ducky Wucky had a happy home for another season. He batted .307.

By contrast, the home-town kid catching, Garagiola, fell under the microscopic analysis on radio of former catcher Gabby Street. The old Sarge analyzed Garagiola's throwbacks to the mound or to second base to the point that every Tom, Dick and Harry Caray was examining the kid's arm. And Dyer didn't help in an unguarded moment when he was quoted back east as saying, "I've got one catcher who can't throw (Garagiola), one who can't hit (Del Rice) and one who can't catch (Del Wilber.)"

There still was—and would continue to be—a big difference in the position Breadon had created by selling Walker Cooper. When the Dodgers won for Burt Shotton, named to replace a Durocher suspended by Chandler, they managed to win seven of the last 10 from the Cardinals, dividing the season series. And in their five-game edge over the 89-65 Redbirds, catcher Bruce Edwards' 80 runs batted in were more than the combined three St. Louis mitt-and-mask men.

For Breadon, that slow start and fast finish, creating a race, brought out his best gate, 1,248,013, one that would be the second largest before the Cardinals moved downtown to Busch Stadium. Breadon long since had given up an idea of his own 43,500-seat stadium. Inflation during and after the war had driven up the cost on construction from $40 to $100 a seat. Beside Singin' Sam was Sad Sam. His health was failing and, based on what he had seen when digging out beyond Lady Bee Britton back there before World War I and more recent troubles with the Yankees, he didn't want a woman to inherit the ball club. When the Yankees' Jacob Ruppert died, the brewer-sportsman had a mistress, but the Yankees had to be sold to meet the inheritance tax and, as a result, Larry MacPhail, Dan Topping and Del Webb got the ball club cheaply.

Only Fred Saigh would know how long and hard Breadon had thought before deciding to sell his love. With 78 percent ownership, he now had $2,600,000 in profits, including more than one million in the ball park fund for a place he wouldn't build, Uncle Sam—the real Uncle Sam—wanted him to build up or pay up. That's when he met Fred Saigh, a little man who had gone a long way from the son of a small-town Springfield, Illinois grocer to a lawyer who at 40 was a wizard at handling downtown real estate. Neat physically, Fred was tidy in his thinking, a sharp man. Asked by Houston people to see about the Cardinals—manager Dyer and friends would have liked to own the parent club of their Texas League Buffaloes—Saigh (pronounced "Sigh") found Breadon more interested in capital gains than in selling to strangers, but he wasn't clubby with the little Lebanese from Northwestern law school by way of Bradley Tech.

Now, conversationally one Irishman mentioned another he liked, a former star St. Louis University athlete, jut-jawed, Robert E. Hannegan, who had gone far in politics. First as St. Louis Democratic chairman, next as Internal Revenue commissioner for St. Louis and finally nationally with IRS and as National Democratic chairman, Bob Hannegan helped maneuver Harry Truman into the White House and a date with destiny. Truman, as President, named Hannegan Postmaster-General.

Nice title, nice honor, but not too much money, and Hannegan, a pretty good semi-pro ball player, was a fan of the Cardinals, a friend of Breadon and also ill. He listened, fascinated, as Saigh conceived a wonderful way to pay Breadon his capital gains price of $3,500,000.

They would form a new corporation and, using Saigh's two big downtown buildings as collateral, they would borrow the money short term. The Cardinals,

LEGAL WORK: Fred Michael Saigh, attorney of Lebanese background, and Robert Emmet Hannegan, as Irish as his name, formed the right kind of combination to attract and buy out Cardinals' owner Sam Breadon in November, 1947. Hannegan, stepping down as Postmaster General under Harry Truman, was named president, Saigh vice-president, though he owned 70 percent of the stock. When Hannegan's struggle with high blood pressure worsened a year later, Saigh bought him out. Bob died in October, 1949 at age 46.

meaning Breadon, owned ball parks in Rochester, Columbus and Houston. They would inherit the cash drawer with its $2,600,000 assets and quickly pay off the bankers. Cost: Little more than $60,000 for the short-term loan.

At the last minute, faced by the obvious affection of many who had worked for him, including Miss "Moiphy", Breadon wanted to call it off, but Hannegan already had quit his cabinet post! So, Sam Breadon stepped down after 27 years as president, most of them as majority owner with nine pennants and six world championships.

Within two years Breadon would be dead of cancer, at first angry when he learned Hannegan had sold out to Saigh, who, as vice-president, really controlled 70 percent to president Hannegan's 30 percent. Hannegan sold out after the 1948 season for $1,000,000 and a handsome return for, in effect, a $15,000 investment. Hannegan, gravely ill, died of blood pressure within a year at 46, relieved that Mrs. Hannegan and her sons would be well-fixed financially.

RAIN, RAIN, GO AWAY: Owner Fred Saigh and manager Eddie Dyer check the weather for a delayed full-house night game with Brooklyn in 1949. From the Dodgers' boss, Branch Rickey, Saigh learned that if it rained, the answer was to double up next possible date with two games for the price of two, afternoon and night.

They finished second again in 1948, this time behind the Cape Cod Cardinals, i.e., Billy Southworth's Boston Braves. Their 85-69 left them six and a half games behind rather than far back only because Musial had his greatest year. When Dr. Hyland removed the appendix and performed a tonsilectomy, too, Stan felt strong from the time he picked up his bat in spring training. He had a remarkable .376 season in which he batted .415 on the road.

Becoming thereafter a home-run hitter, Musial hit 39 and missed by one rained out at New York of becoming the only hitter in the century to lead everything—average (.376), runs (135), hits (230), doubles (46), triples (18), runs batted in (131), long hits (103), and slugging percentage (.702).

"As Musial goes, so go the Cardinals, " Marty Marion would sing out. True, especially when Kurowski ran into a career-crippling period with his sore arm and the pitching wasn't robust except for Brecheen's spectacular 20-7 record and league-leading 2.34 ERA.

The pitching might have been more robust if Murry Dickson had listened to his hunting pal at dinner one midsummer night after Dickson had been beaten by too many home runs at Brooklyn. He complained about the lively ball and shorter fences, but Brecheen shook his head. "Murry," he said, "you're trying to coast and you can't. Go as long as you can as hard as you can."

An eavesdropping reporter took note of home runs allowed and victories thereafter. Dickson, though under .500 for the season, was much better the rest of the way. So it was a shock when he was sold to Pittsburgh for $125,000 before the 1949 season and just after Saigh took control from Hannegan. The lame excuse was that Hannegan had done a favor for his Democratic chair successor, new Pittsburgh owner Frank McKinney. If so—and manager Dyer didn't like it—the political pander made a Democratic donkey out of the Cardinals.

Before the transaction, McKinney advised Pirate manager Bill Meyer that he had a choice, big George Munger or little Murry Dickson and that, of course, Bill would want Munger with a four-season 43-26 record compared with Dickson's .500 50-50. The wily Meyer said, smiling, "No, Frank, I'll take the little one." The little one was a bone in the throat to the Cardinals, beating them five of seven times in a 12-14 season in which the Redbirds, picked fourth, ran another tight race with the Dodgers, managed by Shotton again, and appeared to have the edge, but when you lose by one game, those that get away haunt you.

For instance, a game against the Giants where recent Mexican League returnee, Cuban Adrian Zabala balked just as Nippy Jones hit a two-run homer. Under the rules then, the first decision prevailed, not the more punishing one to the transgressor. And in a game at Pittsburgh, where a new Pirate hot shot, Dino Restelli, got under plate umpire Larry Goetz's skin by jumping out of the batter's box. Goetz directed the Cardinals' Gerry Staley to deliver the ball. Wool-gathering, with Garagiola screaming at him to hurry, Staley checked the runners. Meanwhile, recognizing Goetz wasn't fooling, Restelli stepped back in and delivered the soft pitch for a game-winning, two run-double. Afterward, Goetz sizzled, "I can't throw the damn ball for them."

Dizzy Dean's comment on Zabala's balk pitch for the homer that didn't count: "Dawgonnit, I pitched too soon. Now you can call back your home-runs balls."

With Saigh out in front, helping commissioner Chandler lift the suspension on contract-jumping players, Max Lanier came back and helped with a 1-0 victory over Brooklyn's Don Newcombe as part of the day-night, separate-admission games Saigh had picked up from Branch Rickey. Jackie Robinson, winning a three-way batting race with Musial and Slaughter for the championship, was thrown out just before a rejuvenated Garagiola singled off replacement Eddie Miksis's glove. Pollet was back with 20-game efficiency, joining Lanier, Brecheen and Brazle in a staff deep in lefthanders. Big Munger was 15-8 and Ted Wilks living up to Garagiola's nickname as "The Cork," winning and saving in relief. Jones and Schoendienst helped in hitting, but it was largely Musial and Slaughter, both of them devastating the Dodgers.

With five games to go, the Cardinals were two up on the defeat side. As they rode through rain to Pittsburgh, visiting writers traveling with St. Louis press, traveling secretary Leo Ward pointed out that if the Redbirds were rained out of their last five games, Brooklyn couldn't win even if the Dodgers didn't lose again. Cute thought, possible then because of different rules on making up rainouts, but all the water did was to rain on the parade in the first fold-up of the Cardinals, proudly known as a come-from-behind ball club.

With Saigh selling World Series tickets after a tremendous 1,430,676 attendance at small Sportsman's Park, Dyer decided to send his three lefthanded starters—Lanier, Brecheen and Pollet—to rest up for the final three-game series with the Cubs. At Pittsburgh, with rain setting back one game, Meyer told a St. Louis reporter he hoped the Cardinals would win, "But I don't think

POWER PLAYER: George (Whitey) Kurowski, handicapped by osteomyelitis in his boyhood, underwent surgery that shortened his right arm, but not enough to keep him from becoming a pretty good third baseman defensively and a hard-hitting player. Stocky, thick-legged, Kurowski could run, too, as a star with championship St. Louis teams that were in the World Series four times in his first five years.

they will, certainly not here. When Slaughter slid into second Labor Day in St. Louis, shaking up Danny Murtaugh, he awakened our club. Besides, your guys look tired to me."

To Dyer, too. Eddie called up second baseman Solly Hemus from Houston to give the weary Schoendienst a rest, but in infield practice a bad-hopping grounder broke Hemus's nose. Red, who had tailed back obviously because of a tubercular bug, had to play.

First night, against Munger, who had a way of finding troubles in big ones, rookie Tom Saffell hit the right-field foul pole for only his second homer of the season—a 6-4 grand slam! Afterward, Dickson, making post-season hunting plans with Chicago-bound Brecheen, said he hoped the Cardinals would win, "but you're not going to beat me." They didn't—not for the fifth time—7-2.

Now out of first place, the Cardinals could regain a tie at Chicago, but Lanier, who had won five in a row, faltered and so did Munger in relief. A journeyman named Monk Dubiel beat them, 6-5. On the next-to-last day, Chicago scored three quick runs off Brecheen, an old nemesis, but the Redbirds, pressing, couldn't hit a herky-jerky nuthin'-ball lefthander, Bob Chipman. They left too many men on base and lost 3-1. One behind on the last day, there was hope when the Dodgers' Newcombe blew an early five-run lead. Tension off, the Cardinals romped, 15-5, with two homers and a single by Musial, but it was too late when clutch-hitting Carl Furillo delivered for the Dodgers in the tenth at Philadelphia, 9-7.

Merry Magician: Murry Dickson, little and wiry, was a steady, strong-armed pitcher, breezy with comments that he put "woofle dust" on the ball, but a winner for – and yes– against the Cardinals. Below, the smiling yet unhappy trio who jumped to the Mexican League in 1946. From the left, infielder Lou Klein and pitchers Fred Martin and Max Lanier.

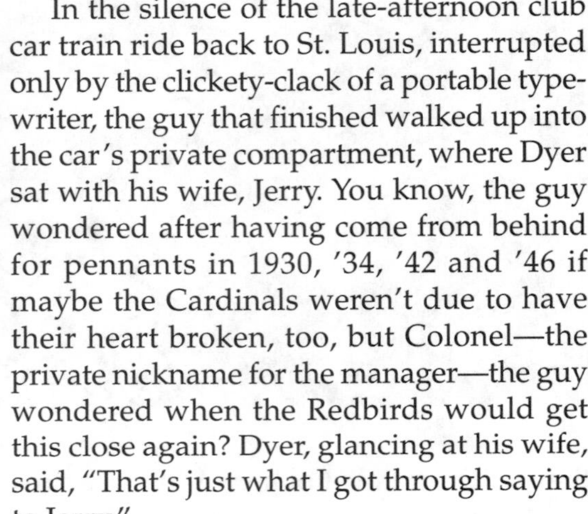

In the silence of the late-afternoon club car train ride back to St. Louis, interrupted only by the clickety-clack of a portable typewriter, the guy that finished walked up into the car's private compartment, where Dyer sat with his wife, Jerry. You know, the guy wondered after having come from behind for pennants in 1930, '34, '42 and '46 if maybe the Cardinals weren't due to have their heart broken, too, but Colonel—the private nickname for the manager—the guy wondered when the Redbirds would get this close again? Dyer, glancing at his wife, said, "That's just what I got through saying to Jerry."

The answer—18 years.

The Fifties were a period of frustration for the Cardinals because they didn't have what Branch Rickey would call "quantitative quality." In other words, thanks to Sam Breadon's scouting retrenchment in World War II and post-war sale of talent, the cupboard was bare.

Eddie Dyer felt the impact even more than Fred Saigh. First baseman Nippy Jones' bad back flared up. Promising young righthander Cloyd (Junior) Boyer suffered arm trouble. Staff leader Howard Pollet faltered and just when marriage had settled Joe Garagiola into a most promising career at the plate and behind it—he was hitting .347—he tripped over Jackie Robinson's foot on a play at first base and fell heavily. Subpar left-clavicle surgery, not performed by ailing Dr. Hyland, headed him toward early retirement.

For Garagiola, of course, his decision in 1954 to walk away from the world champion New York Giants as backup catcher—he turned down a $16,000 contract for $12,000 to go into radio—proved a launching pad to stardom on radio, TV and the banquet circuit.

Musial won the batting championship in 1950 with what—for him!—was a so-so .348 with 28 homers and 109 RBIs. The fifth-place finish, their first in the second division since 1938, finished Dyer. Aware the Cardinals had dropped nearly 400,000 attendance with their 78-75 season, Dyer was prepared to go quietly when he saw broadcaster Harry Caray hovering in a ball-park waiting room. Extremely self-conscious about what he regarded as royal second guessing, Dyer balked. He told Saigh that if Caray sat in on his sentencing, the manager and the boss would have it out. Caray stayed in the ante-room.

Coach Terry Moore and minor-league manager Johnny Keane were rumored as likely successors, but Saigh surprised by choosing 33-year-old shortstop Marty Marion, fading fast physically because of persistent back problems, not helped by his nervous housekeeping attempt to pick up infield pebbles. "Mr. Shortstop" long since had lost his edge to the Dodgers' PeeWee Reese. In Dyer's last year he played only 106 games and batted .247.

Marion, deciding to sit it out as a player, brought back Ray Blades as a coach, impressed in the minors by Blades' ability to give and to steal signs. He also brought up a coach, popular long-time organization handyman , Dominic (Mike) Ryba. Marty, relaxed, had a smiling way by which he could criticize players openly in the press without rancor. His ball club improved by three victories to 81 and two spots to third place, but they were 15 games behind New York and Brooklyn in the historic two-team race won by Bobby Thomson's dramatic playoff home run. Marty's man Stan Musial won another batting championship—.355, 32, 108—and young sinkerball righthander Gerry Staley won 19 games, but, like Dyer, Marion ran into hard luck with young pitchers.

Before he, too, went down with injuries, handsome young righthander, "Baby Joe" Presko, as nicknamed by the *Star-Times* W. Vernon Tietjen, was beating Brooklyn at Sportsman's Park with his easy-does-it delivery and singing fast ball, seeking his sixth straight victory. Trouble was, in a game of missed opportunities that symbolized their frustrations, they got 15 hits and only one run. Presko and even player-smart Red Schoendienst were picked off base. And with runners on first and third, Garagiola inexplicably froze on a hot grounder to Gil Hodges at first base, so he was doubled up when Hodges threw to Roy Campanella for a tag-out and Campy fired back to Hodges. So, in the ninth with two out and one on, Hodges hit a long game-winning homer for a 2-1 Brooklyn victory. Next day, at the trading deadline, Garagiola was traded to Pittsburgh, along with Pollet, Ted Wilks, outfielder Bill Howerton and infielder Dick Cole. The deal for outfielder Wally Westlake and pitcher Cliff Chambers didn't particularly help either side.

Marion's dismissal after one season was surprising. Explaining, Saigh suggested that the runaway race up top, had hurt at the gate, too, because the Cardinals finished closer behind Philadelphia in 1950 when old Redbird Dick Sisler's final-day homer won for the Phillies. To Saigh, Marion lacked fire and, in addition, an unwillingness to spend more time in the office with the owner, in effect, serving as his own general manager. Then the burr-under-the-saddle truth surfaced. Said Saigh, "I still don't know how we could have lost 18 of 22 to the Dodgers!"

THE LONG OF IT AT SHORT: Lanky, rangy Marty Marion greets shortstop Tommy Thevenow, hero of the Cardinals' 1926 World Series, at a 25th-anniversary celebration of the Redbirds' first title team. A broken leg Thevenow suffered in 1927 hurt his career incredibly. In 1951, troubled by an aching back, Marion as manager did not play. Released, he joined the Browns in '52.

When the Giants prevailed in the "Little Miracle of Coogan's Bluff," as the 1951 race was labeled, one spunky little man, Saigh, was impressed by another, Eddie Stanky. Labeled "The Brat," as a hustling, walk-wheedling leadoff man, Stanky indeed fit Rickey's description of the pint-sized player's "intangibles." Stanky might not be able to hit or field or throw, as Rickey exaggerated, but he had a big heart and a winning habit and little tolerance for those who wouldn't play the team game. To get him, even though he had hit only .247 with 14 homers and 127 walks and was past 35, Saigh had to give up lefty Max Lanier and fleet, light-hitting outfielder Chuck Diering.

Taking over a franchise to which he had been a noisy, bothersome enemy with Chicago, Brooklyn, Boston and New York wasn't easy. Eddie deluded himself that he could play second base and Red Schoendienst shortstop. Once earlier maybe for Red, who really didn't have a shortstop's arm. Eddie couldn't carry Red's glove at second base and soon realized it. So he spent himself working with a cheerful, pug-nosed kid Marion had called the "Mighty Mouse"—Solly Hemus. Hemus, using an old-fashioned second baseman's basic squat fielding technique, never was a first-rate shortstop defensively, but he became Stanky's alter ego, a walk-wheedler challenged by the manager to reach base 250 times and he did with 268 on hits, walks and as a human pin cushion with pitches. With a tip by Musial to use a thinner-handled bat, he also achieved the Redbird high of 15 homers by a shortstop. With his emphasis on taking one shot at hitting behind the runner, Stanky improved offense and was rewarded when two old foes, Schoendienst and Slaughter reached the magic .300. Stanky wouldn't use them the last day of the season. "They worked too hard for me—even if they don't like me—to jeopardize in the statistics what they did on the field," said Stanky nobly.

Stanky wasn't at his best handling players, most certainly veterans, or pitchers, either, though he honestly didn't have too much, but he got considerable mileage out of an old reliever, lefthanded Al Brazle, and a young one, righthander Eddie Yuhas. They were Cardinal counterparts of the Giants' Hoyt Wilhelm and Dodgers' Joe Black in a farther stride by knights of the bullpen begun by Ray Blades' breakthrough in 1939, the Yankee-Dodger use of Joe Page and Hugh Casey in the 1947 World Series and Jim Konstanty's Most Valuable Player award for the Phillies' 1950 pennant-winners.

Manly Stanley: The man of many hours in those years when the Cardinals didn't win, Stan Musial is giving a public relations batting tip to Fred Saigh, who ran the Redbirds from 1949 through '52.

Yuhas (12-2 and six saves) would last only one year. Brazle, 12-5 with 16 saves, was a leathery-looking, square-shouldered Colorado cowboy. Even though a roly-poly righthanded slugger like Roy Campanella tattooed fences whenever old Boots and Saddles served up his soft stuff, Brazle's sidearmed sinker and expecially his curve were difficult for disciplined lefthanded hitters, i.e., Dixie Walker, Tommy Holmes and Earl Torgeson.

As subsequent years would indicate, Stanky didn't see the relief magic in Gerry Staley, who would tire as a starter, and he also didn't see beyond the incredible slow-slower-slowest deliveries of a pasty-faced young righthander, Stu Miller, who narrowly missed throwing three straight shutouts. Miller became a great short-order reliever—elsewhere.

Trouble was, in 1952 the staff was lean and green, none greener than a long, lanky kid with the colorful name of Wilmer (Vinegar Bend) Mizell, nicknamed for the Alabama town from which he emerged. Mizell, a rangy Will Rogers with his conversational drawl and droll commentaries, ultimately wound up in Congress, but, originally, it looked as if it would take an act of Congress to get him through the bigs that seemed as tall as his southern pines.

Mizell made his major-league debut on an April night in 1952 that figures in red-letter remembrances in the history of the Redbirds. First, arriving from Washington to see his highly publicized phenom, clubowner Saigh learned he had been indicted for income-tax evasion. Next, wild at first, Mizell lost to the Reds, 2-1. Finally—and this was virtually man-bites-dog news—an umpire threatened a player! In a squabble with Stanky's playing clone, Hemus, plate umpire Scotty Robb got in a shouting match with the gesturing Stanky. Suddenly, the ump pushed the manager, whipped off his mask and stepped back as if to measure Muggsy with the weapon. Stanky was as stunned as league president Warren Giles, present at the game. Giles fined Hemus $25, Stanky $50 and Robb an "amount in excess of both," probably $100. Indignant, Robb promptly quit, quickly caught on in the American League and soon decided he didn't like it there, either.

With Musial winning a third straight

batting title, embarrassed he hadn't driven in more than 91 runs with his .336 average and 21 homers, Stanky's team won 88 games, the most until close pennant contention 11 years later.

While Redbird fans were discouraged by the eight-game distance between pennant-winning Brooklyn and their third-place club, their neighbors—and ball park proprietors—were able to double their embarrassing gate beyond a half-million. With burrhead Bill Veeck having bought the Browns from the brothers DeWitt, Bill and Charley, Veeck tried to charm crowds and to annoy Saigh.

Somehow the Sport Shirt, as open-collared Veeck as in "wreck" was called, delighted in surprising fans with everything, of which the use of a midget pinch-hitter was tops. He delighted, too, in trying to needle, cajole and anger the Cardinals' owner by scooping up discards. First, he hired Marty Marion, presumably as a player, and then when Saigh fingered Harry Brecheen as his pitching coach, Veeck gave The Cat more money to stay as an obviously over-the-hill pitcher. Soon, Marion became manager who played little for the Browns, inheriting the club when Veeck did in St. Louis what his father had done as general manager in Chicago. That is, fire Rogers Hornsby, a popular public choice as pilot that boomeranged. Brecheen, moving to Baltimore, became a great pitching coach for the Orioles.

Saigh, no softie, wouldn't have bowed to Veeck, who was well aware that his old sportswriting friend, Russ Lynch of the Milwaukee *Journal*, had led the movement by which Milwaukee built a major-league ball park on an if-come basis. At the time, this was a boldest of moves, undoubtedly encouraged by Veeck, formerly a popular owner of the minor-league Brewers. You know, fellas, build it. If nobody else will come, I probably will.

Suddenly, unexpectedly in the view of legal eagles in St. Louis, Saigh was given a 15-month sentence to go with a $15,000 fine atop his income-tax penalty. Federal Judge Roy Harper once had been business manager at an old Cardinals' farm club at Caruthersville, Mo. Saigh was asked to sell the Cardinals by the new commissioner, Ford Frick, whom he recently had helped move up from league president to Happy Chandler's chair. He reluctantly agreed. Emerging from a meeting in New York, Frick said in his soft gravel, "This is the biggest day in this little man's life."

FRED'S SAIGH: For Fred Saigh, it was indeed a sad moment, but for Anheuser-Busch a big one when the brewery bought the Cardinals at an early-morning session in February, 1953. To his right, August A. Busch Jr., Adalbart Von Gontard and John L. Wilson, all representing A-B. The fifth man is National League president Warren Giles.

The unhappiest, too, and—for baseball—one of the most significant. No major league franchise had moved in the half-century from when Milwaukee moved to St. Louis in the American League in 1902, but now there soon would be a game of musical chairs, one which broke hearts in many traditional towns and created new ones in a regional-to-national expansion of big-league baseball. A what-have-you-done-for-me-lately attitude still makes many a city more nervous than St. Louis was in early 1953.

For too long, St. Louis had enjoyed the luxury of both the National and American Leagues, one of five cities that soon would be only two with moves from Boston and Philadelphia, both larger. So there was no panic, but inner-circle concern because Milwaukee for one and Houston for another spoke out. Quietly, Saigh turned down $750,000 more from Houston and $500,000 more from Milwaukee to sell to Anheuser-Busch for $3,750,000.

Resentfully over the years, Saigh was annoyed by orchestration that the brewery saved the ball club, and, worse, that the president of the brewery, August A. Busch Jr. was "clubowner". The clubowner was, of course, stockholders, among them Saigh, probably wiser than anyone to the goodwill and public-relations aspects of owning a ball club. He bought 28,000 shares of brewery stock. Over a half-century's ownership of the Cardinals, which cost them $3,750,000, king Budweiser and its alcoholic buddies went from celebration of five million barrels a year to 85-million plus barrels.

Through success, under father and son, inflation and stock splits, Saigh's shares of stock reached 1,089,000, today worth nearly $60 million. With a selling price of $150,000,000 in 1996—and it's apparent he could have asked for more—the third August Busch, Gussie's son and even more efficient successor—the brewery hit a financial grand-slam, but St. Louis, in return, got a stadium jewel still deservedly named Busch Stadium and warmth for the Busch who died at 90 in 1989, having lived hard and fast. Affectionately, he became good ol' Gussie.

THE DAY THE BIRD BECAME A BIG EAGLE: Grinning, August A. Busch, Jr. (right) becomes president of the Cardinals with Anheuser-Busch purchase of the ball club, February 20, 1953. The happy man in the center is National League president Warren Giles. Most unhappy at the left is Fred Saigh, asked to sell by commisioner Ford Frick after an income-tax conviction. Saigh, recognizing even more than the brewery the P.R. value of the Cardinals, immediately bought 28,000 shares of brewery stocks.

Truly a local legend and a national figure, August Adolphus Busch Jr.—why the heck didn't they call him August *Anheuser* Busch?—was prominent, yet aloof to the man in the street until Anheuser-Busch bought the ballclub. An avid horseman, a rugged outdoorsman, he loved to hear the stags at bay bang horns at mating time in the rich family estate. It's only slight exaggeration that Gussie didn't know a foul ball from a mallard. Oh, sure, socially he had known Frankie Frisch and Leo Durocher of the Gas House Gang and he hunted with Red Schoendienst and the redhead's neophyte firearm neighbor, Stan Musial, but he soon was captivated by a steely blue-eyed guy he inherited as manager, Eddie Stanky.

Meanwhile back at the ranch, where previously Busch would have liked to be, things moved faster than Gussie getting a first walk-through rusty, rundown Sportsman's Park with gimpy Bill Veeck, still pretty nimble on his prosthesis. Yardstick ruler in hand, Veeck went along when Busch touched all the toilets and creaky crannies. Afterward, Busch rasped, "I'd rather have my ball club play in Forest Park than play here." City inspectors, aware of the brewery's vulnerability, talked about stopgap safety measures being necessary. Veeck was offered $800,000 for the old ball yard, $1,100,000 if he left town. That didn't sit well with Brownie fans and American League beer drinkers, but Veeck already had answered the siren summons of Milwaukee's Lynch and the Wisconsin burgomeisters. Trouble was, Lou Perini heard it, too.

Perini owned the Boston Braves and had pumped enough in for Southworth and the Cape Cod Cardinals to win a rare pennant in 1948, but the Braves backslid into distant second place behind the Red Sox in New England affections. With fewer than 300,000 attendance in 1952, and a seventh-place finish, Perini trumped Veeck's bid. His minor-league farm club, the American Association Brewers, gave him territorial rights in Milwaukee. With the March blessing of the National League, barely a month before the season opened, he got it.

The Boston Braves would become the Milwaukee Braves, en route to Atlanta a decade later. Next year, without Veeck, frozen out of an immediate move to Baltimore, by starched-collar American League executives who didn't like him, the lame-duck Browns became Orioles. Soon followed in 1955 by the Philadelphia Athletics who became the Kansas City A's en route to Oakland. And when Walter O'Malley, who had squeezed out Branch Rickey, took Brooklyn to Los Angeles in 1958 and persuaded Horace Stoneham to go from New York to San Francisco, stop the music!

Busch stepped onto baseball's merry-go-round. He soon was captivated by the conventionality—he liked cheese sandwiches as much as he did caviar—and by the baseball intelligence of Stanky, a great teacher. Other than this prejudiced view of a guy who began fighting Stanky and then admiring him, The Brat won a deserved prize of the Cardinals' long-time guru of baseball instruction, George Kissell, as the best teacher. Enough said!

By happenstance, the other Sudsville, Milwaukee, was the site of the Braves' first home game there and Busch's first of ownership. Gussie, who didn't fly then, took a train to Milwaukee where he huddled at a chilly opener won by Warren Spahn from the Cardinals, as usual, 3-2, on a tenth-inning homer hit by rookie Bill Bruton. Bruton batted more than 600 times that season and didn't homer again. Busch's first home game was a near disaster, too, saved only by rookie Harvey Haddix, a 20-game winner in a season of limited pitching. With a night-game opener, a tradition begun in 1950 by Saigh, Busch watched in horror as pre-game aerial bombs didn't burst, tenor Phil Regan couldn't sing the Anthem because of a sore throat and Gov. Phil Donnelly had a sore arm and couldn't throw out the first ball. Happily Haddix, called "The Kitten" as almost the spitting fuzzy cousin of "The Cat" shut out the Cubs.

With inexperienced pitching and the presence of other rookies like the Three Polish Falcons—first baseman Steve Bilko, third baseman Ray Jablonski and left fielder Rip Repulski—they dropped five more victories to 83 and dropped to a tie with the Phillies for fourth. Brewery ownership was no immediate panacea for attendance, 880,242, not even with those orphaned Browns playing before huge crowds of empty seats. It didn't help, either, when the mighty Musial had a horrible slump, as low as .250 in June before a spectacular surge to .337-30-113.

GOOD LUCK, GUSSIE: August A. Busch Jr. (center) gets a welcome at the Cardinals' spring training camp the first year the brewery bought the ball club. From the left, manager Eddie Stanky, Enos Slaughter, Busch, Red Schoendienst and Stan Musial.

As a result, roomie Red Schoendienst, getting a timely week's rest because of an injury, almost won the batting title with a .342 season. In the All-Star game at Cincinnati, Slaughter, 37 at a time rosters had few older players, starred in a 5-1 victory over Casey Stengel's American Leaguers. He walked, singled twice, stole a base and executed a sliding catch of a low line drive. Said Ol' Case, "I hafta say he's still an amazin' man as he was when I was in the league."

Obviously, with that typical Yankee idea of a late season acquisition that had helped nail down a record five straight world championships, the Yankees (1) did their shopping early, (2) Busch spent $2,500,000 to improve Sportsman's Park with more and better rest rooms, bigger box seats and an arboretum in center field, (3) the Cardinals' attendance in the now one-team town increased about 250,000 to 1,039,698, (4) Stan Musial hit a record five homers in a doubleheader and (5) the Cardinals acquired their first major-league-level black players. One was ready, Brooks (The Bull) Lawrence. The first, Tom Alston, unfortunately, wasn't.

With Busch eager for better talent and also to end St. Louis' resistance to the color line, baseball men in the organization worked hurriedly, peeling off $100,000-plus

A Broadening Thought: The *Post-Dispatch*'s Bob Broeg, seated, offered his ample derriere to measure new stadium seats when the brewery renovated Sportsman's Park in 1954, rechristened Busch Stadium. Box seats were widened from 18 inches to 21, as published in the ball club's house organ, *Cardinal News*. Standing (from the left), Ellis Veech, East St. Louis sports editor; Nat Hall, ball-club ticket manager; Jim Scott, INS reporter; Dick Meyer, brewery vice-president and Cardinals' general manager, and Al Banister, stadium supervisor.

purchase prices for tall Tom Alston, a first baseman with San Diego of the Pacific Coast League. They also bought a soft-serving Mexican lefthander, Memo Luna, best known in a one-game big-league venture for having a father as mayor of a town south of the border. Alston, gangling, fast, a nice guy with a brilliant glove, was physically under par—it looked as if the bat swung Tall Tom—and he had mental distresses that affected him, too. His .246 in 66 games didn't help much in a sag to sixth place, 72-82, but The Bull helped.

Brooks Ulysses Lawrence, son of a Pittsburgh policeman, came along just after the first black pitcher, Bill Greason, proved inadequate. The burly Lawrence, whose aggressiveness delighted an aggressive man, Stanky, won 15 games, lost only six, but with only Haddix effective among starters, pitching once more was short. This time Dick Meyer, Busch's valuable righthand man at the brewery, had stepped in at the ball park and acquired Alex Grammas from Cincinnati to play shortstop. (Cost: $100,000 and pitcher Jack Crimian.)

Colorful Busch liked colorful characters and the Cardinals got one at an early-season exhibition at Rochester. At a look-see of the Red Wings' first baseman, Joe Cunningham, Stanky told the Rochester GM, Bing Devine, a bright man with a bright future, to wrap him up. Immediately moving to first base with the Cardinals so that Musial once again could move to the outfield, the lefthanded-hitting Cunningham hit three homers his first two games, two off masterful southpaw Warren Spahn. Jersey Joe then was a shy guy from Saddle Brook, N.J., but not for long.

Musial, who later would keep Cunningham in the outfield, where Joe excitedly made easy catches look hard, had a most unusual day for an unusual man May 2, 1954, a day the spruced up ball park's pressbox was filled with writers headed back from the Kentucky Derby the day before. Before the game, New York *Post* writer Arch Murray, aware Willie Mays had come back from service to the Giants, wondered who Stanky thought was the best ball player in the league. Eddie pointed to Musial. "Still No. 6" he said. That day Musial hit five home runs in a doubleheader, including three in the first game, and his best shot, one he didn't properly pull, was hauled down by Mays at the center field fence.

The improved new look to Sportsman's Park, rechristened Busch Stadium after the face-lift, was the scene of an extraordinary reaction at the first pre-season exhibition game played there. A player traded to the champion New York Yankees cried! Making a long story short, at spring training that year a gaunt, beetle-browed outfielder from Omaha, Wally Moon, had shown up at St. Petersburg instead of the minor-league camp. A classic boo-boo by the guy with a Master's Degree from Texas A & M, but great for him, but not for Enos Slaughter. Stanky agreed, with Meyer's blessing, that he could afford to give up the veteran for whatever the proper offer.

The Yankees offered a Triple-A outfielder, Bill Virdon, who like Moon, would win Rookie-of-the-Year recognition and long-time service, but that was unforeseen and far ahead when Slaughter took the news hard. Sixteen years after he came up as the boy from the boondocks, "Country" felt betrayed. When he wept with face hidden behind glistening bald head before the game, he met Musial across the street afterward.

They both cried.

Slaughter, sought by Casey Stengel, helped Ol' Case to three more pennants before, at 43, he wound up at Milwaukee in 1959, six seasons after the Cardinals traded him. St. Louis retired the Old War Horse's No. "9" as a baseball Hall of Famer in 1996.

Strange bedfellows with the highly successful Yankees, who most quickly had copied the Cardinals' farm system program, the Redbirds peeled off $85,000 from eager-beaver Busch's brewery buckerinoes for Vic Raschi, a giant of past Bronx Bomber success. In New York he had a 110-40 record, including three 20-win seasons and a rich reputation in the big ones. To the regret of Stanky, who admired his competitive tenacity if not his dwindling stuff, Raschi gave up two noteworthy hits his first two starts. Second day, 1954 at Milwaukee, he gave up a double to a willowy outfield rookie with a quick snap of the wrists, the kid's first hit. A few days later against the same Braves at Busch Stadium, Raschi gave up a home run to that willowy outfield rookie—the first of 755 for Henry Aaron!

Managing, Stanky had his moments of redemption as, for instance, when Wallace Wade Moon, named for a famed defensive coach of champion Alabama and Duke teams, hit a home run in his first time at bat in the majors. He hit .304 for, as mentioned, National League Rookie of the Year. Overall, though, Stanky suffered. In a rain-delayed doubleheader with the Phillies at Sportsman's Park, a free-for-all fight delayed one game, with Terry Moore, fired as coach by Stanky and then managing Philadelphia, trying to find Eddie in the pile-up. When The Brat had Cot Deal deliberately stall and miss the plate in the fifth inning of the second game, umpire Babe Pinelli awarded a forfeit to the Phillies. The fans booed Stanky, cheered Moore.

When league president Warren Giles came to town for a hearing, during which he suspended Stanky for five days and fined him $100, Giles explained the farce with a capital "F". All concerned, including the umpire, thought lights could not be turned on to complete a game that began after 6 o'clock. (The second game began at 6:45). The weird time-table had been designed by former commissioner Happy Chandler to pacify Baptists, but, as Giles noted, it had been changed. If, Giles noted dryly, the Cardinals had protested a misinterpretation of the rules, he would have had to uphold the protest, void the forfeit and declare the game resumed. The Cardinals' vice-president, Bill Walsingham, inherited by Saigh and then Busch from his uncle, Sam Breadon, had muffed it along with the veteran Pinelli.

Stanky apologized, but the sensitive folks at the brewery's burgeoning public-relations firm, Fleishman-Hillard, were worried. When the Cardinals in 1955 neared Memorial Day, with Stanky using rookie Ken Boyer at third base, Virdon in center field and Larry Jackson pitching, the manager thought he had a youth movement ahead. Serving as GM then, with Dick Meyer recalled by the brewery as too important to A-B, Bing Devine brought years of responsibility to the job and understand-

BOO-HOO: Bosco Enos Slaughter was glum in 1954 (below), happy when the Redbirds retired '9' in 1996.

ing of Stanky.

Trouble was, Stanky got into a fuss at Cincinnati with another little gamecock, Reds' coach Dick Bartell. When Cincy scored the winning run in the tenth inning of a doubleheader opener, Rowdy Richard gave Stanky an obscene gesture as the manager cut across the field to the clubhouse. Not too many fans saw it, but Stanky saw red. In the clubhouse, with lunch meat, bread and condiments spread out on the table for between game consumption, Eddie backhanded the picnic spread. Unfortunately, the yellow mayonnaise jar banked off tan mustard and into the ketchup, cutting Stanky's hand as red as the condiment.

This was, as Mr. Dickens said, the worst of times, anyway, because that weekend ailing trainer Harrison J. (Doc) Weaver died in St. Louis. Big Bucko Weaver, who played fullback for coach Branch Rickey, was an osteopath who came in to visit an old friend back in 1927, took a trip with the ball club as a lark and stayed. He was muscle-massage-morale man and, as mentioned an inventor, too. With an open date Monday, many key players and Weaver's capable replacement, Bob Bauman, who had decided to stay in St. Louis rather than go with the Browns to Baltimore, would take a train to the funeral. Stanky and the rest of the club would go on to Chicago, with the manager trying to conceal that bandaged cut hand.

Frustrating Success: In 1955 the Cardinals hit a record club homerun total, 143, of which Wally Moon had 19, Rip Repulski (seated at left), 23; Bill Virdon, 17; Stan Musial, 33; and Red Schoendienst, 11; but the Cards finished seventh in an eight-club league.

Aware of the misplays by the tender greenpea players, accounting for a 17-19 record, a sympathetic story written by a guy who appreciated Stanky's baseball acument was, in effect, the final straw. A day after it appeared in the *Post-Dispatch* and as the Cardinals finished a two-game series, Stanky was canned en route to St. Louis. A cub of "The Lion," as he called Leo Durocher, Eddie had picked up a few of The Lip's flaws as well as the good ones. Included was taunting that turned the Cubbies into bad nasty Bears.

Over a beer when he learned he was out, Stanky said softly, "And I would have managed this club next year for nothing," an exaggeration probably in the promising young team's outlook as well as in a professional's value of his services. Stanky still was enough of a pet of Busch that, uniquely, Gussie permitted the exiting manager to serve, in effect, as master of ceremonies at a press conference in which Harry Walker, player-manager at Rochester, took over the job. Talkative and talented, The Hat had problems, including the fact that he couldn't hit or play enough to inspire major leaguers as he had in the minors.

If Walker made any mistake, it was overworking players with morning workouts after day games and, additionally, in calling up too many Rochester players who didn't have major-league credentials. Even Musial, for whom he had the highest respect, dropped off to .319 in a tumble down to seventh place with a 68-86 record reflected in attendance of only 849,130. Musial did hit 33 homers of the Cardinals' team-record 143, a mark that lasted until 1997. The total in '55 included 23 by Rip Repulski, 19 by Wally Moon, 18 by Ken Boyer, 17 by Bill Virdon and 11 by Red Schoendienst. There would be an asterisk, of course, because for the first and only time from 1929 to the ball park's end in 1966, the right-field screen did not impede home runs. At Stanky's request in '54, publicist Jim Toomey charted fly balls that would have landed in the rightfield pavilion if there hadn't been the 20-foot screen above the 11-foot wall. The result, 35 for the Cardinals and 18 for the foes, indicated a legitimate reason to take a home-field advantage. However, in 1955 the visitors hit 28 into the screenless area to only 24 for the Redbirds. Included by the opposition was two in one game by ping hitter Richie Ashburn, whose many walk-wheedling, bunting and fouling-off skills did not include homers. He hit only three, duly—and quickly—noted by Frank Lane when the flamboyant Trader Horn of the diamond came aboard after the 1955 season.

Hiring Lane as GM was unfortunate, expecially when he requested and received unlimited power, but Gussie Busch was desperate, tired of what he didn't do well—lose. So he listened when *The Sporting News* J.G. Taylor Spink, who years earlier had helped Miller Huggins go the other way, urged the brewer sportsman to bring in Lane. Frantic Frank, as they called him, was a self-styled "park rat" from Cincinnati. He didn't believe in working unless it was in sports. A physical fitness fadist and a showoff who insisted on refereeing the coldest football games in short sleeves, he got by whistle-blowing in college and pros until he came out of the Navy, a most handsome officer, and into baseball with the Kansas City Blues, then as president of the American Association. At Chicago, with Paul Richards, he used shrewd deals to turn the White Sox from pretenders into contenders.

Lane, insisted Spink, was the man. Maybe, if the Cardinals' front-office field men, Walter Shannon and Joe Mathes, hadn't decided to "force feed" kids into the bigs, cutting short preparation, so that the ball club was losing. Lane, taking over, listed only six players as "untouchable"—Schoendienst, Boyer, Virdon, Moon, Haddix and Musial. Hah! Before the 1956 season was two months gone, three of the untouchables were gone, and Trader Lane burned to send off the franchise player, Musial.

Lane quickly fired manager Walker, who thought he was short-cutting preparation with his morning workouts. Frank brought in a former Seattle schoolboy wonder, 37-year-old Fred Hutchinson, a ruggedly handsome former pitcher best known for his competitive zeal and his temper. When he managed earlier at Detroit, where he had been a pitcher, Hutch's calling card included dismantling dressing rooms. Whenever, for instance, the Yanks followed the Tigers into a town, Yogi Berra didn't have to read the paper to determine from the clubhouse furniture whether Detroit had won or lost. He recognized the kindling wood.

First, Lane and Hutchinson scored with the fans by bringing back Terry Moore as a coach and adding two more St. Louis favorites, Johnny Hopp and the Browns' Al (Boots) Hollingsworth. Just as quickly, Lane went from public penthouse to outhouse by removing the traditional bird-and-bat insignia from the uniform front leaving only a scrolled "Cardinals." He substituted blue socks with white stripes for the road uniforms that had red hose with blue and white stripes. To "stabilize" the young club, he picked up veteran Ellis Kinder, a former

MASSAGE MEN: Cardinal's trainer Bob Bauman, well-remembered for his massage-and-morale efforts with the old Browns and St. Louis University athletic teams, and colorful Dr. Harrison J. (Doc) Weaver, whom Bauman succeeded as Redbirds' trainer in 1955.

Browns pitcher who had made it big. He also picked up another old favorite, Walker Cooper, as a player-coach-pinch hitter. He traded for an over-the-hill slugger, the Cubs' Hank Sauer, then raised brows by dealing Lawrence to the Reds for little lefty Jackie Collum. The Bull won 19 for the third-place Reds.

Although exhibition games don't count, Hutchinson's team won 21 of 32 and began the season briskly. Opening day, though he intended to play Don Blasingame at shortstop, Hutchinson decided to let holdover Grammas play there, hoping not to pressure the kid. With Bill Sarni catching Vinegar Bend Mizell, the Cardinals won the opener on a two-run hit by Musial off lefty Joe Nuxhall, 4-2. And they were in first place a couple of weeks later, 13-and-7, when the trading itch hit the baseball ivory-hunter. First, he sent pitchers Harvey Haddix, Stu Miller and Ben Flowers to the Phillies for an old ex-Redbird, Murry Dickson, and also Herman Wehmeier. The big good-natured Cincinnati Dutchman, Wehmeier, was a nice guy with one weakness. He couldn't beat the Cardinals—zero and 14—but Lane had put him where they couldn't beat him.

Go Get 'Em, Podnuhs: Dizzy Dean, all nearly 300 pounds of him, was doing his national Game-of-the-Week on television when he greeted the McDaniel brothers, Lindy (left) and Von in a 1957 game in St. Louis. Von, 18, just out of high school, joined Lindy in what really was only one season of recreating the Dean brothers.

When Lane sent pepperpot Hemus to Philadelphia for Bobby Morgan, the explanation was that he wanted a better shortstop, but both the Dodgers and Phils had found that as a shortstop, Morgan was a pretty good second baseman. Slowly, surely, painting himself into a corner, Frantic Frank dealt shortstop Grammas. The backup shortstop to Blasingame went to Cincinnati with pinch-hitter-outfielder Joe Frazier for infielder-outfielder Chuck Harmon. Harmon's first comment when he came to the Cardinals was a downer. "I thought," he said "I was going to the minors."

Within hours, having watched young Bobby DelGreco hit two homers in a game for Pittsburgh, Lane traded Rookie-of-the-Year center fielder Virdon to Pittsburgh, where Bill immediately hit .317 and became a defensive mainstay for winning Pirate ball clubs. DelGreco was a good-field, no-hit bust. The loss of Grammas had immediate concern because Blasingame soon proved he was no shortstop and, as mentioned, Morgan wasn't either. So something had to give, and it was one of the Redbirds' most popular players ever, Schoendienst. The Giants were willing to deal Alvin Dark, a gifted all-around athlete who had teamed in a slick second-base combination with Eddie Stanky for the Braves and Giants. The ball club and brewery were bombarded with protests as Red went for Dark in a multiple-player deal that also sent catcher Bill Sarni, pitchers Dick Littlefield and Gordon Jones for catcher Ray Katt and Don Liddle. Oh, yes, Lane explained lamely, the Giants wouldn't have made the deal if he hadn't thrown in Jackie Brandt. At the time of limited farm-system talent, Brandt was the apple of every front-office and minor-league official. In fairness, the 20-year-old Brandt never achieved full expectations in an 11-season career, but he could run, hit, field and throw. A little flaky, for stardom, maybe, but at the time the deal was a psychological blow.

The biggest blow was avoided when Lane was sniffing toward a deal with Philadelphia, Musial for Robin Roberts, a future Hall of Fame player for a future Hall of Fame pitcher. It never happened because Musial's business partner, Julius (Biggie) Garagnani, picked up a phone and told an Anheuser-Busch official that Stan wouldn't report. Of course, he would have had to play because peonage still was the name of the game, but Busch insisted to Lane that Musial was untouchable. Face-saving Frank asked to be allowed to make the announcement.

As the Cardinals slid down into a fourth-place finish, 76-78, young Ken Boyer at third base hit .305 with 26 homers, starring at the All-Star game in Washington, where he and Musial both homered. Stan's season-long average was the lowest to that point in his career, .310, but his 27 homers included a league-leading 109 RBIs. At the All-Star game luncheon at D.C.'s prestigious Touchdown Club, Musial was presented with a handsome giant hall clock, a gift from *The Sporting News* for having finished first in a Player-of-the-Decade poll taken among players, managers, coaches, scouts, umpires, clubowners, baseball writers and broadcasters. Flattered, Stan the Man hit a home run of acceptance when he said with thanks, "I can't hit like Williams, field like DiMaggio, throw like Feller or run like Robinson."

Musial and his associates had one graceful end to the season, to the bitter disgust of the Milwaukee Braves. With the Braves one up over Brooklyn the last weekend of the season at St. Louis, the Dodgers swept so that the Braves lost and then needed a Saturday night victory to stay in the race. Warren Spahn lost because DelGreco fielded sensationally for the Cardinals in center field and Musial tagged Spahn for a double and scored when Rip Repulski singled off Eddie Mathews' glove.

One historical footnote. Opening series the next year, 1957, DelGreco, who had played phenomenally in center field that black Saturday night for the Braves, dropped the first fly ball Milwaukee hit to him. Oh, such language from the Braves!

Now under the restraint of having to clear deals with the boss first, Lane seemed to have made sensible moves for 1957. He obtained the Phillies' favorite boo bird, outfielder Del Ennis, for the last of the Polish Falcons, Rip Repulski. From Chicago he obtained temperamental pitcher Sam Jones for Tom Poholsky. The Cardinals almost won in 1957 with a performance Lane correctly labeled "courageous and aggressive," bouyed by two 15-game winning pitchers, Larry Jackson and former bonus baby Lindy McDaniel. Ennis delivered power, 24 homers and 107 RBIs. Cunningham hit .318 and Musial, at 37, delivered in a Cinderella story almost as remarkable as the fairy tale about 18-year-old Von McDaniel.

VOICES OF THE GAME: When Jack Buck joined Harry Caray in broadcasting Cardinal games in 1954, Stan Musial hit five home runs in a doubleheader. Cracked Buck, "Does he do that every Sunday, Harry?" Caray was an exciting commentator from 1945 to 1970, then made an even bigger splash at Chicago before his death in 1998.

Von McDaniel, tall, pink-cheeked, a 4-H boy from Oklahoma cotton corner near the Red River into Texas, came up out of high school early in 1957, fresh from a weary red-clay ball field. Like older brother Lindy, who had come up two years earlier, he was saddled with a $50,000 bonus, one that would freeze him to the major-league roster. For a time with the Cardinals, he was expected to do two things-little or nothing. But even though sensitive to kid's emotions as one who had been a schoolboy wonder from Seattle, Hutchinson stuck him in a game hopelessly lost at Philadelphia. He pitched four perfect innings. So now he was in the bullpen again at Brooklyn, another anticipated loss, when the Redbirds rallied to take the lead at Ebbets Field. Surely, Hutch now would switch to experience. The manager stuck with the kid, leading by one in the seventh inning. Suddenly in the ninth, PeeWee Reese beat out a bunt. Dark hurried in from shortstop, already a bible-study leader for young Fellowship of Christian athletes. At bat was big, lefthanded-hitting Duke Snider, headed to the Hall of Fame.

"Do you know who this is?" Dark inquired

"Sure" solemnly, "Mr. Snider."

Mr. Snider grounded out, preserving victory. A few nights later, with Hutchinson trying to conceal his pitching choice, Hutch did not fool a capacity crowd at St. Louis, but young McDaniel did. He beat the Dodgers on a two-hitter, 2-0, and, helping stimulate the ball club and the public, he posted a 7-and-5 record that included a one-hitter over Pittsburgh.

By the All-Star game, played in St. Louis, the Cardinals led a close five-club race by two and a half lengths. Winking, Casey Stengel suggested aloud they (the Yankees) might be back in October. By early August, still in front with an eight-game winning streak, the Cardinals lost momentum when the Phillies' Harry Anderson hit a two-run homer off Jackson with two out in the ninth. Stone cold, the Cardinals lost nine straight. The two other contenders lost, also, and second-place Milwaukee won 10 in a row. Suddenly, the Braves had a nine-game lead.

When the weary Redbirds limped into Milwaukee, Hutchinson told the ball club to skip the midnight curfew. "Maybe," he suggested smiling, "the McDaniels might indulge with a double-thick malted milk" Further, to loosen up the ball club, the manager posted a phony lineup the next night that included the diminutive equipment

Verily: Because of Stan Musial and not enough else in the 1950s, the jockey carried the horse, Musial's hitting and box office attraction helping upbeat the down years. Right, Amadee?

manager, Butch Yatkeman, and others, including pitcher Bob Miller, 18, like Von McDaniel, frozen to the roster because of a bonus. At Milwaukee, with Musial thundering, the Cardinals won three out of four, making it a race again. They hung tough even though Musial, rebounding to a seventh batting title Gussie Busch had forecast, was hurt in late August in Philadelphia. There, trying to protect Wally Moon on a hit-and-run, Stan swung at a pitch high and outside, difficult to pull, and tried to jerk it behind the runner. The savagery of the awkward swing, creating undue pressure, yanked the left arm out of the socket, fractured the bone of the shoulder socket and tore most of the heavy muscle over both the collarbone and the shoulder blade. The chipped fracture and assorted hurts indicated Musial would miss the last five weeks of the season.

The season had been unusual for Stan the Man. Beforehand, he had accepted a $5000 salary cut. Over the winter he had quit smoking, a now-and-then habit that increased when Hank Sauer replaced the departed Schoendienst as his roommate. Like Ted Williams, acknowledging the development of the quick-darting slider inside, Musial altered his batting stance. Opening day, ordinarily a slow starter, he had gone 4 for 4 at Cincinnati. Afterward, he confided that to accommodate the slider darting in toward the fists, he had altered his stride from deep in the batting box, striding more directly toward the pitcher than, previously, to the plate. "I've left the outside corner unprotected," said Musial. "They'll probably discover it."

They didn't. By the time he was hurt, Musial already was well ahead of heavy-hitting young Henry Aaron, who would beat him out of his fourth MVP award. Eager to help in the pennant race, batting leader Musial convinced Hutchinson he could hit. Sixteen days later, just poking the ball, he pinch-singled. When Musial noted Joe Cunningham rarely had to make a difficult throw from first base, he offered to return there with Cunningham moving back to the outfield. First game back at Pittsburgh, he poked at the ball and got three hits, two of them doubles. With Musial providing a big help, the 1957 Cardinals won 13 of 17 after Labor Day and were only two and a half out.

Just before the showdown at Milwaukee, a critical Cardinal loss eased the pressure for Fred Haney's ball club, led by Red Schoendienst, who had been acquired from the Giants in a pivotal mid-season deal. Herm Wehmeier led the Reds into the ninth inning when Jerry Lynch homered to tie the score and light-hitting shortstop Roy McMillan won the game with another in the tenth—Mac's first and only homer of the season. So the end came a few days before the end, a game at Milwaukee that went into extra innings, Musial singled and doubled off the Braves' Lew Burdette before Aaron put it away in the eleventh with a home-run total the same as his uniform number—"44". The pennant-winning homer was the first and only given up over the season in brilliant relief by Billy Muffett.

Hutchinson walked up to Musial in the quiet visitors clubhouse, shook his hand and said "Stan, you're still my MVP. Take off the last three days so I can look at some kids. Those other guys couldn't catch you in the batting race if they took all winter."

Musial, hitting .351, drove in 102 runs out of 171 in scoring position, an incredible statistic, and won recognition by *The Sporting News* as Player-of-the-Year. After the injury that forced him to punch at the ball, rather than take a king-sized swing, he'd gone 16 of 31. The last hit was a pinch single that clinched second place, ahead of the Los Angeles-bound Brooklyn Dodgers. The Giants, sixth, would go from New York to San Francisco.

Surprisingly, too, Lane announced he would go to Cleveland, apparently uneasy after having hailed the "heroic ball club that wouldn't quit" in an 87-67 season and 1,183,575 satisfied customers. Frank Lane was a good fellow, really. If you divided and then subtracted Frantic Frank's profanity in the pressbox, nearby where he sat on the roof, a sun worshipper, squinting with little more vision than Mr. Magoo, listening to the radio. First and always an engaging personality, handsome hair dyed and his body exercised to make him look younger than his years, whatever they were. Ball players had to learn that Frank really didn't mean it when he'd shout sarcastically as one of his men swung and missed, "My God, how can the ball stand it." Or if one missed a play, "Hang a lantern on the ball" He travelled always with a radio in his ear and a stack of newspaper sports sections under an arm. He got away to Cleveland without dealing one of Gussie Busch's Clydesdales for a pinto pony.

SIR GALAHAD: Bing Devine – formally Vaughn P. Devine – was a Redbird Knothole Gang member who twice general-managed the Cardinals and won a reputation for his relationship with players, the press, the public and – most of the time – his boss, Gussie Busch.

His successor, Bing Devine, a front-office legacy of Dick Meyer, as Lane's assistant, didn't smoke or drink, either, no merit badge in the mind of fast-living boss Busch. Devine also avoided swearing, usually, but he admired and acquired from Lane the belly to deal players, traditionally developing pitchers he swapped for regulars who would win the long-awaited pennant.

Devine's first deal as general manager—uniquely three pitchers for two outfielders—prefaced his policy as the Cardinals' first home-town general manager, a 40-year-old former Knothole Gang member. Vaughan Palmore Devine—nicknamed "Bing"—had parents who loved baseball as much as he did. They would vacation summers on the road where the Redbirds were playing so that the blond, skinny kid could gawk at his heroes. One, particularly nice to him, was outfielder Watty Watkins of the 1930 and '31 pennant winners. By the time Devine stepped up in place of Lane, he had been back in the Cardinals' front-office for a few years. He had played college basketball and baseball at Washington University. Even played a couple of games at second base for the club he was business-managing, Johnson City, Tenn., in the Appalachian League. He loved the challenge even though, dryly, he suggested the manager gave him the "take" sign on a full-count.

As Lane's assistant, he frowned on one of Frantic's last proposed deals, third baseman Ken Boyer to Pittsburgh for Frank

Thomas, and at the first meeting of general managers at the Colorado Springs winter meeting, he rejected another deal involving Boyer. The big third baseman, moving to center field to help the cause in 1957, actually had been subpar at bat. Confided Devine, "The Phillies have made a very fair offer—(outfielder) Richie Ashburn and a return of (pitcher) Harvey Haddix for Boyer. But I'm betting what little reputation I've got that Boyer, returned to third base, will be a star."

On a so-so team in 1958, Boyer was a star, and stayed one. Modeling himself after Musial, whom he idolized, Ken hit .307 with 23 homers and 90 runs batted in, figures he would approach or often pass through the years, capped by a Most Valuable Player award in 1964 when he led the Cardinals to the long-elusive pennant and world championship. At the moment of the big deal Devine didn't make, Bing and manager Hutchinson agreed on a swap of pitchers Willard Schmidt, Marty Kutyna and Ted Wieand for two Cincinnati outfielders, Joe Taylor, who like the St. Louis trio will be little remembered, and a fleet 20-year-old kid whose name would be remembered on the field and off it.

Homer Helper: Greg Masson (center) figured in Stan Musial's amusing Cleveland episode. Equipment manager Butch Yatkeman (left) and catcher Vern Rapp (right) also pictured.

Curt Flood!

At the pivotal position—shortstop—Dark slowed. Pitching created a problem, too. Lindy McDaniel faltered and had to be optioned out briefly. Brother Von, the fairy-tale figure of 1957, turned into a pitching pumpkin. Wisely, neither Hutchinson nor Devine had figured on him too much, but he was a bust, probably a physical victim of the first idle moments in his life and also caught up in a crushing letdown mentally. Every year, working the harvest between basketball and baseball seasons down there in the sparse country, the kid never had known anything except fitness, but he went to a religious college after that sensational first season and sat on his duff, studying. So when he got to the heavy humidity of Florida and encountered the arm weakness to which veteran pitchers become accustomed, he panicked. He tried to throw harder. He lost his control and his confidence. So he was in just two official games, one start, two hits, five walks and a 13.50 ERA away from that storybook story's nightmare ending. He couldn't pitch in the minors, either.

So the story, as usual, was Musial, his accomplishments and his "inner conceit," Branch Rickey's apt description of the drive within even the most humble of athletes. It slipped out now and then on Stan the Man. For instance, after seeing the Indians' Al Rosen and Larry Doby demonstrate their home-run power at the 1954 All-Star game at Cleveland. When the Cardinals played an exhibition game at the giant lakefront stadium thereafter, Musial had been lured into a home-hitting contest for charity. Musial asked traveling batting practice catcher Greg Masson to pitch to him and said that if he won, he'd give Greg $100. Masson, making less than $5000, beamed.

In the contest Rosen and Doby hit a couple of "homers" each over the fence, while Musial hit seven over and one against the barrier. When the mayor of Cleveland gave him a small trophy, Stan walked into the clubhouse, peeled off $100 and gave it to Masson. The catcher grinned. "Stan," he said, "you're a great hitter, but a lousy economist. Spending 100 bucks for a 10-buck loving cup!"

With the Cardinals—and Musial—appearing on the West Coast for the first time with first-week opening of the Giants at San Francisco and the Dodgers at Los Angeles, Musial put on quite a show. Given a handsome hand from the fans at Seals Stadium, where the wind from right field handicapped lefthanded hitters, the Man swung with the reduced clout of his previous year's injury. He doubled and singled twice the first night, and went 7-for-11 for the series. At Los Angeles, where the Dodgers were playing in the rectangular Coliseum, with left field a pitching putt away and right field a trolley ride distant, the Dodgers' Duke Snider moaned at the batting cage about the injustice to lefthanded hitters. "If you can't lick it, Duke, join it," said Musial, who hit four straight singles to left in the Redbirds' first game there and for the series—again!—7 for 11.

Even though Musial was a blistering .483 batter, the Cardinals had floundered with 14 defeats in the first 17 games. With a premature party thrown for Musial by restaurant partner Biggie Garagnani, Stan was two hits short of the 3000 mark before a two-game train trip to Chicago. First game, he doubled. Afterward, he said wistfully to coach Terry Moore that he wished he could walk four times the next day so that 3000 could be achieved in a return to St. Louis. Moore told Hutchinson. Hutch called an emergency press conference in the bar at Chicago's old Knickerbocker Hotel. He pointed out that he could lie and say Musial had a sick stomach, but that, hell, he wouldn't use him that day unless necessary so that, Hutch put it, "Only about 6000 will get to see it here when they've got a 30,000 packed house in St. Louis."

Hutch was right-on. A crowd of little more than 6000 at Wrigley Field, forewarned, watched the next afternoon when the Cardinals and Sam Jones trailed, 3-1, and Hutch found it "necessary." Pinch-hitting, Musial hit a run-scoring double, the first player since the Boston Braves' Paul Waner in 1942 to reach 3000 hits. The Redbirds continued to rally and won, 5-3.

Hutchinson, caught up in the emotion, lifted Musial for a pinch-runner. Stan, stepping over photographers, rushed to a box seat and kissed an attractive blonde. A cameraman wondered if he knew her? "My wife" was the answer as part of the light touches that occurred before and on the last organized train trip the Cardinals ever took. Aboard the Illinois Central on an unforgettable late-afternoon trip, the chef had whipped up a special cake. Broadcaster Harry Caray gave Musial attractive "3000" cuff links. Musial brought winning pitcher Jones a giant bottle of champagne. En route, at Clinton, Ill., and Springfield, the train stopped like a political bandwagon as Musial stepped out to speak to crowds and sign autographs briefly. Ultimately, The Man catnapped. With a near-midnight arrival at Union Station, jammed as if it still were a war-traffic hub, Musial spoke to the crowd and drew two repeated cheers, including one in which he said he knew now how Charles A. Lindbergh must have felt when he returned from his flight to Paris in 1927. "What did *he* hit?" one guy guffawed. Musial won the day—and the night—when he summed it up, "No school tomorrow, kids!"

Trying to help with more power production, let down and physically weary, Musial hit only .337 with just 17 homers and 62 RBIs. The Cardinals sagged to a tie for fifth, 72-82, and Busch fired Hutchinson late in the season. No genius, Hutch, but a motivator—heck, watching him take out his anger on inanimate objects was enough to scare anybody to do the right thing! Fred Hutchinson went on to win a pennant for Bill DeWitt at Cincinnati in 1961. En route to perhaps another in the photo finish of '64, he died of cancer at only 45.

For a St. Louis replacement, Busch picked a ball player who had written a bread-and-butter note, proving it's wise to be nice to your elders and your financial superiors. When Solly Hemus left the Cardinals, dealt to Philadelphia a couple of years earlier, he had written Gussie a thank-you note for his years wearing the birds-on-the-bust.

Solomon Joseph Hemus, a Catholic whose first name suggested he was Jewish, was as a captivating person as he was a holler-guy player, self-made and humorous. Although Busch obviously was stretching

CAPTAIN COURAGEOUS: Ken Boyer as captured by David Lipman for juvenile book market. Below, a magazine cover perennial, the Man Stan.

MAGIC WORDS: The magic moment was Stan Musial's achieving the coveted 3000-hit goal on May 23, 1958 at Chicago's Wrigley Field. The magic words were Stan the Man's when the Cardinals' early-evening train was delayed en route by celebrating stops in Illinois. With a packed house at Union Station near midnight, including children, Musial chirped into a mike, "No school tomorrow, kids!"

it, picking a 35-year-old player with no previous experience, some thought he would be a better-humored Eddie Stanky, his mentor. Trouble was, Hemus had an aging Musial, a bad ball club and an inability to get along with the umpires. Solly Joe, as many call him in Houston, where he earned and retained personal popularity, had an edge as manager because he inherited the job of taking the Cardinals to Japan for the biannual trip to play Japan's professional players. Players surprised by his choice responded by playing the kind of hustling ball that won the admiration of promoter Yetsuo Higa and discriminating Nippon fans. For Musial, who wearily didn't really want to go, the trip was a delight, not a disappointment. He hit for average, but not for what he knows they wanted to see—power.

Like many players of old, Musial had relied on spring training to get him in shape, merely pushing away from the dinner plate and desserts in the off-season. A bit heavier, thick at the waist, he was urged to take it easy in spring training, 1959. Wrong!

Accustomed to playing a little in all games, to please fans, he was rested too often. He wasn't ready, especially his legs. By the season opener, Hemus hoped to return Musial to the outfield and to play better-fielding Joe Cunningham at first. Cunningham was a .345 hitter that year, but he had to return to the outfield because Musial's lack of conditioning was evident out there. Fact is, the Redbirds were full of first basemen when Eddie Stanky, back with the Cardinals in charge of player development, recommended Bill White. White was obtained from the Giants for colorful toothpick-chewing Sam Jones, White, forced also for a time to move to the outfield, responded with a.302 average.

Another first baseman—yeah, they had four!—was "The Judge," George Crowe, acquired from the Reds. Crowe was a pinch-hitting whiz, .301, and conductor of the clubhouse kangaroo court. "And," recalled Musial, "he taught me something else. The Judge taught me how to stay in shape when you're on the bench."

Coincidentally also having his worst year was rival Ted Williams, who hit only .254. Musial batted a point higher, but with just 14 homers and 44 RBIs. The Cardinals sagged to seventh with a 71-83 record and the poorest attendance in several years, 929,963. And that fleet kid Flood wasn't getting enough playing time, either.

In mid-August, Devine wanted to know Musial's plans. Quit or stay? Old No. "6", coming up to 39 in November, said he wanted to stay. "I had bad advice," he said, "but it's my fault. Solly has rested me when I felt I needed it, but, encouragingly, they're not throwing the fast ball by me." The decision reached, Musial played seldom the rest of the season. Two pitchers who didn't believe his season was miserable were the Cubs' Glen Hobbie and the Giants' Jack Sanford. He spoiled no-hitters for both.

Musial began his comeback in the gymnasium, taught and teased by trainer Bob Bauman's bosom buddy, Walter (Doc) Eberhardt, long-time director of physical fitness at St. Louis University. Musial lost an inch at the waist before spring training, where he ran and played regularly, weak at first and then feeling wonderfully. Opening day, playing left field in the Giants' first game at Candlestick Park, Musial went hitless as newcomer Leon (Daddy Wags) Wagner hit a home in a 3-1 loss to Sam Jones. Devine had said, when dealing Jones, that he might help the Giants to a pennant.

Toothpick Sam almost did it in 1960, a year of vindication for the Redbirds and for Musial.

Hemus, casting about after an 0-and-5 start, ran pitchers in and out, using nine starters the first three weeks, including Lindy McDaniel, back from the minors, and headed for one of the greatest relief seasons. Although not hitting for average, but delivering men on base, Musial was benched at .260, then was told by Hemus, struggling with a 10-and-16 team, that he would start the second game of a doubleheader against the Cubs' Don Cardwell.

Trouble was, in the opener, the Redbirds gained their first road victory of the season in 13 games. Superstitiously, Hemus stuck with the same righthanded-hitting lineup for the second game. Musial's comment to the manager was, "You were just kidding me, Solly." A pressbox wag, aware of Cardwell's success against righthanded hitters, suggested he might pitch a three-hitter. Correction, a no-hitter, the first suffered by the Cardinals since Hod Eller of Cincinnati in 1919!

Musial played only four of the next 12 games, getting three hits in one, then a call from the Associated Press' Joe Reichler in New York indicating that Stan had been benched "indefinitely." With the story out, the player was called to Grant's Farm for a discussion with Busch, Meyer, Devine and Hemus. They hemmed and hawed about Hemus's deciding to go with younger, "different" lineups. The good soldier's response was only that he thought he could help the club in left field, where they had tried a medley relay of Wagner, Ellis Burton, Moose Moryn and John Glenn. No, no, not that John Glenn!

Finally, Bob Nieman, best known for having been the only player to break into the majors with homers his first two times up for the old St. Louis Browns in 1951, began to hit. If Nieman then hadn't been hurt, a lot of St. Louis baseball history, the Cardinals' and Musial's might have been written differently.

In town, Pittsburgh's manager Danny Murtaugh, headed toward the Pirates' first pennant in 33 years, was happy Devine had turned over a lefthander who might help the Buccos, Vinegar Bend Mizell, getting in exchange a second baseman who helped the Cardinals a lot for years—Julian Javier.

Murtaugh wondered what was wrong "with the Polack?" Nothing, but he just wasn't playing. Too bad, Danny wished he had Musial, but he was certain Stan never would leave the Cardinals. The other guy wasn't so sure. He asked. Stan the Man said he never thought he'd say it, but, yes, with that one more chance at a World Series. Quickly, calling off-the-record from Pittsburgh, general manager Joe L. Brown of the Pirates agreed with Murtaugh that he couldn't give up a budding young prospect for a player nearly 40, but it wasn't a problem picking up Musial's salary, back down to $75,000. It was that Brown couldn't do that to Bing Devine.

"Too nice a man," said the son of gifted movie comedian Joe E. Brown. "If Musial were released, I'd grab him in a New York minute, but I couldn't do that to Devine with public sentiment obviously behind Musial. So this is an off-the-record explanation of why I pass—reluctantly."

Then Nieman was hurt, but Musial, groomed by coach Johnny Keane's fungo bats and daily sprints in the outfield, was ready. Not even a month on the bench had dulled his desire, either. In his first game in the outfield since the second day of the 1959

HAIL TO THE CHIEF: Bill White, timely-hitting first baseman for the Cardinals on their 1964 world champion team, became a long-time broadcaster for the New York Yankees and then president of the National League. White once had a record-tying 14 hits in two consecutive doubleheaders.

FAREWELL, FELLAS: Hutchinson, a man's man and ladies' favorite, too, as a rugged manager, was fired late in his third season, 1958. They wouldn't let him go without a farewell signature. From the left, Del Ennis, Hobie Landrith and Gene Green, obviously not too happy, either.

season, he got only one hit off Robin Roberts, but he covered ground and threw out a man at the plate. His average down to .238 through unsuccessful pinch-hitting appearances, Stan (The Grand Man) simply exploded. For the next three weeks, leading the Cardinals out of the second division, he hit so hard and often—20 for 41—that his average at the All-Star game was .300. Gratefully, Hemus said, "In the last three weeks, Musial has delivered the most big hits I've seen any player get in years."

At the suggestion of National League publicist Dave Grote, National League All-Star manager Walter Alston of the Dodgers picked Musial for the last open spot on the roster. In blazing heat at Kansas City, Stan pinch-singled off Detroit's Frank Lary in a 5-3 victory for the Nationals. With two All-Star games then necessary to buy up expensive back service in the pension plan, Musial walked into Yankee Stadium for the first time since the 1943 World Series. Pinch-hitting against former teammate Gerry Staley, then a sinkerball relief specialist for the defending American League pennant-winning Chicago White Sox, he lined the ball into the upper deck. Musial's All-Star homer, his sixth, still was two ahead of anybody else in 1998.

That day an unusual thing happened. Seated next to each other, a manager and an umpire hugged each other. Mayo Smith and Larry Goetz, taking a busman's holiday, had tears in their eyes. The information, relayed to Musial, brought him a smile. He remembered his first full season when Brooklyn's flame-throwing Van Lingle Mungo knocked him down with two straight pitches. Getting up, he tripled on the next pitch, and plate umpire Goetz, walking out to dust the dish, yelled to Mungo, "Hey, Van, you sure scared the ____ out of that kid, didn't you?"

The 1960 Cardinals almost scared the ____ out of the Pirates, too, combining an ability to beat Pittsburgh so often that in smiling visits to the Golden Triangle close by his home town, Donora, Musial found relations frowned and strained. He beat the young Buccos three times in one short stretch with homers in August when the race really narrowed, twice in ninth and the third time in the fourteenth. Too hot not to cool down, the Cardinals finished a close third behind Milwaukee and the championship-bound Bucs. Boyer was the big bopper with .304, 32 homers and 90 RBIs. Musial, starting only 88 of his 116 games, hit .275 with 17 homers and 63 RBIs. The pitching strength was Larry Jackson's 18-13 and especially Ernie Broglio' s 21-9 when "Earnshaw," as Hemus called him, was aided by the bullpen magic of McDaniel. Lindy's efforts were superb back then before the role of a one-inning "closer" and with newly recorded "saves" more strict than later.

With his overhanded forkball dipping deep, McDaniel had the following: Sixty-five games, two starting, with a 12-4 won-loss record and only 85 hits allowed in 116 innings with just 24 walks and 105 strikeouts. His 26 saves were tops. His earned-run average of 2.09 most definitely would have been lower except for one complete game and a short early start.

At a time "their" Hal Smith (Pittsburgh's) was a Series hero with a last game series homer obscured only by Bill Mazeroski's, "our" Hal Smith, also a catcher, succumbed to the jinx men in the mask had experienced over the years. Pickles Dillhoefer died in the 1920s, potential Hall of Famer Bill DeLancey contracted career-ending tuberculosis in the '30s, Joe Garagiola suffered an injury to a promising career in the '50s and Bill Sarni experienced a heart attack shortly before Smith's. Smith was ruled out early in the 1961 season, a blow for manager Hemus and the ball club. Briefly a few years later he made a tentative return. Over the years, cherubic, yet hard-nosed, Smitty was almost as funny as the songs he said he wrote, i.e., "I'm Madly in Love With What's Her Name" and "Sittin', Spittin' and Whittlin'." Scouting for the Cardinals in the Southwest, St. Louis's Hal Smith found in a cruel delayed diagnosis years later that the heart attack sympton had been a medical false alarm!

An alarm that wasn't false occurred in a spring-training accident at Vero Beach, Florida. Traditionally the staff leader, though perhaps only third best on a championship ball club, Larry Jackson was hit by the butt end of a bat broken with powerful Duke Snider swinging. If the jagged end had impaled Jackson, the hot potato from Idaho would have been past tense. Instead, he was sidelined with a broken jaw. Devine, trying to assemble a winner, had brought up a bonus lefthander, Ray Sadecki, and a young righthander named Bob Gibson on whom coach Johnny Keane was high. Keane had managed the former Creighton basketball star on the Omaha American Association ball club. And Devine had reined in a free agent unusually in 1960. Curt Simmons, once one of the whizziest Philadelphia Whiz Kids with a flame-thrower fast ball, hadn't been the same since he ran a lawn mower over his toes. Just when the Cubs' Lou Boudreau was rained out of a chance of watching Simmons work out in Philadelphia, Devine made a phone call to the pitcher from a Maryland gas station and agreed to terms sight unseen.

So Simmons, Sadecki and Gibson were in rotation with a slumping Broglio as the 1961 Cardinals floundered. On the Fourth of July, just after Bill White had banged three homers in the difficult lefthanded-hitting park, Los Angeles Coliseum, Devine fired Hemus as manager. The ball club's record was 33-41. Alarmed, cruelly at first, Hemus screamed "foul", indicating that his long-time friend and minor-league manager, Keane, had second-guessed him to the front office. Wasn't so. Keane, a highly principled man from South St. Louis who had studied for the priesthood, had been in the sight-lines since Fred Saigh owned the club a decade earlier. He had his own ideas, too. First, he told Jackson, with whom Hemus had used gingerly in relief roles, that Larry would start at San Francisco and go all the way, if necessary, to get more competitive

BULL'S EYE:
The same sweet swing by which Ken Boyer, captain of the 1964 Cardinals, hit a grand-slam off the Yankees' Al Downing for a 4-3 victory in the pivotal fourth game of the 1964 World Series. Boyer, his number "14" retired after his death at only 51 in 1982, was a third baseman with Hall of Fame credentials.

innings. Next, he told Flood, only an occasional light-hitting center fielder, that the job was his, period. Finally, Keane's presence soothed Gibson, who had resented Hemus, who called him "Bridges," confusing him with a lefthanded black pitcher, Marshall (Sheriff) Bridges.

Things picked up quickly. Jackson, battered early, hung in and won a high-scoring game. Flood, playing center field and with the wisdom finally not to swing for the fences, began hitting with a .322 second only to Boyer's .329 of 24 homers and 95 RBIs. Jackson and Sadecki won 14 games, Gibson 13. With almost a reverse of the record under Hemus—47-33—they finished 80-74, but that was good for only sixth place. The gate was an embarassing 855,305.

Musial was embarrassed, hitting .288 with 15 homers and 70 RBIs, to have done less for Keane than for Hemus. A reporter wondered on the last day of the season if Keane planned to use Musial less in 1962 at nearly age 42? The answer had a Hitchcock snapper. "Less? No, more!" said Keane. "I just told Stan that if 1962 is going to be his last year, let's go all-out. I'm going to try to play him enough to qualify for the batting championship."

HOOLIE: Julian Javier, pronounced as if his son had to be called "Hoolian Havier Hunior," was a standout Cardinal second baseman for nearly a dozen years, from the time he was acquired in 1960 by Bing Devine. If Hoolie had hit righthanders just half as good as he ate up lefthanders, he would have been like his old manager, Red Schoendienst, a Hall of Famer.

Trying to provide another good righthanded bat, elusive since Walker Cooper's day and Kurowski's, Devine gave up Joe Cunningham for the Chicago White Sox's colorful veteran, Orestes (Minnie) Minoso. Minnie came at a time when there were revolutionary changes in training. Bill White had complained that black players still were second-class citizens in Florida, unable to live in the club's hotel. Gussie Busch was upset for them. The result was to arrange for two adjoining motels to create a happy camp for which even wealthier players agreed to join ranks, and come in off the beaches. If harmony with a capital "H" spelled success, the 1962 Cardinals would have lived up to their opening seven-game winning streak, equalling the record high from 1899 when Cy Young and the Cleveland Spiders switched to Redbird red. Teaching wives conducted classes. Game rooms were available for kids and for adults. A first-rate move every night was picked by publicist Al Fleishman, founder of the company that bears his name and Busch's confidante. Fleishman glowed with supervisory approval. Trouble was, Al couldn't hit or field for a swift, awkward Puerto Rican, Julio Gotay, at the critical shortstop position. And neither he nor the best sawbones could help it early when Minoso ran into the green outfield concrete at Busch Stadium, fracturing his skull and a wrist.

With the National League expanded to 10 clubs, a result of New York getting the Mets and Houston also joining, more minor league players helped dilute pitching talent, just as occurred the year before when the Yankees welcomed American League expansion with 221 home runs, including 61 by Roger Maris. For the '62 Cards, White hit .324 with 24 homers and 102 RBIs. Boyer's .298 included 24 homers and 98 RBIs. And Musial did so well he didn't want to quit. Stan broke in with 3 for 3 against New York's Mets. He got a shot in the ego after he did what happened rarely at the time. He often flied to left field with a runner on third rather than pop up. But on a May day at Cincinnati with a chance to tie a game, he popped up against Dave Sisler. Playing only the first game of doubleheaders then, he sat barebacked in front of his locker, head down, when manager Keane walked by and slapped him on the back. "You're playing the second game, Stan, and you're going to get four hits." Overjoyed, Musial played, got three hits and won the game in the ninth, 3-0, with a homer off Moe Drabowsky.

Just before the All-Star break, he hit a

game-winning pinch homer back at New York's Polo Grounds on a Saturday. Next day, the last before the trip to Washington, he interspersed home runs with walks so that he officially had four straight homers when he whipped one around the cozy right field foul pole off lefty Willard Hunter. "I'll never forget the look on that kid's face because the pitch had been way inside, but I'd learned to try to hook the ball fair or merely suffer a foul strike," Musial said with a smile.

At Washington, Stan was invited to President John F. Kennedy's box for the All-Star game at D.C. Stadium. There, Musial reminded JFK that a few years earlier in a chance meeting in Milwaukee, Kennedy had kidded Musial that folks thought Stan was too old to play ball and JFK too young to be president. Musial remembered.

"I think, Mr. President, that we both fooled them," he said. When Musial went up to pinch-hit, Kennedy leaned over to baseball buff Dave Powers of his staff and said, "I hope the 'old man' gets a hit." He did.

Although settled into a sixth-place finish in the 10-team league with an 84-78 record, Keane's Cards figured in the pennant race in a manner reminiscent of championship days of old. First, before leaving for the West Coast, they won one in St. Louis when Gibson, swinging hard in batting practice, chipped an ankle. Moved up, Simmons beat the Dodgers, but Los Angeles still led in the final week.

The old rivals got a break, with the Cardinals playing Alvin Dark's Giants at Candlestick Park. There, owner Horace Stoneham of the Giants insisted on an annual reunion with Musial and ex-Giant Red Schoendienst, back with the Cardinals as a pinch-hitter and coach. They drank extra innings, a common occurrence with the sportsman-clubowner, and before permitting the players' reluctant departure, Stoneham said he'd like to ask Musial to "take it easy" but he noted that the last time he asked that at Musial's restaurant (in 1954), Stan hit five homers the next day. "Yeah, don't ask that," said Stan the Man. That day he capped an incredible .330 season at nearly age 42 with 19 homers and 82 RBIs—the last 5 for 5 day of his career.

Young catcher Gene Oliver's three-run homer gave the Cards a 7-4 victory as they flew toward Los Angeles, then three up with four games to play before losing a night game to Houston. Still, just one more to tie for the pennant and only one if the second-place Giants lost one. San Fran lost a weekend game against Houston, but—

Larry Jackson won the opener Friday night in 10 innings, 3-2. Next night, bouncing back with a 12-9 record, Ernie Broglio pitched a two-hitter and won, 2-0, when long-armed Frank Howard dropped a foul called fair as he crossed the right field line. The final day, necessary to avoid a playoff the Dodgers would lose to the Giants, Simmons was back with that herky-jerky delivery and changing speeds. He beat Johnny Podres when Oliver hit an eighth-inning change-up, 1-0.

TWILIGHT OF A STAR: Stan Musial, saluted by his favorite cartoonist, Amadee Wohlschlaeger of the St. Louis *Post-Dispatch*, gets another bow before an All-Star game.

Huddling, Devine and Keane decided what they needed most to compete was a shortstop and an outfielder and they had a plan, but—oops —there was another head in the huddle, the bushy-browed bean of 81-year-old Branch Rickey, hired as a "senior consultant" after having threatened the majors with the Continental League, one that didn't play only because of expansion to Houston and a franchise back to where it never should have left—New York.

Rickey's return to St. Louis, 21 years after he left with highest championship honors, the St. Louis Swifties of 1942, was a result of (1) Busch's understanding desire to win one and (2) his willingness to listen to persuasion, this by one of Mr. Rickey's many synchophants, Bob Cobb, owner of the old Pacific Coast League Hollywood Stars and the famed Brown Derby restaurants. Trouble was, the man they had aptly

One for the Road: Stan Musial signs what proves to be his last major league contract prior to the 1963 season. Seated next to the slugger, past 42, was Redbird president August A. Busch Jr. and Sam Breadon's long-time private secretary, Mary Murphy – "Miss Moiphy." Behind them is Redbird general manager Bing Devine.

called Mahatma in New York, remembered Devine only as he had known him, a virtual office boy as a front-office P.R. assistant back in 1939, a year before Der Bingle went into the farm system as business manager. Mr. Rickey recommended Musial retire and when many interrupted indignantly, including boss Busch who put it grandly, "Since when do you ask a .330 hitter to retire?" B.R. backtracked and said he thought he had heard Musial mention retirement.

To fulfill the Cardinals' needs, as Keane and Devine saw them, the general manager put together a complicated three-way deal by which they would get lefthanded-hitting George Altman from the Cubs and shortstop Dick Groat from the Pirates. From the Cubs, who would get Larry Jackson and Lindy McDaniel, Don (No-Hit) Cardwell would go to Pittsburgh with Gotay. Nope, insisted Rickey, no Gotay. Finally, with Dick Meyer talking to Busch, the deed was done. A year later Jackson would have a 24-game season for the Cubs and McDaniel would regain relief stability. And Altman with the Cardinals must have been nearly as disappointing as the nervous high-strung Gotay was at Pittsburgh, where poor Julio must have led the league in antacids. For the Cardinals, Groat, the former Duke All-American player who had been the National's MVP in 1960, came in with a good bat and a gifted way to make up for his lack of speed at shortstop. The infield, as a result, was superb, all picked to start in the All-Star game for the NL because the Pirates' Bill Mazeroski at second base was injured.

They had All-Star years. Ken Boyer hit .295 with 24 homers and 111 RBIs. Hit-and-run master Groat hit .319 and drove in 70 runs. White's contribution was a .304 average, 27 homers and 109 runs driven in. Javier, hitting .263 with nine homers and 46 RBIs, was so good that—to name three noble names—Devine, Bob Gibson and Schoendienst—all thought that overall, defensively, he was even better than double-play dandy Mazeroski.

One pitcher short when Sadecki flattened out behind Gibson and Broglio, 18-game winers, and Simmons, who won 15, Devine made a deal at the trading deadline for the Milwaukee Braves' Lew Burdette, Warren Spahn's partner in championship seasons. Good try, but no cigar. Burdette was only 3-and-8 with the Cardinals, but they still hung in there, helped finally by a great winning streak and an old song after the muggy, last August rainy-day club picnic at Busch's beautiful bailiwick, Grant's Farm. There, Musial confirmed what he had told Devine privately at breakfast in Milwaukee where, wryly, he noted he had beat Spahn in a Senior Citizens' night game. Bing asked what he wanted to do? Bow out was the honest answer. Said Musial, "I can't do enough defensively or on the bases any more and, hitting, I can't concentrate well enough. I'm doing what I never did—taking called third strikes." At Busch's place, with players and families there, Musial looked weary in the wilting hot day, the beads on his face either perspiration or tears. Stan the Man said, "I'd like to go out once more with a winner. Our 1942 team was farther behind. We still have a chance."

The *Post-Dispatch* sports editor, reminiscing about more glamorous pennant rallies, brought up the good-luck charm, "Pass the Biscuits, Mirandy." Back there in 1946, Dr. Robert F. Hyland had scouted up a record from a radio station. Now, none was available for Doc Hyland's Sherlock son, Bob, general manager of KMOX and CBS radio vice-president. Hyland Junior finally went to Spike Jones' gold record in Hollywood for a print. So night and day, Mirandy passed her biscuits again on KMOX, and night and day the Cardinals ripped off probably their greatest streak, if not longest. They won 10, lost one and then won nine. So the 19-of-20 propelled the ball club from seven games out to just one behind Walter Alston's Dodgers. L.A., beaten in late-season surges by Cincinnati and San Francisco the two previous years, had become poised under pressure. The three-game packed-house series was one of the best played in St. Louis—and all lost by the home team.

The first game was a scoreless duel between Broglio and Johnny Podres until the sixth inning when brilliant Curt Flood, fooled by a ball hit off slugger Tommy Davis' fists, misjudged a fly for a precious run. An inning later with one of the greatest ovations ever, Musial hit the 475th—and final—home run of his career, tying the score. The storybook tale should have brought victory to the elder statesman who had recently had become probably the first grandfather ever to hit a home run in celebration of Jeffrey Stanton Musial. Now, though, with Broglio out for a pinch-hitter, little veteran lefty Bobby Shantz faltered in the ninth. The Dodgers scored two, and reliever Ron Perranoski protected Podres' 3-1 victory. That one was pivotal because the next night the Cardinals faced the great Sandy Koufax. He held the Cardinals hitless until Musial singled in the seventh and, breaking a 28-inning scoreless streak by Curt Simmons, L.A. won, 4-0. So the race was in jeopardy even before the Dodgers produced the coup d'etat. Revved up Gramps Musial got two hits behind Bob Gibson, who led into the eighth, 5-1. Los Angeles rallied and then tied in the ninth on a kid pinch-hitter called up from Oklahoma City. Dick Nen might later become better known as the palindrome father of a palindrome son, Robb Nen, Florida Marlins' star relief closer in 1997. Back there when Robb was a future bright spot, Dick Nen hit a game-tying home run in the ninth and when Perranoski shrugged off a leadoff triple by Groat in an overtime inning, L.A. won in the thirteenth, 6-5. The race was over, richly won by the better team. The Dodgers had won 12 of 18 from the Cardinals even though Musial, hitting just .255, batted .325 against the old foe. The Dodgers finished up with 99 victories, then handed the Yankees an embarrassing four-game sweep in the World Series.

For the Cardinals, winning their most games, 93, since the last-day near miss in 1949, a capacity crowd in a season of the best attendance since 1957—1,170,556—shoehorned into that rechristened stadium for Musial's last game. Busch generously made the game available for local television, then a rare occasion. Wearing a Boy Scout kerchief before the game when honored at home plate, Musial and all heard commissioner Ford Frick suggest that when he would be elected into the Hall of Fame shortly, "They list no records, but merely state, 'Here stands baseball's greatest warrior, here stands baseball's greatest knight." With a statue planned for the northeast corner of the new stadium, funded by St. Louis baseball writers at a retirement dinner for number "6", Frick's farewell salute seemed an apt inscription for the bronze. The original "The Boy and The Man," favored by Musial and others, bypassed for one erected in 1968.

First things first, meaning an upbeat exit, Musial singled his last two times against Cincinnati Sept. 23, 1963, as the Cardinals won by the same 3-2 score they had prevailed 22 years earlier in his first game against Boston. Stanley Frank Musial, the poor immigrant's son who struck it rich as a man playing a boy's game,

THE BOY AND THE MAN: That's what St. Louis baseball writers and artist Amadee envisioned of the statue planned for Stan Musial and paraded in large, color mockup in a drive around Sportsman's Park. With neckerchief, Stan is greeted by boss Gussie Busch. Musial bowed out with base hits his last two times at bat.

finished with 3630 hits and many records, some broken, but not the fans' affection for their favorite harmonica player.

With refreshing frankness, Musial would say later, "The Cardinals couldn't win in 1964 with me in left field." No, and without most folks, including Charley James, former Missouri U. football player who had been a stand-in for a couple of years. By the trading deadline, the Redbirds floundered as badly as the world champion Dodgers, spiraling down to fifth place. Keane coveted a fast young Chicago outfielder, Lou Brock, who obviously had power when he met the ball. Brock, highly touted, had hit only .255 and .258 as a so-so outfielder whose power (24 homers the first season) was reflected in a gargantuan drive into the 483-feet bleachers at the Polo Grounds. Trouble was, the Cubs' management, which had given $30,000 to the kid from Monroe City, La., luring him from Southern University, were about as frustrated with Brock as the Cardinals were with misbehaving Broglio, a roller-coaster righthander off to a stumbling 4-and-7 start. From the West Coast, headed for Houston, Devine swung a three-for-three deal with the Cubs' John Holland. "It's done," he told Keane on the plane. "Good," said the manager, who did what managers so often do with a new toy. Brock, getting off a late plane from Chicago the next afternoon, was rushed into the game as a late-inning pinch-hitter in Houston's sultry, mosquito-laden temporary big-league park. He struck out. A Houston fan, obviously a holdover from the Cardinals' days in the Texas League, growled, "Who could have made that deal?"

Louis Clark Brock: Champion base-stealer, 3000-hit batter, classic contributor in World Series play, hitting often for power and first-time Hall of Fame inductee, 1985.

Devine, seated nearby with assistant Art Routzong, said wryly, "Yeah, who could have made that deal?"

But, of course, it was spectacular almost overnight. Keane, urging the St. Louis press not to pressure Brock, moved the 24-year-old outfielder from troublesome sun-drenched right field at Wrigley Field to left field. He gave him the green light on the bases, and told him to relax. That's just what the teacher might have ordered back home in Monroe City when, briefly a Peck's Bad Boy, little Lou threw a spitball at a girl in the classroom, missed and hit "teacher". The dear madam banished him to the library to research ball players—Joe DiMaggio, Don Newcombe, Jackie Robinson and the man he would replace, Musial—and helped kindle the kid's interest. Louis Clark Brock, reared in a large family by his mother, learned to become "a positive person". He learned enough about mathematics, his major at Southern U., to take the Cubs' bonus offer his senior year.

Despite his immediate efforts for a sixth-place ball club, the Cardinals still were far behind fast-moving Philadelphia at the All-Star break. Fact is, the day after the game at new Shea Stadium and the site of New York's World's Fair, Curt Simmons lost a tough game there when the Mets' Frank

Thomas hit a two-run homer off his pet change-up. That night the Cardinals finished the first half of their season with a 40-41 record. Traveling with the team , a guy sought to seek out their summary of the sub-par first half of the season. Maybe an off-the-record interview? Gibson, typically, wouldn't talk. One would only if he were listed on-the-record. That would be a standup guy, Bill White, headed for years as a big-league president as National League president. "I'm the reason," said White, "I haven't driven in half the runs I did last year."

Virtually under the reporter's nose that night, but in the quiet of the clubhouse, Dick Groat pleaded mea culpa for having popped off earlier when manager Keane withdrew from the heady shortstop the automatic hit-and-run privilege that also had been an Alvin Dark mainstay. Now and then, caught up in his artistry, Dark would throw his bat at a 3-and-1 pitch, to protect a runner in motion. Keane had become provoked in a game at Los Angeles where Groat worked the hit-and-run repeatedly with hard-working catcher Tim McCarver, fouling off ball after ball with McCarver in motion. So, hereafter, the manager would give the sign. His pride hurt, Groat told too many before facing up to the unpleasant display of personal selfishness that prompted him to apologize to Keane and to his fellow players, but, unfortunately, one to whom he had complained was Eddie Mathews, Milwaukee's great third baseman, then dating August A. Busch Jr.'s daughter, Elizabeth, whom he briefly would marry.

Liz told dear dad, a man to whom loyalty was spelled with a capital "L". Gussie was fed up, understandably, with years of disappointment, now with his promising club floundering. Actually they had begun to improve. Devine had brought up Mike Shannon from Atlanta, then a farm club, to play right field, where the aggressive guy who thought he'd have been a Heisman Trophy winner if he stayed with football had a strong heart and a productive second-half bat. And to shore up the bullpen, Bing brought up veteran George (Barney) Schultz. If only briefly, the knuckleball righthander would become a Superman. He saved 11 victories in 30 appearances with a 1.65 earned-run average. So with White launching a savage second-half surge, shaking off a shoulder injury to produce 70 RBIs in the last 80 games, Capt. Ken Boyer, Curt Flood, Groat and McCarver had the offense to back up 20-game winner Sadecki, Gibson, Simmons and two valuable aids, Ron Taylor and Roger Craig.

When Busch talked with Devine and Keane, he persisted. Didn't they have something they wanted him to know? No, all was well. They were puzzled, but Busch thought they were withholding the Groat matter from him. Innocently, because it had been blown over a month earlier, they didn't think of it as an issue. Why bother the boss? Wrong conclusion. Busch's burr-in-the-saddle didn't come out until later. At the time, miffed, and annoyed at business manager Routzong's anaysis of athletes in an area where Busch didn't think he belonged, Gussie wanted Devine to fire Routzong. Bing declined. Then, sounding like an umpire ejecting a player, Busch's decision was that you're gone, too. Keane was in the gunsights, but that could wait until the end of the season. Leo Durocher, coaching then for the Dodgers, always had been senior consultant Rickey's man. Leo, apparently escorted down to Grant's Farm with Los Angeles in town, acknowledged he had been approached about the job, but denied that heart-balm payment had been made in view of wondrous developments that made the job offer highly unlikely.

First, as a replacement for Devine, Mr.

CENSORED: Catcher Tim McCarver, much later a national television figure in baseball, lets an umpire have it in an argument at Busch Stadium. Oddly, manager Johnny Keane, a one-time student of the priesthood and who knew all the words, is silent or, maybe, catching his breath.

Umpire's Helper: First-base coach Joe (El Birdos) Schultz (3) assists with a 'safe' call on Tim McCarver in '64 with Todd Stottlemyre's father, Mel, covering first base for the Yanks.

Rickey knew just the man, Bob Howsam, a former Denver beekeeper who was son-in-law of Colorado senator Edwin Johnson. Howsam had banked heavily on Denver's franchise in Rickey's proposed Continental League until the third major league was shot down with franchises in the National for Houston and New York. Howsam—Busch always called him "Houseman"—would go on to a remarkable front-office career in Cincinnati, helping build on Bill DeWitt's talent with sharp deals of his own that created the Big Red Machine of the 1970s, but he was miscast in St. Louis, merely a spectator as the unlikely happened. For Keane, accustomed to constant conferences with Devine, the general manager's lack of communication was disheartening, yet a meaningful snub for a guy awaiting the guillotine. For the players, Devine's departure had a remarkable reaction of resentment, but still, there just didn't seem a chance to overtake Philadelphia. Ten games behind the Phils in late July, the Redbirds straightened up and flew right at a torrid .687 club—46-21—but it wouldn't have been enough if Gene Mauch's Phils hadn't hit the skids in a 10-game losing streak, precipitated when Cincinnati's Chico Ruiz recklessly stole home with mighty Frank Robinson at bat.

That 1-0 loss to the Reds in the opener of a three-game sweep came about with the Cardinals idle, a half-length farther out than the Reds, then managed by coach Dick Sisler, elevated to the job as the tragically dying Fred Hutchinson had to step down. Sisler's Reds just had delivered what looked like a knockout blow to the Cardinals at Crosley Field. First night, with Simmons leading 4-0, rain washed out the game in the fifth inning. Next night, Gibson, carrying six straight complete-game victories and a 6-0 lead, lost in the ninth on a three-run homer by Robinson. Even after Sadecki won 2-0, the Cards again blew a six-run lead, 9-6, their seventh loss in nine games at the Cincinnati snakepit. Suddenly, with Ruiz's bold steal at about the time Mauch lost confidence in third starter Art Mahaffey, relying heavily on his big pair, Jim Bunning and Chris Short, the Phils' lead was whittled to six and a half games with 12 to play.

The Cardinals began their move when Simmons beat the Mets at New York on a six-hitter, 3-1. The Mets beat ex-teammmate Craig, 2-1, but then Gibson and Sadecki won a doubleheader at Pittsburgh, 4-2 and 4-0 as they swept five in a row at Forbes Field, including beating big Bob Veale, the Pirates' overpowering lefthander. With only four hits they won a 5-3 game, then Simmons won 6-3, and Craig shut out the Buccos, 5-0. When Cincinnati beat the Mets twice and Philadelphia lost a fourth straight to Milwaukee, 13-8, despite three homers by All-Star game hero Johnny Callison, the Reds were first, the Cardinals one behind Philadelphia as the Cardinals came back to town and the floundering Phillies, too.

A year previously, the Cardinals had been bested in a big series. Gibson achieved the Cards' sixth straight, beating Short 5-1. The following night, as Pittsburgh's Bob Friend halted the Reds' nine-game winning streak on an 11-hit shutout, 2-0, Sadecki's 4-2 win over the Phils put the Cardinals in a tie with Cincinnati for first. The Cardinals' eighth straight and the 10th nail in Philadelphia's coffin, 8-5, Simmons over Bunning, produced first place as the Reds left 18 men on base in a 16-inning, 1-0 loss to the Pirates on a squeeze bunt by rookie catcher Jerry May.

An open date for the Cardinals and

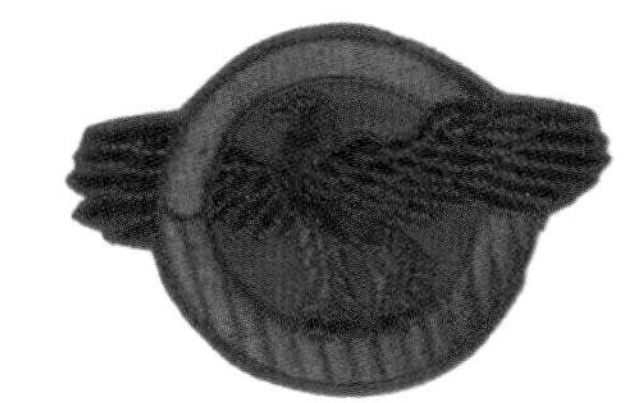

THE "PATCH"WORK OF HISTORY: From top to bottom and left to right, major leaguers saluted Doubleday Centennial on sleeve insignias, 1939; the 100th year anniversary patch was worn in 1969; the 125th year anniversary patch is in relation to Cincinnati's first professional team, 1869; finally, the Cards' 1958 post-season trip to Japan was commemorated with this sleeve adornment. Second row, all big-league ball clubs advertised "Health" in World War II years; the "J.M." patch is a nod to umpire Jerry McSherry, 1996; Jackie Robinson's patch recognizes the 50th anniversary of the breaking of the color barrier and was worn on the 1997 uniform. The Cardinals celebrated their National League centennial in 1992, and the animated right-handed hitting Redbird (obtained by Fred Saigh), was used on the uniform sleeve by Frank Lane in 1956. Last row, Grover Cleveland Alexander's woolen sweater of 1926 includes his Hall of Fame award and good luck charms on its lapel. The celebrated "ruptured duck," the honorable discharge given to all World War II service men and the Mudcat band uniform, 1938 (designed by Pepper Martin).

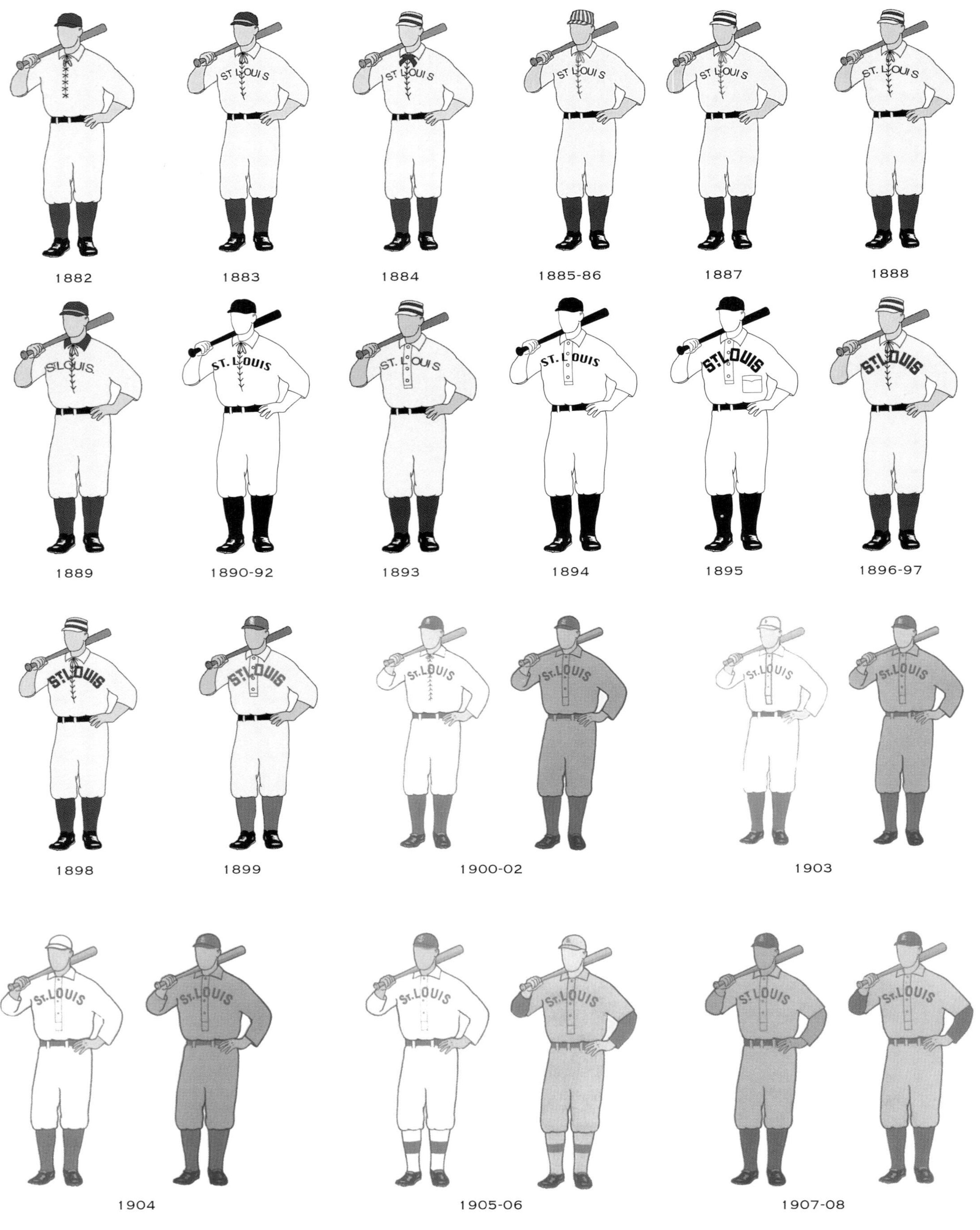
1882
1883
1884
1885-86
1887
1888
1889
1890-92
1893
1894
1895
1896-97
1898
1899
1900-02
1903
1904
1905-06
1907-08

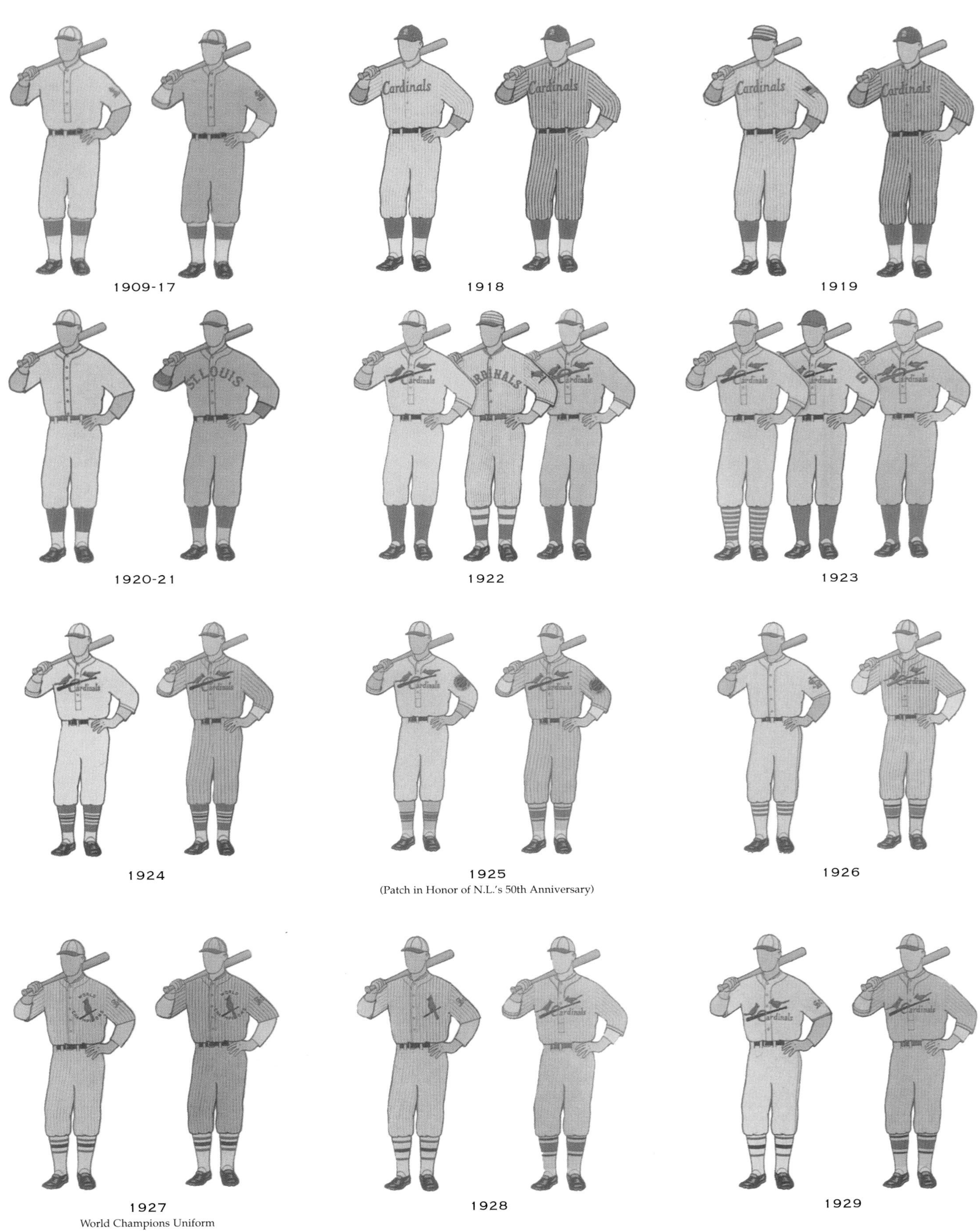

1909-17

1918

1919

1920-21

1922

1923

1924

1925
(Patch in Honor of N.L.'s 50th Anniversary)

1926

1927
World Champions Uniform

1928

1929

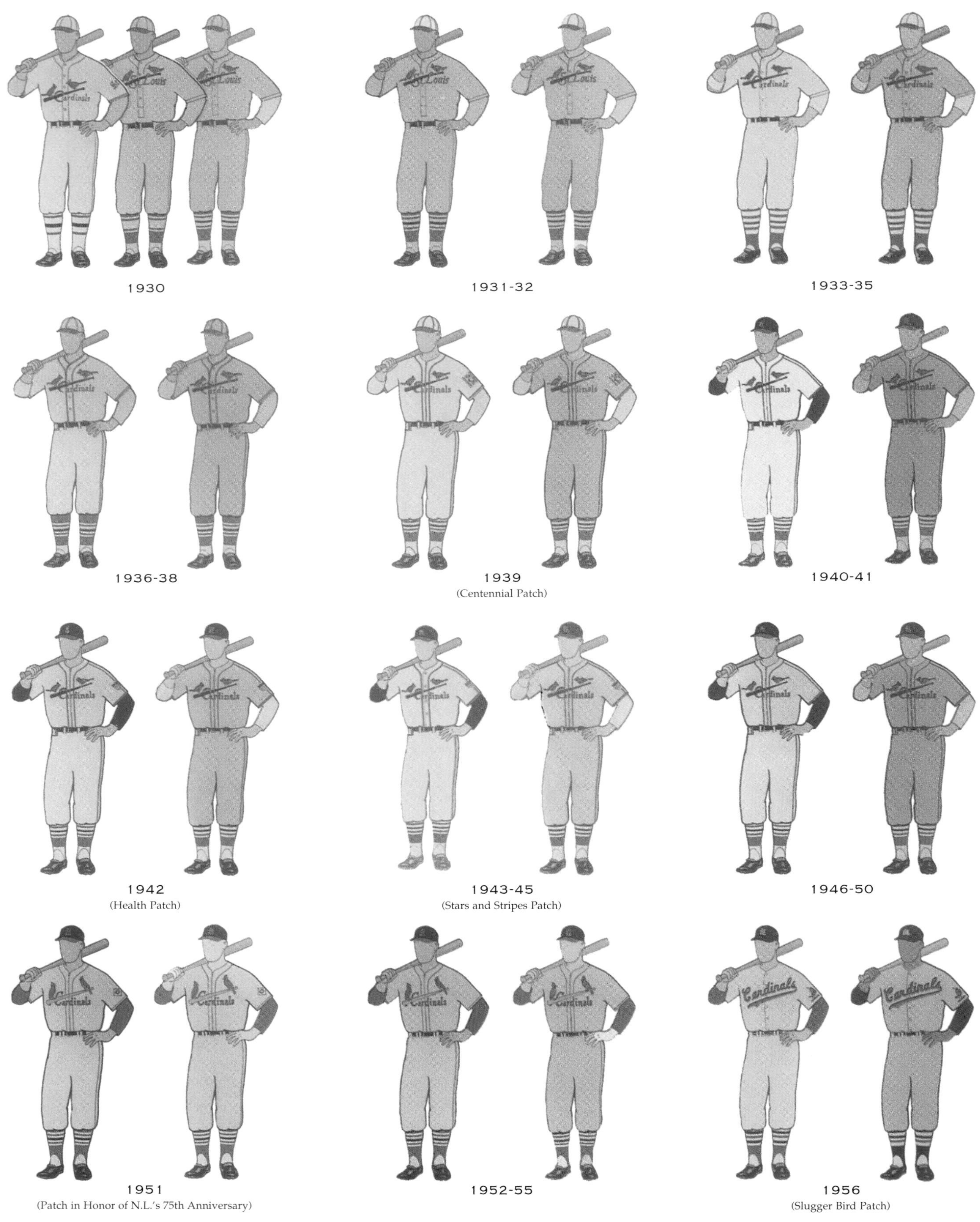
1930
1931-32
1933-35
1936-38
1939
(Centennial Patch)
1940-41
1942
(Health Patch)
1943-45
(Stars and Stripes Patch)
1946-50
1951
(Patch in Honor of N.L.'s 75th Anniversary)
1952-55
1956
(Slugger Bird Patch)

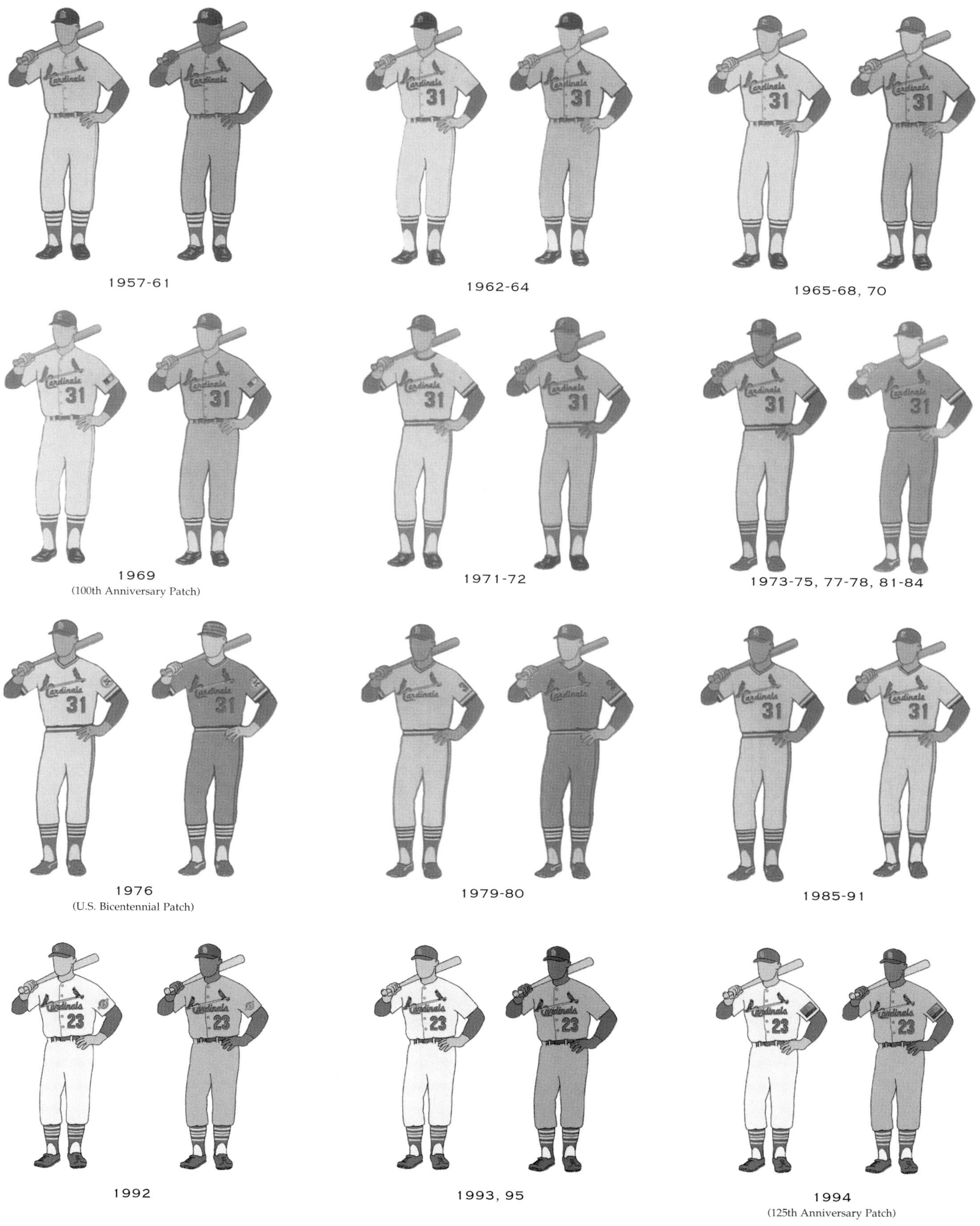

1957-61

1962-64

1965-68, 70

1969
(100th Anniversary Patch)

1971-72

1973-75, 77-78, 81-84

1976
(U.S. Bicentennial Patch)

1979-80

1985-91

1992

1993, 95

1994
(125th Anniversary Patch)

Cardinals
23
Cardinals
23

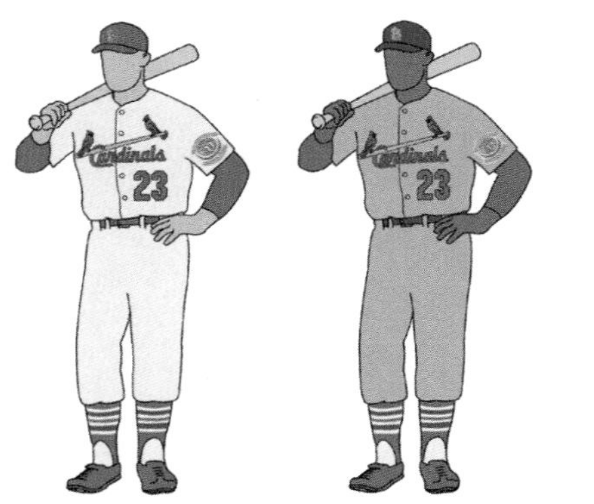

1996
(30th Anniversary Patch Busch Stadium)

Cardinals
Cardinals

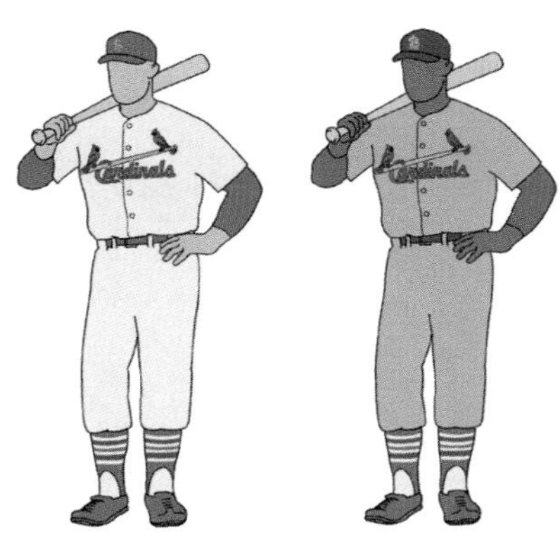

1997
(JM Patch worn on right sleeve)

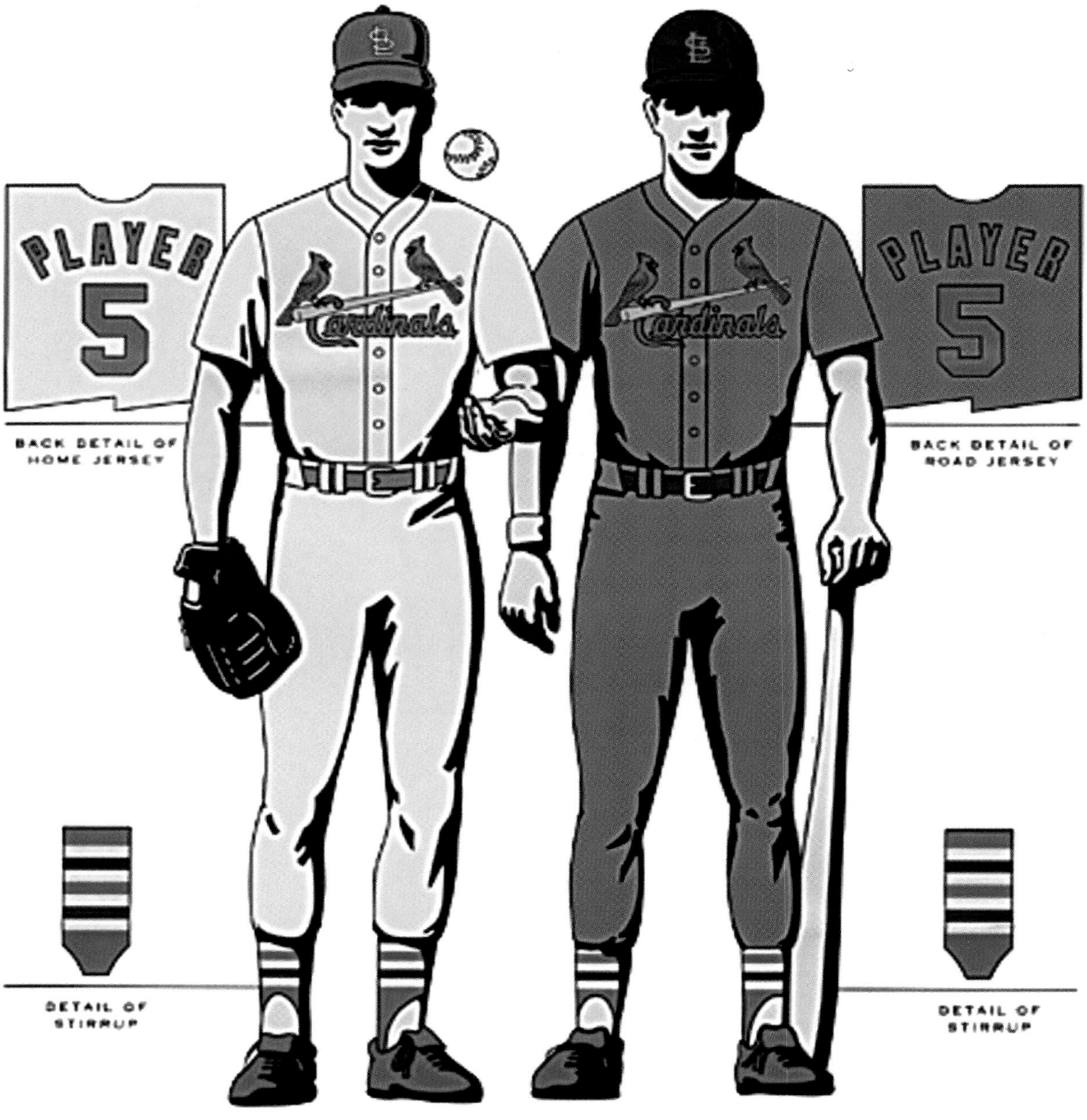
PLAYER
5
BACK DETAIL OF
HOME JERSEY
Cardinals
Cardinals
PLAYER
5
BACK DETAIL OF
ROAD JERSEY
DETAIL OF
STIRRUP
DETAIL OF
STIRRUP

1998

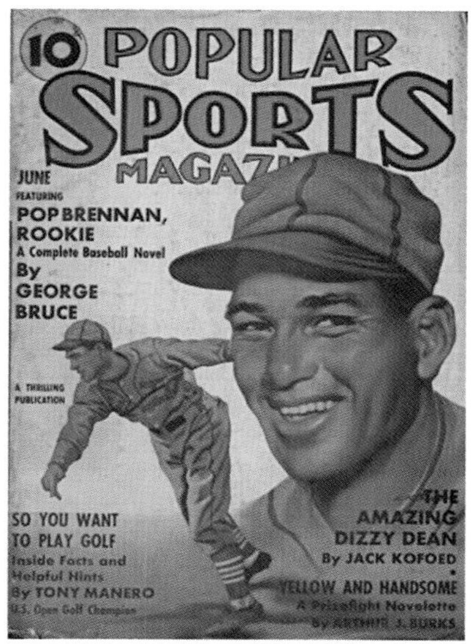
10
POPULAR
SPORTS
JUNE
FEATURING
POP BRENNAN, ROOKIE
A Complete Baseball Novel
By GEORGE BRUCE
A THRILLING PUBLICATION
SO YOU WANT TO PLAY GOLF
Inside Facts and Helpful Hints
By TONY MANERO
U.S. Open Golf Champion
THE AMAZING DIZZY DEAN
By JACK KOFOED
YELLOW AND HANDSOME
A Prizefight Novelette

DIERDORF
COSTAS
GIBSON
SHANNON
BUCK
KMOX RADIO
Mike Shannon's
Steaks and Seafood
Downtown St. Louis

STAN MUSIAL AND BIGGIE'S
Steak and Lobster House
ST. LOUIS, MISSOURI

ST. LOUIS
Cardinals

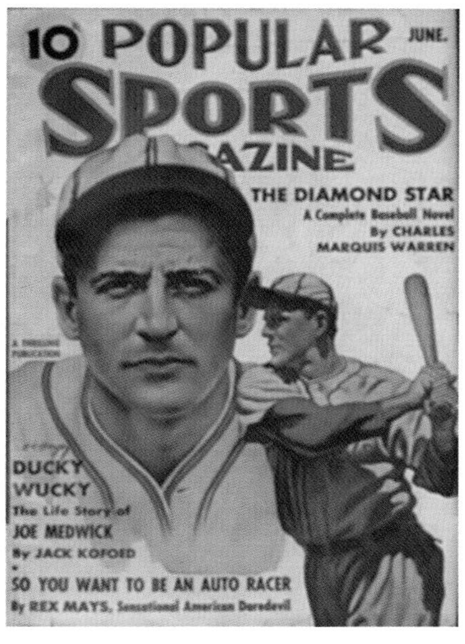
10¢ POPULAR
JUNE.
SPORTS
THE DIAMOND STAR
A Complete Baseball Novel
By CHARLES MARQUIS WARREN
DUCKY WUCKY
The Life Story of
JOE MEDWICK
By JACK KOFOED
SO YOU WANT TO BE AN AUTO RACER
By REX MAYS, Sensational American Daredevil

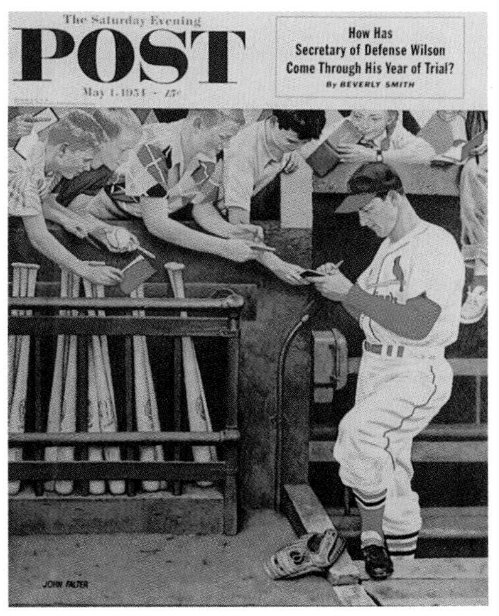
The Saturday Evening
POST
How Has Secretary of Defense Wilson Come Through His Year of Trial?
By BEVERLY SMITH

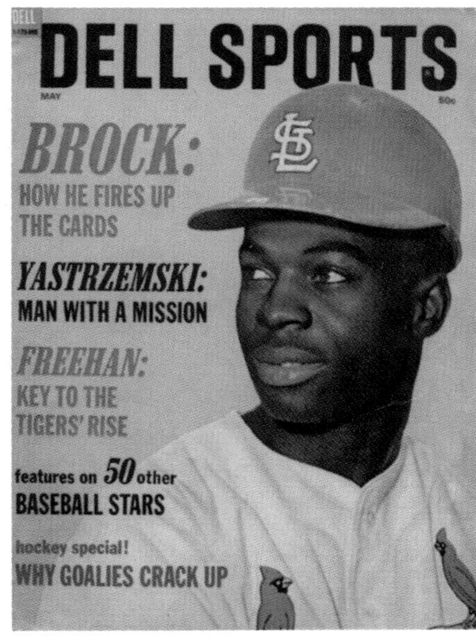
DELL SPORTS
MAY
50¢
BROCK:
HOW HE FIRES UP THE CARDS
YASTRZEMSKI:
MAN WITH A MISSION
FREEHAN:
KEY TO THE TIGERS' RISE
features on 50 other
BASEBALL STARS
hockey special!
WHY GOALIES CRACK UP

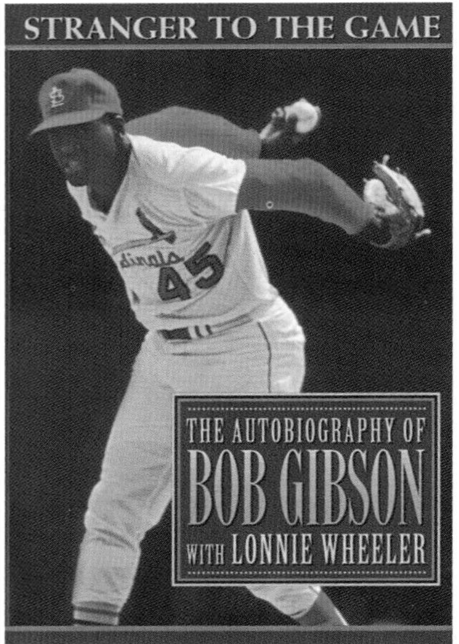

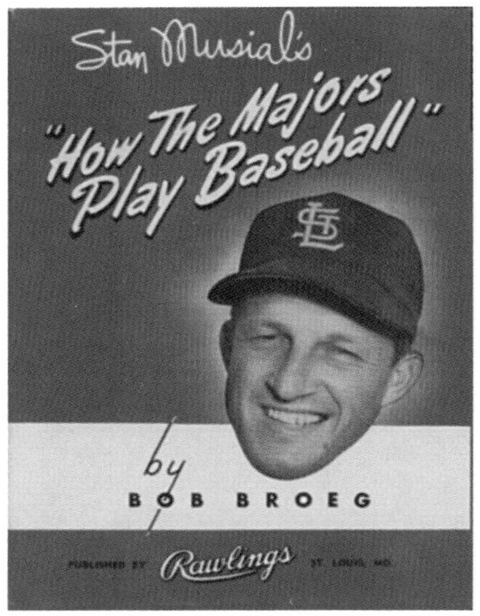

ST. LOUIS CARDINALS

Certificate of Membership

IN THE ASSOCIATION OF HONORARY BATBOYS

Whereas,

has clearly demonstrated his loyalty to the St. Louis Cardinals, and

Whereas,

the St. Louis Cardinals desire to officially recognize such support,

Therefore, the St. Louis Cardinals take great pleasure in issuing this certificate of membership in their association of honorary batboys. This membership includes a guarantee that at no time will the member's loyalty to the St. Louis Cardinals be traded to any other Major League baseball club. The St. Louis Cardinals hope that our present mutually satisfactory relationship will be a permanent one.

WITNESS MY HAND AND SEAL

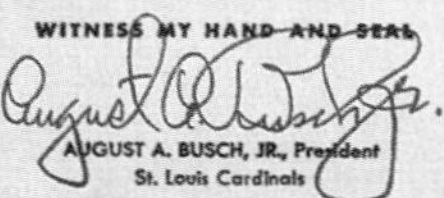

AUGUST A. BUSCH, JR., President
St. Louis Cardinals

Phillies gave the Reds a chance to move withing a half-game of the lead, and National League president Warren Giles set up playoffs not only for two teams or three, but also four because the fourth-place Giants had a championship chance.

In the third-to-last game, lefty Al Jackson, pitching for the lowly Mets, ended the Cardinals' eight-game winning streak by beating Gibson, 1-0. That night, providing a reprieve for themselves, the Phillies ended their losing streak, nosing out the Reds, 4-3.

With Cincinnati and Philadelphia idle on Saturday, the Mets shellacked Sadecki, 15-5, in a game that put the Reds back into a first-place tie, creating a possibility of three-way tie. Fourth-place San Fran was eliminated in a 17-7 slugfest loss at Chicago.

The final day, Simmons wasn't sharp, but Redbird bats boomed. Curt Flood finished a .311 season with a homer. White, winding up 102 RBIs and a .303 average, hit his 21st. Capt. Boyer, whose 24 homers and 119 league-leading homers would net him MVP, delivered key hits. So did the man who made Devine's last deal a Brink's holdup, Brock, finishing .348 with 23 homers and 33 stolen bases. Gibson came out of the bullpen to help and Barney Schultz, too. When McCarver drifted back for a game-ending pop foul—kerplop!—the first pennant in 18 years. Forty and 41 the first half of the season, 53-28 the second, and a victory total that hadn't been quite good enough in 1963—93!

The 1964 World Series against the New York Yankees, managed by the home-town favorite who got away, Yogi Berra, was a great one between two teams that weren't great. The Yanks had nudged in at the finish with aging aspects, but, as always, the great reputation. One part of that reputation,10-game Series winner Ed (Whitey) Ford joined injured shortstop Tony Kubek on the sidelines. "The Chairman," as they called the crafty lefthander, wouldn't be seen again after blowing a two-run lead in a four-run sixth, an inning in which Mike Shannon unloaded a long two-run homer. A double by Tim McCarver routed Ford, and off Al Downing pinch-hitter Carl Warwick began a great Series with a single and Flood tripled. The 9-5 victory might have set up a big one in the second game between Gibson and Mel Stottlemyre because it was tied in the sixth when plate umpire Bill McKinley insisted that an inside pitch had hit Joe Pepitone. The break led to a run. The Yanks would score two more later off Gibson—and this never would happen again in an incredible World Series career—Gibby left before the final four runs. Score: New York 8, St. Louis 3.

For one who watched World Series one way or another for 70 years, the center-cut three games on the '64 World Series were among the most interesting and exciting. At New York, Simmons dueled Jim Bouton, better known later as the controversial author of "Ball Four," but then a great pitcher. With Simmons driving in his only run, the veteran lefty went out for a pinch-hitter in the ninth, tied 1-1. Bouton got the side out. In his book Jim would chide the manners and morals of Mickey Mantle, but now as Mantle faced Barney Schultz in the home half, he got the best and the beast out of The Switcher. Mantle, timing Schultz's knuckler, hit a tremendous home run high into right-field stands, winning the game, 2-1, and breaking a tie with Babe Ruth for Series homers. This one was a Ruthian whopper, a Mantle masterpiece.

Next day, a Sunday, the Yankees threw their best Sunday punch at Sadecki, who had been no problem in the first game, either. This time he gave up three runs with only one out, leading to a classic stretch of relief pitching by Roger Craig and then Ron Taylor. Craig, later a pennant-winning manager at San Francisco, shut out the Yanks on two hits through the fifth and then Canadian-born Taylor, a mechanical engineer who turned into a doctor and Toronto's team physician,

MR. OFFENSE & MR. DEFENSE: Lou Brock (left) and Bob Gibson share the spotlight in the 1967 World Series, one of three in which they starred for the Cardinals. The seventh-game press conference is at Fenway Park. The tall, spectacled writer trying to listen at the rear is the *Chicago Tribune*'s Dave Condon.

was even better in his four hitless innings. In one amusing moment in what seemed like a laugher for the Bombers, Mantle stood at second base when Groat wondered if Mick had seen Moon Man Shannon leap high in front of the low-slung fence, far below Mantle's gargantuan game-winner the day before. No, chuckling, Mickey hadn't seen it. Off guard, Mantle was picked off second!

Still, the fun was all on New York's side until the sixth inning when Ken Boyer, reaching down for a breaking ball with the bases loaded, hooked a long drive in the left field seats. As K. Boyer rounded the bases on what would be a game-winning grand-slam, 4-3, younger brother Clete Boyer of the Yankees stood in the third-base path to the bag, forcing Ken to go around him. He did with a slap on the fanny.

Comrades in Arms: Capt. Ken Boyer (left), third baseman and Most Valuable Player in the league, gets a bear hug from Bob Gibson after Gibby won the final game of the 1964 World Series, Boyer's one and only and Gibby's first of three pennant winners and two title teams.

A slap on the fanny well might have been the difference in the fifth game. Gibson led Stottlemyre into the ninth when Pepitone hit a hot smash that hit the big righthander's right buttock as he wheeled through in his follow-through. The ball glanced crazily toward the third-base foul line, Gibson after it with the hot pursuit of a brilliant basketball player. Scooping it up with his bare hand, throwing across his body as he fell away, Gibby pegged a strike to White. On a bang-bang play, American League umpire Al Smith called Pepitone out and, though Berra argued, television replays showed Smith was right. For Gibson and the Cardinals, this was good because Tom Tresh immediately followed with a two-run homer that with one more aboard would have won the game. Tied in the tenth, McCarver faced Pete Mikkelsen and, seeking merely a sacrifice fly, he lofted a three-run homer that won it, 5-2.

Back in St. Louis, hitting like the Bombers of old, the Yankees clobbered Simmons and replacements Schultz and Gordon Richardson, including homers by Roger Maris, Mantle and a grand-slam by Pepitone. The 8-3 score sent it down to a showdown between Gibson and Stottlemyre, each working with two days rest.

With Brock hitting a home run and Boyer another among three hits, Gibson got a 6-0 lead, cut in half by Mantle's three-run homer in the sixth, but Gibby struggled into the ninth when, tired, he gave up a home run to Clete Boyer and another to Phil Linz. With the clock having struck 12 for Cinderella Schultz, Keane made up his mind. He sat back. Bobby Richardson, hitting better than he fielded, had a Series record 13 hits and behind him was home-run king Maris.

"But I made a pledge to the man's heart," the manager would relate later. "I'd go all the way with Gibson."

Forcing one raising fast ball, Gibby got Richardson to pop high toward right behind second baseman Dal Maxvill, who had played well as Julian Javier's Series replacement. As Maxie camped under the ball, Groat jeered, "Don't forget to catch the ball." He did, and the Cardinals were world champions.

The next 24 hours were the wackiest with, as described by the first page of the *Post-Dispatch,* summing up the news that October day—China Drops First H-Bomb... Khrushchev Ousted by Soviets... Berra Fired as Manager... Keane Quits Cardinals. Berra's ouster, instigated by pressure from the press that still worshipped in Casey Stengel's comical touch and Ralph Houk's military pressure, made it a big question when Keane immediately jumped to the Yanks, suggesting to some he had been approached previously. Maybe, but it's true that he knew he was headed for release until the remarkable reversal of the 1964 race.

Keane's decision to go with the Yanks seemed questionable in the judgment of one who recognized a Titanic tilt to the one-time flagship of baseball. The suggestion in the *Post-Dispatch* was that the opening at Pittsburgh seemed better. Harry Walker took it and The Hat received two 90-game seasons as a third-place manager. Keane, managing an unmanageable team, dipped to a most unlikely Yankee position, sixth place with a 77-85 record, criticized constantly. When he lost 16 of the first 20 in 1966, he was succeeded by the "Major", meaning war-time hero Houk. In the former backup catcher's eight seasons, they got out of the second division just once. Keane died of a heart attack at 46, shortly after his dismissal. Of a broken heart, perhaps.

Baseball is a tough game even for a man of Branch Rickey's magic and mastery. The Mahatma was disclosed to have written an "if" memo, late in the 1964 season suggesting that if by a certain date the Cardinals weren't closer to the lead, changes should be made. Among them was the disposition of Mike Shannon and another was recommendation to Busch and Howsam that Julian Javier be benched at second base, where he was a great pennant-winning fielder who didn't hit righthanded pitching too well. Mr. Rickey recommended taking a second-base look at Ed Pacheco, catching for the Tulsa farm club. Obviously a wild pitch that prompted Busch to fire the old genius whose recommendations had embarrassed both men.

Rickey finished his handsome book, "The American Diamond," illustrated by gifted Robert Riger. The book came out and was reviewed in a *Post-Dispatch* column, noting B.R.'s choice of ill-fated Bill DeLancey among the three potentially best catchers he ever had seen. DeLancey had died of tuberculosis in 1947, 12 years after his short career ended. The book was reviewed the same night Mr. Rickey accepted induction into the Missouri Sports Hall of Fame with his prized pupil, the great George Sisler, and his late newspaper confidante, Taylor Spink of *The Sporting News*. Rickey talked of three degrees of courage. He illustrated the physical and the mental and was giving a parable of spiritual courage when he stepped back at the lectern of the hotel in Columbia, Mo. He said,"I don't believe I can continue." The words in November, 1965 were his last as he slipped into a coma and died three weeks later.

THREE OF A KIND: And all greats — Ken Boyer receives his 1964 MVP award from Benchwarmer Bob Burnes, chairman of the St. Louis baseball writers. In the center, another editor, Lowell Reidenbaugh of the *Sporting News*.

In his return to the Redbirds, Rickey created a public-relations problem, but so did Busch when Keane walked away from an expected ho-hum announcement of a contract renewal. With the aid of his instinctive PR person, Al Fleishman and others, including Dick Meyer, Gussie came up with a bell-ringer as manager.

Red Schoendienst!

The boyhood Huckleberry Finn was a fan favorite, an instinctive 7-come-11 player who had endeared himself when he chose to return to the Cards as a pinch-hitter and coach rather than go to the expansion Los Angeles Angels as a regular in 1961. The reward was the job for which close friend and former road roommate Stan Musial had it right. "I think," said Stan the Man, "that Red will be like Walter Alston and last a long time as manager."

Schoendienst's first season was a disaster for him and for Howsam, who had angered many by trying to take credit obliquely for Devine's success. Only Curt Flood (.311) and Bill White (24 homers) held up offensively. The pitchers backed away from .500, notably Curt Simmons (9-15)

PHANTOM FEET: Master second baseman Julian Javier of three pennant-winning Cardinals shows the swiftness of foot that made him a "phantom" when the foe sought to take him out in a potential double play.

and Ray Sadecki (6-15), but Bob Gibson surged into 20 victories for the first time. In the 80-81 season, seventh in the 10-club league, Howsam tried to help when he dealt for Houston lefthander Hal Woodeshick. Woody didn't help too much, but a young Cuban lefthander Howsam sent Houston, Mike Cuellar, would later go on to use his tantalizing screwball to win 20 games four times for the Baltimore Orioles and appear in five World Series. Howsam—and the Cardinals—got tough luck another way when baseball installed football's long successful reverse-order draft. As the world champions, the Cardinals drafted last among the 20 major-league clubs and came up with a New Jersey righthander with an unforgettable name: Joe DiFabio.

For 1966, a season that figured to be historic if only because the Cardinals would go into a new stadium, the jewel of downtown, Howsam decided his infield was getting long in the tooth. He dispatched Ken Boyer to the New York Mets and Groat and White to Philadelphia. White resented the general manager's suggestion that he was "older" than listed (32), but a torn achilles tendon handicapped him in Philly. Neither Boyer nor Groat was effective. Unfortunately, one of the players obtained in the Boyer deal from New York was a plumber, literally, Charley Smith. Smitty was better behind a monkey wrench than behind a glove. He didn't last, but the new shortstop, a skinny home-town kid with a master's degree in engineering and a masterful glove, Dal Maxvill, proved the importance of a no-hit player at a critical position.

The hit of the second-division season was the new stadium, originally named modestly Busch Memorial Stadium, then later labeled Busch Stadium because it was August Adolphus Busch Jr. who was the key figure in the combination by which St. Louis built a symmetrical stadium for baseball and pro football, which came in 1960 when the football Cardinals transferred from Chicago.

Urged by maximum help from city and business leaders—if St. Louis raised $20,000,000 million of capital, Equitable Life Assurance would lend $35,000,000—Busch rammed through resisting brewery stockholders a sizable $5,000,000 leadoff amount. They noted the $2,500,000 spent to upgrade old Sportsman's Park and wouldn't $1,000,000 be enough or $2,000,000? Squinting around his cigarette, Busch frowned and growled, no, blankety-blank, no. It had to be $5,000,000. In addition, Busch gave away the store, agreeing for 30 years to give up parking and ball-park concessions, offering the difference between plus-or-minus in profits. When the football Cardinals were asked to do the same, they hemmed and hawed and then pointed a gun at the head of the Civic Center Redevelopment Canter. They refused to sign their lease until concessions were made or they would go to Atlanta.

Fact is, Fulton County belatedly and hurriedly built a stadium, one that in construction and upkeep would become archaic and was later destroyed. Meanwhile, Busch Stadium, more tenderly built and given constant spit-and-polish improvements under later brewery ownership, was still a physical attraction at the end of the Twentieth Century.

When delay in building the stadium indicated that the first 12 games would have to be played at the old ball park, Howsam came up with a clever plan, honoring a different Redbird star and also the Browns'

George Sisler. A bronze-style coin was given each game with the living featured guest honored on the field.

The May Sunday the last game was played, won by the Giants with Willie Mays hitting the last home run, a dramatic deal was consummated, happily for the Cardinals. At a time Redbird offense was thin—actually Mike Shannon's .288 and 16 homers, Tim McCarver's .274 with 12 were the only consistent contribution in 1966—they needed a big bat. One seemed possible if (1) they could make a deal for Orlando Cepeda and (2) the Baby Bull, as they had nicknamed in San Francisco, was not a wounded cow. Cepeda, actually briefly more popular than the mighty Mays when he joined the Giants, had sulked because manager Herman Franks wanted him to play the outfield rather than the new and even more powerful first baseman, Willie McCovey.

The open rift created speculation. One included Durocher's Chicago Cubs, seeking Cepeda for Wrigley Field, offering lefthander Dick Ellsworth. Franks was a St. Louis and Brooklyn teammate of Durocher. The suggestion was that Herman was willing to help Leo get a little bit more from Stoneham. A dangerous assumption, compounded by the fact that Howsam, thinking the same thing, dragged his feet on a speculated trade, Ray Sadecki for Cepeda. Howsam fiddled while Busch and Meyer burned, aware that Bing Devine, now working as vice-president of the Mets, had been tricked into an on-the-record comment that, sure, he'd make that trade.

So with the Giants winning that final game at old Sportsman's Park, Cardinals' team physician Dr. I. C. Middleman examined Cepeda's balky knee and was convinced that the tender and loving care of trainer Bob Bauman would bring the music out of Cha-Cha's stereo and his bat. The deal was reluctantly done. Cepeda hit a team-high .303 with 17 home runs.

When Busch Stadium opened in mid-May, against the Atlanta Braves, Felipe Alou, the eldest of the brothers three, hit two home runs, making Busch Stadium seem to be what it wasn't—a home run hitter's park—and Mike Shannon homered for the Cardinals. They won in the twelfth, 4-3, on a base hit by Brock.

The tendency in the new park—shorter in the left-center power alley, shorter in dead center and longer in right-center and at the foul line—was to judge how many flies to right would have been "screen balls", singles or doubles off the 354-foot meshed area in right to right center. A favorite target was McCarver, who hit only 12 home runs, but led in the league in triples with 13, unusual for a catcher.

Unusual, too, was the ability of a big young Redbird lefthander, Larry Jaster, to face Los Angeles five times and shut them out five times, matching a record set by Grover Cleveland Alexander back in the dead ball days. Jaster, 11-5 that season, led with five shutouts. Actually he had only two others in 80 career starts in the majors.

With a sixth-place season, 83-79, producing a record 1,712,980 gate, a tribute largely to the beauty of new Busch Stadium, Howsam surprised by moving over to Cincinnati, where, as mentioned, he did tremendously, helped by success in deals with the Cardinals. Boldly, Busch picked front-office neophyte Stan Musial as general manager, and, to paraphrase broadcaster Jack Buck's famous line, that proved to be a winner!

Musial had the personality to attract attention and help of many, including technical aspects from the ball club's publicity director, Jim Toomey. And when he needed further help, Musial could go to the best—Bing Devine, then president of the New York Mets. Typically, going "1 for 1" as a general manager, Musial was good and lucky. After the season, Red Schoendienst had coach Joe Schultz take right fielder Mike Shannon up to

FOR THE LOVE OF MIKE: Mike Shannon (right), who could've won a Heisman Trophy if he had stayed with football at Missouri, paved the way for pennants with Roger Maris when he moved from right field to third base. Here, Mike gets instructions from Red Schoendienst, a Hall of Fame infielder.

Fairgrounds Park and hit ground balls to him. Yes, Shannon, a natural athlete, could fill the hole at third base. Now if only they could get Roger Maris from the Yankees to play right field!

At 32, damaged goods with a weak wrist, the record home-run king of 61, set six years earlier, had a salary too rich for the Yankees at the time, $75,000. Howsam made the last move a winning one. The Cards gave up the third-base plumber, Smith and cash.

Uncertain about playing, Maris had a dandy carrot dangled before him by Busch: an Anheuser-Busch distributorship in Ocala-Gainesville in Florida. He signed and loved it, the next two seasons, peaceful years that squeezed out the sour reminisces from his baseball memories. Rog didn't hit too much and really no longer could provide the long ball, but the two-time former American League Most Valuable Player proved himself a team-player. Neither Rog nor Shannon, who would become a close friend, hit for average in 1967, but they did it timely. Maris played right field with great skill, Shannon played third with the vigor of Pepper Martin and more skill.

Led at bat by Orlando Cepeda and in clubhouse, too, with his stereo, the 1967 Cardinals breezed as "El Birdos," the ungrammatical Spanish-flavored nickname hung on them by coach Joe Schultz. Not figured in the pennant picture, they were in it from opening night when the great Gibson shut out Juan Marichal and San Francisco, 5-0.

O-O-O-O-O:
Lefty Larry Jaster, little more than a journeyman, opened many eyes, including those of chief Baltimore scout Jim Russo when he shut out Los Angeles a record-tying five times in 1966, suggesting to Russo that the Orioles could beat the Dodgers in the 1966 World Series with fast balls. They did.

Musial had only to make one move, picking up Jack Lamabe from Devine and the Mets in July when Gibson was hurt.

Astonishingly, the ball club won the pennant with 101 victories even though no pitcher won more than 16 games, though obviously Gibson would if he hadn't been hurt. The leader was a rookie retread, bespectacled Dick Hughes, 16-6. Next was the snubnosed stocky righthander, Nelson Briles, who came out of the bullpen when Gibby was hurt. Nellie was 14-5. Another who won 14 was a lean, lanky lefty, just 22, who had joined the Cardinals from Tulsa in August 1966, for the Hall of Fame exhibition game, getting a look-see. That day when Ted Williams and Casey Stangel were inducted into the national baseball Hall of Fame, they got another look at one who would have a similar date in Cooperstown—Steve Carlton.

Obviously, enough pitchers were over .500. Gibson was 13-7 in his short season. Ray Washburn, coming back from shoulder surgery, was 10-7. Southpaws Al Jackson and Larry Jaster were 9-4 and 9-7. Witty reliever Ron Willis was 6-5 and even though Joe Hoerner did no better than break even, he symbolized the free-wheeling attitude of the club. Un-huh, free-wheeling and literally, like late in the pennant-winning season when the Cardinals couldn't find their bus driver for a ride from Atlanta's Fulton County Stadium to their hotel. Hoerner leaped in behind the wheel and gave his teammates a ride back to the hotel, merely knocking down a driveway "Entrance" sign. At least, as the light-hearted lefty put it, it wasn't the "Exit" sign.

Curt Flood (.335) led in team hitting, and Brock hit 21 homers and stole 76 bases. Julian Javier, having the kind of year that if it had been consistent would have made him a Hall of Fame candidate, batted .281. Workhorse Tim McCarver hit .295 with 14 homers earning him second place in the league's Most Valuable Player voting. Front and center, the league's last unanimous

MVP until Philadelphia's Mike Schmidt in 1980, was Cha-Cha Cepeda, who had labored long with a weighted boot to strengthen his knee. Limping, the Baby Bull could outrun most players and, a slick glove man at first base, the good-natured, good-looking big guy hit .325 with 24 home runs and 111 RBIs.

Early, Leo Durocher's Cubs, more surprising in their climb than the Cardinals, made a run at the Redbirds, but with coach Pete Reiser sending Ted Savage into a big out at the plate, El Birdos won a key game and took off. The only question was whether they could recover after Gibson suffered a broken leg in July struck with a line drive off Roberto Clemente's bat. Not even Gibson could pitch with a broken leg, but he tried. But when Briles stepped forward, the only question for manager Schoendienst was whether Gibson, returning to the mound in September, could be ready for the World Series. He was—ready for one of the most impressive pitching performances in Series history—and yet pressed hard by teammate Lou Brock for the sports car then given to the Series MVP. The peach of a pair had to be at their best because Carl Yastrzemski, winning the American League pennant for the Boston Red Sox on the last day of the season, had the career year of his 23 in the majors. Yaz was a Triple Crown Winner—.326, 44, 121—and then blistered Redbird pitching in the Series. He hit .400 with two doubles, three homers and five RBIs.

The Sox got a bad Series break for the opener because 22-game winner Jim Lonborg had been necessary to win the last-day pennant-clincher. So Dick Williams, the St. Louisan who managed Boston, went with Jose Santiago, a 12-and-4 pitcher, and almost got away with it. Fact is, Santiago even hit a home run. But future Hall of Fame selections Gibson and Brock combined their talent in the opener, helped by the professionalism of Maris, twice noting the infield playing back for him and hitting run-scoring ground balls to the right side. One scored Brock after his single and a double by Flood in the third inning. The second made Gibson a six-hit victor, 2-1, when Brock singled in the seventh, stole second base and scored as both Flood and Maris grounded out. Boston's aces, Lonborg and Yastrzemski, took over the second game. The pitcher had a no-hitter until Javier doubled in the eighth for the Cardinals'only hit. Meanwhile, with Yaz teeing off on Hughes in the fourth inning, the Sox won, 5-0.

When the Series moved to St. Louis, Briles came through with a strong pitching performance and won, 5-2, over Gary Bell and associates with Brock's triple and Flood's single producing one run in the first inning. Two more followed in the second on a single by McCarver and a homer by Shannon. When Gibson breezed to a five-hitter in the next game, 5-0, a result of a four-run first against Santiago, the Sox needed a big one—another big one—from Lonborg and got it, 3-1, a three-hitter in which Maris homered for the Cardinals' only run. The big kid, Carlton, gave up an unearned run, left for a pinch-hitter in the sixth, and the Bosox got the last two off Willis and Lamabe.

AMONG THE SOUVENIRS: This one, recorded seconds after Bob Gibson (bareheaded at right center) whiffed George Scott to end with a flourish the 1967 World Series. Gibby the Great, shortly after ending his convalescence from a mid-season broken leg, won three games – and a sports car.

The return of the Series to Boston brought out the muscle in the Sox as if Ted Williams and Jimmy Foxx still were on sportsman Tom Yawkey's payroll. Off Hughes and successors, Rico Petrocelli hit two homers. Yastrzemski and Reggie Smith one each. Brock homered in the Series-tying 8-4 loss.

With the Cardinals frozen out of a nearby hotel and farmed out to a motel in nearby Quincy, a long ride from Fenway, the seventh-game morning tabloid headline crowed "LONBORG AND CHAMPAGNE." They could have mentioned Gibson "burned on toast" because, served late in the small crowded motel restaurant, Gibby was offered only a piece of dry, burnt toast. He stormed out to the bus without touching it. A St. Louis writer who had suffered the pangs of an ulcer, knowing the need for a little something to eat, fretted until he recognized a cafeteria, called a halt to the bus driver and hopped off, portable typewriter in hand. The mission was a couple of carry-out ham-and-egg sandwiches, taken by cab to Fenway Park and then delivered to equipment manager Butch Yatkeman at the visitors' clubhouse.

So with a Lonborg handicapped working with two days, Gibson with three, the Cardinals got two runs in the third. Maxvill tripled, Flood and Maris singled, and a wild pitch added a second run. Two more came in the fifth, the first a homer by Gibson, the other on Brock's single, his two stolen bases and a sacrifice fly by Maris. The sixth was a knockout. McCarver doubled, Shannon reached on an error and, in a typical bunting situation, Javier hammered a three-run homer. With Gibson allowing only three hits and striking out 10, the verdict was in, 7-2, even before the great grinning righthander sat sipping champagne and eating a sandwich in the clubhouse.

"I only had one before the game," he told the crestfallen scribe, who had suggested in the pressbox that Gibson's gumption got him through the seventh inning, the ham through the eighth and the eggs in the ninth.

No-No: No-hit games are rare indeed, but in 1968, just after the Cardinals clinched the National League pennant, San Francisco's Gaylord Perry (left) held the Redbirds' hitters. Next day the Redbirds' Ray Washburn (right) did the same thing to the Giants.

Another egg was on the face of KMOX's Bob Hyland after Gibson was awarded the sports car for his three victories, dressed up with only 14 hits, just five walks and 26 strikeouts with a 1.00 ERA. Brock, hitting .414, had 12 hits, including two doubles, a triple, a homer, three runs scored and a record seven stolen bases. Magnanimously, Hyland, the fan perhaps more than the businessman, told Brock to go out and pick a car at the radio station's expense. True-Blue Lou chose a Cadillac Eldorado!

As general manager, Musial, hitting a grand slam with the team that won 101 games and drew the first season in excess of 2,000,000, naively was too good a guy promising World Series seats. Only the sharp suggestion of assistant ticket manager Mike Bertani, temporarily winning fire marshall approval for adding a folding chair in each of the Stadium's spacious ailes, permitted a record 54,692 for each of the three Series games at Busch.

With the unexpected death of business-partner friend, 53-year-old Julius (Biggie) Garagnani, restaurateur, promoter, politician, Musial felt the need to get back to the shop and away from the long telephone hours of a general manager. Why not Bing Devine? A forgive-and-forget guy, who recognized he'd been mislaid by the red herring of the Dick Groat matter in 1964, Busch approved the deal. Der Bingle, giving up the presidency of the Mets, to the delight of a wife and family who seldom made it east, finally was rewarded for his first official pennant, easier with a 97-65 record than the year before. This was, 1968, the Year of the Pitcher in the big leagues and, Detroit's Denny McLain not withstanding, Pack Robert (Hoot) Gibson was the pitcher!

Gibson, born in an Omaha ghetto after his father died, was bit on the ear by a rat as a baby, but, chances are the rodent got a frozen lip because Gibby emerged as a tremendous competitor, challenged by an older brother as an asthmatic kid with rickets and with a heart murmur. "Josh", his personal hero. A great all-around athlete, Gibson was a Creighton University basketball star who played with the Harlem Globetrotters. When he was a star with the

ROGER WHO?: Next to the man on the left, home-run king Roger Maris of the Yankees and Cardinals would run a distant second in the national spotlight. The fan looking down in the Redbirds' dugout in the 1968 World series, lost to the Detroit Tigers, is Frank Sinatra.

Cardinals, the professional basketball Hawks had a young man, Paul Silas, who would set an NBA record for rebounds. Silas paid Gibson quite a tribute. "I'm a couple of inches taller than he is, but he beat me bloody for rebounds in an Alumni-Varsity game," said Silas. "What a competitor!"

Yeah, and at his nastiest best with high-and-tight intimidating pitching and a biting slider in 1968, a year he lost nine times only because it was that kind of low-score year. He won 22 games, 13 of them by shutouts, just three fewer than Grover Cleveland Alexander's record of 16 in the deadball era, 1916. That's not all. Gibson won 15 games in a row and over one 90-inning period he permitted just two earned runs. He finished 28 of 34 starts, allowed only 198 hits in 305 innings. He walked 68, struck out 268 and established a 1.12 earned-run average, lowest ever for a 300-inning pitcher.

Reflecting the year, Flood was the only .300 hitter, 34 points below his 1967 average, and even Cepeda hit an embarrassing .248. Among the pitchers, Briles won 19 games, Carlton 13 and Ray Washburn 14, one of which was most interesting for more reasons than one. When the Cardinals clinched the pennant in San Francisco, they over-indulged and were bleary-eyed, as celebrating teams will do now and then. The next hungover night they were held hitless by Gaylord Perry. Annoyed, the champion Redbirds responded the next day when Washburn also threw a no-hitter.

The day before the first World Series game, broadcasting on national radio, Sandy Koufax talked to the *Post-Dispatch* 's Dave Lipman, a sports writer en route to the managing editor's chair. Koufax noted that Gibson pitched with nearly as much arthritic pain as Sandy had with his left before painfully calling it quits. "You know," said Koufax, "McLain, a great pitcher and colorful with his organ playing, has got most of the news with his 31 victories, but I know Gibson. He's going to eat McLain alive tomorrow."

Indeed, for lunch. With what would be regarded as the most impressive strikeout total ever, considering that the occasion was bright daylight and the opposition baseball's best-hitting ball club, the 17-strikeout effort in the spotlight of the World Series was remarkable and inspiring. Gibby the Great's performance in the 4-0 victory, one in which that other Series standout Brock homered, was two strikeouts higher than Koufax's for Los Angeles against the Yankees in 1963. When batterymate McCarver rushed out to tell him he had reached 15, as reflected on the message scoreboard, Gibson snarled at Timmy to get the blankety-blank behind the plate. As bench jockey Gibson would chide in clubhouse humor to McCarver, "The only thing you know about pitching is that you couldn't hit it."

The Cardinals couldn't hit pugdy lefthander Mickey Lolich in the second game when the future doughnut king of Detroit, 17-8 in the regular season, gained an 8-1 victory over Briles on home runs by Norm Cash, Willie Horton and the chubby chucker himself.

Back at Detroit, the Tigers got an early lead off Washburn when Al Kaline hit a two-run homer in the third. Kaline, a future Hall of Famer, got into the lineup because of manager Mayo Smith's guts in moving Mickey Stanley from center field to shortstop and moving Jim Northrup to center. In Kaline's one and only Series chance, the talented player hit .379 with two homers and eight RBIs. The Cards overcame Kaline's clout, getting three-run homers by McCarver and Cepeda to win the third game, 7-3. For game four, Gibson vs. McLain again. The weather bothered Gibson more than the Tigers' bats. The game was delayed in starting for 35 minutes and halted again for 74 minutes in the third inning. The waiting and starting over

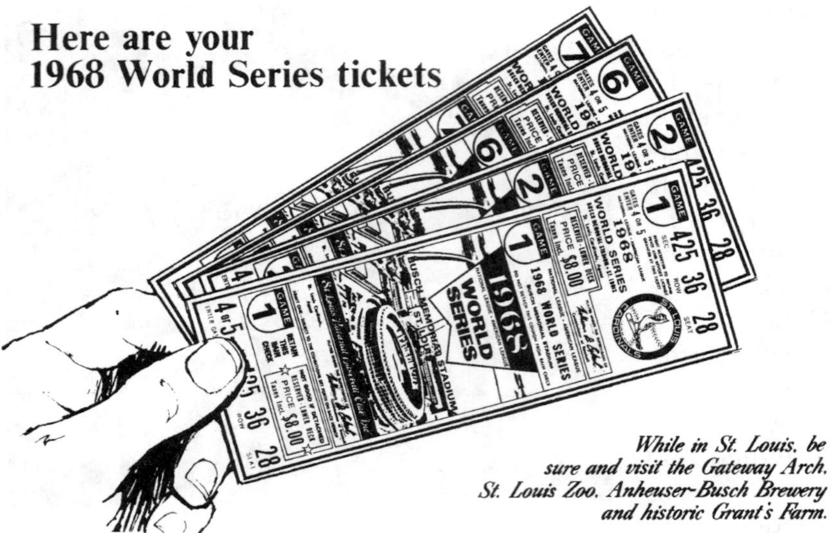

couldn't have helped Gibson down the road, but it wasn't evident in their knockout of McLain in a 10-1 romp led by Brock's single, double, triple and four runs batted in. Gibby also hit a homer, a record two for a pitcher in Series play.

The Series swung on the fifth game, one in which it appeared the Cardinals would wrap it up early, a result of a three-run first inning on Cepeda's homer off Lolich. By the seventh, the lead was only a run, but St. Louis appeared ready to put it away. Brock doubled with one out, then surprisingly was thrown out at the plate on a disputed call after Javier singled to left. The theory, probably logical, was that with Detroit two runs behind, Smith would have pinch-hit for Lolich in the home half, but, leery of his bullpen, Mayo let Mickey hit. In the Redbirds' outfield, both Brock and Flood urged rightfielder Ron Davis to move in for the righthanded-hitting pitcher. Davis didn't hear or didn't care. Lolich's high pop fly fell into right for a surprising single. Here, Schoendienst replaced Briles with Hoerner. Dick McAullife bad-hopped a single over Javier's head, Stanley walked and old pro Kaline delivered a key two-run base hit. Cash's single added an insurance run and a 5-3 Tiger triumph.

With McLain getting a shot of cortisone for an aching arm and having worked fewer than three innings in the fourth game, the Tigers chewed up the Cardinals in the sixth game, 13-1, a result of a parade of pitchers, Washburn and seven others. They were victims of a 10-run inning, the most since the Philadelphia A's overcame an eight-run deficit against the Chicago Cubs in the 1929 World Series.

So now it came down to the OK Corral, the Cardinals who never lost a seventh-game shoot out, Gibson vs. Lolich in a game that silver dollars to one of Mickey's sugar doughnuts, figured to be much closer than the Tigers kept the Cardinals to their bases. Actually it seemed almost arrogant in that final game. They already had stolen 11 bases, but Brock took such a l-o-n-g lead in the sixth inning after his record-tying 13th hit. Picked off, Brock broke for second, retired only because Cash made an accurate over-the-shoulder throw. An instant later, Flood, taking an even longer lead, was picked off and retired.

With two out in the Tigers' seventh, Cash looped a single to right and Horton grounded a base hit to left. Next up, Northrup hit a line drive to center, making a home-town fan wish only that the ball wouldn't sink for a hit. Relieved, it stayed up, straight for Flood, but, perhaps bothered by white-shirted background, Curt broke in briefly, then tried to wheel back, slipping with his spikes churning up the turf. Too late, he got back as the ball bounced against the center-field bleachers for a two-run triple. The misjudged ball did it, 4-1, in a game in which the Cardinals' only run had been a ninth-inning homer by Shannon.

The stunning blow of that first-time seventh-game loss in seven tries found Flood stubbornly not acknowledging any misplay, and Gibson pointing out, softly, that he owed too many too often to Flood to complain. Gibby had been a hero in defeat after seven straight complete-game World Series, a record 35 strikeouts with his 1.67 earned-run average. Brock had been even more so with a phenomenal .464 in which his record-matching 13 hits had been good for 24 bases—three doubles, a triple and two homers—with six runs scored, five driven in and matching his own World Series stolen base record, seven. To second-guess Brock for not sliding in a pivotal fifth-game

Goliath By David: David Lipman's juvenile-age book on Gibby the Great.

play—he didn't believe he could avoid catcher Bill Freehan's plate-blocking foot—would be even worse than second-guessing Bing Devine for a trade announced as the Cardinals showered hurriedly for an off-season trip to Japan.

With Maris retiring, Devine had given up outfielder Bobby Tolan and pitcher Wayne Granger to Cincinnati for veteran outfielder Vada Pinson. At the moment most media members in the Cardinals' clubhouse automatically yielded the Redbirds a third straight pennant in 1969, a season the National League would expand to12 clubs, adding Montreal and San Diego, and go to a League Championship Series. They had the first leg, but not with the Cardinals competing.

With Pinson suffering a broken bone in a leg early in the year, a disappointing .255 season for him and for the Cardinals as a fourth-place club in the split-division league, Musial observed that he shied when approached by Howsam for deals. "He and too many (front-office) people he had taken from us knew our strengths better than we did the Reds' weaknesses." Bold Devine was burned when Bobby Tolan, the fleet Redbird lefthanded-hitting reserve outfielder who had hung in against southpaw pitching, blossomed as a regular with the Reds. So did the rangy Granger in relief. Devine made one other deal, a good one, prompted in part by Cepeda's having leveled off at bat, but also because the carefree character was so deep in financial problems that the creditors were threatening to invade the dugout.

Meanwhile, at Atlanta, Joe Torre was having a salary dispute with Braves' general manager Paul Richards. So the Cardinals obtained the versatile Torre, once needled as just a "fat kid" by elder brother Frank, himself a World Series first baseman for the Milwaukee-based Braves. Stung, Joe had trimmed down and was skilled enough as a catcher to play first base and third, too. Torre's immediate contribution was .289 with 13 homers and 101 RBIs. Javier held up with .288 and Brock .298 and again leading in stolen bases with 53.

Gibson was the staff leader with 20-13 and a 2.18 ERA after having stormed angrily when the pitching mound was lowered from 15 inches to 10 and umpires criticized for having widened the strike zone for Gibby's slider and other pitchers. The great competitor didn't take kindly to the suggestion that, heck, he caused the trouble in large part with too many 1-0 games, creating fewer runs than goals were scored in hockey. Gibson was so upset that he went out and won 23 games in 1970, but that's ahead of the story of the 87-75 season in '69 and an attendance drop of nearly 400,000 to 1,682,583.

If Gussie Busch liked less the profit—and, for sure, they were making money then in baseball—he had become disenchanted in his relationship with the players. He had taken great pride in establishing the first $1,000,000 payroll, trumpeted by *Sports Illustrated*'s showing his first-team unit on the magazine's cover. (If, like Rip Van Winkle, you just came out of your deepest sleep, everything is relative, as Einstein might have said or Mr. Rickey. When Busch paid $75,000 to Maris, that was $3000 more than the entire first nine of Frankie Frisch's Gas House Gang was paid in tough times 1934. And, of course, at the other modern extreme in a different day of different dol-

DISPUTE: In a key play in the pivotal fifth game of the 1968 World Series, Lou Brock, trying to score standing up from second on a single, was thrown out surprisingly on a great throw from Willie Horton to Bill Freehan.

lars, the ante for staying in the race in 1998 was about 50 times more costly than dear Gussie's proud first million-buck payroll.)

Back to the ranch, or rather, to Grant's Farm, Busch was annoyed at the reaction of his favorite player, Curt Flood, for whom the boss pestered management early for more playing time. The talented center fielder also had won brownie points with the boss by giving Gussie a handsome painted old blowup sketch of a favorite small photo of the Big Eagle. Impressed, Busch commissioned Flood to do the same for other members of his vast family.

After the upset loss to Detroit in 1968, Flood, his average dipping from .335 to .301 in the Year of the Pitcher, wanted a handsome raise from $72,000. He wanted $100,000— Flood insisted saucily, "and I don't mean $99,999.99, either." He didn't get what he wanted, settling for $90,000, but he lost what he had, the close affection of the man who had helped him through family scrapes, too. So he dipped to .285 in 1969, burning the candle at both ends. Flood and another favorite, McCarver, were dealt to Philadelphia for Richie Allen in a seven-player deal. Labeled as temperamental, a two-fisted drinker, Dick Allen was accepted with the considerable warmth of St. Louis fans, given a standing ovation opening night. Even though he missed the entire last month of the '70 season, he hit 34 homers, an impressive total at Busch Stadium.

Curtly Speaking: Curt Flood could speak his mind as well as chase down fly balls about as good as anyone – and hit, too – but his refusal to adhere to the reserve clause after a 1969 trade from St. Louis to Philadelphia was costly. A year's layoff with little regard for training made him an old young man who retired at 33, shortly before the career-long player peonage was lifted.

Flood, stunned, knew that in face-lifting at the ball park artificial turf would be installed in 1970. A Dutch uncle friend as a writer had suggested that with the faster infield, the defense pinched up the middle by Houston manager Harry Walker and copied by others, wouldn't be so successful. Yeah, and Curt had his own portrait-painting business in St.Louis. So he refused to report to Philadelphia. Flood's assault against the reserve clause, soon eliminated, made Curt a martyr to the cause for players who were bound by baseball's player renewal clause. Unfortunately, too, not caring for himself physically after a year away—he could have been baseball's first $100,000 "singles" hitter—he agreed to a trade to Washington and a generous salary from Bob Short. Only 13 games into the 1971 season, Curtis Charles Flood retired, a once-fast masterful center fielder with a career .293 average, seven times a .300 hitter and maybe just a couple of more from Hall of Fame election. Said a Washington doctor, "He's got the oldest 33-year-old body of any player I ever examined."

McCarver, by contrast, spent another decade catching, largely with the Phillies, famed as the private caddy for Steve Carlton and for accomplishing more than probably any Redbird in radio and television except Joe Garagiola and Bob Uecker nationally, almost as strong as Mike Shannon regionally. Uecker, helped by success in TV sitcoms, too, was a strong-armed former defensive catcher, McCarver's caddy with the 1964 Cardinals, and a no-hit player who parlayed batting deficiency into his delightful humor.

The 1970 season wasn't funny to the Cardinals from the outset. First, third baseman Mike Shannon was seriously ill with a kidney disease by which the body urinated protein. For a time, Mike's life was touch-and-go or, to use one of the Moon Man's pet radio expressions, from the git-go. Black Mike recovered a lot better than the ball club, fourth with a 76-86 season in which Gibson's 23 victories were the only plus among staff won-and-lost records. One downer, 10-19 by Steve Carlton, would have unfortunate ramifications.

Aware that Richie Allen had taken a monthly sabbatical in September—except for one final appearance at Philadelphia's Connie Mack Stadium when he played under the influence and hit a homer—an annoyed Devine planned to deal him. Richie, his own worst enemy, had been accepted with trepidation by Schoendienst as manager, but at Allen's departure Red was sorry to lose Dick's big bat. From the Dodgers the Cardinals got a second baseman, Ted Sizemore, to replace an aging Javier.

In 1971, with other new or recent names in the lineup—Joe Hague at first base, Matty Alou and Jose Cruz in the outfield and Reggie Cleveland and Jerry Reuss among pitchers—Carlton was very good as the staff leader with 20-9. At bat, Torre, always a good hitter, was great. Playing the entire season at third base without once flipping on a catcher's mask or first baseman's mitt, he was the NL's MVP as the Redbirds finished second in the Eastern Division, seven games behind Pittsburgh. Torre, hitting to right-center like a Rogers Hornsby or Joe Medwick, batted a league-leading .363 with 24 homers and finished first in RBIs with 137.

A modest drop in attendance to 1,604,671 even with a 90-72 record didn't help Busch's pride or disposition, particularly when the young lefthanders, Carlton and Reuss, held out the following spring. In advance of finance-strangling multiple-year deals of recent times in baseball, contracts longer than a season were few then. As a result, a player was basically paid more or less on what he did the previous year. Busch was impressed with Carlton's 20-9 record in 1971, but, huumph, what about the 10-19 in '70? Gussie didn't want to give Steve as much as the guy called "Lefty" wanted. The 22 year-old Reuss, 14-14 in '71, tried to insist he be able to take his wife on trips with the ball club. In training camp, sounding like Der Poss Bresident of old, Busch ordered Devine to get rid of them for the best he could. Der Bing for too long took the rap, too loyal to point the finger at Busch or, come to think of it, maybe smart enough.

With Phillies' righthander Rick Wise having come off a 17-14 season, his best, the bespectacled 29-year-old righthander wanted more money than John Quinn would give him. Why, in one game he not only had pitched a no-hitter, but he'd also won the game with a pair of home runs. So the deal was made—just moments before Carlton phoned Devine to say that he'd fly in and would accept the club's offer!

Barely .500 for two seasons with the Cardinals and floundering down the pennant stretch in 1973, Wise soon went over to the American League for most of his last nine seasons, a 188-181 pitcher. Carlton? Well, Steve looked as if he would be a lefthanded Cy Young. In 1969 he had struck out 19 Mets in a late season game against the surprising division and league winners. Now he went over to Philadelphia and immediately perpetrated one of the most amazing performances ever, winning 27 games for a last-place ball club that won only 59. Thereafter, usually with McCarver hunkering down for him, Lefty would achieve five more 20-game seasons and win four Cy Young awards. With his slider biting down and out, he became a strikeout pitcher with the second most lifetime, 4136. He won 329 games, ninth most in history, and pitched the once futile Phils into five League Championship Series and to the 1980 World Series championship. He was a first-ballot Hall of Famer in 1994. Busch, who died five years earlier at 90 after Steve bowed out as a pitcher at 44, lamented late in life, before Whitey Herzog's bluster and success warmed the old man's heart, "I hate to be remembered only as the guy who traded Steve Carlton."

STEVEN NORMAN CARLTON: Ninth-highest winning pitcher ever, 329 games including 27 for the last-place Philadelphia team that won only 59 in 1972, four-time 20-game winner was also a four-time Cy Young award winner with 19 strikeouts for the Cardinals in 1969. First-time Hall of Fame inductee, 1994.

Or the guy who executed the early exit of Reuss, dealt to Houston for an engaging young righthander, Scipio Spinks, briefly a hero with his pitching and his toy-sized gorilla, Mighty Joe Young. Caught up in the headlines of success, poor Scipio tried to stretch a base-running gamble, running through a third-base coach's stop sign and into the formidable knee-protected pads of Johnny Bench. Sayanaro! For the record, Reuss, proving another annoying Methusaleh of the mound to Busch and the Cardinals, lasted 22 seasons in the majors,

THE MAD HUNGARIAN: Self-styled, wearing a fierce Fu Manchu mustache, Al Hrabosky tried to pitch as mean as he looked in a 13-year big-league career before arm trouble got him. Hrabosky's career season was 1975 with the Cardinals – a 13-1 record, 1.61 ERA in 65 games and 22 saves. Al bounced back as a colorful TV commentator for the Redbirds.

won 220 games until age 42, pitching in six championship series and was a member of the Dodgers' 1981 world champions. In reflection, it's tough to think in a quarter-century look-see into the past that the Cardinals had an excuse for their fourth-place finish in 1972 and deserve a basic bow for their near-misses in 1973 and '74, the last upbeat period before the White Rat Herzog come back to town.

In '72, finishing fourth in the Eastern Division with a 75-81 record and a 1,196,194 attendance, Devine was able to keep Schoendienst on the job and Busch satisfied. Alou, Brock and that heavy-haired young catcher, Ted Simmons, were .300 hitters and Simba really the only home-run threat with 16. Torre hit only 11 in a .289 season on 81 RBIs. Among the pitchers, only the king of the hill, Gibson, had a winning record, 19-11 and a 2.45 ERA. A year later, 1973, if Gibson hadn't been hurt, the Cardinals might have written the most outstanding reversal in any race.

From a stumbling start, their worst ever, 5-and-20, the Redbirds rose like a phoenix from their ashes to a point where, unbelievably, they were in first place early in August, 11 games over .500, five in front. At Cooperstown, bathing in the hotel's pool, Hall of Famer Joe Medwick happily relayed radio results of a series in New York, but that day Gibson was hurt. When Gibson suffered that broken leg back in 1967, Nelson Briles had rushed to the rescue, looking and acting like a bulldog. This time, Rick Wise, Reggie Cleveland and others backed off from responsibility as if it were land-mined. Slowly, the Cardinals came back to .500. Second-place Pittsburgh, too. So Yogi Berra's New York Mets came on to win the division only three games over .500, 82-79, but then upset heavily favored Cincinnati in the LCS and carried the Oakland A's to a seventh game of the World Series. At season's end, Gibson tried out the knee after surgery and pitched well enough and long enough to beat Carlton, but over the winter directed toward active rehabilitiation, he was unable to follow through because of marital troubles.

So the gimpy-kneed 38-year-old wasn't the Gibson of old. The ball club was better, however, because Devine almost bitterly had unloaded Wise and Cleveland to Boston in an off-season deal that brought switch-hitting Reggie Smith for power in the outfield and added Lynn McGlothen to the pitching staff. McGlothen was a staff leader with 16 victories. Reliever Al Hrabosky—the "Mad Hungarian"—was as menacing as his Fu Manchu mustache and, pounding the ball in his glove behind the mound and then into the catcher's mitt, he went 8-and-1 with nine saves.

Offensively, the handsome Smith, troubled in Boston and arriving with a chip on his shoulder, found St. Louis as salubrious as Brock, Maris, Cepeda, Allen and other unhappy campers had discovered the friendly bank of Father Mississippi. Reg hit .303 with 23 homers, 100 RBIs. Simba Simmons, the other switcher, had 20 homers and 103 runs driven in. And Lou Brock, hitting .305 climbed the highest mountain. True-Blue Lou, who raised chants of "Lou, Lou, Lou" that sounded like a chorus of boos, shattered Maury Wills' stolen-base record.

Brock topped Wills' 104 with 118 stolen bases, and only the inability of Sizemore and others, hitting behind him, to move the ball to right field kept Brock from scoring more than 105 runs. Three times he had tallied more. The lean and lanky center fielder, rookie Bake McBride, who ran like Brock, broke in with .309 and scored a run historic if only because it broke up the second longest game ever in major-league baseball, a 25-inning marathon at Shea Stadium that lasted through most of the night. Taking a long lead, McBride sped around the bases on an overthrow at first base. The run kept the '74 race as close as one second from another. Slick-fielding, light-hitting Ken Reitz had sent the game into overtime, where Claude Osteen pitched a full-game in relief. When it ended, Jack Buck had Reitz as Star-of-the-Game hero for KMOX and the radio network. Buck's commentary was like a Gibson-pitched game—good and fast—because he said, "And now the star of the game, Ken Reitz. Congratulations, Ken, good night—and good morning!"

Gibson now pitched fast, but not good, a victim of age and inability to put full weight on the left foot for his emphatic follow-through. He was 11-and-13, but in the final week when a playoff could be achieved with Pittsburgh if both won their final games, Gibby had one more chance. He served up a decisive two-run homer to Montreal's Mike Jorgensen in a backbreaker lost 3-2. So now Pittsburgh would have to lose. The next night when the Pirates played the Cubs at Pittsburgh, the Cardinals were rained out in Montreal. If the Pirates lost and the Cards could win a make-up game, there could still be a playoff for the division title.

Busch and gin-rummy buddies had gathered at the Bevo Mill, a former brewery landmark, for a few drinks, dinner, a little gin-rummy and a telecast that seemed fair and warmer when Chicago led. That is, until the the Pirates rallied to win in extra innings when a low-breaking pitch by Rick Reuschel eluded catcher Steve Swisher.

Silently, wearily, now as old as his years, Gussie addressed personal friend Ben Kerner, former owner of the basketball Hawks, "Drive me home, Hawk," said Mr. Busch. There wasn't a word spoken all the way down Gravois Road to Grant's Farm. For Big Eagle Busch—again!—there would be no tomorrow.

Nor for the faithful followers, 1,695,394 of whom saw the 1975 Cardinals finish a distant third behind Pittsburgh, 10 games better than St. Louis's 82-80. It was the last season for Gibson the Great, down to 3-and-10 with those rickety, injured legs not able to hold up for him at nearly 40. With no stopper, even though Bob Forsch and McGlothen won 15 games and Hrabosky had a remarkable year in relief—11-2 and 22 saves—the Cardinals came up short offensively, too, though Brock was Brock with a .309 average and 56 stolen bases. The fleet Baker, McBride, batted .300, but the power came from Smith, moved to first base, and the catcher, Simmons. Reggie hit .302 with 19 homers and 76 RBIs. Ted hit a whopping .332 with 18 homers and100 RBIs.

Busch took care of Gibson grandly after a 251-174 career, barely under the difficult .600 winning percantage, plus a Most Valuable Player award in 1968 and the Cy Young that year and in 1970. He had a 17-year career with a 2.91 earned-run average and 3117 strikeouts in 3885 innings, but—above all—stardom in the spotlight of the World Series. In the blue-ribbon classic, to coin a cliche, Gibby had seven consecutive complete-game victories in nine Series decisions. When Gibson went into the Hall of

ST. LOUIS SWIFTIES: Not the fabulous nicknamed 1942 Cardinals, but Lou Brock and James (Cool Papa) Bell. The legendary speed merchant of black-league baseball presents to Brock the record 105th steal of Lou's 118 in 1974.

Fame the first year eligible, Busch was there, reflecting the happier side of the Big Eagle, torn then by player demands after early having been a patsy. At a time no player got $200,000 a season—Aaron of Atlanta and Allen of the White Sox were the only two before free-agency and inflation blew off the lid—Gibson and Brock were top-salaried at about $160,000.

But Busch could get grumpy over requests, for instance, Simmons'. Simba, aptly nicknamed because of a flowing mane, was an outstanding hitter and pretty good receiver, as durable as perhaps any receiver since Yogi Berra. When he held out one year and Busch opposed the height of the raise, Simba simply wouldn't sign his contract. This was an alarm at a time the reserve clause had been challenged unsuccessfully by Flood and a favorable arbitrator's ruling, shutting down the peonage, wasn't too far ahead. Obviously Simmons or his agent—more likely the player—wouldn't accept the figure. So he was the first player to withhold his signature and, potentially, the first to sit out a season since the New York Giants' Edd Roush wasted the second-to- last season of a golden career in 1931.

THE SWITCHER: Ted (Simba) Simmons, a big leaguer briefly at 19 and a .300 hitter at 22, had 2456 hits, most of them as a catcher in a career that lasted until he was nearly 40. The "turn-around hitter," as they used to call men who batted both left and righthanded, had eight seasons above .300, five with more than 20 homers, three with 100 RBIs and five more with above 90.

If Simmons didn't sign, under contract restrictions, they could renew his contract with a maximum 20 per cent cut. The Cardinals didn't deduct pay in their March 10 renewal but, as noted, Simmons didn't sign. He went out, played, and kept his mouth shut, probably aware that a guy didn't have to be a Philadelphia lawyer to conclude that "renew the contract for one year," didn't mean forever. In advance of a court case, for which baseball would hold its breath, Busch's righthand man and Devine's adviser at the brewery, Dick Meyer, crafted a two-year deal, the first on which would placate the Big Eagle, the second of which would satisfy Simba. Crisis resolved.

The 1976 season was one of transition for the Cardinals, involved in a promising youth movement, and the last as manager for Red Schoendienst, whose 12 seasons had almost doubled Branch Rickey's previous club record as field foreman. The pitching was almost as bad as a one-sided, trading-deadline deal that sent Reggie Smith to the Dodgers for a catcher Joe Ferguson, and a couple of kids. By mid-June the club hadn't been able to resolve a contractual problem with Smith, not playing well, either. So he went to Los Angeles for Ferguson, accompanied by a couple of nonentities. Moodily, Ferguson moved to the outfield now and then, hitting .201. A year later, he was gone. In the colorful language of Branch Rickey, an addition by subtraction. Ferguson, that is, not Smith. At L.A., Smith hit .307 with 32 homers and 104 RBIs.

Two names to be remembered came up in 1976, 21-year-old rookie firstbaseman Keith Hernandez and late-season shortstop Garry Templeton, but not soon enough or good enough to avoid the nosedive to fifth in the six-team Eastern Division with a 72-90 record, the most defeats since a seventh-place finish in 1916, and an attendance barely past 1,200,000. Busch, though he liked Schoendienst, liked to win more and he liked a firm hand. He thought he had the answer in one of two candidates Devine suggested. One, Joe Altobelli of Rochester, would become a World Series-winner at Baltimore. Busch wanted a sterner man and got one in Vern Rapp, a St. Louis graduate of Cleveland High School and former farm-system catcher. Vern had served for years as manager under Bob Howsam in the minors. Howsam was a spit-and-polish disciplinarian. So was Rapp, which meant right down his South Side alley, Vern's and boss Busch. Based on where they've been and where they were going, it would be a bum rap—pardon the pun!—to blame Rapp because, actually, the Redbirds improved under the chunky, tow-headed, home-town manager. They finished third in the East—it didn't help Busch to know that Steve Carlton and the Phillies were first—and their 83-79 record upgraded attendance 450,000 to 1,659,287.

It helped at the box office, of course, that Brock, once timed at 3.5 seconds with a 13-stride steal and pop-up slide, chased—and caught—Ty Cobb's career stolen base record just as he previously had caught Maury Wills' single-season mark. Steal No. 893, one more than Tyrus the terrific, came at San Diego in late August.

Meanwhile, younger players were doing good things for a ball club that was short of pitching except for Forsch's 20-7. In addition to Simmons' annual sturdy contribution to the cause—.318, 21, 95—the impact came from a peach of a pair, Templeton and Hernandez.

Handsome Hernandez, given a good $30,000 bonus even though he didn't go high in the draft, had impressed two of Devine's esteemed baseball men, Harry Walker and Bob Kennedy, as "another Stan Musial." Not quite, of course, but a good hitter to all fields, not fast afoot, yet quick and certainly one of the finest-fielding first baseman ever. He hit .291 with 15 homers and 91 runs batted in.

Better things were to come. Templeton, arriving the previous year at 20, looked early to be possibly the best Cardinal player ever—obviously a heady analysis—but when you get a switch-hitter batting .300 from either side of the plate, extremely fast, strong-armed and playing the key shortstop position, you've got a diamond, the Hope diamond. That first full season was .322 with 200 hits, including a league-leading 13 triples. Truth is, with Hernandez flipping Garry's low throws out of the dirt with grace and artistry, Templeton had only himself to blame if anything happened. The fleet fellow became the only player other than Detroit's Sam Crawford early in the century to lead in triples three times, en route to a potential first. He was also the first player to get 100 hits a season from either side of the plate and had a league-leading 211 hits with 13 triples in 1979. That's about the time young Tempy—or "Jump Steady," as the folks back home called him—commented haughtily about the All-Star game, "If I ain't startin', I ain't departin.'" Could the foreign substances by then have cut into his ability and judgment? Hernandez's, too?

JUMPING JOY: Most deservedly for Bob Forsch after he pitched his first of a Redbird record two no-hitters, on April 16, 1978, against Philadelphia. Forsch became an elder statesman on the mound for the Cardinals, spending 14 of his 16 season in the majors in the raiment of the Redbirds. He was 20-7 in 1977.

Rapp, who rode the herd hard, was successful, but he wasn't popular with the players or others. In spring training in 1978, he seemed to be trying to relax, but when the Cardinals got off to a slow start—what's new?—his 6-and-11 record and other aspects of life caught up with him. One was a session in which he called Simmons a "loser." Sleepy-eyed Simba, faced with the problems of more base-stealers than baseball had known for years, was too durable, too hard-nosed and, yes, hard hitting to be labeled negatively. One night, glumly, the catcher mentioned it to Jack Buck.

Buck, a member of the Cardinals' broadcast team from 1954 through publication of this saga of St. Louis baseball, has achieved even greater stature than predecessor Harry Caray, partly because he's more compassionate, but the sentimental Irishman, enraged, made public his displeasure about the "loser" label. Buck's cutting comments about the commentator, i.e., the manager, helped cut out the commentator, fired by the Big Eagle. The successor was the former third-base star and captain, Ken Boyer, then managing Louisville. Boyer's finish—62-81

in his games—left the Cardinals fifth, 69-93, and with only 1,278,175 who saw the sag.

Early in 1979, Devine engineered a deal with San Diego for outfielder George Hendrick, sending pitcher Eric Rasmussen, and he'd also acquired a big righthanded Serb, Pete Vuckovich, for a staff that was short despite low-score games by another acquisition, Silvio Martinez, and the promise of a young righthander John Fulgham. The ball club perked up to third, 86-78, and attendance responded with a 400,000 hike to 1,627,259, aided by Hernandez's career year, .344 in which he won the batting championship and shared the National League's Most Valuable Player with pennant-winning Pittsburgh's popular Willie (Pops) Stargell. Hernandez hit 11 homers and drove in 111 runs. With new second baseman Ken Oberkfell hitting .300, the lineup had three other .300 hitters—Hendrick, Templeton and in a dramatic climax to his career, Brock.

Brock's average and his base hits had dwindled before the season at 40 that he gracefully acknowledged beforehand would be his last. Old teammate Boyer was concerned."I want very much to see Lou get 3000 hits," he confided, "but I can't lose ball games or my job if he can't deliver." Brock's private analysis was that he wanted the milestone for obvious reasons, "but mainly," he said, "to prove that I've been a hitter as well as a base-stealer."

Magically rejuvenated, Brock was able to play in 120 games in which he batted .304, responding with 123 hits and total of 3024. The historic 3000 hit came in mid-August at Busch Stadium against righthander Dennis Lamp of the Cubs, the club that gave Brock away in the biggest heist since Brinks. With more than 46,000 standing to cheer, Lamp low-bridged Brock dangerously with a high-and-tight pitch that narrowly could have left True-Blue Lou one hit short, but number "20" bounced up, brushed himself off—and hit a crippling line drive off the pitcher's hand. As Lamp went down in pain, the ball squirted into foul territory for a base hit.

As Stan Musial came out, grinning to make the presentaton to Brock as James (Cool Papa) Bell had when he got his record steal, overjoyed True-Blue Lou could only recall, "Funny, I fantasized about hitting the big one up the middle." When they got around to him for "orchestrating my own exit," as he put it, boss Busch, himself an old salt, gave a big pleasure boat to Louis Clark Brock—"King Louie of St. Louie"—and then what many others would have liked to do: Busch bear-hugged Brock.

Scoreboard Tells It: When Lou Brock lined a base hit off Chicago righthander Dennis Lamp's hand, just after Lamp had decked him on August 13, 1979, a gaggle of guys from the Cardinals' clubhouse congregated for congratulations at first base. The 40-year-old Brock, finishing with a high note of .304 average and 3023 hits, also broke Ty Cobb's career stolen-base record that season. Lou's 938 was later topped by Rickey Henderson.

Stick-up man Devine, who filched Brock for his 15-year brilliance into the baseball Hall of Fame, automatic like Gibson first time around in 1985, was fired before the season-ending ceremonies. By now, eased out of control at the brewery, 80-year-old Mr. Busch suddenly was surrounded by a guard at the palace, Grant's Farm. One, lawyer Lou Susman, the beer baron's executor, apparently didn't like Devine too much. Perhaps Der Bingle, reading the writing on the outfield walls, had offended the old man when Montreal offered a long-term contract and he talked about more than a hand shake back home. Anyway, Devine was done, in September, replaced by a young man he had taken from their mutual alma mater, Washington University, and brought the Bears' baseball coach into professional baseball. With Devine's guidance, John Claiborne got a sample of front-office baseball jobs, including an invitation to work for a time with Oakland's Charley Finley because the eccentric master of the mule deliberately worked short staffed. To learn the most in the least time, Devine suggested Oakland and Finley for Claiborne. If, as some thought, Claiborne had suggested that maybe he could come in as Devine's assistant, chances are he'd have been told to take a hike. So Claiborne took the Cardinals into a new decade, fair and warmer for the ball club, as cold as the reception to most of his deals.

With reliever Mark Littell hurt, the shortage of a finisher in the bullpen was never more evident than opening night, 1980. At Busch Stadium, Boyer permitted Vuckovich to go all the way in a tense duel with Pittsburgh, one in which the Pirates filled the bases with none out in the ninth, and the mustachioed guy gutted it out to a shutout victory. By deals and free-agent acquisitions, then a new thing as players began to take over the asylum, Claiborne gave long-term, high salaried contracts to Bernie Carbo, Darold Knowles, Steve Swisher and Mike Phillips and lost some without compensation, too.

In a big move to aid the offense, confident that no-hit artist Bob Forsch would rebound, he gave up pitching talent, including one-time ERA leader John Denny along with outfielder Jerry Mumphrey, for Cleveland outfielder Bobby Bonds, an impressive 30-30 player with the Giants, hitting homers and with stolen bases, but who had a bad wrist and a batting average to match, .203. Maybe he was older than his listed age, 34. Anyway, a year later the Cardinals couldn't give him away. The Cards of 1980 had many good things, including .300 seasons from Hernandez, Oberkfell, Templeton, Hendrick, Simmons and handyman Dane Iorg. Hendrick hit 25 homers and drove in 109 runs. Simmons hit 21 with 98 RBIs, but they still finished fourth with a 74-88 record and almost a 300,000 drop in attendance to 1,385,147. And they had more changes than a striptease artist.

Stunningly, Boyer was dropped as manager in June with the team at 18-33, still a victim of a need of a bullpen closer and, shortly, horribly, a victim of cancer. Big number "14" , then managing the Cardinals' Louisville farm club, died at only 51 in September 1982. For the record, Solly Hemus assisted his old teammate and ex-player financially—and anonymously. Soon, the Cardinals retired Boyer's 14, but

MATINEE IDOL: Handsomely mustached Keith Hernandez, a good hitter and a great-fielding first baseman, was lost to the Cardinals prematurely because of off-the-field problems, but not before he shared the 1979 Most Valuable Player award with Pittsburgh's Willie Stargell. Hernandez later starred with the New York Mets.

Jump Steady:
That was a home-town nickname for Garry Templeton, who looked as if he were headed to the Hall of Fame when the strong-armed, sure-fielding and fleet shortstop led the National League three straight years in triples and became the first switch-hitter with 100 hits a season from each side of the plate, but off-the-field problems and a gimpy knee dimmed his baseball future.

they probably would have honored "24", too, because that was the number of a 49-year-old cottontop who took them to new heights in a cluster like the '40s and '60s, one then that seemed in the distant past, especially to a man Gussie Busch's age, 82. He wanted to win "just one more."

So it was a wedding made in heaven when Dorrell Norman Elvert Herzog, whose dear Mom must not have been able to spell too well, was recruited from the unemployment ranks to succeed Boyer. Whitey—they called him inelegantly the"White Rat"—was preparing to play in former broadcaster Bud Blattner's golf tournament at the Lake of the Ozarks when Susman phoned. The Big Eagle wanted the White Rat to get the Redbirds to fly high, just as he so recently had done for the Kansas City Royals. There, in five-plus seasons he had won three straight division titles, three times bowing to the Yankees in the League Championship Series. After a second-place finish in 1979, he apparently had hastened his departure by saying something indelicate to or about sportsman owner Ewing Kauffman's wife.

So, in effect, Busch was getting a man like himself, a stand-up guy. Whitey was from nearby New Athens, Ill., where, he quipped, they had more saloons than grocery stores. Herzog grew up worshipping the Cardinals, selling St. Louis newspapers. A high-school basketball whiz, he was good enough in baseball to play eight seasons as a lefthanded-hitting outfielder for Washington, Kansas City, Baltimore and Detroit. Later coaching for Casey Stengel with the Mets, he'd been too much like the outspoken manager himself. Bing Devine, then running the Mets, valued Whitey's evaluation and rescued him from release. Whitey ran the New York Nationals' farm system. Cocksure, confident, grandly articulate if at times ungrammatical, Herzog sat across the table from Busch at Grant's Farm and, finally, played his cards as he would later in gin rummy with Busch. Said Herzog:

"You haven't won for a dozen years, Mr. Busch. Why don't you let me do it my way?"

Taking over in June as manager, Whitey was a break-even field foreman (38-35) when Claiborne was fired as general manager on Labor Day. Busch wanted the new manager to take the dual job as the first since Branch Rickey in 1925. Herzog accepted with the condition he could temporarily turn over the ball club to the faithful old redhead, Schoendienst, back as a coach. Red finished out the club's subpar season, 14 games under .500, by winning 18 and losing 19. Herzog, meanwhile, began the most remarkable face-lifting in baseball history probably since the Robison brothers switched their whole Cleveland club to St. Louis back in 1899. Here's what Herzog did:

(1) Signed catcher Darrell Porter from Kansas City as a $700,000-a-year free agent; (2) Dealt promising kid catcher Terry Kennedy, reserve infielder Mike Phillips, catcher Steve Swisher and young pitchers John Urrea, John Littlefield, Kim Seaman and Al Olmsted to San Diego for pitcher Rollie Fingers, first baseman-catcher Gene Tenace, pitcher Bob Shirley and minor-league catcher Bob Geren; (3) Traded first baseman-outfielder Leon Durham, third-baseman Ken Reitz and third baseman-out-

fielder Ty Waller to the Chicago Cubs for pitcher Bruce Sutter; (4) Traded catcher Ted Simmons and pitchers Pete Vuckovich and Fingers to Milwaukee for outfielder Sixto Lezcano, pitchers Lary Sorensen and Dave LaPoint and outfielder David Green.

Simplified—go ahead, Whitey, catch your breath!—the deal would bring a defensive catcher who could hit, Porter, at the sacrifice of some of Simmons's power and, mainly, strengthen the bullpen weakness that unfrocked Boyer. Actually, acquiring both Fingers and Sutter—one in the Hall of Fame and the other apparently headed there—Herzog had more game-saving ability than he could afford. So before Fingers could tweak his long villainous mustache, Rollie was gone, but Sutter stayed for a time—and starred.

Seeking speed to go with defense, ingredients of the run-sheep-run baseball he would bring back to the home of the reckless Gas House Gang and St. Louis Swifties, Herzog let go base-clogging Reitz at third base, planning to move Oberkfell there and play a kid named Tommy Herr at second base. Herzog gambled and lost about replacing Vuckovich, but he profited from friend Bing Devine's deal for Hendrick. Silent George's unwillingness to talk to the media became almost a fun game. Even though his strike-shortened season was limited to 93 games, Hendrick hit 18 homers and drove in 61 runs. Forsch led in victories in the bobtailed season with 10 and Sutter, winning three in relief, saved 25.

The season was good, but also frustrating. A rousing April after a losing spring training brought them into contention—even though Porter suffered arm trouble—and only a slight slump before the players' walkout on June 11 cost them first place to Philadelphia when commissioner Bowie Kuhn, eyeing the large-market ball clubs in first place, declared leaders as first-half winners. So when the 30-20 Redbirds again lagged late in the resumed season, they were a half-game behind Montreal in the second-half. St. Louis's record, 59-43, was the best in the Eastern Division and Cincinnati's 66-42 was tops in the West, but neither the Redbirds nor Reds were included in the playoffs.

Could the hard-luck ball club of 1981 be the team to beat in '82? The bookies didn't think so. They favored Montreal and Philadelphia in the East. After all, Herzog had lost a potential Hall of Famer when gifted Garry Templeton indulged enough in foreign substances to become a problem, one the brewery and manager wanted out. Like a masterful golfer, he longed to spend summer hours golfing when not fishing—Herzog chipped out of the rough before convincing boss Busch to let him go back to only managing. His successor as general manager was Joe McDonald, one-time Brooklyn bat boy and former Mets' GM.

Still seeking more speed, Whitey waited until the Phillies, needing a catcher, dealt Lonnie Smith to Cleveland for Bo Diaz. Then Herzog dealt pitchers Silvio Martinez and Lary Sorenson to the Indians for Smith. The Phillies wouldn't have wanted to deal with a division rival. Lonnie was no great shakes as an outfielder, but he could hit and ran so fast he fell so often that they called him "Skates".

Disappointed that Lezcano hadn't been able to shake off a wrist injury suffered at Philadelphia, Herzog traded Sixto to San Diego for pitcher Steve Mura, who helped

WINNING COMBINATION: Whitey Herzog (left) was hired by August A. Busch Jr., and noting the Cardinals hadn't won in a dozen years, wanted to do it his way. They struck up great drink-sipping sessions over a little gin rummy and mainly baseball conversation. Only one admonition from the Big Eagle: "Let me know about it before you give it to the press." Three pennants and a title before Busch died in 1989 and Herzog quit in '90.

Buffalo Stampede: That's what it seemed when big, burly Glenn Brummer, Cardinals' third-string catcher, stole home to win a big game for the pennant-bound Cardinals in August, 1982. Glenn is shown here presenting the stolen goods – home plate – to Jerry Vickery, then Director of the Cardinals Hall of Fame. The young man at the right is Jerry too. But we call him Charley.

early in 1982, and Whitey also shipped seldom-seen southpaw Bob Sykes to the Yankees for a lightly regarded outfielder at Nashville named Willie McGee. Yes, George Steinbrenner was steamed about the way that one worked out.

Incredibly, the one by which talented Templeton had to go—the final straw had been an obscene gesture to the Cardinal fans—turned out to achieving Dr. Jekyll for Mr. Hyde. At San Diego, great-fielding, banjo-batting Ozzie Smith had been involved in a holdout, so San Diego manage-

ment was annoyed, too. The Templeton-for-Smith deal gave San Diego a great shortstop who merely finished pretty good, his career hampered by a balky knee, and grass that took away artificial turf hits, including those patented triples. The Cardinals got a pretty good player who became great, perhaps the finest-fielding shortstop, a self-made hitter, a personable player, colorfully acrobatic, a winner and hopefully an early Hall of Fame choice.

So the Cardinals had the Cough Drop Kids, the unrelated Smiths, Lonnie and Ozzie, teamed as regular-playing top contributors to the Cardinals' cause in a year in which Herzog used his 25 players so well. To a long-time Redbird follower and researcher, he seemed to be the ball club's No. 1 manager. One of his trades the year before, the acquisition of pitcher Joaquin Andujar from Houston for outfielder Tony Scott, produced a staff-leading 15-10 record in 1982 with a good 2.46 earned-run average and a hot streak at the finish. Old Reliable Bob Forsch was a 15-game winner, too, and among those who helped was journalism student John Stuper and the crafty lefthanded veteran, Jim Kaat. And Sutter, winning nine, also had a league-leading 36 saves. Offensively, only Skates Smith hit .300 and only Hendrick and Porter hit for some power, as reflected in 19 home runs and 12, but the Go-Go Guys were far ahead in stolen bases with 200.

Opening night at Houston, beating the king of strikeouts and no-hitters, Nolan Ryan, 14-3, the Cardinals got a big night with a homer and seven doubles, reflecting the speed of the "gappers", i.e., doubles and triples in the outfield slots. Even though the home opener was lost to Pittsburgh, 11-7, despite a grand-slam homer by Skates Smith, the Cardinals soon catapulted into a 12-game winning streak, the longest since the club record 14 set by the Gas House Gang in a season of a sad finish, 1935. With a steady drive to a 92-70 season, one that attracted the club's first home attendance past 2,000,000—2,111,906—the Cardinals were good and lucky as well as fast on the bases and defensively.

When fourth-outfielder Dave Green pulled a hamstring in a May collision at first base, Herzog beckoned to Louisville for a young outfielder who came with an embarrassed, heads-down look. The scared-rabbit switch-hitter, Willie McGee, became a good hitter, great team player and a legend. And the Cardinals even won one when third-string catcher Glenn Brummer, built like a buffalo and running like one, stole home to win a game—with two out and two strikes on the hitter. Broken bones couldn't deter Ken Oberkfell and the new second baseman, Tommy Herr, was trussed up. When the Wizard of Oz, as they already had begun to call Ozzie Smith, was hurt in September, Mike Ramsey filled in nicely.

So they deserved the Eastern Division championship, won by three games over Philadelphia, the club they beat in the showdown game of the season. Alarmingly, shut out by nemesis Steve Carlton in mid-September, they fell a half-game behind the Phillies and suddenly faced the moment of truth. Would those near-miss moments of 1927, '35, '49, '71, '73 and '74 come back to haunt them?

The moment of truth actually came when, leading 2-0 behind Stuper, the bearded prophet and profit, Sutter, stalked in from the bullpen, bases loaded with one out, and faced home-run king and Hall of Fame-bound Mike Schmidt. Gulp!

Sutter served up that finger-tip fast ball, dipping like a forkball, and the mighty Schmidt tapped back to Bruce. Double play, pitcher to home to first, and the Cardinals ripped off eight straight wins. The division was won on Sept. 27 at Montreal, where McGee hit a three-run inside-the-park-homer, running like a scalded cat, and Sutter came in to clinch the game and the division. So for the first time the Cardinals had won a division, but they still were a critical best-of-five League Championship Series away from the World Series.

Atlanta came to town for the first of two, managed by former Redbird and future Cardinal manager Joe Torre. The Braves got a bad break in the first game, which was rained out in the fourth inning with them leading 1-0, behind knuckleball veteran and future Hall of Famer Phil Niekro. Knucks couldn't come back the next night. Chances are, he would have no chance because Forsch, pitching better than in his no-hitter, three-hit the Braves, 1-0. In the next game, a medley relay of Stuper, Sutter and associates came up to the ninth where Atlanta's Gene Garber had a chance to walk Oberkfell, a .600 hitter against Garber. They pitched to Obie. He did it again. His single won, 4-3. With a Sunday special in Atlanta, McGee hit Rick Camp for a three-run triple and later homered. Andujar, the self-styled "one tough Dominican", might not have needed Sutter's perfect seven-out effort for a 6-2 sweep.

The American League foe in the World Series was Milwaukee, labeled Harvey's Wallbangers, a tribute to manager Kuenn and his men of muscle. They proved it at the outset when, led by young third baseman Paul Molitor's record five hits, lefty Mike Caldwell breezed to a 10-0 victory. The second-game outlook was not promising, either, when rookie Stuper trailed Hall of Fame electee (1998) Don Sutton into the sixth inning, 4-2. Darrell Porter, staking a bid for the Series MVP award to go with the one he won in the playoffs, doubled in the tying runs. Reliever Pete Ladd's borderline fourth ball to Lonnie Smith in the eighth walked in the winning run, 5-4.

The Series moved to Sudsville for the first time since 1958 when the Braves lived there, not the Brewers. Milwaukee saw one of baseball's greatest Series accomplishments in the third game. Shy-guy Willie McGee crunched two homers off Vuckovich, 6-2, then made two great catches, one depriving the Brewers of two runs.

Afterward then and as he would repeat later, Herzog put it in perspective."If that had happened in New York or by a New York player, it would be immortalized."

The Cardinals paid a price when Andujar, hit by a hot shot off Simmons' bat, was carried off in the seventh inning, and their outlook became as black as the crepe ribbons they wore on their uniforms in trib-

SUTTER'S GOLD: Bearded prophet and profit, Bruce Sutter, ace reliever acquired by Whitey Herzog from the Cubs, celebrates the 1982 world championship with another acquisition, Darrell Porter, hitting standout of the playoffs and Series.

ute to recently deceased Ken Boyer. They blew a 5-1 lead in the seventh inning of the fourth game when Dave LaPoint, covering first, dropped a throw. The misplay opened the floodgates to a 7-5 Milwaukee victory.

Quipped Herzog sourly about the portly LaPoint, "If it was a cheeseburger, he wouldn't have dropped it!" In game five, Robin Yount had his second four-hit game of the Series, spearheading Caldwell's second victory over Forsch, 6-4.

Milwaukee needed just one more, but it rained on the Brewers' parade or, rather, St. Louis paraded after a delay of two and a half hours. Hernandez homered and drove in four runs. Porter also homered, and super-sub Dane Iorg, getting a National League taste of the American League's designated-hitting delicacy, hit two doubles and a triple. The Great Dane batted .500 in five games. John Stuper went all the way despite the delay in the 13-1 series-tying victory. They couldn't be stopped now.

Nice Kitty:
Jim (Kitty) Kaat, long-time lefty with Hall of Fame credentials, wound up his 25-year career as a Cardinal in 1983, en route to post-career broadcasting. Kaat tipped the Redbirds to Cesar Cedeno as a down-the-stretch lifesaver in 1985.

They weren't, either, though Milwaukee obviously would have been tougher if relief ace Rollie Fingers hadn't been hurt. They probably would have gone to him when they led after the Brewers took a 3-1 lead in the first half of an unforgettable sixth inning. With one out in the Cardinals' half, the Cough Drop Kids delivered. Ozzie Smith singled and Lonnie Smith doubled over third base. Lionhearted Vuckovich didn't want to come out, but it was time. Manager Kuenn replaced him with a lefthander, Bob McClure. Righthanded-hitting Gene Tenace, batting for Oberkfell, walked to fill the bases. They now were playing with the White Rat's deck. Hernandez, a late bloomer with eight RBIs in the last three games, singled to right-center, tying the score. Now it was Hendrick, who earlier had cut down a run with a key throw to third base. Basically a pull-hitter, Silent George was a team player. Pitched outside, he flicked a go-ahead single to right.

Supported by shouts of "Bruce, Bruce" in the 44-degree weather, big number "42" strode in, back erect and wiped the suds off the Brewers. Backed by two more runs, 6-3, he worked down to a Series-ending swinging strike past Gorman Thomas. Whitey's Go-Go Guys, beating the wizard of odds, had gone over the rainbow to win the world championship, the Cardinals' ninth in 13 tries.

Amid the clamor of the foot-stomping song "Celebration," Darrell Porter put it best. Over the hub-bub of hurrah, Porter, in a twangy Ozark drawl, caught by the *Post-Dispatch* 's Kevin Horrigan, yelled happily, "Hoo-ee! I been to two county fairs and a goat roast—and I ain't never seen nothin' like this." Porter had more that helped to the fairy-tale finish of Whitey Herzog's shakewell success. With the White Rat in KayCee, Porter had been an aggressive, take-charge guy given to an occasional sniff of the magic dragon and a snort of moonshine, but Darrell had seen the light. He'd quit abusing himself. When he came to the Cardinals, a close American League observer said, "I'm afraid you're getting a marshmallow." A wincing description and perhaps true. In five years with the Cardinals, Porter wasn't the take-charge guy he had been at Kansas City, but in that Series showdown in 1982, hitting .556, he had been the show.

One of the most talented men in the Redbird show was Hernandez, a matinee-idol player and a Fancy Dan at first base. So it was a shock near mid-season, 1983, when the dimpled darling was dealt to the New York Mets for a couple of pitchers, Neil Allen and Rick Ownbey. Sure, the pitching was struggling then, but the club was holding tough, five games over .500 when Lonnie Smith, a victim of weird base-running and outfield lapses, turned himself in for drug rehabilitation. Rehabbed nearly a month, Skates hit .321. With use of foreign substance, could the guilty include Hernandez? Keith was so adamant that wise media folks feared libel or slander, but Herzog knew as did Busch and the brewery. So they removed the source from the scene, sending Hernandez off to new success at

New York before Keith and Joaquin Andujar sang like canaries in plea-bargaining involving a Pittsburgh cocaine-dealer.

Too late for the Cardinals and good news for the Mets and New York fans who welcomed Hernandez as a conquering hero. In his absence Hendrick moved to first base, hitting 18 homers with 97 RBIs. The young second baseman, Herr, batted .323, and another gifted newcomer, Andy Van Slyke, moved into the outfield where David Green hit .284 and Willie McGee .286. The offense was good enough and the defense great, but pitching short in a season of Forsch's second no-hit game and one in which, just like 1966 when Steve Carlton came aboard for a successful look-see at Cooperstown, Danny Cox pitched the Hall of Fame game against Baltimore and won promotion to the varsity.

Man-on-the-spot Allen won his first start against the Mets in mid-June, 6-0, and actually won five of his first six, then lost four and fell in disfavor. Only a half-game out in an even race Labor Day, Herzog's Hessians fell back as Philadelphia won 11 in a row. The undefending world champs finished fourth, 79-83, but warm aftermath of the '82 Series and a strong showing until September produced the club's largest attendance, 2,317,914.

The 1984 Cardinals stole 220 bases, but, as the saying goes, you can't steal first. They lacked consistency and firepower—David Green led with only 15 homers, Porter with 11—and the only noteworthy average was a late-season acquisition of a thick-thighed kid brought up after Ken Oberkfell was traded

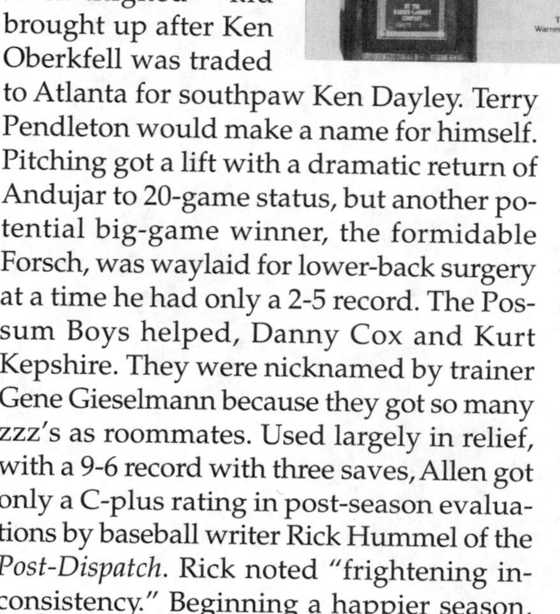

to Atlanta for southpaw Ken Dayley. Terry Pendleton would make a name for himself. Pitching got a lift with a dramatic return of Andujar to 20-game status, but another potential big-game winner, the formidable Forsch, was waylaid for lower-back surgery at a time he had only a 2-5 record. The Possum Boys helped, Danny Cox and Kurt Kepshire. They were nicknamed by trainer Gene Gieselmann because they got so many zzz's as roommates. Used largely in relief, with a 9-6 record with three saves, Allen got only a C-plus rating in post-season evaluations by baseball writer Rick Hummel of the *Post-Dispatch*. Rick noted "frightening inconsistency." Beginning a happier season, 1985, one to remember, Allen blew the first two games of the season. At a time the bullpen was highly suspect, as will be related, the high-salaried pitcher of low respect lost the opener on a tenth-inning homer by Gary Carter at New York, 6-5,

BULLPEN BY COMMITTEE: Aptly named by Kip Ingle, then Cardinal public relations' director, the 1985 foursome – Rick Horton, Bill Campbell, Ken Dayley, and Jeff Lahti – worked admirably with game-saver Bruce Sutter gone to a higher bid. In the September run to the division title, LCS and Series, Todd Worrell joined the committee and helped spectacularly.

Gutsy Guy:
A bag o' bones shortstop, good-field, no-hit Dal Maxvill helped Cardinals as a player and as a general manager, too, though handicapped at times by salary budget restraints. Maxie, who had a master's degree is engineering, was a feisty fella, occasionally terse and tart.

then the next game walked in the winning run in the eleventh. Soon, like sorely missed relief ace Bruce Sutter, Allen was gone.

Although the '84 Cards improved their won-and-lost record to 87-78 and third place, they finished farther back because the cow jumped over the moon and hell froze over. Chicago's long-suffering Cubs won the Eastern division with a 96-65 record. The Cubbies feasted on the Birdies, too, winning 13 of 18, including a game so unforgettable that Ryne Sandberg remembered it fondly when retiring in 1997. Sandberg, playing second base at Wrigley Field like Rogers Hornsby and Billy Herman, completely overwhelmed the Cardinals and the great Sutter in a game for which Willie McGee should have been the attraction. Hitting for the cycle as the first Redbird since Lou Brock nine years earlier, Willie's single, double, triple and homer drove in six runs. Sandberg, facing the matchless Sutter in the eighth, hit a two-run homer to tie the score and in the eleventh Ryno lifted another split-fingered pitch over the left-field ivy at Wrigley for a 12-11 triumph.

Otherwise, virtually unhittable as well as unbeatable, Sutter had an incredible 1.45 earned-run average with 45 saves in 71 appearances, winning five and losing seven. The bow-legged pot-bellied game-saver suddenly was lost when Ted Turner of Atlanta waved a reported six-year, no-trade contract of $10,000,000. Parenthetically, with Sutter soon hurt and his magic gone, Turner would have to salt-and-pepper a contract that over annuities for 36 years would pay Bruce $43,600,000. Similarly, Turner would have to eat without malice or mustard an earlier blockbuster given to another ailing former Redbird relief ace, Al Hrabosky. But the super-station genius soon would laugh a ha-ha as heavy investments and a good farm system turned the Braves into the top team of the 1990s in the National League.

Meanwhile, Herzog, seeking a power hitter and improved lefthanded pitching, dealt by numbers to San Francisco for slugger Jack Clark, in frequent salary displeasure. He sent lefty LaPoint, outfielder-first baseman David Green, shortstop Jose Gonzalez (Uribe) and first baseman Gary Rajsich. For lefthanded pitcher John Tudor at Pittsburgh and handyman Brian Harper, he dealt Hendrick and a kid catcher, Steve Barnard. Former general manager Bing Devine gave an old questioning friend an endorsement, cutting through warm bodies to the cold fact, "Wouldn't you rather have a Clark and a Tudor than LaPoint and Hendrick?"

Herzog, his ball club picked to finish last in the National League East after Sutter followed the money to Atlanta, was smitten by Clark's power potential and also by Tudor's ability as a lefthanded pitcher able to win more games than he lost at Boston's Fenway Park, a previous stop. "I said we could finish anywhere from first to sixth (last), but now I say we won't finish last."

Indeed, and with new faces in the front office. Fred Kuhlmann, long-time counsel for Anheuser-Busch, moved over to the ball club as chief executive officer. And after Busch's ego, Susman, sought Tim McCarver as general manager, the former catcher headed to a celebrated career as a television commentator, declined and recommended Dal Maxvill. Susman chose Maxie, then a coach for Joe Torre with the Braves. What did Devine think?

"Why shouldn't he be a good general manager," Der Bingle said. "He's always done everything better than any of us expected." Devine would know. A bag o' bones infielder, too, Dal Maxvill had played at Devine's alma mater, Washington University, as a good-field, no-hit player. When Winnipeg as a farm club needed a quick-fix shortstop, Bing thought of Dal, then working on his Master's in engineering. Why not give it a try? Self-made, Maxie improved. When he reached the majors and was about to quit, discouraged, Devine did an unusual thing. He persuaded a couple of sportswriter friends of Maxvill to urge him to stick it out because he already was in shape from spring training. Maxvill reconsidered, staying in the minors until called up later in 1962. With more mental than muscle, Maxvill lasted 14 years in the majors and on four pennant-winners. So an early chore—with money left over because Sutter walked away—general manager Maxvill was able to craft a four-year deal for $10,000,000 for another little man who would take his talent a stride farther at shortstop—Ozzie Smith.

As mentioned, the 1985 Cardinals stumbled at the start with two rapid failures in relief by Allen, indicating utter weakness in the bullpen, by now sophisticated with a starter, reliever, setup man and closer. Happily, rejected by Philadelphia, Jeff Lahti came back as masterful in middle innings. Lefty Ken Dayley was good early and late and, ultimately, down the stretch, came giant righthander Todd Worrell. Before long, the Cardinals tub-thumper at the time described it right. Kip Ingle called them the "bullpen by committee."

Fourth in mid May, the Cardinals got a break when handy outfielder Tito Landrum was hurt, and the club called up Vince Coleman from Louisville "just until Landrum is ready," said Herzog, who ate his words cheerfully. Coleman went 1-for-3 the first game, stole two bases, then went 4-for-5 in the second game. By season's end Vince was invincible with 110 stolen bases, a record for a rookie.

With Andujar hot early, en route to 21 victories, Tudor corrected a pitching fault with one phone call from an old Massachusetts batterymate. Losing the first seven of eight decisions, Tudor became as spectacular as his 2.93 earned-run average with a 21-9 record and 10 shutouts. Andujar, the one tough Dominican, fingered a strikeout with a pointed smoking-gun gesture, a showman's swaggering attitude. Tudor, trim, quiet and emotionless, mixed incredible changing speeds to paint outside corners, then could bust one inside that was made to look faster by his pattycake pitches.

At the All-Star break, before following Andujar into drydock, Kepshire beat San Diego, 2-1, giving St. Louis a 52-33 record, two and a half games in front, but three straight losses to the Dodgers was a downer. Fortunately in the fourth game, Terry Pendleton doubled and Steve Braun pinch-homered for a 4-2 victory in 10 innings. A night later at Candlestick Point, Pendleton and Braun starred again, 4-3, and they went on a seven-game winning streak.

The Go-Go Guys were something to behold—if you could hold them. At Wrigley Field in a double steal, Coleman and McGee, Vince over-slid third base, then got into a rundown between third and home, eluded a tag, and Willie hustled around to third. The official scorer had a time figuring that one—four steals on the same play!

When Jack Clark was hurt in late August at a time the Cardinals had a three-game lead, former Redbird Jim Kaat at Cincinnati suggested to Herzog that the Cards might be able to make a deal for sulking, high salaried Cesar Cedeno, pining as he rode the pines of the Reds' bench. The 34-year-old Cedeno was like money in the bank and that tall, powerful kid, Worrell, was called up the next day, but, still, the Redbirds toppled out of first place Sept. 10 at New York. They averted disaster there when Tu-

JACK THE RIPPER: Jack Clark delivers the knockout blow in the sixth game of the 1985 League Championship Series with the Los Angeles Dodgers, teeing off a ninth-inning three-run homer off Tom Niedenfuer.

dor duelled Dwight (Doc) Gooden scoreless into the tenth, then won, 1-0, when Cedeno homered off Jesse Orosco.

"The Heat Is On," throbbed the song played constantly by NBC's St. Louis television outlet, KSDK. The song, sung by Glenn Frey for "Beverly Hills Cops", caught on and so did the Go-Go Guys, winning 14 of the next 15 games, including a memorable weekend series against the Expos at Busch Stadium. First game, McGee's single preceded successive triples by Cedeno and Pendleton and a squeeze bunt by Ozzie Smith, topping Montreal, 5-3. Next day on national TV, the returning Clark hit a two-run homer in a 7-6 rally. And on Sunday, they came from behind again to win on a two-run homer by Herr in the ninth, 6-5.

Quipped humorist Andy Van Slyke, "It's not over, but you can start taking the nails out of the box and getting the hammer ready."

The coffin wasn't nailed tight, though, until just after the Mets had won two in St. Louis, including Darryl Strawberry's 13th-inning tape measure homer off Dayley,1-0. Then Danny Cox and the Cardinals took the pivotal 4-3 game in which Hernandez, following settlement of a nasty divorce case that afternoon, went 5-for-5. The Cards officially wrapped up the division two days later when Tudor won his 11th straight, 7-1 over the Cubs, and Cedeno homered to finish his Cinderella contribution at a rousing .434.

To win 101 games, three more than New York and the Cardinals' most since the war season of 1944, some career years were made other than those established, namely by Tudor, Andujar, and Danny Cox, 18-9, 2.88. Among the players, Willie McGee won his first batting championship, .353, with 82 runs batted in, and Herr had the finest season by a St. Louis second baseman since Frank Frisch drove in more runs in 1930. Herr, hitting .302, drove in 110 runs with only eight homers.

Even though the Cardinals had led the league with 745 runs scored and more than doubled any other club with 314 stolen bases, they soon were two games down in the best-of-five LCS with Los Angeles. Fernando Valenzuela topped Tudor, 4-1, and then Orel Hershisher won 8-2 over Andujar, who had won just one game after Aug. 23.

Back home, with Cox pitching well and Dayley displaying impeccable post-season skill, the Cardinals beat Bob Welch, 4-2, a result of Herr's homer and Coleman's speed, but when a fluke accident the next night caught Coleman's leg in an automatic tarpaulin, the outlook was as ugly as the accident. Coleman's fill-in, Tito Landrum, went 4-for-5 helping Tudor to a 12-2 truimph over Jerry Reuss.

The fifth game will live as long as Jack Buck's recorded "Go crazy, folks" is regarded as a quintessential call for the highly unlikely. The unlikely occurred with Ozzie Smith leading off the last of the ninth with the game tied 2-2. Now, Smith, stronger and sturdier, had hit .276 in a batting climb to respectability, but he'd hit only six home runs, all righthanded, and the switcher was batting lefthanded against Tom Niedenfuer. Fact is, in eight National League seasons, Smith never had hit a homer lefthanded! So it was an annoyance to a pressbox observer when Oz swung hard and fouled off the first pitch. When he again swung hard at the second pitch, fouling it off rather than just trying to make contact, the one guy said to the next guy, "Who does he think he is? Babe Ruth?" Yeah, because Smith hit the next pitch against a right-field concrete barrier above the yellow home-run marker. Homer! Game's over, 3-2, and, as Buck told his audience, "Go crazy, folks! That's a w-i-n-n-e-r!"

They went crazy two days later in L.A., too, in a game in which Smith's triple off Niedenfuer—again!—just had tied the score before the Dodgers' Mike Marshall untied it with a homer off Todd Worrell. With one out in the St. Louis ninth, McGee singled and stole second. Treating Ozzie like the Babe, Niedenfuer walked him. When Herr grounded out, first base was open, but Tommy Lasorda decided to pitch to Clark. Jack the Ripper's three-run homer won the pennant, 7-5.

The Cardinals almost stole the World Series from Kansas City with a powder-puff offense. They lost it in part because an umpire missed a call—by a mile of, if you will, one full stride. A legitimate steal.

This was highly publicized as the I-70 Series because of the highway ribbon from St. Louis to KayCee. There, in the opener, Tudor gave the Royals a royal treatment, 3-1, aided by that husky young reliever, Worrell, and a remarkable play from the roly-poly third baseman Pendleton. The third baseman hustled to make a tremendous catch of a foul fly and, whirling, cut down a runner at the plate with a bull's eye throw. Next night, the Cardinals were good and lucky. They were shut down for eight innings by lefty Charlie Leibrandt, 2-0, but they rallied in the ninth and made the whole thing look disarmingly easy. McGee bad-hopped a grounder for a double that kept the inning alive when Clark, on a full-count pitch, singled in a run. Next, Tito Landrum looped a double to right. Wisely, Kansas City manager Dick Howser ordered Cedeno passed intentionally, filling the bases. Here, Pendleton stroked an opposite-field double that cleared the bases. Final, 4-2.

Even though young Series hero Bret Saberhagen beat Andujar in the shift to St. Louis, the Cardinals were close to making their Missouri metropolitan neighbors say "uncle" after Tudor's shutout pitching was accompanied by homers by McGee and Landrum, 3-0. Forsch dropped the fifth game, 6-1.

In a brilliant duel between Danny Cox and Leibrandt in the sixth game, the Cardinals took a 1-0 lead in the eighth inning when pinch-hitter Brian Harper bounced a run-scoring single to center. A guy had to gasp. Why, the run-shy Redbirds would bat only .185 and score just 13 runs in the ultimate seven games. Yep, they'd just stole the Series...

But—hold the phone!—beginning with a second guess against Herzog, who switched to righthander Worrell as a closer even as southpaw Ken Dayley had zeroed in as unhittable. Dayley worked five scoreless innings in four games of the League Championship Series with Los Angeles, including the championship final. Against KayCee in three games, he had four scoreless innings, fanning two in the eighth. But Herzog feared a righthanded designated hitter, Hal McRae, so he went to Worrell.

100 years and 11 days after umpire Dave Sullivan's call caused Charles Comiskey to pull his team from the field—first up, pinch-hitting, Jorge Orta grounded to Clark's right. The first baseman fed the ball to Worrell covering first. The giant stretched up for the throw, stepped on the bag and Orta, a stride behind, stepped on Todd's shoe. American League umpire Don Denkinger hesitated, then dropped his hands down—in a safe sign! Hot at the time, Herzog years later had a cold analysis of what he should have done. Said Whitey, "I should have gone to the commissioner seated nearby and, because of the flagrant mistake, asked him to take a look at instant replay and to change the decision. If he wouldn't, I should have pulled my team off the field and taken the consequences." Pretty considerable consequences, no

'THE PLAY':
Then and now, *the play* was the one umpire Don Denkinger missed in the sixth game of the 1985 World Series, setting up Kansas City's rally that won the game. The Royals won in seven. Here, taking a throw from Jack Clark, Todd Worrell strides onto first base, a half-step *ahead* of Jorge Orta's foot, but first-base umpire Denkinger ruled 'Safe.' A two-run uprising then turned a 1-0 Redbird lead into a 2-1 KC win.

doubt, including a forfeited loss and a suspension if he still had a job, which would have been doubtful under Anheuser-Busch's spit-and-polish concern about proper procedure.

To return to the scene of the crime, Orta, the man flagrantly out, was safe, the decision made worse by instant replay. So when Steve Balboni, next up, arched a high foul near the first-base box, Clark, no Hernandez or Gil Hodges at first base, had to cut to his right from the bag rather than trot diagonally in from a deeper position with no one on base. Hasseled by catcher Porter's presence, Clark missed connections with the foul. So, reprieved, Balboni singled to left. A sacrifice bunt put two runners in scoring position. An intentional pass was in order, filling the bases for the Great Dane, former Redbird Dane Iorg. Iorg flared a broken-bat basehit into right field, scoring the tying and winning runs, 2-1, the decisive run scoring as Porter made a feeble effort to block the plate.

The seventh game, won by the Royals 11-0, was an even greater travesty than Detroit's Battle of Produce Row in 1934 when the Gas House Gang tanked them in the seventh game. Tudor, failing finally, punched a clubhouse electric fan and came off a bloody gouged hand's second best. With Denkinger unfortunately the plate umpire, he wasn't the right man for the wrong pitcher, Andujar, who got a heave-ho in relief. This was a black mark on the Cardinals' post-season escutcheon.

IN*VINCE*-ABLE: That's what Vince Coleman was for the Cardinals after joining them in the 1985 season, including league-leading stolen bases of 110, 107, 109, 81, 65 and 77 until he went to the New York Mets in 1991. In this '87 LCS Series game, Coleman does what comes naturally, avoiding a tag by the Giants' Will Clark.

If there was any consolation in the defeat, the Cardinals could admit that it was a deserved victory for the Royals. Dick Howser, the Royals' manager who previously had seen Kansas City come from behind an identical three games-to-one deficit to Toronto, became terminally ill shortly after the World Series, a victim of a brain tumor.

The dear old Redbirds played 1986 as if they were terminally ill every way except at the box office, dropping just a couple of hundred thousands in attendance—to 2,471,817—despite the fewest runs since 1908, 601, and the worst batting average, .236, since 1916. The reformed "out" man, Ozzie Smith, was the leading hitter at .280. With Andujar gone, as anticipated, for a hyperkenetic Oakland catcher, Mike Heath, who tried too hard and failed, it's amazing that a team of wounded hearts and physical injuries could finish third in the East with 79-82.

The 1987 Cardinals, labeled a pressbox poet as the "Purple Martin Redbirds," in tribute to their injuries, fore and aft, meaning in '86 and then in '87, combined to put on such a good show that they finished first with 95-67 record and—this one no doubt would shock Sam Breadon and Branch Rickey if they weren't already dead—home attendance of 3,072,121. The old French fur-trading post had come a long way from those early days when they didn't get over 300,000 until the year the circus came to town with Cy Young in 1899.

Herzog didn't have a Cy Young—not even half of one in '87—because his top victory total, 11, was shared by Danny Cox, Bob Forsch and Greg Mathews—but he undoubtedly would have had more from Tudor if the stylish artist hadn't been felled early by husky New York Mets' catcher, Barry Lyons, who dived into the St. Louis dugout and broke Tudor's right knee. Sidelined much of the season, Tudor still returned with a 10-2 record.

Like the stock market company's slogan, the Cards earned it in 1987. Tommy Herr hustled back to the hills of Pennsylvania to find a tighter body. Ozzie Smith put himself in the hands of a fitness wiz. McGee underwent knee surgery. Forsch turned down large offers from Japan to stay with the club for which he was a latter-day Pop Haines. Dayley underwent surgery. The front office starred—to a point. They resisted Tim Wallach as a hitter from Montreal, a tempting offer, when they needed one. They wouldn't give up Pendleton and Mathews, but to get a catcher they paid dearly to Pittsburgh—and picked up a $1,300,000 contract—when they acquired Tony Pena for catcher Mike LaValliere, rookie pitching standout Mike Dunne and the village humorist, Andy Van Slyke. Slick Van Slyke, the quick-quipping, fleet, talented outfielder and whatever else you might want, helped crystalize Pittsburgh as an emerging hitter. Pena helped early, but not too much or too long.

Highly touted Jim Lindeman, the man behind Clark in the batting order, flattened out, unfortunately, but a productive bench included outfielders Curt Ford and the "secret weapon" as broadcaster Mike Shannon called infielder Jose Oquendo, the first player since Minnesota's Cesar Tovar in 1968 to play every position.

Lo, the hitless wonders of late 1985 and '86 became wonderful hitters. Led by Jack the Ripper Clark at first base, they spreadeagled the field into mid-season. They led at the halfway mark with a 53-29 record, nine games up. No wonder Herzog got a new contract through 1990 and Maxvill through '88. By the All-Star break several days later, a result of a nine-game winning streak, they were 56-30, 10 up.

Included were the kind of come-from-behind victories that thrill the spirits and whirl the turnstiles. Included was a two-night double dip over the Dodgers. The Cards won the first two, both 5-4, in a rain-delayed opener of what became a matinee marathon with a 10-inning second game in the wee hours. Next night they did it again to L.A., 6-3 and in the tenth, 8-7. Before Clark was hurt—the Ripper hit 36 homers and a league-leading 136 RBIs in only 131 games—firepower was adequate. Pendleton had 12 homers and 96 RBIs and McGee 11 with 105 ribbies. But even though Smith reached .303, and Coleman stole 105 bases, ability to score became a problem in a humpty-dumpty fall. A seven-game losing streak after the All-Star game led to a descent of barely .500 ball (25-24) so that they were only four up over New York, five over Montreal. Now it was Shea Stadium, where the Cardinals in '85 had floundered in September, and Clark's injury of a sprained ankle and torn ligaments suffered in a slide Sept. 9 was virtually season-ending.

The Mets were only a game and a half behind and led into the ninth inning when Pendleton struck probably the blow of the season. Trailing 4-1, the Redbirds scored a run on McGee's two-out single. Then, inching up in the box against Roger McDowell's sinkerball, Pendleton hit a game-tying homer. In the tenth, breaking out of a 1-for-21 slump, Herr beat Orosco with a two-run single, 6-4.

TRIUMPHANT TRIO: Two of the reasons Whitey Herzog (center) was Manager-of-the-Year in a pennant-winning 1985 season was Willie McGee (left), Most Valuable Player winner after a .353 batting championship, and Vince Coleman, Rookie-of-the-Year with 110 stolen bases.

Aided by the return of Tudor, a month earlier than anticipated, and the convalescence of Cox, the Cards hung on into the final week, facing cheek-to-jowl encounters with the fast-closing Expos and the Mets. If Montreal won two in a makeup doubleheader, there could be a Canadian sunset to the Cardinals' chances. If Montreal won two that night and New York one, the race could be down to a half-game.

For the double dip, Herzog must have spoken to the devil because he picked his two kid roommates, Joe Magrane and Greg Mathews, and he couldn't have picked better.

Magrane had won only three games in three months when he got chin-deep in trouble in the first inning. Two on, one out, he faced tough Tim Wallach. Wallach struck out, and the Big Cat, Andres Galarraga, was retired. Trouble in paradise again in the sixth. Fortunately with none on, Wallach doubled, and Galarraga hit a screamer down the third-base line, where the gallant humpty-dumpty, Pendleton, made a great backhanded stab, spun about by the blow, and insurance-policy Dan Driessen made a good grab at first. Then in the home half, Vince Coleman singled and the past master

GOOD AND FUNNY: Three Redbird pitching stars, left to right, Danny Cox, John Tudor and Bob Forsch, ham it up after the 1985 Cardinals won 101 games. Cox won 18, elder statesman Forsch 9 and Tudor, obtained from Pittsburgh, won 21 with 10 shutouts and a 1.93 ERA.

of team play, Ozzie Smith, grounded a hit-and-run single that sent Mercury flying to third base. Coleman scored the game's only run, 1-0, on a sacrifice fly by Herr.

The second game also was scoreless into the sixth when rapid-running Redbird legs caught up with Bryn Smith. Tony Pena blooped a base hit to right and as two Expos collided, the fast-moving catching veteran reached second. Next up, after faking a bunt, Mathews hit away and with the infield charging, grounded to Casey Candaele, but Pena beat his throw to third. When Coleman also grounded to Candaele, Pena scored, opening the door to a three-run inning, one that was saved for Mathews by Todd Worrell the last three innings, 3-0.

After the double schneider, Herzog glowed, "Six hits in two games, only four runs, hardly conducive to winning one game, not two." With New York also losing that night, Cox offered a rare complete game the next evening with Driessen, a latter-day Cesar Cedeno, knocking in three runs. The 8-2 sweep of the Expos clinched the division. As frosting to the foe, the bitter rival Mets, who earlier had hinted the Cardinals were "scared," i.e. choked, sat in the upper deck football pressbox and witnessed their own funeral.

For the League Championship Series, the Cardinals drew the San Francisco Giants, managed by an old friend and wily foe, Roger Craig. The Humm Babies, nicknamed for Craig's own humming habit, had another fan, windy Candlestick Park, where they had won most of their seven victories in 12 games against the Cards, giving them an arrogance best summarized by the ponderous left fielder, Jeffrey Leonard. For Herzog, shortened to eight able pitchers, the Series became a pain in the neck as large as Hac-Man Leonard or the one first-game starter Cox suffered. Danny was a no-show in the opener, but Mathews, stepping to the front, not only allowed only an earned run and a homer to Leonard, but the 25-year-old lefty did it at the plate, too. Mathews' two-run single was a key blow in a 5-3 victory over Rick Reuschel. With foggy, nasty Candlestick beckoning, San Fran took an inferential edge here when lefthander Dave Dravecky pitched a dandy two-hitter and won 5-0. Tudor was beaten on home runs by Will Clark and by Leonard. Hac-Man hot-dogged it with a fancy flap-down trot around the bases, tucking his left arm to his side when running the bases and riling the crowd.

At Candlestick, in the late-afternoon, third-game gloaming, Pendleton twisted an ankle and the Giants twisted Magrane off the mound early, scoring four runs, including another homer by Leonard. Old pro Forsch provided the big guy a private calling card, nicking Hac-Man with a pitch. The Cardinals finally got on the scoreboard in the seventh when the oft-maligned Jim Lindeman hit a two-run homer off lefty Atlee Hammaker. Suddenly, shades of old, the Redbirds rallied against Hammaker and Don Robinson. Ford and Driessen hit pinch homers, Coleman singled in a pair and Ozzie added a key bunt. When Lindeman hit a tie-breaking sacrifice fly, Worrell protected the stirring 6-5 win. That one was so important because, impressively, the Giants won the next two at the 'Stick, as they called the Point. They beat Cox, 4-2, and after starter Mathews was forced out early with a strained right quadriceps, they beat the gutty Forsch in relief, 5-3.

Back at Busch Stadium, Tudor and the gallant Dravecky, headed to a shocking loss of his left arm because of cancer, dueled into the eighth with St. Louis up, 1-0, only because Candy Maldonado lost a line drive in the lights, permitting Pena to reach. Tony scored when the valuable Oquendo hit a fly to Maldonado. Tudor had held Leonard, happily to the delight of fans who chorused "Jeff-rey" to the big guy, fair enough, unsportsmanslike when they hit him with a golf ball, cow bell and beer. The poor bloke really hadn't been the Giant who called St. Louis "a cow town." The villian was center fielder Chili Davis. When Tudor handed the baton to the bullpen in the eighth, Herzog served up a two-headed pitcher, using both Todd Worrell and Ken Dayley at the same time, maneuvering Dayley into the game and moving Worrell to right field even though that field had been Maldonado's downfall and the Giants'. The ruse worked, creating need for a seventh game.

No wonder the *Post-Dispatch*'s Rick Hummel graded Herzog A-plus for what he suggested "might have been his best year as Cardinal manager." For the big game, big Cox was the big man. A complete-game pitcher successful except when pitching to Hac-Man Leonard, Danny shut out the Giants in the clincher, 6-0, aided by a three-run homer by the Puerto Rican handy dandy, Oquendo, a timely third-birthday present for his daughter just as impressive as the 22-consecutive inning shutdown of Giants' power, an LCS record.

To face Minnesota in the World Series, the St. Louis lineup looked fresh out of Louisville—or, as it would be the future, Memphis—because talented, slick-fielding Pendleton was unavailable and the mighty Clark's cameo was a one-two-strike strikeout. The huge indoor stadium favored the Twins with bandbox playing dimensions and air-conditioning that seemed to have varying home-town velocity. Heck, Tom Kelly's guys didn't need Redbird batter signs. The sights and sound of the Decibel Dome were enough.

They proved it quickly, too, winning 10-1 and 8-4 before the Cardinals got them outdoors. At Busch Stadium, Tudor's pitching and Coleman's running won the third game, 3-1. And, bless Tommy Lawless' heart, which had to be strong, too, the reserve infielder unloaded a three-run homer off Series hero Frank Viola, 7-2. Lawless was surprised himself. He stood at home plate in a fashion that could have violated Viola's peace of mind, then flipped the bat haughtily as if he did it every day. Actually only two other times in 531 major-league times at bat. When Cox outpitched Bert Blyleven in the fifth game, 4-2, aided again by Coleman's base-stealing speed, they were one up, but, going back to the dome, was like an advance to the rear. They already had shown against Detroit in 1968 and Kansas City in '85 that they no longer had black magic in a seven-game series.

If, as suggested, Minnesota helped swipe battery signals from the scoreboard, beating Tudor and associates, 11-5, then got favorable umpiring breaks in a final-game victory over Magrane and Cox, 4-2, the Cardinals had no excuses and needed no alibi. The junior varsity had gone about as far as it could go against future Redbird Gary Gaetti and Minny's men of muscle.

Ah, if they had only had Clark, but—wait!—something went drastically wrong between the time Black Jack shook hands with general manager Dal Maxvill on a proposed big increase and limped home. After all, he had knocked in most of his 106 runs in the first half of the season in which the Cardinals fought to hang on.

Suddenly Clark didn't return phone calls or agent Tom Reich, a good friend of the Yankees' George Steinbrenner. Maybe Jack the Ripper really didn't like it because

THE MIGHTY BUCK: Jack Buck broke in as junior to Harry Caray on Cardinal broadcasts in 1954. "That's a Winner" Buck – his game-winning signature and title of his autobiography – has had a quarter-century partner in former championship rightfielder-third baseman Mike Shannon. For the love of Mike, Shannon has a restaurant a long outfield fly north of Busch Stadium.

tough time of it that year at Los Angeles.

St. Louis gave up the prize package of the recent past, John Tudor. Guerrero came with too little much too late. Why, they couldn't even win for Magrane, the National League's earned-run average leader, 2.18. Joe was 5-and-9 and they, the ball club, finished fifth, 10 games behind the Mets. "Nothing went right," grumped Herzog, "and we didn't win in September" not only a factor that leafless fall, but of nine defeats in the last 11 games.

General manager Maxvill and field foreman Herzog tried their best before the 1989 season at a time free agency offered a get-well formula if you had the right kind of medicine. Whether the front ofice had too tight a budget or not—titular leader Gussie Busch was aged, ailing and feeble—the fact is that they came up short in bids for free-agent pitchers Mark Langston, Bruce Hurst and Mike Moore.

A scrappy guy who would on occasion speak his mind—enough to avoid live radio call-in shows—Maxvill thought the Cardinals had been used too often in the free-agent freeze-out, but, amazingly, with the roller-coaster activity of the Redbirds in the exciting pennant period, they almost did it and, yes, before the Cardinals' record home attendance—3,080,980. This was one of Herzog's better managerial jobs because even though only one Redbird regular hit aggressively, they overcame pre-season injuries to Mathews and Cox and also missed McGee for more than a month, but DeLeon won 16 games and Magrane 18 before fading in September. Frank DiPino, a free-agent cut adrift by the Cubs, was 9-0 and Milt Thompson, an outfielder obtained from the Phillies for outfielder Curt Ford and catcher Steve Lake, was a solid contributor, but the man front-and-center, as forecasted by Ozzie Smith, was Pedro Guerrero.

"Pete" to the tribe was, as the Oz said not unkindly, a loud-mouthed leader. Not particularly gifted defensively at any position, Guerrero played 162 games at first base, hit .311 with a league-leading 42 doubles, 17 homers and 117 RBIs. He led by example and when clutch-hitting Pete un-

"1" ONE OF A KIND: Ozzie Smith, of course, whose career number – "1" – was retired after the 1996 season in which he helped the Cardinals to another pennant. Acquired 15 years earlier in what amounted to a swap of shortstops – good for great, Smith for Templeton – the Wizard rose to the challenge, continued spectacular afield and developed from an automatic out to a pretty good hitter and base-stealer. He became one of the most popular Redbirds ever.

Ozzie Smith earned more. Slack-jawed Jack didn't even like personable batting champion Tony Gwynn at San Diego after that one year he went to the Yanks for roughly the $1,500,000 St. Louis had offered.

Maxvill tried elsewhere for that big righthanded bat. For Bob Horner, bulky blonde former Atlanta slugger who had spent his aching back, Maxie persuaded the hulking athlete to play in the States after a stint in Japan. He was out of the lineup more than in, unable to help. Even Tom Brunansky, obtained from the Twins for Tommy Herr, couldn't help enough with 22 homers. Fact is, everything was down in a season in which Jose DeLeon was the only winner in double figures, 13, after he had been obtained from the White Sox for popular Ricky Horton, Lance Johnson and cash. In August, the Cardinals obtained veteran hard-hitting Pedro Guerrero, having a furled a three-run, opposite-field homer at Chicago in early September, everyone came to attention.

Sure, the White Rat traditionally had his ball clubs in contention around Labor Day, good for the boxoffice as well as the standings, but the Dominican's homer in the 11-8 barn-burner meant that the Redbirds were only a half-game down with 22 to play. Ah, old times!

False alarm! The next day, the Cardinals led by a run into the ninth in raw, chilly windy Wrigley Field when Dwight Smith led off with a base hit. Playing right field, Brunansky tried a trick play with a nimble Pena hustling from the plate down the first-base line. Bruno cut the throw in behind the runner making his turn, but alertly, Smith went to his left, not back to his right, and beat Pena's throw to second. Smith scored the tying run on a single and then in the tenth, with no injured Worrell able to provide basic righthanded relief, Luis Salazar singled home the winning run off Ken Dayley. That 3-2 win strengthened the lead, and young Ken Hill, a greenpea rushed to the majors, was beaten in the windup. Chicago was a comfortable three-and-a-half in front.

With no successor acquired to replace Worrell—and general manager Maxvill got criticized for this one—the Cardinals were swept by Pittsburgh and lost 13 of their last 22 games and finished third with an 86-76 record.

Hours before the Cardinals' only victory in their last six games—7-5 over the division-winning Cubs—Busch died September 29 at nearly 90 out there at Grant's Farm. One legend was gone. Another would soon follow. Much of the fun for the White Rat had been those bull-sessions with the boss in the cozy gameroom of the French renaissance mansion. Over gin with Gussie, filling him in on baseball gossip and waltzing by him decisions necessary to do it Whitey's way was a winning way. Lawyer Lou Susman, Busch's executor, was a strong man of strong opinions—he didn't want either Herzog or Maxvill to bring back Bing Devine as a scout or consultant—but he ultimately went to Chicago for business purposes. Maybe the new A-B honcho, Gussie's incredibly efficient son, August A. Busch III—didn't like Lou, either.

About the 1989 season, Herzog wondered how they could have won without Worrell because of bashful batting. Maxvill's rejoinder, with logic and sarcasm, was that he couldn't see any ball club with a good relief pitcher willing to give up the precious commodity. Sports columnist Bernie Miklasz of the *Post-Dispatch* had a different and dark view. Miklasz noted it had been not only the end of a season, but of a decade and probably of Vince Coleman, no longer invincible. The Cardinals had lost their game-breaking speed, falling under 200 stolen bases for the first time in eight years. The columnist noted they had scored three or fewer runs 88 times, and left Miklasz to suggest, "This isn't a slump. It could be a transition."

Uh-huh, and under a couple of different managers in 1990. Except for wonderful Willie McGee, who hit a league-leading .335 in 112 games before he went to Oakland, and a grand career-climaxing performance by John Tudor, reacquired from Los Angeles, it was a dank and dark season as where the Cardinals finished—last place.

Free agency was involved to the point that in McGee's case, facing it, Maxvill dealt him to Oakland in August for three players, including young outfielder Felix Jose, and Willie helped a championship manager named LaRussa. Tudor, walking away from L.A. as an uncompensated free agent, spun

POWDER RIVER: That's what Lee Smith played with the hitters in his two-plus St. Louis seasons of many as a great game-saver. Big Lee won 10 games in relief two years, 1988-1989, and saved a league-leading 47 and 43. Overall, he had the most career saves.

a 12-4 season and 2.40 ERA. Then the cunning master walked into retirement at 34, head high but hurting, with a quality record—117 victories, only 72 defeats for a seldom-achieved .600 percentage (.619).

Not even Herzog could leave so gracefully. Acquiring Lee Smith from the Boston Red Sox for Tom Brunansky had helped, but the players floundered and got sullen. When a weary Fernando Valenzuela threw a no-hitter at them, Whitey told the truth. "They were pathetic," he said. By then, an observer hoped Herzog would ask for a sabbatical, but he chose to offer to quit. First time around, management said, no, thanks, but presumably they thought about it, meaning Maxvill, Kuhlmann and the brewery.

Gee, nobody in responsibility ever would say the beer was flat. So they reconsidered and apparently offered a golden-parachute separation, one that would enable the White Rat to spend more time at his favorite fishing hole or honing his lefthanded golf swing—and not speak critically. For a guy who heard Herzog's radio farewell of muted frustration, he left to a 70-year observer as No. 1 manager overall, a master at handling a squad and manipulating. Maxvill went to the tried and true for his interim manager, Red Schoendienst, one of the most colorful Redbirds ever. Baseball's Huckleberry Finn, backed by 12 years previously as pilot, fit as nicely as a grounder into his talented glove. Truth is, as a coach he would wear the uniform virtually into the next century, longer than any other previous major leaguer.

The '90 Cards, 33-47 under Herzog, won 13 of 24 for the Old Redhed, but by now Maxie had the man he wanted, Joe Torre, a former teammate for whom he had coached at Atlanta when Torre had a division champion. Torre had spent six seasons managing the Mets back home, son of a Brooklyn cop, and he'd had three at Atlanta, which might have seemed enough. Once needled sneeringly as "a little fat kid" by his older brother and idol, Frank, Joe had disciplined himself into a good versatile career, the peak of which had been that .363 season with the Cardinals. He had his way even though he had broadcasting security with the Angels and the climate for Disneyland and a new wife who preferred the weather there.

So he came, aged 50, with a smile in his heart more often than on his dark-eyed scowling face. Taking over, he managed a 24-34 record for a ball club that finished last for the first time since 1918. That they trailed in the NL East with 22 more defeats than victories (70-92), couldn't have been too comforting either for the manager or general manager. They faced a challenge to keep nine free agents at a time the purse strings were tightening.

One was Coleman, who had responded with a pretty good year with a .292 average and 77 stole bases, a combination that made him an offensive catalyst as a leadoff man, but Vince went to high bidder, New York Mets. Pendleton, the third baseman who came off a disappointing .230 season, wanted just too much money. He listened to Redbird advice at Atlanta, shortened his swing and hit .319. McGee already was gone, rather than pay a whopping long-term contract, and, as mentioned, Tudor retired. So they would have to do it with a youth movement, one that seemed far-fetched in spring training where Torre emphasized the Cardinals' championship tradition.

"This is," he said, "a team that wins, a

Spoon-Fed: Charlie Spoonhour (right), basketball coach at St. Louis University by way of Southwest Missouri, is a deep-dish Cardinal fan from his boyhood days in Arkansas. So he suits up with the Redbirds here and gives his "advice" to Joe Torre, then Cardinal manager.

team of Bob Gibson and Lou Brock and Stan Musial and many others in the Hall of Fame, too. And of Ozzie Smith." Baseball is not a pep-talk game, as Eddie Dyer had suggested so many years before, but Torre sounded like that other frowning-faced paisano when he added: "This is not a fifth or sixth-place club. All I ask is that you consider the past and the present and look to the future, yours and the club, and give me all you've got. You can win."

They did from a 4-1 opening-day victory for Bryn Smith, an overall free-agent disappointment, and for Lee Smith, the 6-6, 270-pound genial giant Maxvill had kept with a three-year $8,000,000 contract. Maxie could be tough as, for instance, the contract he crafted for Ozzie Smith by which the master shortstop had to achieve a number of appearances to qualify for a renewal. Admirably, Ozzie did. In 1991, ranking up there with Lee Smith, who shattered Bruce Sutter's club record of 45 saves with 47, the Wizard of Oz was No. 1 in ability as well as in uniform number. The Smiths helped most in a startling climb to second place, dimmed only because Pittsburgh was hot under Jim Leyland, 14 games ahead of the 84-78 Redbirds, themselves considerably better with 14 more victories than in 1990.

One move that helped strengthen the '91 team was the one made by Todd Zeile, like Pepper Martin and Mike Shannon before him, moving to third base. Zeile's was from behind the plate. The sophomore player's move permitted a better catcher, Tom Pagnozzi, to hunker behind the plate. And it didn't hurt Zeile's solid contribution of a .280 average, 11 homers and 81 RBIs. Outfielder Felix Jose—the temptation was to call him Jose Felix—helped when he came over from Oakland in the McGee deal, batting .305 with 77 ribbies. Trouble was, offensively, the Redbirds were shut out 14 times. Still, they regained 200-steal status. With a spotty attack, they didn't have enough pitching, especially with Magrane sidelined. Three pitchers were over .500—B. Smith, Ken Hill and Omar Olivares, but just barely—and snakebit DeLeon, his own error of pitching judgment, couldn't win more than he lost even with a 2.77 ERA.

THE BIGGER THEY ARE: The harder they fall, as witnessed by big Phillies' former catcher, Darren Daulton, dazed enough to drop the ball when trying to block out the Redbirds' rapid-running Ray Lankford, a standout developed by the organization.

Dramatically at season's end, aware they couldn't afford a lucrative contract for aged, gimpy Guerrero, the Cardinals bade Pete farewell. His power was primarily in the past tense, but in that windup with fans chanting, "Pedro, Pedro!," Guerrero unloaded a two-run homer, scoring Ray Lankford. The fleet Lankford, in his first full season, had hit .251 with a league-leading 15 triples. The other new outfielder, a hometown rookie named Bernard Gilkey, hadn't done as well, but he showed promise.

Largely on the advice of Maxvill and Torre the brewery spent money to cut down the distances to outfield fences, moving in the walls, beautifying them, installing another expensive rug of artificial turf and upgrading the gift shop and museum. With the symmetrical stadium reasonable at the foul lines, Anheuser-Busch arranged to trim the distances eight feet to the power alleys in left-center and right-center, to shorten center field from 414 feet to 402—it had been 426 to center at old Sportsman's Park—and to lower the height of the Busch Stadium walls from 10 feet to eight.

Thoughtfully, hopefully, Maxvill and Torre brought in Andres Galarraga from Montreal in exchange for Ken Hill. With the Expos, Ken became king of the Hill, but Galarraga early suffered a broken wrist that cut heavily into his playing time and the quality of his performances, though he improved as the season progressed. He played only 95 games and hit just .243, but he had 10 homers and, as always, was the Big Cat around first base. With Johnny Mize, the feline synonym term was derisive. With the Big Venezuelan it was actual and a tribute. So when the 1992 season ended with another third-place finish—again too far behind the Pirates and a couple arrear Montreal—Galarraga or a greedy agent forced the Cardinals' hand, seeking a large raise and long-term contract for a good hitter whose last two seasons with the Expos also had been diminishing. A day before the expansion draft for expansion came up, Galarraga signed with Colorado, where Cardinal hitting coach Don Baylor was named manager. Would it be presumptuous to wonder whether Baylor, first runner-up to Torre for the Redbirds' job, had encouraged the Big Cat to make it difficult for the Cardinals to retain him? Out there in the thin air of the mountains, Galarraga immediately won the batting title at .370 and 22 homers en route to more.

Oz and Octogenarian: Amadee Wohlschlaeger (right), semi-retired chief artist and sports cartoonist of the St. Louis *Post-Dispatch,* was sketching big-league ball players even before Ozzie Smith was born. Amadee had a little more trouble with spelling than the Oz did with ground balls, so the gifted artist dropped his polysyllabic surname and became – Amadee!

With limited time and performance from Galarraga in 1992, young Lankford hit .293 with 20 homers and 97 runs driven in. Felix—uh, Jose—hit .295 with 14 homers and 75 RBIs. Gilkey batted .305. Milt Thompson was a helpful .293, steady Ozzie .295 and Geronimo Pena, never living up to his promise, hit .305 with seven homers in limited play. And, oh, yes, a football player named Brian Jordan got into some ball games. For the young pitching staff, with Mike Perez looking like a future closer, big Lee Smith saved 43. The staff leader for a club that had one fewer victory and one more defeat, 83-79, was a soft-serving righthander, Tewksbury, 16-5 with a 2.16 earned-run average.

Tewksbury led with victories again in 1993 with17, but Magrane returned really only as a shell and young starters Donovan Osborne, Rheal Cormier and Allen Watson were a help, and Rene Arocha, a defected Cuban acquired in a special draft, never quite achieved his expectations. Offensively, Maxvill acquired a high-salaried former Mets' infielder, Gregg Jefferies, in a deal that sent Felix Jose to Kansas City, and he also got another big hitter, Mark Whiten, from Cleveland for righthander Mark Clark. Jefferies, a dirty-suit player, meaning he hustled and perspired, had defensive deficiencies most anywhere, but he hit .342 with 14 homers and 93 RBIs.

Whiten, a strong-armed outfielder, was a hot-and-cold hitter who was white hot at Cincinnati the day he became the first St. Louis player—and one of the rare ones—to hit four homers in a game, driving in 12 runs that tied Sunny Jim Bottomley's 69-year-old record. Whiten hit 25 homers in a .293 season.

Zeile's .277 average included 17 homers and 103 runs driven in. Gilkey, with sidekick Lankford under par, muscled up to .305 with 16 homers and 70 RBIs. And that young pro-football defensive halfback, Brian Jordan, nagged by injuries more on the diamond than on the gridiron, hit 10 homers in just 293 times at bat. With a .309 batting average, B.J. had a bright future—if they could keep him Redbird red rather than Atlanta Falcon black.

If you will, this season of 87 victories, the most since the 1987 pennant season, reflected baseball at its appealing height, St. Louis and elsewhere, because even though Torre's team finished third again and 10 games behind the Phillies, the attendance of 2,844,326 was just about a half-million more than the previous few years since the 3,000,000 in 1989. Then the inmates took over the asylum, the players now just as clubowners controlled unfairly in the penny-pinching past, the shutdown occurred with only 94 games played in 1994. St. Louis, reflecting to a degree the resentment elsewhere over cancellation that included the World Series, didn't draw that well for a couple of more seasons until Tony LaRussa brought home a division champion in 1996.

In that bobtailed sorry third-place season in 1994, 53-61, all individual totals were shortened. Still, Jefferies hit 12 homers, Zeile and Lankford 19, Whiten 14 and mystery man Pena 11 in 83 games. The mystery was why the Dominican of immense talent didn't do better. Yet, remember, he's the kind of hard-luck character who even cut short one season by stepping on his glove when fielding a ground ball and was badly hurt.

In that abbreviated '94 season, Tewskbury led with victories again, 12, twice as many as the nearest members of the staff, Allan Watson and Rick Sutcliffe, but the shaky ace who had lingered long in the minors would fly the Redbirds' perch for the highest bidder, a pain in the posterior for men trying to compete and for the brewery, which now had a bottomline approach. The sport had been a business. This was, in effect, a tough time to be a Mark Sauer, a Fred Kuhlmann, a Stu Meyer or a Joe Torre. August A. Busch III, with his father no longer alive, played musical chairs with his front man downtown at the Civic Center Redevelopment Corporation and the Cardinals.

The brewery had bought the huge complex for which Gussie Busch was the leader of a drive that enhanced downtown. To buy control, A-B got back rights to concessions and parking for which the senior Busch generously had agreed to relinquish for 30 years. In the process of taking over Civic Center, young Busch used the traditional spit-and-polish approach that rivals the quality of Budweiser as a backbone of the brewery's preminence. At a time Busch Stadium was 25 years old—in the midst of the revolving front-office activity—August paid an infrequent visit to the ball park and over a glass of beer with a guy dumb enough not to be an A-B stockholder, he was told that Anheuser-Busch reminded the other fellow of the U.S. Navy. August the Third—or, rather, "Three Sticks" as some call him privately—raised a brow. Why? "Because, August," the other guy said, "if it doesn't move, like the Navy, you paint it," Busch III liked the comment and the compliment to the Entertainment Division's prime property.

The Entertainment Division got into the picture after the 1990 season. Young Mark Sauer, 45, an accounting whiz by way of the University of Illinois and Columbia University, had been vice-president of Civic Center, second only to Fred Kuhlmann. Kuhlmann, at 68, chief legal counsel at A-B, had been reassigned in 1984 as senior vice-president and CEO of the center and in 1989, at Gussie Busch's death, president of the Cardinals. Sauer, enjoying the fanaticism of baseball no end, was crushed in March, 1991 when the junior Busch and se-

FOR PETE'S SAKE: Pedro (Pete) Guerrero came to the Cardinals in 1989, a year of pitching shortage, especially in the bullpen, and almost helped win a pennant with a .311 batting average, 42 league-leading doubles, 17 homers and 117 RBIs.

And The Winner Is...: The St. Louis Amateur Baseball Hall of Fame's Rising Star Award, sponsored by Mike Shannon, is presented annually to the area's top high school talent.

nior boss asked him to transfer back to the financially ailing Entertainment Division. He declined and was given a see-you-later-alligator-or-dolphin-dismissal. Sauer went that year to Pittsburgh as president of the financially struggling Pirates and did such a good job with a bad cause that he later came back to St. Louis with the hockey Blues.

Kuhlmann, a baseball fan, too, was the intermediary for Maxvill and Torre with the brewery, seeking as much leeway as possible with a tighter budget. Kuhlmann stepped down in 1992 as president of the ball club for which Sam Breadon and August A. Busch, Jr. had served for more than a half century. Hopefully, Stuart Meyer, 61, legal eagle of things labor, could help. Meyer, like Kuhlmann a nice man, could do little to solve baseball's unique arrangement where the players have the best of both worlds, individual contractors protected by a union. Stu couldn't help improve the ball club's own budget appreciably. He suffered an embarrassment when his publicly recommended contract extensions for Maxvill and Torre were rescinded by August the Third. In a year he was further embarrassed by having to deny players the courtesy of the deadheaded plane flight to St. Louis, after the 1994 strike caught the Cards in Florida, Meyer stepped into retirement, but not before his choice of a successor as president was approved—Mark Lamping.

Lamping, 38, was a cherubic, stocky, former St. Louis high school and college soccer player. He was also the spitting image of his late father, John Lamping, a contractor who had been an outstanding center-linebacker at Cleveland High School, pretty good catcher, and an honor student. Young Lamping, a Vianney and Rockhurst College graduate, had joined Anheuser-Busch in 1981. At the brewery, Lamping rose rapidly in sports marketing, working closely with World Cup soccer, the Olympics and all professional sports, including baseball. Just in February of that 1994 he had resigned to become commissioner of the Continental Basketball Association, moving its headquarters to St. Louis. Even though Mark once had quit A-B, August Busch approved his return.

Taking over in September, 1994, when there was no baseball, Lamping faced decisions, one of which was anticipated when Maxvill closed out his general manager's desk before they met. Dal hadn't ingratiated himself with the Top Gun when, failing to convince Busch that their contract agreement with Torre required an extension before the last official season, he suggested heatedly that if August didn't like baseball, why the blankety-blank didn't he sell the damn thing. So Torre was, in effect, a lame duck manager when Lamping followed the official dismissal of Maxvill with a month-and-a-half search for his choice as general manager. He found his name in blonde 46-year-old Walt Jocketty, a University of Minnesota graduate 20 years earlier. Before joining new franchise Colorado in 1993, he had put in 14 seasons with the Oakland Athletics, hired by tough-to-please Charles O. Finley as minor-league director and scouting supervisor. For 10 years, he overhauled the A's fading farm system and developed such players as Jose Canseco, Walt Weiss and a man with whom he—and St. Louis—would have a happy wedding. Mark McGwire!

As general manager, Jocketty got off a shaky start when he dealt Mark Whiten and Rheal Cormier to Boston for a home-town third baseman, Scott Cooper, and picked up lefthander Danny Jackson as a free agent. And Jefferies, who still might be best as a designated hitter, took the free-agency tram to Philadelphia. Great Scott, Cooper hit a home run in his first game wearing the Cardinal uniform he'd idolized as a kid, but, somehow, Coop went downhill to a frustrating .230. With young Tripp Cromer hitting only at .226 at shortstop and Jose Oquendo back at second with .220, first baseman John Mabry's .307 wouldn't have been enough even if he had hit for the power of Lankford with 25 homers and Jordan 22. Gilkey had 17. But the pitching was as poor as Jackson's outlook and production when Danny was stricken with cancer and dived to 2-and-12. Not even the yeoman effort of veteran Tom Henke in the

Missouri farm boy's retirement season as a great closer, with 36 saves, could keep the Cardinals from a fourth-place finish, 62-81 in the late-starting 1995 season.

En route, the Cardinals lost a manager and, briefly, got one when farm director Mike Jorgensen over for 42-54 after Torre had said good-bye with a 20-27 record. Dismissed as a manager for the third time, Joe had the distinction of having managed the Cardinals the longest, seven fragmentary seasons, without having returned a winner. Torre hadn't been in a World Series as a player, either, but good things do come at times to people who wait. With former newspaperman Artie Richman as his cheerleader to boss George Steinbrenner, stormy George hired Joe to manage the great home-area Yankees. Torre led the Yanks to the title and, in addition, had such a dramatic season—with Brother Rocco dying and oldest brother Frank getting an eleventh-hour heart transplant—that they made a television story about the travails of Torre. If Joe Torre was doubly blessed in 1996, the Cardinals and St. Louis didn't do too bad, and, in fact, missed by just one elusive victory of bringing up a sixth World Series between two old famed foes with St. Lou one up on New Yawk.

By the time Jocketty got the name he wanted as manager, Tony LaRussa, a man of the highest credentials and results, one with whom he was acquainted, August Busch announced through a spokesman that the brewery—with no special rush—hoped to sell the ball club. With no action achieved until March 1996, it's to be presumed that August approved a handsome six-figure salary for LaRussa and high coaching salaries by a ball club, unlike most others, that paid coaches comparative pittance.

As a manager in the majors from late 1979 when he was 35, the 51-year-old LaRussa owned five playoff teams, winning three League Championship Series. He finished first three straight years in the American League West, four in five seasons. His three World Series included a four-game sweep over San Francisco in 1989, the year thunder came up across the bay, i.e., an infamous earthquake. For LaRussa, Italian born in Spanish-flavored Tampa, Fla., base-

NOSTALGIA: In a tribute to Jackie Robinson a half-century earlier, the 1997 Cardinals played a regular-season game dressed in the attire of the St. Louis Stars, Negro National League champions when they left town in 1931. Here, Willie McGee and handyman Danny Scheaffer model the blue-on-white uniforms.

ball was a big thing from the time he signed with the Kansas City A's the night he graduated from high school in 1962. His playing career as a light-hitting infielder was limited through six seasons, but by then the thinking man's player had graduated from Florida State University law school in 1978. A year later he joined four others—John Montgomery Ward, Branch Rickey, Hugh Jennings and Miller Huggins—as the only lawyer-managers in baseball history.

ONE FINE BUCK: Joe Buck figures early to be one of broadcasting's best as baseball announcer for KMOX and the Cardinals' network, winning national attention on pro football, too, with FOX sports and even with his first horse-racing assignment in 1998. Joe is the son of Hall of Fame broadcaster Jack Buck and singing-dancing actress Carole Lindsey. His maternal grandfather, Joe Lintzenich, was an outstanding punter with St.Louis University and the Chicago Bears.

Before doffing his playing uniform, LaRussa played and coached for a Cardinals' Triple-a farm club at New Orleans in 1977. He moved a year later as manager at Knoxville, then one at Iowa before being beckoned to finish the 1979 season with the Chicago White Sox. In 1983, winning 99 games, LaRussa lost out in the final game of the LCS to Baltimore when Tito Landrum, in effect "on loan" to the Orioles from the Redbirds, hit a Series-winning homer and then returned to St. Louis. Catching genius Dave Duncan came along as pitching coach, Andy Benes, Gary Gaetti and Ron Gant signed to free-agent contracts—Gant five years at $5,000,000 each—and Tony Fossas and Rick Honeycutt and Dennis Eckersley were acquired to bolster the bullpen. Why, the '96 Cardinals might have not only the best team, but oldest with Rick nearing 44 and Eck 42. And wonderful Willie McGee returned.

Before the 1996 season opened, they cut the Cards with a new deck, and the joker was wild. From the first time since Fred Saigh sold out to Anheuser-Busch in March 1953, the Cardinals in March, 43 years later were under new ownership, the kind August Busch III carefully had sought. August was not a baseball fan, but a business man. As a young spirited kid, like his father before him, he was active in sports, but not the old national pastime. He liked speed, motor sports and he flew his own helicopter. He had the quaint notion that a man heading an international company and expanding it deserved more money than guys who played for him. Mainly, he knew the difference between black ink and red. And the Redbirds had begun to bleed red. So he wanted out for himself and for prosperous A-B stockholders. Yet he wanted men to succeed him who had a similar affection for the old French fur-trading post and the game that began the year Custer lost out. He got them. They came 16 ownership partners strong, led by a name familiar to all in baseball and mainly in St. Louis—DeWitt.

The senior DeWitt, one of the most versatile front-office men in baseball, was the son of a North St. Louis butcher, consigned with selling bleacher peanuts at old Sportsman's Park until brother Charley, two years older at 14, convinced Branch Rickey he had the new office boy he was seeking. Under Rickey, William Orville DeWitt was office boy, receptionist and adoped son, encouraged to study nights for a law degree. By 23, he was treasurer of the Cardinals. By 1936, he was general manager of the rival Browns, built a winning wartime ball club with little money in 1944, then planned to seek permission to move to Los Angeles. The majors' scheduled meeting was cancelled the morning after the Japanese dropped their calling card at Pearl Harbor.

With an assist from their second boss, Dick Muckerman, for whom the DeWitt brothers had worked, the one-time peanut vendors acquired the Browns for about $800,000 in 1949. They were forced to sell stars as they kept Muckerman intact. Charley, who in tough times officated *Post-Dispatch* junior ball games for 50 cents, was traveling secretary. He made every night New Year's Eve, proving that the Brownies weren't cheapskates as well as poor. They religiously paid bills in cash, to gain advantage of a 10 percent discount. Frustrated, the DeWitts sold the Browns at a profit to flamboyant Bill Veeck early in 1951. Bill DeWitt's odyssey after a consulting period with Veeck included a brief period assisting general manager George Weiss of the New York Yankees and then as administrator of a fund for ailing ball clubs. Next was a whistle-stop session as president of the Detroit Tigers.

"They didn't like me there," said Bill tartly, "because I made them take down the dime slots from the women's restroom toilets, costing somebody some money." While there, he contrived in a bit of contretemps unlike a man of dignity, swapping managers with Trader Frank Lane at Cleveland. In another controversial deal with Lane, DeWitt got the better of it himself and for the Tigers' immediate future when he dealt infielder Harvey Kuenn for Cleveland's popular outfield slugger, Rocky Colavito. The senior DeWitt, hailed to floundering Cincinnati, made his mark and life there and his family's, too. Bill's wife, a horsewoman socialite of a St. Louis lumber family, Margaret Holekamp, gave him three children, two of whom closely resembled her. One, son William O. DeWitt, Jr., had one mark of distinction with the Brownies. At age 10, in 1951, his customized uniform was worn by midget Eddie Gaedel—number "1/8"—and is displayed at the baseball Hall of Fame in Cooperstown.

By that time, representing the Powell Crosley Foundation and then adroit acquisition of club ownership, the senior DeWitt had a teen-aged son fascinated by baseball and eager to learn. Father-and-son associations included participation in Cincinnati's Riverfront Coliseum and hockey club. As president with a pleasant immediate present—a pennant—DeWitt rebuilt the Reds, then sold them at a handsome profit to a group that would include as general manager and president the Cardinals' former GM, Bob Howsam. Only now and then would DeWitt complain about the new regime's failure to note the running start. Late in life he was relaxed, happy, wealthy and a member of the baseball Hall of Fame's Veterans committee. ("How the hell can they complain about so many New York and St. Louis players in Cooperstown when they were good enough to win pennants for the Yanks, Giants, Dodgers and Cardinals?" he would blurt, banjo-eyed and then giggle into his growling laugh.)

One of his late ventures was to serve as a baseball authority sandwiched between a national bank and big investment firm when Gussie Busch sought to buy the Cardinals from the brewery. The effort failed. DeWitt, declining to name the figures, conceded that his evaluation on the Redbirds had been considerable less than the price tag recommended by the bankers and by the brokers. "I suspect," he said, slyly, "Mr. Busch didn't really want to own the ball club that much."

Years later when August Busch finalized his view to sell and even before an official of Anheuser-Busch announced A-B's desire to terminate baseball ash from brewery beechwood, Fred Hanser heard the word and immediately called Bill DeWitt, Jr. in Cincinnati.

Hanser, 43, partner in an impressive law firm for close to 20 years, was a classmate of the younger DeWitt at St. Louis' Country Day School where they had prepped, teammates in baseball with Bill as a rangy pitcher and Hanser a stocky second baseman and all-around athlete. He even played football briefly at Yale, where he earned a degree in economics in 1963 and then a law degree from home city's Washington University. Like close friend Bill, Hanser, son of a doctor, was a lifelong baseball fan with a special interest in the Cardinals. His lively mother's grandfather, Adolph Diez, was a former Cardinal investor whose willed baseball watch was Fred's. So Hanser called DeWitt with interest and with willingness, if it could be achieved, to give up his law practice and move into the ball park offices. For Bill

GRAND-SLAM GAETTI: Gary Gaetti, close by St. Louis at Centralia, Ill., was an early Redbird fan who helped beat them in the 1987 Series as Minnesota's third baseman. Gaetti's grand-slam off incomparable Greg Maddux was a big blow in the 1996 NLCS with Atlanta. When the Braves humiliated the Cards in the seventh game, old-timer Gary played that night like a kid trying to win a varsity letter.

Teammates, Then and Now: Primary stockholders of the sweet 16 who stepped forth to buy the Cardinals were (left to right) Frederick O. Hanser, William O. DeWitt Jr. and Andrew N. Baur. DeWitt is chairman of the board and general partner, Hanser, principal organizer, is chairman and Baur is secretary-treasurer. Drew watched Bill and Fred as athletic teammates at Country Day School and then succeeded them as a Codasco player.

DeWitt Jr.—really no longer Billy—he'd held investments in the Baltimore Orioles, the latter-day highly successful ex-Browns, and also the Cincinnati Reds and Texas Rangers. He was on the board of pro football's Cincinnati Bengals and the community's hockey club.

The peach of a pair became a most interested threesome when the next to join force was a banker, Andrew Baur—"Drew"—to virtually all who know him—and another baseball fan, 41 and a couple of years younger than DeWitt and Hanser. He had watched them play at Country Day before becoming Codasco's first baseman, rangy, with one compaint. "I could field, but I couldn't hit," Baur said. Drew, son of Andrew H. Baur, had graduated from Washington and Lee in Lexington, Va., with an A.B. in 1966 and a business major from Georgia State University in 1970. He had become chairman and CEO of Southwest Bank, a St. Louis institution.

DeWitt, Hanser and Baur formed with 13 others, Gateway Group, Inc. The other rooting investors are Stephen F. Brauer, St. Louis; Robert H. Castellini, Cincinnati; G. Waite Humphrey, Jr., Pittsburgh; Nick D. Kladis, Chicago; Donna DeWitt (Dee-Dee) Lambert, St. Louis and Bill DeWitt's sister; Michael McDonnell, Memphis; David C. Pratt, St. Louis; Michael E. Pulitzer, St. Louis; Mercer Reynolds, Cincinnati; Richard H. Sulphin, Cincinnati; Dudley S. Taft, Cincinnati; John K. Wallace, Jr., St. Louis, and W.J. and T.L. Williams, Cincinnati.

With DeWitt majority stockholder and chairman of the board and general partner, Hanser president and director, and Baur as secretary-treasurer, Gateway Group, Inc. didn't get its official blessing from baseball until March 21, 1996, but the previous Christmas, two days before Santa Claus, they announced the purchase from Anheuser-Busch for a reported $150,000,000, which included the franchise, ball park and four parking garages. Selling the 12-block project at a price regarded as reasonable, August Busch threw into the project an $8,000,000 improvement, including a return to grass and other old-fashioned amenities that enabled old Al Fleishman's public-relations alma mater, Fleishman-Hillard, to propose a new slogan: "Baseball like it oughta be."

For the Codasco cohorts and financial associates, the LaRussa era got off with a 7-6 loss at Shea Stadium, but next day early dividends included a first victory for Todd Stottlemyre, who had seen many games in New York when his father Mel was a winner for the Yankees. Todd's 5-3 win was protected by Eckersley's first of 30 saves. And, speaking of 30, Gant hit his first of 30 homers in a three-RBI game.

A week later, Alan and Andy Benes, the first brothers to toe the Redbird slab since the McDaniels in 1958, got into the winner's circle on successive days in well-pitched games against Montreal, 4-1, and Philadelphia, 2-1. The brothers Benes loomed as large in the outlook at their size—24-year-old Alan, a rookie from Creighton University, 6-5 and 215, and six-year veteran Andy, an alumnus of home-town Evansville University an even larger 6-6 and 245 pounds. But size and shape are only part of the mix in the long pennant run and when Andy bowed to Colorado in the high-rise altitude of the Rockies in mid-May, the elder Benes was only 1-and-7, and the reeling Redbirds were nine games under .500, 17-26, fifth in the division and four games behind Houston—and headed to the Texas metropolis.

Pennants aren't won in a day or in a series, and, truth is, Andy Benes rebounded from that stumbling start to 10 consecutive victories, the most since John Tudor crafted 11 in a row in 1985. And, more important at the moment, successive victories by Donovan Osborne, Stottlemyre and Alan Benes over the Astros left the race what it would be most of the season—close! Despite the reprieve from being far back, which a loss to Houston would have produced, the Cardinals were allergic to .500 until near the end of June at Pittsburgh when, facing gifted Denny Neagle, a name to remember, Osborne beat Pittsburgh, 6-1. The 39-39 record tied for first place in a Central Division in which it seemed no team was interested in winning.

For Duke Osborne, originally a first-round draft choice in 1990, the climb through injury that cost him the entire '94 season for surgical shoulder repair, his tide-turning win was one of 13, most by a lefthander since Joe Magranes' 18 in 1989. Osborne's obscure nickname "Duke" is an inside joke. Osborne's father, a John Wayne fan, named him "Donovan" after Wayne's John Ford swashbuckler, "Donovan's Reef". The needling admirer wondered why Pop Osborne hadn't settled for Wayne's swaggering nickname—"Duke".

Next day after the Duke or Don or Donovan beat Neagle, a pitcher to be reckoned in playoffs after Atlanta bought his expensive contract, the winner in relief was Frederick Wayne (Rick) Honeycutt. The 6-5 win putting the Cards over .500 was one of two scored by the grand 42-year-old gaffer in 61 games of a 2.85 ERA. Age was served in the acquisition of the 20-year, six club pickup from the Yanks for a kiss and a promise, i.e., "future cash considerations."

Stottlemyre won the next one in the pull away from the .500 magnetic field, providing in his 14 victories and losing efforts a bulldog spirit that seemed to catch the club's fancy, and the fans, proving a winner for Jocketty, who gave up outfielder Allen Battle and three young pitchers for him.

From Stottlemyre's win into July, the Cardinals burst forth like the Fourth with eight victories in nine games. They passed the All-Star game five up, then won six straight to open a four-game lead, but a five-game losing streak dropped them abruptly. By the end of August, they were down two and a half games. They were, however, engaged in a sweet September song, in the midst of a six-game winning streak that included three straight against Houston head to head, as in days of old when as the St. Louis Swifties they needed most a series against the Brooklyn Dodgers. They knocked Houston on their Astros.

The result was a rousing 10 victories in 12 tries, more than a difference in a division race won by six lengths. With a flourish to the finish, as part of a five-game winning streak that ended the season's final day, Andy Benes beat Pittsburgh there, 7-1 to wrap up the division title. And in their first experience with a wild-card possibility, where they could have made the playoffs possibly by finishing second, LaRussa's lads won going away. They finished with an 88-74 record and brought their new owners an attendance of 2,654,716.

This was an upbeat sentimental farewell to future Hall of Famer Ozzie Smith as a magnificient fielder who became a pretty good hitter, one with numerous Gold Gloves and other decorations. Haughty about it, even after gracefully announcing his retirement along the way, the Wizard of Oz declined to move to second base,

TWIN ATTRACTIONS: *Fowlball* magazine and Todd Stottlemyre, a peach of a pair at Busch Stadium. The publication is a gift at the ball park. Stottlemyre, whose father, Mel, pitched against the Cardinals for the Yankees in the 1964 World Series, has followed in the old man's sizable shoes as a steady starter.

where the need was great, but in 82 games, hitting .282, he manifested team-play artistry as a contact hitter. In final ceremonies they honored "1" of a kind by retiring his number, just as previously that season Lamping and the new owners demonstrated sentimental understanding by retiring the "2" of Hall of Famer Red Schoendienst and the "9" of Hall of Famer Enos Slaughter.

AYE, AYE, SKIPPER: Tony LaRussa, a thinking man's man – and winning manager – at Chicago and Oakland, too.

Pressed into a conflicting situation, Royce Clayton, acquired from the Giants for Allen Watson and two others, played extremely well at shortstop in a .277 season of 33 stolen bases and, as result, permitted LaRussa's kid-glove diplomacy. Playing first base and outfield, John Mabry hit .297 with 13 homers and 74 RBIs, indicating Mabry hit for higher average if not for more power. Not hitting for average, but productively was Ron Gant with 30 homers and 82 runs driven in. Lankford, until suffering a late-season injury that required rotator-cuff surgery and a delay into the 1997 season, had a smashing .275 of 150 hits that included 65 extra-base hits, 27 of them homers, with 86 RBIs. Catcher Tom Pagnozzi chipped in with .270, 13 homers, 55 RBIs and the confidence of LaRussa and Duncan. And 38-year-old Gary Gaetti was an old pro at third and at the plate. He had .274-27-80 totals. Fourth outfielder Bernard Gilkey, whom they felt they couldn't keep with the salary cap, went to New York with a season so successful he spoiled Mets fans for '97, a year of injuries and regrets.

In St. Louis, acquired as a minor-league free agent as a steal, was an old favorite, Willie Deane McGee. At 38, the gifted switch-hitter, twice batting champion and a World Series hero, came back dramatically with more plate appearances than he envisioned and more productive, too. Willie the Wonder, playing 123 games, hit .307 with a .350 mark as a pinch-hitter.

Far and away the leader offensively was right fielder Brian Jordan. B.J., batting .310 with 17 homers and 104 RBIs had runs driven in that were timely with a capital "T". His runs batted in average—.438 with men in scoring position—was the best in the majors and, so important, that its full significance wasn't felt until Flash Jordan wasn't able physically to do it again.

Pitching? There seemed no difference for former AL pitchers who came over to the NL with a strike zone so presumably lower, though occasionally and unfortunately as wide as one ample arbiter's derriere. Andy Benes, returning from a brief sojourn with Seattle after his previous seasons at San Diego, led with 18 victories and when rookie brother Alan contributed 13, the Benes brothers had 31, the most since Dizzy Dean won 30 and brother Paul 19 for 49 when Me 'n Paul won the Gas House Gang's 1934 pennant and Series. The Deans also had 47 in '35.

Stottlemyre won 14, Osborne 13, Mark Petkovsek 11, usually out of the bullpen. T.J. Mathews was more reliable than his 2-6 record, enough to draw future attention in the Mark McGwire deal, and the triumverate of bullpen old folks—Eckersley, Honeycutt and Fossas—were like an iceberg, the tip of their value out of sight beyond their combined 2-11 won-and-lost record. And Eck, by heck, was almost as great as in his salad seasons as the American League's finest.

Major league baseball's introduction of the "wild card" a year earlier, a gimmick that honestly made the National Football League except for its television impact, proved to be a bell ringer for baseball, too. As winners in the realigned Central Division, the Cardinals with 88 actually had fewer victories than any of the five other division winners in the bigs. Fact is, their opponent in the first round, not decided until the last day, was San Diego, which showed spirit and character by beating out Los Angeles on the final day—even though it meant the Padres would play the Redbirds rather than the mighty champion Atlanta Braves.

Over the season LaRussa's Redbirds had won eight of 12 from San Diego, whipping a horrible hex out there with four of six, but the Padres were slightly favored in the Division Series, best of five. It began in St. Louis with a whopping 54,193 that saw the pride and joy of Centralia, Ill., Gary Gaetti, unload a three-run homer off Joey Hamilton in the first inning. Seasoned Rickey Henderson hit a homer off Stottlemyre in the sixth inning, and Todd battled into the seventh, then got good but not great relief from Honeycutt and Eckersley, called on unusually to finish the eighth. The 3-1 win at home gave the Birds wings. Importantly, though touched by batting master Tony Gwynn for two hits, they shut out San Diego's hot MVP threat, slugger Ken Caminiti.

The second game was tighter, better and even more well-attended with 56,752 squeezing into Gussie's legacy for an exciting tug o' war, Andy Benes vs. Scott Sanders. Gant unloaded a three-run homer in the fourth, breaking a 1-1 tie and when Benes falterered in the eighth for a tense tie, the Cardinals scored a victory on only five hits, 5-4, when Pagnozzi hit a fielder's grounder too soft to achieve an out against the fleet Jordan. B.J., playing in the post-season liked the man whose number "3" he wore, Frankie Frisch, scored the winning run of the playoff at San Diego, the site of a delightful third straight. Caminiti, who had zeroed in with a homer in the second game, teed off on Osborne as the Padres took a two-run lead, and his second homer off Honeycutt in the eighth tied the score and spoiled a magnificent six inning middle-relief job by Mark Petkovsek. With the game in the balance in the ninth, here came Mr. Jordan with a two-run blast off Trevor Hoffman, providing St. Louis with a 7-5 victory and a three-game rout in their first Division Series.

For the first Series in the double-layer playoff, Jordan and Gant, who unfortunately would be the most missed a year later, B.J. overall and Ron for his bat, were the stars against the Padres. Jordan's total was .333 with three RBIs, Gant's even better at .400 with four hits good for eight total bases and four RBIs. And Ozzie Smith, in his one and only experience in the new division Series, batted .333 as did his shortstop successor, Royce Clayton. Pitching was particularly solid in the bullpen, especially from Eckersley, Honeycutt, Petkovsek and Mathews. Starters, it figured, would have to be better in the League Championship Series with Atlanta, laden with Cy Young talent, Greg Maddux, John Smoltz and Tommy Glavine. And in the run to the wire, Ted Turner's bucks had bought Denny Neagle from starving Pittsburgh as another starting toy for manager Bobby Cox.

With the 1996 Cy Young winner Smoltz showing why, the Braves won the opener over Andy Benes at home, 4-2, and that was bad news because in the regular season the only place the Cards had prevailed over the team of the '90s was at Fulton County Stadium. The score was 4-2 with slick Chipper Jones contributing a perfect "4 for 4" for

PASS IN REVIEW: They let Ozzie Smith's past – and presence – bring out the ball club for the final regular season game, 1996, in which the superstar shortstop's uniform number was retired.

Cover Boys:
In the Cardinals' monthly magazine, Ray Lankford and Matt Morris, top contributors in 1997.

Atlanta, and Jordan, who lives there, contributing a triple in five St. Louis hits.

The Redbirds hung in tough against the perfect traditionalist Maddux in the second game, leading 3-2 after Marquis Grissom hit a two-run homer off Stottlemyre in the third inning. Stotts was wild, but strong, walking three and striking out eight. Suddenly he and all got a tremendous lift in the seventh inning when Gaetti's only hit was a grand-slam blow off Maddux. So with Gant's earlier three hits and Jordan two, the Cardinals evened the series, 8-3.

When they returned to St. Louis in storybook weather for a storybook game, a crowd of 56,769, nearly dittoed the next two days, saw Gant unload twice on the ball club that had let him go to Cincinnati, fearful he hadn't recovered from injuries. His two-run homer off Glavine and another in the sixth were the difference, 3-2, in a game won by Osborne assisted by LaRussa's senior citizen bullpen.

The victory was the first of the year over the Braves in St. Louis, but encore seemed unlikely in the next game in which Ryan Klesko and Mark Lemke hit homers off Andy Benes, a shutout victim until in the seventh when Cox pulled a quick thumb on Neagle, a two-hit pitcher. By the time greenpea Dmitri Young came up in the glaring spotlight as a pinch-hitter for good-field, no-hit Mike Gallego of the weak second-base link, righthander Greg McMichael had toed the slab for the Braves. Cards' bench intelligence told Young that McMichael threw excessive change-ups. The switch-hitter waited, got a let-up and drove it deep to the left-center field fence for a triple. And when Clayton singled, the game went into the eighth a surprising tie. Here, Jordan struck again, hitting a game-winning homer off McMichael, 4-3, with Honeycutt and Eckersley in form.

Suddenly, headily, the underdogs were ahead of the top dogs. Soberingly, behind Smoltz's seven-hit pitching, the bulging two-game advantage in the best-of-seven season was down to a game. The Braves clobbered Stottlemyre, Jackson and associates, 14-0.

Now once-upon-a-happier period, the Cardinals of old would put on their road grays and go into enemy lines and throttle them, but even though rookie Alan Benes pitched admirably in five innings of three hits and only two runs, Benes and the Birds were faced with the embarrassed corner-cutting dart thrower, Maddux, and he owned a 2-0 lead when he weakened in the eighth, allowing six scattered hits, two by Willie McGee. He walked none and struck out seven. Big Mark Wohlers closed it out 3-1, after an extra run off Stottlemyre.

Befitting their status as in the best ball club in the National League if not both—see their upset loss to the Yankees in the World Series!—Cox's cohorts came out for the seventh game that was almost as ugly as the World Series of 1985 except that this time, i.e., minus Joaquin Andujar!—nobody threw a fit, not even the heavily viewed TV dugout shots of manager LaRussa. The 22-hit assault was over even before the Braves scored a touchdown against Osborne in the first inning—"6"—en route to a 15-0 wrap-up.

So Clayton's .350, McGee's .333, Gant's homer-heights and Jordan's were lost in the letdown, including Gaetti's grand-slam off Maddux, but the flowing-haired third-base veteran played like a rah-rah kid still trying to make the varsity. He flung himself around for batted balls, left and right, long after the surprising, delightful season ended on a sour scoreboard note.

The St. Louis baseball writers at their annual winter dinner honored many, just as the Associated Press originally had named LaRussa as its Manager of the Year in the National League, an honor he had achieved previously in the American. LaRussa got to his feet and "guaranteed" another Division Championship in 1997. Gosh, the gloomy old football coaches, beginning with Amos Alonzo Stagg, would turn over in their graves, though baseball managers traditionally are optimistic publicly if not nearly so certain as LaRussa was. As Tony well knows, baseball is a funny game, courtesy of Joe Garagiola's book talk, and the ball is round, but it takes funny bounces through injuries, sags, slump, and career highs—and lows.

For one thing, the 1997 Cardinals stumbled at the start, losing their first six games and were matched too often too early with the team they trimmed in 1996, Houston. With former Redbird pitcher Larry Dierker surprisingly taken from the press booth to the dugout as manager and their prominent first baseman and second baseman, Jeff Bagwell and Craig Biggio, leading the charge, physically and emotionally, Houston won nine out of 12 from the team Dierker knew they had to beat.

Overall, it wasn't pleasant, the fifth-place season of 73-89 in which the Cardinals drew their eighth-best attendance of 2,656,357, a half-million more than on the road. The baseball atmosphere of Busch Stadium never was better than in the plaza of champions, a semi-circle of championship monuments, surrounding the Stan Musial statue at the northeast (Walnut and Broadway) corner of the ball park. With President Mark Lamping the catalyst, Anheuser-Busch generously contributed $8,000,000 more in improvements that created a kids pavilion at the back of the bleachers, a Homer's Landing area that replaced seats with a newly placed bullpen and other things. Under DeWitt, Hanser, Baur and their financial associates, the new owners approved also for a reduction of seats, construction of a giant manual center-field scoreboard and pennants of the past in 1997—representing championship ball clubs and retired numbers. Even when faced with grim responsibility of losing money by hiking a heavy payroll, they agreed to pay for further improvements for 1998 and beyond. The drive for intimacy is a new look to an old concept as reflected in new stadiums. For instance, by Camden Yards in Baltimore and Jacobs Park in Cleveland.

Because of experimental limited interleague play, St. Louis got to see the American League's Central Division Indians in 1997, losing two out of three; the Chicago White Sox, winning two out of three, and the Minnesota Twins, victims in three straight. On the road, they won two out of three in a return trip of the I-70 Series at Kansas City, but then lost three straight to Milwaukee, long home of the Braves and

FORE!: They had better duck, as in golf, when Mark McGwire swings away toward the "Mac Attack Pack," the slogan of Busch Stadium bleacherites who always bring their own helmets.

later the Brewers who return to the NL in 1998.

For a disappointing '97, a season in which they treated .500 as a landmine, an obvious mark between teams going somewhere or going nowhere, the Cardinals had too few pluses, too many minuses and, apparently, too many injuries. So, for example, a gritty, gentlemanly guy, Willie McGee, the fans's favorite, had to play more than expected. The old pro hit .300 in 122 games. Delino DeShields, acquired by Jocketty as a free agent from Los Angeles, was a pleasant surprise, returning to his batting form, .295 and stealing 55 bases, even if at times his play at second base was spotty. DeShields and Clayton teamed well, rising above the injury that sidelined Tom Pagnozzi virtually all year and took far too many games away from Osborne and John Mabry.

THE EYES HAVE IT: *TV Guide*, nationally established weekly for boob-tube viewers, saluted the Cardinals before the 1996 playoff system with a catchy cover that included as players St. Louis's Andy Benes (left) and Hall of Fame prospect Ozzie Smith.

Others also were hurt, but one who rose out of the ashes after a shoulder injury was center fielder Ray Lankford, who hit 31 homers and drove in 98 runs. It's too bad that the RBIs weren't 100 and that slump at the end tagged him five points below .300. Lankford received the St. Louis baseball writers' Man-of-the-Year award, named for J. G. Taylor Spink, and young Matt Morris, looking as comfortable as if he had been there before, turned in a 12-9 record with a good 3.90 earned-run average. He became local Rookie-of-the-Year.

Before Todd Stottlemyre's arm wore down, requiring precautionary rest, Stott was 12-9, too, with a 3.88 ERA. Andy Benes, hurt early and late, was 10-7 with 3.10. Brother Alan, laid up longer, was 9-9 with the best starter's ERA, 2.89. Basically, among starters, except for Osborne, who missed far too much time with too many nagging injuries, the starters were good and unlucky. Good enough, usually, to keep the ball club into contention, unlucky because the Redbirds struggled too often to score more than two runs a game. And unless you're a Bob Gibson, a Dizzy Dean, a Sandy Koufax or, yeah, a Greg Maddux, you can't win with fewer than two.

Plagued by too many strikeouts and too little contact hitting, cutting down base-advancing team ball, the Cardinals missed most the hot season B. J. Jordan had in 1996. Maybe Jordan wouldn't have been so spectacular again with men on base or the bases loaded, but afflicted with a wrist injury that affected his swing, and a bad back, the kid with leadership qualities contributed in only 47 games, batting .247 without a homer and only 10 RBIs. Playing 139 games, Ron Gant hit only .229 with just 16 homers and 62 runs batted in. His strikeout total was a horrific 162. Catcher Tom Pagnozzi's virtual season-long absence was paramount. So when you get Osborne with only a 3-7 record and 4.93 ERA for just 14 games, you've got the 1-2-3-4 reasons for the decline—Jordan, Gant, Pagnozzi and Osborne—followed by the rest of the top 10, often combining injuries with disappointment. In this judgment they would be John Mabry, Alan Benes, Andy Benes, Todd Stottlemyre, Gary Gaetti—and attitude!

Attitude would best be summarized by hitters' resistance to cut down their swings, to make contact, to hit behind the runner and other niceties of team play—and winning baseball. The Cardinals are traditionally taught better in the minor-league circuit headed by guru George Kissell.

If you think it's possible to end a colorful history of a colorful ball club with a downbeat, even with the loss of Andy Benes, you don't have to be someone for whom the glass of life is always half full to be excited by the immediate and early outlook, headed for the next century, by the presence of Mark McGwire. The Cardinals lured the powerful slugger from Oakland on the last day of July with the A's having trouble financially keeping him. Bill DeWitt Jr. later met up with American League president Gene Budig. Condescendingly, Budig praised DeWitt for having tried to help down the stretch with a far outside chance by acquiring a rent-a-player slugger for a couple of million dollars. "Of course," said Budig, "we expect to have him back (in the American League) next year." That's what just about every Tom, Dick and Harriet thought, young and old. Gee, it's great to have that big good-looking red-headed guy swinging the most impressive home-run bat—for opportunity—since Babe Ruth, but, heck, he'll go to the highest bidder, perhaps King George Steinbrenner of the Yankees or Peter Angelos of the Orioles or maybe the Rockies would like to see if he could hit one over the roof at high-altitude Colorado. Or maybe the Chicago Tribune would gulp and decide how many Big Mac would hit at Wrigley Field, where back in 1930 Hack Wilson hit 56 and, yeah, where Orlando Cepeda said he could have "hit 50 ceench."

McGwire, son of a California dentist, attended the University of Southern California for a time as a pitcher, encouraged to try first base by several, including a man who became a dear friend, Joe Armstrong, who ran an Anchorage, Alaska summer semi-pro team for whom college kids played. At first base, McGwire would prove Lou Gehrig, Jimmy Foxx and Hank Greenberg reincarnate as a long-ball hitter. As a rookie for Oakland in 1987, he hit a record first-year man's total, 49, and blithely walked away from a chance to hit 50, achieved by few, because his wife was giving birth to the apple of the sentimental young man's life, son Matthew. "You'll always have another chance to hit 50 homers, but never a second chance to be there for your first born," said McGwire, divorced, who has no other son. Plagued by back troubles at times—he hit 42 in just 139 games in '92—Mark McGwire scaled that 50-homer heights at Oakland in 1996, but the team in city by the Bay was losing money, attendance and enthusiasm.

So he accepted the trade gracefully when Jocketty gave up promising T.J. Mathews and a few other players for what all thought would be temporary. Briefly, breaking into the National League, McGwire did nothing except, like the Babe before him, catch other players' attention with his gargantuan clouts in batting practice. Soon, beginning to hit where they counted, spectators wandered in early, the way it was years ago for 3 p.m. games when you could drop in at lunch. Gates opened early. On Tuesday, September 16, Jocketty and the Cardinals called an astonishing press conference. Big Mac—at 6-5 with 240 pounds giving him an armored breast-plate look—would stay with the Cardinals for three years and maybe a fourth. He could have robbed the store, but in the present day when the average bloke gets well past $1,000,000 a year, his request for $9,000,000 was one with which those middle-aged Redbird fans could live happily. Oh, yes, annually he would give away $1,000,000 of the sum to establish a foundation for physically and sexually abused kids and contribute, too, to the Cardinal Care that LaRussa and associate Ed Lewis brought in to aid Dr. Ted Savage's inner-city baseball program.

Standing there in the glare of lights, Big Mac did all right until he tried to explain his program, having previously praised St. Louis as a place both he and his dear son liked. "It's going to be something new for me," he said. "I'm real excited. It's going, hopefully, to deal with sexually and physically abused children...children..."

He blinked, gulped and stared in silence for 33 seconds, a long time, until a whisper brought him back, a smile to his teary eyes. As aptly put by Tom Timmerman in the *Post-Dispatch*, "And at that moment, as his emotions overcame him, as he lost his ability to speak and the tears welled into his eyes, Mark McGwire went from being popular to being loved."

Well-said, and followed that night remarkably when Big Mac stepped up to the plate for the first time as a confirmed Cardinal. The crowd was on its feet, applauding, as he stepped to the plate and still applauding as he did his thing, semi-crouched with the bat swishing low like the wiggle-waggle of a golfer at the driving tee.

ANNIVERSARY SPECIAL: For their 40th annual baseball writers' dinner – held on exact date of their first one, Jan. 20, 1958 – St. Louis scribes served an expanded souvenir program that, among others, featured Stan Musial's greatest season in '58 and the accomplishments in '97 of Ray Lankford as Player-of-the-Year and Mark McGwire for historic 58 homers.

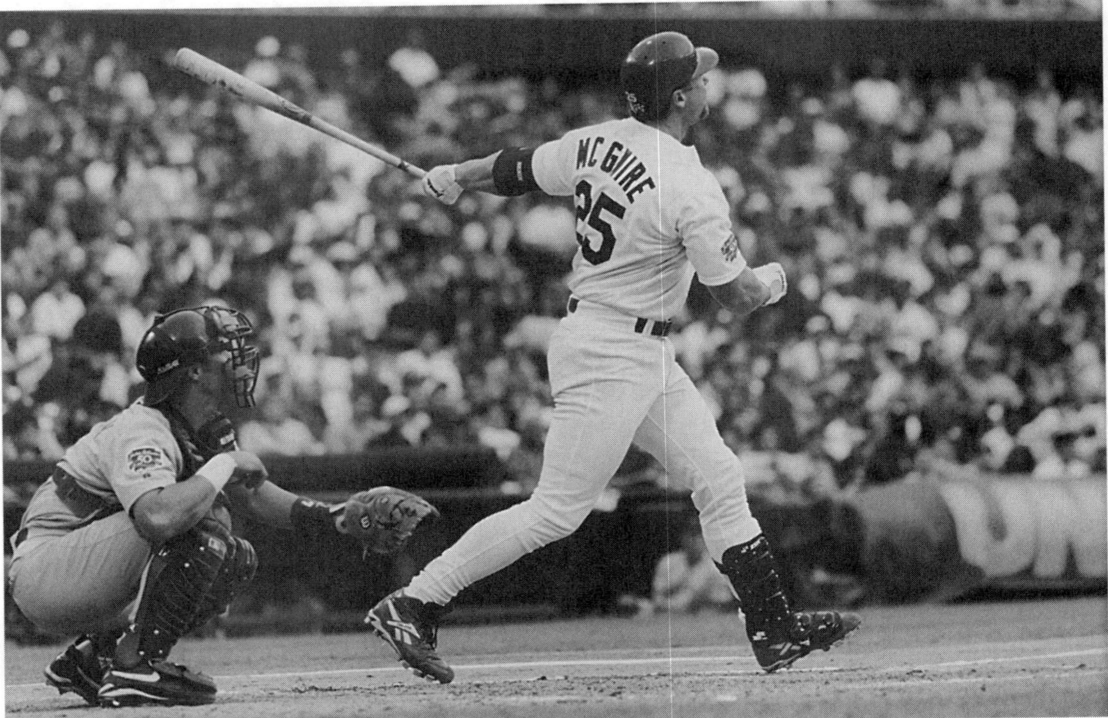

"58!": A magic number for righthanded hitters, only two of whom previously had reached that figure until, as caught by the lens of *Fowlball* Magazine's Jim Mense, Mark McGwire teed off in the final game of the 1997 season. Big Mac matched Jimmy Foxx, Philadelphia A's, 1932, and Hank Greenberg, Detroit, 1938. Only two players, lefthanded-hitting Babe Ruth and Roger Maris, ever hit more in a season, and only the Babe and Big Mac ever posted back-to-back seasons of 50 home runs.

If he yelled the traditional warning lingo of the links—"Fore!"—it would have been apt because it could have meant "four" as in "four bases." And, of course, duck out there in the bleachers, folks. Happily he rewarded the applauding crowd with a long, majestic drive.

Mark McGwire went on to hit 24 home runs for the Cardinals in 51 games, a total that reached his two-league 58 the last day of the season, two beyond Wilson's National League record, a total for the future. Only Jimmy Foxx and Hank Greenberg as righthanded hitters ever hit so many and only Roger Maris and Babe Ruth hit more in a season. But the big one so far was the second one that red-letter September day of significance for the Redbirds when he said he had come to stay and then to punctuate the glamorous story by hitting a virtual home run for abused kids and then hitting a real one for the fans that night. No wonder the next time Board Chairman Bill DeWitt No. 2 met Gene Budig, the American League President winced and said, "Congratulations, but tell Mark he'll receive no Christmas card."

For the Cardinals, with Mark McGwire, an all-around athlete and gifted first baseman dedicated to winning first, the weather for the Redbird future, barring the unexpected, became fair and warmer.

The All-Time Roster

ST. LOUIS CARDINALS
NATIONAL LEAGUE CHAMPIONS
1931

ABBOTT, ODY CLEON
Nickname: Ody, Toby
In St. Louis: 1910
M.L. Debut: 9/10/10

ABERNATHY, THEODORE WADE
Nickname: Ted
In St. Louis: 1970
Number: 40
M.L. Debut: 4/13/55

ADAMS, CHARLES BENJAMIN
Nickname: Babe
In St. Louis: 1906
M.L. Debut: 4/18/06

ADAMS, EARL JOHN
Nickname: Sparky
In St. Louis: 1930-33
Number: 1
M.L. Debut: 9/18/22

ADAMS, ELVIN CLARK
Nickname: Buster
In St. Louis: 1939, 43, 45-46
Number: 12, 18, 14
M.L. Debut: 4/27/39

ADAMS, JAMES J.
Nickname: Jim
In St. Louis: 1890
M.L. Debut: 4/21/1890

ADAMS, JOSEPH EDWARD
Nickname: Wagon Tongue, Joe
In St. Louis: 1902
M.L. Debut: 4/26/02

ADDUCI, JAMES DAVID
Nickname: Jim
In St. Louis: 1983
M.L. Debut: 9/12/83

ADKINSON, HENRY MAGEE
Nickname: Henry
In St. Louis: 1895
M.L. Debut: 9/25/1895

AGEE, TOMMIE LEE
Nickname: Tommie
In St. Louis: 1973
M.L. Debut: 9/14/62

AGOSTO, JUAN ROBERTO (GONZALEZ)
Nickname: Juan
In St. Louis: 1991-92
Number: 49
M.L. Debut: 9/7/81

AINSMITH, EDWARD WILBUR
Nickname: Eddie, Dorf
In St. Louis: 1921-23
M.L. Debut: 8/9/10

ALBA, GIBSON ALBERTO (ROSADO)
Nickname: Gibson
In St. Louis: 1988
M.L. Debut: 5/3/88

ALBERTS, FREDRICK JOSEPH
Nickname: Cy
In St. Louis: 1910
M.L. Debut: 9/17/10

ALEXANDER, GROVER CLEVELAND
Nickname: Pete
In St. Louis: 1926-29
M.L. Debut: 4/15/11

ALEXANDER, WILLIAM HENRY
Nickname: Nin
In St. Louis: 1884
M.L. Debut: 6/7/1884

ALICEA, LUIS RENE (DE JESUS)
Nickname: Luis
In St. Louis: 1988, 91-94, 96
Number: 18
M.L. Debut: 4/23/88

ALLEN, ETHAN NATHAN
Nickname: Ethan
In St. Louis: 1933
Number: 24
M.L. Debut: 6/21/26

ALLEN, NEIL PATRICK
Nickname: Neil
In St. Louis: 1983-85
Number: 13
M.L. Debut: 4/15/79

ALLEN, RICHARD ANTHONY
Nickname: Richie, Dick
In St. Louis: 1970
Number: 15
M.L. Debut: 9/3/63

ALLEN, RONALD FREDERICK
Nickname: Ron
In St. Louis: 1972
Number: 16
M.L. Debut: 8/11/72

ALOU, MATEO ROJAS
Nickname: Matty
In St. Louis: 1971-73
Number: 17
M.L. Debut: 9/26/60

ALSTON, THOMAS EDISON
Nickname: Tom
In St. Louis: 1954-57
Number: 10, 22
M.L. Debut: 4/13/54

ALSTON, WALTER EMMONS
Nickname: Walt, Smokey
In St. Louis: 1936
Number: 21
M.L. Debut: 9/27/36

ALTMAN, GEORGE LEE
Nickname: George
In St. Louis: 1963
Number: 26
M.L. Debut: 4/11/59

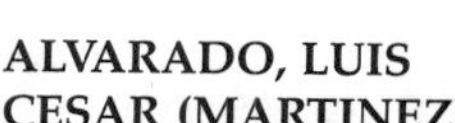

ALVARADO, LUIS CESAR (MARTINEZ)
Nickname: Pimba
In St. Louis: 1974, 76
Number: 1, 14
M.L. Debut: 9/13/68

ALYEA, GARRABRANT RYERSON
Nickname: Brant
In St. Louis: 1972
Number: 21
M.L. Debut: 9/11/65

AMARO, RUBEN SR. (MORA)
Nickname: Ruben
In St. Louis: 1958
Number: 19
M.L. Debut: 6/29/58

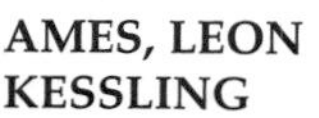

AMES, LEON KESSLING
Nickname: Red
In St. Louis: 1915-19
M.L. Debut: 9/14/03

ANDERSON, DWAIN CLEAVEN
Nickname: Dwain
In St. Louis: 1972-73
Number: 19
M.L. Debut: 9/3/71

ANDERSON, GEORGE JENDRUS
Nickname: Andy
In St. Louis: 1918
M.L. Debut: 5/26/14

ANDERSON, JOHN CHARLES
Nickname: John
In St. Louis: 1962
Number: 35
M.L. Debut: 8/17/58

ANDERSON, MICHAEL ALLEN
Nickname: Mike
In St. Louis: 1976-77
Number: 27
M.L. Debut: 9/2/71

ANDERSON, NORMAN CRAIG
Nickname: Criag
In St. Louis: 1961
Number: 47
M.L. Debut: 6/23/61

ANDERSON, FERRELL JACK
Nickname: Ferrell, Andy
In St. Louis: 1953
Number: 38
M.L. Debut: 4/16/46

ANDREWS, JOHN RICHARD
Nickname: John
In St. Louis: 1973
Number: 37
M.L. Debut: 4/8/73

ANDREWS, NATHAN HARDY
Nickname: Nate
In St. Louis: 1937, 39
Number: 29, 22
M.L. Debut: 5/1/37

ANDUJAR, JOAQUIN
Nickname: One Tough Dominican, Jack
In St. Louis: 1981-85
Number: 30, 47
M.L. Debut: 4/8/76

ANKENMAN, FREDERICK NORMAN
Nickname: Pat
In St. Louis: 1936
Number: 29
M.L. Debut: 4/16/36

ANTONELLI, JOHN LAWRENCE
Nickname: John
In St. Louis: 1944-45
Number: 18, 22
M.L. Debut: 9/16/44

ARNDT, HARRY J.
Nickname: Harry
In St. Louis: 1905-07
M.L. Debut: 7/2/02

ARNOLD, SCOTT GENTRY
Nickname: Scott
In St. Louis: 1988
Number: 41
M.L. Debut: 4/7/88

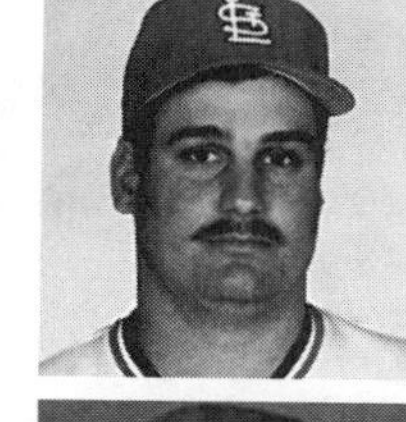

AROCHA, RENE (MAGALY)
Nickname: Rene
In St. Louis: 1993-95
Number: 43
M.L. Debut: 4/9/93

ARROYO, LUIS ENRIQUE
Nickname: YoYo
In St. Louis: 1955
Number: 38
M.L. Debut: 4/20/55

ARROYO, RUDOLPH
Nickname: Rudy
In St. Louis: 1971
Number: 43
M.L. Debut: 6/1/71

AUST, DENNIS KAY
Nickname: Dennis
In St. Louis: 1965-66
Number: 35
M.L. Debut: 9/6/65

AYALA, BENIGNO (FELIX)
Nickname: Benny
In St. Louis: 1977
M.L. Debut: 8/27/74

AYBAR, MANUEL ANTONIO
Nickname: Manny
In St. Louis: 1997
Number: 38
M.L. Debut: 8/4/97

BACKMAN, LESTER JOHN
Nickname: Les
In St. Louis: 1909-10
M.L. Debut: 7/3/09

BAILEY, PHILIP CORY
Nickname: Cory
In St. Louis: 1995-96
Number: 39
M.L. Debut: 9/1/93

BAILEY, WILLIAM F.
Nickname: Bill
In St. Louis: 1921-22
M.L. Debut: 9/17/07

BAIR, CHARLES DOUGLAS
Nickname: Doug
In St. Louis: 1981-83, 85
Number: 43, 40
M.L. Debut: 9/13/76

BAIRD, HOWARD DOUGLAS
Nickname: Doug
In St. Louis: 1917-19
M.L. Debut: 4/18/15

BAKENHASTER, DAVID LEE
Nickname: Dave
In St. Louis: 1964
Number: 43
M.L. Debut: 6/20/64

BAKER, STEVEN BYRNE
Nickname: Steve
In St. Louis: 1983
Number: 41
M.L. Debut: 5/25/78

BAKER, WILLIAM PRESLEY
Nickname: Bill
In St. Louis: 1948-49
Number: 15
M.L. Debut: 5/4/40

BALDWIN, ORSON F.
Nickname: Ollie
In St. Louis: 1908
M.L. Debut: 9/6/08

BALL, ARTHUR
Nickname: Art
In St. Louis: 1894
M.L. Debut: 8/1/1894

BANNON, JAMES HENRY
Nickname: Jimmy, Foxy Grandpa
In St. Louis: 1893
M.L. Debut: 6/15/1893

BARBEAU, WILLIAM JOSEPH
Nickname: Jap
In St. Louis: 1909-10
M.L. Debut: 9/27/05

BARBER, BRIAN SCOTT
Nickname: Brian
In St. Louis: 1995-96
Number: 52
M.L. Debut: 8/12/95

BARCLAY, GEORGE OLIVER
Nickname: George, Deerfoot
In St. Louis: 1902-04
M.L. Debut: 4/17/02

BARE, RAYMOND DOUGLAS
Nickname: Ray
In St. Louis: 1972-74
Number: 42, 40
M.L. Debut: 7/30/72

BARFOOT, CLYDE RAYMOND
Nickname: Clyde, Foots
In St. Louis: 1922-23
M.L. Debut: 4/13/22

BARGAR, GREG ROBERT
Nickname: Greg
In St. Louis: 1986
Number: 43
M.L. Debut: 7/17/83

BARKLEY, SAMUEL E.
Nickname: Sam
In St. Louis: 1885
M.L. Debut: 5/1/1884

BARLOW, MICHAEL ROSWELL
Nickname: Mike
In St. Louis: 1975
Number: 24, 27
M.L. Debut: 6/18/75

BARNES, FRANK
Nickname: Frank
In St. Louis: 1957-58, 60
Number: 27, 36
M.L. Debut: 9/22/57

BARNES, WILLIAM HENRY
Nickname: Skeeter
In St. Louis: 1987
Number: 59
M.L. Debut: 9/6/83

BARRETT, CHARLES HENRY
Nickname: Red
In St. Louis: 1945-46
Number: 13
M.L. Debut: 9/15/37

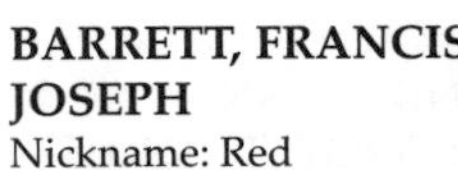

BARRETT, FRANCIS JOSEPH
Nickname: Red
In St. Louis: 1939
Number: 18
M.L. Debut: 10/1/39

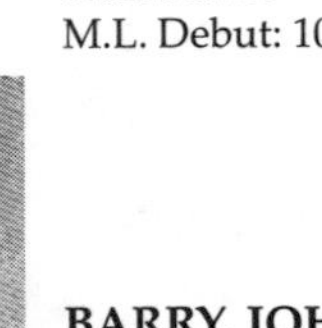

BARRY, JOHN C.
Nickname: Shad
In St. Louis: 1906-08
M.L. Debut: 5/30/1899

BARTOSCH, DAVID ROBERT
Nickname: Dave
In St. Louis: 1945
Number: 8
M.L. Debut: 4/28/45

BATCHELOR, RICHARD A.
Nickname: Rich
In St. Louis: 1993, 96
Number: 44
M.L. Debut: 9/3/93

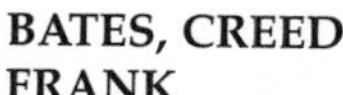

BATES, CREED FRANK
Nickname: Frank
In St. Louis: 1899
M.L. Debut: 10/7/1898

BATTLE, ALLEN ZELMO
Nickname: Allen
In St. Louis: 1995
Number: 35
M.L. Debut: 4/26/95

BAUTA, EDUARDO (GALVEZ)
Nickname: Eddie
In St. Louis: 1960-63
Number: 33, 38
M.L. Debut: 7/6/60

BAUTISTA, JOSE JOAQUIN (ARIAS)
Nickname: Jose
In St. Louis: 1997
Number: 33
M.L. Debut: 4/9/88

BAXTER, JOHN MORRIS
Nickname: John
In St. Louis: 1907
M.L. Debut: 4/19/07

BEALL, JOHN WOOLF
Nickname: Johnny
In St. Louis: 1918
M.L. Debut: 4/17/13

BEARD, RALPH WILLIAM
Nickname: Ralph
In St. Louis: 1954
Number: 39
M.L. Debut: 6/29/54

BEAUCHAMP, JAMES EDWARD
Nickname: Jim
In St. Louis: 1963, 70-71
Number: 17, 16
M.L. Debut: 9/22/63

BEAZLEY, JOHN ANDREW
Nickname: Johnny
In St. Louis: 1941-42, 46
Number: 21, 27
M.L. Debut: 9/28/41

BECK, ZINN BERTRAM
Nickname: Zinn
In St. Louis: 1913-16
M.L. Debut: 9/14/13

BECKLEY, JACOB PETER
Nickname: Jake, St. Jacob, Eagle Eye
In St. Louis: 1904-07
M.L. Debut: 6/20/1888

BECKMANN, WILLIAM ALOYSIUS
Nickname: Bill
In St. Louis: 1942
Number: 27
M.L. Debut: 5/2/39

BEEBE, FREDERICK LEONARD
Nickname: Fred
In St. Louis: 1906-09
M.L. Debut: 4/17/06

BEECHER, EDWARD
Nickname: Ed, Scrap Iron
In St. Louis: 1897
M.L. Debut: 9/26/1897

BEERS, CLARENCE SCOTT
Nickname: Clarence
In St. Louis: 1948
Number: 37
M.L. Debut: 5/2/48

BELL, DAVID MICHAEL
Nickname: David
In St. Louis: 1995-97
Number: 27
M.L. Debut: 5/3/95

BELL, HERMAN S.
Nickname: Hi
In St. Louis: 1924, 26-27, 29-30
M.L. Debut: 4/16/24

BELL, LESTER ROWLAND
Nickname: Les
In St. Louis: 1923-27
M.L. Debut: 9/18/23

BELLMAN, JOHN HUTCHINS
Nickname: John, Happy Jack
In St. Louis: 1889
M.L. Debut: 4/23/1889

BELTRAN, RIGOBERTO
Nickname: Rigo
In St. Louis: 1997
Number: 53
M.L. Debut: 5/21/97

BENES, ALAN PAUL
Nickname: Alan
In St. Louis: 1995-97
Number: 41
M.L. Debut: 9/19/95

BENES, ANDREW CHARLES
Nickname: Andy
In St. Louis: 1996-97
Number: 40
M.L. Debut: 8/11/89

BENES, JOSEPH ANTHONY
Nickname: Joe, Bananas
In St. Louis: 1931
M.L. Debut: 5/9/31

BENNETT, JUSTIN TITUS
Nickname: Pug
In St. Louis: 1906-07
M.L. Debut: 4/12/06

BENSON, VERNON ADAIR
Nickname: Vern
In St. Louis: 1951-53
Number: 25, 19
M.L. Debut: 7/31/43

BENTON, SIDNEY WRIGHT
Nickname: Sid
In St. Louis: 1922
M.L. Debut: 4/18/22

BERBLINGER, JEFFREY J.
Nickname: Jeff
In St. Louis: 1997
Number: 56
M.L. Debut: 9/2/97

BERGAMO, AUGUST SAMUEL
Nickname: Augie
In St. Louis: 1944-45
Number: 17
M.L. Debut: 4/25/44

BERLY, JOHN C.
Nickname: Jack
In St. Louis: 1924
M.L. Debut: 4/22/24

BERNARD, JOSEPH CARL
Nickname: Joe, J.C.
In St. Louis: 1909
M.L. Debut: 9/23/09

BERTAINA, FRANK LOUIS
Nickname: Frank
In St. Louis: 1970
Number: 21
M.L. Debut: 8/1/64

BERTE, HARRY THOMAS
Nickname: Harry
In St. Louis: 1903
M.L. Debut: 9/17/03

BESCHER, ROBERT HENRY
Nickname: Bob
In St. Louis: 1915-17
M.L. Debut: 9/5/08

BETCHER, FRANKLIN LYLE
Nickname: Franklin
In St. Louis: 1910
M.L. Debut: 5/21/10

BETTS, HAROLD MATTHEW
Nickname: Hal, Chubby, Ginger
In St. Louis: 1903
M.L. Debut: 9/22/03

BETZEL, CHRISTIAN FREDERICK
Nickname: Bruno
In St. Louis: 1914-18
M.L. Debut: 9/13/14

BIBBY, JAMES BLAIR
Nickname: Jim
In St. Louis: 1972-73
Number: 48
M.L. Debut: 9/4/72

BIERBAUER, LOUIS W.
Nickname: Lou
In St. Louis: 1897-98
M.L. Debut: 4/17/1886

BILKO, STEVEN THOMAS
Nickname: Steve
In St. Louis: 1949-54
Number: 5
M.L. Debut: 9/22/49

BILLINGS, RICHARD ARLIN
Nickname: Dick
In St. Louis: 1974-75
Number: 12, 16
M.L. Debut: 9/11/68

BIRD, FRANK ZEPHERIN
Nickname: Dodo
In St. Louis: 1892
M.L. Debut: 4/16/1892

BLADES, FRANCIS RAYMOND
Nickname: Ray
In St. Louis: 1922-28, 30-32
Number: 7,17
M.L. Debut: 8/19/22

BLAKE, HARRY COOPER
Nickname: Harry, Dude
In St. Louis: 1899
M.L. Debut: 7/7/1894

BLAKE, JOHN FREDERICK
Nickname: Sheriff
In St. Louis: 1937
Number: 27
M.L. Debut: 6/29/20

BLANK, FRANK IGNATZ
Nickname: Coonie
In St. Louis: 1909
M.L. Debut: 8/15/09

BLASINGAME, DON LEE
Nickname: Don, The Blazer
In St. Louis: 1955-59
Number: 3,11
M.L. Debut: 9/20/55

BLATNIK, JOHN LOUIS
Nickname: Johnny, Chief
In St. Louis: 1950
Number: 35
M.L. Debut: 4/21/48

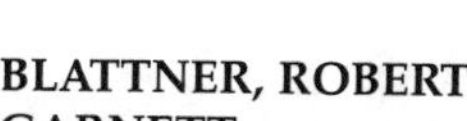

BLATTNER, ROBERT GARNETT
Nickname: Buddy
In St. Louis: 1942
Number: 2
M.L. Debut: 4/18/42

BLAYLOCK, GARY NELSON
Nickname: Gary
In St. Louis: 1959
Number: 44
M.L. Debut: 4/10/59

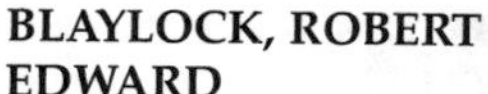

BLAYLOCK, ROBERT EDWARD
Nickname: Bob
In St. Louis: 1956, 59
Number: 24
M.L. Debut: 7/22/56

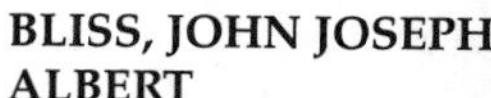

BLISS, JOHN JOSEPH ALBERT
Nickname: Jack
In St. Louis: 1908-12
M.L. Debut: 5/10/08

BLOOMFIELD, CLYDE STALCUP
Nickname: Clyde, Bud
In St. Louis: 1963
Number: 19
M.L. Debut: 9/25/63

BOARDMAN, CHARLES LOUIS
Nickname: Charlie
In St. Louis: 1915
M.L. Debut: 9/26/13

BOEVER, JOSEPH MARTIN
Nickname: Joe
In St. Louis: 1985-86
Number: 36
M.L. Debut: 7/19/85

BOHNE, SAMUEL ARTHUR
Nickname: Sammy
In St. Louis: 1916
M.L. Debut: 9/9/16

BOKELMANN, RICHARD WERNER
Nickname: Dick
In St. Louis: 1951-53
Number: 25
M.L. Debut: 8/3/51

BOLDEN, WILLIAM HORACE
Nickname: Bill, Big Bill
In St. Louis: 1919
M.L. Debut: 6/27/19

BOLLWEG, DONALD RAYMOND
Nickname: Don
In St. Louis: 1950-51
Number: 40
M.L. Debut: 9/28/50

BONDS, BOBBY LEE
Nickname: Bobby
In St. Louis: 1980
Number: 00
M.L. Debut: 6/25/68

BONNER, FRANK J.
Nickname: Frank, The Human Flea
In St. Louis: 1895
M.L. Debut: /26/1894

BOOKER, RODERICK STEWART
Nickname: Rod
In St. Louis: 1987-89
Number: 5, 10
M.L. Debut: 4/29/87

BORBON, PEDRO (RODRIGUEZ)
Nickname: Pedro
In St. Louis: 1980
M.L. Debut: 4/9/69

BORDAGARAY, STANLEY GEORGE
Nickname: Frenchy
In St. Louis: 1937-38
Number: 14
M.L. Debut: 4/17/34

BORDERS, PATRICK LANCE
Nickname: Pat
In St. Louis: 1996
Number: 38
M.L. Debut: 4/6/88

BOSETTI, RICHARD ALAN
Nickname: Rick
In St. Louis: 1977
Number: 21
M.L. Debut: 9/9/76

BOTTOMLEY, JAMES LEROY
Nickname: Sunny Jim
In St. Louis: 1922-32
Number: 5, 4
M.L. Debut: 8/18/22

BOWMAN, ROBERT JAMES
Nickname: Bob
In St. Louis: 1939-40
Number: 26
M.L. Debut: 4/21/39

BOYER, CLOYD VICTOR
Nickname: Junior
In St. Louis: 1949-52
Number: 24
M.L. Debut: 4/23/49

BOYER, KENTON LLOYD
Nickname: Ken
In St. Louis: 1955-65
Number: 14
M.L. Debut: 4/12/55

BOYLE, JOHN ANTHONY
Nickname: Jack, Honest Jack
In St. Louis: 1887-89, 91
M.L. Debut: 10/8/1886

BRADFORD, CHARLES WILLIAM
Nickname: Buddy
In St. Louis: 1975
Number: 12
M.L. Debut: 9/9/66

BRADSHAW, TERRY LEON
Nickname: Terry
In St. Louis: 1995-96
Number: 55
M.L. Debut: 5/4/95

BRAIN, DAVID LEONARD
Nickname: Dave
In St. Louis: 1903-05
M.L. Debut: 4/24/01

BRANCH, HARVEY ALFRED
Nickname: Harvey
In St. Louis: 1962
Number: 40
M.L. Debut: 9/18/62

BRANDT, JOHN GEORGE
Nickname: Jackie
In St. Louis: 1956
Number: 21
M.L. Debut: 4/21/56

BRASHEAR, ROY PARKS
Nickname: Roy
In St. Louis: 1902
M.L. Debut: 4/25/02

BRATCHER, JOSEPH WARLICK
Nickname: Joe, Goobers
In St. Louis: 1924
M.L. Debut: 8/26/24

BRAUN, STEPHEN RUSSELL
Nickname: Steve
In St. Louis: 1981-85
Number: 26
M.L. Debut: 4/6/71

BRAZLE, ALPHA EUGENE
Nickname: Al, Cotton
In St. Louis: 1943, 46-54
Number: 27, 36, 16, 11
M.L. Debut: 7/25/43

BRECHEEN, HARRY
Nickname: Harry, Harry the Cat
In St. Louis: 1940, 43-52
Number: 32
M.L. Debut: 4/22/40

BREITENSTEIN, THEODORE P.
Nickname: Ted, Theo
In St. Louis: 1891-96, 1901
M.L. Debut: 4/28/1891

BREMER, HERBERT FREDERICK
Nickname: Herb, Butch
In St. Louis: 1937-39
Number: 11, 13
M.L. Debut: 9/16/37

BRESNAHAN, ROGER PHILLIP
Nickname: The Duke of Tralee
In St. Louis: 1909-12
M.L. Debut: 8/27/1897

BRESSLER, RAYMOND BLOOM
Nickname: Rube
In St. Louis: 1932
M.L. Debut: 4/24/14

BRESSOUD, EDWARD
Nickname: Ed
In St. Louis: 1967
Number: 11
M.L. Debut: 6/14/56

BREWER, RODNEY LEE
Nickname: Rod
In St. Louis: 1990-93
Number: 58, 33
M.L. Debut: 9/5/90

BRIDGES, EVERETT LAMAR
Nickname: Rocky
In St. Louis: 1960
Number: 30
M.L. Debut: 4/17/51

BRIDGES, MARSHALL
Nickname: Sheriff
In St. Louis: 1959-60
Number: 30
M.L. Debut: 6/17/59

BRIGGS, GRANT
Nickname: Grant
In St. Louis: 1892
M.L. Debut: 4/17/1890

BRILES, NELSON KELLEY
Nickname: Nellie
In St. Louis: 1965-70
Number: 34
M.L. Debut: 4/19/65

BRINKMAN, EDWIN ALBERT
Nickname: Ed
In St. Louis: 1975
Number: 5
M.L. Debut: 9/6/61

BROCK, JOHN ROY
Nickname: John
In St. Louis: 1917-18
M.L. Debut: 8/10/17

BROCK, LOUIS CLARK
Nickname: Lou
In St. Louis: 1964-79
Number: 20
M.L. Debut: 9/10/61

BRODIE, WALTER SCOTT
Nickname: Steve
In St. Louis: 1892-93
M.L. Debut: 4/21/1890

BROGLIO, ERNEST GILBERT
Nickname: Ernie
In St. Louis: 1959-64
Number: 32
M.L. Debut: 4/11/59

BRONKIE, HERMAN CHARLES
Nickname: Dutch
In St. Louis: 1918
M.L. Debut: 9/20/10

BROSNAN, JAMES PATRICK
Nickname: Jim, Professor
In St. Louis: 1958-59
Number: 37
M.L. Debut: 4/15/54

BROTTEM, ANTON CHRISTIAN
Nickname: Tony
In St. Louis: 1916, 18
M.L. Debut: 4/17/16

BROUGHTON, CECIL CALVERT
Nickname: Cal
In St. Louis: 1885
M.L. Debut: 5/2/1883

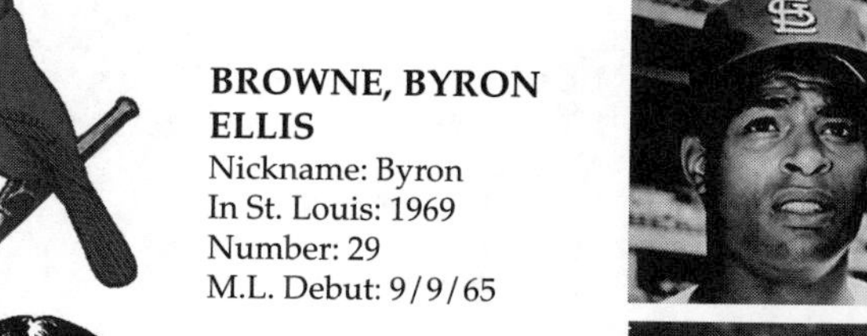

BROWN, CHARLES EDWARD
Nickname: Buster, Yank
In St. Louis: 1905-07
M.L. Debut: 6/22/05

BROWN, EDWARD P.
Nickname: Ed
In St. Louis: 1882
M.L. Debut: 8/19/1882

BROWN, JAMES DONALDSON
Nickname: Don, Moose
In St. Louis: 1915
M.L. Debut: 9/13/15

ST. LOUIS CARDINALS
NATIONAL LEAGUE CHAMPIONS
1931

BROWN, JAMES ROBERSON
Nickname: Jimmy
In St. Louis: 1937-43
Number: 15, 3
M.L. Debut: 4/23/37

BROWN, MORDICAI PETER CENTENNIAL
Nickname: Three Finger, Minor
In St. Louis: 1903
M.L. Debut: 4/19/03

BROWN, THOMAS TARLTON
Nickname: Handsome
In St. Louis: 1895
M.L. Debut: 7/6/1882

BROWN, WILLIARD
Nickname: Big Bill, California Brown
In St. Louis: 1894
M.L. Debut: 5/10/1887

BROWNE, BYRON ELLIS
Nickname: Byron
In St. Louis: 1969
Number: 29
M.L. Debut: 9/9/65

BROWNING, CALVIN DUANE
Nickname: Cal
In St. Louis: 1960
Number: 23
M.L. Debut: 6/12/60

BROWNING, LOUIS ROGERS
Nickname: Pete, The Gladiator
In St. Louis: 1894
M.L. Debut: 5/2/1882

BRUMMER, GLENN EDWARD
Nickname: Glenn
In St. Louis: 1981-84
Number: 11
M.L. Debut: 5/25/81

BRUNANSKY, THOMAS ANDREW
Nickname: Tom, Bruno
In St. Louis: 1988-90
Number: 23
M.L. Debut: 4/9/81

BRUNET, GEORGE STUART
Nickname: Lefty
In St. Louis: 1971
Number: 34
M.L. Debut: 9/14/56

BRUNO, THOMAS MICHAEL
Nickname: Tom
In St. Louis: 1978-79
Number: 49
M.L. Debut: 8/1/76

BRYANT, RONALD RAYMOND
Nickname: Ron, Bear
In St. Louis: 1975
Number: 32
M.L. Debut: 9/29/67

BUCHA, JOHN GEORGE
Nickname: Johnny
In St. Louis: 1948-50
Number: 24, 15
M.L. Debut: 5/2/48

BUCHEK, GERALD PETER
Nickname: Jerry
In St. Louis: 1961, 63-65
Number: 17, 11
M.L. Debut: 6/30/61

BUCHER, JAMES QUINTER
Nickname: Jim
In St. Louis: 1938
M.L. Debut: 4/18/34

BUCKELS, GARY S.
Nickname: Gary
In St. Louis: 1994
M.L. Debut: 7/23/94

BUCKLEY, RICHARD D.
Nickname: Dick
In St. Louis: 1892-94
M.L. Debut: 4/20/1888

BUELOW, FREDERICK W.
Nickname: Fritz
In St. Louis: 1899-1900
M.L. Debut: 9/28/1899

BURBRINK, NELSON EDWARD
Nickname: Nels
In St. Louis: 1955
Number: 18
M.L. Debut: 6/5/55

BURCH, ALBERT WILLIAM
Nickname: Al, Cotton
In St. Louis: 1906-07
M.L. Debut: 6/19/06

BURDA, EDWARD ROBERT
Nickname: Bob
In St. Louis: 1962, 71
Number: 24, 10
M.L. Debut: 8/25/62

BURDETTE, SELVA LEWIS
Nickname: Lew
In St. Louis: 1963-64
Number: 33
M.L. Debut: 9/26/50

BURGESS, THOMAS ROLAND
Nickname: Tom, Hockey Legs
In St. Louis: 1954
Number: 28
M.L. Debut: 4/17/54

BURK, CHARLES SANFORD
Nickname: Sandy
In St. Louis: 1912-13
M.L. Debut: 9/12/10

BURKE, JAMES TIMOTHY
Nickname: Sunset Jimmy
In St. Louis: 1899, 1903-05
M.L. Debut: 10/6/1898

BURKE, JOSEPH A.
Nickname: Joe
In St. Louis: 1890
M.L. Debut: 9/19/1890

BURKE, LEO PATRICK
Nickname: Leo
In St. Louis: 1963
Number: 18
M.L. Debut: 9/7/58

BURKETT, JESSE CAIL
Nickname: Jesse, The Crab
In St. Louis: 1899-1901
M.L. Debut: 4/22/1890

BURKHART, KENNETH WILLIAM
Nickname: Ken
In St. Louis: 1945, 48
Number: 10
M.L. Debut: 4/21/45

BURNETT, JOHN P.
Nickname: Jack
In St. Louis: 1907
M.L. Debut: 7/2/07

BURNS, EDWARD JAMES
Nickname: Ed
In St. Louis: 1912
M.L. Debut: 6/25/12

BURNS, JAMES
Nickname: Farmer, Slab
In St. Louis: 1901
M.L. Debut: 7/6/01

BURNS, TODD EDWARD
Nickname: Todd
In St. Louis: 1993
M.L. Debut: 5/31/88

BURRELL, HARRY J.
Nickname: Harry
In St. Louis: 1891
M.L. Debut: 9/13/1891

BURRIS, BETRAM RAY
Nickname: Ray
In St. Louis: 1986
Number: 35
M.L. Debut: 4/8/73

BURTON, ELLIS NARRINGTON
Nickname: Ellis
In St. Louis: 1958, 60
Number: 11
M.L. Debut: 9/18/58

BUSBY, MICHAEL JAMES
Nickname: Mike
In St. Louis: 1996-97
Number: 62
M.L. Debut: 4/7/96

BUSH, GUY TERRELL
Nickname: Guy, The Mississippi Mudcat
In St. Louis: 1938
M.L. Debut: 9/17/23

BUSHONG, ALBERT JOHN
Nickname: Doc
In St. Louis: 1885-87
M.L. Debut: 7/19/1875

BUSSE, RAYMOND EDWARD
Nickname: Ray
In St. Louis: 1973
Number: 5
M.L. Debut: 7/24/71

BUTLER, ARTHUR EDWARD
Nickname: Art
In St. Louis: 1914-16
M.L. Debut: 4/14/11

BUTLER, JOHN ALBERT
Nickname: John
In St. Louis: 1904
M.L. Debut: 9/28/01

BUTLER, JOHN STEPHEN
Nickname: Johnny, Trolley Line
In St. Louis: 1929
M.L. Debut: 4/18/26

BYERLY, ELDRED WILLIAM
Nickname: Bud
In St. Louis: 1943-45
Number: 27
M.L. Debut: 9/26/43

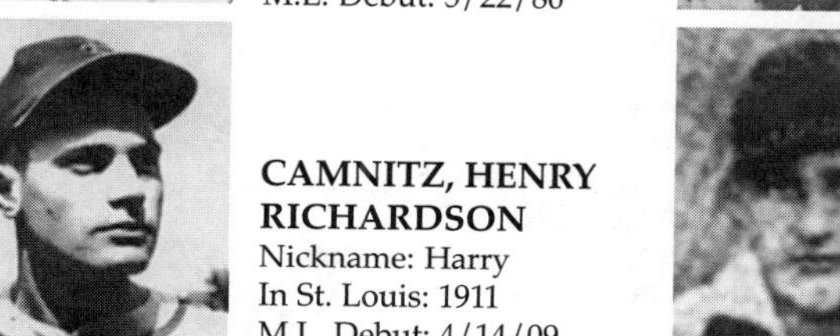

BYERS, JAMES WILLIAM
Nickname: Bill, Big Bill
In St. Louis: 1904
M.L. Debut: 4/15/04

Byers has trouble with Corbett's fast ones.

BYRNE, ROBERT MATTHEW
Nickname: Bobby
In St. Louis: 1907-09
M.L. Debut: 4/11/07

CABRERA, ALFREDO A.
Nickname: Al
In St. Louis: 1913
M.L. Debut: 5/16/13

CALHOUN, JOHN CHARLES
Nickname: Jack, Red
In St. Louis: 1902
M.L. Debut: 6/27/02

CALLAHAN, JAMES W.
Nickname: Jim
In St. Louis: 1898
M.L. Debut: 9/3/1898

CALLAHAN, WESLEY LEROY
Nickname: Wes
In St. Louis: 1913
M.L. Debut: 9/7/13

CAMACHO, ERNEST CARLOS
Nickname: Ernie
In St. Louis: 1990
Number: 62
M.L. Debut: 5/22/80

CAMNITZ, HENRY RICHARDSON
Nickname: Harry
In St. Louis: 1911
M.L. Debut: 4/14/09

CAMP, LLEWELLYN ROBERT
Nickname: Lew
In St. Louis: 1892
M.L. Debut: 8/26/1892

CAMPAU, CHARLES COLUMBUS
Nickname: Count
In St. Louis: 1890
M.L. Debut: 7/7/1888

CAMPBELL, DAVID WILSON
Nickname: Dave
In St. Louis: 1973
Number: 18
M.L. Debut: 9/17/67

CAMPBELL, JAMES ROBERT JR.
Nickname: Jim
In St. Louis: 1970
Number: 10
M.L. Debut: 4/11/70

CAMPBELL, WILLIAM JAMES
Nickname: Billy
In St. Louis: 1905
M.L. Debut: 4/17/05

CAMPBELL, WILLIAM RICHARD
Nickname: Bill
In St. Louis: 1985
M.L. Debut: 7/14/73

CAMPISI, SALVATORE JOHN
Nickname: Sal
In St. Louis: 1969-70
Number: 30
M.L. Debut: 8/15/69

CANNIZZARO, CHRISTOPHER
Nickname: Chris
In St. Louis: 1960-61
Number: 34
M.L. Debut: 4/17/60

CANSECO, OSVALDO (CAPAS)
Nickname: Ozzie
In St. Louis: 1992-93
Number: 46
M.L. Debut: 7/18/90

CAPILLA, DOUGLAS EDMUND
Nickname: Doug
In St. Louis: 1976-77
Number: 26
M.L. Debut: 9/12/76

CARABALLO, RAMON (SANCHEZ)
Nickname: Ramon
In St. Louis: 1995
Number: 10
M.L. Debut: 9/9/93

CARBO, BERNARDO
Nickname: Bernie
In St. Louis: 1972-73, 79-80
Number: 12, 1, 11
M.L. Debut: 9/2/69

CARDENAL, JOSE ROSARIO DOMEC
Nickname: Jose
In St. Louis: 1970-71
Number: 1
M.L. Debut: 4/14/63

CARLETON, JAMES OTTO
Nickname: Tex
In St. Louis: 1932-34
Number: 18, 15
M.L. Debut: 4/17/32

CARLTON, STEVEN NORMAN
Nickname: Steve, Lefty
In St. Louis: 1965-71
Number: 32
M.L. Debut: 4/12/65

CARMEL, LEON JAMES
Nickname: Duke
In St. Louis: 1959-60, 63
Number: 43, 28
M.L. Debut: 9/10/59

CARPENTER, CRIS HOWELL
Nickname: Cris
In St. Louis: 1988-92
Number: 44
M.L. Debut: 5/14/88

CARPENTER, WARREN WILLIAM
Nickname: Hick
In St. Louis: 1892
M.L. Debut: 5/1/1879

CARR,CHARLES LEE GLENN
Nickname: Chuck
In St. Louis: 1992
Number: 43
M.L. Debut: 4/28/90

CARROLL, CLAY PALMER
Nickname: Hawk
In St. Louis: 1977
Number: 33
M.L. Debut: 9/2/64

CARROLL, SAMUEL CLIFFORD
Nickname: Cliff
In St. Louis: 1892
M.L. Debut: 8/31/1882

CARSEY, WILFRED
Nickname: Kid
In St. Louis: 1897-98
M.L. Debut: 4/8/1891

CARTWRIGHT, EDWARD CHARLES
Nickname: Ed, Jumbo
In St. Louis: 1890
M.L. Debut: 7/10/1890

CARUTHERS, ROBERT LEE
Nickname: Parisian Bob
In St. Louis: 1884-87, 92
M.L. Debut: 9/7/1884

CASTIGLIONE, PETER PAUL
Nickname: Pete
In St. Louis: 1953-54
Number: 1
M.L. Debut: 9/10/47

CATER, DANNY ANDERSON
Nickname: Danny
In St. Louis: 1975
Number: 7
M.L. Debut: 4/14/64

CATHER, THEODORE PHYSICK
Nickname: Ted
In St. Louis: 1912-14
M.L. Debut: 9/23/12

CEDENO, CESAR (ENCARNACION)
Nickname: Cesar
In St. Louis: 1985
Number: 7
M.L. Debut: 6/20/70

CEPEDA, ORLANDO MANUEL (PENNE)
Nickname: Cha-Cha, The Baby Bull
In St. Louis: 1966-68
Number: 28, 30
M.L. Debut: 4/15/58

CHAMBERLAIN, ELTON P.
Nickname: Icebox
In St. Louis: 1888-90
M.L. Debut: 9/13/1886

CHAMBERS, CLIFFORD DAY
Nickname: Cliff, Lefty
In St. Louis: 1951-53
Number: 28
M.L. Debut: 4/24/48

CHAMBERS, JOHNNIE MONROE
Nickname: John
In St. Louis: 1937
Number: 31
M.L. Debut: 5/4/37

CHAMBERS, WILLIAM CHRISTOPHER
Nickname: Bill
In St. Louis: 1910
M.L. Debut: 7/11/10

CHANT, CHARLES JOSEPH
Nickname: Charlie
In St. Louis: 1976
Number: 28
M.L. Debut: 9/12/75

CHARLES, RAYMOND
Nickname: Chappy, Charles Shuh Achenbach
In St. Louis: 1908-09
M.L. Debut: 4/15/08

CHENEY, THOMAS EDGAR
Nickname: Tom
In St. Louis: 1957, 59
Number: 38
M.L. Debut: 4/21/57

CHILDS, CLARENCE ALGERNON
Nickname: Cupid
In St. Louis: 1899
M.L. Debut: 4/23/1888

CHILDS, GEORGE PETER
Nickname: Pete
In St. Louis: 1901
M.L. Debut: 4/24/01

CHITTUM, NELSON BOYD
Nickname: Nels
In St. Louis: 1958
Number: 27
M.L. Debut: 8/17/58

CHLUPSA, ROBERT JOSEPH
Nickname: Bob
In St. Louis: 1970-71
Number: 40
M.L. Debut: 7/16/70

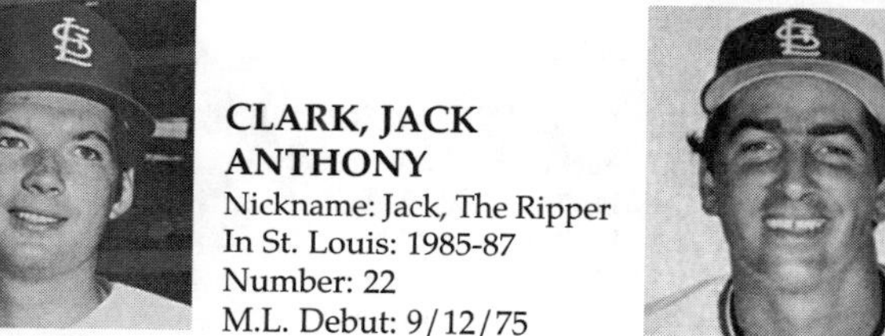

CIAFFONE, LAWRENCE T.
Nickname: Larry, Symphony
In St. Louis: 1951
Number: 34
M.L. Debut: 4/17/51

CICOTTE, ALVA WARREN
Nickname: Al, Bozo
In St. Louis: 1961
Number: 33
M.L. Debut: 4/22/57

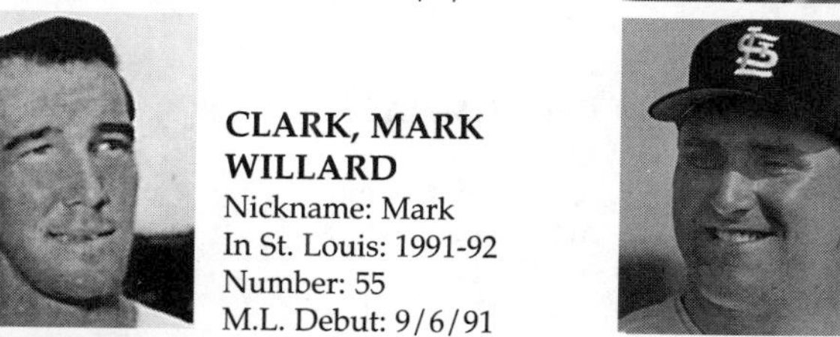

CIMOLI, GINO NICHOLAS
Nickname: Gino
In St. Louis: 1959
Number: 22
M.L. Debut: 4/19/56

CIMORELLI, FRANK THOMAS
Nickname: Frank
In St. Louis: 1994
Number: 58
M.L. Debut: 4/30/94

CITARELLA, RALPH ALEXANDER
Nickname: Ralph
In St. Louis: 1983-84
Number: 43
M.L. Debut: 9/13/83

CLAREY, DOUGLAS WILLIAM
Nickname: Doug
In St. Louis: 1976
M.L. Debut: 4/20/76

CLARK, DANIEL CURRAN
Nickname: Danny
In St. Louis: 1927
M.L. Debut: 4/12/22

CLARK, JACK ANTHONY
Nickname: Jack, The Ripper
In St. Louis: 1985-87
Number: 22
M.L. Debut: 9/12/75

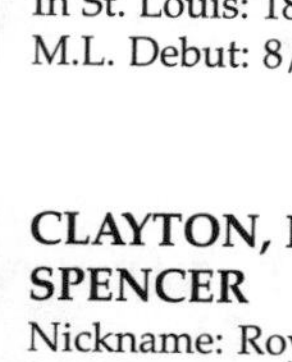

CLARK, JAMES FRANCIS
Nickname: Jim
In St. Louis: 1911-12
M.L. Debut: 9/2/11

CLARK, MARK WILLARD
Nickname: Mark
In St. Louis: 1991-92
Number: 55
M.L. Debut: 9/6/91

CLARK, MICHAEL JOHN
Nickname: Mike
In St. Louis: 1952-53
Number: 22
M.L. Debut: 7/27/52

CLARK, PHILLIP JAMES
Nickname: Phil
In St. Louis: 1958-59
Number: 22, 36
M.L. Debut: 4/15/58

CLARKE, JOSHUA BALDWIN
Nickname: Josh, Pepper
In St. Louis: 1905
M.L. Debut: 6/15/1898

CLARKE, STANLEY MARTIN
Nickname: Stan
In St. Louis: 1990
Number: 61
M.L. Debut: 6/7/83

CLARKSON, ARTHUR HAMILTON
Nickname: Dad
In St. Louis: 1893-95
M.L. Debut: 8/20/1891

CLAYTON, ROYCE SPENCER
Nickname: Royce
In St. Louis: 1996-97
Number: 11
M.L. Debut: 9/20/91

CLEMENS, DOUGLAS HORACE
Nickname: Doug
In St. Louis: 1960-64
Number: 38, 40, 22
M.L. Debut: 10/2/60

CLEMENTS, JOHN J.
Nickname: Jack
In St. Louis: 1898
M.L. Debut: 4/22/1884

CLEMONS, LANCE LEVIS
Nickname: Lance
In St. Louis: 1972
Number: 47
M.L. Debut: 8/12/71

CLEMONS, VERNE JAMES
Nickname: Verne, Tubby, Stinger
In St. Louis: 1919-24
M.L. Debut: 4/22/16

CLENDENON, DONN ALVIN
Nickname: Donn
In St. Louis: 1972
Number: 16
M.L. Debut: 9/22/61

CLEVELAND, REGINALD LESLIE
Nickname: Reggie
In St. Louis: 1969-73
Number: 22
M.L. Debut: 10/1/69

CLONINGER, TONY LEE
Nickname: Tony
In St. Louis: 1972
Number: 25
M.L. Debut: 6/15/61

CLOUGH, EDGAR GEORGE
Nickname: Ed, Spec
In St. Louis: 1924-26
M.L. Debut: 8/28/24

COLE, RICHARD ROY
Nickname: Dick
In St. Louis: 1951
Number: 15
M.L. Debut: 4/27/51

COLEMAN, JOHN
Nickname: John
In St. Louis: 1895
M.L. Debut: 9/25/1895

COLEMAN, PIERCE D.
Nickname: Percy
In St. Louis: 1897
M.L. Debut: 7/2/1897

COLEMAN, VINCENT MAURICE
Nickname: Vince
In St. Louis: 1985-90
Number: 29
M.L. Debut: 4/18/85

COLES, DARNELL
Nickname: Darnell
In St. Louis: 1995
Number: 7
M.L. Debut: 9/4/83

COLLINS, DAVID SCOTT
Nickname: Dave
In St. Louis: 1990
Number: 15
M.L. Debut: 6/7/75

COLLINS, JAMES ANTHONY
Nickname: The Ripper
In St. Louis: 1931-36
Number: 8, 12, 14
M.L. Debut: 4/18/31

COLLINS, PHILLIP E.
Nickname: Phil, Fidgety Phil
In St. Louis: 1935
Number: 28
M.L. Debut: 10/7/23

COLLINS, WILLIAM J.
Nickname: Bill
In St. Louis: 1892
M.L. Debut: 10/5/1889

COLLUM, JACK DEAN
Nickname: Jackie
In St. Louis: 1951-53, 56
Number: 32
M.L. Debut: 9/21/51

COLUCCIO, ROBERT PASQUAILI
Nickname: Bob
In St. Louis: 1978
M.L. Debut: 4/15/73

COMISKEY, CHARLES ALBERT
Nickname: Commy, The Old Roman
In St. Louis: 1882-89, 91
M.L. Debut: 5/2/1882

CONNOR, JOSEPH FRANCIS
Nickname: Joe
In St. Louis: 1895
M.L. Debut: 9/9/1895

CONNOR, ROGER
Nickname: Roger
In St. Louis: 1894-97
M.L. Debut: 5/1/1880

CONROY, TIMOTHY JAMES
Nickname: Tim
In St. Louis: 1986-87
Number: 39, 40
M.L. Debut: 6/23/78

CONWELL, EDWARD JAMES
Nickname: Ed, Irish
In St. Louis: 1911
M.L. Debut: 9/22/11

COOK, PAUL
Nickname: Paul
In St. Louis: 1891
M.L. Debut: 9/13/1884

COOLBAUGH, SCOTT ROBERT
Nickname: Scott
In St. Louis: 1994
Number: 53
M.L. Debut: 9/2/89

COOLEY, DUFF GORDON
Nickname: Duff, Sir Richard
In St. Louis: 1893-96
M.L. Debut: 7/27/1893

COONEY, JAMES EDWARD
Nickname: Jimmy, Scoops
In St. Louis: 1924-25
M.L. Debut: 9/22/17

COOPER, MORTON CECIL
Nickname: Mort
In St. Louis: 1938-45
Number: 25, 13
M.L. Debut: 9/14/38

COOPER, SCOTT KENDRICK
Nickname: Scott
In St. Louis: 1995
Number: 34
M.L. Debut: 9/5/90

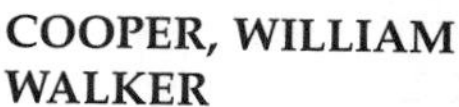

COOPER, WILLIAM WALKER
Nickname: Walker
In St. Louis: 1940-45, 56-57
Number: 15, 30
M.L. Debut: 9/25/40

COPELAND, MAYS
Nickname: Mays
In St. Louis: 1935
Number: 15
M.L. Debut: 4/27/35

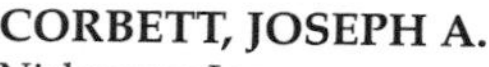

CORBETT, JOSEPH A.
Nickname: Joe
In St. Louis: 1904
M.L. Debut: 8/23/1895

CORHAN, ROY GEORGE
Nickname: Roy, Irish
In St. Louis: 1916
M.L. Debut: 4/20/11

CORMIER, RHEAL PAUL
Nickname: Rheal
In St. Louis: 1991-94
Number: 52
M.L. Debut: 8/15/91

CORRALES, PATRICK
Nickname: Pat, Ike
In St. Louis: 1966
Number: 7
M.L. Debut: 8/2/64

CORRIDON, FRANK J.
Nickname: Frank, Fiddler
In St. Louis: 1910
M.L. Debut: 4/15/04

COSMAN, JAMES HENRY
Nickname: Jim
In St. Louis: 1966-67
Number: 42
M.L. Debut: 10/2/66

COSTELLO, JOHN REILLY
Nickname: John
In St. Louis: 1988-90
Number: 50
M.L. Debut: 6/2/88

COUTLER, THOMAS LEE
Nickname: Tom, Chip
In St. Louis: 1969
Number: 35
M.L. Debut: 6/18/69

COVENEY, JOHN PATRICK
Nickname: Jack
In St. Louis: 1903
M.L. Debut: 9/19/03

COX, DANNY BRADFORD
Nickname: Danny
In St. Louis: 1983-90
Number: 34
M.L. Debut: 8/6/83

COX, WILLIAM DONALD
Nickname: Bill
In St. Louis: 1936
M.L. Debut: 6/6/36

CRABTREE, ESTEL CRAYTON
Nickname: Estel, Crabby
In St. Louis: 1933, 41-42
Number: 27, 11
M.L. Debut: 4/18/29

CRAIG, ROGER LEE
Nickname: Roger
In St. Louis: 1964
Number: 41
M.L. Debut: 7/17/55

CRANDALL, JAMES OTTIS
Nickname: Doc
In St. Louis: 1913
M.L. Debut: 4/24/08

CRAWFORD, CLIFFORD RANKIN
Nickname: Pat
In St. Louis: 1933-34
Number: 11
M.L. Debut: 4/18/29

CRAWFORD, FORREST A.
Nickname: Forrest
In St. Louis: 1906-07
M.L. Debut: 7/30/06

CRAWFORD, GLENN MARTIN
Nickname: Glenn, Shorty
In St. Louis: 1945
Number: 35
M.L. Debut: 4/22/45

CRAWFORD, WILLIE MURPHY
Nickname: Willie, Murph
In St. Louis: 1976
Number: 5
M.L. Debut: 9/16/64

CREEK, PAUL DOUGLAS
Nickname: Doug
In St. Louis: 1995
Number: 72
M.L. Debut: 9/17/95

CREEL, JACK DALTON
Nickname: Jack, Tex
In St. Louis: 1945
Number: 19
M.L. Debut: 4/22/45

CREELY, AUGUST L.
Nickname: Gus
In St. Louis: 1890
M.L. Debut: 10/9/1890

CREGER, BERNARD ODELL
Nickname: Bernie
In St. Louis: 1947
Number: 16
M.L. Debut: 4/29/47

CRESPI, FRANK ANGELO JOSEPH
Nickname: Creepy
In St. Louis: 1938-42
Number: 24, 19, 7
M.L. Debut: 9/14/38

CRIGER, LOUIS
Nickname: Lou
In St. Louis: 1899-1900
M.L. Debut: 9/21/1896

CRIMIAN, JOHN MELVIN
Nickname: Jack
In St. Louis: 1951-52
Number: 25-26
M.L. Debut: 7/3/51

CRITCHLEY, MORRIS ARTHUR
Nickname: Morrie
In St. Louis: 1882
M.L. Debut: 5/8/1882

CROMER, ROY BUNYAN
Nickname: Tripp
In St. Louis: 1993-95
Number: 44, 7
M.L. Debut: 9/7/93

CROOKS, JOHN CHARLES
Nickname: Jack
In St. Louis: 1892-93, 98
M.L. Debut: 9/26/1889

CROSBY, EDWARD CARLTON
Nickname: Ed
In St. Louis: 1970, 72-73
Number: 14, 4
M.L. Debut: 7/12/70

CROSS, JOFFRE JAMES
Nickname: Jeff
In St. Louis: 1942, 46-48
Number: 2, 35, 3
M.L. Debut: 9/27/42

CROSS, LAFAYETTE NAPOLEON
Nickname: Lave
In St. Louis: 1898-1900
M.L. Debut: 4/23/1887

CROSS, MONTFORD MONTGOMERY
Nickname: Monte
In St. Louis: 1896-97
M.L. Debut: 9/27/1892

CROTTY, JOSEPH P.
Nickname: Joe
In St. Louis: 1882
M.L. Debut: 5/4/1882

CROUCH, WILMER ELMER
Nickname: Bill
In St. Louis: 1941, 45
Number: 34, 22
M.L. Debut: 5/9/39

CROWE, GEORGE DANIEL
Nickname: George
In St. Louis: 1959-61
Number: 18
M.L. Debut: 4/16/52

CRUISE, WALTON EDWIN
Nickname: Wall
In St. Louis: 1914, 16-19
M.L. Debut: 4/14/14

CRUMLING, EUGENE LEON
Nickname: Gene
In St. Louis: 1945
Number: 35
M.L. Debut: 9/11/45

CRUZ, CIRILIO (DILAN)
Nickname: Tommy
In St. Louis: 1973
Number: 17
M.L. Debut: 9/4/73

CRUZ, HECTOR LOUIS (DILAN)
Nickname: Heity
In St. Louis: 1973, 75-77
Number: 11, 25
M.L. Debut: 8/11/73

CRUZ, JOSE (DILAN)
Nickname: Cheo
In St. Louis: 1970-74
Number: 38
M.L. Debut: 9/19/70

CUELLAR, MIGUEL ANGEL (SANTANA)
Nickname: Mike
In St. Louis: 1964
Number: 35
M.L. Debut: 4/18/59

CULVER, GEORGE RAYMOND
Nickname: George
In St. Louis: 1970
Number: 39
M.L. Debut: 9/7/66

CUMBERLAND, JOHN SHELDON
Nickname: John
In St. Louis: 1972
Number: 36
M.L. Debut: 9/27/68

CUNNINGHAM, JOSEPH ROBERT
Nickname: Smokey Joe
In St. Louis: 1954, 56-61
Number: 28
M.L. Debut: 6/30/54

CUNNINGHAM, RAYMOND LEE
Nickname: Ray
In St. Louis: 1931-32
M.L. Debut: 9/16/31

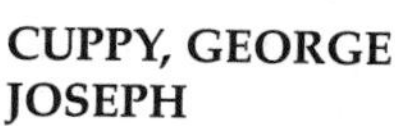

CUPPY, GEORGE JOSEPH
Nickname: Nig
In St. Louis: 1899
M.L. Debut: 4/16/1892

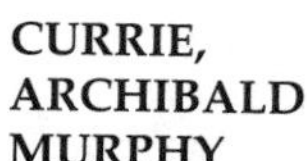

CURRIE, ARCHIBALD MURPHY
Nickname: Murphy
In St. Louis: 1916
M.L. Debut: 8/31/16

CURRIE, CLARENCE FRANKLIN
Nickname: Clarence
In St. Louis: 1902-03
M.L. Debut: 4/25/02

CURTIS, JOHN DUFFIELD
Nickname: John
In St. Louis: 1974-76
Number: 22
M.L. Debut: 8/13/70

CUTHBERT, EDGAR EDWARD
Nickname: Ned
In St. Louis: 1882-83
M.L. Debut: 5/20/1871

D'ACQUISTO, JOHN FRANCIS
Nickname: John
In St. Louis: 1977
Number: 34
M.L. Debut: 9/2/73

DALE, EMMETT EUGENE
Nickname: Gene
In St. Louis: 1911-12
M.L. Debut: 9/19/11

DAMASKA, JACK LLOYD
Nickname: Jack
In St. Louis: 1963
Number: 19
M.L. Debut: 7/3/63

DANIELS, PETER J.
Nickname: Pete, Smiling Pete
In St. Louis: 1898
M.L. Debut: 4/19/1890

DARINGER, ROLLA HARRISON
Nickname: Rolla
In St. Louis: 1914-15
M.L. Debut: 9/19/14

DARK, ALVIN RALPH
Nickname: Alvin, Blackie
In St. Louis: 1956-58
Number: 11
M.L. Debut: 7/14/46

DARLING, CONRAD
Nickname: Dell
In St. Louis: 1891
M.L. Debut: 7/3/1883

DAVALILLO, VICTOR JOSE
Nickname: Vic
In St. Louis: 1969-70
Number: 17
M.L. Debut: 4/9/36

DAVANON, FRANK GERALD
Nickname: Jerry
In St. Louis: 1969-70, 74, 77
Number: 26
M.L. Debut: 4/11/69

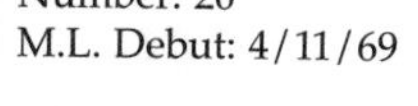

DAVIS, CURTIS BENTON
Nickname: Curt, Coonskin
In St. Louis: 1938-40
Number: 27
M.L. Debut: 4/21/34

DAVIS, GEORGE WILLIS
Nickname: Kiddo
In St. Louis: 1934
Number: 4
M.L. Debut: 6/15/26

DAVIS, JAMES BENNETT
Nickname: Jim
In St. Louis: 1957
Number: 26
M.L. Debut: 4/18/54

DAVIS, JAMES J.
Nickname: Jumbo
In St. Louis: 1889-90
M.L. Debut: 7/27/1884

DAVIS, JOHN HENRY ALBERT
Nickname: Daisy
In St. Louis: 1884
M.L. Debut: 5/6/1884

DAVIS, RONALD EVERETTE
Nickname: Ron
In St. Louis: 1968
Number: 14
M.L. Debut: 8/1/62

DAVIS, VIRGIL LAWRENCE
Nickname: Spud
In St. Louis: 1928, 34-36
Number: 8
M.L. Debut: 4/30/28

DAVIS, WILLIAM HENRY
Nickname: Willie
In St. Louis: 1975
Number: 5
M.L. Debut: 9/8/60

DAWLEY, WILLIAM CHESTER
Nickname: Bill
In St. Louis: 1987
Number: 48
M.L. Debut: 4/15/83

DAY, CHARLES FREDERICK
Nickname: Boots
In St. Louis: 1969
Number: 11
M.L. Debut: 6/15/69

DAY, CLYDE HARRY
Nickname: Pea Ridge
In St. Louis: 1924-25
M.L. Debut: 9/19/24

DAYLEY, KENNETH GRANT
Nickname: Ken
In St. Louis: 1984-90
Number: 46
M.L. Debut: 5/13/82

DEAL, ELLIS FERGUSON
Nickname: Cot
In St. Louis: 1950, 54
Number: 38, 22
M.L. Debut: 9/11/47

DEAN, JAY HANNA
Nickname: Dizzy, Jerome Herman
In St. Louis: 1930, 32-37
Number: 17
M.L. Debut: 9/28/30

DEAN, PAUL DEE
Nickname: Daffy
In St. Louis: 1934-39
Number: 21, 22
M.L. Debut: 4/18/34

DEASLEY, THOMAS H.
Nickname: Pat
In St. Louis: 1883-84
M.L. Debut: 5/18/1881

DECINCES, DOUGLAS VERNON
Nickname: Doug
In St. Louis: 1987
Number: 12
M.L. Debut: 9/9/73

DECKER, FRANK
Nickname: Frank
In St. Louis: 1882
M.L. Debut: 6/25/1879

DECKER, GEORGE A.
Nickname: George, Gentleman George
In St. Louis: 1898
M.L. Debut: 7/11/1892

DEFATE, CLYDE HERBERT
Nickname: Tony
In St. Louis: 1917
M.L. Debut: 4/18/17

DEGROFF, EDWARD ARTHUR
Nickname: Rube
In St. Louis: 1905-06
M.L. Debut: 9/22/05

DEJESUS, IVAN
Nickname: Ivan
In St. Louis: 1985
Number: 11
M.L. Debut: 9/13/74

DELAHANTY, JOSEPH NICHOLAS
Nickname: Joe
In St. Louis: 1907-09
M.L. Debut: 9/30/07

DELANCEY, WILLIAM PINKNEY
Nickname: Bill
In St. Louis: 1932, 34-35, 40
Number: 9, 15
M.L. Debut: 9/11/32

DELANEY, ARTHUR DEWEY
Nickname: Art, Swede
In St. Louis: 1924
M.L. Debut: 4/16/24

DELEON, JOSE (CHESTARO)
Nickname: Jose
In St. Louis: 1988-92
Number: 48
M.L. Debut: 7/23/83

DELEON, LUIS ANTONIO (TRICOCHE)
Nickname: Luis
In St. Louis: 1981
Number: 49
M.L. Debut: 9/6/81

DEL GRECO, ROBERT GEORGE
Nickname: Bobby
In St. Louis: 1956
Number: 9
M.L. Debut: 4/16/52

DELKER, EDWARD ALBERTS
Nickname: Eddie
In St. Louis: 1929, 31-32
M.L. Debut: 4/28/29

DELL, WILLIAM GEORGE
Nickname: Wheezer
In St. Louis: 1912
M.L. Debut: 4/22/12

DELUCIA, RICHARD ANTHONY
Nickname: Rich
In St. Louis: 1995
Number: 41
M.L. Debut: 9/8/90

DEMAREE, JOSEPH FRANKLIN
Nickname: Frank
In St. Louis: 1943
Number: 17
M.L. Debut: 7/22/32

DEMONTREVILLE, LEON
Nickname: Lee
In St. Louis: 1903
M.L. Debut: 7/10/03

DENNIS, DONALD RAY
Nickname: Don
In St. Louis: 1965-66
Number: 29
M.L. Debut: 6/18/65

DENNY, JOHN ALLEN
Nickname: John
In St. Louis: 1974-79
Number: 36
M.L. Debut: 9/12/74

DERRINGER, SAMUEL PAUL
Nickname: Paul, 'Oom Paul, Duke
In St. Louis: 1931-33
Number: 20
M.L. Debut: 4/16/31

DERRY, ALVA RUSSELL
Nickname: Russ
In St. Louis: 1949
M.L. Debut: 7/4/44

DESA, JOSEPH
Nickname: Joe
In St. Louis: 1980
Number: 7
M.L. Debut: 9/6/80

DESHIELDS, DELINO LAMONT
Nickname: Delino
In St. Louis: 1997
Number: 7
M.L. Debut: 4/9/90

DEVLIN, JAMES H.
Nickname: Jim
In St. Louis: 1888-89
M.L. Debut: 6/28/1886

DICKERMAN, LEO LOUIS
Nickname: Leo
In St. Louis: 1924-25
M.L. Debut: 4/21/23

DICKSON, MURRY MONROE
Nickname: Murry
In St. Louis: 1939-40, 42-43, 46-48, 56-57
Number: 22, 36
M.L. Debut: 9/30/39

DIERING, CHARLES EDWARD ALLEN
Nickname: Chuck
In St. Louis: 1947-51
Number: 32
M.L. Debut: 4/15/47

DIERKER, LAWRENCE EDWARD
Nickname: Larry
In St. Louis: 1977
Number: 49
M.L. Debut: 9/22/64

DIFELICE, MICHAEL WILLIAM
Nickname: Mike
In St. Louis: 1996-97
Number: 37
M.L. Debut: 9/1/96

DILLARD, ROBERT LEE
Nickname: Pat
In St. Louis: 1900
M.L. Debut: 4/24/1900

DILLHOEFER, WILLIAM MARTIN
Nickname: Pickles
In St. Louis: 1919-21
M.L. Debut: 4/16/17

DIMMEL, MICHAEL WAYNE
Nickname: Mike
In St. Louis: 1979
Number: 21
M.L. Debut: 9/2/77

DIPINO, FRANK MICHAEL
Nickname: Frank
In St. Louis: 1989-90, 92
M.L. Debut: 9/14/81

DISTEL, GEORGE ADAM
Nickname: Dutch
In St. Louis: 1918
M.L. Debut: 6/21/18

DIXON, STEVEN ROSS
Nickname: Steve
In St. Louis: 1993-94
Number: 41
M.L. Debut: 9/7/93

DOAK, WILLIAM LEOPOLD
Nickname: Bill, Spittin' Bill
In St. Louis: 1913-24, 29
M.L. Debut: 9/1/12

DOCKINS, GEORGE WOODROW
Nickname: Lefty
In St. Louis: 1945
Number: 23
M.L. Debut: 5/5/45

DOLAN, ALBERT J.
Nickname: Cozy
In St. Louis: 1914-15
M.L. Debut: 8/15/09

DOLAN, JOHN
Nickname: John
In St. Louis: 1893
M.L. Debut: 9/5/1890

DOLAN, THOMAS J.
Nickname: Tom
In St. Louis: 1883-84, 88
M.L. Debut: 9/30/1879

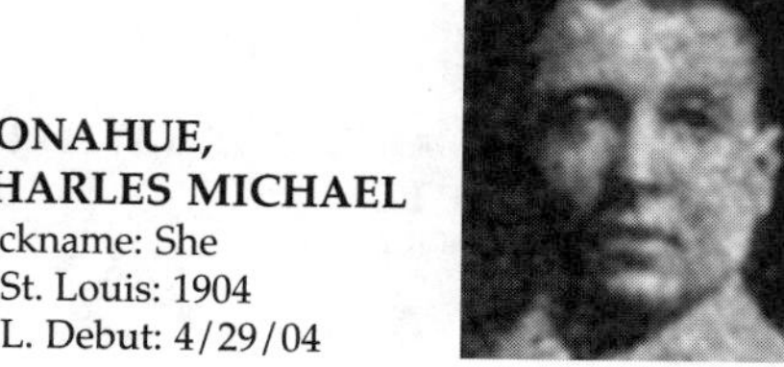

DONAHUE, CHARLES MICHAEL
Nickname: She
In St. Louis: 1904
M.L. Debut: 4/29/04

DONAHUE, FRANCIS ROSTELL
Nickname: Red
In St. Louis: 1895-97
M.L. Debut: 5/6/1893

DONLIN, MICHAEL JOSEPH
Nickname: Mike, Turkey Mike, Highlonesome
In St. Louis: 1899-1900
M.L. Debut: 7/19/1899

DONNELLY, JAMES B.
Nickname: Jim
In St. Louis: 1890, 98
M.L. Debut: 7/11/1884

DONNELLY, SYLVESTER URBAN
Nickname: Blix
In St. Louis: 1944-46
Number: 3, 20
M.L. Debut: 5/6/44

DONOVAN, PATRICK JOSEPH
Nickname: Patsy
In St. Louis: 1900-03
M.L. Debut: 4/19/1890

DORR, CHARLES ALBERT
Nickname: Bert
In St. Louis: 1882
M.L. Debut: 8/24/1882

DOUGLASS, WILLIAM BINGHAM
Nickname: Klondike
In St. Louis: 1896-97
M.L. Debut: 4/23/1896

DOUTHIT, TAYLOR LEE
Nickname: Taylor, Tay
In St. Louis: 1923-31
M.L. Debut: 9/14/23

DOWD, THOMAS JEFFERSON
Nickname: Tommy, Buttermilk Tommy, Pink Coat
In St. Louis: 1893-98
M.L. Debut: 4/8/1891

DOWLING, DAVID BARCLAY
Nickname: Dave
In St. Louis: 1964
Number: 29
M.L. Debut: 10/3/64

DOYLE, JEFFREY DONALD
Nickname: Jeff
In St. Louis: 1983
M.L. Debut: 9/13/83

DOYLE, JOHN ALOYSIUS
Nickname: John
In St. Louis: 1882
M.L. Debut: 7/26/1882

DOYLE, WILLIAM CARL
Nickname: Carl
In St. Louis: 1940
Number: 27
M.L. Debut: 8/5/35

DRABOWSKY, MYRON WALTER
Nickname: Moe
In St. Louis: 1971-72
Number: 28
M.L. Debut: 8/7/56

DRESSEN, LEE AUGUST
Nickname: Lee
In St. Louis: 1914
M.L. Debut: 4/21/14

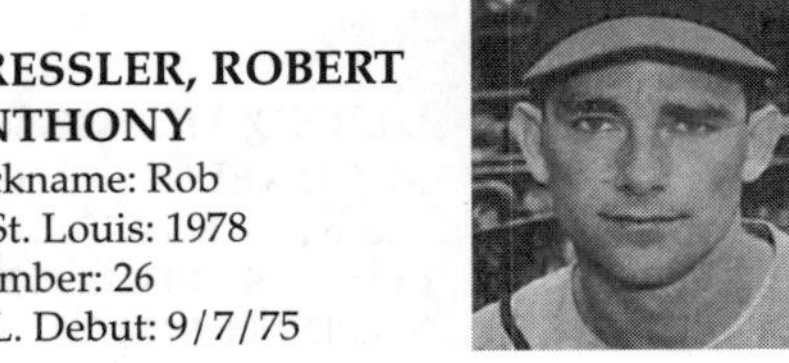

DRESSLER, ROBERT ANTHONY
Nickname: Rob
In St. Louis: 1978
Number: 26
M.L. Debut: 9/7/75

DRIESSEN, DANIEL
Nickname: Dan
In St. Louis: 1987
Number: 23
M.L. Debut: 6/9/73

DRISSEL, MICHAEL P.
Nickname: Mike
In St. Louis: 1885
M.L. Debut: 9/5/1885

DRUHOT, CARL A.
Nickname: Carl
In St. Louis: 1906-07
M.L. Debut: 4/18/06

DUFFEE, CHARLES EDWARD
Nickname: Charlie, Homerun
In St. Louis: 1889-90
M.L. Debut: 4/17/1889

DULIBA, ROBERT JOHN
Nickname: Bob
In St. Louis: 1959-60
Number: 24, 33
M.L. Debut: 8/11/59

DUNCAN, TAYLOR MCDOWELL
Nickname: Taylor
In St. Louis: 1977
Number: 16
M.L. Debut: 9/15/77

DUNHAM, HENRY HUSTON
Nickname: Wiley
In St. Louis: 1902
M.L. Debut: 5/24/02

DUNLAP, GRANT LESTER
Nickname: Grant, Snap
In St. Louis: 1953
Number: 10
M.L. Debut: 4/21/53

DUNLEAVY, JOHN FRANCIS
Nickname: Jack
In St. Louis: 1903-05
M.L. Debut: 5/30/03

DURHAM, DONALD GARY
Nickname: Don
In St. Louis: 1972
Number: 46
M.L. Debut: 7/16/72

DURHAM, JOSEPH VANN
Nickname: Joe, Pop
In St. Louis: 1959
Number: 20
M.L. Debut: 9/10/54

DURHAM, LEON
Nickname: Bull
In St. Louis: 1980, 89
Number: 16, 10
M.L. Debut: 5/27/80

DUROCHER, LEO ERNEST
Nickname: Lippy
In St. Louis: 1933-37
Number: 2
M.L. Debut: 10/2/25

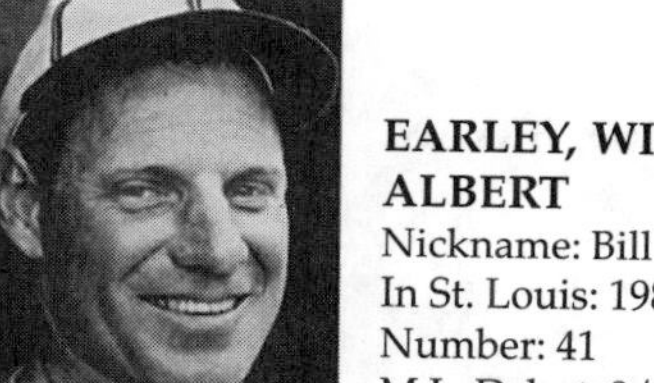

DURYEA, JAMES NEWTON
Nickname: Jim, Cyclone Jim
In St. Louis: 1891
M.L. Debut: 4/20/1889

DUSEK, ERVIN FRANK
Nickname: Erv, Four Sack
In St. Louis: 1941-42, 46-51
Number: 17, 19, 7, 25
M.L. Debut: 9/18/41

DWYER, JAMES EDWARD
Nickname: Jim, Pig Pen
In St. Louis: 1973-75, 77-78
Number: 11, 25
M.L. Debut: 6/10/73

DWYER, JOHN FRANCIS
Nickname: Frank
In St. Louis: 1892
M.L. Debut: 9/20/1888

DYER, EDWIN HAWLEY
Nickname: Eddie
In St. Louis: 1922-27
M.L. Debut: 7/8/22

EAGAN, WILLIAM
Nickname: Bad Bill
In St. Louis: 1891
M.L. Debut: 4/8/1891

EARLE, WILLIAM MOFFAT
Nickname: Billy, The Little Globetrotter
In St. Louis: 1890
M.L. Debut: 4/27/1889

EARLEY, WILLIAM ALBERT
Nickname: Bill
In St. Louis: 1986
Number: 41
M.L. Debut: 9/22/86

EARNSHAW, GEORGE LIVINGSTON
Nickname: George, Moose
In St. Louis: 1936
Number: 33
M.L. Debut: 6/3/28

EASTON, JOHN S.
Nickname: Jack
In St. Louis: 1891-92
M.L. Debut: 9/23/1889

EASTWICK, RAWLINS JACKSON
Nickname: Rawly
In St. Louis: 1977
Number: 26
M.L. Debut: 9/12/74

ECHOLS, JOHN GRESHAM
Nickname: Johnny
In St. Louis: 1939
Number: 4
M.L. Debut: 5/24/39

ECKERSLEY, DENNIS LEE
Nickname: Dennis, Eck
In St. Louis: 1996-97
Number: 43
M.L. Debut: 4/12/75

ECKERT, ALBERT GEORGE
Nickname: Al, Obbie
In St. Louis: 1935
Number: 20
M.L. Debut: 4/21/30

EDELEN, BENNY JOE
Nickname: Joe
In St. Louis: 1981
Number: 44
M.L. Debut: 4/18/81

EDWARDS, JOHN ALBAN
Nickname: Johnny
In St. Louis: 1968
Number: 7
M.L. Debut: 6/27/61

EGAN, ALOYSIUS JEROME
Nickname: Wish
In St. Louis: 1905-06
M.L. Debut: 9/3/02

EHRET, PHILLIP SYDNEY
Nickname: Red
In St. Louis: 1895
M.L. Debut: 7/7/1888

ELLIOTT, HARRY LEWIS
Nickname: Harry
In St. Louis: 1953, 55
Number: 11
M.L. Debut: 8/1/53

ELLIS, GEORGE WILLIAM
Nickname: Rube
In St. Louis: 1909-12
M.L. Debut: 4/15/09

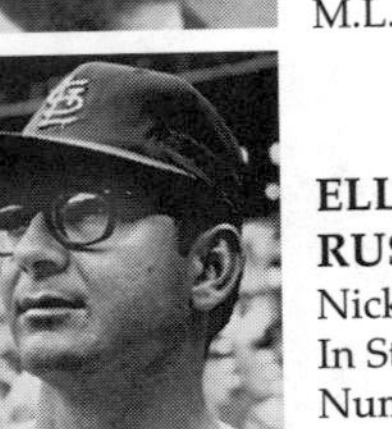

ELLIS, JAMES RUSSELL
Nickname: Jim
In St. Louis: 1969
Number: 33
M.L. Debut: 8/11/67

ELY, WILLIAM FREDERICK
Nickname: Bones
In St. Louis: 1893-95
M.L. Debut: 6/19/1884

ENDICOTT, WILLIAM FRANKLIN
Nickname: Bill
In St. Louis: 1946
Number: 24
M.L. Debut: 4/21/46

ENNIS, DELMER
Nickname: Del
In St. Louis: 1957-58
Number: 7
M.L. Debut: 4/28/46

ENWRIGHT, CHARLES MASSEY
Nickname: Charlie
In St. Louis: 1909
M.L. Debut: 4/19/09

EPPS, HAROLD FRANKLIN
Nickname: Hal
In St. Louis: 1938, 40
Number: 17
M.L. Debut: 9/9/38

ERAUTT, EDWARD LORENZ SEBASTIAN
Nickname: Eddie
In St. Louis: 1953
Number: 25
M.L. Debut: 4/16/47

ESPER, CHARLES H.
Nickname: Duke
In St. Louis: 1897-98
M.L. Debut: 4/18/1890

ESSEGIAN, CHARLES ABRAHAM
Nickname: Chuck
In St. Louis: 1959
Number: 29
M.L. Debut: 4/15/58

EVANS, LOUIS RICHARD
Nickname: Steve
In St. Louis: 1909-13
M.L. Debut: 4/16/08

EVANS, ROY
Nickname: Roy
In St. Louis: 1897
M.L. Debut: 5/15/1897

EVERSGERD, BRYAN DAVID
Nickname: Bryan
In St. Louis: 1994
Number: 62
M.L. Debut: 4/30/94

EWING, GEORGE LEMUEL
Nickname: Bob, Long Bob
In St. Louis: 1912
M.L. Debut: 4/19/02

EWING, REUBEN
Nickname: Rueben
In St. Louis: 1921
M.L. Debut: 6/21/21

FAGIN, FREDERICK H.
Nickname: Fred
In St. Louis: 1895
M.L. Debut: 6/25/1895

FAIRLY, RONALD RAY
Nickname: Ron
In St. Louis: 1975-76
Number: 15
M.L. Debut: 9/9/58

FALCONE, PETER
Nickname: Pete
In St. Louis: 1976-78
Number: 41
M.L. Debut: 4/13/75

FALLON, GEORGE DECATUR
Nickname: George, Flash
In St. Louis: 1943-45
Number: 7
M.L. Debut: 9/27/37

FANOK, HARRY M.
Nickname: Harry, The Flame Thrower
In St. Louis: 1963-64
Number: 30
M.L. Debut: 4/16/63

FARRELL, EDWARD STEPHEN
Nickname: Doc
In St. Louis: 1930
M.L. Debut: 6/15/25

FARRELL, JOHN SEBASTIAN
Nickname: John, Little Johnny
In St. Louis: 1902-05
M.L. Debut: 4/16/01

FASZHOLZ, JOHN EDWARD
Nickname: Jack, Preacher
In St. Louis: 1953
Number: 41
M.L. Debut: 4/25/53

FENWICK, ROBERT RICHARD
Nickname: Bobby, Bloop
In St. Louis: 1973
Number: 18
M.L. Debut: 4/26/72

FERGUSON, JOSEPH VANCE
Nickname: Joe
In St. Louis: 1976
Number: 13
M.L. Debut: 9/12/70

FERRARESE, DONALD HUGH
Nickname: Don, Midget
In St. Louis: 1962
Number: 36
M.L. Debut: 4/11/55

FIALA, NEIL STEPHEN
Nickname: Neil
In St. Louis: 1981
Number: 51
M.L. Debut: 9/3/81

FIGUEROA, BIENVENIDO (DELEON)
Nickname: Bien
In St. Louis: 1992
Number: 50
M.L. Debut: 5/17/92

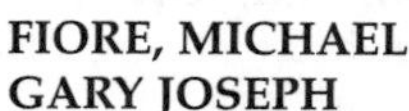

FIORE, MICHAEL GARY JOSEPH
Nickname: Mike, Lefty
In St. Louis: 1972
M.L. Debut: 9/21/69

FISHBURN, SAMUEL E.
Nickname: Sam
In St. Louis: 1919
M.L. Debut: 9/30/19

FISHER, CHAUNCEY BURR
Nickname: Chauncey, Peach
In St. Louis: 1901
M.L. Debut: 9/20/1893

FISHER, EDDIE GENE
Nickname: Eddie
In St. Louis: 1973
Number: 48
M.L. Debut: 6/22/59

FISHER, GEORGE ALOYS
Nickname: Showboat
In St. Louis: 1930
M.L. Debut: 4/24/23

FISHER, ROBERT TAYLOR
Nickname: Bob
In St. Louis: 1918-19
M.L. Debut: 6/3/12

FITZGERALD, MICHAEL PATRICK
Nickname: Mike
In St. Louis: 1988
M.L. Debut: 6/23/88

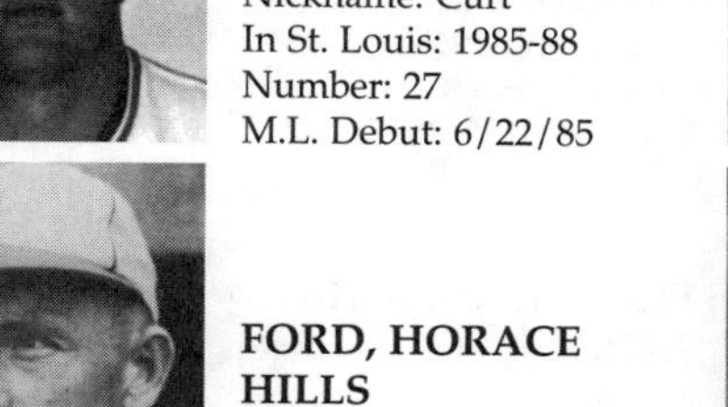

FLACK, MAX JOHN
Nickname: Max
In St. Louis: 1922-25
M.L. Debut: 4/16/14

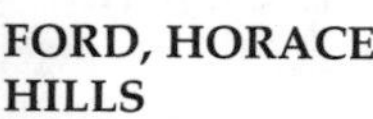

FLANIGAN, THOMAS ANTHONY
Nickname: Tom
In St. Louis: 1958
Number: 44
M.L. Debut: 4/14/54

FLOOD, CURTIS CHARLES
Nickname: Curt
In St. Louis: 1958-69
Number: 42, 21
M.L. Debut: 9/9/56

FLOOD, TIMOTHY A.
Nickname: Tim
In St. Louis: 1899
M.L. Debut: 9/24/1899

FLOWERS, BENNETT
Nickname: Ben
In St. Louis: 1955-56
Number: 37
M.L. Debut: 9/29/51

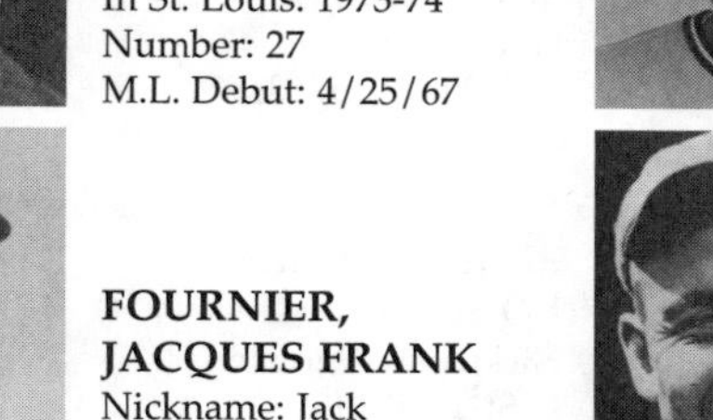

FLOWERS, D'ARCY RAYMOND
Nickname: Jake
In St. Louis: 1923, 26, 31-32
Number: 23
M.L. Debut: 9/7/23

FOLKERS, RICHARD NEVIN
Nickname: Rich
In St. Louis: 1972-74
Number: 28
M.L. Debut: 6/10/70

FORD, CURTIS GLENN
Nickname: Curt
In St. Louis: 1985-88
Number: 27
M.L. Debut: 6/22/85

FORD, HORACE HILLS
Nickname: Hod
In St. Louis: 1932
M.L. Debut: 9/8/19

FORSCH, ROBERT HERBERT
Nickname: Bob
In St. Louis: 1974-88
Number: 31
M.L. Debut: 7/7/74

FOSSAS, EMILIO ANTONIO (MOREJON)
Nickname: Tony
In St. Louis: 1995-97
Number: 48
M.L. Debut: 5/15/88

FOSTER, ALAN BENTON
Nickname: Alan
In St. Louis: 1973-74
Number: 27
M.L. Debut: 4/25/67

FOURNIER, JACQUES FRANK
Nickname: Jack
In St. Louis: 1920-22
M.L. Debut: 4/13/12

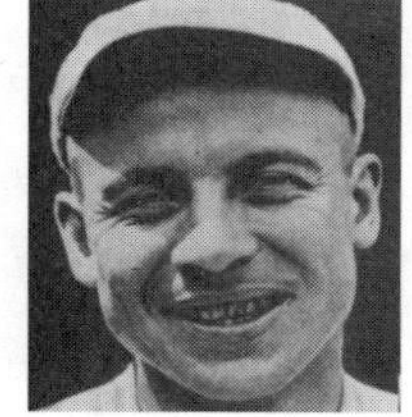

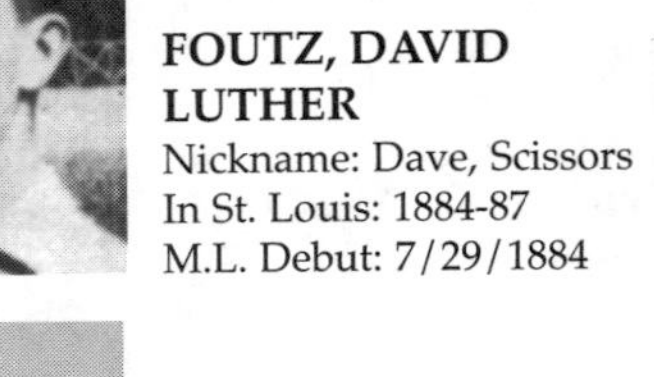

FOUTZ, DAVID LUTHER
Nickname: Dave, Scissors
In St. Louis: 1884-87
M.L. Debut: 7/29/1884

FOWLER, JESSE PETER
Nickname: Jesse
In St. Louis: 1924
M.L. Debut: 7/29/24

FRANCIS, EARL COLEMAN
Nickname: Earl
In St. Louis: 1965
Number: 36
M.L. Debut: 6/30/60

FRANCONA, JOHN PATSY
Nickname: Tito
In St. Louis: 1965-66
Number: 23
M.L. Debut: 4/17/56

FRANK, CHARLES
Nickname: Charlie
In St. Louis: 1893-94
M.L. Debut: 8/8/1893

FRANKHOUSE, FREDERICK MELOY
Nickname: Fred
In St. Louis: 1927-30
M.L. Debut: 9/11/27

FRANKLIN, MICAH ISHANTI
Nickname: Micah
In St. Louis: 1997
Number: 68
M.L. Debut: 5/13/97

FRANKS, HERMAN LOUIS
Nickname: Herman
In St. Louis: 1939
Number: 12, 13, 15
M.L. Debut: 4/27/39

FRASCATORE, JOHN VINCENT
Nickname: John
In St. Louis: 1994-95, 97
Number: 50
M.L. Debut: 7/21/94

FRASER, WILLIAM PATRICK
Nickname: Willie
In St. Louis: 1991
Number: 46
M.L. Debut: 9/10/86

FRAZIER, GEORGE ALLEN
Nickname: George
In St. Louis: 1979-80
Number: 43, 39
M.L. Debut: 5/25/78

FRAZIER, JOSEPH FILMORE
Nickname: Joe, Cobra Joe
In St. Louis: 1954-56
Number: 24
M.L. Debut: 8/31/47

FREED, ROGER VERNON
Nickname: Roger
In St. Louis: 1977-79
Number: 7
M.L. Debut: 9/18/70

FREEMAN, JULIUS BENJAMIN
Nickname: Julie
In St. Louis: 1888
M.L. Debut: 10/10/1888

FREESE, EUGENE LEWIS
Nickname: Gene, Augie
In St. Louis: 1958
Number: 24
M.L. Debut: 4/13/55

FREIGAU, HOWARD EARL
Nickname: Howard, Ty
In St. Louis: 1922-25
M.L. Debut: 9/13/22

FREY, BENJAMIN RUDOLPH
Nickname: Benny
In St. Louis: 1932
M.L. Debut: 9/18/29

FRISCH, FRANK FRANCIS
Nickname: Frankie, The Fordham Flash
In St. Louis: 1927-37
Number: 3
M.L. Debut: 6/14/19

FRISELLA, DANIEL VINCENT
Nickname: Danny, Bear
In St. Louis: 1976
Number: 34
M.L. Debut: 7/27/67

FROMME, ARTHUR HENRY
Nickname: Art
In St. Louis: 1906-08
M.L. Debut: 9/14/06

FULGHAM, JOHN THOMAS
Nickname: John
In St. Louis: 1979-80
Number: 41
M.L. Debut: 6/19/79

FULLER, HENRY W.
Nickname: Harry
In St. Louis: 1891
M.L. Debut: 4/8/1891

FULLER, WILLIAM BENJAMIN
Nickname: Shorty
In St. Louis: 1889-91
M.L. Debut: 7/19/1888

FULLIS, CHARLES PHILIP
Nickname: Chick
In St. Louis: 1934-36
Number: 4, 31
M.L. Debut: 4/13/28

FULMER, CHARLES JOHN
Nickname: Chick
In St. Louis: 1884
M.L. Debut: 8/23/1871

FUSSELBACK, EDWARD L.
Nickname: Ed
In St. Louis: 1882
M.L. Debut: 5/3/1882

FUSSELMAN, LESTER LEROY
Nickname: Les
In St. Louis: 1952-53
Number: 17
M.L. Debut: 4/16/52

GAETTI, GARY JOSEPH
Nickname: Gary, Rat
In St. Louis: 1996-97
Number: 8
M.L. Debut: 9/20/81

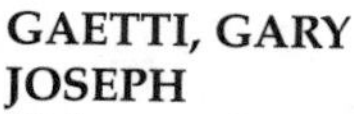

GAGLIANO, PHILIP JOSEPH
Nickname: Phil
In St. Louis: 1963-70
Number: 16
M.L. Debut: 4/16/63

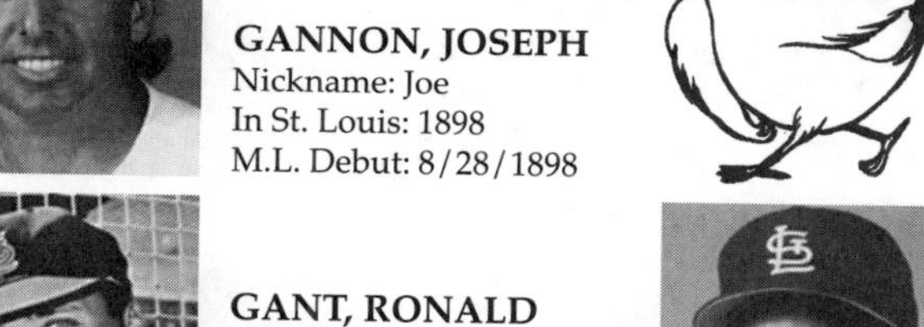

GAINER, DELLOS CLINTON
Nickname: Del, Sheriff
In St. Louis: 1922
M.L. Debut: 10/2/09

GAISER, FREDERICK JACOB
Nickname: Fred
In St. Louis: 1908
M.L. Debut: 9/3/08

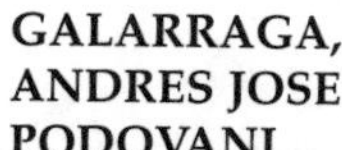

GALARRAGA, ANDRES JOSE PODOVANI
Nickname: Andres, Big Cat
In St. Louis: 1992
Number: 41
M.L. Debut: 8/23/85

GALLEGO, MICHAEL ANTHONY
Nickname: Mike
In St. Louis: 1996-97
Number: 22
M.L. Debut: 4/11/85

GALLOWAY, JAMES CATO
Nickname: Bad News
In St. Louis: 1912
M.L. Debut: 8/24/12

GALVIN, JAMES FRANCIS
Nickname: Pud, Gentle Jeems, The Little Steam Engine
In St. Louis: 1892
M.L. Debut: 5/22/1875

GANNON, JOSEPH
Nickname: Joe
In St. Louis: 1898
M.L. Debut: 8/28/1898

GANT, RONALD EDWIN
Nickname: Ron
In St. Louis: 1996-97
Number: 5
M.L. Debut: 9/6/87

GARAGIOLA, JOSEPH HENRY
Nickname: Joe
In St. Louis: 1946-51
Number: 17, 23
M.L. Debut: 5/26/46

GARDELLA, DANIEL LEWIS
Nickname: Danny
In St. Louis: 1950
Number: 29
M.L. Debut: 5/14/44

GARDNER, MILES GLENN
Nickname: Glenn
In St. Louis: 1945
Number: 15
M.L. Debut: 7/21/45

GARIBALDI, ARTHUR EDWARD
Nickname: Art
In St. Louis: 1936
Number: 30
M.L. Debut: 6/20/36

GARMAN, MICHAEL DOUGLAS
Nickname: Mike
In St. Louis: 1974-75
Number: 43
M.L. Debut: 9/22/69

GARMS, DEBS C.
Nickname: Debs, Tex
In St. Louis: 1943-45
Number: 9
M.L. Debut: 8/10/32

GARRETT, RONALD WAYNE
Nickname: Wayne, Red
In St. Louis: 1978
Number: 11
M.L. Debut: 4/12/69

GEDMAN, RICHARD LEO
Nickname: Rich
In St. Louis: 1991-92
Number: 29
M.L. Debut: 9/7/80

GELBERT, CHARLES MAGNUS
Nickname: Charley
In St. Louis: 1929-32, 35-36
Number: 11, 4, 7
M.L. Debut: 4/16/29

GENINS, FRANK C.
Nickname: Frank, Frenchy
In St. Louis: 1892
M.L. Debut: 7/5/1892

GETTEL, ALLEN JONES
Nickname: Al
In St. Louis: 1955
Number: 31
M.L. Debut: 4/20/45

GETTINGER, LEWIS THOMAS LAYTON
Nickname: Lewis
In St. Louis: 1889-90
M.L. Debut: 9/21/1889

GETZEIN, CHARLES H.
Nickname: Charlie, Pretzels
In St. Louis: 1892
M.L. Debut: 8/13/1884

GEYER, JACOB BOWMAN
Nickname: Rube
In St. Louis: 1910-13
M.L. Debut: 4/24/10

GIANNELLI, RAYMOND JOHN
Nickname: Ray
In St. Louis: 1995
M.L. Debut: 5/4/91

GIBSON, ROBERT
Nickname: Bob, Hoot
In St. Louis: 1959-75
Number: 58, 31, 45
M.L. Debut: 4/15/59

GILBERT, WILLIAM OLIVER
Nickname: Billy
In St. Louis: 1908-09
M.L. Debut: 4/25/01

GILHAM, GEORGE LOUIS
Nickname: George
In St. Louis: 1920-21
M.L. Debut: 9/24/20

GILHOOLEY, FRANK PATRICK
Nickname: Frank, Flash
In St. Louis: 1911-12
M.L. Debut: 9/18/11

GILKEY, OTIS BERNARD
Nickname: Bernard
In St. Louis: 1990-95
Number: 23
M.L. Debut: 9/4/90

GILL, JAMES C.
Nickname: Jim
In St. Louis: 1889
M.L. Debut: 6/27/1889

GILLENWATER, CARDEN EDISON
Nickname: Carden
In St. Louis: 1940
M.L. Debut: 9/22/40

GILLPATRICK, GEORGE F.
Nickname: George
In St. Louis: 1898
M.L. Debut: 5/22/1898

GILSON, HAROLD
Nickname: Hal, Lefty
In St. Louis: 1968
Number: 47
M.L. Debut: 4/14/68

GIUSTI, DAVID JOHN
Nickname: Dave
In St. Louis: 1969
Number: 39
M.L. Debut: 4/13/62

GLASSCOCK, JOHN WESLEY
Nickname: Jack, Old Battle Ax, Pebbly Jack
In St. Louis: 1892-93
M.L. Debut: 5/1/1879

GLAVIANO, THOMAS GIATANO
Nickname: Tommy, Rabbit
In St. Louis: 1949-52
Number: 12, 11
M.L. Debut: 4/19/49

GLEASON, JOHN DAY
Nickname: Jack
In St. Louis: 1882-83
M.L. Debut: 10/2/1879

GLEASON, WILLIAM G.
Nickname: Will
In St. Louis: 1882-87
M.L. Debut: 5/2/1882

GLEASON, WILLIAM J.
Nickname: Youngster, Kid
In St. Louis: 1892-94
M.L. Debut: 4/20/1888

GLENN, BURDETTE
Nickname: Bob
In St. Louis: 1920
M.L. Debut: 7/27/20

GLENN, HARRY MELVILLE
Nickname: Harry, Husky
In St. Louis: 1915
M.L. Debut: 4/14/15

GLENN, JOHN
Nickname: John
In St. Louis: 1960
Number: 22
M.L. Debut: 6/16/60

GODBY, DANNY RAY
Nickname: Danny
In St. Louis: 1974
Number: 24
M.L. Debut: 8/10/74

GOLDEN, ROY KRAMER
Nickname: Roy
In St. Louis: 1910-11
M.L. Debut: 9/7/10

GOLDSBY, WALTON HUGH
Nickname: Walt
In St. Louis: 1884
M.L. Debut: 5/28/1884

GOLDSMITH, HAROLD EUGENE
Nickname: Hal
In St. Louis: 1929
M.L. Debut: 6/23/26

GONZALEZ, JOSE ALTAGRACIA (URIBE)
Nickname: Jose
In St. Louis: 1984
Number: 5
M.L. Debut: 9/13/84

GONZALEZ, MIGUEL ANGEL (CORDERO)
Nickname: Mike
In St. Louis: 1915-18, 24-25, 31-32
Number: 15
M.L. Debut: 9/28/12

GONZALEZ, JULIO CESAR (HERNANDEZ)
Nickname: Julio
In St. Louis: 1981-82
Number: 14
M.L. Debut: 4/8/77

GOODENOUGH, WILLIAM B.
Nickname: Bill
In St. Louis: 1893
M.L. Debut: 8/31/1893

GOODFELLOW, MICHAEL J.
Nickname: Mike
In St. Louis: 1887
M.L. Debut: 6/13/1887

GOODWIN, MARVIN MARDO
Nickname: Marv
In St. Louis: 1917, 19-22
M.L. Debut: 9/7/16

GORE, GEORGE F.
Nickname: George, Piano Legs
In St. Louis: 1892
M.L. Debut: 5/1/1879

GORMAN, HERBERT ALLEN
Nickname: Herb
In St. Louis: 1952
M.L. Debut: 4/19/52

GORMAN, JOHN F.
Nickname: Jack, Stoopin Jack
In St. Louis: 1883
M.L. Debut: 7/1/1883

GORNICKI, HENRY FRANK
Nickname: Hank
In St. Louis: 1941
Number: 33
M.L. Debut: 4/17/41

GOTAY, JULIE ENRIQUE (SANCHEZ)
Nickname: Julio
In St. Louis: 1960-62
Number: 27,19
M.L. Debut: 8/6/60

GRABOWSKI, ALFONS FRANCIS
Nickname: Al, Hook
In St. Louis: 1929-30
M.L. Debut: 9/11/29

GRADY, MICHAEL WILLIAM
Nickname: Mike, Michaelangelo
In St. Louis: 1897, 1904-06
M.L. Debut: 4/24/1894

GRAMMAS, ALEXANDER PETER
Nickname: Alex
In St. Louis: 1954-56, 59-62
Number: 4, 10
M.L. Debut: 4/13/54

GRANGER, WAYNE ALLAN
Nickname: Wayne
In St. Louis: 1968, 73
Number: 29
M.L. Debut: 6/5/68

GRANT, JAMES TIMOTHY
Nickname: Mudcat
In St. Louis: 1969
Number: 22
M.L. Debut: 4/17/58

GRATER, MARK ANTHONY
Nickname: Mark
In St. Louis: 1991
Number: 50
M.L. Debut: 6/12/91

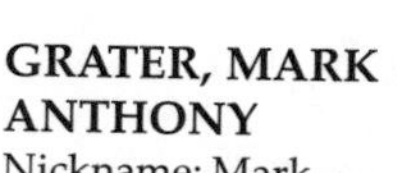

GRAY, RICHARD BENJAMIN
Nickname: Dick
In St. Louis: 1959-60
Number: 27
M.L. Debut: 4/15/58

GREASON, WILLIAM HENRY
Nickname: Bill, Booster
In St. Louis: 1954
Number: 34
M.L. Debut: 5/31/54

GREEN, BERTRUM SCARBOROUGH
Nickname: Scarborough
In St. Louis: 1997
Number: 22
M.L. Debut: 8/2/97

GREEN, DAVID ALEJANDRO (CASAYA)
Nickname: David
In St. Louis: 1981-84, 87
Number: 27, 22,18
M.L. Debut: 9/4/81

GREEN, GENE LEROY
Nickname: Gene
In St. Louis: 1957-59
Number: 24, 12, 1
M.L. Debut: 9/10/57

GREIF, WILLIAM BRILEY
Nickname: Bill
In St. Louis: 1976
Number: 38
M.L. Debut: 7/19/71

GRIESENBECK, CARLOS PHILLIPE TIMOTHY
Nickname: Tim
In St. Louis: 1920
M.L. Debut: 9/11/20

GRIEVE, THOMAS ALAN
Nickname: Tom
In St. Louis: 1979
Number: 3
M.L. Debut: 7/5/70

GRIFFIN, TOBIAS CHARLES
Nickname: Sandy
In St. Louis: 1893
M.L. Debut: 5/26/1884

GRIFFITH, CLARK CALVIN
Nickname: Clark, General, Griff, The Old Fox
In St. Louis: 1891
M.L. Debut: 4/11/1891

GRIM, ROBERT ANTON
Nickname: Bob
In St. Louis: 1960
Number: 46
M.L. Debut: 4/18/54

GRIMES, BURLEIGH ARLAND
Nickname: Burleigh, Ol'Stubblebeard
In St. Louis: 1930-31, 33-34
Number: 20, 31
M.L. Debut: 9/10/16

GRIMES, JOHN THOMAS
Nickname: John
In St. Louis: 1897
M.L. Debut: 7/28/1897

GRIMM, CHARLES JOHN
Nickname: Charlie, Jolly Cholly
In St. Louis: 1918
M.L. Debut: 7/30/16

GRINER, DONALD DEXTER
Nickname: Dan, Rusty
In St. Louis: 1912-16
M.L. Debut: 8/17/12

GRISSOM, MARVIN EDWARD
Nickname: Marv
In St. Louis: 1959
Number: 42
M.L. Debut: 9/10/46

GROAT, RICHARD MORROW
Nickname: Dick
In St. Louis: 1963-65
Number: 24
M.L. Debut: 6/19/52

GRODZICKI, JOHN
Nickname: Johnny, Grod
In St. Louis: 1941, 46-47
Number: 34, 33
M.L. Debut: 4/18/41

GRZENDA, JOSEPH CHARLES
Nickname: Joe
In St. Louis: 1972
Number: 31
M.L. Debut: 4/26/61

GUERRERO, MARIO MIGUEL (ABUD)
Nickname: Mario
In St. Louis: 1975
Number: 19
M.L. Debut: 4/8/73

GUERRERO, PEDRO
Nickname: Pete
In St. Louis: 1988-92
Number: 28
M.L. Debut: 9/22/78

GUETTERMAN, ARTHUR LEE
Nickname: Lee
In St. Louis: 1993
M.L. Debut: 9/12/84

GULAN, MICHAEL WATTS
Nickname: Mike
In St. Louis: 1997
Number: 53
M.L. Debut: 5/14/97

GUMBERT, HARRY EDWARD
Nickname: Harry, Gunboat
In St. Louis: 1941-44
Number: 42, 19
M.L. Debut: 9/12/35

GUNSON, JOSEPH BROOK
Nickname: Joe
In St. Louis: 1893
M.L. Debut: 6/14/1884

GUTTERIDGE, DONALD JOSEPH
Nickname: Don
In St. Louis: 1936-40
Number: 22, 5
M.L. Debut: 9/7/36

GUZMAN, SANTIAGO DONOVAN
Nickname: Santiago
In St. Louis: 1969-72
Number: 36
M.L. Debut: 9/30/69

HABENICHT, ROBERT JULIUS
Nickname: Bob, Hobby
In St. Louis: 1951
Number: 22
M.L. Debut: 4/17/51

HABYAN, JOHN GABRIEL
Nickname: John
In St. Louis: 1994-95
Number: 32
M.L. Debut: 9/29/85

HACKETT, JAMES JOSEPH
Nickname: Jim, Sunny Jim
In St. Louis: 1902-03
M.L. Debut: 9/14/02

HADDIX, HARVEY
Nickname: Harvey, The Kitten
In St. Louis: 1952-56
Number: 42
M.L. Debut: 8/20/52

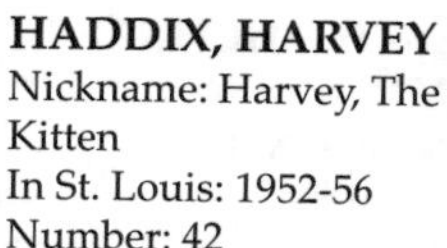

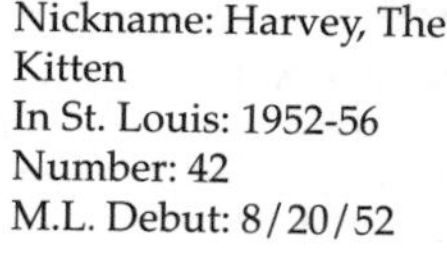

HAFEY, CHARLES JAMES
Nickname: Chick
In St. Louis: 1924-31
Number: 5
M.L. Debut: 8/28/24

HAGEMAN, KURT MORITZ
Nickname: Casey
In St. Louis: 1914
M.L. Debut: 9/18/11

HAGEN, KEVIN EUGENE
Nickname: 1983-84
Number: 35
M.L. Debut: 6/4/83

HAGUE, JOE CLARENCE
Nickname: Joe
In St. Louis: 1968-72
Number: 12
M.L. Debut: 9/19/68

HAHN, DONALD ANTONE
Nickname: Don
In St. Louis: 1975
M.L. Debut: 4/8/69

HAHN, FREDERICK ALOYS
Nickname: Fred
In St. Louis: 1952
Number: 41
M.L. Debut: 4/19/52

HAID, HAROLD AUGUSTINE
Nickname: Hal
In St. Louis: 1928-30
M.L. Debut: 9/5/19

HAIGH, EDWARD E.
Nickname: Ed
In St. Louis: 1892
M.L. Debut: 8/14/1892

HAINES, JESSE JOSEPH
Nickname: Jesse, Pop
In St. Louis: 1920-37
Number: 16
M.L. Debut: 7/20/18

HALL, CHARLES LOUIS
Nickname: Charley, Sea Lion
In St. Louis: 1916
M.L. Debut: 7/12/06

HALL, ROBERT RUSSELL
Nickname: Russ
In St. Louis: 1898
M.L. Debut: 4/15/1898

HALLAHAN, WILLIAM ANTHONY
Nickname: Bill, Wild Bill
In St. Louis: 1925-26, 29-36
Number: 22
M.L. Debut: 4/16/25

HALLMAN, WILLIAM WILSON
Nickname: Bill
In St. Louis: 1897
M.L. Debut: 4/23/1888

HAMILTON, DAVID EDWARD
Nickname: Dave
In St. Louis: 1978
Number: 26
M.L. Debut: 5/29/72

HANEY, FRED GIRARD
Nickname: Fred, Pudge
In St. Louis: 1929
M.L. Debut: 4/18/22

HANEY, WALLACE LARRY
Nickname: Larry
In St. Louis: 1973
Number: 7
M.L. Debut: 7/27/66

HARDING, LOUIS EDWARD
Nickname: Lou, Jumbo
In St. Louis: 1886
M.L. Debut: 10/5/1886

HARLEY, RICHARD JOSEPH
Nickname: Dick
In St. Louis: 1897-98
M.L. Debut: 6/2/1897

HARMON, CHARLES BYRON
Nickname: Chuck
In St. Louis: 1956-57
Number: 24
M.L. Debut: 4/17/54

HARMON, ROBERT GREEN
Nickname: Bob, Hickory Bob
In St. Louis: 1909-13
M.L. Debut: 6/23/09

HARPER, BRIAN DAVID
Nickname: Brian
In St. Louis: 1985
Number: 25
M.L. Debut: 9/29/79

HARPER, CHARLES WILLIAM
Nickname: Jack
In St. Louis: 1900-01
M.L. Debut: 9/18/1899

HARPER, GEORGE WASHINGTON
Nickname: George
In St. Louis: 1928
M.L. Debut: 4/15/16

HARRELL, RAYMOND JAMES
Nickname: Ray, Cowboy
In St. Louis: 1935, 37-38
Number: 20, 28
M.L. Debut: 4/16/35

HARRIS, VICTOR LANIER
Nickname: Vic
In St. Louis: 1976
Number: 4
M.L. Debut: 7/21/72

HART, ROBERT LEE
Nickname: Bob, Billy
In St. Louis: 1890
M.L. Debut: 7/13/1890

HART, WILLIAM FRANKLIN
Nickname: Bill, Uncle Billy
In St. Louis: 1896-97
M.L. Debut: 7/26/1886

HARTENSTEIN, CHARLES OSCAR
Nickname: Chuck, Twiggy
In St. Louis: 1970
M.L. Debut: 9/11/65

HARTMAN, FREDERICK ORRIN
Nickname: Fred, Dutch
In St. Louis: 1897, 1902
M.L. Debut: 7/26/1894

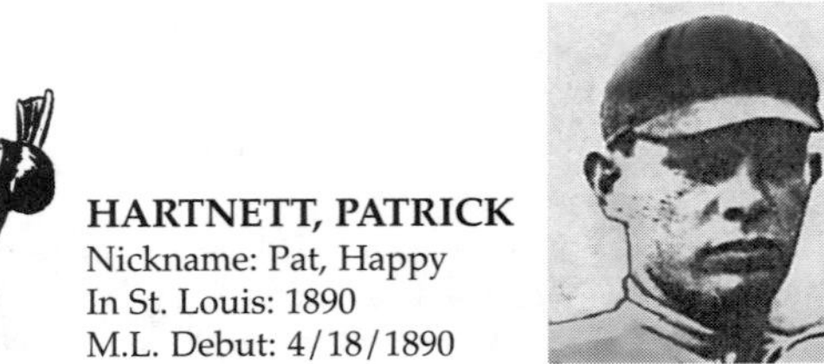

HARTNETT, PATRICK
Nickname: Pat, Happy
In St. Louis: 1890
M.L. Debut: 4/18/1890

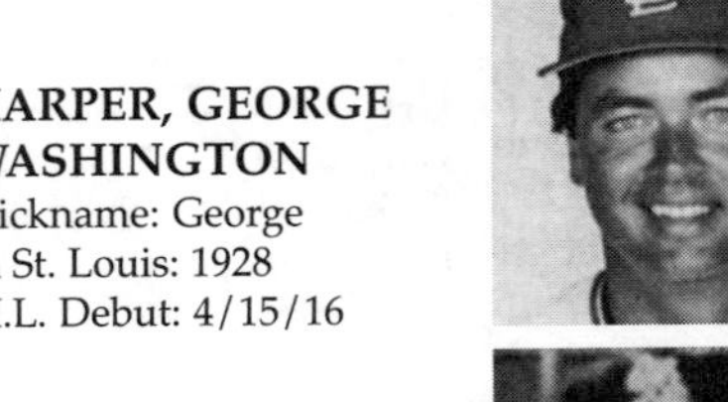

HASSLER, ANDREW EARL
Nickname: Andy
In St. Louis: 1984-85
Number: 44
M.L. Debut: 5/30/71

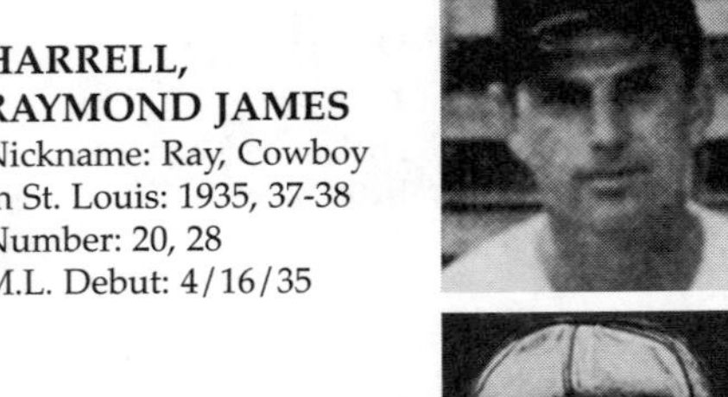

HATTON, GRADY EDGEBERT
Nickname: Grady
In St. Louis: 1956
Number: 28
M.L. Debut: 4/16/46

HAUSER, ARNOLD GEORGE
Nickname: Arnold , Pee Wee, Stub
In St. Louis: 1910-13
M.L. Debut: 4/21/10

HAWKE, WILLIAM VICTOR
Nickname: Bill, Dick
In St. Louis: 1892-93
M.L. Debut: 7/28/1892

HAWLEY, EMERSON P.
Nickname: Pink
In St. Louis: 1892-94
M.L. Debut: 8/13/1892

HAZELTON, WILLARD CARPENTER
Nickname: Doc
In St. Louis: 1902
M.L. Debut: 4/17/02

HEALY, FRANCIS XAVIER PAUL
Nickname: Francis
In St. Louis: 1934
Number: 27
M.L. Debut: 4/29/30

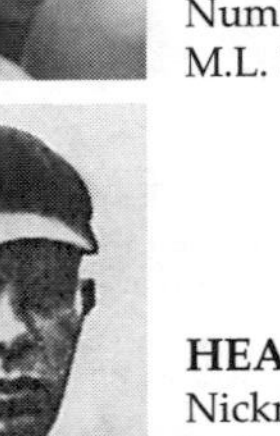

HEARN, BUNN
Nickname: Bunny
In St. Louis: 1910-11
M.L. Debut: 9/17/10

HEARN, JAMES TOLBERT
Nickname: Jim
In St. Louis: 1947-50
Number: 34
M.L. Debut: 4/17/47

HEATH, MICHAEL THOMAS
Nickname: Mike
In St. Louis: 1986
Number: 5
M.L. Debut: 6/3/78

HEATHCOTE, CLIFTON EARL
Nickname: Cliff
In St. Louis: 1918-22
M.L. Debut: 6/4/18

HEIDEMANN, JACK SEALE
Nickname: Jack
In St. Louis: 1974
Number: 11
M.L. Debut: 5/2/69

HEIDRICK, R. EMMET
Nickname: Emmet, Snags
In St. Louis: 1899-1901
M.L. Debut: 9/14/1898

HEINKEL, DONALD ELLIOT
Nickname: Don
In St. Louis: 1989
Number: 30
M.L. Debut: 4/7/88

HEINTZELMAN, THOMAS KENNETH
Nickname: Tom
In St. Louis: 1973-74
Number: 5
M.L. Debut: 8/12/73

HEISE, CLARENCE EDWARD
Nickname: Clarence, Lefty
In St. Louis: 1934
Number: 27
M.L. Debut: 4/22/34

HEISE, ROBERT LOWELL
Nickname: Bob
In St. Louis: 1974
M.L. Debut: 9/12/67

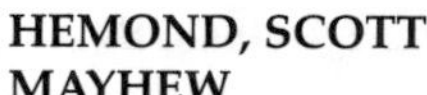

HEMOND, SCOTT MAYHEW
Nickname: Scott
In St. Louis: 1995
Number: 26
M.L. Debut: 9/9/89

HEMPHILL, CHARLES JUDSON
Nickname: Charlie, Eagle Eye
In St. Louis: 1899
M.L. Debut: 6/27/1899

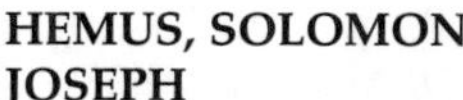

HEMUS, SOLOMON JOSEPH
Nickname: Solly
In St. Louis: 1949-56, 59
Number: 22, 7
M.L. Debut: 4/27/49

HENDRICK, GEORGE ANDREW
Nickname: George, Silent George
In St. Louis: 1978-84
Number: 27, 25
M.L. Debut: 6/4/71

HENDRICK, HARVEY
Nickname: Harvey, Gink
In St. Louis: 1932
M.L. Debut: 4/20/23

HENKE, THOMAS ANTHONY
Nickname: Tom, The Terminator
In St. Louis: 1995
Number: 50
M.L. Debut: 9/10/82

HENSHAW, ROY KNIKELBINE
Nickname: Roy
In St. Louis: 1938
Number: 31
M.L. Debut: 4/15/33

HERNANDEZ, KEITH
Nickname: Keith, Mex
In St. Louis: 1974-83
In St. Louis: 18, 37
M.L. Debut: 8/30/74

HERNDON, LARRY DARNELL
Nickname: Larry
In St. Louis: 1974
Number: 46
M.L. Debut: 9/4/74

HERR, EDWARD JOSEPH
Nickname: Ed
In St. Louis: 1888, 90
M.L. Debut: 4/16/1887

HERR, THOMAS MITCHELL
Nickname: Tommy
In St. Louis: 1979-88
Number: 28
M.L. Debut: 8/13/79

HERTWECK, NEAL CHARLES
Nickname: Neal
In St. Louis: 1952
M.L. Debut: 9/27/52

HEUSSER, EDWARD BURLTON
Nickname: Ed, The Wild Elk of the Wasatch
In St. Louis: 1935-36
Number: 32,14
M.L. Debut: 4/25/35

HEYDON, MICHAEL EDWARD
Nickname: Mike, Ed
In St. Louis: 1901
M.L. Debut: 10/12/1898

HICKMAN, JAMES LUCIUS
Nickname: Jim
In St. Louis: 1974
Number: 24
M.L. Debut: 4/14/62

HICKS, JAMES EDWARD
Nickname: Jim
In St. Louis: 1969
Number: 24
M.L. Debut: 10/2/64

HIGGINBOTHAM, IRVING CLINTON
Nickname: Irv
In St. Louis: 1906, 08-09
M.L. Debut: 8/11/06

HIGGINS, DENNIS DEAN
Nickname: Dennis
In St. Louis: 1971-72
Number: 37
M.L. Debut: 4/12/66

HIGGINS, THOMAS EDWARD
Nickname: Eddie, Irish, Doc
In St. Louis: 1909-10
M.L. Debut: 5/14/09

HIGGINS, WILLIAM EDWARD
Nickname: Bill
In St. Louis: 1890
M.L. Debut: 8/9/1888

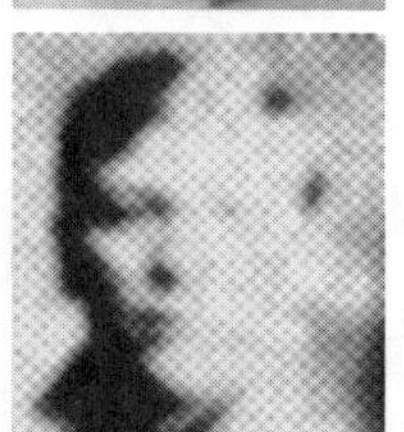

HIGH, ANDREW AIRD
Nickname: Andy, Handy Andy
In St. Louis: 1928-31
Number: 15
M.L. Debut: 4/12/22

HILDEBRAND, PALMER MARION
Nickname: Palmer, Pete
In St. Louis: 1913
M.L. Debut: 5/14/13

HILGENDORF, THOMAS EUGENE
Nickname: Tom
In St. Louis: 1969-70
Number: 19
M.L. Debut: 8/15/69

HILL, CARMEN PROCTOR
Nickname: Carmen, Bunker, Specs
In St. Louis: 1929-30
M.L. Debut: 8/24/15

HILL, HUGH ELLIS
Nickname: Hugh
In St. Louis: 1904
M.L. Debut: 5/1/03

HILL, KENNETH WADE
Nickname: Ken, Thrill
In St. Louis: 1988-91, 95
Number: 56,43
M.L. Debut: 9/3/88

HILL, MARC KEVIN
Nickname: Marc
In St. Louis: 1973-74
Number: 16
M.L. Debut: 9/28/73

HILTON, HOWARD JAMES
Nickname: Howard
In St. Louis: 1990
Number: 42
M.L. Debut: 4/9/90

HIMES, JOHN HERB
Nickname: Jack
In St. Louis: 1905-06
M.L. Debut: 9/18/05

HITT, BRUCE SMITH
Nickname: Bruce
In St. Louis: 1917
M.L. Debut: 9/23/17

HOBBIE, GLEN FREDERICK
Nickname: Glen
In St. Louis: 1964
Number: 40
M.L. Debut: 9/20/57

HOCK, EDWARD FRANCIS
Nickname: Ed
In St. Louis: 1920
M.L. Debut: 7/8/20

HODNETT, CHARLES
Nickname: Charlie
In St. Louis: 1883
M.L. Debut: 5/3/1883

HOELSKOETTER, ARTHUR H.
Nickname: Art, Holley, Hoss
In St. Louis: 1905-07
M.L. Debut: 9/10/05

HOERNER, JOSEPH WALTER
Nickname: Joe
In St. Louis: 1966-69
Number: 43
M.L. Debut: 9/27/63

HOGAN, MARTIN F.
Nickname: Marty
In St. Louis: 1894-95
M.L. Debut: 8/6/1894

HOGAN, ROBERT EDWARD
Nickname: Eddie
In St. Louis: 1882
M.L. Debut: 7/5/1882

HOLBERT, AARON KEITH
Nickname: Aaron
In St. Louis: 1996
Number: 68
M.L. Debut: 4/14/96

ST. LOUIS CARDINALS
NATIONAL LEAGUE CHAMPIONS
1931

HOLLAND, HOWARD ARTHUR
Nickname: Mul
In St. Louis: 1929
M.L. Debut: 5/25/26

HOLLY, EDWARD WILLIAM
Nickname: Ed
In St. Louis: 1906-07
M.L. Debut: 7/18/06

HOLM, ROSCOE ALBERT
Nickname: Wattie
In St. Louis: 1924-29, 32
Number: 24
M.L. Debut: 4/15/24

HOLMES, HOWARD ELBERT
Nickname: Ducky
In St. Louis: 1906
M.L. Debut: 4/18/06

HOLMES, JAMES WILLIAM
Nickname: Ducky
In St. Louis: 1898
M.L. Debut: 8/8/1895

HONEYCUTT, FREDERICK WAYNE
Nickname: Rick
In St. Louis: 1996-97
Number: 32
M.L. Debut: 8/24/77

HOOD, DONALD HARRIS
Nickname: Don
In St. Louis: 1980
Number: 26
M.L. Debut: 7/16/73

HOPKINS, JOHN WINTON
Nickname: Sis, Buck
In St. Louis: 1907
M.L. Debut: 7/22/07

HOPP, JOHN LEONARD
Nickname: Johnny, Hippity
In St. Louis: 1939-45
Number: 12,40
M.L. Debut: 9/18/39

HOPPER, WILLIAM BOOTH
Nickname: Bill, Bird Dog
In St. Louis: 1913-14
M.L. Debut: 9/11/13

HORNER, JAMES ROBERT
Nickname: Bob
In St. Louis: 1988
Number: 5
M.L. Debut: 6/16/78

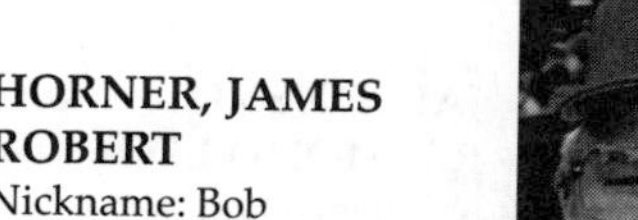

HORNSBY, ROGERS
Nickname: Rogers, Rajah
In St. Louis: 1915-26, 33
Number: 4
M.L. Debut: 9/10/15

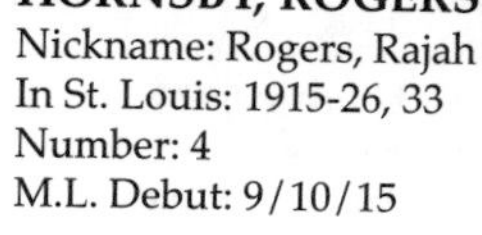

HORSTMANN, OSCAR THEODORE
Nickname: Oscar
In St. Louis: 1917-19
M.L. Debut: 4/18/17

HORTON, RICKY NEAL
Nickname: Ricky
In St. Louis: 1984-87, 89-90
Number: 49
M.L. Debut: 4/7/84

HOUSEHOLDER, PAUL WESLEY
Nickname: Paul
In St. Louis: 1984
Number: 37
M.L. Debut: 8/26/80

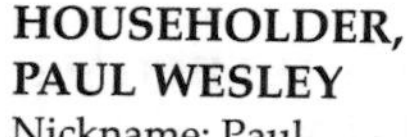

HOUSEMAN, JOHN FRANKLIN
Nickname: Johnny
In St. Louis: 1897
M.L. Debut: 9/11/1894

HOWARD, DOUGLAS LYNN
Nickname: Doug
In St. Louis: 1975
Number: 37
M.L. Debut: 9/6/72

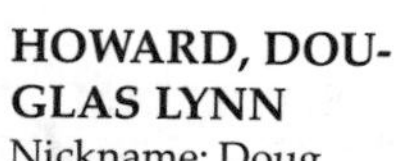

HOWARD, EARL NYCUM
Nickname: Earl
In St. Louis: 1918
M.L. Debut: 4/18/18

HOWE, ARTHUR HENRY JR.
Nickname: Art
In St. Louis: 1984-85
Number: 7
M.L. Debut: 7/10/74

HOWELL, ROLAND BOATNER
Nickname: Roland, Billiken
In St. Louis: 1912
M.L. Debut: 6/14/12

HOWERTON, WILLIAM RAY
Nickname: Bill, Hopalong
In St. Louis: 1949-51
Number: 36
M.L. Debut: 9/11/49

HOY, WILLIAM ELLSWORTH
Nickname: Dummy
In St. Louis: 1891
M.L. Debut: 4/20/1888

HRABOSKY, ALAN THOMAS
Nickname: Al, The Mad Hungarian
In St. Louis: 1970-77
Number: 39
M.L. Debut: 6/16/70

HUDGENS, JAMES PRICE
Nickname: Jimmy
In St. Louis: 1923
M.L. Debut: 9/14/23

HUDLER, REX ALLEN
Nickname: Rex, Hurricane, The Wonder Dog
In St. Louis: 1990-92
Number: 10
M.L. Debut: 9/9/84

HUDSON, CHARLES
Nickname: Charlie
In St. Louis: 1972
Number: 30
M.L. Debut: 5/21/72

HUDSON, NATHANIAL P.
Nickname: Nat
In St. Louis: 1886-89
M.L. Debut: 4/18/1886

HUELSMAN, FRANK ELMER
Nickname: Frank
In St. Louis: 1897
M.L. Debut: 10/3/1897

HUGGINS, MILLER JAMES
Nickname: Miller, Hug, The Mighty Mite
In St. Louis: 1910-16
M.L. Debut: 4/15/04

HUGHES, RICHARD HENRY
Nickname: Dick
In St. Louis: 1966-68
Number: 31
M.L. Debut: 9/11/66

HUGHES, TERRY WAYNE
Nickname: Terry
In St. Louis: 1973
Number: 14
M.L. Debut: 9/2/70

HUGHES, THOMAS EDWARD
Nickname: Tom
In St. Louis: 1959
M.L. Debut: 9/13/59

HUGHEY, JAMES ULYSSES
Nickname: Jim, Cold Water Jim
In St. Louis: 1898, 1900
M.L. Debut: 9/29/1891

HULETT, TIMOTHY CRAIG
Nickname: Tim
In St. Louis: 1995
M.L. Debut: 9/15/83

HULSWITT, RULDOLPH ED-WARD
Nickname: Rudy
In St. Louis: 1909-10
M.L. Debut: 6/16/1899

HUMPHREYS, ROBERT WILLIAM
Nickname: Bob
In St. Louis: 1963-64
Number: 47
M.L. Debut: 9/8/62

HUNT, BENJAMIN FRANKLIN
Nickname: Ben, High Pocket
In St. Louis: 1913
M.L. Debut: 8/24/10

HUNT, JAMES RANDALL
Nickname: Randy
In St. Louis: 1985
Number: 10
M.L. Debut: 6/4/85

ST. LOUIS CARDINALS
NATIONAL LEAGUE CHAMPIONS
1931

HUNT, OLIVER JOEL
Nickname: Joel, Jodie
In St. Louis: 1931-32
M.L. Debut: 4/27/31

HUNT, RONALD KENNETH
Nickname: Ron
In St. Louis: 1974
Number: 32
M.L. Debut: 4/16/63

HUNTER, HERBERT HARRISON
Nickname: Herb
In St. Louis: 1921
M.L. Debut: 4/29/16

HUNTZ, STEPHEN MICHAEL
Nickname: Steve
In St. Louis: 1967, 69
Number: 14
M.L. Debut: 9/19/67

HUNTZINGER, WALTER HENRY
Nickname: Walter, Shakes
In St. Louis: 1926
M.L. Debut: 9/29/23

HURDLE, CLINTON MERRICK
Nickname: Clint
In St. Louis: 1986
Number: 13
M.L. Debut: 9/18/77

HUTCHINSON, IRA KENDALL
Nickname: Ira
In St. Louis: 1940-41
Number: 27, 30
M.L. Debut: 9/24/33

HUTCHINSON, WILLIAM FORREST
Nickname: Bill, Wild Bill
In St. Louis: 1897
M.L. Debut: 6/10/1884

HYATT, ROBERT HAMILTON
Nickname: Ham
In St. Louis: 1915
M.L. Debut: 4/15/09

HYNES, PATRICK J.
Nickname: Pat
In St. Louis: 1903
M.L. Debut: 9/27/03

IORG, DANE CHARLES
Nickname: Dane
In St. Louis: 1977-84
In St. Louis: 19
M.L. Debut: 4/9/77

ST. LOUIS CARDINALS
CHAMPIONS NATIONAL LEAGUE
1928

IRWIN, WALTER KINGSLEY
Nickname: Walt, Lightning
In St. Louis: 1921
M.L. Debut: 4/24/21

JABLONSKI, RAYMOND LEO
Nickname: Ray, Jabbo
In St. Louis: 1953-54, 59
Number: 16
M.L. Debut: 4/14/53

JACKSON, ALVIN NEIL
Nickname: Al
In St. Louis: 1966-67
Number: 38
M.L. Debut: 6/1/59

JACKSON, DANNY LYNN
Nickname: Danny
In St. Louis: 1995-97
Number: 29
M.L. Debut: 9/11/83

JACKSON, LAWRENCE CURTIS
Nickname: Larry
In St. Louis: 1955-62
Number: 39
M.L. Debut: 4/17/55

JACKSON, MICHAEL WARREN
Nickname: Mike
In St. Louis: 1971
M.L. Debut: 5/10/70

JACOBS, ANTHONY ROBERT
Nickname: Tony
In St. Louis: 1955
Number: 1
M.L. Debut: 9/19/48

JACOBS, WILLIAM ELMER
Nickname: Elmer
In St. Louis: 1919-20
M.L. Debut: 4/23/14

JAMES, BERTON HULON
Nickname: Bert, Jesse
In St. Louis: 1909
M.L. Debut: 9/18/09

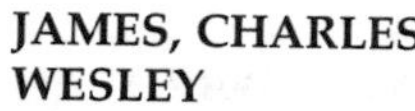

JAMES, CHARLES WESLEY
Nickname: Charlie
In St. Louis: 1960-64
Number: 23
M.L. Debut: 8/2/60

JANVRIN, HAROLD CHANDLER
Nickname: Hal, Childe Harold
In St. Louis: 1919-21
M.L. Debut: 7/9/11

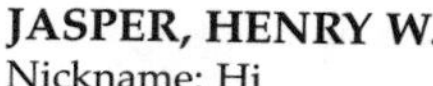

JASPER, HENRY W.
Nickname: Hi
In St. Louis: 1916
M.L. Debut: 4/19/14

JASTER, LARRY EDWARD
Nickname: Larry
In St. Louis: 1965-68
Number: 39
M.L. Debut: 9/17/65

JAVIER, MANUEL JULIAN (LIRANZO)
Nickname: Julian, Hoolie, The Phantom
In St. Louis: 1960-71
Number: 25
M.L. Debut: 5/28/60

JEFFCOAT, HAROLD BENTLEY
Nickname: Hal,
In St. Louis: 1959
Number: 36
M.L. Debut: 4/20/48

JEFFERIES, GREGORY SCOTT
Nickname: Gregg
In St. Louis: 1993-94
Number: 12, 25
M.L. Debut: 9/6/87

JOHNSON, ADAM RANKIN SR.
Nickname: Adam, Tex
In St. Louis: 1918
M.L. Debut: 4/20/14

JOHNSON, ALEXANDER
Nickname: Alex
In St. Louis: 1966-67
Number: 12
M.L. Debut: 7/25/64

JOHNSON, DARRELL DEAN
Nickname: Darrell
In St. Louis: 1960
Number: 8
M.L. Debut: 4/20/52

JOHNSON, JERRY MICHAEL
Nickname: Jerry
In St. Louis: 1970
Number: 21
M.L. Debut: 7/17/68

JOHNSON, KENNETH LANCE
Nickname: Lance
In St. Louis: 1987
Number: 21
M.L. Debut: 7/10/87

JOHNSON, KENNETH WANDERSEE
Nickname: Ken, Hook
In St. Louis: 1947-50
Number: 35
M.L. Debut: 9/18/47

JOHNSON, ROBERT WALLACE
Nickname: Bob
In St. Louis: 1969
Number: 29
M.L. Debut: 4/19/60

JOHNSON, SILAS KENNETH
Nickname: Si
In St. Louis: 1936-38
Number: 18, 12
M.L. Debut: 5/2/28

JOHNSON, SYLVESTER
Nickname: Syl
In St. Louis: 1926-33
Number: 23, 30
M.L. Debut: 4/24/22

JOHNSON, WILLIAM RUSSELL
Nickname: Billy, Bull
In St. Louis: 1951-53
Number: 1
M.L. Debut: 4/22/43

JONES, ALBERT EDWARD
Nickname: Cowboy, Bronco
In St. Louis: 1899-1901
M.L. Debut: 6/24/1898

JONES, GORDON BASSETT
Nickname: Gordon
In St. Louis: 1954-56
Number: 45
M.L. Debut: 8/6/54

JONES, HOWARD
Nickname: Howie, Cotton
In St. Louis: 1921
M.L. Debut: 9/5/21

JONES, MAURICE MORRIS
Nickname: Red
In St. Louis: 1940
In St. Louis: 19
M.L. Debut: 4/16/40

JONES, SAMUEL
Nickname: Sam, Sad Sam, Toothpick Sam
In St. Louis: 1957-58, 63
Number: 23
M.L. Debut: 9/22/51

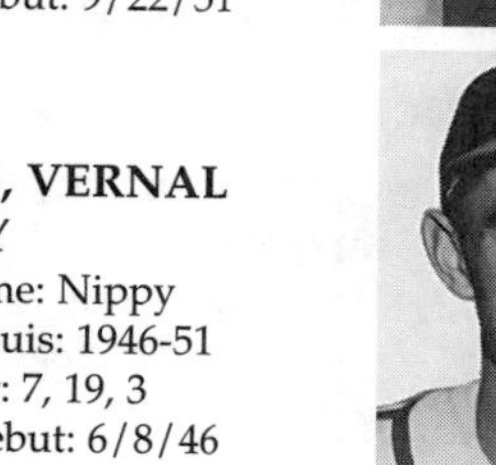

JONES, VERNAL LEROY
Nickname: Nippy
In St. Louis: 1946-51
Number: 7, 19, 3
M.L. Debut: 6/8/46

JONES, WILLIAM TIMOTHY
Nickname: Tim
In St. Louis: 1988-93
Number: 22, 8
M.L. Debut: 7/26/88

JONNARD, CLARENCE JAMES
Nickname: Bubber
In St. Louis: 1929
M.L. Debut: 10/1/20

JORDAN, BRIAN O'NEAL
Nickname: Brian
In St. Louis: 1992-97
Number: 3
M.L. Debut: 4/8/92

JORGENSEN, MICHAEL
Nickname: Mike
In St. Louis: 1984-85
In St. Louis: 19
M.L. Debut: 9/10/68

JOSE, DOMINGO FELIX (ANDUJAR)
Nickname: Felix
In St. Louis: 1990-92
Number: 40, 34
M.L. Debut: 9/2/88

JUDY, LYLE LEROY
Nickname: Lyle, Punch
In St. Louis: 1935
Number: 10
M.L. Debut: 9/17/35

JURISCH, ALVIN JOSEPH
Nickname: Al
In St. Louis: 1944-45
Number: 29
M.L. Debut: 4/26/44

JUTZE, ALFRED HENRY
Nickname: Skip
In St. Louis: 1972
Number: 18
M.L. Debut: 9/1/72

KAAT, JAMES LEE
Nickname: Jim, Kitty
In St. Louis: 1980-83
Number: 36
M.L. Debut: 8/2/59

KANE, WILLIAM JERIMIAH
Nickname: Jerry
In St. Louis: 1890
M.L. Debut: 5/2/1890

KARGER, EDWIN
Nickname: Ed, Loose
In St. Louis: 1906-08
M.L. Debut: 4/15/06

KASKO, EDWARD MICHAEL
Nickname: Eddie
In St. Louis: 1957-58
Number: 10
M.L. Debut: 4/18/57

KATT, RAYMOND FREDERICK
Nickname: Ray
In St. Louis: 1956, 58-59
Number: 15
M.L. Debut: 9/16/52

KAUFMAN, ANTHONY CHARLES
Nickname: Tony
In St. Louis: 1927-28, 30-31, 35
Number: 20, 25
M.L. Debut: 9/23/21

KAVANAGH, MARTIN JOSEPH
Nickname: Marty
In St. Louis: 1918
M.L. Debut: 4/18/14

KAZAK, EDWARD TERRANCE
Nickname: Eddie
In St. Louis: 1948-52
Number: 21, 1
M.L. Debut: 9/29/48

KEELY, ROBERT WILLIAM
Nickname: Bob
In St. Louis: 1944-45
Number: 2, 18
M.L. Debut: 7/25/44

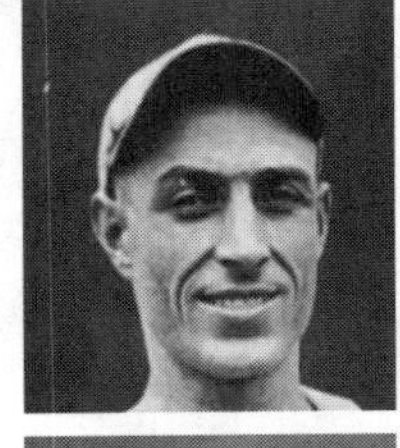

KEEN, HOWARD VICTOR
Nickname: Vic
In St. Louis: 1926-27
M.L. Debut: 8/13/18

KEENER, JEFFERY BRUCE
Nickname: Jeff
In St. Louis: 1982-83
Number: 44
M.L. Debut: 6/8/82

KEISTER, WILLIAM HOFFMAN
Nickname: Bill, Wagon Tongue
In St. Louis: 1900
M.L. Debut: 5/20/1896

KELLEHER, JOHN PATRICK
Nickname: John
In St. Louis: 1912
M.L. Debut: 7/31/12

KELLEHER, MICHAEL DENNIS
Nickname: Mick
In St. Louis: 1972-73, 75
Number: 25, 28
M.L. Debut: 9/1/72

KELLNER, ALEXANDER RAYMOND
Nickname: Alex
In St. Louis: 1959
Number: 34
M.L. Debut: 4/29/48

KELLUM, WINFORD ANSLEY
Nickname: Win
In St. Louis: 1905
M.L. Debut: 4/26/01

KELLY, JOHN B.
Nickname: John
In St. Louis: 1907
M.L. Debut: 4/11/07

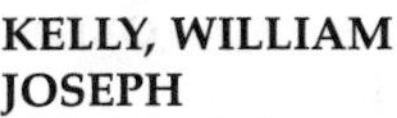

KELLY, WILLIAM JOSEPH
Nickname: Bill
In St. Louis: 1910
M.L. Debut: 5/2/10

KEMMLER, RUDOLPH
Nickname: Rudy
In St. Louis: 1886
M.L. Debut: 7/26/1879

KENNEDY, JAMES EARL
Nickname: Jim
In St. Louis: 1970
Number: 24
M.L. Debut: 6/14/70

KENNEDY, TERRANCE EDWARD
Nickname: Terry
In St. Louis: 1978-80
Number: 16
M.L. Debut: 9/4/78

KEOUGH, MATTHEW LON
Nickname: Matt
In St. Louis: 1985
Number: 33
M.L. Debut: 9/3/77

KEPSHIRE, KURT DAVID
Kurt
In St. Louis: 1984-86
Number: 50
M.L. Debut: 7/4/84

KERINS, JOHN NELSON
Nickname: John
In St. Louis: 1890
M.L. Debut: 5/1/1884

KERNEK, GEORGE BOYD
Nicknamd: George
In St. Louis: 1965-66
Number: 30, 14
M.L. Debut: 9/5/65

KESSINGER, DONALD EULON
Nickname: Don
In St. Louis: 1976-77
Number: 11
M.L. Debut: 9/7/64

KILGUS, PAUL NELSON
Nickname: Paul
In St. Louis: 1993
Number: 36
M.L. Debut: 6/7/87

KIMBALL, NEWELL W.
Nickname: Newt
In St. Louis: 1940
Number: 25
M.L. Debut: 5/7/37

KIME, HAROLD LEE
Nickname: Hal, Lefty
In St. Louis: 1920
M.L. Debut: 6/19/20

KIMMICK, WALTER LYONS
Nickname: Wally
In St. Louis: 1919
M.L. Debut: 9/13/19

KINDER, ELLIS RAYMOND
Nickname: Ellis, Old Folks
In St. Louis: 1956
Number: 16
M.L. Debut: 4/30/46

KING, CHARLES FREDRICK
Nickname: Silver
In St. Louis: 1887-89
M.L. Debut: 8/28/1886

KING, CHARLES GILBERT
Nickname: Charlie, Chick
In St. Louis: 1959
M.L. Debut: 8/27/54

KING, CURTIS ALBERT
Nickname: Curtis
In St. Louis: 1997
Number: 57

KING, JAMES HUBERT
Nickname: Jim
In St. Louis: 1957
Number: 9
M.L. Debut: 4/17/55

KING, LYNN PAUL
Nickname: Lynn, Dig
In St. Louis: 1935, 36, 39
Number: 24, 5, 17
M.L. Debut: 9/21/35

KINLOCK, WALTER
Nickname: Walt
In St. Louis: 1895
M.L. Debut: 8/1/1895

KINSLOW, THOMAS
Nickname: Tom
In St. Louis: 1898
M.L. Debut: 6/4/1886

KINZER, MATTHEW ROY
Nickname: Matt
In St. Louis: 1989
Number: 59
M.L. Debut: 5/18/89

KINZIE, WALTER HARRIS
Nickname: Walt
In St. Louis: 1884
M.L. Debut: 7/17/1882

KIRCHER, MICHAEL ANDREW
Nickname: Mike
In St. Louis: 1920-21
M.L. Debut: 8/8/19

KISSINGER, WILLIAM FRANCIS
Nickname: Bill, Shang
In St. Louis: 1895-97
M.L. Debut: 5/30/1895

KLEIN, LOUIS FRANK
Nickname: Lou
In St. Louis: 1943, 45-46, 49
Number: 2,7,29
M.L. Debut: 4/21/43

KLEINKE, NORBERT GEORGE
Nickname: Nub
In St. Louis: 1935, 37
Number: 24
M.L. Debut: 4/25/35

KLINE, RONALD LEE
Nickname: Ron
In St. Louis: 1960
Number: 44
M.L. Debut: 4/21/52

KLING, RUDOLPH A.
Nickname: Rudy
In St. Louis: 1902
M.L. Debut: 9/21/02

KLUSMAN, WILLIAM F.
Nickname: Billy, Bull
In St. Louis: 1890
M.L. Debut: 6/21/1888

KLUTZ, CLYDE FRANKLIN
Nickname: Clyde
In St. Louis: 1946
Number: 39
M.L. Debut: 4/20/42

KNICELY, ALAN LEE
Nickname: Alan
In St. Louis: 1986
Number: 23
M.L. Debut: 8/12/79

KNIGHT, ELMA RUSSEL
Nickname: Jack
In St. Louis: 1922
M.L. Debut: 9/20/22

KNODE, KENNETH THOMPSON
Nickname: Mike
In St. Louis: 1920
M.L. Debut: 6/28/20

KNOUFF, EDWARD
Nickname: Ed, Fred
In St. Louis: 1887-88
M.L. Debut: 7/1/1885

KNOWLES, DAROLD DUANE
Nickname: Darold
In St. Louis: 1979-80
Number: 34
M.L. Debut: 4/18/65

KOENIGSMARK, WILLIAM THOMAS
Nickname: Will
In St. Louis: 1919
M.L. Debut: 9/10/19

KOLB, GARY ALAN
Nickname: Gary
In St. Louis: 1960, 62-63
Number: 22, 20
M.L. Debut: 9/7/60

KONETCHY, EDWARD JOSEPH
Nickname: Ed, Big Ed, Koney
In St. Louis: 1907-13
M.L. Debut: 6/29/07

KONSTANTY, CASIMIR JAMES
Nickname: Jim
In St. Louis: 1956
Number: 25
M.L. Debut: 6/18/44

KOPSHAW, GEORGE KARL
Nickname: George
In St. Louis: 1923
M.L. Debut: 8/4/23

KOY, ERNEST ANYZ
Nickname: Ernie, Chief
In St. Louis: 1940-41
Number: 19
M.L. Debut: 4/19/38

KRAUSSE, LEWIS BERNARD JR.
Nickname: Lew
In St. Louis: 1973
Number: 29
M.L. Debut: 6/16/61

KREHMEYER, CHARLES L.
Nickname: Charles
In St. Louis: 1884
M.L. Debut: 7/8/1884

KRIEGER, KURT FERDINAND
Nickname: Kurt, Dutch
In St. Louis: 1949, 51
Number: 24, 30
M.L. Debut: 4/21/49

KRIST, HOWARD WILBER
Nickname: Howie, Spud
In St. Louis: 1937-38, 41-43, 46
Number: 26, 29
M.L. Debut: 9/12/37

KRUEGER, ARTHUR WILLIAM
Nickname: Otto, Oom Paul
In St. Louis: 1900-02
M.L. Debut: 9/16/1899

KUBIAK, THEODORE RODGER
Nickname: Ted
In St. Louis: 1971
Number: 1
M.L. Debut: 4/14/67

KUEHNE, WILLIAM J.
Nickname: Willie
In St. Louis: 1892
M.L. Debut: 5/1/1883

KUROSAKI, RYAN YOSHITOMO
Nickname: Ryan
In St. Louis: 1975
M.L. Debut: 5/20/75

KUROWSKI, GEORGE JOHN
Nickname: Whitey
In St. Louis: 1941-49
Number: 1
M.L. Debut: 9/23/41

KUZAVA, ROBERT LEROY
Nickname: Bob, Sarge
In St. Louis: 1957
Number: 46
M.L. Debut: 9/21/46

LAGA, MICHAEL RUSSELL
Nickname: Mike
In St. Louis: 1986-88
Number: 35
M.L. Debut: 9/1/82

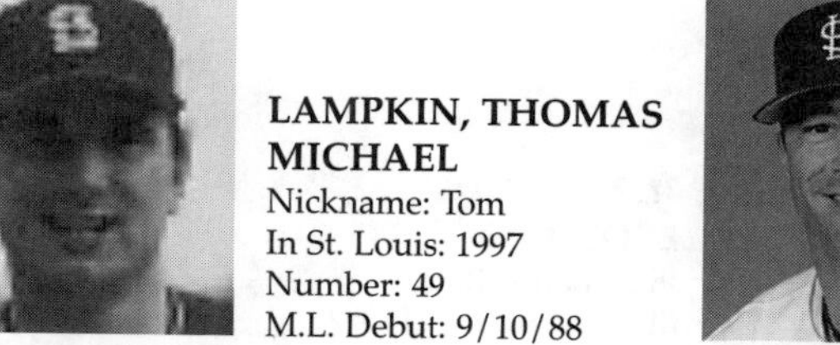

LAGROW, LERRIN HARRIS
Nickname: Lerrin
In St. Louis: 1976
Number: 44
M.L. Debut: 7/28/70

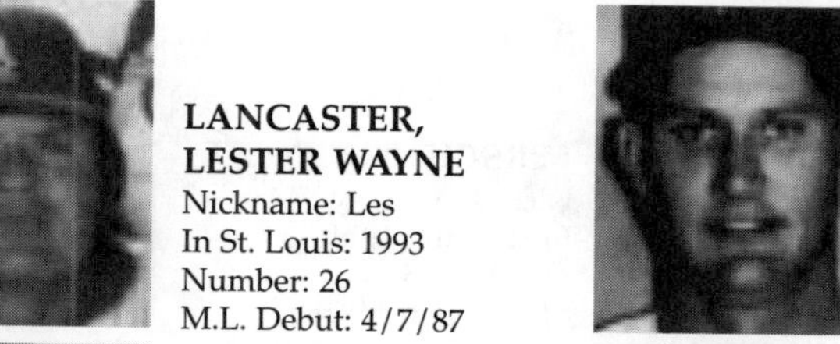

LAHTI, JEFFREY ALLEN
Nickname: Jeff
In St. Louis: 1982-86
Number: 32
M.L. Debut: 6/27/82

LAKE, EDWARD ERVING
Nickname: Eddie, Sparky
In St. Louis: 1939-41
Number: 1
M.L. Debut: 9/26/39

LAKE, STEVEN MICHAEL
Nickname: Steve
In St. Louis: 1986-88
Number: 25
M.L. Debut: 4/9/83

LALLY, DANIEL J.
Nickname: Bud
In St. Louis: 1897
M.L. Debut: 8/19/1891

LAMABE, JOHN ALEXANDER
Nickname: Jack
In St. Louis: 1967
Number: 23
M.L. Debut: 4/17/62

LAMLINE, FREDERICK ARTHUR
Nickname: Dutch
In St. Louis: 1915
M.L. Debut: 9/18/12

LAMPKIN, THOMAS MICHAEL
Nickname: Tom
In St. Louis: 1997
Number: 49
M.L. Debut: 9/10/88

LANCASTER, LESTER WAYNE
Nickname: Les
In St. Louis: 1993
Number: 26
M.L. Debut: 4/7/87

LANDRITH, HOBERT NEAL
Nickname: Hobie
In St. Louis: 1957-58
Number: 16
M.L. Debut: 7/30/50

LANDRUM, DONALD LEROY
Nickname: Don
In St. Louis: 1960-62
Number: 24
M.L. Debut: 9/28/57

LANDRUM, TERRY LEE
Nickname: Tito
In St. Louis: 1980-87
Number: 21
M.L. Debut: 7/23/80

LANG, DONALD CHARLES
Nickname: Don
In St. Louis: 1948
Number: 29
M.L. Debut: 7/4/38

LANIER, HUBERT MAX
Nickname: Max
In St. Louis: 1938-46, 49-51
Number: 30, 23, 21, 40
M.L. Debut: 4/20/38

LANKFORD, RAYMOND LEWIS
Nickname: Ray
In St. Louis: 1990-97
Number: 16
M.L. Debut: 8/21/90

LAPALME, PAUL EDMORE
Nickname: Paul, Lefty
In St. Louis: 1955-56
Number: 35
M.L. Debut: 5/28/51

LAPOINT, DAVID JEFFREY
Nickname: Dave, Snacks
In St. Louis: 1981-84, 87
Number: 47, 39
M.L. Debut: 9/10/80

LAPOINTE, RALPH ROBERT
Nickname: Ralph
In St. Louis: 1948
Number: 16
M.L. Debut: 4/15/47

ST. LOUIS CARDINALS
CHAMPIONS NATIONAL LEAGUE
1926

LARMORE, ROBERT MCKAHAN
Nickname: Bob, Red
In St. Louis: 1918
M.L. Debut: 5/14/18

LARY, LYNFORD HOBART
Nickname: Lyn, Broadway
In St. Louis: 1939
Number: 2
M.L. Debut: 5/11/29

LASSETTER, DONALD O'NEAL
Nickname: Don
In St. Louis: 1957
Number: 31, 46
M.L. Debut: 9/21/57

LATHAM, WALTER ARLINGTON
Nickname: Arlie, The Freshest Man on Earth
In St. Louis: 1883-89, 96
M.L. Debut: 7/5/1880

LAVALLIERE, MICHAEL EUGENE
Nickname: Mike, Spanky
In St. Louis: 1985-86
Number: 10
M.L. Debut: 9/9/84

LAVAN, JOHN LEONARD
Nickname: Doc
In St. Louis: 1919-24
M.L. Debut: 6/22/13

ST. LOUIS CARDINALS
NATIONAL LEAGUE CHAMPIONS
1931

LAVIN, JOHN
Nickname: Johnny
In St. Louis: 1884
M.L. Debut: 9/10/1884

LAWLESS, THOMAS JAMES
Nickname: Tom
In St. Louis: 1985-88
Number: 12
M.L. Debut: 7/15/82

LAWRENCE, BROOKS ULYSSES
Nickname: Brooks, Bull
In St. Louis: 1954-55
Number: 31
M.L. Debut: 6/24/54

LEAHY, THOMAS JOSEPH
Nickname: Tom
In St. Louis: 1905
M.L. Debut: 5/18/1897

LEE, LERON
Nickname: Leron
In St. Louis: 1969-71
Number: 37
M.L. Debut: 9/5/69

LEE, MANUEL LORA
Nickname: Manny
In St. Louis: 1995
Number: 18
M.L. Debut: 4/10/85

LENTINE, JAMES MATTHEW
Nickname: Jim
In St. Louis: 1978-80
Number: 21
M.L. Debut: 9/3/78

**?????
LEONARD**
In St. Louis: 1892
M.L. Debut: 9/12/1892

LERSCH, BARRY LEE
Nickname: Barry
In St. Louis: 1974
Number: 15
M.L. Debut: 4/8/69

LESLIE, ROY REID
Nickname: Roy
In St. Louis: 1919
M.L. Debut: 9/6/17

LEWANDOWSKI, DANIEL WILLIAM
Nickname: Dan
In St. Louis: 1951
M.L. Debut: 9/22/51

LEWIS, FREDERICK MILLER
Nickname: Fred
In St. Louis: 1883-84
M.L. Debut: 7/21/1881

LEWIS, JOHNNY JOE
Nickname: Johhny
In St. Louis: 1964
Number: 28
M.L. Debut: 4/14/64

LEWIS, WILLIAM HENRY
Nickname: Bill, Buddy
In St. Louis: 1933
Number: 31
M.L. Debut: 6/3/33

LEZCANO, SIXTO JAOQUIN (CURRAS)
Nickname: Sixto
In St. Louis: 1981
Number: 16
M.L. Debut: 9/10/74

LIDDLE, DONALD EUGENE
Nickname: Don
In St. Louis: 1956
Number: 21
M.L. Debut: 4/17/53

LILLARD, ROBERT EUGENE
Nickname: Gene
In St. Louis: 1940
M.L. Debut: 5/8/36

LILLIS, ROBERT PERRY
Nickname: Bob
In St. Louis: 1961
Number: 35
M.L. Debut: 8/30/58

LINDELL, JOHN HARLAN
Nickname: Johnny
In St. Louis: 1950
Number: 5
M.L. Debut: 4/18/41

LINDEMAN, JAMES WILLIAM
Nickname: Jim
In St. Louis: 1986-89
Number: 15
M.L. Debut: 9/3/86

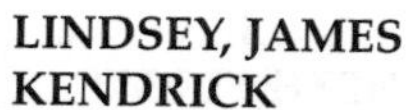

LINDSEY, JAMES KENDRICK
Nickname: Jim
In St. Louis: 1929-34
Number: 19, 20, 31
M.L. Debut: 5/1/22

LINT, ROYCE JAMES
Nickname: Royce
In St. Louis: 1954
Number: 25
M.L. Debut: 4/13/54

LINTZ, LARRY
Nickname: Larry
In St. Louis: 1975
Number: 25
M.L. Debut: 7/14/73

LINZY, FRANK ALFRED
Nickname: Fred
In St. Louis: 1970-71
Number: 35
M.L. Debut: 8/14/63

LITTELL, MARK ALAN
Nickname: Mark, Country
In St. Louis: 1978-82
Number: 32, 34
M.L. Debut: 6/14/73

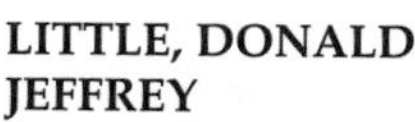

LITTLE, DONALD JEFFREY
Nickname: Jeff
In St. Louis: 1980
Number: 43
M.L. Debut: 9/6/80

LITTLEFIELD, JOHN ANDREW
Nickname: John
In St. Louis: 1980
Number: 50
M.L. Debut: 6/8/80

LITTLEFIELD, RICHARD BERNARD
Nickname: Dick
In St. Louis: 1956
Number: 45
M.L. Debut: 7/7/50

LITTLEJOHN, CHARLES CARLISLE
Nickname: Carlisle
In St. Louis: 1927-28
M.L. Debut: 5/11/27

LITWHILER, DANIEL WEBSTER
Nickname: Danny
In St. Louis: 1943-44, 46
Number: 8, 42
M.L. Debut: 4/25/40

LIVINGSTON, PATRICK JOSEPH
Nickname: Paddy
In St. Louis: 1917
M.L. Debut: 9/2/01

LIVINGSTON, SCOTT LOUIS
Nickname: Scott
In St. Louis: 1997
Number: 29
M.L. Debut: 7/19/91

LOCKE, LAWRENCE DONALD
Nickname: Bobby
In St. Louis: 1962
Number: 36
M.L. Debut: 9/18/59

LOCKMAN, CARROLL WALTER
Nickname: Whitey
In St. Louis: 1956
Number: 2
M.L. Debut: 7/5/45

LOFTUS, THOMAS JOSEPH
Nickname: Tom
In St. Louis: 1883
M.L. Debut: 8/17/1877

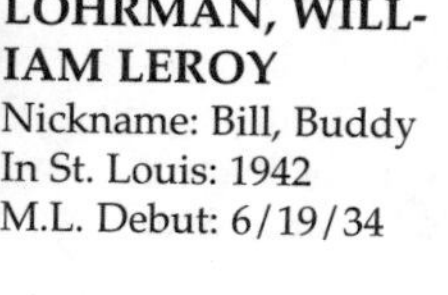

LOHRMAN, WILLIAM LEROY
Nickname: Bill, Buddy
In St. Louis: 1942
M.L. Debut: 6/19/34

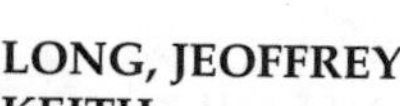

LONG, JEOFFREY KEITH
Nickname: Jeoff
In St. Louis: 1963-64
Number: 10
M.L. Debut: 7/31/63

LONG, THOMAS AUGUSTUS
Nickname: Tommy
In St. Louis: 1915, 17
M.L. Debut: 9/11/11

LOPATKA, ARTHUR JOSEPH
Nickname: Art
In St. Louis: 1945
Number: 24
M.L. Debut: 9/12/45

LOPEZ, AURELIO ALEJANDRO (RIOS)
Nickname: Aurelio
In St. Louis: 1978
Number: 39
M.L. Debut: 9/1/74

LOTZ, JOSEPH PETER
Nickname: Joe, Smokey
In St. Louis: 1916
M.L. Debut: 7/15/16

LOVENGUTH, LYNN RICHARD
Nickname: Lynn, Dig
In St. Louis: 1957
Number: 40
M.L. Debut: 4/18/55

LOVETT, JOHN
Nickname: John
In St. Louis: 1903
M.L. Debut: 5/22/03

LOWDERMILK, GROVER CLEVELAND
Nickname: Grover, Slim
In St. Louis: 1909, 11
M.L. Debut: 7/3/09

LOWDERMILK, LOUIS BAILEY
Nickname: Lou
In St. Louis: 1911-12
M.L. Debut: 4/20/11

LOWE, JONATHAN SEAN
Nickname: Sean
In St. Louis: 1997
Number: 34
M.L. Debut: 8/29/97

LOWREY, HARRY LEE
Nickname: Peanuts, Pinchy
In St. Louis: 1950-54
Number: 29, 37
M.L. Debut: 4/14/42

LUCID, CORNELIUS CECIL
Nickname: Con
In St. Louis: 1897
M.L. Debut: 5/1/1893

LUDWICK, ERIC DAVID
Nickname: Eric
In St. Louis: 1996-97
Number: 54
M.L. Debut: 9/1/96

LUDWIG, WILLIAM LAWRENCE
Nickname: Bill, Buddy
In St. Louis: 1908
M.L. Debut: 4/16/08

LUNA, GUILLERMO ROMERO
Nickname: Memo
In St. Louis: 1954
Number: 40
M.L. Debut: 4/20/54

LUSH, ERNEST BENJAMIN
Nickname: Ernie
In St. Louis: 1910
M.L. Debut: 7/20/10

LUSH, JOHN CHARLES
Nickname: Johnny
In St. Louis: 1907-10
M.L. Debut: 4/22/04

LYONS, DENNIS PATRICK ALOYSIUS
Nickname: Denny
In St. Louis: 1891, 95
M.L. Debut: 9/18/1885

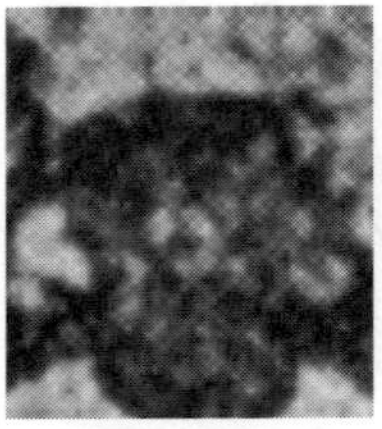

LYONS, GEORGE TONY
Nickname: George, Smooth
In St. Louis: 1920
M.L. Debut: 9/6/20

LYONS, HARRY P.
Nickname: Harry
In St. Louis: 1887-88
M.L. Debut: 8/29/1887

LYONS, HERSCHEL ENGLEBERT
Nickname: Hersh
In St. Louis: 1941
Number: 42
M.L. Debut: 4/17/41

LYONS, WILLIAM ALLEN
Nickname: Bill
In St. Louis: 1983-84
Number: 30
M.L. Debut: 7/20/83

MABE, ROBERT LEE
Nickname: Bob
In St. Louis: 1958
Number: 32
M.L. Debut: 4/18/58

MABRY, JOHN STEVEN
Nickname: John
In St. Louis: 1994-97
Number: 47
M.L. Debut: 4/23/94

MACKENZIE, KENNETH PURVIS
Nickname: Ken
In St. Louis: 1963
Number: 28
M.L. Debut: 5/2/60

MACKINSON, JOHN JOSEPH
Nickname: John
In St. Louis: 1955
Number: 28
M.L. Debut: 4/16/53

MACLIN, LONNIE LEE
Nickname: Lonnie
In St. Louis: 1993
Number: 51
M.L. Debut: 9/7/93

MACON, MAX CULLEN
Nickname: Max
In St. Louis: 1938
Number: 16
M.L. Debut: 4/21/38

MAGEE, LEO CHRISTOPHER
Nickname: Lee
In St. Louis: 1911-14
M.L. Debut: 7/4/11

MAGEE, WILLIAM J.
Nickname: Bill
In St. Louis: 1901
M.L. Debut: 5/18/1897

MAGLIE, SALVATORE ANTHONY
Nickname: Sal, The Barber
In St. Louis: 1958
Number: 43
M.L. Debut: 8/9/45

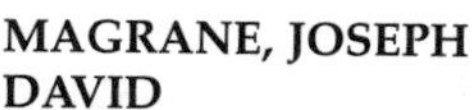

MAGRANE, JOSEPH DAVID
Nickname: Joe
In St. Louis: 1987-90, 92-93
Number: 41, 32
M.L. Debut: 4/25/87

MAHAFFEY, ARTHUR
Nickname: Art
In St. Louis: 1966
Number: 30
M.L. Debut: 7/30/60

MAHONEY, GEORGE W.
Nickname: Mike, Big Mike
In St. Louis: 1898
M.L. Debut: 5/18/1897

MAILS, JOHN WALTER
Nickname: Duster, The Great, Walter
In St. Louis: 1925-26
M.L. Debut: 9/28/15

MALLORY, JAMES BAUGH
Nickname: Jim, Sunny Jim
In St. Louis: 1945
Number: 18
M.L. Debut: 9/8/40

MANCUSO, AUGUST RODNEY
Nickname: Gus, Blackie
In St. Louis: 1928, 30-32, 41-42
Number: 9, 14
M.L. Debut: 4/30/28

MANN, LESLIE
Nickname: Les, Major
In St. Louis: 1921-23
M.L. Debut: 4/30/13

MANRIQUE, FRED ELOY (REYES)
Nickname: Fred
In St. Louis: 1986
Number: 5
M.L. Debut: 8/23/81

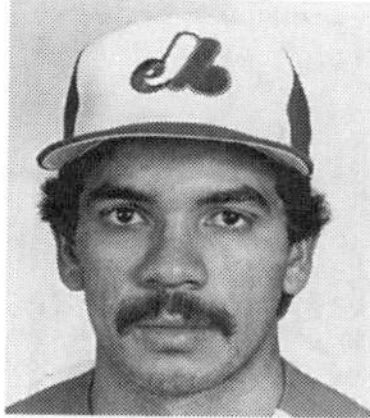

MANSELL, THOMAS E.
Nickname: Tom, Brick
In St. Louis: 1883
M.L. Debut: 5/1/1879

MARANVILLE, WALTER JAMES VINCENT
Nickname: Rabbit
In St. Louis: 1927-28
M.L. Debut: 9/10/12

MARBET, WALTER WILLIAM
Nickname: Walt
In St. Louis: 1913
M.L. Debut: 6/17/13

MARION, MARTIN WHITEFORD
Nickname: Marty, Slats, The Octopus, Mr. Shortstop
In St. Louis: 1940-50
Number: 4
M.L. Debut: 4/16/40

MARIS, ROGER EUGENE
Nickname: Roger
In St. Louis: 1967-68
Number: 9
M.L. Debut: 4/16/57

MAROLEWSKI, FRED DANIEL
Nickname: Fred, Fritz
In St. Louis: 1953
M.L. Debut: 9/19/53

MARRERO, ELIESER
Nickname: Eli
In St. Louis: 1997
Number: 26
M.L. Debut: 9/2/97

MARSHALL, CHARLES ANTHONY
Nickname: Charlie
In St. Louis: 1941
Number: 33
M.L. Debut: 6/14/41

MARSHALL, JOSEPH HANLEY
Nickname: Joe, Home Run Joe
In St. Louis: 1906
M.L. Debut: 9/7/03

MARSHALL, WILLIAM RIDDLE
Nickname: Doc
In St. Louis: 1906-08
M.L. Debut: 4/15/04

MARTIN, FRED TURNER
Nickname: Freddie
In St. Louis: 1946, 49-50
Number: 34, 39, 41, 39
M.L. Debut: 4/21/46

MARTIN, JOHN LEONARD ROOSEVELT
Nickname: Pepper, The Wild Horse of the Osage
In St. Louis: 1928, 30-40, 44
Number: 2, 28, 1, 11, 10
M.L. Debut: 4/16/28

MARTIN, JOHN ROBERT
Nickname: John
In St. Louis: 1980-83
Number: 33
M.L. Debut: 8/27/80

MARTIN, MORRIS WEBSTER
Nickname: Morrie, Lefty
In St. Louis: 1957-58
Number: 25
M.L. Debut: 4/25/49

MARTIN, STUART MCGUIRE
Nickname: Stu
In St. Louis: 1936-40
Number: 6
M.L. Debut: 4/14/36

MARTINEZ, ORLANDO (OLIVA)
Nickname: Marty
In St. Louis: 1972
Number: 11
M.L. Debut: 5/2/62

MARTINEZ, SILVIO RAMON (CABRERA)
Nickname: Silvio
In St. Louis: 1978-81
Number: 35
M.L. Debut: 4/9/77

MARTINEZ, TEODORO NOEL (ENCARNACION)
Nickname: Teddy
In St. Louis: 1975
Number: 19
M.L. Debut: 7/18/70

MASON, ERNEST
Nickname: Ernie
In St. Louis: 1894
M.L. Debut: 7/17/1894

MATHEWS, GREGORY INMAN
Nickname: Greg
In St. Louis: 1986-88, 90
Number: 53
M.L. Debut: 6/3/86

MATHEWS, TIMOTHY JAY
Nickname: T.J.
In St. Louis: 1995-97
Number: 51, 33
M.L. Debut: 7/28/95

MATTICK, WALTER JOSEPH
Nickname: Wally, Chink
In St. Louis: 1918
M.L. Debut: 4/11/12

MAUCH, GENE WILLIAM
Nickname: Gene, Skip
In St. Louis: 1952
Number: 36
M.L. Debut: 4/18/44

MAUPIN, HARRY CARR
Nickname: Harry
In St. Louis: 1898
M.L. Debut: 10/5/1898

MAXVILL, CHARLES DALLAN
Nickname: Dal
In St. Louis: 1962-72
Number: 27
M.L. Debut: 6/10/62

MAY, FRANK SPRUIELL
Nickname: Jakie
In St. Louis: 1917-21
M.L. Debut: 6/26/17

MCADAMS, GEORGE D.
Nickname: Jack
In St. Louis: 1911
M.L. Debut: 7/22/11

MCAULEY, JAMES EARL
Nickname: Ike
In St. Louis: 1917
M.L. Debut: 9/10/14

MCBRIDE, ARNOLD RAY
Nickname: Bake
In St. Louis: 1973-77
Number: 21
M.L. Debut: 7/26/73

MCBRIDE, GEORGE FLORIAN
Nickname: George, Smooth
In St. Louis: 1905-06
M.L. Debut: 9/12/01

MCBRIDE, PETER WILLIAM
Nickname: Pete
In St. Louis: 1899
M.L. Debut: 9/20/1898

MCCAFFREY, HARRY CHARLES
Nickname: Harry
In St. Louis: 1882-83
M.L. Debut: 6/15/1882

MCCARTHY, JOSEPH N.
Nickname: Joe
In St. Louis: 1906
M.L. Debut: 9/27/05

MCCARTHY, THOMAS FRANCIS MICHAEL
Nickname: Tommy
In St. Louis: 1888-91
M.L. Debut: 7/10/1884

MCCARTY, GEORGE LEWIS
Nickname: Lew
In St. Louis: 1920-21
M.L. Debut: 8/30/13

MCCARVER, JAMES TIMOTHY
Nickname: Tim
In St. Louis: 1959-61, 63-69, 73-74
Number: 9, 20, 15
M.L. Debut: 9/10/59

MCCAULEY, JAMES A.
Nickname: Jim
In St. Louis: 1884
M.L. Debut: 9/17/1884

MCCAULEY, PATRICK M.
Nickname: Pat
In St. Louis: 1893
M.L. Debut: 9/5/1893

MCCLURE, ROBERT CRAIG
Nickname: Bob
In St. Louis: 1991-92
Number: 22
M.L. Debut: 8/13/75

MCCOOL, WILLIAM JOHN
Nickname: Billy
In St. Louis: 1970
Number: 43
M.L. Debut: 4/24/64

MCCORMICK, JAMES AMBROSE
Nickname: Jim
In St. Louis: 1892
M.L. Debut: 9/10/1892

MCCURDY, HARRY HENRY
Nickname: Harry, Hawk
In St. Louis: 1922-23
M.L. Debut: 7/4/22

MCDANIEL, LYNDALL DALE
Nickname: Lindy
In St. Louis: 1955-62
Number: 41
M.L. Debut: 9/2/55

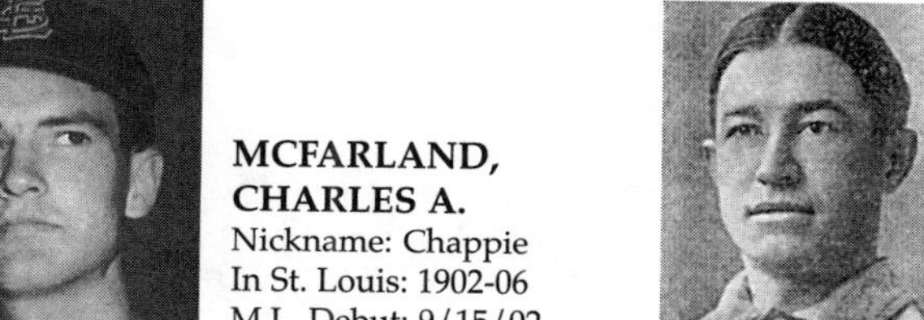

MCDANIEL, MAX VON
Nickname: Von
In St. Louis: 1957-58
Number: 45
M.L. Debut: 6/13/57

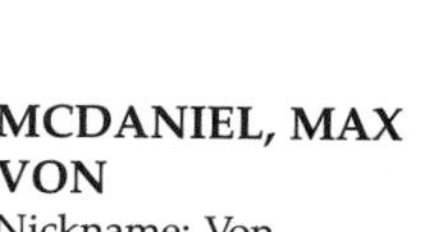

MCDERMOTT, MAURICE JOSEPH
Nickname: Mickey, Maury
In St. Louis: 1961
Number: 38
M.L. Debut: 4/24/48

MCDERMOTT, MICHAEL JOSEPH
Nickname: Mike
In St. Louis: 1897
M.L. Debut: 4/20/1895

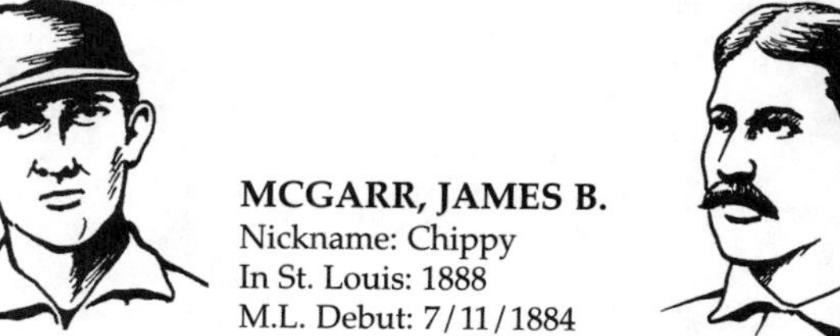

MCDOUGAL, JOHN AUCHANBOLT
Nickname: Sandy
In St. Louis: 1905
M.L. Debut: 6/12/1895

MCDOUGAL, JOHN H.
Nickname: John, Dewey
In St. Louis: 1895-96
M.L. Debut: 4/24/1895

MCENANEY, WILLIAM HENRY
Nickname: Will
In St. Louis: 1979
Number: 47
M.L. Debut: 7/3/74

MCFADDEN, GUY G.
Nickname: Guy
In St. Louis: 1895
M.L. Debut: 8/24/1895

MCFARLAND, CHARLES A.
Nickname: Chappie
In St. Louis: 1902-06
M.L. Debut: 9/15/02

MCFARLAND, EDWARD WILLIAM
Nickname: Ed
In St. Louis: 1896-97
M.L. Debut: 7/7/1893

MCGANN, DENNIS LAWRENCE
Nickname: Dan, Cap
In St. Louis: 1900-01
M.L. Debut: 8/8/1896

MCGARR, JAMES B.
Nickname: Chippy
In St. Louis: 1888
M.L. Debut: 7/11/1884

MCGEE, WILLIAM HENRY
Nickname: Bill, Fiddler Bill
In St. Louis: 1935-41
Number: 19, 24, 29
M.L. Debut: 9/29/35

MCGEE, WILLIE DEAN
Nickname: Willie
In St. Louis: 1982-90, 96-97
Number: 51
M.L. Debut: 5/10/82

MCGEEHAN, DANIEL DESALES
Nickname: Dan
In St. Louis: 1911
M.L. Debut: 4/22/11

MCGILL, WILLIAM VANESS
Nickname: Willie, Kid
In St. Louis: 1891
M.L. Debut: 5/8/1890

MCGINLEY, JAMES WILLIAM
Nickname: Jim
In St. Louis: 1904-05
M.L. Debut: 9/22/04

MCGINNIS, GEORGE WASHINGTON
Nickname: Jumbo
In St. Louis: 1882-86
M.L. Debut: 5/2/1882

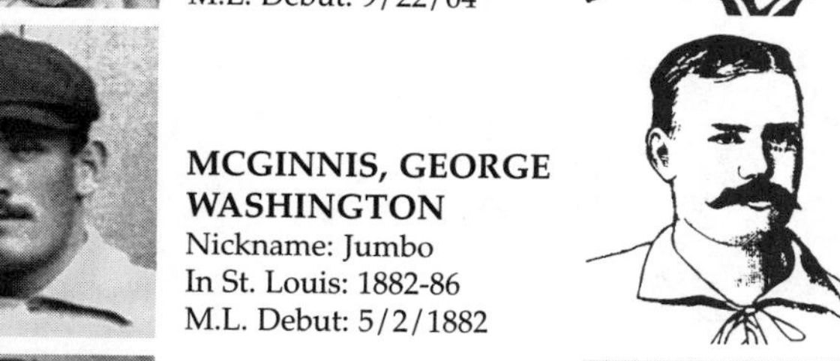

MCGLOTHEN, LYNN EVERETT
Nickname: Lynn, Dig
In St. Louis: 1974-76
Number: 47
M.L. Debut: 6/25/72

MCGLYNN, ULYSSES SIMPSON GRANT
Nickname: Stoney
In St. Louis: 1906-08
M.L. Debut: 9/20/06

MCGRAW, JOHN JOSEPH
Nickname: John, Little Napoleon, Mugsy
In St. Louis: 1900
M.L. Debut: 8/26/1891

MCGRAW, ROBERT EMMETT
Nickname: Bob
In St. Louis: 1927
M.L. Debut: 9/25/1891

MCGRAW, THOMAS VIRGIL
Nickname: Tom
In St. Louis: 1997
Number: 61

MCGRIFF, TERENCE ROY
Nickname: Terry
In St. Louis: 1994
Number: 54
M.L. Debut: 7/11/87

MCGRILLIS, MARK A.
Nickname: Mark
In St. Louis: 1892
M.L. Debut: 9/17/1892

MCGWIRE, MARK DAVID
Nickname: Mark, Mac
In St. Louis: 1997
Number: 25
M.L. Debut: 8/22/86

MCHENRY, AUSTIN BUSH
Nickname: Austin, Mac
In St. Louis: 1918-22
M.L. Debut: 6/22/18

MCIVOR, EDWARD OTTO
Nickname: Otto
In St. Louis: 1911
M.L. Debut: 4/18/11

MCKEAN, EDWIN JOHN
Nickname: Ed, Mack
In St. Louis: 1899
M.L. Debut: 4/16/1887

MCLAURIN, RALPH EDGAR
Nickname: Ralph
In St. Louis: 1908
M.L. Debut: 9/5/08

MCLEAN, JOHN BANNERMAN
Nickname: Larry
In St. Louis: 1904, 13
M.L. Debut: 4/26/01

MCNERTNEY, GERALD EDWARD
Nickname: Jerry
In St. Louis: 1971-72
Number: 15
M.L. Debut: 4/16/64

MCQUAID, MORTIMER MARTIN
Nickname: Marty
In St. Louis: 1891
M.L. Debut: 8/15/1891

MCSORLEY, JOHN BERNARD
Nickname: Trick
In St. Louis: 1886
M.L. Debut: 5/6/1875

MCSWEENEY, PAUL A.
Nickname: Paul
In St. Louis: 1891
M.L. Debut: 9/20/1891

MCWILLIAMS, LARRY DEAN
Nickname: Larry
In St. Louis: 1988
Number: 49
M.L. Debut: 7/17/78

MEADOWS, HENRY LEE
Nickname: Lee, Specs
In St. Louis: 1915-19
M.L. Debut: 4/19/15

MEDWICK, JOSEPH MICHAEL
Nickname: Joe, Ducky, Mickey, Muscles
In St. Louis: 1932-40, 47-48
Number: 7, 21, 12
M.L. Debut: 9/2/32

MEEK, FRANK J.
Nickname: Dad
In St. Louis: 1889-90
M.L. Debut: 5/10/1889

MEJIA, MIGUEL
Nickname: Miguel
In St. Louis: 1996
Number: 35
M.L. Debut: 4/4/96

MEJIA, ROBERTO ANTONIO (DIAZ)
Nickname: Roberto
In St. Louis: 1997
Number: 67
M.L. Debut: 7/15/93

MEJIAS, SAMUEL ELIAS
Nickname: Sam
In St. Louis: 1976
Number: 7
M.L. Debut: 9/6/76

MELENDEZ, LUIS ANTONIO (SANTANA)
Nickname: Luis
In St. Louis: 1970-76
Number: 26
M.L. Debut: 9/7/70

MELTER, STEPHEN BLAZIUS
Nickname: Steve
In St. Louis: 1909
M.L. Debut: 6/27/09

MENZE, THEODORE CHARLES
Nickname: Ted
In St. Louis: 1918
M.L. Debut: 4/23/18

MERCER, JOHN LOCKE
Nickname: John
In St. Louis: 1912
M.L. Debut: 6/25/12

MERRITT, LLOYD WESLEY
Nickname: Lloyd
In St. Louis: 1957
Number: 43
M.L. Debut: 4/22/57

MERTES, SAMUEL BLAIR
Nickname: Sandow
In St. Louis: 1906
M.L. Debut: 6/30/1896

MESNER, STEPHAN MATHIAS
Nickname: Steve
In St. Louis: 1941
Number: 5
M.L. Debut: 9/23/38

METZGER, CLARENCE EDWARD
Nickname: Butch
In St. Louis: 1977
Number: 34
M.L. Debut: 9/8/74

MICKELSON, EDWARD ALLEN
Nickname: Ed
In St. Louis: 1950
Number: 22
M.L. Debut: 9/18/50

MIERKOWICZ, EDWARD FRANK
Nickname: Ed, Butch, Mouse
In St. Louis: 1950
Number: 40
M.L. Debut: 8/31/45

MIGGINS, LAWRENCE EDWARD
Nickname: Larry, Irish
In St. Louis: 1948, 52
Number: 41, 23
M.L. Debut: 10/3/48

MIKKELSEN, PETE JAMES
Nickname: Pete
In St. Louis: 1968
Number: 46
M.L. Debut: 4/17/64

MIKSIS, EDWARD THOMAS
Nickname: Eddie
In St. Louis: 1957
Number: 4
M.L. Debut: 6/17/44

MILLARD, FRANK E.
Nickname: Frank
In St. Louis: 1890
M.L. Debut: 5/4/1890

MILLER, CHARLES BRADLEY
Nickname: Dusty
In St. Louis: 1890, 99
M.L. Debut: 9/23/1889

MILLER, CHARLES MARION
Nickname: Charlie
In St. Louis: 1913-14
M.L. Debut: 9/19/13

MILLER, EDWARD ROBERT
Nickname: Eddie, Eppie
In St. Louis: 1950
Number: 33
M.L. Debut: 9/9/36

MILLER, ELMER
Nickname: Elmer
In St. Louis: 1912
M.L. Debut: 4/26/12

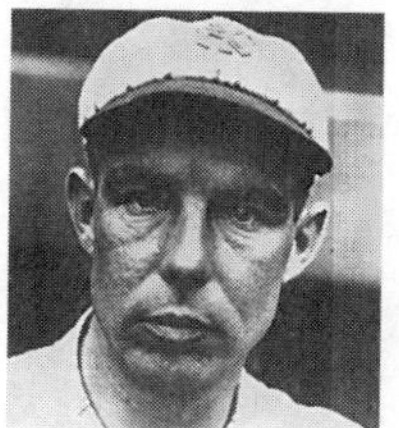

MILLER, FRANK A.
Nickname: Kohly
In St. Louis: 1892
M.L. Debut: 9/16/1892

MILLER, GEORGE FREDERICK
Nickname: Doggie, Calliope, Foghorn
In St. Louis: 1894-95
M.L. Debut: 5/1/1884

MILLER, JOHN BARNEY
Nickname: Dots
In St. Louis: 1914-17, 19
M.L. Debut: 4/16/09

MILLER, ROBERT LANE
Nickname: Bob
In St. Louis: 1957, 59-61
Number: 26, 49, 35, 36
M.L. Debut: 6/26/57

MILLER, STUART LEONARD
Nickname: Stu
In St. Louis: 1952-54, 56
Number: 36
M.L. Debut: 8/12/52

MILLIGAN, JOHN
Nickname: Jocko
In St. Louis: 1888-89
M.L. Debut: 5/1/1884

MILLS, COLONEL BUSTER
Nickname: Buster, Bus
In St. Louis: 1934
Number: 10
M.L. Debut: 4/18/34

MILTON, SAMUEL LAWRENCE
Nickname: Larry, Tug
In St. Louis: 1903
M.L. Debut: 5/7/03

MINOSO, SATURNINO ORESTES ARMAS
Nickname: Minnie
In St. Louis: 1962
Number: 9
M.L. Debut: 4/19/49

MITCHELL, CLARENCE ELMER
Nickname: Clarence
In St. Louis: 1928-30
M.L. Debut: 6/2/11

MITCHELL, ROBERT MCKASHA
Nickname: Bobby
In St. Louis: 1882
M.L. Debut: 9/6/1877

MIZE, JOHN ROBERT
Nickname: Johnny, The Big Cat, Skippy
In St. Louis: 1936-41
Number: 10
M.L. Debut: 4/16/36

MIZELL, WILMER DAVID
Nickname: Vinegar Bend
In St. Louis: 1952-53, 56-60
Number: 33, 17
M.L. Debut: 4/22/52

MOFORD, HERBERT
Nickname: Herb
In St. Louis: 1955
Number: 40
M.L. Debut: 4/12/55

MOLLWITZ, FREDERICK AU-GUST
Nickname: Fritz, Zip
In St. Louis: 1919
M.L. Debut: 9/26/13

MOON, WALLACE WADE
Nickname: Wally
In St. Louis: 1954-58
Number: 20
M.L. Debut: 4/13/54

MOONEY, JIM IRVING
Nickname: Jim
In St. Louis: 1933-34
Number: 21, 28
M.L. Debut: 8/14/31

MOORE, DONNIE RAY
Nickname: Donnie
In St. Louis: 1980
Number: 56
M.L. Debut: 9/14/75

MOORE, EUGENE JR.
Nickname: Gene, Rowdy
In St. Louis: 1933-35
Number: 21, 24, 10
M.L. Debut: 9/19/31

MOORE, LLOYD ALBERT
Nickname: Whitey
In St. Louis: 1942
Number: 35
M.L. Debut: 9/27/36

MOORE, RANDOLPH EDWARD
Nickname: Randy
In St. Louis: 1937
Number: 22
M.L. Debut: 4/12/27

MOORE, TERRY BLUFORD
Nickname: Terry, T, Captain
In St. Louis: 1935-42, 46-48
Number: 11, 2, 8
M.L. Debut: 4/16/35

MOORE, TOMMY JOE
Nickname: Tommy
In St. Louis: 1975
Number: 27
M.L. Debut: 9/15/72

MORALES, JULIO RUBEN (TORRES)
Nickname: Jerry
In St. Louis: 1978
Number: 25
M.L. Debut: 9/5/69

MORAN, CHARLES BARTHELL
Nickname: Charley, Uncle Charley
In St. Louis: 1903, 08
M.L. Debut: 9/9/03

MORAN, WILLIAM L.
Nickname: Bill
In St. Louis: 1892
M.L. Debut: 5/7/1892

MORE, FORREST T.
Nickname: Forrest
In St. Louis: 1909
M.L. Debut: 4/15/09

MORGAN, EDWIN WILLIS
Nickname: Eddie, Pepper
In St. Louis: 1936
Number: 30
M.L. Debut: 4/14/36

MORGAN, JOSEPH MICHAEL
Nickname: Joe
In St. Louis: 1964
Number: 10
M.L. Debut: 4/14/59

MORGAN, MICHAEL THOMAS
Nickname: Mike
In St. Louis: 1995-96
Number: 36
M.L. Debut: 6/11/78

MORGAN, ROBERT MORRIS
Nickname: Bobby
In St. Louis: 1956
Number: 42
M.L. Debut: 4/18/50

ST. LOUIS CARDINALS
NATIONAL LEAGUE CHAMPIONS
1931

MORIARITY, EU-GENE JOHN
Nickname: Gene
In St. Louis: 1892
M.L. Debut: 6/18/1884

MORRIS, JOHN DANIEL
Nickname: John
In St. Louis: 1986-90
Number: 33
M.L. Debut: 8/5/86

MORRIS, JOHN WALTER
Nickname: Walter
In St. Louis: 1908
M.L. Debut: 8/31/08

MORRIS, MATTHEW CHRISTIAN
Nickname: Matt
In St. Louis: 1997
Number: 35
M.L. Debut: 4/4/97

MORSE, PETER RAYMOND
Nickname: Hap
In St. Louis: 1911
M.L. Debut: 4/18/11

MORTON, CHARLES HAZEN
Nickname: Charlie
In St. Louis: 1882
M.L. Debut: 5/2/1882

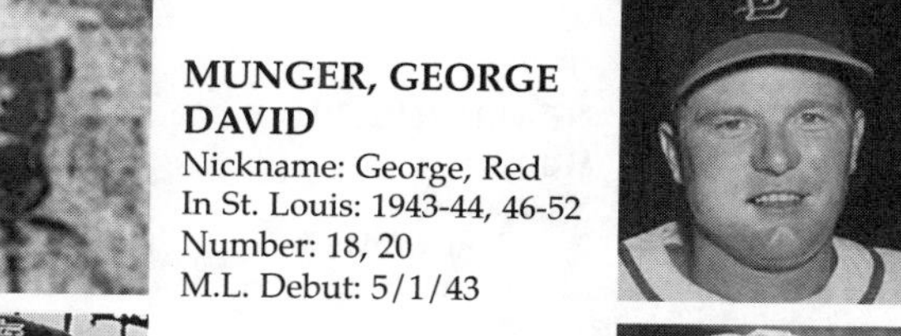

MORYN, WALTER JOSEPH
Nickname: Walt, Moose
In St. Louis: 1960-61
Number: 28
M.L. Debut: 6/29/54

MOWREY, HARRY HARLEN
Nickname: Mike
In St. Louis: 1909-13
M.L. Debut: 9/24/05

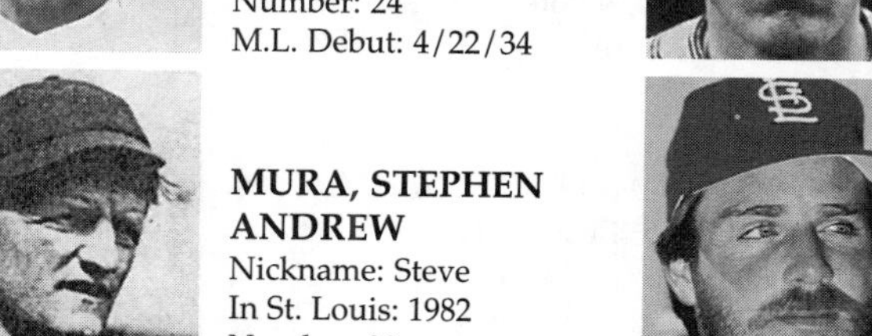

MOYER, JAMIE
Nickname: Jamie
In St. Louis: 1991
Number: 41
M.L. Debut: 6/16/86

MUELLER, CLARENCE FRANCIS
Nickname: Heine
In St. Louis: 1920-26
M.L. Debut: 9/25/20

MUFFET, BILLY ARNOLD
Nickname: Billy, Muff
In St. Louis: 1957-58
Number: 38, 22
M.L. Debut: 8/3/57

MULLANE, ANTHONY JOHN
Nickname: Tony, Count, The Apollo of the Box
In St. Louis: 1883
M.L. Debut: 8/27/1881

MUMPHREY, JERRY WAYNE
Nickname: Jerry
In St. Louis: 1974-79
Number: 29
M.L. Debut: 9/10/74

MUNGER, GEORGE DAVID
Nickname: George, Red
In St. Louis: 1943-44, 46-52
Number: 18, 20
M.L. Debut: 5/1/43

MUNNS, LESLIE ERNEST
Nickname: Les, Big Ed, Nemo
In St. Louis: 1936
Number: 24
M.L. Debut: 4/22/34

MURA, STEPHEN ANDREW
Nickname: Steve
In St. Louis: 1982
Number: 38
M.L. Debut: 9/5/78

MURCH, SIMEON AUGUSTUS
Nickname: Simmy
In St. Louis: 1904-05
M.L. Debut: 9/20/04

MURCHISON, THOMAS MALCOLM
Nickname: Tim
In St. Louis: 1917
M.L. Debut: 6/21/17

MURDOCH, WILBUR EDWIN
Nickname: Wilbur
In St. Louis: 1908
M.L. Debut: 8/29/08

MURPHY, EDWARD J.
Nickname: Ed
In St. Louis: 1901-03
M.L. Debut: 4/23/1898

MURPHY, HOWARD
Nickname: Howard
In St. Louis: 1909
M.L. Debut: 8/4/09

MURPHY, JOHN PATRICK
Nickname: John
In St. Louis: 1902
M.L. Debut: 9/10/02

MURPHY, JOSEPH AKIN
Nickname: Joe
In St. Louis: 1886-87
M.L. Debut: 4/28/1886

MURPHY, MICHAEL JEROME
Nickname: Mike
In St. Louis: 1912
M.L. Debut: 5/17/12

MURPHY, MORGAN EDWARD
Nickname: Morg
In St. Louis: 1896-97
M.L. Debut: 4/22/1890

MURPHY, ROBERT ALBERT JR.
Nickname: Rob
In St. Louis: 1993-94
Number: 46
M.L. Debut: 9/13/85

MURPHY, THOMAS ANDREW
Nickname: Tom
In St. Louis: 1973
Number: 34
M.L. Debut: 6/13/68

MURRAY, JOHN JOSEPH
Nickname: Red
In St. Louis: 1906-08
M.L. Debut: 6/16/06

MUSIAL, STANLEY FRANK
Nickname: Stan, Stan The Man
In St. Louis: 1941-44, 46-63
Number: 19, 6
M.L. Debut: 9/17/41

MYERS, HENRY HARRISON
Nickname: Hy
In St. Louis: 1923-25
M.L. Debut: 8/30/09

MYERS, JAMES ALBERT
Nickname: Bert
In St. Louis: 1896
M.L. Debut: 4/25/1896

MYERS, LYNNWOOD LINCOLN
Nickname: Lynn
In St. Louis: 1938-39
Number: 21, 1
M.L. Debut: 7/13/38

NAGY, MICHAEL TIMOTHY
Nickname: Mike
In St. Louis: 1973
Number: 49
M.L. Debut: 4/21/69

NAHEM, SAMUEL RALPH
Nickname: Sam, Subway Sam
In St. Louis: 1941
Number: 37
M.L. Debut: 10/2/38

NARON, SAMUEL
Nickname: Sam
In St. Louis: 1935, 42-43
Number: 33, 18
M.L. Debut: 9/15/35

NASH, KENNETH LELAND
Nickname: Ken
In St. Louis: 1914
M.L. Debut: 7/4/12

NAYMICK, MICHAEL JOHN
Nickname: Mike
In St. Louis: 1944
Number: 32
M.L. Debut: 9/24/39

NEALE, JOSEPH HUNT
Nickname: Joe
In St. Louis: 1890-91
M.L. Debut: 6/21/1886

NELSON, GLENN RICHARD
Nickname: Rocky
In St. Louis: 1949-51, 56
Number: 19, 7
M.L. Debut: 4/27/49

NELSON, MELVIN FREDERICK
Nickname: Mel
In St. Louis: 1960, 68-69
Number: 35, 47
M.L. Debut: 9/27/60

NICHOLS, ARTHUR FRANCIS
Nickname: Art
In St. Louis: 1901-03
M.L. Debut: 9/16/1898

NICHOLS, CHARLES AUGUSTUS
Nickname: Kid, Nick
In St. Louis: 1904-05
M.L. Debut: 4/23/1890

NICOL, GEORGE EDWARD
Nickname: George
In St. Louis: 1890
M.L. Debut: 9/23/1890

NICOL, HUGH N.
Nickname: Hugh
In St. Louis: 1883-86
M.L. Debut: 5/3/1881

NIEBERGALL, CHARLES ARTHUR
Nickname: Charlie, Nig
In St. Louis: 1921, 23-24
M.L. Debut: 6/17/21

NIEDENFUER, THOMAS EDWARD
Nickname: Tom
In St. Louis: 1990
Number: 41
M.L. Debut: 8/15/81

NIEHAUS, RICHARD J.
Nickname: Dick
In St. Louis: 1913-15
M.L. Debut: 9/9/13

NIEHOFF, JOHN ALBERT
Nickname: Bert
In St. Louis: 1918
M.L. Debut: 10/4/13

NEIMAN, ROBERT CHARLES
Nickname: Bob
In St. Louis: 1960-61
Number: 4
M.L. Debut: 9/14/51

NIETO, THOMAS ANDREW
Nickname: Tom
In St. Louis: 1984-85
Number: 23
M.L. Debut: 5/10/84

NILAND, THOMAS JAMES
Nickname: Tom, Honest Tom
In St. Louis: 1896
M.L. Debut: 4/19/1896

NOONAN, PETER JOHN
Nickname: Pete
In St. Louis: 1906-07
M.L. Debut: 6/20/04

NOREN, IRVING ARNOLD
Nickname: Irv
In St. Louis: 1957-59
Number: 8, 25
M.L. Debut: 4/18/50

NORMAN, FREDIE HUBERT
Nickname: Fred
In St. Louis: 1970-71
Number: 47
M.L. Debut: 9/21/62

NORTH, LOUIS ALEXANDER
Nickname: Lou
In St. Louis: 1917, 20-24
M.L. Debut: 8/22/13

NORTHEY, RONALD JAMES
Nickname: Ron, The Round Man
In St. Louis: 1947-49
Number: 5
M.L. Debut: 4/14/42

NOSSEK, JOSEPH RUDOLPH
Nickname: Joe
In St. Louis: 1969-70
Number: 24
M.L. Debut: 4/18/64

NUNN, HOWARD RALPH
Nickname: Howie
In St. Louis: 1959
Number: 57
M.L. Debut: 4/11/59

NYE, RICHARD RAYMOND
Nickname: Rich
In St. Louis: 1970
Number: 22
M.L. Debut: 9/16/66

OAKES, ENNIS TELFAIR
Nickname: Rebel
In St. Louis: 1910-13
M.L. Debut: 4/14/09

OBERBECK, HENRY A.
Nickname: Henry
In St. Louis: 1883
M.L. Debut: 5/7/1883

OBERKFELL, KENNETH RAY
Nickname: Ken, Obie
In St. Louis: 1977-84
Number: 24, 10
M.L. Debut: 8/22/77

O'BRIEN, DANIEL JOGUES
Nickname: Dan
In St. Louis: 1978-79
Number: 34, 26
M.L. Debut: 9/4/78

O'BRIEN, JOHN THOMAS
Nickname: Johnny
In St. Louis: 1958
M.L. Debut: 4/19/53

O'CONNOR, JOHN JOSEPH
Nickname: Jack, Peach Pie, Rowdy Jack
In St. Louis: 1899-1900
M.L. Debut: 4/20/1887

O'CONNOR, PATRICK FRANCIS
Nickname: Paddy
In St. Louis: 1914
M.L. Debut: 4/17/08

O'DEA, JAMES KENNETH
Nickname: Ken
In St. Louis: 1942-46
Number: 16
M.L. Debut: 4/21/35

O'FARRELL, ROBERT ARTHUR
Nickname: Bob
In St. Louis: 1925-28, 33, 35
Number: 8, 29
M.L. Debut: 9/5/15

OGRODOWSKI, AMBROSE FRANCIS
Nickname: Brusie
In St. Louis: 1936-37
Number: 9
M.L. Debut: 4/14/36

O'HARA, WILLIAM ALEXANDER
Nickname: Bill
In St. Louis: 1910
M.L. Debut: 4/15/09

O'HARA, THOMAS F.
Nickname: Tom
In St. Louis: 1906-07
M.L. Debut: 9/19/06

O'LEARY, CHARLES TIMOTHY
Nickname: Charlie
In St. Louis: 1913
M.L. Debut: 4/14/04

OLIVA, JOSE (GALVEZ)
Nickname: Jose
In St. Louis: 1995
Number: 42
M.L. Debut: 7/1/94

OLIVARES, EDWARD (BALZEC)
Nickname: Ed
In St. Louis: 1960-61
Number: 17, 24
M.L. Debut: 9/16/60

OLIVARES, OMAR (PALQU)
Nickname: Omar
In St. Louis: 1990-94
Number: 55, 26, 00
M.L. Debut: 8/18/90

OLIVER, EUGENE GEORGE
Nickname: Gene
In St. Louis: 1959, 61-63
Number: 29
M.L. Debut: 6/6/59

OLIVO, DIOMEDES ANTONIO (MALDONADO)
Nickname: Diomedes
In St. Louis: 1963
Number: 41
M.L. Debut: 9/5/60

OLMSTEAD, ALAN RAY
Nickname: Al
In St. Louis: 1980
Number: 49
M.L. Debut: 9/12/80

O'NEAL, RANDALL JEFFREY
Nickname: Randy
In St. Louis: 1987-88
Number: 39
M.L. Debut: 9/12/84

O'NEIL, DENNIS
Nickname: Denny
In St. Louis: 1893
M.L. Debut: 6/18/1893

O'NEILL, JAMES EDWARD
Nickname: Tip
In St. Louis: 1884-89, 91
M.L. Debut: 5/5/1883

O'NEILL, JOHN JOSEPH
Nickname: Jack
In St. Louis: 1902-02
M.L. Debut: 4/21/02

O'NEILL, MICHAEL JOYCE
Nickname: Mike
In St. Louis: 1901-04
M.L. Debut: 9/20/01

OQUENDO, JOSE MANUEL
Nickname: Jose, The Secret Weapon
In St. Louis: 1986-95
Number: 11
M.L. Debut: 5/2/83

ORDAZ, LUIS JAVIER
Nickname: Luis
In St. Louis: 1997
Number: 52
M.L. Debut: 9/1/97

ORENGO, JOSEPH CHARLES
Nickname: Joe
In St. Louis: 1939-40
Number: 4, 18
M.L. Debut: 4/18/39

O'ROURKE, JAMES PATRICK
Nickname: Charlie
In St. Louis: 1959
Number: 25
M.L. Debut: 6/16/59

O'ROURKE, JOSEPH LEO SR.
Nickname: Patsy
In St. Louis: 1908
M.L. Debut: 4/16/08

O'ROURKE, TIMOTHY PATRICK
Nickname: Tim, Voiceless Tim
In St. Louis: 1894
M.L. Debut: 5/27/1890

ORSATTI, ERNEST RALPH
Nickname: Ernie
In St. Louis: 1927-35
Number: 5, 6, 12
M.L. Debut: 9/4/27

OSBORNE, DONOVAN ALAN
Nickname: Donovan
In St. Louis: 1992, 93, 95-97
Number: 31
M.L. Debut: 4/9/92

OSTEEN, CLAUDE WILSON
Nickname: Claude
In St. Louis: 1974
Number: 34
M.L. Debut: 7/6/57

OSTEEN, JAMES CHAMPLIN
Nickname: Champ
In St. Louis: 1908-09
M.L. Debut: 9/18/03

OTTEN, JAMES EDWARD
Nickname: Jim
In St. Louis: 1980-81
Number: 34, 40
M.L. Debut: 7/31/74

OTTEN, JOSEPH G.
Nickname: Joe
In St. Louis: 1895
M.L. Debut: 7/5/1895

OWEN, ARNOLD MALCOLM
Nickname: Mickey
In St. Louis: 1937-40
Number: 8, 14
M.L. Debut: 5/2/37

OWNBEY, RICHARD WAYNE
Nickname: Rick
In St. Louis: 1984, 86
Number: 40
M.L. Debut: 8/17/82

PABST, EDWARD D.A.
Nickname: Ed
In St. Louis: 1890
M.L. Debut: 9/26/1890

PACKARD, EUGENE MILO
Nickname: Gene
In St. Louis: 1917-18
M.L. Debut: 9/27/12

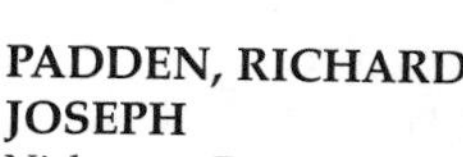

PADDEN, RICHARD JOSEPH
Nickname: Brains
In St. Louis: 1901
M.L. Debut: 7/15/1896

PADGETT, DON WILSON
Nickname: Don, Red
In St. Louis: 1937-41
Number: 4, 16
M.L. Debut: 4/23/37

PAGNOZZI, THOMAS ALAN
Nickname: Tom
In St. Louis: 1987-97
Number: 19
M.L. Debut: 4/12/87

PAINE, PHILLIPS STEERE
Nickname: Phil, Flip
In St. Louis: 1958
Number: 44
M.L. Debut: 7/14/51

PAINTER, LANCE TELFORD
Nickname: Lance
In St. Louis: 1997
Number: 28
M.L. Debut: 5/19/93

PALACIOS, VINCENTE (DIAZ)
Nickname: Vincente
In St. Louis: 1994-95
Number: 58
M.L. Debut: 9/4/87

PALMER, LOWELL RAYMOND
Nickname: Lowell
In St. Louis: 1972
Number: 44
M.L. Debut: 6/21/69

PAPAI, ALFRED THOMAS
Nickname: Al
In St. Louis: 1948-50
Number: 36, 41
M.L. Debut: 4/24/48

PAPI, STANLEY GERARD
Nickname: Stan
In St. Louis: 1974
Number: 29
M.L. Debut: 4/11/74

PAPPAS, ERIK DANIEL
Nickname: Erik
In St. Louis: 1993-94
Number: 12
M.L. Debut: 4/19/91

PARENT, FREDERICK ALFRED
Nickname: Freddy
In St. Louis: 1899
M.L. Debut: 7/14/1899

PARIS, KELLY JAY
Nickname: Kelly
In St. Louis: 1982
Number: 35
M.L. Debut: 9/1/82

PARKER, HARRY WILLIAM
Nickname: Harry
In St. Louis: 1970-71, 75
Number: 34, 31
M.L. Debut: 8/8/70

PARKER, ROY WILLIAM
Nickname: Roy
In St. Louis: 1919
M.L. Debut: 9/10/19

PARMELEE, LE ROY EARL
Nickname: Roy, Bud, Tarzan
In St. Louis: 1936
Number: 15
M.L. Debut: 9/28/29

PARRETT, JEFFREY DALE
Nickname: Jeff
In St. Louis: 1995-96
Number: 49
M.L. Debut: 4/11/86

PARROTT, THOMAS WILLIAM
Nickname: Tom, Tacky Tom
In St. Louis: 1896
M.L. Debut: 6/18/1893

PARTENHEIMER, STANWOOD WENDELL
Nickname: Stan, Party
In St. Louis: 1945
Number: 32
M.L. Debut: 5/27/44

PASQUELLA, MICHAEL JOHN
Nickname: Mike, Toney
In St. Louis: 1919
M.L. Debut: 7/9/19

PATTERSON, DARYL ALAN
Nickname: Daryl
In St. Louis: 1971
Number: 48
M.L. Debut: 4/10/68

PATTON, HARRY CLAUDE
Nickname: Harry
In St. Louis: 1910
M.L. Debut: 8/22/10

PAULETTE, EUGENE EDWARD
Nickname: Gene
In St. Louis: 1917-19
M.L. Debut: 6/16/11

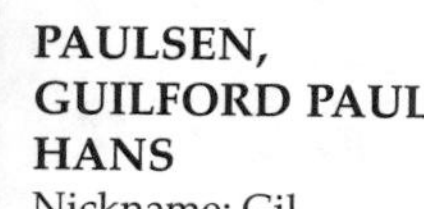

PAULSEN, GUILFORD PAUL HANS
Nickname: Gil
In St. Louis: 1925
M.L. Debut: 10/3/25

PAYNTER, GEORGE WASHINGTON
Nickname: George
In St. Louis: 1894
M.L. Debut: 8/12/1894

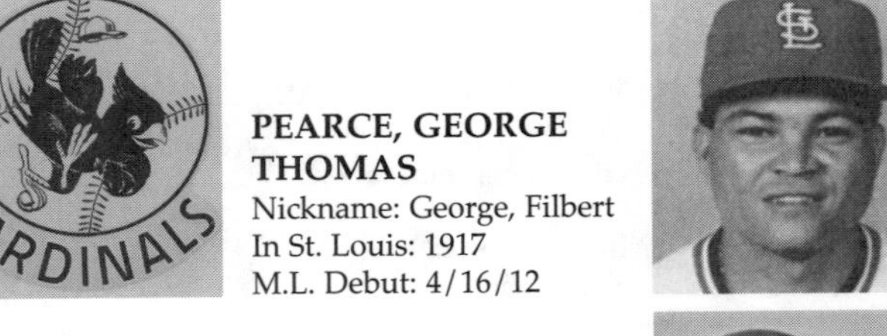

PEARCE, GEORGE THOMAS
Nickname: George, Filbert
In St. Louis: 1917
M.L. Debut: 4/16/12

PEARS, FRANK H.
Nickname: Frank
In St. Louis: 1893
M.L. Debut: 10/6/1889

PEARSON, ALEXANDER FRANKLIN
Nickname: Alex
In St. Louis: 1902
M.L. Debut: 8/1/02

PEEL, HOMER HEFNER
Nickname: Homer
In St. Louis: 1927, 30
M.L. Debut: 9/13/27

PEETE, CHARLES
Nickname: Charlie, Mule
In St. Louis: 1956
M.L. Debut: 7/17/56

PEITZ, HENRY CLEMENT
Nickname: Heinie
In St. Louis: 1892-95, 1913
M.L. Debut: 10/15/1892

PEITZ, JOSEPH
Nickname: Joe
In St. Louis: 1894
M.L. Debut: 7/15/1894

PENA, ANTONIO FRANCESCO (PADILLA)
Nickname: Tony
In St. Louis: 1987-89
Number: 26
M.L. Debut: 9/1/80

PENA, GERONIMO (MARTINEZ)
Nickname: Geronimo
In St. Louis: 1990-95
Number: 21
M.L. Debut: 9/5/90

PENA, ORLANDO GREGORIO (QUEVARA)
Nickname: Orlando
In St. Louis: 1973-74
Number: 36
M.L. Debut: 8/24/58

PENDLETON, TERRY LEE
Nickname: Terry
In St. Louis: 1984-90
Number: 9
M.L. Debut: 7/18/94

PEPPER, RAYMOND WATSON
Nickname: Ray
In St. Louis: 1932-33
Number: 29
M.L. Debut: 4/15/32

PERDUE, HERBERT RODNEY
Nickname: Hub, The Gallatin Squash
In St. Louis: 1914-15
M.L. Debut: 4/19/11

PEREZ, MICHAEL IRVIN (ORTEGA)
Nickname: Mike
In St. Louis: 1990-94
Number: 63, 42
M.L. Debut: 9/5/90

PERRITT, WILLIAM DAYTON
Nickname: Pol
In St. Louis: 1912-14
M.L. Debut: 9/7/12

PERRY, GERALD JUNE
Nickname: Gerald
In St. Louis: 1991-95
M.L. Debut: 8/11/83

PERRY, WILLIAM PATRICK
Nickname: Pat, Atlas
In St. Louis: 1985-87
Number: 37
M.L. Debut: 9/12/85

PERTICA, WILLIAM ANDREW
Nickname: Bill
In St. Louis: 1921-23
M.L. Debut: 8/7/18

PETERS, STEVEN BRADLEY
Nickname: Steve
In St. Louis: 1987-88
Number: 36
M.L. Debut: 8/11/87

PETKOVSEK, MARK JOSEPH
Nickname: Mark
In St. Louis: 1995-97
Number: 46
M.L. Debut: 6/8/91

PFEFFER, EDWARD JOSEPH
Nickname: Jeff
In St. Louis: 1921-24
M.L. Debut: 4/16/11

PHELPS, EDWARD JAYKILL
Nickname: Ed, Yaller
In St. Louis: 1909-10
M.L. Debut: 9/3/02

PHILLIPS, HOWARD EDWARD
Nickname: Ed, Eddie
In St. Louis: 1953
Number: 3
M.L. Debut: 9/10/53

PHILLIPS, MICHAEL DWAINE
Nickname: Mike
In St. Louis: 1977-80
Number: 5
M.L. Debut: 4/5/73

PHYLE, WILLIAM JOSEPH
Nickname: Bill
In St. Louis: 1906
M.L. Debut: 9/17/1898

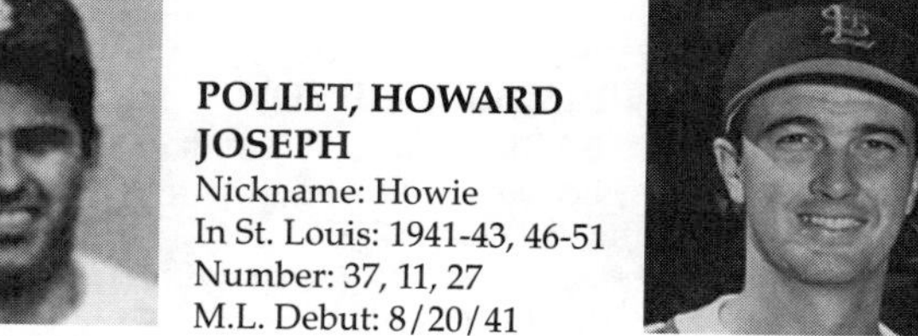

PICHE, RONALD JACQUES
Nickname: Ron
In St. Louis: 1966
Number: 37
M.L. Debut: 5/30/60

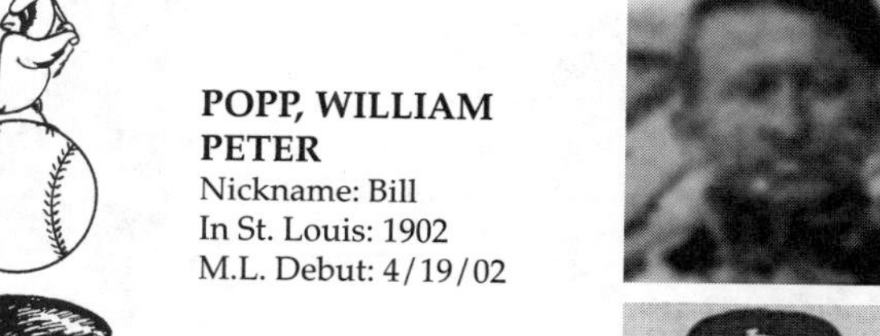

PICKETT, CHARLES ALBERT
Nickname: Charlie
In St. Louis: 1910
M.L. Debut: 6/21/10

PINCKNEY, GEORGE BURTON (PINKNEY)
Nickname: George
In St. Louis: 1892
M.L. Debut: 8/16/1884

PINSON, VADA EDWARD
Nickname: Vada
In St. Louis: 1969
Number: 28
M.L. Debut: 4/15/58

PIPPEN, HENRY HAROLD
Nickname: Cotton
In St. Louis: 1936
Number: 20
M.L. Debut: 8/28/36

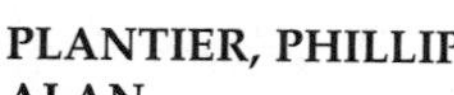

PLANTIER, PHILLIP ALAN
Nickname: Phil
In St. Louis: 1997
Number: 23
M.L. Debut: 8/21/90

PLODINEC, TIMOTHY ALFRED
Nickname: Tim
In St. Louis: 1972
M.L. Debut: 6/2/72

POHOLSKY, THOMAS GEORGE
Nickname: Tom
In St. Louis: 1950-51, 54-56
Number: 10, 29, 23
M.L. Debut: 4/20/50

POLLET, HOWARD JOSEPH
Nickname: Howie
In St. Louis: 1941-43, 46-51
Number: 37, 11, 27
M.L. Debut: 8/20/41

POPP, WILLIAM PETER
Nickname: Bill
In St. Louis: 1902
M.L. Debut: 4/19/02

PORTER, DARRELL RAY
Nickname: Darrell
In St. Louis: 1981-85
Number: 15
M.L. Debut: 9/2/71

PORTER, J.W.
Nickname: Jay
In St. Louis: 1959
Number: 44
M.L. Debut: 7/30/52

POTTER, MICHAEL GARY
Nickname: Mike
In St. Louis: 1976-77
Number: 40, 43
M.L. Debut: 9/6/76

POTTER, NELSON THOMAS
Nickname: Nels, Nellie
In St. Louis: 1936
Number: 20
M.L. Debut: 4/25/36

POWELL, JOHN JOSEPH
Nickname: Jack, Red
In St. Louis: 1899-1901
M.L. Debut: 6/23/1897

POWER, TED HENRY
Nickname: Ted
In St. Louis: 1989
Number: 42
M.L. Debut: 9/9/81

PRESKO, JOSEPH EDWARD
Nickname: Joe, Little Joe, Baby Joe
In St. Louis: 1951-54
Number: 21, 32
M.L. Debut: 5/3/51

PROLY, MICHAEL JAMES
Nickname: Mike
In St. Louis: 1976
Number: 46
M.L. Debut: 4/10/76

PUCCINELLI, GEORGE LAWRENCE
Nickname: George, Count, Pooch
In St. Louis: 1930, 32
M.L. Debut: 7/17/30

PURKEY, ROBERT THOMAS
Nickname: Bob
In St. Louis: 1965
Number: 28
M.L. Debut: 4/14/54

PUTTMAN, AMBROSE NICHOLAS
Nickname: Ambrose, Putty, Brose
In St. Louis: 1906
M.L. Debut: 9/4/03

QUEST, JOSEPH L.
Nickname: Joe
In St. Louis: 1883-84
M.L. Debut: 8/30/1871

QUINLAN, THOMAS FINNERS
Nickname: Finners
In St. Louis: 1913
M.L. Debut: 9/6/13

QUINN, JOSEPH J.
Nickname: Joe, Ol' Reliable, Uncle Joe
In St. Louis: 1893-96, 98, 1900
M.L. Debut: 4/26/1884

QUIRK, JAMES PATRICK
Nickname: Jamie
In St. Louis: 1983
Number: 16
M.L. Debut: 9/4/75

QUISENBERRY, DANIEL RAYMOND
Nickname: Dan, Quiz
In St. Louis: 1988-89
Number: 40
M.L. Debut: 7/8/79

RADEBAUGH, ROY
Nickname: Roy
In St. Louis: 1911
M.L. Debut: 9/22/11

RADER, DAVID MARTIN
Nickname: Dave
In St. Louis: 1977
Number: 14
M.L. Debut: 9/5/71

RAFFENSBERGER, KENNETH DAVID
Nickname: Ken, Raffy
In St. Louis: 1939
Number: 23
M.L. Debut: 4/15/39

RAGGIO, BRADY JOHN
Nickname: Brady
In St. Louis: 1997
Number: 64
M.L. Debut: 4/14/97

RAJSICH, GARY LOUIS
Nickname: Gary
In St. Louis: 1984
Number: 33
M.L. Debut: 4/9/82

RALEIGH, JOHN AUSTIN
Nickname: John
In St. Louis: 1909-10
M.L. Debut: 8/4/09

RAMIREZ, MILTON (BARBOZA)
Nickname: Milt
In St. Louis: 1970-71
Number: 41
M.L. Debut: 4/11/70

RAMSEY, MICHAEL JEFFREY
Nickname: Mike
In St. Louis: 1978, 80-84
Number: 33, 4, 5
M.L. Debut: 9/4/78

RAMSEY, THOMAS A.
Nickname: Toad
In St. Louis: 1889-90
M.L. Debut: 9/5/1885

RAND, RICHARD HILTON
Nickname: Dick
In St. Louis: 1953, 55
Number: 16
M.L. Debut: 9/16/53

RASCHI, VICTOR JOHN ANGELO
Nickname: Vic, The Springfield Rifle
In St. Louis: 1954-55
Number: 17
M.L. Debut: 9/23/46

RASSMUSSEN, ERIC RALPH
Nickname: Eric
In St. Louis: 1975-78, 82-83
Number: 42, 34
M.L. Debut: 7/21/75

RAUB, THOMAS JEFFERSON
Nickname: Tom
In St. Louis: 1906
M.L. Debut: 5/3/03

RAYFORD, FLOYD KINNARD
Nickname: Floyd
In St. Louis: 1983
Number: 12
M.L. Debut: 4/17/80

RAYMOND, ARTHUR LAWRENCE
Nickname: Bugs
In St. Louis: 1907-08
M.L. Debut: 9/23/04

REBEL, ARTHUR ANTHONY
Nickname: Art
In St. Louis: 1945
Number: 8
M.L. Debut: 4/19/38

REDDING, PHILLIP HAYDEN
Nickname: Phil
In St. Louis: 1912-13
M.L. Debut: 9/14/12

REED, MILTON D.
Nickname: Milt
In St. Louis: 1911
M.L. Debut: 9/9/11

REED, RONALD LEE
Nickname: Ron
In St. Louis: 1975
Number: 38
M.L. Debut: 9/26/66

REEDER, WILLIAM EDGAR
Nickname: Bill
In St. Louis: 1949
Number: 33
M.L. Debut: 4/23/49

REESE, JAMES HERMAN
Nickname: Jimmy
In St. Louis: 1932
Number: 9
M.L. Debut: 4/19/30

REILLY, THOMAS HENRY
Nickname: Tom
In St. Louis: 1908-09
M.L. Debut: 7/27/08

REINHART, ARTHUR CONRAD
Nickname: Art
In St. Louis: 1919, 25-28
M.L. Debut: 4/26/19

REIS, HARRIE CRANE
Nickname: Jack
In St. Louis: 1911
M.L. Debut: 9/9/11

REITZ, KENNETH JOHN
Nickname: Kenny, The Zamboni
In St. Louis: 1972-75, 77-80
Number: 44
M.L. Debut: 9/5/72

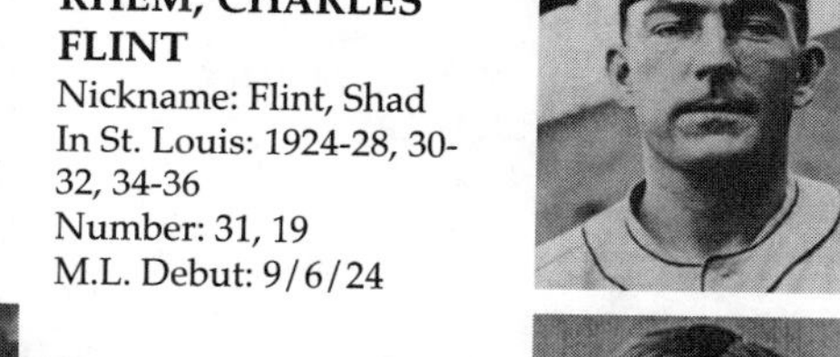

REPASS, ROBERT WILLIS
Nickname: Bob
In St. Louis: 1939
Number: 23
M.L. Debut: 9/18/39

REPULSKI, ELDON JOHN
Nickname: Rip
In St. Louis: 1953-56
Number: 8
M.L. Debut: 4/14/53

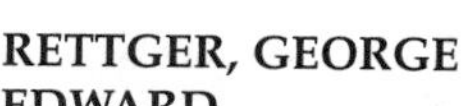

RETTGER, GEORGE EDWARD
Nickname: George
In St. Louis: 1891
M.L. Debut: 8/13/1891

REUSS, JERRY
Nickname: Jerry
In St. Louis: 1969-71
Number: 49
M.L. Debut: 9/27/69

REYNOLDS, KENNETH LEE
Nickname: Ken
In St. Louis: 1975
Number: 24
M.L. Debut: 9/5/70

REYNOLDS, ROBERT ALLEN
Nickname: Bob, Bullet
In St. Louis: 1971
M.L. Debut: 9/19/69

RHEM, CHARLES FLINT
Nickname: Flint, Shad
In St. Louis: 1924-28, 30-32, 34-36
Number: 31, 19
M.L. Debut: 9/6/24

RHOADS, ROBERT BARTON
Nickname: Bob, Dusty
In St. Louis: 1924-28, 30-32, 34, 36
Number: 31, 19
M.L. Debut: 9/6/24

RHODES, CHARLES ANDERSON
Nickname: Charlie, Dusty
In St. Louis: 1906, 08-09
M.L. Debut: 7/26/06

RIBANT, DENNIS JOSEPH
Nickname: Dennis
In St. Louis: 1969
M.L. Debut: 8/9/64

RICE, HAROLD HOUSTEN
Nickname: Hal, Hoot
In St. Louis: 1948-53
Number: 16, 1, 39
M.L. Debut: 4/29/48

RICE, DELBERT W.
Nickname: Del
In St. Louis: 1945-55, 60
Number: 11, 18
M.L. Debut: 5/2/45

RICHARD, LEE EDWARD
Nickname: Lee, Bee Bee
In St. Louis: 1976
Number: 3
M.L. Debut: 4/7/71

RICHARDSON, GORDON CLARK
Nickname: Gordie
In St. Louis: 1964
Number: 22
M.L. Debut: 7/26/64

RICHARDSON, WILLIAM HENRY
Nickname: Bill
In St. Louis: 1901
M.L. Debut: 9/20/01

RICHERT, PETER GERARD
Nickname: Pete
In St. Louis: 1974
Number: 34
M.L. Debut: 4/12/62

RICHMOND, DONALD LESTER
Nickname: Don
In St. Louis: 1951
Number: 38
M.L. Debut: 9/16/41

RICKETTS, DAVID WILLIAM
Nickname: Dave
In St. Louis: 1963, 65, 67-69
Number: 38, 10
M.L. Debut: 9/25/63

RICKETTS, RICHARD JAMES
Nickname: Dick
In St. Louis: 1959
Number: 47
M.L. Debut: 6/14/59

RICKS, JOHN
Nickname: John
In St. Louis: 1891, 94
M.L. Debut: 9/21/1891

RIEGER, ELMER JAY
Nickname: Elmer
In St. Louis: 1910
M.L. Debut: 4/20/10

RIGGERT, JOSEPH ALOYSIUS
Nickname: Joe
In St. Louis: 1914
M.L. Debut: 5/12/11

RIGGS, LEWIS SIDNEY
Nickname: Lew
In St. Louis: 1934
Number: 29
M.L. Debut: 2/28/34

RINCON, ANDREW JOHN
Nickname: Andy
In St. Louis: 1980-82
Number: 46
M.L. Debut: 9/15/80

RING, JAMES JOSEPH
Nickname: Jimmy
In St. Louis: 1927
M.L. Debut: 4/13/17

RIVIERE, ARTHUR BERNARD
Nickname: Tink
In St. Louis: 1921
M.L. Debut: 4/15/21

ROBERTS, CLARENCE ASHLEY
Nickname: Skipper
In St. Louis: 1913
M.L. Debut: 6/12/13

ROBINSON, JOHN HENRY
Nickname: Hank, Rube
In St. Louis: 1914-15
M.L. Debut: 9/2/11

ROBINSON, WILBERT
Nickname: Wilbert, Uncle Robbie
In St. Louis: 1900
M.L. Debut: 4/19/1886

ROBINSON, WILLIAM H.
Nickname: Yank
In St. Louis: 1885-89, 91
M.L. Debut: 8/24/1882

ST. LOUIS CARDINALS
NATIONAL LEAGUE CHAMPIONS
1931

ROCHE, JOHN JOSEPH
Nickname: Jack, Red
In St. Louis: 1914-15, 17
M.L. Debut: 5/24/14

RODRIGUEZ, RICHARD ANTHONY
Nickname: Rich
In St. Louis: 1994-95
Number: 33
M.L. Debut: 6/30/90

ROE, ELWIN CHARLES
Nickname: Preacher
In St. Louis: 1938
Number: 19
M.L. Debut: 8/22/38

ROETTGER, WALTER HENRY
Nickname: Wally
In St. Louis: 1927-29, 31
M.L. Debut: 5/1/27

ROJAS, OCTAVIO VICTOR (RIVAS)
Nickname: Cookie
In St. Louis: 1970
Number: 11
M.L. Debut: 4/10/62

ROJEK, STANLEY ANDREW
Nickname: Stan
In St. Louis: 1951
Number: 19
M.L. Debut: 9/22/42

ROLLING, RAYMOND COPELAND
Nickname: Ray
In St. Louis: 1912
M.L. Debut: 9/6/12

ROMANO, JOHN ANTHONY
Nickname: Johnny, Honey
In St. Louis: 1967
Number: 1
M.L. Debut: 9/12/58

ROMONOSKY, JOHN
Nickname: John
In St. Louis: 1953
M.L. Debut: 9/6/53

RONAN, EDWARD MARCUS
Nickname: Marc
In St. Louis: 1993
Number: 67
M.L. Debut: 9/21/93

ROOF, EUGENE LAWRENCE
Nickname: Gene
In St. Louis: 1981-83
Number: 29
M.L. Debut: 9/3/81

ROQUE, JORGE (VARGAS)
Nickname: Jorge
In St. Louis: 1970-72
Number: 10
M.L. Debut: 9/4/70

ROSEMAN, JAMES JOHN
Nickname: Chief
In St. Louis: 1890
M.L. Debut: 5/1/1882

ROTHROCK, JOHN HOUSTON
Nickname: Jack
In St. Louis: 1934-35
Number: 6
M.L. Debut: 7/28/25

ROYER, STANLEY DEAN
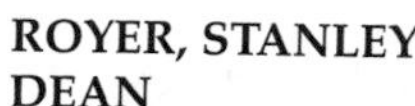
Nickname: Stan
In St. Louis: 1991-94
Number: 5
M.L. Debut: 9/11/91

RUCKER, DAVID MICHAEL
Nickname: Dave
In St. Louis: 1983-84
Number: 36
M.L. Debut: 4/12/81

RUDOLPH, KENNETH VICTOR
Nickname: Ken
In St. Louis: 1975-76
Number: 9
M.L. Debut: 4/20/69

RUSSELL, JACK ERWIN
Nickname: Jack
In St. Louis: 1940
Number: 28
M.L. Debut: 5/5/26

RUSSELL, PAUL A.
Nickname: Paul
In St. Louis: 1894
M.L. Debut: 7/29/1894

RYAN, JOHN BERNARD
Nickname: John, Jack
In St. Louis: 1901-03
M.L. Debut: 9/2/1889

RYAN, JOHN J.
Nickname: John, Mike
In St. Louis: 1895
M.L. Debut: 7/25/1895

RYBA, DOMINIC JOSEPH
Nickname: Mike
In St. Louis: 1935-38
Number: 19
M.L. Debut: 9/22/35

SABO, CHRISTOPHER ANDREW
Nickname: Chris, Spuds
In St. Louis: 1995
M.L. Debut: 4/4/88

SADECKI, RAYMOND MICHAEL
Nickname: Ray
In St. Louis: 1960-66, 75
Number: 37
M.L. Debut: 5/19/60

SADOWSKI, ROBERT FRANK
Nickname: Bob, Sid
In St. Louis: 1960
Number: 19
M.L. Debut: 9/16/60

SALAS, MARK BRUCE
Nickname: Mark
In St. Louis: 1984
Number: 10
M.L. Debut: 6/19/84

SALLEE, HARRY FRANKLIN
Nickname: Slim, Scatter
In St. Louis: 1908-16
M.L. Debut: 4/16/08

SAMULS, SAMUEL EARL
Nickname: Ike
In St. Louis: 1895
M.L. Debut: 8/3/1895

SANCHEZ, ORLANDO (MARQUEZ)
Nickname: Orlando
In St. Louis: 1981-83
Number: 23
M.L. Debut: 5/6/81

SANDERS, GABE RAYMOND FLOYD
Nickname: Ray
In St. Louis: 1942-45
Number: 5
M.L. Debut: 4/14/42

SANDERS, WARREN WILLIAMS
Nickname: War
In St. Louis: 1903-04
M.L. Debut: 4/18/03

SANTANA, RAFAEL FRANCISCO (DE LA CRUZ)
Nickname: Rafael, Ralph
In St. Louis: 1983
Number: 14
M.L. Debut: 4/5/83

SANTORINI, ALAN JOEL
Nickname: Al
In St. Louis: 1971-73
Number: 34
M.L. Debut: 9/10/68

SARNI, WILLIAM FLORINE
Nickname: Bill
In St. Louis: 1951-52, 54-56
Number: 16, 15
M.L. Debut: 5/9/51

SAUER, EDWARD
Nickname: Ed, Horn
In St. Louis: 1949
M.L. Debut: 9/17/43

SAUER, HENRY JOHN
Nickname: Hank
In St. Louis: 1956
Number: 10
M.L. Debut: 9/9/41

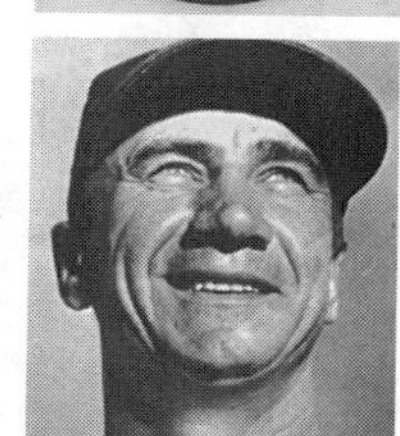

SAVAGE, THEODORE EDMUND
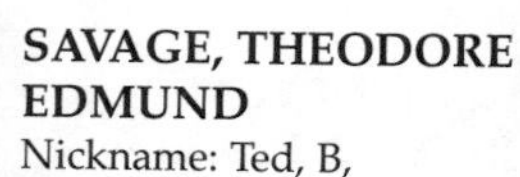
Nickname: Ted, B, Ephesian Savage
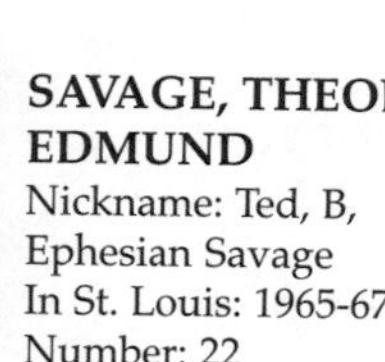
In St. Louis: 1965-67
Number: 22
M.L. Debut: 4/9/62

SAWATSKI, CARL ERNEST
Nickname: Carl, Swats
In St. Louis: 1960-63
Number: 1
M.L. Debut: 9/29/48

SCARSONE, STEVEN WAYNE
Nickname: Steve
In St. Louis: 1997
Number: 38
M.L. Debut: 5/15/92

SCHAFFER, JIMMIE RONALD
Nickname: Jimmy
In St. Louis: 1961-62
Number: 4
M.L. Debut: 5/20/14

SCHANG, ROBERT MARTIN
Nickname: Bobby
In St. Louis: 1927
M.L. Debut: 9/23/14

ST. LOUIS CARDINALS
CHAMPIONS NATIONAL LEAGUE
1928

SCHAPPERT, JOHN
Nickname: Jack
In St. Louis: 1882
M.L. Debut: 5/3/1882

SCHEFFING, ROBERT BODEN
Nickname: Bob, Grumpy
In St. Louis: 1951
Number: 30
M.L. Debut: 4/27/41

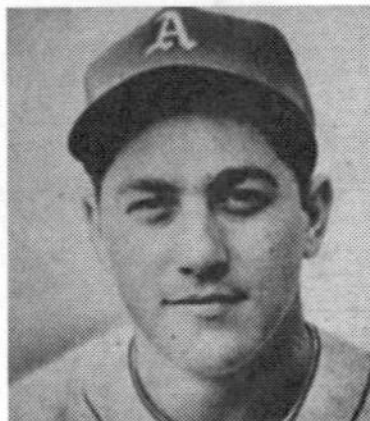

SCHEIB, CARL ALVIN
Nickname: Carl
In St. Louis: 1954
Number: 31
M.L. Debut: 9/6/43

SCHEINBLUM, RICHARD ALAN
Nickname: Richine
In St. Louis: 1974
In St. Louis: 19
M.L. Debut: 9/1/65

SCHINDLER, WILLIAM GIBBONS
Nickname: Bill
In St. Louis: 1920
M.L. Debut: 9/3/20

SCHMIDT, FREDERICK ALBERT
Nickname: Freddy
In St. Louis: 1944, 46-47
Number: 11, 37, 29
M.L. Debut: 4/25/44

SCHMIDT, WALTER JOSEPH
Nickname: Walter
In St. Louis: 1925
M.L. Debut: 4/13/16

SCHMIDT, WILLARD RAYMOND
Nickname: Willard
In St. Louis: 1952-53, 55-57
Number: 44
M.L. Debut: 4/19/52

SCHOENDIENST, ALBERT FRED
Nickname: Red
In St. Louis: 1945-56, 61-63
Number: 6, 2
M.L. Debut: 4/17/45

SCHOFIELD, JOHN RICHARD
Nickname: Dick, Ducky
In St. Louis: 1953-58, 68, 71
Number: 19, 11
M.L. Debut: 7/3/53

SCHRECKENGOST, OSSEE FREEMAN
Nickname: Ossee
In St. Louis: 1899
M.L. Debut: 9/8/1897

SCHRIVER, WILLIAM FREDERICK
Nickname: Pop
In St. Louis: 1901
M.L. Debut: 4/29/1886

SCHUBLE, HENRY GEORGE
Nickname: Heinie
In St. Louis: 1927, 36
Number: 30
M.L. Debut: 7/8/27

SCHULTE, JOHN CLEMENT
Nickname: Johnny
In St. Louis: 1927
M.L. Debut: 4/18/23

SCHULTZ, CHARLES BUDD
Nickname: Buddy
In St. Louis: 1977-79
Number: 22
M.L. Debut: 9/3/75

SCHULTZ, GEORGE WARREN
Nickname: Barney
In St. Louis: 1955, 63-65
Number: 36, 33
M.L. Debut: 4/12/55

SCHULTZ, JOHN
Nickname: John
In St. Louis: 1891
M.L. Debut: 8/7/1891

SCHULTZ, JOSEPH CHARLES SR.
Nickname: Joe, Germany
In St. Louis: 1919-24
M.L. Debut: 9/28/12

SCHULZ, WALTER FREDERICK
Nickname: Walt
In St. Louis: 1920
M.L. Debut: 9/24/20

SCHUPP, FERDINAND MAURICE
Nickname: Ferdie
In St. Louis: 1919-21
M.L. Debut: 4/19/13

SCOFFIC, LOUIS
Nickname: Lou, Weasel
In St. Louis: 1936
Number: 31
M.L. Debut: 4/16/36

SCOTT, ANTHONY
Nickname: Tony
In St. Louis: 1977-81
Number: 30
M.L. Debut: 9/1/73

SCOTT, GEORGE WILLIAM
Nickname: George
In St. Louis: 1920
M.L. Debut: 9/13/20

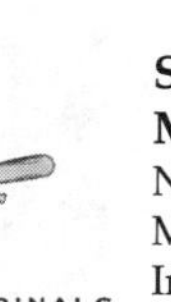

SEAMAN, KIM MICHAEL
Nickname: Kim
In St. Louis: 1979-80
Number: 48
M.L. Debut: 9/28/79

SEGUI, DIEGO PABLO (GONZALEZ)
Nickname: Diego
In St. Louis: 1972-73
Number: 35
M.L. Debut: 4/12/62

SELL, LESTER ELWOOD
Nickname: Epp
In St. Louis: 1922-23
M.L. Debut: 9/1/22

SELPH, CAREY ISOM
Nickname: Carey
In St. Louis: 1929
M.L. Debut: 5/25/29

SESSI, WALTER ANTHONY
Nickname: Walt, Watsie
In St. Louis: 1941, 46
Number: 38
M.L. Debut: 9/18/41

SEWARD, GEORGE E.
Nickname: George
In St. Louis: 1882
M.L. Debut: 5/19/1875

SEXTON, JIMMY DALE
Nickname: Jimmy
In St. Louis: 1983
M.L. Debut: 9/2/77

SHANNON, THOMAS MICHAEL
Nickname: Mike, Moonman
In St. Louis: 1962-70
Number: 28, 18
M.L. Debut: 9/11/62

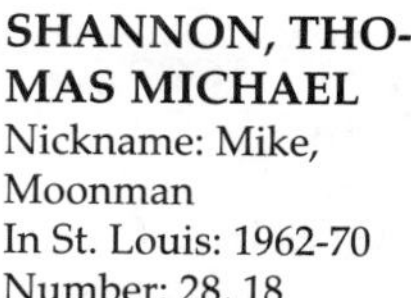

SHANNON, WALTER CHARLES
Nickname: Wally
In St. Louis: 1959-60
Number: 25
M.L. Debut: 7/9/59

SHANNON, WILLIAM PORTER
Nickname: Spike
In St. Louis: 1904-06
M.L. Debut: 4/15/04

SHANTZ, ROBERT CLAYTON
Nickname: Bobby
In St. Louis: 1962-64
Number: 34
M.L. Debut: 5/1/49

SHAW, ALBERT SIMPSON
Nickname: Al
In St. Louis: 1907-09
M.L. Debut: 9/28/07

SHAW, DONALD WELLINGTON
Nickname: Don
In St. Louis: 1971-72
Number: 44
M.L. Debut: 4/11/67

SHAY, DANIEL C.
Nickname: Danny
In St. Louis: 1904-05
M.L. Debut: 4/30/01

SHEA, GERALD J.
Nickname: Gerry
In St. Louis: 1905
M.L. Debut: 10/1/05

SHEAFFER, DANNY TODD
Nickname: Danny
In St. Louis: 1995-97
Number: 12
M.L. Debut: 4/9/87

SHECKARD, SAMUEL JAMES TILDEN
Nickname: Jimmy
In St. Louis: 1913
M.L. Debut: 9/14/1897

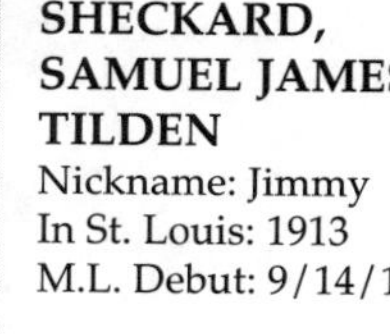

SHEEHAN, TIMOTHY JAMES
Nickname: Biff
In St. Louis: 1895-96
M.L. Debut: 7/22/1895

SHEPHARDSON, RAYMOND FRANCIS
Nickname: Ray
In St. Louis: 1924
M.L. Debut: 9/19/24

SHERDEL, WILLIAM HENRY
Nickname: Bill, Wee Willie
In St. Louis: 1918-30, 32
M.L. Debut: 4/22/18

SHERRILL, TIMOTHY SHAWN
Nickname: Tim
In St. Louis: 1990-91
Number: 56
M.L. Debut: 8/14/90

SHIELDS, CHARLES JESSAMINE
Nickname: Charlie
In St. Louis: 1907
M.L. Debut: 4/23/02

SHIELDS, VINCENT WILLIAM
Nickname: Vince
In St. Louis: 1924
M.L. Debut: 9/20/24

SHINNERS, RALPH PETER
Nickname: Ralph
In St. Louis: 1925
M.L. Debut: 4/12/22

SHIRLEY, ROBERT CHARLES
Nickname: Bob
In St. Louis: 1981
Number: 32
M.L. Debut: 4/10/77

SHOTTON, BURTON EDWIN
Nickname: Burt, Barney
In St. Louis: 1919-23
M.L. Debut: 9/13/09

SHOUN, CLYDE MITCHELL
Nickname: Clyde, Hardrock
In St. Louis: 1938-42
Number: 36, 24
M.L. Debut: 8/7/35

SHOUPE, JOHN F.
Nickname: John
In St. Louis: 1882
M.L. Debut: 5/3/1879

SHUGART, FRANK HARRY
Nickname: Frank, B, Frank Harry Shugarts
In St. Louis: 1893-94
M.L. Debut: 8/23/1890

SIEBERT, RICHARD WALTHER
Nickname: Dick, Ducky
In St. Louis: 1937-38
Number: 22
M.L. Debut: 9/7/32

SIEBERT, WILFRED CHARLES
Nickname: Sonny
In St. Louis: 1974
Number: 42
M.L. Debut: 4/26/64

SIMMONS, CURTIS THOMAS
Nickname: Curt
In St. Louis: 1960-66
Number: 31
M.L. Debut: 9/28/47

SIMMONS, TED LYLE
Nickname: Ted, Simba
In St. Louis: 1968-80
Number: 23
M.L. Debut: 9/21/68

SIMPSON, RICHARD CHARLES
Nickname: Dick
In St. Louis: 1968
Number: 12
M.L. Debut: 9/21/62

SISLER, RICHARD ALLAN
Nickname: Dick
In St. Louis: 1946-47, 52-53
Number: 15
M.L. Debut: 4/16/46

SIZEMORE, THEODORE CRAWFORD
Nickname: Ted
In St. Louis: 1971-75
Number: 41
M.L. Debut: 4/7/69

SKINNER, ROBERT RALPH
Nickname: Bob
In St. Louis: 1964-66
Number: 19
M.L. Debut: 4/13/54

SLADE, GORDON LEIGH
Nickname: Gordon, Oskie
In St. Louis: 1933
Number: 14
M.L. Debut: 4/21/30

SLATTERY, JOHN TERRANCE
Nickname: Jack
In St. Louis: 1906
M.L. Debut: 9/28/01

SLAUGHTER, ENOS BRADSHER
Nickname: Enos, Country
In St. Louis: 1938-42, 46-53
Number: 9
M.L. Debut: 4/19/38

SMILEY, WILLIAM B.
Nickname: Bill
In St. Louis: 1882
M.L. Debut: 10/13/1874

SMITH, BOBBY GENE
Nickname: Bobby, Gene
In St. Louis: 1957-59, 62
Number: 15, 24, 35
M.L. Debut: 4/16/57

SMITH, BRYN NELSON
Nickname: Bryn
In St. Louis: 1990-92
Number: 36
M.L. Debut: 9/8/81

SMITH, CARL REGINALD
Nickname: Reggie
In St. Louis: 1974-76
Number: 7
M.L. Debut: 9/18/66

SMITH, CHARLES WILLIAM
Nickname: Charley
In St. Louis: 1966
Number: 1
M.L. Debut: 9/8/60

SMITH, EARL SUTTON
Nickname: Earl, Oil
In St. Louis: 1928-30
M.L. Debut: 4/24/19

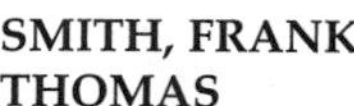

SMITH, FRANK THOMAS
Nickname: Frank
In St. Louis: 1955
Number: 25
M.L. Debut: 4/18/50

SMITH, FRED VINCENT
Nickname: Fred
In St. Louis: 1917
M.L. Debut: 4/17/13

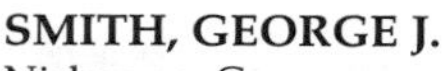

SMITH, GEORGE J.
Nickname: Germany
In St. Louis: 1898
M.L. Debut: 4/17/1884

SMITH, HAROLD RAYMOND
Nickname: Hal
In St. Louis: 1956-61
Number: 18, 2, 9
M.L. Debut: 5/2/56

SMITH, JACK
Nickname: Jack
In St. Louis: 1915-26
M.L. Debut: 9/30/15

SMITH, JUDSON GRANT
Nickname: Jud
In St. Louis: 1893
M.L. Debut: 5/21/1893

SMITH, KEITH LAVARNE
Nickname: Keith
In St. Louis: 1979-80
Number: 3
M.L. Debut: 8/2/77

SMITH, LEE ARTHUR JR.
Nickname: Lee, Big Lee
In St. Louis: 1990-93
Number: 47
M.L. Debut: 9/1/80

SMITH, LONNIE
Nickname: Lonnie
In St. Louis: 1982-85
Number: 27
M.L. Debut: 9/2/78

SMITH, OSBORNE EARL
Nickname: Ozzie, The Wizard
In St. Louis: 1982-96
Number: 1
M.L. Debut: 4/7/78

SMITH, ROBERT GILCHRIST
Nickname: Bob
In St. Louis: 1957
M.L. Debut: 4/29/55

SMITH, THOMAS EDWARD
Nickname: Tom
In St. Louis: 1898
M.L. Debut: 6/6/1894

SMITH, WALLACE H.
Nickname: Wally
In St. Louis: 1911-12
M.L. Debut: 4/17/11

SMITH, WILLIAM GARLAND
Nickname: Bill
In St. Louis: 1958-59
Number: 30
M.L. Debut: 9/13/58

SMITH, WILLIE EVERETT
Nickname: Willie
In St. Louis: 1994
Number: 70
M.L. Debut: 4/25/94

SMOOT, HOMER VERNON
Nickname: Homer, Doc
In St. Louis: 1902-06
M.L. Debut: 4/17/02

SMYTH, JAMES DANIEL
Nickname: Red
In St. Louis: 1917-18
M.L. Debut: 8/11/15

SNYDER, FRANK ELTON
Nickname: Frank, Pancho
In St. Louis: 1912-19, 27
M.L. Debut: 8/25/12

SOFF, RAYMOND JOHN
Nickname: Ray
In St. Louis: 1986-87
Number: 47
M.L. Debut: 7/17/86

SOLOMON, EDDIE JR.
Nickname: Eddie, Buddy
In St. Louis: 1976
Number: 24
M.L. Debut: 9/2/73

SORENSEN, LARY ALAN
Nickname: Lary
In St. Louis: 1981
Number: 39
M.L. Debut: 6/7/77

SOSA, ELIAS (MARTINEZ)
Nickname: Elias
In St. Louis: 1975
Number: 38
M.L. Debut: 9/8/72

SOTHORON, ALLEN SUTTON
Nickname: Allen
In St. Louis: 1924-26
M.L. Debut: 9/17/14

SOUTHWORTH, WILLIAM HARRISON
Nickname: Billy
In St. Louis: 1926-27, 29
M.L. Debut: 8/4/13

SPEIER, CHRIS EDWARD
Nickname: Chris
In St. Louis: 1984
Number: 5
M.L. Debut: 4/7/71

SPENCER, DARYL DEAN
Nickname: Big Dee
In St. Louis: 1960-61
Number: 20
M.L. Debut: 9/17/52

SPIEZIO, EDWARD WAYNE
Nickname: Ed
In St. Louis: 1964-68
Number: 26
M.L. Debut: 7/23/64

SPINKS, SCIPIO RONALD
Nickname: Scipio
In St. Louis: 1972-73
Number: 24
M.L. Debut: 9/16/69

SPRAGUE, EDWARD NELSON SR.
Nickname: Ed
In St. Louis: 1973
Number: 48
M.L. Debut: 4/10/68

SPRING, JACK RUSSELL
Nickname: Jack
In St. Louis: 1964
Number: 22
M.L. Debut: 4/16/55

SPRINZ, JOSEPH CONRAD
Nickname: Joe, Mule
In St. Louis: 1933
Number: 31
M.L. Debut: 7/16/30

STAINBACK, GEORGE TUCKER
Nickname: Tuck
In St. Louis: 1938
M.L. Debut: 4/17/34

STALEY, GERALD LEE
Nickname: Gerry
In St. Louis: 1947-54
Number: 14
M.L. Debut: 4/20/47

STALEY, HENRY ELI
Nickname: Harry
In St. Louis: 1895
M.L. Debut: 6/23/1888

STALLARD, EVAN TRACY
Nickname: Tracy
In St. Louis: 1965-66
Number: 40
M.L. Debut: 9/24/60

STALLCUP, THOMAS VIRGIL
Nickname: Virgil, Red
In St. Louis: 1952-53
Number: 3
M.L. Debut: 4/18/47

STANDRIDGE, ALFRED PETER
Nickname: Pete
In St. Louis: 1911
M.L. Debut: 9/19/11

STANKY, EDWARD RAYMOND
Nickname: Eddie, Muggsy, The Brat
In St. Louis: 1952-53
Number: 12
M.L. Debut: 4/21/43

STANTON, HARRY ANDREW
Nickname: Harry
In St. Louis: 1900
M.L. Debut: 10/14/1900

STARR, RAYMOND FRANCIS
Nickname: Ray, Iron Man
In St. Louis: 1932
M.L. Debut: 9/11/32

STEELE, ROBERT WESLEY
Nickname: Bob
In St. Louis: 1916-17
M.L. Debut: 4/17/16

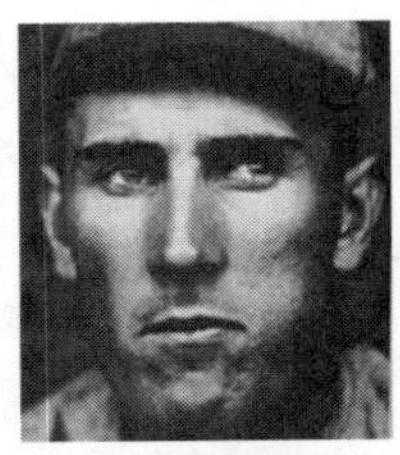

STEELE, WILLIAM MITCHELL
Nickname: Bill, Big Bill
In St. Louis: 1910-14
M.L. Debut: 9/10/10

STEIN, WILLIAM ALLEN
Nickname: Bill
In St. Louis: 1972-73
Number: 32
M.L. Debut: 9/6/72

STENZEL, JACOB CHARLES
Nickname: Jake
In St. Louis: 1898-99
M.L. Debut: 6/16/1890

STEPHENS, CARL RAY
Nickname: Ray
In St. Louis: 1990-91
Number: 54
M.L. Debut: 9/20/90

STEPHENSON, ROBERT LLOYD
Nickname: Bobby Gene
In St. Louis: 1955
Number: 21
M.L. Debut: 4/14/55

STEWART, JOHN FRANKLIN
Nickname: Stuffy
In St. Louis: 1916-17
M.L. Debut: 9/3/16

STINSON, GORREL ROBERT
Nickname: Bob
In St. Louis: 1971
Number: 19
M.L. Debut: 9/23/69

STIVETTS, JOHN ELMER
Nickname: Jack, Happy Jack
In St. Louis: 1889-91
M.L. Debut: 6/26/1889

STOBBS, CHARLES KLEIN
Nickname: Chuck
In St. Louis: 1958
Number: 38
M.L. Debut: 9/15/47

STOCK, MILTON JOSEPH
Nickname: Milt
In St. Louis: 1919-23
M.L. Debut: 9/29/13

STONE, DARRAH DEAN
Nickname: Dean
In St. Louis: 1959
Number: 45
M.L. Debut: 9/13/53

STONE, WILLIAM ARTHUR
Nickname: Tige
In St. Louis: 1923
M.L. Debut: 8/23/23

STORKE, ALAN MARSHALL
Nickname: Alan
In St. Louis: 1909
M.L. Debut: 9/24/06

STOTTLEMYRE, TODD VERNON
Nickname: Todd
In St. Louis: 1996-97
Number: 30
M.L. Debut: 4/6/88

STOUT, ALLYN MCCLELLAND
Nickname: Allyn, Fish Hook
In St. Louis: 1931-33
Number: 21
M.L. Debut: 5/16/31

STREET, CHARLES EVARD
Nickname: Gabby, Old Sarge
In St. Louis: 1931
M.L. Debut: 9/13/04

STRICKER, JOHN A.
Nickname: Cub
In St. Louis: 1892
M.L. Debut: 5/2/1882

STRIEF, GEORGE ANDREW
Nickname: George
In St. Louis: 1883-84
M.L. Debut: 5/1/1879

STRIPP, JOSEPH VALENTINE
Nickname: Joe, Jersey Joe
In St. Louis: 1938
Number: 17
M.L. Debut: 7/2/28

STRUVE, ALBERT
Nickname: Al
In St. Louis: 1884
M.L. Debut: 6/22/1884

STUART, JOHN DAVIS
Nickname: John, Stud
In St. Louis: 1922-25
M.L. Debut: 7/27/22

STUPER, JOHN ANTON
Nickname: John
In St. Louis: 1982-84
Number: 48
M.L. Debut: 6/1/82

SUDHOFF, JOHN WILLIAM
Nickname: Willie, Wee Willie
In St. Louis: 1897-1901
M.L. Debut: 8/20/1897

SUGDEN, JOSEPH
Nickname: Joe
In St. Louis: 1898
M.L. Debut: 7/20/1893

SULLIVAN, DANIAL C.
Nickname: Dan, Link
In St. Louis: 1885
M.L. Debut: 5/2/1882

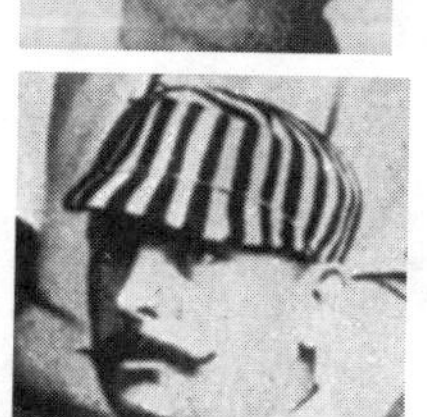

SULLIVAN, HARRY ANDREW
Nickname: Harry
In St. Louis: 1909
M.L. Debut: 8/11/09

SULLIVAN, SUTER G.
Nickname: Suter
In St. Louis: 1898
M.L. Debut: 7/24/1898

SULLIVAN, THOMAS JEFFERSON
Nickname: Sleeper, Old Iron Hands
In St. Louis: 1882-83
M.L. Debut: 5/3/1881

SULLIVAN, JOSEPH DANIEL
Nickname: Joe
In St. Louis: 1896
M.L. Debut: 4/27/1893

SUMMERS, WILLIAM
Nickname: Kid
In St. Louis: 1893
M.L. Debut: 8/5/1893

SUNKEL, THOMAS JACOB
Nickname: Tom, Lefty
In St. Louis: 1937, 39
Number: 28
M.L. Debut: 8/26/37

SURKONT, MATTHEW CONSTANTINE
Nickname: Max
In St. Louis: 1956
Number: 25
M.L. Debut: 4/19/49

SUTCLIFFE, RICHARD LEE
Nickname: Rick
In St. Louis: 1994
Number: 40
M.L. Debut: 9/29/76

SUTHERLAND, GARY LYNN
Nickname: Gary
In St. Louis: 1978
Number: 21
M.L. Debut: 9/17/66

SUTTER, HOWARD BRUCE
Nickname: Bruce
In St. Louis: 1981-84
Number: 42
M.L. Debut: 5/9/76

SUTTHOFF, JOHN GERHARD
Nickname: Jack, Sunny Jack
In St. Louis: 1899
M.L. Debut: 9/15/1898

SUTTON, JOHNNY IKE
Nickname: Johnny
In St. Louis: 1977
Number: 35
M.L. Debut: 4/7/77

SWEENEY, MARK PATRICK
Nickname: Mark
In St. Louis: 1995-97
Number: 23
M.L. Debut: 8/4/95

SWEENEY, PETER JAY
Nickname: Pete
In St. Louis: 1889-90
M.L. Debut: 9/28/1888

SWINDELLS, CHARLES JAY
Nickname: Charlie, Swin
In St. Louis: 1904
M.L. Debut: 9/7/04

SWISHER, STEVEN EUGENE
Nickname: Steve
In St. Louis: 1978-80
Number: 2, 9
M.L. Debut: 6/14/74

SYKES, ROBERT JOSEPH
Nickname: Bob
In St. Louis: 1979-81
Number: 42, 38
M.L. Debut: 4/9/77

SYLVESTER, LOUIS J.
Nickname: Lou
In St. Louis: 1887
M.L. Debut: 4/18/1884

TAMARGO, JOHN FELIX
Nickname: John
In St. Louis: 1976-78
Number: 12
M.L. Debut: 9/3/76

TATE, LEE WILLIE
Nickname: Lee, Skeeter
In St. Louis: 1958-59
Number: 19
M.L. Debut: 9/12/58

TAUSSIG, DONALD FRANKLIN
Nickname: Don
In St. Louis: 1961
Number: 27
M.L. Debut: 4/23/58

TAYLOR, CARL MEANS
Nickname: Carl
In St. Louis: 1970
Number: 44
M.L. Debut: 4/11/68

TAYLOR, CHARLES GILBERT
Nickname: Chuck
In St. Louis: 1969-71
Number: 42
M.L. Debut: 5/27/69

TAYLOR, EDGAR RUBEN
Nickname: Rube
In St. Louis: 1903
M.L. Debut: 8/8/03

TAYLOR, JOE CEPHUS
Nickname: Joe, Cash
In St. Louis: 1958
Number: 21
M.L. Debut: 8/26/54

TAYLOR, JOHN BUDD
Nickname: Jack, Brewery Jack
In St. Louis: 1898
M.L. Debut: 9/16/1891

TAYLOR, JOHN W.
Nickname: Jack, Brakeman
In St. Louis: 1904-06
M.L. Debut: 9/25/1898

TAYLOR, RONALD WESLEY
Nickname: Ron
In St. Louis: 1963-65
Number: 39
M.L. Debut: 4/11/62

TEACHOUT, ARTHUR JOHN
Nickname: Bud
In St. Louis: 1932
M.L. Debut: 5/12/30

TEBEAU, OLIVER WENDELL
Nickname: Patsy
In St. Louis: 1899-1900
M.L. Debut: 9/20/1887

TEMPLETON, GARRY LEWIS
Nickname: Garry, Jump Steady
In St. Louis: 1976-81
Number: 1, 19
M.L. Debut: 8/9/76

TENACE, FURY GENE
Nickname: Gene, B, Fiore Gino Tennaci
In St. Louis: 1981-82
Number: 18
M.L. Debut: 5/29/69

TERLECKY, GREGORY JOHN
Nickname: Greg
In St. Louis: 1975
Number: 35
M.L. Debut: 6/12/75

TERRY, SCOTT RAY
Nickname: Scott
In St. Louis: 1987-91
Number: 37
M.L. Debut: 4/9/86

TERWILLIGER, RICHARD MARTIN
Nickname: Dick
In St. Louis: 1932
Number: 31
M.L. Debut: 8/18/32

TEWKSBURY, ROBERT ALAN
Nickname: Bob, Tewks
In St. Louis: 1989-94
Number: 39
M.L. Debut: 4/11/86

THACKER, MORRIS BENTON
Nickname: Moe
In St. Louis: 1963
Number: 29
M.L. Debut: 4/20/58

THEVENOW, THOMAS JOSEPH
Nickname: Tommy
In St. Louis: 1924-28
M.L. Debut: 9/4/24

THIELMAN, JOHN PETER
Nickname: Jake
In St. Louis: 1905-06
M.L. Debut: 4/23/05

THOMAS, ROY JUSTIN
Nickname: Roy
In St. Louis: 1978-80
Number: 43, 42
M.L. Debut: 9/21/77

THOMAS, THOMAS R.
Nickname: Tom, Savage Tom
In St. Louis: 1899-1900
M.L. Debut: 9/20/1894

THOMPSON, JOHN GUSTAV
Nickname: Gus
In St. Louis: 1906
M.L. Debut: 8/31/03

THOMPSON, MICHAEL WAYNE
Nickname: Mike
In St. Louis: 1973-74
Number: 46
M.L. Debut: 5/19/71

THOMPSON, MILTON BERNARD
Nickname: Milt
In St. Louis: 1989-92
Number: 25
M.L. Debut: 9/4/84

THORNTON, JOHN
Nickname: John
In St. Louis: 1892
M.L. Debut: 8/14/1889

TIEFENAUER, BOBBY GENE
Nickname: Bobby
In St. Louis: 1952, 55, 61
Number: 44, 34
M.L. Debut: 7/14/32

TINNING, LYLE FORREST
Nickname: Bud
In St. Louis: 1935
Number: 19
M.L. Debut: 4/20/32

TOLAN, ROBERT
Nickname: Bobby
In St. Louis: 1965-68
Number: 17
M.L. Debut: 9/3/65

TONEY, FRED ALEXANDRA
Nickname: Fred
In St. Louis: 1923
M.L. Debut: 4/15/11

TOPORCER, GEORGE
Nickname: Specs
In St. Louis: 1921-28
M.L. Debut: 4/13/21

TORRE, JOSEPH PAUL
Nickname: Joe
In St. Louis: 1969-74
Number: 9
M.L. Debut: 9/25/60

TORREZ, MICHAEL AUGUSTINE
Nickname: Mike
In St. Louis: 1967-71
Number: 48
M.L. Debut: 9/10/67

TOTH, PAUL LOUIS
Nickname: Paul
In St. Louis: 1962
Number: 42
M.L. Debut: 4/22/62

TREKELL, HARRY ROY
Nickname: Harry
In St. Louis: 1913
M.L. Debut: 8/16/13

TRIPLETT, HERMAN COAKER
Nickname: Coaker
In St. Louis: 1941-43
Number: 20
M.L. Debut: 4/19/38

TROST, MICHAEL J.
Nickname: Mike
In St. Louis: 1890
M.L. Debut: 8/21/1890

TROTTER, WILLIAM FELIX
Nickname: Bill
In St. Louis: 1944
Number: 14
M.L. Debut: 4/23/37

TUCKER, THOMAS JOSEPH
Nickname: Tommy, Foghorn
In St. Louis: 1898
M.L. Debut: 4/16/1887

TUDOR, JOHN THOMAS
Nickname: John
In St. Louis: 1985-88, 90
Number: 30
M.L. Debut: 8/16/79

TUERO, OSCAR MONZON
Nickname: Oscar
In St. Louis: 1918-20
M.L. Debut: 5/30/18

TUNNELL, BYRON LEE
Nickname: Lee
In St. Louis: 1987
Number: 42
M.L. Debut: 9/4/82

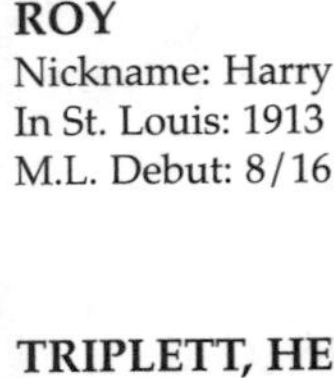

TURNER, GEORGE A.
Nickname: Tuck
In St. Louis: 1896-98
M.L. Debut: 8/18/1893

TWINEHAM, ARTHUR W.
Nickname: Old Hoss
In St. Louis: 1893-94
M.L. Debut: 9/11/1893

TYSON, MICHAEL RAY
Nickname: Mike
In St. Louis: 1972-79
Number: 4, 10
M.L. Debut: 9/5/72

UECKER, ROBERT GEORGE
Nickname: Bob
In St. Louis: 1964-65
Number: 9
M.L. Debut: 4/13/62

UNDERWOOD, THOMAS GERALD
Nickname: Tom
In St. Louis: 1977
Number: 40
M.L. Debut: 8/19/74

URBAN, JACK ELMER
Nickname: Jack
In St. Louis: 1959
Number: 24
M.L. Debut: 6/13/57

URBANI, THOMAS JAMES
Nickname: Tom
In St. Louis: 1993-96
Number: 34
M.L. Debut: 4/21/93

URREA, JOHN GODOY
Nickname: John
In St. Louis: 1977-80
Number: 38
M.L. Debut: 4/10/77

URY, LOUIS NEWTON
Nickname: Lou, Old Sleep
In St. Louis: 1903
M.L. Debut: 9/9/03

VALENZUELA, BENJAMIN BELTRAN
Nickname: Benny, Papelero
In St. Louis: 1958
Number: 24
M.L. Debut: 4/27/58

VALENZUELA, FERNANDO (ANGUAMEA)
Nickname: Fernando
In St. Louis: 1997
Number: 34
M.L. Debut: 9/15/80

VAN DYKE, WILLIAM JENNINGS
Nickname: Bill
In St. Louis: 1892
M.L. Debut: 4/17/1890

VAN NOY, JAY LOWELL
Nickname: Jay
In St. Louis: 1951
Number: 36
M.L. Debut: 6/18/51

VAN SLYKE, ANDREW JAMES
Nickname: Andy, Slick
In St. Louis: 1983-86
Number: 18
M.L. Debut: 6/17/83

VANCE, CLARENCE ARTHUR
Nickname: Dazzy
In St. Louis: 1933-34
Number: 18, 19
M.L. Debut: 4/16/15

VANN, JOHN SILAS
Nickname: John
In St. Louis: 1913
M.L. Debut: 6/11/13

VERBAN, EMIL MATTHEW
Nickname: Emil, Dutch, The Antelope
In St. Louis: 1944-46
Number: 3
M.L. Debut: 4/18/44

VERGEZ, JOHN LOUIS
Nickname: Johnny
In St. Louis: 1936
M.L. Debut: 4/14/31

VICK, HENRY ARTHUR
Nickname: Ernie
In St. Louis: 1922, 24-26
M.L. Debut: 6/29/22

VILLANUEVA, HECTOR (BALASQUIDE)
Nickname: Hector
In St. Louis: 1993
Number: 29
M.L. Debut: 6/1/90

VINES, ROBERT EARL
Nickname: Bob
In St. Louis: 1924
M.L. Debut: 9/3/24

VIRDON, WILLIAM CHARLES
Nickname: Bill
In St. Louis: 1955-56
Number: 9
M.L. Debut: 4/12/55

VISNER, JOSEPH PAUL
Nickname: Joe, B, Joseph Paul Vezina
In St. Louis: 1891
M.L. Debut: 7/4/1885

VON OHLEN, DAVID
Nickname: Dave
In St. Louis: 1983-84
Number: 38
M.L. Debut: 5/13/83

VOSS, WILLIAM EDWARD
Nickname: Bill
In St. Louis: 1972
Number: 17
M.L. Debut: 9/14/65

VUCKOVICH, PETER DENNIS
Nickname: Pete
In St. Louis: 1978-80
Number: 40, 46
M.L. Debut: 8/3/75

WADE, BENJAMIN STYRON
Nickname: Ben
In St. Louis: 1954
Number: 10
M.L. Debut: 4/30/48

WAGNER, LEON LAMAR
Nickname: Leon, Daddy Wags
In St. Louis: 1960
Number: 22
M.L. Debut: 6/22/48

WALKER, DUANE ALLEN
Nickname: Duane
In St. Louis: 1988
Number: 21
M.L. Debut: 5/25/82

WALKER, HARRY WILLIAM
Nickname: Harry, The Hat
In St. Louis: 1940-43, 46-47, 50-51, 55
Number: 6, 10, 5, 17, 1

WALKER, JAMES ROY
Nickname: Roy
In St. Louis: 1921-22
M.L.Debut: 9/16/12

WALKER, JOSEPH RICHARD
Nickname: Joe, Speed
In St. Louis: 1921
M.L. Debut: 9/15/23

WALKER, OSCAR
Nickname: Oscar
In St. Louis: 1882
M.L. Debut: 9/17/1875

WALKER, ROBERT THOMAS
Nickname: Tom
In St. Louis: 1976
Number: 34
M.L. Debut: 4/23/72

WALKER, WILLIAM HENRY
Nickname: Bill
In St. Louis: 1933-36
Number: 10, 18
M.L. Debut: 9/13/27

WALLACE, MICHAEL SHERMAN
Nickname: Mike
In St. Louis: 1975-76
Number: 32
M.L. Debut: 6/27/73

WALLACE, RHODERICK JOHN
Nickname:Bobby, Rhody
In St. Louis: 1899-1901, 17-18
M.L. Debut: 9/15/1894

WALLER, ELLIOTT TYRONE
Nickname: Ty
In St. Louis: 1980
M.L. Debut: 9/6/80

WALLING, DENNIS MARTIN
Nickname: Denny
In St. Louis: 1988-90
Number: 21
M.L. Debut: 9/7/75

WARD, RICHARD OLE
Nickname: Dick, Ole
In St. Louis: 1935
Number: 10, 27
M.L. Debut: 5/3/34

WARMOTH, WALLACE WALTER
Nickname: Cy
In St. Louis: 1916
M.L. Debut: 5/3/34

WARNEKE, LONNIE
Nickname; Lon, The Arkansas Humming Bird
In St. Louis: 1937-42
Number: 18, 21
M.L. Debut: 8/31/16

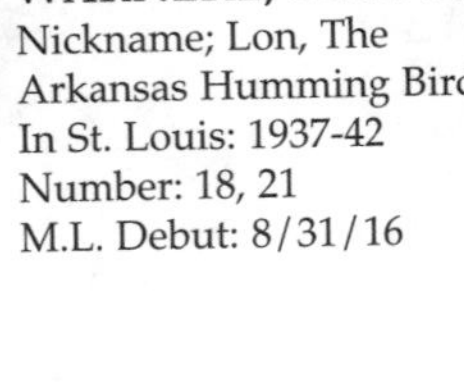

WARNER, JOHN JOSEPH
Nickname; Jack
In St. Louis: 1905
M.L. Debut: 4/23/1895

WARWICK, CARL WAYNE
Nickname: Carl
In St. Louis: 1961-62, 64-65
Number: 24, 42, 27, 17
M.L. Debut: 4/11/61

WARWICK, FIRMAN NEWTON
Nickname: Bill
In St. Louis: 1925-26
M.L. Debut: 7/18/21

WASHBURN, RAY CLARK
Nickname: Ray
In St. Louis: 1961-69
Number: 44
M.L. Debut: 9/20/61

WASLEWSKI, GARY LEE
Nickname: Gary
In St. Louis: 1969
Number: 19
M.L. Debut: 6/11/67

WATERBURY, STEVE CRAIG
Nickname: Steve
In St. Louis: 1976
Number: 48
M.L. Debut: 9/14/76

WATKINS, GEORGE ARCHIBALD
Nickname: George, Watty
In St. Louis: 1930-33
Number: 38
M.L. Debut: 7/8/93

WATSON, ALLEN KENNETH
Nickname: Allen
In St. Louis: 1993-95
Number: 38
M.L. Debut: 7/8/93

WATSON, MILTON WILSON
Nickname: Milt, Mule
In St. Louis: 1916-17
M.L. Debut: 7/26/16

WEAVER, ARTHUR COGGSHALL
Nickname: Art, Six O'Clock
In St. Louis: 1902-03
M.L. Debut: 9/14/02

WEBB, JAMES LAVERNE
Nickname: Skeeter
In St. Louis: 1932
Number: 1
M.L. Debut: 7/20/32

WEHMEIER, HERMAN RALPH
Nickname: Herm
In St. Louis: 1956-58
Number: 37
M.L. Debut: 9/7/45

WEILAND, ROBERT GEORGE
Nickname: Bob, Lefty
In St. Louis: 1937-40
Number: 20
M.L. Debut: 9/30/28

WELCH, CURTIS BENTON
Nickname: Curt
In St. Louis: 1885-87
M.L. Debut: 5/1/1884

WELLS, JACOB
Nickname: Jake
In St. Louis: 1890
M.L. Debut: 8/10/1888

WERDON, PERCIVAL WHERITT
Nickname: Perry, Moose
In St. Louis: 1892-93
M.L. Debut: 4/24/1884

WERLE, WILLIAM GEORGE
Nickname: Bill, Bugs
In St. Louis: 1952
Number: 20, 22
M.L. Debut: 4/22/49

WESTLAKE, WALDON THOMAS
Nickname: Wally
In St. Louis: 1951-52
Number: 17
M.L. Debut: 4/15/47

WEYHING, AUGUST
Nickname: Gus, Rubber, Winged Gus, Cannonball
In St. Louis: 1900
M.L. Debut: 5/21/1887

WHEELER, HARRY EUGENE
Nickname: Harry
In St. Louis: 1884
M.L. Debut: 6/19/1878

WHEELER, RICHARD
Nickname: Dick
In St. Louis: 1918
M.L. Debut: 6/17/18

WHELAN, JAMES FRANCIS
Nickname: Jim
In St. Louis: 1913
M.L. Debut: 4/24/13

WHISENANT, THOMAS PETER
Nickname: Pete
In St. Louis: 1955
Number: 10
M.L. Debut: 4/16/52

WHISTLER, LEWIS W.
Nickname: Lew
In St. Louis: 1937
Number: 22
M.L. Debut: 7/10/37

WHITE, ADEL
Nickname: Ade
In St. Louis: 1937
Number: 22
M.L. Debut: 7/10/37

WHITE, ERNEST DANIEL
Nickname: Ernie
In St. Louis: 1940-43
Number: 2, 32, 28
M.L. Debut: 5/9/40

WHITE, HAROLD GEORGE
Nickname: Hal
In St. Louis: 1953-54
Number: 26
M.L. Debut: 4/22/41

WHITE, JEROME CARDELL
Nickname: Jerry
In St. Louis: 1986
Number: 25
M.L. Debut: 9/16/74

WHITE, WILLIAM DEKOVA
Nickname: Bill
In St. Louis: 1959-65, 69
Number: 12, 26, 7
M.L. Debut: 5/7/56

WHITE, WILLIAM DIGHTON
Nickname: Bill
In St. Louis: 1888
M.L. Debut: 5/3/1884

WHITEHEAD, BURGESS U.
Nickname: Burgess, Whitey
In St. Louis: 1933-35
Number: 14
M.L. Debut: 4/30/33

WHITEN, MARK ANTHONY
Nickname: Mark
In St. Louis: 1993-94
Number: 22
M.L. Debut: 7/12/90

WHITFIELD, FRED DWIGHT
Nickname: Fred
In St. Louis: 1962
Number: 17
M.L. Debut: 5/27/62

WHITNEY, ARTHUR WILSON
Nickname: Art
In St. Louis: 1891
M.L. Debut: 5/1/1880

WHITROCK, WILLIAM FRANKLIN
Nickname: Bill
In St. Louis: 1890
M.L. Debut: 5/3/1890

WHITTED, GEORGE BOSTIC
Nickname: Possum
In St. Louis: 1912-14
M.L. Debut: 9/16/12

WICKER, FLOYD EULISS
Nickname: Floyd
In St. Louis: 1968
Number: 37
M.L. Debut: 6/23/68

WICKER, ROBERT KITRIDGE
Nickname: Bob
In St. Louis: 1901-03
M.L. Debut: 8/11/01

WIGHT, WILLIAM ROBERT
Nickname: Bill, Lefty
In St. Louis: 1958
Number: 45
M.L. Debut: 4/17/46

WIGINGTON, FRED THOMAS
Nickname: Fred
In St. Louis: 1923
M.L. Debut: 4/20/23

WILBER, DELBERT QUENTIN
Nickname: Del, Babe
In St. Louis: 1946-49
Number: 23, 10
M.L. Debut: 4/21/46

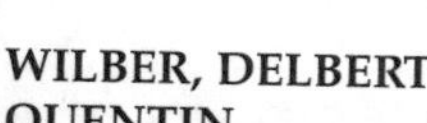

WILHELM, JAMES HOYT
Nickname: Hoyt
In St. Louis: 1957
Number: 25
M.L. Debut: 4/19/52

WILKS, THEODORE
Nickname: Ted, Cork
In St. Louis: 1944-51
Number: 28
M.L. Debut: 4/15/44

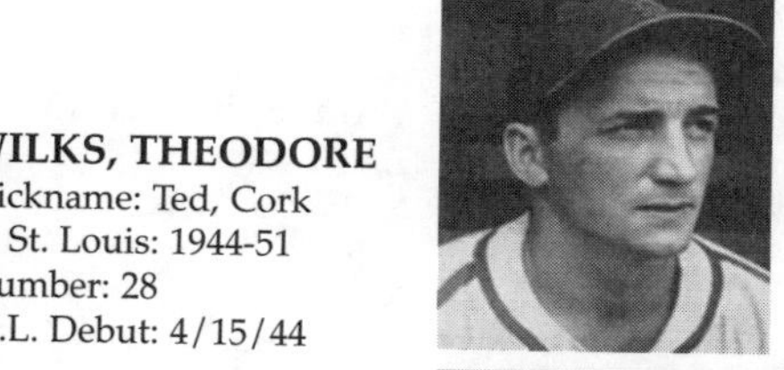

WILLIAMS, JAMES FRANCIS
Nickname: Jimy
In St. Louis: 1966-67
Number: 24
M.L. Debut: 4/26/66

WILLIAMS, OTTO GEORGE
Nickname: Otto
In St. Louis: 1902-03
M.L. Debut: 10/5/02

WILLIAMS, REES GEPHARDT
Nickname: Steamboat
In St. Louis: 1914
M.L. Debut: 7/12/14

WILLIAMS, STANLEY WILSON
Nickname: Stan
In St. Louis: 1971
Number: 24
M.L. Debut: 5/17/58

WILLIAMS, NATHANIEL HOWARD
Nickname: Howie
In St. Louis: 1928
M.L. Debut: 7/7/28

WILIE, DENNIS EARNEST
Nickname: Denney
In St. Louis: 1911-12
M.L. Debut: 7/27/11

WILLIS, JOSEPH DENK
Nickname: Joe, Big Joe
In St. Louis: 1911-13
M.L. Debut: 5/3/11

WILLIS, RONALD EARL
Nickname: Ron
In St. Louis: 1966-69
Number: 36
M.L. Debut: 9/20/66

WILLIS, VICTOR GAZAWAY
Nickname: Vic
In St. Louis: 1910
M.L. Debut: 4/20/1898

WILSON, CHARLES WOODROW
Nickname: Charlie, Swamp Baby
In St. Louis: 1932-33, 35
Number: 33
M.L. Debut: 4/14/31

WILSON, CRAIG
Nickname: Craig
In St. Louis: 1989-92
Number: 12
M.L. Debut: 9/6/89

WILSON, FRANK EALTON
Nickname: Zeke
In St. Louis: 1899
M.L. Debut: 4/23/1895

WILSON, JAMES
Nickname: Jimmie, Ace
In St. Louis: 1928-33
Number: 8, 12, 9
M.L. Debut: 8/17/23

WILSON, JOHN OWEN
Nickname: Owen, Chief
In St. Louis: 1914-16
M.L. Debut: 9/10/32

WINFORD, JAMES HEAD
Nickname: Jim, Cowboy
In St. Louis: 1932, 34-37
Number: 19, 27
M.L. Debut: 9/10/32

WINGO, IVEY BROWN
Nickname: Ivy
In St. Louis: 1911-14
M.L. Debut: 4/20/11

WINSETT, JOHN THOMAS
Nickname: Tom, Long Tom
In St. Louis: 1935
M.L. Debut: 4/20/30

WISE, RICHARD CHARLES
Nickname: Rick
In St. Louis: 1972-73
Number: 40
M.L. Debut: 4/18/64

WITHROW, RAYMOND WALLACE
Nickname: Corky
In St. Louis: 1963
Number: 29
M.L. Debut: 9/6/63

WOLF, WILLIAM VAN WINKLE
Nickname: Chicken
In St. Louis: 1892
M.L. Debut: 5/2/1882

WOLTER, HARRY MEIGS
Nickname: Harry
In St. Louis: 1907
M.L. Debut: 5/14/07

WOOD, JOHN B.
Nickname: John
In St. Louis: 1896
M.L. Debut: 5/9/1896

WOODBURN, EUGENE STEWART
Nickname: Gene
In St. Louis: 1911-12
M.L. Debut:7/27/11

WOODESHICK, HAROLD JOSEPH
Nickname: Hal
In St. Louis: 1965-67
Number: 46
M.L. Debut: 9/14/56

WOODSON, TRACY MICHAEL
Nickname: Tracy
In St. Louis: 1992-1993
Number: 54
M.L. Debut: 4/7/87

WOODWARD, FRANK RUSSELL
Nickname: Frank
In St. Louis: 1919
M.L. Debut: 4/17/18

WOOLDRIDGE, FLOYD LEWIS
Nickname: Floyd
In St. Louis: 1955
Number: 41
M.L. Debut: 5/1/55

WORRELL, TODD ROWLAND
Nickname: Todd
In St. Louis: 1985-89, 92
Number: 38
M.L. Debut: 8/28/85

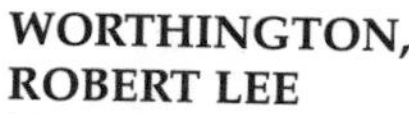

WORTHINGTON, ROBERT LEE
Nickname: Red
In St. Louis: 1934
M.L. Debut: 4/14/31

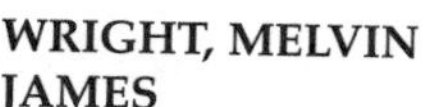

WRIGHT, MELVIN JAMES
Nickname: Mel
In St. Louis: 1954-55
Number: 17
M.L. Debut: 4/17/54

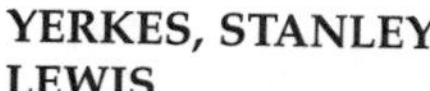

YERKES, STANLEY LEWIS
Nickname: Stan, Yank
In St. Louis: 1901-03
M.L. Debut: 5/3/01

YOCHIM, RAYMOND AUSTIN ALOYSIUS
Nickname: Ray
In St. Louis: 1948-49
Number: 39
M.L. Debut: 5/2/48

YOUNG, DENTON TRUE
Nickname: Cy, Foxy Grandpa
In St. Louis: 1899-1900
M.L. Debut: 8/6/1890

YOUNG, DMITRI DELL
Nickname: Dmitri
In St. Louis: 1996-97
Number: 24
M.L. Debut: 8/29/96

YOUNG, GERALD ANTHONY
Nickname: Gerald
In St. Louis: 1994
Number: 15
M.L. Debut: 7/8/87

YOUNG, JOSEPH B.
Nickname: Joe
In St. Louis: 1892
M.L. Debut: 6/10/1892

YOUNG, LEMUEL FLOYD
Nickname: Pep
In St. Louis: 1941, 45
Number: 6, 7
M.L. Debut: 4/25/33

YOUNG, NORMAN ROBERT
Nickname: Babe
In St. Louis: 1948
Number: 10
M.L. Debut: 9/26/36

YOUNG, ROBERT GEORGE
Nickname: Bobby
In St. Louis: 1948
Number: 3
M.L. Debut: 7/28/48

YOUNGBLOOD, JOEL RANDOLPH
Nickname: Joel
In St. Louis: 1977
Number: 19
M.L. Debut: 4/13/76

YUHAS, JOHN EDWARD
Nickname: Eddie
In St. Louis: 1952-53
Number: 37, 43
M.L. Debut: 4/17/52

YVARS, SALVADOR ANTHONY
Nickname: Sal
In St. Louis: 1953-54
Number: 17, 21
M.L. Debut: 9/27/47

ZACHARY, WILLIAM CHRISTOPHER
Nickname: Chris
In St. Louis: 1971
Number: 36
M.L. Debut: 4/11/63

ZACHER, ELMER HENRY
Nickname: Elmer, Silver
In St. Louis: 1910
M.L. Debut: 4/30/10

ZACKERT, GEORGE CARL
Nickname: George, Zeke
In St. Louis: 1911-12
M.L. Debut: 9/22/11

ZEARFOSS, DAVID WILLIAM TILDEN
Nickname: Dave
In St. Louis: 1904-05
M.L. Debut: 4/17/1896

ZEILE, TODD EDWARD
Nickname: Todd
In St. Louis: 1989-95
Number: 27
M.L. Debut: 8/18/89

ZELLER, BARTON WALLACE
Nickname: Bart
In St. Louis: 1970
Number: 29
M.L. Debut: 5/21/70

ZIES, WILLIAM
Nickname: Bill
In St. Louis: 1891
M.L. Debut: 8/9/1891

ZIMMERMAN, EDWARD DESMOND
Nickname: Eddie, Zimmie
In St. Louis: 1906
M.L. Debut: 9/29/06

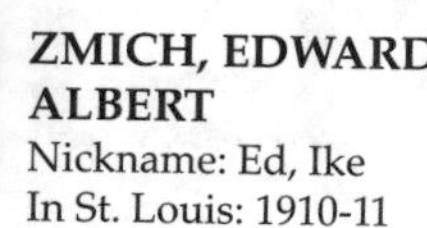

ZMICH, EDWARD ALBERT
Nickname: Ed, Ike
In St. Louis: 1910-11
M.L. Debut: 7/23/10

BASE BALL TODAY !

AMERICAN ASSOCIATION CHAMPION
ST. LOUIS BROWNS

VS.

NATIONAL LEAGUE CHAMPION
ANSON'S BABIES OF CHICAGO

REMEMBER THIS DAY !!!
OCTOBER 23, 1886
TODAY'S THE DAY COMMY AND HIS CREW SEND
ANSON AND HIS SNIVELING CRYBABIES,
CRYING WEE-WEE-WEE ALL THE WAY HOME.

VONDY'S BROWNS
TODAY BECOME
CHAMPIONS OF THE WORLD

BASE BALL TODAY !

The Hall of Fame Gallery

By Bob Broeg

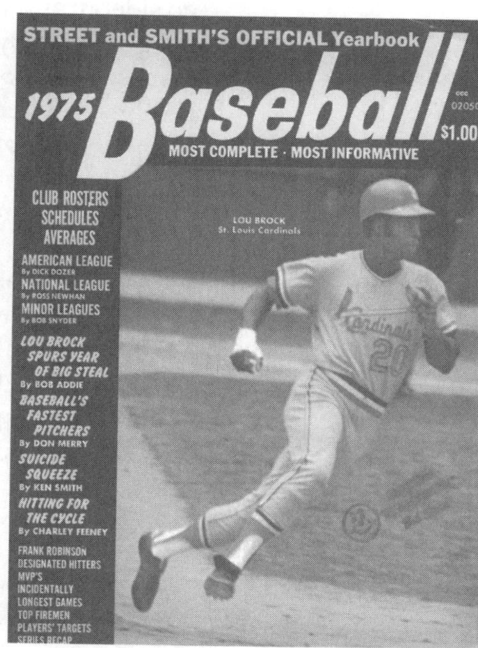

SOME OF THE BEST OF THE BEST: Top Row, Jim Bottomley, Frank Frisch, Cy Young; Middle Row, Steve Carlton, Frank Frisch advertisement, Dizzy Dean; Bottom Row, Lou Brock's record 105th Steal and press coverage of the event.

GROVER CLEVELAND ALEXANDER

Grover Cleveland Alexander—alcoholic, epileptic, his own worst enemy and one of the greatest pitchers ever—won 373 games, matching the National League record, but he's still best remembered for a game he saved back there on a raw, rainy October afternoon in 1926, a tall, knock-kneed player with a peanut-sized cap perched on his head and his red woolen warmup jacket over his arm. He moseyed from Yankee Stadium's left field bullpen into baseball immortality. The story is so well known that it became the basis for a 1952 movie featuring a handsome young man who had a date with White House destiny—Ronald Reagan.

Alexander's story was a good one. One of too many boys in a large family near the sand hills of St. Paul, Neb., he showed such control hurling rocks that many a time he brought home a rabbit or squirrel he had hit between the eyes. He was much better out there skimming rocks than failing to show up often enough for work as a telephone lineman. The phone-company straw boss gave him the good recommendation that it would be best to get that baseball nonsense out of his head. The sandy-haired kid with no sideburns burned up the New York State League with Syracuse in '10, winning 29 games and a $500 "theft" by Philadelphia Phillies' owner Horace Fogel. Mr Fogel promptly assured Alexander he'd make $210 a month if he made the club.

Hah! "Dode" Alexander, as they'd called him back home, broke in as sensationally as any rookie, posting a 28-13 record. He had great speed then, throwing shortarmed with a three-quarter delivery, and he soon became the very best. Although the ball still didn't have the juice that would be prevalent after the Babe hit 54 homers his first year with the Yankees, 1920, Alexander's 16 shutouts in the 1916 season still are remarkable. With his three-season 94-35 record and the highest ERA of only 1.83, Alex threw a scare into the frugal Phils as much as the impact of World War I and the Phillies' fear that the childless pitcher soon could be lost to the military and maybe hurt or crippled.

So the Phils sold Alexander to Chicago, where William Wrigley guaranteed $500 a month for a three-year period to his new bride, Aimee Arranta, an attractive woman who would be played by Doris Day in the Alexander movie. Overseas in the military, Pete lost hearing in one ear, shellshocked, and epilepsy surfaced. To his death, separated twice by dear Aimee, Alex suffered spells that could be attributed either to the big guns or to a youthful blow to the head that had left him double-visioned for a long time. Most definitely, the soothing glow of alcohol helped even though it might have shortened his career, but most certainly affected a life that ended one drab day in 1950, back home in Nebraska, where he wasn't too welcome. He was only 63.

As control of himself wavered, Alexander's control of the ball improved. With his fast ball diminishing, he relied on pinpoint control, ability to nick the outside corner with a short, short curve or to turn the ball over in what amounted to a screwball. So his record of eight-plus seasons of 125-77 was good if not Alexander great.

Trouble was, new manager Joe McCarthy, up from the minors in 1926, found Alex insubordinate and a distraction to Marse Joe's idea of harmony. McCarthy asked general manager Bill Veeck Sr. to get rid of the 39-year-old gaffer.

In one of baseball's great moments, with teetotaler Rickey away, manager Hornsby asked boss Breadon to claim Alexander on waivers, then $4500. When no lower club claimed, the Cardinals got the player, a pennant, a world championship and a nice hunk of romantic St. Louis baseball history. With a 3-2 victory over the Cubs the first weekend, Alexander was better than his 9-7 contribution. He pitched and won the second and sixth games of the World Series. At New York, Hornsby, who didn't drink, asked Alexander to take it easy because he just might need him in the seventh game. Pete nodded, but cautioned that he be asked to warm up just once.

Suddenly in the seventh inning, the Yankees rallied against Jesse Haines, whose knuckles had become raw from extensive use of his pet pitch. Bases loaded, two out, one run up with hard-hitting rookie second baseman Tony Lazzeri at bat. Hornsby wigwagged not for either Flint Rhem or Art Reinhart, warming up. He wanted Alexander. Reserve catcher Ernie Vick nudged old Pete. Stretching, Alexander stood, removed the woolen jacket and without a warmup slowly took the Grand Circle route toward the mound, aware Lazzeri pawed impatiently as a rookie.

Lazzeri's strikeout was so dramatic that it is described at Cooperstown on the Hall of Fame plaque, Alexander's, not Tony's. Two innings later, after Ruth walked as the only Yankee baserunner against Alexander, the Babe went out stealing. Grover Cleveland Alexander, a grand geezer, was baseball's greatest hero.

"Old Low and Away," as Haines referred to the great pitcher, because of his corner-cutting control work, won 21 games for the Cardinals in 1927, 16 more in a pennant-winning 1928 season in which the Babe, Lou Gehrig and the Yankees creamed the Cardinals.

When Alexander went off the deep end in 1929, after one rest cure, he gained his ninth victory, one that apparently left him first in National League history. Later, they found that Christy Mathewson also had won one more game for a tying total of 373.

Makes a baseball historian wonder if the carrot still had been there, how much longer Pete Alexander could have kept the thirst for victory paramount instead of the other thirst.

WALTER ALSTON

As a big-league ball player, Walter Alston will be remembered as a guy who batted zero and almost fielded the same, but as a manager he will be remembered seriously as one who won his way into the baseball Hall of Fame.

Brought up the final month of the 1936 season, the 24-year-old Alston got into only the final game of the season. Rip Collins was hurt and Johnny Mize was ejected by an umpire. In a 6-3 loss to Lon Warneke and the Chicago Cubs, costing St. Louis sole possession of second place behind the New York Giants, Alston didn't help Dizzy Dean and the fading Gas House Gang. With only two fielding chances, he muffed one. In his only time at bat he struck out.

Over the years then and later, until he achieved financial stability, Walt Alston was a school teacher in Darr, Ohio, close by the Miami University at Oxford. His intelligence, presence and personal reserve won over Branch Rickey after both had gravitated to the Brooklyn farm system, where Walt became a minor-league manager. By the time B.R.'s successor, Walter O'Malley, decided not to heed the two-year demands of Chuck Dressen, the Dodgers' pennant-winning manager of 1952 and '53, the puzzled cry at Ebbets Field was, "Walter Who?"

But Walter Emmons (Smokey) Alston had the quiet ability to lead over the cool reception of Jackie Robinson—Walt had managed Roy Campanella and Don Newcombe in the minors—and he did immediately what no other manager of Dem Beloved Bums ever had done. His second year, 1955, he won a world championship, Brooklyn's one and only. Thereafter, working constantly with a one-year handshake at a time, Alston won seven pennants and four championships over a 23-year period. He stepped into retirement gracefully in 1976 at 65.

The Hall of Fame teacher was selected for Cooperstown shortly before his death in 1984.

JAKE BECKLEY

Jake Beckley came along too late to know Samuel Clemens before Mark Twain probed and piloted the Mississippi from Hannibal, home-town of the famed writer

and the Hall of Fame ball player, but both men have a distinction more significant to the athlete than to the author. Both wore mustaches, an "in" thing in Sam's day and Jake's, too, but Beckley persevered to wear the upper lip adornment, which he wore as one of the final four until in more recent times Oakland's rebellious Charley Finley offered incentives to his players to flout longstanding regulations against facial hair.

Back in Beckley's durable day—and he played for 20 years from 1888—some of the stashes were as magnificent as Rollie Fingers', but by the time manager Kid Nichols bought good ol' Jake from Cincinnati in 1904, a couple of older timers had lip or chin adornment. Beckley, a big man by his generation's standards, was a solid hitter in a career from Pittsburgh through New York through Cincinnati to St. Louis. His career average of .306 was misleading because he batted over .300 13 times. Included was .324 for one year, 1890, when the Player's League rebellion nearly brought the low-paying National League to its haughty heels.

Beckley's career hits of 2831—close to magic 3000 at a time Cap Anson was the first achieving it—included 242 triples, fourth high. Distinctively, back in 1897, Jake hit three home runs in a game for Cincinnati, last to achieve it until the lively-ball home-run surge of 1922, but then Jake always could hit.

Jacob Peter Beckley didn't have the arm to play second base, but he found a happy home at first, where he played 2337 games, behind only Eddie Murray.

Hmmm, wonder if Jake knew personally or as well of as his more illustrious hometown native, the humorist who loved the river that ran by their town? Twain, born in 1835, died in 1910, a member of everybody's Hall of Fame. Beckley, 1867-1918, was picked for baseball's Hall of Fame in 1971.

JIM BOTTOMLEY

Sunny Jim Bottomley was famous for his disposition, his appealing good looks to the ladies, his ability to hit in the pinches, including a still-standing record of RBIs in one game—and the fact that he was the majors' first farm-system player to win a Most Valuable Player award for the team that scouted and signed him.

A farm kid from the coal-mining community of Nakomis, Ill., near St. Louis, James Leroy Bottomley wrote Branch Rickey for a tryout. B.R.'s scouts looked at the lefthanded-hitting first baseman and brought him to town. Bottomley was so naive that when he saw a long, slender bat in the rack, he had a question.

"Who," said the 20-year-old kid to pitcher Bill Sherdel, "is this Mr. Fungo?"

The cracker-barrel philosopher grew up to understand pennant races, appearing on four winners with the Redbirds. When trainer Harrison (Doc) Weaver lamented the need one time for a winning streak, Sunny Jim set him straight. "Naw, Doc," he drawled, "you win two, lose one, win two, lose one and one day you've got 100 victories and you throw the others away."

Bottomley, joining the Cardinals late in the 1922 season, did well enough that Rickey happily unloaded the salary of veteran Jacques Fournier. Bottomley didn't disappoint. He hit .371 the next season, then began a string of six straight seasons of 100-plus RBIs.

En route to the Hall of Fame in 1974, he harvested 12 RBIs in a six-hit game at Brooklyn in '24 and established a league-leading 227 hits and 44 doubles in 1925, a .367 season. But he was absolutely at his best the year he won the MVP, 1928. That year his .325 average of 187 hits included 93 for extra bases.

His .628 slugging percentage included 42 doubles and the league lead in triples,

20, homers, 31, and RBIs, 136. Bottomley's second base playing partner, Frankie Frisch, himself labeled a "money player," lauded Sunny Jim. "He's the best clutch hitter I ever saw," Frisch said. "With Jim hitting fourth, Chick Hafey fifth, I learned to steal bases seldom ahead of them."

Bottomley was a colorful performer, big and fast. His appeal to women fans included more than his cap cocked rakishly over his left eye. He had a swaggering, easy-does-it approach afield and a deceptive swing at bat. Addressing the ball at the plate, choking a heavy bat, he seemed to swing leisurely, yet powerfully.

That pull-hitting power lost something when the cozy right-field home-run distance at St. Louis's Sportsman's Park was increased in mid-season, 1929. Disgruntled Browns' owner Phil Ball, the ball-park landlord, opted for a towering screen in front of the pavilion, from the 310 foul-line to 354 in right-center.

Bottomley's homers dropped a couple that year, then fell off to nine in 1931, a season of limited play in which Sunny Jim finished with a .348 average, only a fraction of a point behind batting champion Hafey and the incumbent champion, the Giants' Bill Terry.

Terry, rather than former teammate Frisch, who had died the year before in a car accident, made the strongest Hall of Fame appeal for Bottomley, who was enshrined in 1974. Terry spoke as a first-base rival and pennant-competitive foe.

Hurt, Bottomley played less in 1932, crowded by long-waiting replacement Ripper Collins. He and his larger salary were dealt to Cincinnati in 1933, but the perceptive Rickey had seen enough. As a shell, Bottomley came back to the Browns in 1936, playing briefly then and in '37 as managerial successor to old championship teammate Rogers Hornsby.

Disappointingly in retirement, Sunny Jim lasted only one season (1939) as Johnny O'Hara's partner on radio broadcasts of Cardinal and Browns home games. Ultimately, back in the cattle country of Bourbon and Sullivan, Mo., he also scouted for the Cubs. A prize cow he had been given when he left the Brownies, unable to make chicken salad out of chicken feathers, was a bovine whose winning name in a contest was apt—"Fielder's Choice."

Bottomley loved to hunt with a judge, Waldo Mayfield, with whom he had roomed when Mayfield was a young lawyer. When Sunny Jim was named late in 1959 to receive the St. Louis baseball writers' first nostalgia award at a January dinner, he heard the good news before dropping dead in December. At the dinner Judge Mayfield accepted for him with similar cracker-barrel wit and warmth.

ROGER BRESNAHAN

Roger Bresnahan ought to be remembered for three things: (1) a romantic memory that had him born in Ireland, (2) development of catching shinguards and chest protector and (3) the fact that you can't sass a lady.

So the Duke of Tralee, as he was called in the fib about Ireland rather than Toledo as his birthplace, became a rare bird in a tightfisted era of baseball when he was paid a couple of years salary not to manage the Cardinals.

Through the early years of the century, teamed with another Irishman he respected, John McGraw, the short, bulky Bresnahan was an aggressive catcher for the New York Giants. In his best season, 1905, he hit .302 and caught every game of the World Series as Christy Mathewson shut out the Philadelphia Athletics three times and Joe McGinnity once.

Doubtless, the Duke could have stayed with McGraw a long time because he was so fast he often led off, a considerable compliment to a catcher, and he was fiery, too. But Mac saw an opportunity to help a young friend approaching 30. Through delightful cloak-and-dagger, McGraw arranged for Bresnahan to slip into St. Louis for an interview with the baseball Robisons.

The price was high—Bresnahan wanted

Roger the Dodger: One of Roger Bresnahan's troubles as manager of the Cardinals from 1909 was that he didn't have the skill or desire to play often enough with the leadership that made the Duke of Tralee one of John McGraw's favorites. Shown here, swinging and losing his bat, he barely played half a season in each of his first four years in St. Louis.

$10,000—and McGraw shrewdly wanted prime roster players in return, but the starstruck St. Louis owners agreed. So Bresnahan hunkered down behind home plate for the Redbirds in 1909 as player-manager.

Truth is, like many a manager stepping out of the playing ranks, the Duke became only a part-time catcher thereafter. His finishes of 7-7-5-and-6 were not good even for a perennial losing franchise, but the race in 1911 had been so close that the Cardinals made money. And, replacing her uncle and father after their early untimely deaths, Helene Hathaway Robison Britton offered a new five-year contact at $10,000-per with a 10 percent share of profits. She placated the Duke, whose associates had offered $500,000 for the ballclub and ballpark.

Mrs. Britton, delightful and attractive, was a graceful woman called "Lady Bee" as she sat in league meetings, following her divorce from Schuyler (Skipper) Britton. Trouble was, St. Louis' "petticoat rule" was accepted more elsewhere than by the rough-and-ready Bresnaham whose language got saltier in questioning sessions by the female boss as part of a disappointing season.

Afterward, indignantly, Lady Bee wanted the Duke of Tralee out. Bresnahan wanted his remaining four years. Lawyer James C. Jones finally settled for half, $20,000, and Bresnahan went to Chicago as a player-coach and finally one-season manager in 1915. A year later Mrs. Britton sold the Cardinals.

Chances are, Bresnahan might have survived, but Lady Bee had promoted to manager a little second baseman Roger had obtained from Cincinnati. Miller Huggins was en route to a great career—good in St. Louis, championship in New York. The Duke of Tralee went back to his real home town, Toledo, and was a political turnkey in Toledo before his death in 1944, just before Cooperstown beckoned too late.

LOU BROCK

P. K. Wrigley, the Chicago chicle-and-chew man, might have doubled his pleasure by making certain his Cubbies played only in the daylight at Wrigley Field, but the mild sports eccentric might have prevented baseball's heist of the century.

Oh, if not the best Brink's steal this side of a holdup, but certainly one of the most one-sided deals, probably even more than the one by which the Chicagos palmed off ancient righthander Jack Taylor to the Cardinals in 1904 for Mordecai (Three-Finger) Brown.

This one, gifting the Cardinals the services of Lou Brock, turned St. Louis into world champions that same season, 1964, and helped add to the Cubs' frustration with a capital "F."

Still, if owner Phil Wrigley had followed his pre-war intentions to spread the lights over Chicago's north side landmark, Brock just might have done what he'd done in his one minor-league season, rip the ball for a .361 average. And most certainly he wouldn't have blanched in the sunshine like Count Dracula when he reported at Clark Street and Addison Ave.

"No one told me Wrigley Field had sun," Brock later would explain, defending an inability to play right field, which he never did like as well as left. They called him "Brock as in rock," a reflection on his outfield ability, never great, but often good enough.

Not, however, when he hit .263 his first season, .258 the next and was battling at .251 at the 1964 trading deadline, when he went to the Cardinals for righthander Ernie Broglio as the highlight players of a deal disappointed and disputed in St. Louis, After all, Broglio had won 21 games in 1960 and 18 in '63.

But if Wrigley didn't know enough to bring Brock in out of the sun, Cardinal manager Johnny Keane knew enough to shoo away the media and to make a point. Why, as Brock said in protest, he was a home run hitter, as witness one of the record shots deep into the center field horseshoe of New York's Polo Grounds.

Not, insisted Keane, if he wanted to play regularly. He had to steal bases. So, Brock would recall merrily, eyes dancing, "I became a basestealer." One of the best ever, as reflected by a National League record 118 stolen bases one year, 1974, and a career total of 938, second high for a 19-year career.

Two things stand out about Lou Brock other than his strong body beautiful. He curbed his swing to become a rare 3000-hit performer his last season, but in the bright spotlight of World Series play, mild Dr. Jekyll turned into savage Mr. Hyde. Pumped up with excitement, he displayed a rare combination of speed and power.

Brock's average for three World Series, .391, highest for any player with 20 or more games played in the classic, is just a tip of the iceberg. So, too, are his record seven stolen bases, set in the 1967 Series and matched in '68. The eye-opener was his display of power—nine hits for 14 total bases against the Yankees in '64, 12 hits for 23 against Boston in '67 and 13 for 25 against Detroit in '68.

The unkindest cut of all is to suggest that if Brock had slid at home plate in the fifth game of the '68 Series lost to Detroit, the Cardinals would have won. Hell's bells, if Brock hadn't been burning up the ball parks, the Cardinals wouldn't have been close to retaining their title.

The 29-year-old athlete stroked a record-tying 13 hits, matching Bobby Richardson's totals against the Cards in Lou's first Series. Included were three doubles, a triple and two home runs. Largely because he was running his way into scoring position, he scored six runs and drove in five.

The one he didn't score in the fifth game, cutting short an inning against the Detroit doughboy, lefty Mickey Lolich, followed a one-out double by Brock and a line drive base hit by Julian Javier. Willie Horton uncorked a strong throw and Brock, standing up, was tagged out by catcher Bill Freehan and the Cardinals failed to add to their 3-2 lead.

Why not slide?

"Because,"explained Brock, "Freehan's foot, up the line in the basepath, permitted him to turn the foot left or right and deflect me away from the plate if I slid. Actually, when I collided with him, he hadn't had time to extend his arms to take the throw. So the tag really was on the plate—safe!"

As suggested, the added run might have encouraged manager Mayo Smith to bat for Lolich in the seventh, but, wary of his bullpen, Smith stayed with Mickey, and the sinkerball southpaw looped a hit that led to a three-run rally, a 5-3 victory and the springboard to an upset.

With Brock batting .464 with an incredible .844 slugging percentage, it seemed fair only to pursue his defensive argument. Truth is, after experiencing a repeated to-and-fro replay of the '68 Series film at Cooperstown's National Baseball Hall of Fame Library, an author suggests that Brock was on the plate when tagged!

So Lolich won the sports car traditionally awarded the Most Valuable Player of the Series, a result of a third Series victory in the windup. Brock also was nosed out of the MVP and the 1967 sports car when he hit .414, breaking Honus Wagner's record of six stolen bases. That one went to teammate Bob Gibson, who won three games with record strikeouts.

But Louis Clark Brock had come a long way from the family of Arkansas cotton choppers who had hard times making ends meet. Good enough to win an athletic scholarship at Southern University in Baton Rouge—if he'd stayed in football the swift powerful back might have been as good as Lou Jr. would prove years later at Southern California—but the chance to help the family financially made baseball an attractive early offer. Selected for the Pan-American games, Brock did well enough to interest a scout for the Cardinals, but the baseball

Happy Birthday, Lou: Here, Lou celebrates with Orlando Cepeda and Phil Gagliano.

gumshoe had to go to Washington to sign pitcher Ray Washburn. The host Cubs came up with the right offer, a $30,000 bonus.

"I went in washing walls at the YMCA and came out with enough money to buy one," he remembered happily, then and after flourishing for St. Cloud in the Northern League, where he hit for average and power.

That's when he went from night to day, to the bright, gusty winds at Wrigley Field where more experienced outfielders have had their share of troubles. He dropped and double-dribbled enough balls to make him overswing at the plate.

When he hit like Bill Terry and Henry Aaron, he unloaded that tape-measure shot at the Polo Grounds, but he didn't hit consistently enough for the pitching-poor Cubs. The Cardinals dangled Broglio, whose conduct had disenchanted Keane. General manager Bing Devine made the eleventh-hour deal.

Next night, pinch-hitting at Houston's old Colts Stadium, Brock struck out, but Keane painted that picture of just get on base, kid, and he did. The Cardinals, 28-30 when they made the move, soon saw No. "20" getting on and often. With a sizzling 65-39 after the trade, they used Brock's .346 hitting and 43 stolen bases as a springboard for their first pennant in 18 years.

"I've had greater seasons and performances, but none thrilled me more than '64," said Brock. "I belonged."

He did, following his first of four 200-hit seasons, with a .300 Series contribution against the Yankees. From there, he posted seven more .300 seasons and, playing durably, his stolen bases mounted as the fans chanted:

"Lou...Lou!"

He never stole as few as that first season in St. Louis until late in his career. He studied pitchers and listened, too. For instance, when black league Hall of Famer James (Cool Papa) Bell urged him to encourage the second spot hitter to drop deeper in the box, requiring the catcher to retreat one precious step.

Brock did the rest, studying pitching tipoffs for a fast start and—he counted them!—11 strides and a courageous pop-up slide into second base that exposed himself to a catcher's late throw, yet shielded the

play from the infielder.

The pop-up slide, the jack-in-the-box propelling himself to his feet from the double-up leg as a springboard, was good and effective, yet occasionally frustrating. As Brock explained, "Umpires working the infield, National League style, rather than behind the infield as they did in the American League, were blocked from view. They would guess—too often wrong."

Playing until 40, though well-conditioned, Brock suffered the inevitable letdown—from 150 hits in 133 games in 1976, to 66 in 92 games two seasons later. Old teammate Ken Boyer, then managing the Cardinals, expressed his fears. "I'd love to see him get 3000 hits, but I can't use him any more or as much if he can't perform."

Brock rose to the occasion first with a pronouncement that 1979 would be his last season and then he "orchestrated" his retirement handsomely. "Orchestrate" was one of the articulate athlete's favorite words, and he was symphonic that final season.

He played so well that he played 120 games, improved his average to .304 and got 123 hits—that magic 3000 and 23 more. And the big one came most dramatically with a home crowd pulling for the popular go-go guy.

First pitch, the Cubs' Dennis Lamp decked the lefthanded leadoff man with a pitch that might have—well, the gasp of fear from the stands was audible up in the pressbox, where well-wishers winced, tearful of what might have happened if the pitch has crashed against the batter's helmet.

Lou Brock got up, dusted himself off and with a touch of the dramatics, he lined the next pitch directly back at the pitcher, glancing the ball painfully off Lamp's right hand toward the third-base dugout.

If you will, a finish with a Hall of Fame flourish.

THREE FINGER BROWN

When the Cardinals finished a sad last in 1903 with a 43-94 record, the lowest won-and-lost percentage (.314) they've had since 1898, panicky club president Frank Robison traded away potentially one of the ball club's best pitchers ever. Robison flouted the efforts of fired manager Patsy Donovan, who had brought up the pitcher from the Indiana mining town of Nyesville. If you don't know the town or how to pronounce it, you've undoubtedly heard or read about Mordecai Peter Centennial Brown. Long for Miner Brown, short for his more famous nickname:

Three Finger Brown!

A righthanded pitcher who had lost his first finger and badly damaged his middle finger in a boyhood threshing machine, Brown was a rookie pitcher with a poor record for a bad ball club. So the elder Robison brother gave him and a couple of other guys for Chicago righthander Jack Taylor. Taylor, twice a 20-game winner for the Cubs at a time of more 20-game winners, was pretty good with a better St. Louis ball club in 1904, but by '06, he was back in Chicago, en route to an early baseball demise.

Brown? All he did was to begin a remarkable career that included six straight 20-game seasons, including nine straight victories over the New York Giants' fabulous Christy Mathewson, including the famous pennant replay in 1908. And that year, a 29-9 season, Miner pitched 11 scoreless innings for two World Series victories in the last World Series the Cubs won. Brownie pitched on four pennant-winning teams in nine seasons in Chicago.

Famed Three-Finger came back to St. Louis with the Federal League Terriers as player-manager in 1914. He won 12 and lost six for the wrong club at the wrong time, traded away at the wrong time by the wrong club, the Cardinals.

JESSE BURKETT

Jesse Burkett was a pain in his own small posterior to umpires and to fans, who called him "The Crab" because of his constant complaining, but John McGraw would have made it worse, profanely worse. Years after the slight Burkett put down a skilled bat that prompted him to two .400 seasons and a 16-year career average of .339, he was asked as former Holy Cross University coach to take a look-see at a promising catcher for old friend McGraw, master of the New York Giants.

Burkett wired back a telegram that the catcher never would make it because his hands were "too small." Long before Gabby Hartnett followed McGraw and Burkett into the baseball Hall of Fame, McGraw would have liked to wring the little man's neck.

So probably would St. Louis—at least the Cardinals' half of the two-team major-league town—when batting champion Burkett jumped to the Browns just after posting a league-leading .382 average in 1901.

The Browns' uniform and, oddly, theoretically weaker American League weren't therapeutic for the aging bones of Burkett, who dipped quickly under .300. He finished in 1905 in Boston, the New England area where he lived long enough to go into the Hall of Fame in 1946 and almost late enough to see the guy whose hands were too small make it. Hartnett got to Cooperstown two years after Burkett's death in 1953.

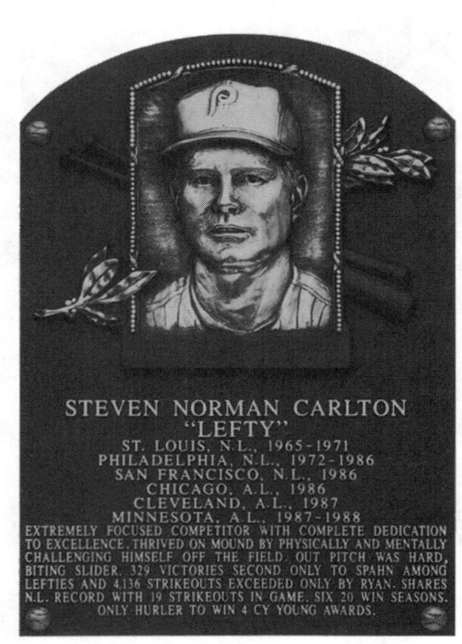

Still, Jesse Cail Burkett must not be regarded too harshly, even by Redbird historical diehards. He was smart enough to play, manage and briefly own the Worcester ball club of the Eastern League. Besides, despite the kind of grousing that didn't sit well with baseball's earlybird umpires and followers, he was nice to sports writers who liked to listen to the 5-8, 155-pound West Virginian discuss the thing he did best—hit.

Just one thing, don't ask "The Crab" to scout. He'd have told Custer there wasn't an Indian in sight—except in Cleveland.

STEVE CARLTON

When the Cardinals beckoned to Tulsa for a pitching look-see against Minnesota in the national baseball Hall of Fame's fund-raising game in 1966, they brought up a big lefthander who just might have stayed right there in Cooperstown—Steve Carlton.

"Lefty," as virtually all called the tall, dark and handsome pitcher, proved to be one of the best ever, four times a Cy Young award winner and author of one of the game's most incredible seasons. For the phutile Philadelphia Phillies, who won only 59 of 162 games in a sad last-place finish in 1972, Carlton was a rousing 27-10.

Big Steve, humming a lively fastball and biting off one of the most jagged sliders ever, was dandy and durable that season and most of the 24 years in which he pitched until he was 44. If he chased a buck too long, presumably at one time a victim of an unscrupulous agent or whether he honestly felt he could match Warren Spahn's record 363 victories for a lefthander, Carlton was most impressive as late as 40. At that time he was only 16 victories shy of his final 329 victories and saddled with just 206 of his 244 defeats. So impressive that he was a first-round shoo-in for the Hall of Fame in 1994.

Carlton was a quick-fix for Cooperstown, where he pitched the game back in '66 that kept him in the majors for nearly a quarter-century, though he proved to be a Greta Garbo of the game, incommunicado with the media because of what he interpreted as early personal slights. Yet articulate and affable, the standoffish southpaw could be charming as well as highly successful.

When the towering 6-foot-4 junior-college kid from Miami came to St. Louis's attention, pitching coach Howard Pollet, himself a former stylish lefthander, urged management to lock the gates at Sportsman's Park to keep from losing the lefty, then just lanky and not a muscular physical faddist.

Steven Norman Carlton never faltered as he helped flesh out a winning pennant staff behind Bob Gibson, posting a 14-9 record in one pennant-winning season, 1967, and 13-11 in '68. He was a low-run loser in the first World Series, hit hard in the second, but he had his best years ahead. Down the stretch in 1969, a third straight season with a good ERA, the 17-11 pitcher struck out 19 New York Mets on a raw, rainy night, yet lost the game on a pair of two-run homers by Ron Swoboda. Carlton's 2.12 ERA efforts got him a two-year contract.

Here, after he nosedived to 10-19, then responded with 20-7, came the breach that led mournful club president Gussie Busch to wonder—even though the brewery had bought the Cardinals and initiated the downtown ball-park move—whether the beer baron would be remembered most as the guy who traded Steve Carlton. Busch, remembering the losing first half of the two-year contract, angrily questioned whether Lefty's request for a sizable increase was right.

Suddenly, his Dutch up, Busch ordered general manager Bing Devine to unload Carlton in spring training. With the Phillies having contract troubles with 20-game righthander Rick Wise, Devine made the deal with Philadelphia's John Quinn. Within an hour, Carlton called Devine and capitulated—too late.

Years later, Bing wondered what might have happened if he had opposed Busch more vigorously. Gussie's right-hand man, Dick Meyer, had the answer. "Carlton," said Meyer, "still would have been traded—after you had been fired."

At Philadelphia, as mentioned, Lefty responded with the 27-game season and 1.97 ERA for a rinky-dink team, then combined with a third baseman named Mike Schmidt, also bound for the Hall of Fame, to turn to Philadelphia patsies into kingpins. Four more 20-game seasons followed, including league-leading totals of 23 in 1977, 24 in a World Championship season, 1980, and 23-11 in '82.

The body beautiful, using former St. Louis teammate Tim McCarver as his catching caddy, worked over or close to 300 innings four times, completed 30 games one time and five times led with strikeouts, topped by 310 that unforgettable first Philly season when he made himself the best talent to get away from the Cardinals since Three-Finger Brown in 1904.

CHARLES COMISKEY

If only Charley Comiskey had paid like he played, which was pretty good, and if he'd treated his hired knickered help with the same regard he got in obtaining them or in helping others, this Hall of Fame alumnus of St. Louis baseball origin could have had a town named for himself, not just a ball park. A prominent baseball pioneer, almost as prominent as the sidesaddle silhouette of his proboscis, Commy would be worshipped rather than just respected. The "Old Roman"—a nickname applicable either because of his grand schnozz or the Irish Catholic background—had tremendous accomplishments.

The young man from Chicago, by way of Dubuque, Ia., played 12 major-league seasons at first base, revolutionizing the style of play if not necessarily the first to play off the bag. As a young manager, he recruited and built the St. Louis Browns into four-time pennant winners of the American Association, then a major league, 1885-88, and conquered his home-town Chicago Nationals in a World Series equivalent.

As a founding father of the American League, second only to ex-Cincinnati newspaperman Ban Johnson, a dear friend who became a bitter foe, Comiskey became owner of the Chicago White Sox and fought the good battle for instant recognition. In 1910 he built "the baseball palace," handsome Comiskey Park, for years a symmetrical standard. A springboard to popularity in the Chicago area was an upset in the 1906 World Series when Comiskey's "Hitless Wonders" knocked off the winningest pennant-winner, the North Side neighbor Cubs, a team that had won 116 regular-sea-

The Old Roman: Actually, a young one with the Browns, for whom Charles A. Comiskey was first baseman and manager for four American Association pennants in St. Louis with the Browns, who converted to the National League. Commy, a rangy man, nicknamed the Old Roman because of his Irish commitment to the Catholic Church, and a sizable nose, has his name immortalized at Chicago's Comiskey Park.

son games.

When the Federal League threatened to destroy weaker teams, Comiskey gave $10,000 to Washington's Clark Griffith, partly to help the Senators and partly, as Old Fox Griff put it, to make certain that Big Train Walter Johnson didn't jump to the Chicago Whales. "Commy didn't relish the idea of having Johnson compete across town as a top pitching attraction," said Griffith. Building another winning ball club, Commy gave Connie Mack $50,000, a huge sum in 1914, for second base super-star Eddie Collins and he peeled off $31,000 to go with three players for Cleveland's slugging outfielder Joe Jackson.

Trouble was, Comiskey paid for talent, but not to it. An exception was Collins, the shrewd, well-educated player who had threatened to quit. "Cocky's" contract was a bone in the throat to other players, especially after they won the 1917 world championship and the '19 pennant. For instance, Jackson, an illiterate regarded by Ty Cobb and Babe Ruth as having the sweetest swing, was paid only $6000 when he certainly was worth twice that much. Collins, by contrast, got $14,500.

So seven players contrived to throw the World Series. An eighth Black Sox, third baseman (Buck Weaver), was involved simply because he didn't snitch on his teammates. Cincinnati scored a huge Series upset. With rumors in 1920 flying like home runs off the bat of Babe Ruth, a pleasant distraction, Comiskey waited until the last weekend, just when Chicago no longer could catch Cleveland. His suspension of his players preceded a comic-opera trial in which the players were freed by a sympathetic jury. Regardless, baseball's first commissioner, a tough federal judge name Kenesaw Mountain Landis, barred all for life, including future certain Hall of Famer Jackson and two others who had a chance, pitcher Eddie Cicotte and the unfortunate Weaver.

Comiskey continued to charm the media with his lavish late-hour parties in an ornate private club at his ball park, but the Chisox didn't prevail again until 1959, long after his death. Comiskey died at 72 in 1931, two years before the first All-Star game was played at his park, eight before he received early Hall of Fame induction.

Charles Albert Comiskey, a rangy athlete encouraged by a priest at a school in Prairie du Chien, Wis., when he was 15, caught on later with a Dubuque semi-pro team, managed by a boyhood friend, Ted Sullivan. St. Louis publisher Al Spink saw Comiskey and recommended him to St. Louis saloon keeper, Chris Von der Ahe, who ran the American Assocation team. Von der Ahe liked the play, style and thinking of the man who knew how to play and how to build a better ball club. With Comiskey managing in 1884, acquiring talent, St. Louis finished second and then won four straight pennants, largely because of the run-sheep-run game Commy built. One year he stole 117 bases himself, but wasn't first on the club or second.

With a lineup that included himself, Yank Robinson, Bill Gleason and Arlie Latham in the infield, Tip O'Neil, Curt Welch and Hughie Nicol in the outfield, Doc Bushong catching and Parisian Bob Caruthers, Dave Foutz and George McGinnis pitching, the Browns won the Association. Cap Anson's Chicago White Stockings, as the Cubs early were known, were National League champions. In '85 they played to a post-season tie, but in '86 the Browns prevailed in a six-game series. Because of a bold winner-take-all policy, promoted by Anson, Von der Ahe got the $13,000 profits, kept half and gave the other half to Commy and the players.

Comiskey staved off the inevitable in 1887 by adding a 19-year-old home-town phenom, Charles Frederick Koenig, best known by his colorful sports sobriquet, Silver King. But Von der Ahe began selling off stars, presumably impressed by Comiskey's magic as well as a chance to get richer. By 1890, Chris had run out of talent and Comiskey, too. With regard for players or at least himself, Commy jumped to the Chicago club of the shortlived Players League, one by which the athletes were closer to caving in the professional league than they knew.

When the Brotherhood surrendered prematurely, Comiskey ducked back to old friend Von der Ahe in 1891, but that was the last year of the American Association. Rather than they stay with St. Louis, one of four Association clubs brought into the NL, Comiskey jumped to Cincinnati. Four years later, tired at 35 and with a losing ball club, the Old Roman followed his ample nose into ownership, first in the Western League that soon became the American League.

Comiskey shot the first cannon in the war with the National League, vulnerable because of a ridiculous $2400-a-player salary limit. Commy persuaded cagey pitcher Clark Griffith to jump from the rival Cubs to the new White Sox. Chicago won the first AL pennant in 1901.

If only the dear Old Roman had done unto other what he did for himself, a pinchpenny proprietor with profitable property would be remembered more fondly.

ROGER CONNOR

If Roger Connor wasn't unique—heck, make that darned ususual—by playing third base lefthanded early in his big-league career, he merited extra attention as the first of the long-ball home-run hitters, an early-day Babe Ruth.

Fact is, even though he played much of his career before pitchers were asked to do it from six feet farther away in 1894, his career homers of 137, though modest by modern standards, were tops until the Babe muscled up.

In Connor's era, actually three-base hits best reflected power, and the genial giant of the Giants—a man 6-3, 220 pounds was huge then—had a career total of 233 , still fifth high.

From St. Louis's standpoint, by the time the Waterbury (Conn.) Irishman came to the Browns, as Chris Von der Ahe still called his Nationals, Rog was in the sundown of his slugging career. Still, he hit .321 for most of the traded season, 1894, and .329 at age 38 in '95.

Then Connor made the "mistake" of letting Von der Ahe sweet-talk him into becoming one of five managers Der Poss Bresident used in a well-rounded season of inefficiency, 1896. St. Louis won 40 and lost 90. Rog's contribution was only 8-and-37, as difficult as trying to play third base lefthanded.

Actually, they say only an injury to his throwing shoulder forced him to move to first base, most certainly a more logical position for lefthander, but hurt feelings might have limited his managing thereafter to the minors, where he moved after fragmentary use in St. Louis in 1897.

Connor put on glasses, better to see and manage with, in his home town of Waterbury in '98, serving briefly as clubowner of the Connecticut League ball club. By the time he stepped into retirement five years later, becoming school superintendent there, the big man still was the big man in the league.

Funny, though, despite his ability to draw walks and to hit for both power and average—with a league-leading .371 one year, 14 homers another and 130 RBIs a different season—Roger Connor had been dead for 45 years before he won Veterans Committee selection to Cooperstown.

DIZZY DEAN

The mayor of St. Louis, on hand to congratulate the manager on a 1930 pennant clinched the day before, watched a lean, lanky, high-cheekboned righthander warm up. To Gabby Street, His Honor Victor J. Miller asked, "Is this Dizzy Dean going to be as good as I hear he is?"

Old Sergeant Street, later Harry Caray's first radio partner on Cardinal broadcasts, put it in life's sidepocket when he responded, "Mr. Mayor, I think he's going to be great, but I don't think we'll ever know from one minute to the next what he's going to do."

"Old Diz," as the gangling guy called himself when he was barely old enough to vote, did become a great pitcher, his career cut short by injury sadly at a time he should have been reaching his peak. And from that time in the last September, 1930 afternoon when he beat Pittsburgh on a three-hitter, 3-1, helping himself with a base hit, until he ballooned into a national broadcaster, he fulfilled the second half of Street's philosophy, too.

Never has anyone, including the Great One, been sure what he'd say or do until he died in 1974 at only 63, overstuffed from too many of dear wife's catfish and hushpuppies and the hottest barbecue anywhere he could find it.

The bulging-bellied giant with a grin almost as wide as his western hat didn't look like a shadow of his slender self, yet he played golf with the sly competitive gamesmanship by which he always won by just enough to make the other guy to want to try another time. Dwight D. Eisenhower was impressed by his golf fame as well as his girth, yet wondered to him if was good for the kids of America to see a hero so outsized.

As always, except when Branch Rickey outtalked him at contract time, Dizzy had the answer. "Mr. President," he explained, "for the first 20 years I didn't get enough to eat, and I ain't caught up yet."

Barely an exaggeration, unusual for the Baron Munchausen of the Mound, but it is true that when he quit school in fourth grade at only 10, to join his paw and brothers chopping cotton, meals were skimpy. So the peacetime army seemed a nice place to get three squares a day.

Trouble was, pitching for his service unit and a semi-pro team in San Antonio, Jay Hanna Dean, nicknamed "Dizzy" by a perceptive sergeant, was so promising in professional promise that father Albert Dean bought him out of the military for $120.

Signed by a Cardinal scout, suddenly free as a bird, Dizzy went berserk in 1930 at St. Joseph, Mo., in the Western League, reportedly renting three hotel rooms at the same time. He won 17 games so fast that there was enough time left to win eight more for Houston in the tough Texas League and, as mentioned, finish with a flourish the day the mayor of St. Louis asked a question of wonderment for which the Cardinal manager gave that right-on-the-button answer.

If Jay Hanna—he supposedly permitted himself to be called Jerome Herman because a friend had lost a boy of the same age and name—had been less than dizzy in the Redbirds' 1931 spring-training camp at Bradenton, Fla., he might have made the roster then. But like a kid with nose pressed against the window at the candy store, 20-year-old Dean began spending his $3000-a-year salary faster than he could get into mischief. He overslept and overspent.

Soon, Rickey directed traveling secretary Clarence Lloyd to limit the lad to $1-a-day salary advance and, ultimately, he was shipped back to Houston, at which point big Redbird reliever Jim Lindsey quipped, "That's the only time I ever saw a ball club lose 30 games in one day."

Back at Houston, Dizzy met his match in an attractive department-store saleswoman. Pat Nash refused to be married at home plate, a ball-club gimmick, but she put her foot down and her hands in Dizzy's pocket, saving $1200 of his $3000 salary. And with the balance-wheel boss at home, Dizzy was an overpowering 26-game pitcher who struck out as many as innings he pitched.

For the next half-dozen years the National League in particular and baseball in general just wasn't the same. Dizzy was almost as good as he thought he was, though in later life he quantified that by suggesting, "I wasn't the best pitcher, but I was amongst 'em."

With a bad second-division ball club in 1932, he won 18 games and sweet-talked himself out of $100 fine for missing a train by promising manager Street a shutout and delivering it. A year later, a 20-game winner again with a ball club that again finished out of the money, he struck out 17 Chicago Cubs, a record at a time choked-gripped batters didn't strike out so much.

Although captain-turned-manager Frisch vowed he wouldn't overwork Dizzy in 1934, the Dutchman was full of kalteraufschnitt. With his 21-year-old younger brother, Dizzy allowed that if they gave them the ball often enough, "Me'n Paul would win 45 games."

Frisch, needing another pitcher and aware of the boxoffice potential, stayed with Paul early and—never "Daffy," as they would like to call the more sober brother—Paul Dean soon joined force. If you wonder why the '34 Gas House Gang won the pennant, with a special bow to switch-hitting Ripper Collins at first base, it was mainly the Dean brothers. They won 49, nearly 52 percent of the team total of 95.

At one stormy period, Dizzy threatened a sitdown strike to improve brother Paul's $3000 salary. Another time when the Deans conveniently missed a train for a mid-season exhibition at Detroit, Frisch stuck them with a fine and made it stick.

Late in a dramatic drive to a pennant, Dizzy pitched a three-hit shutout at Brooklyn and brother Paul followed with a no-hitter. "Jeez, if I'd-a known Paul was gonna do it, I'd-a done it, too," apologized Dizzy. He had held the Dodgers hitless until the eighth inning.

Down the stretch, the Deans pitched virtually every other day, relieving often. Paul, winning 19 games, clinched a title tie the next-to-the-last-day. Ol' Diz wound up remarkable with a final-day 9-0 rout of Cincinnati, giving him a 30-7 season, his first of three straight 300-plus innings pitched seasons and a rousing Most Valuable Player award. Heck, he was close up in MVP voting the other years, too.

Noting that me 'n Paul had won 49 games, four more than he prophesied, the Great One suggested that, for pity's sake, he just didn't know how good they really were. And that, of course, was before Dizzy and Paul won two games each in the World Series.

The Series really was Dizzy's from the time the Cardinals arrived at Navin Field, crossing the field to work out after the Tigers. Diz took the bat out of slugger Hank Greenberg's hands, stepped into the batter's box en mufti, and hit the ball out of the park. "That's the way to do it, podnuh," he recommended to the power hitter.

Before warming up to pitch the opener, Dizzy swiped a tiger skin from a playing-field band, perched it across his back and oom-pahed into a tuba. Then, of course, he won the game. Later he did lose the fifth game, 3-1, after having been hit in the skull with a double-play throw as a pinch-runner the day before.

Happily, brother Paul's pivotal victory gave Dizzy the seventh-game chance he wrested from Frisch. Beforehand, passing behind submarining righthander Elden Auker, warming up for Detroit, he paused and suggested in the ugly vernacular, "You don't expect to get anyone out with that s_____, do you, podnuh?"

THE DEAN OF PITCHERS: Among the best ever from 1932 until he hurt his arm in '37, Dizzy Dean was tremendous for the Cardinals, winning 18 games, 20, 30 , 28, 24 and – until hurt – 13. Soft-serving, he was 7-and-1 for the Cubs in a pennant-winning year, 1938, and later became a greater legend in radio and television.

Dizzy's own ability and speed, turning a one-out single into a double, set up a decisive "7" in the third inning of a game won, 11-0.

With nearly $50,000 in endorsements the Deans shared, plus a doubled salary to $15,500, Dizzy no longer would be hungry except for anything other than victory. In 1935, working even more as a starter and game-saver, he was 28-12 with five saves and only a 21-game Chicago Cubs winning streak in September kept him for an encore effort against Detroit.

A 24-game workhorse once more in 1936, Dizzy was a mid-season 12-7 pitcher with a weakened ball club in '37, a popoff who had made the league back down when huffily he described National League president Ford Frick and umpire Geroge Barr as "a couple of crooks", after a disputed balk call. When asked for a written apology, he huffed, "I ain't signin' nuthin'."

At the All-Star break, he tried to take French leave, following his bags to St. Louis after a trip, but wife Pat and clubowner Sam Breadon persuaded him to change his mind. Breadon flew him to Washington, then a six-hour flight. Unfortunately, Dizzy and his big right toe had a date with destiny and Earl Averill's bat.

A line drive off the bat of Cleveland's Averill broke the toe. Good team man Dean insisted on returning when still favoring the foot with a limp. In his first game back at Boston, he felt something snap in his right shoulder. Never again was Ol' Diz able to "fog" the ball past hitters, a favorite self-description for his high hard one.

Despite his sag to only 13-10 and a damaged goods label, P. K. Wrigley of Chicago peeled off $185,000 large depression dollars as well as three helpful players (pitchers Curt Davis, Clyde Shoun and outfielder Tuck Stainback.) The Cub owner's reward was barely more than a good month's work from the former cotton-chopper at his swaggering best.

Still, several of those assorted 16 victories over three fragmentary seasons came critically in 7-and-1 in a 1938 season in which Gabby Hartnett's Cubs won the pennant. The day before Gabby's famed homer-in-the-gloamin' shot enabled Chicago to nose past Pittsburgh, Hartnett called on the seldom-seen ailing super-star.

"I knew," said Gabby, "they couldn"t scare Dizzy or pressure him, either."

Serving soft stuff deceptively and with good control, Dizzy won that game, 2-1, and then in the World Series almost beat the powerful Yankees with his junk. An infield misplay set up two New York runs so that Dizzy had just a one-run lead in the eighth when Frank Crosetti hit a two-run homer. To Crosetti, as he circled the bases, Dizzy informed him, "if I-da had my old fast ball, you wouldn't-a seen the damn ball."

Stepping on the plate, Crosetti turned and politely said, "Darned if I don't think you're right."

As sportsman Wrigley would reflect later, "No, I never was sorry I got Dizzy. Having him around was like traveling with your own circus band."

The colorful character's colloquial expressions later won him national radio and television limelight, but he had one last baseball hurrah.

Haw-hawing the ineptness of the Browns, for whom he broadcast in 1947, the corpulent 36-year-old Dean, six years in retirement, was urged by the Brownies' Bill DeWitt to show him how it was done, an obnoxious last-day-of-the-season gimmick.

Dizzy Dean slowballed the Chicago White Sox for four scoreless innings, delighting old friends and new, then banged out a base hit, limping. Dear wife Pat Dean put an end to the nonsense, leaning into the dugout and shouting to manager Muddy Ruel:

"Muddy, get my blessed fool out of there before he kills himself."

LEO DUROCHER

To categorize Leo Durocher in the National Baseball Hall of Fame only as a "manager" would be to deny the game's public—and the colorful Gas House Gang—of one of its brashest, noisiest players and, as it should say at Cooperstown, a definite "contributor".

Leo Ernest Durocher, a slick-back, slick-haired, pool shark from Springfield, Mass., was something from the time he got a sniff of Broadway as a two-game player with the Yankees at 20 in 1925 until he died at 86 in the luxury of Palm Springs, California.

In between, a great-fielding, no-hit shortstop who emerged from that label in St. Louis, Durocher helped win the 1934 championship for the Cardinals—even helped christen with the "Gas House" label—and spent 24 major league seasons as a smart, aggressive manager. He was really better than his first-place record of three pennants and a world championship.

Only five of his teams finished in the second division.

Durocher's four-game sweep with his New York Giants over Cleveland's record 111-game pennant-winners in 1954 ranks probably third only to the 1906 all-Chicago Series upset and the 1914 "miracle" Boston Braves' rout of the Philadelphia A's.

Yet Durocher's greatest managerial accomplishment might have been in stirring up the Cubs in the late 1960s at a time not even sunny Wrigley Field could attract enough fans. The Cubbies, long out of the pennant picture, surged from 10th in Lippy Leo's first year (1966) to third two straight seasons, even threatening St. Louis in 1968. Then, by the time fans were coming out to "the friendly confines," as Ernie Banks always put it, they led much of the 1969 season before folding. The New York Mets became the first expansion team to finish first.

If, as suggested, Durocher helped blow it in '69 by using his regulars too often, no one ever considered him "perfect." Fact is, Durocher-admirer Branch Rickey put it well one time when he suggested that Leo has "an infinite capacity for making a bad situation worse."

Yet Rickey admired the booming-voiced athlete's smarts, more than Yankee general manager Ed Barrow did after the 1929 season. Shortly after the death of manager Miller Huggins, who must have seen some of himself in Durocher, Leo stormed the big boss's bastion, insisting on a better contract. To Barrow, Lippy Leo was a popoff whose biggest asset had been caddying for injured Tony Lazerri in the late innings of the 1928 Series romp over the Redbirds.

Barrow promptly sold Durocher to Cincinnati, then the Siberia of the National League, and light-hitting Leo languished there until Rickey, forced to fill the Cardinals' gaping shortstop vacancy, made a pivotal deal with the Reds in 1933, sending pitcher Paul Derringer for Durocher.

The brassy young man, who hadn't been able to hit either way in a brief switch-hitting experience, tried to outtalk Rickey, whom he rudely called "Branch" when few did, but The Lip met his match in the mastery of the oratory. By the time B.R. ticked off Leo's bad debts, overdue alimony and child support, etc., Durocher probably was glad he was making $6000.

Abashed, but unbroken, Durocher became Rickey's pet reclamation project and not just incidentally the glue to the infield as shortstop partner of manager Frank Frisch. With the Cards, the player Babe Ruth sarcastically had labeled the "All-America out" became a .270 hitter the next three seasons. When The Lip hit eight homers in 1935, driving in 78 runs from the eighth spot, then followed with .286, he earned a new nickname: "Capt. Slug," J. Roy Stockton nicknamed Durocher, whose St. Louis marriage to a good-looking dress designer Grace Dozier had paid off his debts and earned the clotheshorse a handsome wardrobe.

MUTUAL ADMIRERS: Shortsop Leo Durocher and third baseman Pepper Martin were linked together in the Gas House Gang era. Of Martin, Lippy Leo would say, "For three weeks he'd bust his gut for you out there, but then you'd better get him relief before he killed himself or collapsed."

Dealt to Brooklyn after a subpar 1937 season—the suggestion is that Frisch thought Durocher envied his job—Leo spent one year feuding with Babe Ruth, the Dodgers' first-base coach in 1938, then was named manager to succeed Burleigh Grimes. The holler-guy and Ebbets Field, home of the Flatbush faithful, were made for each other.

With club president Larry MacPhail's front office help, Durocher turned the borough of Brooklyn and Dodgers from jokes into a ball club that won the 1941 pennant and then couldn't repeat in '42 with 104 victories only because Rickey's St. Louis swansong, the Swifties, won 106. Their Hatfield-and-McCoy rivalry, even more savage than the old Gas House Gang, produced baseball's first pennant playoff, won by the Cardinals in 1946.

With Rickey hailed the "Mahatma," coming over as new head man at Brooklyn, Durocher would have handled the Jackie Robinson situation admirably in 1947, but, as a result of a gambling misunderstanding and a messy marital mixup with actress Laraine Day, Leo was handed a stunning year-long suspension by commissioner A.B.

(Happy) Chandler.

Ultimately, the Machivellian Rickey maneuvered a deal by which Durocher went to the hated rival Giants at the All-Star break in 1948. At the Polo Grounds, still fighting, fussing and stomping the umpires, Lippy insisted on "my kind of team," dealing slow-moving power hitters Johnny Mize, Walker Cooper, Willard Marshall and Sid Gordon. New players included two mid-infield smoothies, Alvin Dark and Eddie Stanky, both with managerial futures.

They hung on the dandy little manager his latter-day nickname—"The Lion"—and the king's come-from-behind Giants won a dramatic pennant on Bobby Thomson's playoff homer in 1951. As mentioned, in '54 they knocked off Al Lopez's unbeatable Indians.

Over the years, coaching now and then, Durocher put in those 24 managerial years reasonably balanced at Brooklyn, New York and Chicago. He probably even would have returned to St. Louis as field foreman, too, if Johnny Keane's Cardinals hadn't rallied to win the 1964 pennant. Lippy Leo already was Gussie Busch's choice.

As a manager, after beginning an on-and-off career in radio, television and as a good, brazen public speaker, Durocher finally hung it up at 68 at Houston in 1973, still in the first division.

Over the years thereafter, hobnobbing with Hollywood greats, including Frank Sinatra, Leo the Lion Durocher yearned for one thing, the Hall of Fame, and had pretty good evidence that he had been railroaded into that 1947 suspension.

But from that French kid's sassy son to a balding fashion place, Du-ro-shay had stepped on many toes, literally the umpires', as well as figuratively others. From the safety of the dugout in bitter battles, Lippy had urged one too many pitchers to "stick it into his ear,"an intimidating threat to hitters.

So when he was dead a couple of years before he finally was tapped for Cooperstown in 1994, he couldn't smell the roses in the garden or sniff the last sweet smell of success.

FRANKIE FRISCH

Twenty years after he danced on the hot spot marked "X", trying to fill the sizable shoes of Rogers Hornsby with the Cardinals, and 10 seasons after he banged out his last major-league hit, a game-winning single, Frankie Frisch received one of his greatest compliments in reference to another future Hall of Fame player, Jackie Robinson.

The time was the 1947 barrier-breaking episode in which Frisch's long-time St. Louis boss, Branch Rickey, brought to Brooklyn a gifted all-around athlete from UCLA, just as Frisch himself often has been referred to as the finest overall at Fordham. When the first big-league black in the century, Robinson, played the Cardinals in his first visit to St. Louis, he was greeted warmly by Redbird manager Eddie Dyer, who had been a topflight football and baseball star at Rice.

Robinson obviously was surprised at the rival manager's warm greeting. To a St. Louis reporter who had overheard the exchange, chiding Dyer, the manager snapped:

"He's a great all-around athlete, a great competitor, reminds me of Frank Frisch. If you get him mad, he'll beat you by himself. I've told my guys to go easy razzing him."

That's why, in Ford Frick's autobiography published in 1973, the late National League president and commissioner not only exonerated the Cardinals from the canard that they actually threatened to strike against Robinson, but he also suggested that "in reality, their (St. Louis) players adjusted more quickly than many of the other players who were more vocally vehement in the clubhouse condemnations."

Chalk one up for the perspicacity of Dyer, a sorearmed student watching from the Redbirds' bench in 1922, Frisch's third full season with the Giants of his native New York, an overnight sparkplug in their drive to four straight pennants. Eddie saw

HOME, SWEET HOME: to Stan Musial and many others from the Civil War, on-and-off for 100 years, a model of beautiful Sportsman's Park. You're watching, in effect, from the old North Side "Y" beyond centerfield. Above the ballpark model, historic sites of persons and places in the Cardinals' own Hall of Fame. (Photo by Dan Donovan) Below, Stan the Man's returned Hall of Fame ring, obtained at Cooperstown, N.Y., in 1969.

STEPPING STONES TO SUCCESS: From left to right, from the top of this page and the next, Redbird World Series and All-Star press-pin keepsakes. Note: No All-Star pin was made in 1940. Also included are three "phantom" pins never used as the 1945, 1949 and 1963 Cardinals did not win. When they missed by a game in '49, owner Fred Saigh sent to Senior ticket holders their tickets as a souvenir stamped with an apology.

ST. LOUIS
PRESS
1931

ST. LOUIS
PRESS
1934

PRESS
ST. LOUIS
1942
ST. L

WORLD SERIES
Cardinals
1963

ST. LOUIS
THE 1967
WORLD SERIES

THE 1968
WORLD SERIES
ST. LOUIS

ST. LOUIS
1945

ST. LOUIS
1949 WORLD SERIES
PRESS

WORLD SERIES
Cardinals
1964

NATIONAL LEAGUE • AMERICAN LEAGUE
WORLD'S CHAMPIONSHIP GAMES • 1949
SPORTSMAN'S PARK - SAINT LOUIS
FIRST ROW 26 BOX
GAME 5
1949
We're really RED Birds now—embarrassed as can be. But here's a World Series ticket as a souvenir. And (surprise!) you get your money back, too. Seriously, thank you for your interest and support. It's grand to know we have so many good fans.
FRED SAIGH. (For the Cardinal family)

ARNHEIM
The Tailor
No. 11 NORTH BROADWAY.
Fine Cashmere Pants to Order, $5.
Stylish Suit to Order, - $20.
Fit and Workmanship Guaranteed.
11 NORTH BROADWAY 11
OPPOSITE COURT HOUSE
Joseph Schnaider
Brewing Co.
Proprietors of Schnaider's Garden.
Bottles of Celebrated Lager Beer for Family Use or Export.
Orders can be Given at Base Ball Park.
Office: 2000 Chouteau Avenue.
NOW YOU GO

WORLDS OFFICIAL SCORE CARD
CHAMPIONSHIP SERIES
DETROIT B.B.C.
CHAMPION LEAGUE CLUB
OFFICIAL SCORE CARD
WORLDS CHAMPIONSHIP SERIES
ST LOUIS BROWNS
CHAMPIONS OF THE ASSOCIATION

OFFICIAL SCORE CARD
WORLDS CHAMPIONSHIP SERIES
NEW YORK B.B.C.
1889
CHAMPION LEAGUE CLUB
WORLDS CHAMPIONSHIP SERIES
OFFICIAL SCORE CARD
ST. LOUIS BROWNS
CHAMPIONS OF THE AMERICAN ASSOCIATION
1886-87-88-89

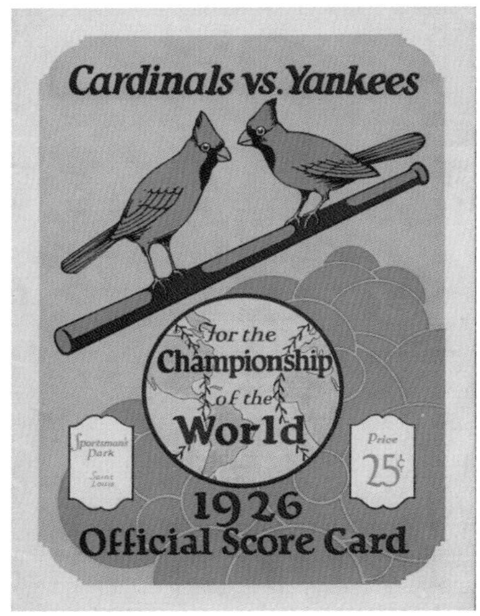
Cardinals vs. Yankees
For the Championship of the World
Sportsman's Park
Price 25¢
1926
Official Score Card

Cardinals vs. Yankees
For the Championship of the World
Sportsman's Park
Price 25¢
1928
Official Score Card

Official Score Card
1930
Sportsman's Park
Price 25¢
For the Championship of the World
St. Louis
vs
Philadelphia

OFFICIAL souvenir PROGRAM
ST. LOUIS vs PHILADELPHIA
for the Championship of the World
SPORTSMAN'S PARK -- 1931

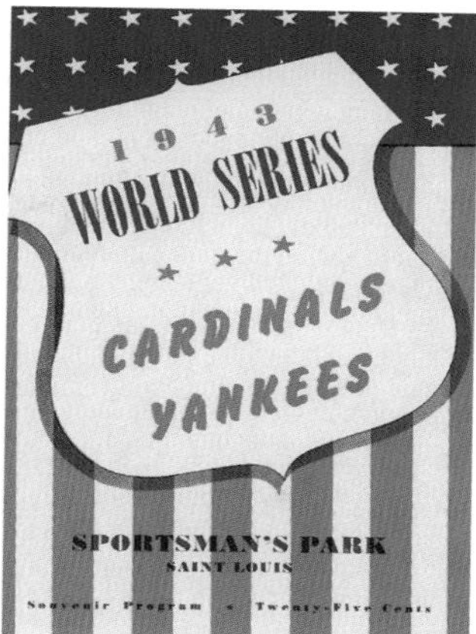

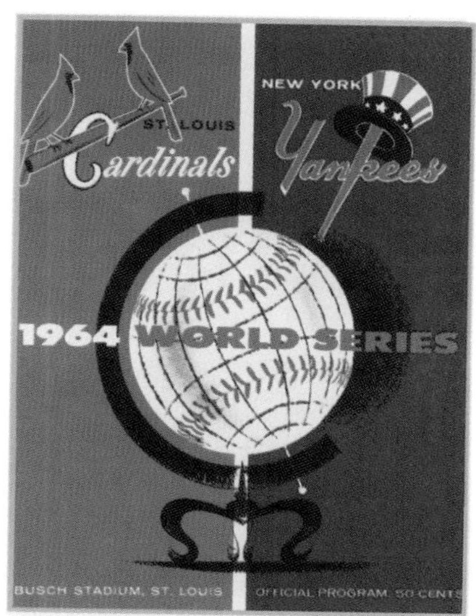

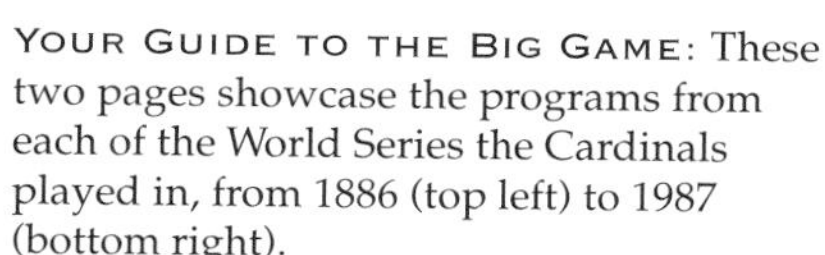
YOUR GUIDE TO THE BIG GAME: These two pages showcase the programs from each of the World Series the Cardinals played in, from 1886 (top left) to 1987 (bottom right).

Sportsman's Park St. Louis
World's Championship Games
1926
National League vs American League
Game 3
Lower Deck Reserved Seat
New Stand
Rain Check
Not good if detached

Notice
Warning

World's Championship Games 1928
Game 3
Admit One
Bleacher
Rain Check
Good this game only
Game No. 3
Price $1.00
Bleacher
Do not detach this Coupon from Check Rain.
1662

World's Championship Games 1930
Game 4
Admit One
Pavilion
Do not detach this Coupon from Rain Check.
Rain Check
Good this game only
Game No. 4
Price $3.00
662
Sportsman's Park St. Louis
Pavilion

World's Championship Games
Sportsman's Park St. Louis
National League vs American League
Game 7
Field Box Seat
Admit One
Rain Check
Not good if detached
Weldon, Williams & Lick, Ft. Smith, Ark.

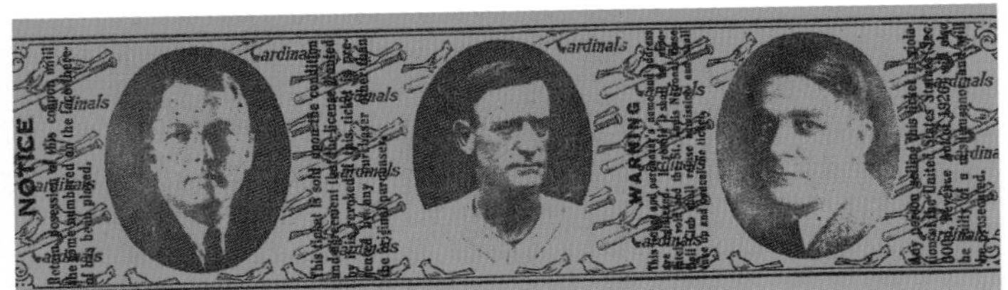

Notice
Warning

World's Championship Games
Sportsman's Park St. Louis
National League vs American League
Game 5
Lower Deck Reserved Seat
Old Stand
Admit One
Rain Check
Not good if detached
Weldon, Williams & Lick, Ft. Smith, Ark.

Notice
Warning

World's Championship Games
National League
American League
1942
Sportsman's Park · St. Louis
Rain Check
Game 1
$5.75
Res. Seat - Lower Stand
Retain this check
Not good if detached
Sec. DD Row 27 Seat 19

For War Relief & Service Fund, Inc., By Kenesaw M. Landis, Commissioner
American League of Professional B. B. Clubs — St. Louis National Baseball Club, Agent
National League vs. American League
World's Championship Games
1943
Rain Check
Sportman's Park St. Louis
Game 4
$5.75
Res. Seat Upper Stand
Retain this check
Not good if detached
Sec. E Row 19 Seat 1

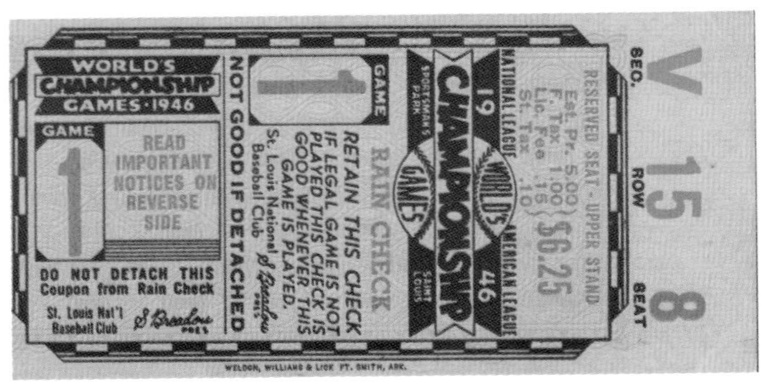

World's Championship Games · 1946
Game 1
Read important notices on reverse side
Do not detach this Coupon from Rain Check
St. Louis Nat'l Baseball Club
Not good if detached
Retain this check
Rain Check
Championship
$6.25
Reserved Seat - Upper Stand
Sec. V Row 15 Seat 8
Weldon, Williams & Lick Ft. Smith, Ark.

1944 World's Championship Games
Game 2
Read important notices on reverse side
Do not detach this Coupon from Rain Check
Not good if detached
Retain this check
Rain Check
World's Championship Games
$6.25
Reserved Seat - Lower Stand
Sec. XX Row 24 Seat 18

ALL PRESENT AND ACCOUNTED FOR: Opposite page: Top, 1926 World Series ticket (face and reverse); Second Row, 1928 and 1930 World Series ticket stubs; Third Row, 1931 World Series ticket (face and reverse); Fourth Row, 1934 World Series ticket (face and reverse); Fifth Row, 1942 and 1943 World Series ticket stubs; Bottom Row, 1944 and 1946 World Series ticket stubs. This page: Right, (from top to bottom), 1964, 1967 and 1968 World Series tickets; Bottom (from left to right) 1982, 1985 and 1987 NLCS and World Series tickets.

HUNTER
ST. LOUIS CARDINALS TRADING CARDS
WHAT'S MY NAME?
WHAT'S MY RECORD?
COMPLETE RECORD
BOYS! GIRLS! Cut out and save these cards. Match up player picture with correct player record and add the correct autograph from Hunter Teenie Smokies packages. Enter the big Hunter Baseball Contest. 200 prizes. Get rules and prize list from your Hunter dealer.
HUNTER

$8
MAJOR LEAGUE BASEBALL
OFFICIAL PROGRAM
LEAGUE Championship SERIES 1996
N
1996
Atlanta Braves
+
St. Louis Cardinals
CS
WHAT A GAME.

CHAMPION JOE MEDWICK STOPS A RALLY
PRESENTED BY JACK ARMSTRONG, ALL-AMERICAN BOY
JACK ARMSTRONG ON THE AIR FOR WHEATIES, FOLKS... ONE OF THE MOST SENSATIONAL CATCHES OF BASEBALL HISTORY TOOK PLACE IN THE ALL-STAR GAME OF 1938, WHEN THAT FAMOUS WHEATIES' CHAMPION, JOE MEDWICK OF THE ST. LOUIS CARDS STOPPED A RALLY OF THE AMERICAN LEAGUERS WHO WERE THREATENING EVEN THOUGH BEHIND 4-TO-0 IN THE 9TH INNING...
WE'LL HAVE TO DO SOME TALL FIELDING TO HOLD THEM DOWN THIS INNING, JOE.
YESSIR....IT'S A REAL MURDERER'S ROW COMING UP... SURE GLAD I HAD MY WHEATIES THIS MORNING.
BOY! WITH DIMAGGIO ON FIRST AND DICKEY AT BAT IT LOOKS AS THOUGH I'D BETTER START CLIMBING THE FENCE IF HE LAYS INTO IT.
IF DICKEY GETS HOLD OF THIS IT CAN START A REGULAR SCORING PARADE.
GOLLY! WILL YOU TAKE A LOOK AT JOE MEDWICK LAYING BACK FOR THAT ONE!
IT'S A HIT!
LOOKS LIKE A HOMER...
HERE THEY GO!
...GUESS BILL DICKEY COLLECTS HIS HOME RUN CASE OF WHEATIES!
BUT LOOK AT DUCKY MEDWICK GO!
I'VE GOT TO GET IT!
GOT IT!
COPYRIGHT 1939 - GENERAL MILLS INC.
BOY! THAT'S ONE CATCH YOU CAN CHALK UP TO A "BREAKFAST OF CHAMPIONS."
BEATING THOSE SLUGGERS 4 TO 1... THAT'S SOMETHING!
YOU SURE STOPPED THAT RALLY, JOE... WHAT'D YOU HAVE, GLUE ON YOUR GLOVE?
MAYBE, AND SOME STEADY TRAINING AND A LOT OF WHEATIES ON MY BREAKFAST TABLE.
JACK ARMSTRONG SAYS...
WITH A LIFETIME BATTING AVERAGE WELL OVER .300, CHAMPION JOE MEDWICK KNOWS A HIT WHEN HE SEES IT!
"IF YOU'RE LOOKING FOR A BREAKFAST FOOD THAT TASTES LIKE A MILLION DOLLARS JUST TRY A BIG BOWLFUL OF WHEATIES"
WE WHEATIES FLAKES ARE TOASTED WHOLE WHEAT READY TO EAT. WE'VE GOT LOTS OF FOOD-ENERGY FOR YOU, PLUS GOOD PROTEINS IRON AND THAT IMPORTANT VITAMIN "B". AND WE'RE READY TO PLEASE YOU ...RIGHT NOW!
WHEATIES
Breakfast of Champions
"Breakfast of Champions"
WHEATIES WITH PLENTY OF MILK AND SOME FRUIT

St. Louis
Cardinals
Cardinals

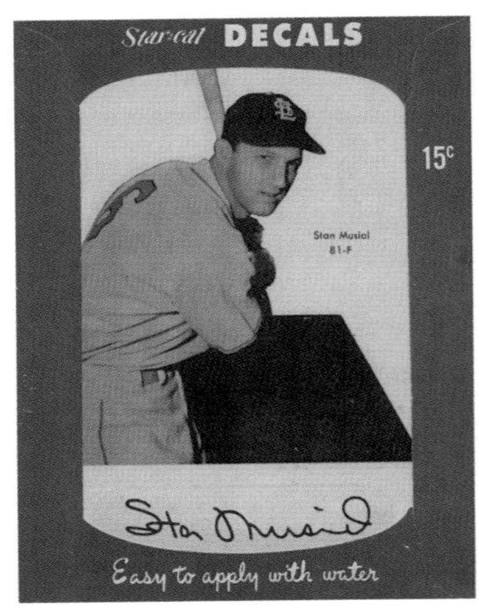
Star-cal DECALS
15¢
Stan Musial
81-F
Stan Musial
Easy to apply with water

Frankie at his inspirational best, including 1923, a .348 season, when the Fordham Flash, not Rogers Hornsby or any other, led the league in hits (223) and total bases (314).

Dyer saw something else, capped by an early-season look-see in 1927, the pivotal point in Frisch's career as a player and the Cardinals as a franchise. When Sam Breadon dropped a lump of coal into the Christmas stocking of Cardinal fans, trading Hornsby after The Rajah had averaged .400 for five seasons and managed the first championship ball club, reaction was so devastating that the Chamber of Commerce denounced the sportsman by resolution, and irate fans festooned Breadon's home and automobile agency with black funeral crepe.

Frisch didn't make them forget Hornsby, but to remember Frisch, pilot light of the colorful Gas House Gang, a ball club that mirrored his own rough-and-ready way to play the game. Rajah Hornsby went into the Hall of Fame in 1942, Flash Frisch in '47 after a war-time voting hiatus at Cooperstown.

Frank Francis Frisch was an amusing anomaly, funny but fiery, an intellectual roughneck. He grew up in a fashionable section of The Bronx, about five miles from the Polo Grounds, where he would enhance the great college reputation at Fordham's Rose Hill, regarded as the Rams' greatest athlete by legendary trainer Jake Weber.

Son of a wealthy German-born linen manufacturer, Frisch grew up with a silver spoon in his mouth, but, in effect, cutting his teeth on a brass cuspidor. He was eloquent in many things, including profanity, and ranked as an outstanding student in chemistry. Herr Frisch, a puzzled parent, was concerned about his son's fanatical interest, especially in "feetball."

Playing football, the swift, chunky halfback played one key game with a broken hand carefully taped in a cigar box by trainer Weber, but Jake couldn't help him earlier. Catching in a boy's game, against his mother's pointed directions, he suffered a broken middle finger on his right hand and tried to hide the injury. Francis was no physician. Infection forced surgery, shortening the longest finger. Happily the handicap did not affect his throwing or hitting.

MONEY PLAYER: Frank Francis Frisch, the Fordham Flash, played in the most World Series by a National League player – eight– and had 58 Series hits in 50 games – and much of the time was the best player and clutch hitter on the New York Giants, 1919-26, and with the Cardinals, 1927-37.

Years later, when he was virtually an overnight star with the Giants, he was spiked badly in an exhibition game, but not permitted by martinet manager John McGraw to get proper attention. As a result, he suffered permanent problems with one infected big toe. So with well-polished ballet-sized shoes, he wore fresh sanitary socks daily, a marked contrast to a uniform dirtied from early use then of the headfirst slide, duly noted one year as a "trend" by the annual Spalding Guide. One of the shoes on Frankie's tiny tootsies was a half-size larger.

Slightly hypochondriac, Frisch moaned about his health even when he didn't groan about his players or gnash his teeth at the unnacceptable—defeat. Fact is, his beer-drinking buddy, umpire John (Beans) Reardon nicknamed him "Happy", shortened to "Hap", but to most players he was the "Dutchman".

The Dutchman did have a physical complaint, painful lower-back lumbago, though when the hard-playing competitor moaned the loudest, teammates suspected he was hinting at a brief mid-summer "vacation". Regenerated by rest, Frisch often could carry a ball club down the stretch, as Eddie Dyer suggested. The Fordham Flash participated in more World Series than any other National Leaguer—eight.

Pulitzer-Prize winning sports syndicated columnist, Red Smith, whose early years were spent covering the Cardinals, remembered with fascination a time when lumbago flattened Frisch as he got out of bed before the third game of the 1931 World Series. "Strapped up like a mummy," Red wrote, "all he did was get seven hits, two of them doubles, steal a base, handle 42 chances without an error and pivot on five double plays."

Smith remembered something else of the funny side of Frisch, that season of the World Series upset over Philadelphia's powerful Athletics. In a late season get-away game hard-luck loser Burleigh Grimes seemed likely to lose, 1-0, George (Watty) Watkins hit a ninth-inning homer to tie the game and the switch-hitting Frisch hit the next pitch to win it, 2-1.

"That was," Red wrote, "the longest home run in history—Frisch talked about it all the way to Boston."

Only four times did Frisch hit 10 or more homers in 19 seasons—topped by 12 the year he led in total bases—but the clutch-hitting "money player" had theatrical ham in him. Big crowds excited him. In the first All-Star game at Chicago's Comiskey Park in 1933, he homered lefthanded off Washington's Alvin Crowder. Next year back home in the '34 game at the Polo Grounds, he hit one righthanded off the Yankees' Lefty Gomez.

With 4 for 7 in All-Star play—and he just dipped below .300 in World Series competition at the dwindling end with 58 hits in 50 games—Frisch saved the best for last. A weary 37 years old, a year older than the record book showed, he struggled with .194 against Detroit, in the '34 Series, but the pilot light ignited the final game 11-0 laugher over the Tigers.

The game was scoreless in the third inning, bases loaded, one out, when Frisch repeatedly fouled off Elden Auker's full count submarine delivery, fearful an American League umpire would punch him out on strikes. Then he stroked a line drive over first base and into the right field corner. Triumphantly, Frisch broke into his trademark gallop, watching Dizzy Dean, Pepper Martin and Jack Rothrock score.

Trembling with excitement, he squatted at second base as manager Mickey Cochrane changed pitchers. To himself, the Flash said, "I'd rather have that hit than bat .800, but, hey, I tripled into a double. Skylarking, watching those guys score, I ought to be on third base. If one of my buzzards had done that, I'd have fined him 50 bucks."

In his first World Series game, 1921, Giants versus Yankees, he had faced tough-guy submariner, Carl Mays, known for the fact that he accidentally killed a batter with a pitch, Cleveland's Ray Chapman, as well as for a 20-game winning habit. That first game in the '21 series at the Polo Grounds, Mays shut out the Giants on five hits. Sassy Mr. Frisch got four of them!

Frisch would ring up remarkable Series averages—.300, .471, .400, .333—in addition to running the bases like a scalded cat and making circus catches. He was a frisky fella, that chest-stopping star whether playing second base or third, from the time McGraw found he didn't have the sure hands to be a shortstop.

Even though that young home-town phenom went 4 for 5 against the International League Baltimore Orioles in a spring exhibition for Fordham, batting crosshanded when he switched to the righthanded stance, McGraw wanted to ship him out. When the player realized his boyhood ambition, surprisingly the kid said no. So he became a rarity. He never wore a minor league suit, player or manager.

Stuck into a late-season series against pennant-bound Cincinnati in 1919, he knocked down a hot smash, pounced on the ball and threw out the batter. Said McGraw, "He'll do."

Frisch did from the virtual git-go, hitting .341 to lead the Giants to that first of four pennants his second full year, 1921, but even then he was so keyed up for the combat that...well, as he put it, he wet his pants. As he put it in the presence of Butch Yatkeman, veteran equipment manager of the Cardinals, "I'd get so emotional that I'd—ah, a little trickle!—and you'd have to get me a new jock strap, Butcher."

Actually, with the nasal, high-pitched voice of the New Yorker, it came out Butch-ah. Whenever Frisch or big boss Breadon talked about the ball club, it was the "Cawdínals" to both natives of the Big Apple.

Frisch came to the Cardinals not because

FRIENDLY FOES: Frantic Frisch (left) was Gabby Street's best player and MVP captain in 1931. A year later, Street thought Frisch was "laying down" on the manager.

McGraw necessarily preferred the slugger to the rapier because, actually, he tried for years to coax Hornsby from the financially strapped Cardinals, aware Frisch played third base even more majestically. But suddenly "his" boy—that's how he regarded Frankie—rebelled against McGraw's method of using his captain as the foil for his cutting clubhouse comments.

So this time when Breadon did the talking rather than the listening, the swap of super-stars was achieved. Actually less one-sided than unhappy St. Louis fans would believe. Or sports editors, too. One, Jim Gould of the St. Louis *Star*, huffed in print that he'd never cover another Cardinals' game.

By the time Frisch and the Cardinals came out of Avon Park, Fla., new manager Bob O'Farrell was convinced. Frisch would recall the first spring city series game against the Browns when he reached down for a potential double-play grounder off George Sisler's bat and, as the saying goes, felt nothing. With the ball bounding between his stocky legs into the outfield for a run-scoring error, Frisch with head down could hear the chant:

"We want Hornsby...we want H-o-r-n-s-b-y."

Frisch, whose recollections ran the gamut from pouting as the unappreciated to a more plausible embarrassment of one who knew he could do better, didn't give the punchline. That is, his eighth-inning hit won that spring game or that he broke in two days later with a triple and homer that beat the Chicago Cubs' Pat Malone, 4-3.

Flash Frisch was a whirling dervish, hitting .337 despite a badly swollen wrist in September, striking out only 10 times, getting 208 hits and a league-leading 48 stolen bases, pawing the dirt to distract pitchers. He'd score from second now and then on an infield out, even tagging up on a long one and taking two bases.

Afield, he was spectacular, knocking down hot smashes with that thick chest, ranging like a fourth outfielder for pop flies and going far to either side, especially behind second, and diving for stops and leaping to his feet. Seventy years later, no infielder in history ever achieved more chances than the 1061 that Frisch contributed in 1927—even though the schedule had been eight games longer for 35 years.

Pittsburgh's Paul Waner, hitting .380 for pennant-winning Pittsburgh, nosed out Frisch for the Most Valuable Player award, which the Flash deserved more than the one he was accorded in 1931. At a private victory party in '31, Branch Rickey asked aloud, "What are we going to do when we lose Frisch?"

Although Frisch could feud with Rickey at times, he respected so much a letter of commendation from B.R. after the pivotal '27 season that he saved the tribute, now included in the old Flash's files at the Hall of Fame library in Cooperstown.

They ought to have there the many books he read voraciously, penning notes of question on the pages. He had a horticulturist's green thumb, one that got him more than one hot afternoon ejection to fuss over his flora and fauna in New York. He could hurry 45 minutes from Broadway to his New Rochelle home. That is, until umpire Reardon, who would think nothing of borrowing Frisch's car one night in St. Louis and then running him, decided he had the answer. He was going to spend the hot afternoon there and so could "Hap."

Frisch could do no wrong with umpires. Oh, they would chase him because he knew all the words, but they respected him as a live-and-let-live guy the next day, one who saved an umpire's job once in embarrassment. Even Bill Klem, who liked him because he did so well against the American League, looked the other way until Frisch, finishing up with managerial jobs at Pittsburgh and Chicago, keeled over one day—kerplop!—bringing the Old Arbitrator to lean over him, scowling:

"If you ain't dead, Frisch, yer outta the game!"

If in these capsules of Hall of Fame players who wore the bird-and-bat raiment of the Redbirds there seems to be a bit too much of funny, fiery Frank Frisch, you'll have to forgive the senior author who pulled rank on the junior.

Still, Frankie Frisch had his flaws, for instance, returning overstuffed and out of shape from a world cruise after the 1931 World Series. The first Cardinal to wear number "3" proved what Rickey had wondered about. Although Frisch insists he didn't "lay down" on manager Gabby Street—and the Dutchman has that printed critique in his diamond dossier at Cooperstown—it was a sore spot for him then and for those who pictured Frisch as did Joe McCarthy, former manager of the Cubs before establishing a dynasty with the New York Yankees.

One day a writer approached Marse Joe and wondered if McCarthy could help him put together the ingredients of a perfect player. McCarthy cut short efforts to apply best-this, best-that superlatives:

"What couldn't Frank Frisch do?"

PUD GALVIN

Pud Galvin was a rarity, a Hall of Fame player actually born in St. Louis, a Christmas Day present in 1856, and a player so far back in the game's lore that he reached the majors actually a year before the National League with the National Association's St. Louis Reds of 1875.

By 1879, short, pudgy Galvin had begun his actual 14-year big-league stretch with Buffalo in the National League. A workhorse at the 45-foot pitching distance and a winner again at 50 feet, the chunky mustachioed man was out of the majors a year before the modern 60-foot-6 distance was establised.

Fittingly, he finished back home, briefly, with the St. Louis Nationals in 1892, winning the last five of his 361 games, a lofty total that didn't get him Cooperstown recognition from the Hall of Fame's Veterans Committee until the century anniversary of his birth. He died at Pittsburgh in 1902 at only 46, by then a victim of weight as well as a finger injury that had forced him out of the games as a player.

James Francis Galvin was called "Gentle Jeems" because he was a nice guy, the "Little Steam Engine" for obvious hard-work efforts, but mainly "Pud", short for "pudding," a slang expression of his distant day, reflecting what Galvin did to the other side.

BOB GIBSON

From ghetto to glory, from rat bites to rickets, from boyhood asthma to adult arthritis in his pitching arm, from abject poverty to affluence, Bob Gibson ran the gamut like the rat that bit him as a boy in Omaha. The rodent had to wind up with a frozen lip because Gibby the Great was one tough customer.

For a guy who once in the distant past had an unfair reputation of fading at the finish, Gibson became pitching royalty in part because of a livewire fast ball and a jagged slider that just would't quit, and also because competitive fire surged through his veins and burned at his vitals.

Like Dizzy Dean before him, as probably the only Cardinal pitcher to match his overall excellence in Redbird uniform, Gibson would spin an enemy batter's cap with high-and-tight pitching. Like Ol' Diz, too, young Gib also hit, ran and fielded so well that Gas House Gang mentor Frankie Frisch thought Gibson could have made the Hall of Fame as a shortstop.

Instead, he got to Cooperstown first time eligible as a pitcher in 1981 after having won 251 games, 56 of them shutouts, including 13 in 1968 when he posted the lowest earned-run average ever of a 300-inning-plus performer. In the Year of the Pitcher, he was THE pitcher, even eating alive Detroit's 31-game winner Denny McLain in the World Series, striking out a record 17 batters. The marvel of his 22-win season, which included only 198 hits and 268 strikeouts in 304 2/3 innings, is that he could have lost seven times, but then that year he paced pitching dominance to the point that baseball lowered the pitching parapet from a 15-inch mound to 10 and attempted also to shrink the width of a strike zone across which his vicious slider swerved.

Gibson, basically only an unhappy man the day or night he pitched, grumbled about the rulesmaker's discriminations, but, bless Pack Robert (Hoot) Gibson's fighting heart, he responded with a 20-game season in 1969 and a second Cy Young award in '70 with 23 victories. That dazzling season in '68 had won for him the Most Valuable Player award, too. In 1971, he pitched a no-hitter against the hard-hitting Pittsburgh Pirates.

If there was a situation in which the great Gibson scintillated, it was the World Series. Between losing his first chance in 1964, a victim of a questionable hit-batsman call, and his last one in '68, a time close friend Curt Flood failed him in center field, Gibby was sensational. He won a record seven straight Series games, all complete, and struck out 92 batters, including a single Series high of 26 in 1967 and topped by 35 in '68.

With a 7-2 won-and-lost mark in blue-ribbon play, Gibson worked 91 complete-game innings in which he yielded just 56 hits, only 17 earned runs, fanned 92 and walked only four. His Series ERA was an incredible 1.89.

It's hard to believe that the king of the pitching hill once was an undernourished kid, left without the father for whom he actually was named—Pack—before Bob was born. Mother Victoria labored valiantly for her seven, the oldest of whom, Leroy, nicknamed "Josh" for the black-league catching great, was the father Gibby never had.

When the wheezing, coughing, asthmatic last born seemed likely to die, Josh promised—and delivered—a baseball glove, but also boxed Bobby's ears when he got into trouble.

As a gifted kid, though troubled by the leg rickets that would trouble him, Gibson was a switch-hitting catcher and shortstop and, playing high school sports with a doctor's permission after discovery of a heart murmur, he starred in basketball. Actually he wanted to take a shot at pro baseball for $3000, but brother Josh, who

Gibby the Great: Pack Robert (Hoot) Gibson, to use the formal first name, hung up his famed "45" after pitching as if he fired from a .45 revolver. His great Hall of Fame career was undoubtedly the greatest ever for a pitcher who wore the Cardinals' red and white. Gibby was a first-round choice for Cooperstown in 1981.

had worked his way through college, opted for Creighton.

There, leaping so high he almost could put his elbow on a basket's rim, the 6-1 Gibson became the Bluejays' first athletic Hall of Fame member. Just short of a degree in philosophy, he signed with the Cardinals' Triple-A Omaha farm club in 1957 for $4000, but he was closer to being ready for pro basketball. He played briefly with the Harlem Globetrotters, quitting only at Redbird general manager Bing Devine's request.

Perhaps too inexperienced, starting too high too soon, the 21-year-old Gibson struggled through the next four-plus seasons, including a couple up and down with the Cardinals. Overall, including the minors, he wasn't .500 on the record when Johnny Keane, replacing Solly Hemus as manager, on Fourth of July, 1961, handed him the ball. Same day the perspicacious pilot also installed Flood in center field to stay.

With better control of the ball and himself, Gibson showed immediate stepping stones as reflected in 13 victories, 15, 18 and finally 19, after saving the 1964 pennant from the bullpen. So Bob was the second-game starter in the '64 World Series against the Yankees, beaten in part after a controversial call that he had hit Joe Pepitone with an inside pitch. The play opened the door to runs that broke a 1-1 tie.

The same Pepitone surfaced again in the key play of Gibson's second start in the fifth game. With Gibby leading in the ninth, 2-0, the lefthanded-hitting Yankee first baseman lined a shot off the pivoting pitcher's right hip. The ball rebounded the wrong way—toward third base—but the cat-like pitcher lunged over to his right, scooped up the ball and made a remarkable fall-away throw to first.

The perfect bang-bang play saved the game and Series. Next up, Tom Tresh hit a home run that would have won the game, but merely tied it. Gibson's batterymate, Tim McCarver, hit a three-run homer in the tenth that gave Gibson his first Series win, 5-2.

Over the years, Gibson would flourish best with four days' rest, but in critical situations he hunkered up as, for instance, the seventh game when he tired badly in the ninth. After yielding a three-run homer earlier to Mickey Mantle, he had shut down the Bombers until Clete Boyer and Phil Linz homered in the ninth.

In the Cardinals' dugout, Keane gritted his teeth. "I'm going all the way with a man's heart," he told himself. Gibson got the Series' hottest hitter, Bobby Richardson, on a Series-clinching pop fly, 7-5.

From that silent vote of confidence, Gibson emerged as a constant 20-game winner and staff stopper, interrupted only in mid-season 1967, when Pittsburgh's Roberto Clemente broke a leg with a savage line drive. Gibson gamely tried to continue before he collapsed.

Las Vegas immediately lowered the odds on the favored Cardinals, but Nelson Briles came out of the bullpen with a hot hand. By then manager, Red Schoendienst wanted only to see Gibson return in September just to be sure —.

Yes, sure that he could pitch and win three games of the World Series against Boston—2-1, striking out 10; 1-0, fanning six, and then 7-2 in the seventh game, a three-hitter with 10 more strikeouts and a homer by Gibson himself.

Gibby nosed out hot-hitting, base-stealing Lou Brock for the sports car MVP trophy, then might have to tussle Brock again for the steering wheel in '68 if Detroit's doughnut dandy, Mickey Lolich, hadn't nipped him in the seventh game, a result of a rare misjudgment of a fly ball by Flood.

No excuses, but Gibson hadn't been helped by two rain delays when winning the fourth game, 10-1, striking out 10 and becoming the first pitcher to hit a second World Series home run. If Gibson hadn't been hurt again in 1973 when there was no Briles to come out of the bullpen and other pitchers backed off without their staff leader, the ball club that began the season with a 5-and-20 record just might have achieved the greatest comeback ever. St. Louis had a five-game lead in early August when Gibby tore a knee sliding back into first base.

He never really recovered from that one, largely because marital problems kept him from a required winter rehabilitation, after he had recovered to win a final-game shutout over former teammate Steve Carlton the final game of the '73 season.

A year later with that gimpy knee, his heart wasn't enough when Montreal's Mike Jorgenson beat him with a two-run game-winning homer the next-to-last game of a race lost to Pittsburgh. At nearly 40, he was only a 3-and-10 whisper of himself in '75 when he drove off with a $30,000 mobile home as a going-away gift from Anheuser-Busch.

Big number "45" no longer could pull the trigger on his .45. A young Atlanta Brave grumbled about that "lucky stiff" after a savage line drive went to a Redbird defender. Quietly, Henry Aaron spoke up, "Son," he said, "if Gibson had his old fast ball, you'd be lucky to get a loud foul."

Although deliberately a distant player from rivals and no fun even for teammates the day or night he pitched, Gibson could be unfortunate too, often aloof about signing autographs. But his respect never suffered as, for instance, when former foe Sandy Koufax predicted his overwhelming performance the day he dazzled Denny McLain, who had received much more ink before the opener of the 1968 World Series. Gibby struck out a record 17.

"You guys," said Koufax, referring to the media, "don't realize Gibson has suffered nearly as much arthritic pain in his elbow as I did, but he's a proud man as well as one who can tolerate pain. He deserves as much credit as McLain did or more, but he didn't get it. Watch!"

Many in baseball describe Gibby the Great as the most competitive man they ever saw. Another source came from a young basketball player, five inches taller, who faced him in a Creighton varsity-alumni basketball game.

"I just didn't have a chance," said admiring Paul Silas, en route to breaking the National Basketball Association record for rebounds.

CLARK GRIFFITH

A sly guy—a small and spry sly guy—Clark Griffith belongs in a St. Louis book as a Hall of Famer for more reason than the fact that he was born in Missouri and began his big-league career with the oldest of the old Browns. He also won his last pennant as a clubowner because he fleeced the later Browns out of a good outfield.

No wonder they call him the "Old Fox" as early as when he was just a kid, then cutting the ball and using all forms of foreign substance to help overcome the fact that he was just 5-6 , only 156 pounds. Certainly he didn't have the height or the heft to throw the ball past hitters, but he had the smarts. Born in a log cabin in western Missouri at Clear Creek in late 1869, after the Civil War had left guerillas, including Jesse James, Clark Calvin Griffith grew up in Bloomington, Ill., but he never lost the guts of his area's birth. As an early job, he had as a young man, Griff hustled tables as a gambling-room croupier in the bad-man West.

Meanwhile, pitching with the St. Louis American Association Browns in 1891 at just 21, he had a winning record of 11-8, but someone made a monumental mistake and dealt him to the Boston American Association team. Even though sidelined briefly there with arm trouble that caused his release, the little righthander returned in 1893 to establish a career that actually lasted two decades of assorted excitement. With Cap Anson's White Stockings, as the Na-

National League Cubs then were called, the cunning character put together six straight 20-win seasons and led the National League in earned-run average in '98 (1.88.) But the feisty little fella had ants in his pants, jumping to the new American League in 1901. There, Griffith had an early jackpot with a 24-win season and the AL's first pennant.

Two years later he was pitcher-manager of the New York Highlanders, the early-day label of the Yankees, and, appearing less often as a pitcher, contributed only seven of his 227 in '04. That's the year when record 41-game winner Jack Chesbro lost the pennant the last day on a wild pitch. Griff, though he would take a token pitching turn until 1914, actually was bench boss from '07 at New York and Cincinnati before sneaking in as manager and part owner at Washington in 1912. There, in D.C., Clark made his biggest mark, first managing, next persuading William Howard Taft and other presidents to throw out the first ball. Clubowning, Griffith didn't have the money and, managing, he had only one pitching immortal, Walter Johnson, but he had the gall—and good luck—to appoint two "boyhood playing managers," Bucky Harris, 27, and Joe Cronin, same age, into rare pennant winners of the Senators. Harris won a world championship in 1924 and a pennant in '25. Cronin won the Capital's last pennant in 1933.

Cronin, that is, and "Unk", as the shortstop called Griffith, actually his father-in-law because Joe married Clark's ward, Mildred Robertson. When Griff's brother-in-law died, he officially adopted nephew Calvin, renamed Griffith, and raised the rest, one of whom, Sherry Robertson actually played several years for his uncle. "Unk" could be cantankerous at times as, for instance, coming out in favor of abolishment of the spitter that had helped him and later voting against night ball, yet quickly installing lights at his own park.

The Old Fox was at his foxiest when he dealt for what Cronin wanted most—a catcher, Luke Sewell, and lefthanded pitchers Earl Whitehill and Walter Stewart, necessary to top the perennial powerhouse Yankees. Stewart came from the St. Louis Browns. So did the regular outfield of Goose Goslin, Fred Schulte and Heine Manush. In '30 Griffith swapped batting-title rivals with Browns' owner Phil Ball, giving up Goslin for Manush, then got back the Goose and Schulte in 1933, just in time for Washington to win and St. Louis to finish last.

This was, if you will, the Old Fox's finest flim-flam. Trouble was, overall, the western card shark just didn't have enough money to compete over the years. He died at 85 in 1955, six years before son-in-law Cronin, as American League president, helped the Senators move to Minneapolis as the Twins.

BURLEIGH GRIMES

Off the field professorial-looking, tweedy, bow-tied, Burleigh Grimes looked—and was—the direct opposite of the square-jawed, scowling guy they called "Ol' Stubblebeard." An intimidator, he threw baseball's last legal spitball in 1934.

The gentle boyhood logger and adult farmer was entirely different when he pulled down his tight-fitting baseball cap and loosened up hitters. Of the 270 games he won for Hall of Fame induction in 1964, long before he died in '92 in his beloved Clear Lake, Wis., the most precious apparently were those nearest to the end. By the time St. Louis's Sam Breadon, goaded by a young reporter, Sam Muchnick of the old St. Louis *Times*, traded for Burleigh in 1930, he was a well-traveled, winning pitcher, on the move often because he wanted more dough.

A short, stocky man, he had overcome two legs broken badly in a youthful logging mishap and had put in his best and longest years at Brooklyn. Grimes was there when baseball barred foreign substances for pitchers, grandfathering 17 who threw the unsanitary spitter. That year, 1920, Grimes had his first of four 20-win seasons for the pennant-winning Dodgers, including a first-game shutout over Cleveland in the World Series, though the Indians beat him twice, once on baseball's first Series grand slam by Elmer Smith.

Throwing the spitter required a moist mouth, so Grimes chewed slippery elm, which irritated his skin, so he didn't shave the day he pitched, creating a Jack Dempsey look of severity that fit his win-at-all-cost mood. Every pitch, Ol' Stubblebeard would bring both hands up to his mouth and expectorate or fake the spit. He had three more 20-win seasons for the Dodgers and a league-leading 25 in 1928 for Pittsburgh.

That one could have been most embarrassing to the Giants' John McGraw, for whom the cranky veteran had only one 19-8 season. McGraw dealt him to the Pirates for another pitcher, Vic Aldridge, who bombed himself out of baseball within a year.

Grimes, meanwhile, had been dealt in 1930 to perennially second-division Boston Braves and didn't like it. That's the message young reporter Sam Muchnick portrayed to Breadon that trading-deadline day. Impulsively, the Cardinal clubowner gave up veteran southpaw Bill Sherdel and young righthander Fred Frankhouse.

The happiest Redbird was team captain Frank Frisch, at whom Grimes repeatedly had thrown as a sassy college kid those early years when Brooklyn and New York were bitter borough rivals. Frisch's ability to hit that low-breaking spitter added to the annoyance. Grimes helped Gabby Street's ball club immediately, but, still, the Cardinals were fourth, 12 1/2 games out with only one more victory than defeat, 53-52, when they exploded in August. They won 39 of their last 49 and had the lead into the final weekend when Breadon called in the pitcher.

"Burleigh, you've been great," said Breadon. "I told you we just might have a chance if you won a dozen games. I need one more."

Grimes gave him No. 13 with only six defeats, a day before road roommate Jesse Haines pitched the clincher. So at nearly 37, Grimes got two World Series chances against Connie Mack's powerful defending champion Philadelphia Athletics. He lost both low-hit games, the 5-2 opener to Lefty Grove when he gave up only five hits, and the fifth game against Grove and George Earnshaw when Jimmy Foxx made the A's fifth hit a ninth inning game-winning homer, 2-0.

A SPITTIN' IMAGE: Spitball ace Burleigh Grimes, a future Hall of Famer, demonstrates his best pitch for the great woman athlete, Mildred (Babe) Didrikson, barnstorming in exhibitions for the 1931 Boston Braves. The Babe, later Mrs. George Zaharias, was a good basketball and great golfer as well as an Olympic track star.

The 1931 Cardinals cakewalked to a pennant with 101 victories even though no pitcher won 20 games. If anyone was better than Grimes, it was lefthander Wild Bill Hallahan, who had become Sweet William. Hallahan, like Grimes, was better than in '30 in the encore Series with Mack's mighty White Elephants, seeking their third straight championship.

Manager Street almost outthought himself in this one, a Series featured by Pepper Martin's batting and base-running brilliance and the pitching of Hallahan and Grimes. Gabby put his first-game faith in rookie Paul Derringer, 18-8, and a two-time loser in the Series.

Grimes, getting his first chance in the third game, held the A's scoreless on only one hit into the ninth when Al Simmons' homer merely spoiled a 5-2 win that would have been a shutout. So Ol' Stubblebeard became the seventh-game showdown pitcher against Earshsaw, even more impressive than Grove.

Two cheap first-inning runs and a two-run homer by Watty Watkins carried the old battler into the ninth with a four-hit, four-run shutout, but Burleigh Armand Grimes was down to his heart now and an empty tank, weakened by age, an incipient appendix attack and just too many innings. Bullpen catcher Mike Gonzalez, slipping up to the dugout presumably for a drink of water, looked into Grimes' watery, squinting blue eyes. Back in the bullpen, Mike got Hallahan onto his feet.

Battling Burleigh got by the two big game-breakers, Simmons and Foxx, but a walk and three hits followed, scoring two. The tying runs were on in the 4-2 game when lefty Hallahan came in to retire lefthanded-hitting Max Bishop on a fly to Series hero Martin.

For Ol' Stubblebeard, that really was his last hurrah. Burleigh underwent surgery for an appendectomy, but Breadon and Branch Rickey, always happy to unload a good salary, especially in tough times, traded Grimes to the Cubs for lefthander Bud Teachout and an over-the-hill Hack Wilson, ticketed for sale to Brooklyn. Grimes didn't help the Cubs much in a pennant season or a feeble Series relief appearance against the Yankees. A couple of years later, back with friend Frisch's Gas House Gang, he couldn't help enough to stay, either.

So his last victory and the last by a spitball pitcher was achieved that same year with the 1934 Yankees. A couple of losing seasons as manager at Brooklyn followed, 1937-38, and years of managing in the minors and scouting, then sunset back in Wisconsin.

CHICK HAFEY

If there's any ball player to whom the economic timing of his era backfired on him it was the man John McGraw said "with two good eyes" would be the best player of his generation—Chick Hafey.

Hafey, probably never so robust as his rangy rawhide frame or vicious line-drives would indicate, overcame strength-sapping sinusitis—or was it, as now, allergies?—and accompanying weak eyesight.

Team surgeon Dr. Robert F. Hyland knew there was something amiss when Hafey was hit by too many pitches. Teammates knew that in certain times of the season, the lanky outfielder couldn't see the red exit light at the end of a players' railroad Pullman. But a good hitter before he put on glasses—first batting champion ever to wear spectacles—Hafey was great with readjustment.

The only problem was a contract that corseted his earnings with only a $1000 increase annually over three years through 1930, even though he put together salad seasons of .329, .337 and .338, plus RBI's up to 125 even though he never played more than 138 games. And, as Rogers Hornsby said admiringly, he'd have had more homers than his tops of 29 if his wicked line drives couldn't climb fast enough to clear outfield concrete walls.

"He's the best righthanded hitter I ever saw," said Hornsby. Obviously, too, Hafey was one of the most powerful throwing and fast, too.

A proud, quiet man who preferred his chicken farm in the scenic mountains above San Francisco, Chick Hafey seethed over the small, mincing stepping stone from $8000 to $9000 to $10,000 through 1930. When he drooled over $15,000 for '30, the stock-market crash of October, 1929 brought the Depression.

Hafey held out the entire spring before signing for $12,500 opening day, then was told to move over to the Cardinals' Danville (Ill.) farm club until management decided he was lineup ready. So they docked him $2400 and when he led the league with a .349 average, he not only wanted that 15 grand, but also the money they had siphoned from his salary.

For 1931, they invited him from California to spring training in Florida. There, an impasse developed so heatedly that Hafey drove back across country, ripping his 1929 midnight-blue Auburn across ribbon-thin desert roads at 90 miles an hour.

Opening day, 1932, Sam Breadon and Branch Rickey sent the batting champion to Cincinnati for cold cash and a couple of warm bodies. Hafey put together two strong seasons at Cincinnati before illness kept him out virtually two full seasons and a token return. He was only 34 when he quit in 1937.

At Cincinnati, they missed his quiet humor, reflected when he couldn't stand the thundering snore of his roommate, big Ernie Lombardi, who drooped over small hotel beds. Hafey tied neckties around big Lom's ankles that hung over lip of the bed, then started a small fire in a waist can and shrieked. Lombardi, leaping up in a fog, tried to force himself out of the room door, lugging the bed behind him.

Hafey's own pull-hitting power with four pennant-winners in St. Louis was so powerful that starting pitchers, tuning up by throwing batting practice, made certain they kept the ball inside so the slugger might not accidentally slash one up the middle.

Phillies' third baseman Fresco Thompson had the right idea one day when Hafey floored him with a double off Thompson's shins. Next time, Fresco played so deep that the fleet Hafey beat out a bunt. When Chick returned to the bench, an ice-cream vendor leaned over the top of the dugout and called out, extending a confection. "Compliments of Mr. Thompson, Mr. Hafey," said the young man to Charles James (Chick) Hafey, "if you'll bunt again, Mr. Thompson said he'd send over another ice-cream bar."

JESSE HAINES

Terry Moore, captain and center fielder of the 1942 and '46 champion Cardinals, was regarded deservedly by other players as inspirational. Truth is, Moore learned his own lesson as a Gas House Gang rookie in 1935—from a 42-year-old "nice guy" pitcher.

Following a tough-luck defeat behind faulty fielding at Cincinnati, Tee Moore walked into a visitor's clubhouse torn up in anger by the guy they called "Pop"—Jess Haines. Master center fielder Moore never forgot, especially after having watched four close-call second-place finishes. "If," he recalled, "a man as old and as experienced as good ol' Pop could be so teed off by losing, I knew this is serious business."

That's the way Terry, then 23, followed it throughout his career, needling younger members. Slyly, Pop Haines himself was pretty good with a pep talk when tempermental Dizzy Dean sulked in a clubhouse in 1934, unwilling to pitch. At 41, in the sundown of a Redbird career record of 18 seasons for a pitcher, Haines sweet-talked Dean privately, reminding Dizzy that, by gosh, it sure would be nice to go out on one more pennant-winner. The soft-soaped super-star said he couldn't let down an old friend.

In the '34 World Series, won by the Gas Housers with two games each from the Dean brothers, Dizzy and Paul, the old-timer got one mop-up role for an inning, and Jesse Joseph (Pop) Haines briefly was as effective as he had been when pitching two winning games in the 1926 World Series and one in '30.

Haines, elected into the Hall of Fame in 1970, had only marginal credentials except in his heart and character. He won 210 games for second-division teams most of his early years, then put together three 20-game seasons, topped by 24 in 1927. And, as mentioned, he was a winner in big games when healthy, shutting out the Yankees in one game of the '26 Series, hitting a homer, and came off the ailing list to close down the powerful Philadelphia A's ín 1930.

Haines threw over the top with a good fast ball and a sinking knuckler, learned from the A's Eddie Rommel. Jesse gripped the ball with his knuckles, not the finger-tips by which the modern knuckler long-since has been incorrectly labeled. His ball skidded across the plate rather than fluttered.

Only when those knuckles were bleeding raw did Jesse give up in the seventh inning of the seventh game of the 1926 Series, his second victory saved by Pete Alexander's historic relief appearance.

Over the years through 1937, when he was 44, the affectionate nickname—"Pop"— became commonplace with the players, press and public. Unusually, Haines was bought by fellow Ohioan, Branch Rickey, from Kansas City of the American Association for $10,000, an amount (ahem!) Rickey just didn't have.

When late career roommate Burleigh Grimes became manager at Brooklyn, Haines went to the Dodgers briefly as pitching coach. Grizzled Ol' Stubblebeard Grimes summed up Pop Haines perhaps better than anyone except that impressed rookie, Terry Moore. At championship reunions, Grimes would rib his old roomie.

"Everyone thought I was a nasty and he was a nice guy," lamented Burleigh, "but he was a hard loser who knocked down as many hitters as I did."

Trouble was, when Grimes managed Brooklyn and Haines coached, they were too old to show young staff members to do it their winning ways. Jesse Hanies soon went back home to Philipsburg, Ohio, to win a county auditor's job he held as long as he had pitched.

ROGERS HORNSBY

The name sounded more like a big-band leader of the Roaring Twenties than a ball player and, deceptively, the man had hazel eyes, rosy cheeks and the cutest dimples, but handsome Rogers Hornsby was a tough-talking Texan whose tart tongue was almost as forceful as his big bat.

For 24 years, beginning with the Cardinals in 1915 at only 19, Hornsby probably was baseball's best pure hitter. His career average, .358, was the best ever for a righthanded hitter, highlighted by one five-year span averaging .400 and with the century's highest single-season figure, .424 in 1924.

Building his body with hard work on a ranch and heartier meals, when he understood manager Miller Huggins' thought he probably would have to be "farmed out," Hornsby fleshed out virtually overnight. He stood deep in the batter's box, bat motionless on his right shoulder and strode directly into the pitch.

Just after rival St. Louis Browns' manager, Fielder Jones, claimed to have developed the "secret" of pitching to Hornsby—"slow curves and low and away"—the kid won his first of seven batting titles. Best to remember Jones as the manager who led the Chicago White Sox's famed Hitless Wonders to the 1906 world championship.

Hornsby's weakness was not really a pitched ball (he didn't like golf because, as he put it, "When I hit a ball, I want someone else to chase it.") but in a rare display of baseball compassion he said he actually felt "sorry" for the opposing pitcher.

Hornsby's weakness playing second base was catching pop flies, a problem explained away tongue-in-cheek because he hit so few himself, but the major flaw was really to say what others might have thought. Although they called him The Rajah, a regal nickname he admired and yet to which he did not conform, he was really Mr. Blunt. Rog must have thought diplomacy was a respiratory disease.

Other than to tell clubowners to mind their own frigging business when they asked him how and why he did things—succeeding Branch Rickey as St. Louis's manager in 1925 he immediately threw away B. R.'s clubhouse blackboard—Hornsby's problem was slow horses if not fast women.

Hornsby's fascination with gambling probably cost him a chance to own a ball club, though he would grumble more about losing in the stock-market crash of 1929. So when he borrowed from his players as manager in 1932 at Chicago, he was relieved by general manager Bill Veeck, Sr. Baseball's first commissioner, Judge Landis, called Hornsby into his office.

Landis was disturbed also that angry Cubs had omitted Hornsby from any of their 1932 World Series shares even though they were second when he was fired in August. The Judge wanted to know and with a profanity even Hornsby could admire.

In his own defense, The Rajah suggested that at least on the race track he got a run for his money rather than in market. Hornsby was aware that the commissioner was touchy for having lost a good bit of baseball's money in a pie-in-the-sky scandal perpetrated by infamous Samuel Isbell.

Hornsby, flat broke, was lucky that Sam Breadon and Rickey of the Cardinals could persuade Landis to let them bring back the 37-year-old faded super-star for part-time play in '33. By mid-season when rival Frank Frisch was named manager, Rickey discreetly sweet-talked the rival Browns to take Hornsby as a big name manager who could play a little.

With the bumbling Browns, Hornsby soon had one of his finest hours when he pinch-hit against the champion Yankees and the great Lefty Gomez. With the braying Bombers chortling aloud, "Here's the great National League hitter, Mr. Hornsby," Rog hit the right field roof with a decisive homer.

Circling the bases, Hornsby touched home plate and blasted the Babe and rest, "Yeah, you ________, that was the great National League hitter, Mr. Hornsby."

Hornsby's run with the Brownies ended almost as abruptly as when the manager first sashayed into a bar across the street from Sportsman's Park and questioned the ethics of the undercover gambling man, Louis (Murph) Calcaterra. Murph decked Hornsby, who thereafter used a clubhouse boy to run his bets.

Once, when he hit big, he offered a cashier's check to repay the Browns' new boss, Donald L. Barnes, a small-loan operator. When Barnes challenged whether the money represented gambling winnings—bingo!—Rog hit the jackpot again. "If it is," he snapped, "it ain't from robbing widows and orphans!"

Presumably blacklisted unofficially from the big leagues, Hornsby was rescued in 1952 by the younger, promotional Bill Veeck, aware that The Rajah still had a magic following. Trouble was, times had caught and passed Hornsby at least in personal relations. When he wanted to relieve a pitcher with the Browns or briefly at Cincinnati in 1953, he would not stride to the mound, hold out his hand for the ball, pat a pitcher on the fanny and send him whistling to the showers. Rog would stand on the dugout steps, whistle to the mound, crook his finger with a baseball version of the old vaudeville hook, then beckon to the bullpen for a replacement.

UH-HUH, SARGE, I FEEL SORRY FOR THE PITCHERS: That was the philosophy of Rogers Hornsby (seated, center) as he talks with manager Gabby Street at spring training in 1933, the year The Rajah returned to the Redbirds. Coach Clyde (Buzzy) Wares listens at the left.

Happiest thereafter when running summer camps for a Chicago newspaper and the mayor—and he genuinely liked kids—Rog went to Wrigley Field or Comiskey Park only when the race tracks were dark. His salty pressbox banter won him another nickname for which even he smiled—Sweet Talk.

Sweet Talk Hornsby, still shunning movies to protect his valuable eyes even when flicks no longer flickered, oddly needed cataract surgery. In recovery, he died of a heart attack early in 1963 at 67, perhaps a teetotaling, smokeless victim of his two favorites—steaks and ice cream.

If he had lived long enough, Hornsby likely would have been baseball's longest-active Designated Hitter. When he delivered a base hit in near darkness in 1933, lining a base hit off flame-throwing Roy (Tarzan) Parmelee, the Giants' Bill Terry said admiringly at first base, "Rog, you proved what I always knew you could do—hit at midnight in the dark."

At 48, managing in the Mexican Winter

League in World War II, The Rajah was asked to pinch-hit with the bases loaded, his side three runs down after having won the opener of a three-game series. When Hornsby answered clubowner Jorge Pasquel's request and hit a game-winning grand-slam homer, the crowd was happy, but senor Pasquel was sad, "Mee-ster Hornsby," he wailed. "now you take suspense out of tomorrow's third game."

You can bet the next flight out of Vera Cruz that Hornsby was en route back to the States. Maybe with Pasquel he even used the same suggestion for an utterly impossible disposition that was similar to the you-know-what-you-can do recommendation to Sam Breadon that created the big breach at the height of his career.

By the time Hornsby applied a tag to Babe Ruth's spikes, completing the 1926 World Series, he recalled the hour as his finest even though his dear mother, Mary Rogers Hornsby, had died back home at Hornsby Bend, insisting her funeral could wait.

Her boy had become quite a man, especially after the Cardinals left cavernous Robison Field (League Park) for Sportsman's Park in 1920. With a reasonably sized park and more frequent use of a whiter ball, Rog went from .370 to .397, .401, .384, .424 and .403. In the most devastating season—.401 in 1922—his 250 hits included 42 homers, 152 RBIs and a National League record 450 total bases.

With farm-system creator Rickey's development not quite ready, boss Breadon relieved B.R. of his field command at Memorial Day in '25, giving the job to Hornsby. Mr. Rickey, seldom outsmarted, angrily wanted out of his stock holdings. Breadon counter-signed for Hornsby's $45,000. In a stormy scene, Rog got back $120,000.

The Rajah's first spring training team went all the way in 1926, St. Louis's first pennant since the American Association Browns of 1885-88. Two deals solidified the ball club, a mid-season move that brought Billy Southworth from New York to play right field and acquisition of aged pitching super-star Grover Cleveland Alexander on waivers.

Old Pete, falling out of favor with Joe McCarthy because of drinking and disrespect, was one of Hornsby's pitching cousins because Rog could hammer the old master's low-and-away delivery, but few others mistreated the 373-career winner. Rog wanted him. Alexander helped win the pennant, won two and saved one dramatically in a World Series upset over the Yankees.

As a player, Hornsby had been hurt and dipped to a .317 average, but now he wanted a $50,000-a-year contract at a time only Babe Ruth earned more. He wanted it for three years, too, a problem even if Breadon already wasn't angry because Hornsby had told him vulgarly how to dispose of a late-season exhibition game.

Although the move wasn't made until a December deal that spoiled Christmas for crushed Cardinal fans, indications are that Breadon early had made up his mind to make the super-star a limited offer he had to refuse. When the Hornsby trade for Frank Frisch was made, Breadon was denounced, but Frisch saved the situation in 1927.

Hornsby, long coveted by John McGraw, rebounded with a .367 average, 25 homers and 167 RBIs, but he displeased clubowner Horace Stoneham with his aloofness and blistered the ears of traveling secretary Jim Tierney for questions about playing-field decisions.

Stunningly, dealt to Boston, Hornsby hit .387 in his one year at Braves Field "against the wind," as admirer Casey Stengel later would remark sarcastically to moaning latter-day Boston players. Ol' Case was enamored, too, over Hornsby's quick-release peg across the chest on a double-play pivot. Hornsby served as player-manager when Jack Slattery was relieved of his duties after 31 games.

With the senior Veeck only one player

away from a pennant winner at Chicago, he wanted Hornsby. Rog persuaded Boston owner Judge Emil Fuchs, who was struggling financially, to take the money and run, five players and $200,000 when that sum would be more than a couple of million later.

At Chicago in 1929, hitting .380 with 40 homers, Hornsby scored 156 runs, drove in 149 and won his second Most Valuable Player award as the Cubs won the pennant.

Well into his 50s, Hornsby could step into a batting cage and hit line drives to all fields, particularly his power alley, right-center, but he never came close to full duty his last eight years as player and pilot. He suffered a broken leg early in 1930, costing the Cubs another pennant and McCarthy the managing job that went to the second baseman. Thereafter, painful heel spurs limited Hornsby's ability and his fielding range.

But not his fascination for horses that were slower than he became, nor his noble view of hypocrisy or his far less acceptable racial intolerance. When Mr. Blunt drove Satchel Paige hard at spring training in Hornsby's shortlived return to the Browns in 1952, Ol' Satch inquired:

"Mr. Rog, are ya trainin' us for baseball or for the U.S. Army?"

MILLER HUGGINS

If Miller Huggins had achieved his dream, i.e., buying the Cardinals when their lady owner wanted out, the Redbirds' entire future might have changed and most certainly the career and perhaps life of a mighty playing mite who proved to be a big man as a manager.

Huggins made a little go a long way as a pasty-faced, pint-sized player, only 5-6 and 140 pounds, who was a walk-wheedling leadoff man for 13 years in the National League, and a good second baseman.

As a manager, the Mighty Mite or, better still, his more familiar nickname, Hug, was a winner with a good ball club in St. Louis and a championship pilot with a good team in New York. At only 50, with his powerful Yankees finally coming up short in 1929, Huggins died of a blood disease.

Many mourned. Babe Ruth, whom he once had fined $5000 when the sum probably had the impact and virtual value of $100,000, cried in remorse and regret.

Miller James Huggins, a law graduate at his native Cincinnati, was traded by the Reds to the Cardinals in 1910, acquired by Roger Bresnahan, whom he replaced as manager after the 1912 season when Bresnahan capped one too many salty-tongue comments to owner Helene Hathaway Robison Britton. Mrs. Britton gave the job to her little 34-year-old second baseman.

Bresnahan not only went out screaming about his contract, which was settled favorably, but he pouted that Huggins had undermined him and tattled to the boss. Close observers couldn't agree, but if it's true that dear Lady Bee and mighty Miller cared for each other, Helene had divorced her playboy husband and Hug was a bachelor.

For the dear lady, Huggins offered no immediate improvement his first year, but despite the presence of a third St. Louis big-league team, the Federals, when two might have been one too many, Huggins and his team rose in 1914. Their third-place finish—excitement was so great in late August that 27,000 crammed into 17,000 seat Robison Field for a midweek double-header with the Giants—was St. Louis's finest since the first National League team came home second in 1876.

Aggravatingly, as true too many times, the ball club waffled back into the second division the next two years, combining with other factors for Mrs. Britton to want out. With an apparent oral option, Huggins went back home, seeking financial backing from the Fleischmann yeast family.

The price, $375,000, was right, but Lady Bee's attorney, James C. Jones, figured with perspicacity that ownership by St. Louis people might be better. Public auction at $50 a pop brought in many fans, including a bright young automobile dealer named Sam Breadon.

At a request of sports editors and baseball writers Jones consulted, the consensus was for Branch Rickey, field and business

MILLER JAMES HUGGINS: Little self-made player, long-time winning manager, Hall of Fame inductee, 1964.

manager of the rival Browns. The Brownie boss, Phil Ball, didn't like Rickey, but his obstinate "no" to Rickey's departure was lost in court. So Huggins, hurt by his own missed chance to operate the Cardinals, used another strong third-place finish in 1917 to face a ruminative crossroads.

American League president Ban Johnson, who hated the National's guts, recommended Huggins to Yankee owner Jake Ruppert. Bolstered by the acquisition of Babe Ruth and others from the Red Sox rummage sale, Huggins put together a Yankee ball club that won six pennants and three world champions his last nine years.

Now if Hug had won the rights to Redbird ownership, assuming certainly no franchise shift at least in his day, Rickey undoubtedly wouldn't have been aboard for the Cardinals, using Breadon's financial windfall to set up an unprecedented farm system. That grow-your-own concept was climaxed by the 1926 pennant winners, first of two that faced Huggins' Yankees.

The first one, 1926, dramatically pitted Huggins against the young infielder he had brought up late in the 1915 season, Rogers Hornsby. It was Hug who encouraged the peppy young Texan even if Rog misunderstood that he ought to be "farmed out" for development. Heck, Hornsby worked the fields so hard and ate so many steaks and drank enough pure milk over the winter that his weight increased to 180 pounds.

By the time Huggins went east, Hornsby was ready to go to the top as a hitter, capping his career with a World Series upset over the Yankees, achieved when he tagged out Babe Ruth on a Series-ending attempt to steal second base.

The Babe gave Huggins many a headache with his actions off the field and contempt of authority. "The little runt,"as the Babe described the might mite, stuck it to Ruth with that $5000 fine in a disastrous seventh-place season, 1925.

Although the Babe ranted and raved, Ruppert stuck behind the manager. Ultimately, the big star understood the little manager. By the time the Babe, Lou Gehrig and associates murdered the Redbirds in a 1928 Series reprise, Huggins was so stiff that he lost his false teeth on the victory train ride back to New York.

A year later Miller James Huggins, who once fortunately lost the Cardinals, unfortunately lost his life.

RABBIT MARANVILLE

One of the reasons that Rabbit Maranville made the baseball Hall of Fame was that he was among the shortest, oldest and funniest ever to play the game, a Peter Pan or, more accurately, a Peck's Bad Boy.

Fact is, playing 23 major league seasons with a National League record for games as a shortstop, 2153, the Springfield (Mass.) Irishman was the smallest this century to reach Cooperstown—5-5 , 155 pounds—and he was forced to quit at nearly age 45 because he'd suffered a broken leg.

A tough cookie as well as obviously durable, but a smart one, dazzling afield with an amusing waist-high catch of pop flies, one that Willie Mays later used in the outfield. Only a .258 career hitter, Walter James Vincent Maranville was at his best in two short World Series, 1914 and 1928, hitting .308 each time.

The Rabbit won his major-league job the hard way, beating out the nephew of the boss, manager George Stallings, then serving as a leader in the Braves' remarkable last-to-first surge in '14.

Fourteen years later, resurrected from the minors by St. Louis's Branch Rickey, Maranville came up just too late to help the Cardinals in 1927, but played enough to shore up shortstop in a pennant-winning '28. "If," beefed second baseman Frank Frisch, "they had brought up the Rab a couple of weeks earlier in '27, we'd have won that one, too."

With a handshake agreement with Rickey to return to Rochester as player-manager, an embittered Maranville was sold back to Boston for 1929. Four years later, as mentioned, until the broken leg forced him out early in 1935, Peter Pan played short and then second base.

Always, though, the Peck's Bad Boy. At St. Louis, playing for a sharp manager, Bill McKechnie, who fancied himself on infield play, Maranville slyly would countermand the manager by belatedly moving third baseman Andy High. '"Usually," High would recall, "with uncanny judgment."

The Rabbit couldn't resist being the merry Maranville of old in the pennant-winning St. Louis season when he watched a teammate, underpaid and a cheapskate or both, slip his wife onto a sleeping car and into his berth just before a midnight departure. Rab tattled to the train conductor and watched with silent glee at morning departure when the railroad guy put the bite on the bashful, embarrassed athlete.

A good-natured guy—honest!—Maranville ran summer baseball camps for a New York newspaper and died at 63 in 1954, just weeks before the baseball writers honored him with Hall of Fame election.

TOMMY McCARTHY

Maybe, just maybe, the oldest version of Hall of Fame old-timer voters must have thought they were seeing double when the guy next to Hugh Duffy looked like the leprechaun center fielder credited with a .440 average in 1894.

Regardless, Tommy McCarthy—Thomas Francis Michael McCarthy—is in the Hall of Fame, so chalk one up for the old American Association St. Louis Browns because it was with Chris Von der Ahe's Brownies that McCarthy and had his best season.

In 1890, his third of four seasons in St. Louis, McCarthy not only hit .350 and stole a league-leading 83 bases, but he also had a cup of coffee or, if you prefer as he would, a stein of beer as one of Von der Ahe's many shortlived managers.

Tommy had one other distinction. He's the only player of the shortlived Union Association to make it to the hallowed Halls of Cooperstown. A rookie at 21, trying unsuccessfully to pitch in the Union, McCarthy couldn't pitch and didn't hit, either, but he got his foot into the outfield of the home-town Boston Beaneaters the next year.

Oh, he was a sly one, that personable Irish lad—same height, 5-7, and size, 165-170 pounds, of the brilliant Duffy—when they were regarded as the "Heavenly Twins" by the Boston faithful. That McCarthy boy, he'd fake a bunt, draw in the third baseman and then spank the ball past him.

Defensively, ah, that Irish lad was a tricky one, too. Playing outfield shallowly and occasionally the infield, he'd let pop flies drop and then scoop 'em up on the short bounce. If you wonder whether that one had a hand—or sleight of hand—in hastening the long-standing infield-fly rule, chances are he did.

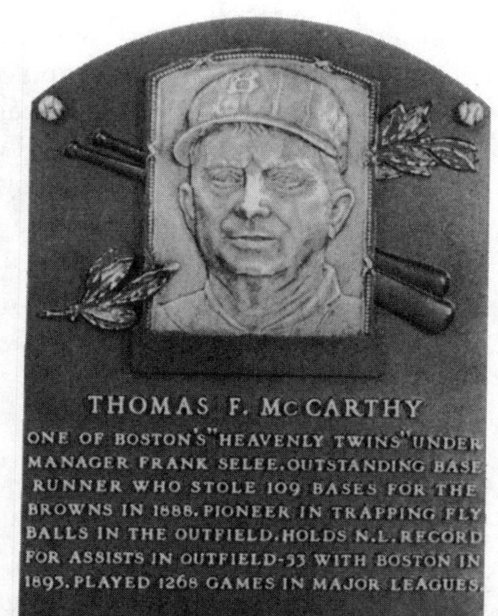

So he figured often in the news, especially coming back from the wild West—St. Louis—after playing on Charley Comiskey's last Association pennant winners in 1888. He didn't help as much with his .274 average as he did the next three years with averages of .291, .350 and .309.

When the Association folded and the National League took in four clubs, they penalized Von der Ahe by stripping him of players he hadn't already sold. So most certainly Boston was interested in the 29-year-old Duffy look-alike.

Mac was overmatched in 1892, the last season of the 55-foot pitching distance, hitting only .242, but he climbed to .346 in 1893 and Duffy went from .301 to .361 when pitchers retreated to the classic 60-foot 6 inches. Next year when Tommy got to .349, little Hughie sprayed around hits for his lofty .440, long recognized as .438.

A couple of years later the Irish twain or, as labeled "Heavenly Twins", were separated with McCarthy finishing at .242 in 1896 at Brooklyn and only a .292 career total. Duffy, three years younger than his 33-year-old shadow, played 10 years more with an overall .324 average.

Long a Fenway fixture as a coach for the Red Sox, Hughie got the Cooperstown call in 1945, nine years before his death at 88. The other fella, McCarthy, after managing in the minors, ran for years a bowling alley and saloon he called "Duffy and McCarthy."

The public never forgot Thomas Francis Michael McCarthy. Neither, obviously, did the Veterans Committee. Dead since 1922, Tommy was elected into the Hall of Fame just a year after his pony pal from Boston's outfield meadows.

JOHN McGRAW

Even though John J. McGraw ceremoniously dumped his Redbird uniform into the Mississippi River, en route back east after his one and only season with the Cardinals, 1900, it was nice that Little Napoleon graced St. Louis with his presence—even though Muggsy thought a St. Louis team had to be 25 percent stronger because of the summer heat.

Actually, McGraw hated St. Louis as much as he did that nickname—"Muggsy"—used to describe a savory political figure in Baltimore, where the stormy little third baseman, gifted and most aggressive, had helped build a championship dynasty. By 1898, Mac even had succeeded to playing manager of the old Orioles.

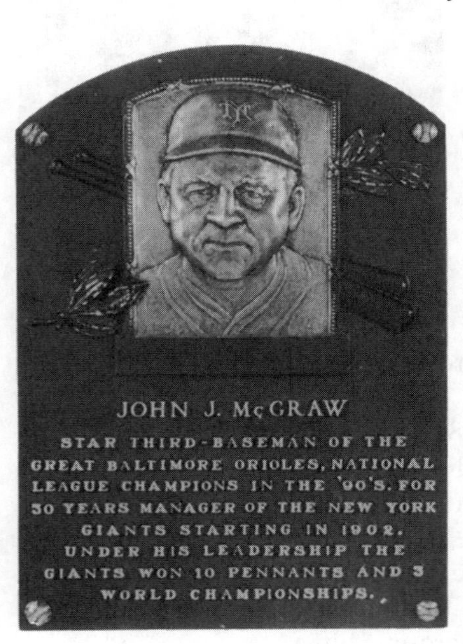

After a realignment, the crabcake capital was muscled out of the majors. Physically ailing, but more annoyed, the .391-hitting future Hall of Famer refused to accept reassignment elsewhere. He agreed only to join the drooling Robison brothers of the new-look Redbirds for $100-a-game and no option on his services. Johnny Mac knew Ban Johnson would expand his Western League into the American League and to Baltimore.

So McGraw and henchman Wilbert Robinson, a catcher, joined the Cardinals at Robison Field, which, unfortunately, then was located across the street from a handsome race track, Fairground Park. If he was out of the lineup with injuries or kicked out of a game early, McGraw spent his free hours trying to figure out win, place and show. He was a lifelong horse bettor.

Playing 99 games worth—$9900 was big money at the turn of the century—McGraw did well enough, batting .344, 11 points higher than his career average for 16 years of service.

In St. Louis, living in a boarding house close by the ball park, typically in a time of limited transportation, McGraw took a shine to a little, four-eyed neighbor kid eager to learn from Mr. McGraw. That kid, Sid C. Keener, became a long-time St. Louis sports editor.

McGraw, giving his uniform the deep six after another disappointing fifth-place season for the Cardinals, went back to Baltimore as player-manager in the new American League, but, shucks, the league wasn't big enough for league president Ban Johnson, strong in his support for the umpires, and for the cocky bantam rooster who liked to take it out on the arbiters.

Within a year, McGraw jumped back into the National League with the New York Giants as manager, beginning a 30-year stretch of nine pennants and three world championships. He became as big as the bright lights on Broadway, where he was a fast-living celebrity. By contrast, in his dugout he was a managerial martinet and, though behind his back, the players might call him "the old man," up front and out center he was addressed by his athletes as "Mr. McGraw!"

Caustic at times, especially to his club captains, but generous with an out-of-the-pocket 20 bucks for a big play, McGraw could be physical with too much to drink or when angry. As, for instance, the time St. Louis photographer Bob Artega, taking a picture of McGraw and his staff for *The Sporting News*, saw coach Dave Bancroft meander too slowly for the impatient manager. McGraw, still in uniform before winding up like Connie Mack in civvies, kicked Bancroft so severely in the seat with spiked shoes that blood seeped through the chastised coach's flannels.

At least no one was wearing the pants of the uniform John Joseph McGraw dumped into the drink when bidding St. Louis farewell as a player.

BILL McKECHNIE

Bill McKechnie was a rare bird, the first major-league manager to win pennants in three cities and one of the few fired after having won a pennant, which he did for the Cardinals in 1928.

A pleasant man, yet firm enough to last for four pennants in 25 years as a skipper, McKechnie was a wily Scot from Wilkinsburg, Pa., nicknamed "Deacon Will" because he spent a quarter-century in the Methodist church choir there.

McKechnie wasn't good enough in an 11-year career as a good-field, no-hit infielder, but he was a thinking man's manager, best known for his development of pitchers. Frank Frisch, who had played for John McGraw at New York, thought McKechnie was masterful at holding back his best pinch-hitter to the most meaningful opportunity.

As far back as 1914, when he broke away as a Yankee benchwarmer, McKechnie joined the Newark Federal League team as player-manager at only 29, but his next managerial chance didn't come until 1922 when the home-town area Pirates hired him in mid-summer to replace George Gibson.

At Pittsburgh, Bill gave the Buccos their first flag since the Jolly Rogers of Fred Clarke 's perennial early-century champions. Trouble was, Clarke returned to the bench as a front-office executive and "coach" who second-guessed McKechnie. As result, the Deacon was fired following a third-place finish in 1926.

Strangely, success taunted and flaunted McKechnie those early managerial years. He had won a world championship over Washington in 1925, but by '27 he was coaching for the Cardinals. Promoted to manager in '28 after Bob O'Farrell was reduced in ranks, McKechnie won the pennant. However, after his Redbirds were whipped four straight games by the Yankees in the World Series, he was relieved of the job.

Embarrassed, clubowner Sam Breadon thought McKechnie had been too impassive in the Series in which Babe Ruth and Lou Gehrig perpetrated the most awesome 1-2 punch in Series history. If Bill made any mistake, it was not walking the midway monsters more often.

Breadon encouraged McKechnie to swap jobs with Billy Southworth at Rochester, but after 90 games with his pennant-winners two games under .500, Breadon flip-flopped the two men. McKechnie returned to St. Louis and won five games more than he lost. Breadon was prepared to retain the manager, but Deacon didn't like the odds.

McKechnie took a long-term contract from the moribund Boston Braves in 1930 and, though his '35 team suffered the humiliation of a miserable last-place finish with a 38-115 record, he impressed observers, trying to making chicken salad out of chicken feathers for eight years. By 1937, he had turned the team into a fifth-place winner with a 79-73 record and got his reward.

Warren Giles, for whom he had worked when Giles general-managed Rochester, replaced Larry MacPhail at Cincinnati. Giles hired McKechnie. Bill's second and third years the Reds won their first pennants in 20 years and added a world championship over Detroit in 1940. The shrewd manager, keeping the grass at Crosley Field high, won it all there behind pitchers Bucky Walters and Paul Derringer just as two veteran pitchers at Boston, Jim Turner and Lou Fette, had come through for him.

McKechnie lasted nine years in Cincinnati, fired reluctantly by Giles after a sixth-place finish in 1946. Cleveland's Bill Veeck, eager to bolster player-manager Lou Boudreau, immediately hired McKechnie as a coach.

When Player-of-the-year Boudreau daringly used outfielder Allie Clark for the one-game pennant playoff against the Red Sox in 1948, Veeck and vice-president Hank Greenberg cautioned against the move. Reflecting years later after the bold venture worked, Boudreau said, "I knew I was right because Bill McKechnie agreed with me."

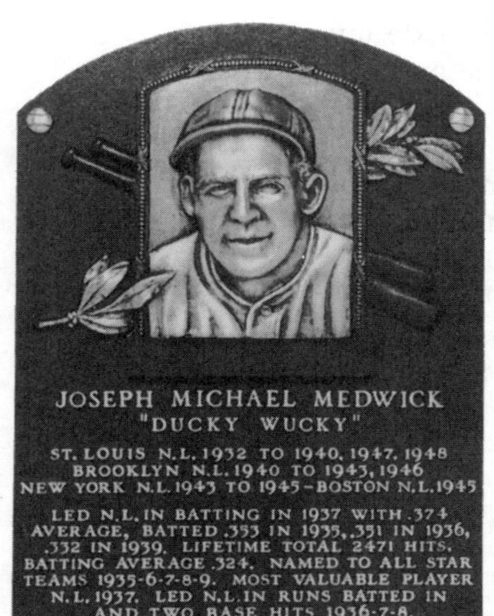

McKechnie lived for years in Bradenton, Fla., where the Pirates' playing field is named for him. Deacon Will was a nice man to the end at 79 in 1965, three years after his Hall of Fame induction. Except one night when a burglar attempted to steal his assets, the gentle former manager floored him with his bed lamp.

"I worked too hard for what I've got," explained William Boyd McKechnie, as they led away the young target, surprised that he had been bounced by old Deacon Will for a trip to jail.

JOE MEDWICK

If, as Frank Frisch conjectured with amusing exaggeration, Joe Medwick had had a bat in his hand when he faced 40,000 frustrated, angry Detroit fans at old Navin Field in 1934, "The odds would have been even."

With that big brown bat in his hands itching to hit anything, including the baseball and an opposing player's chin or a teammate's, Joseph Michael Medwick was indeed a manacing figure. Actually, too, though a stubborn, hot-headed, second-generation Hungarian, he was a practical man, too.

Back there in the seventh inning of the seventh game of the '34 World Series, one in which St. Louis's Gas House Gang twisted the Tigers' tail, Medwick's closest teammate, Leo Durocher, came out to left field to console a player at whom the unhappy defeated fans were throwing everything, including a fit. Said Lippy Leo to Muscles, "Don't let 'em scare you, kid."

Medwick snorted, "Here, you play left field and I'll play shortstop."

A couple of Detroit detectives ate dinner that evening in Medwick's hotel room and then put the 22-year-old slugger on the midnight train to St. Louis. So Medwick didn't have that bat in his hands to make things even with the crowd that thought he deliberately had cut Marvin Owen with his spikes.

Instead, bowing to the mob when he might have threatened to forfeit the game, Judge Landis, himself a tough bird as commissioner, told Medwick to take his 11 Series hits into the clubhouse. Ultimately, Dizzy Dean coasted to an 11-0 cakewalk.

If Medwick resented a chance at missing an opportunity for a record-tying 12th hit, has anger was minor to one a year earlier, his first full season. In a game at New York, teammate Ethan Allen, batting out of turn in Medwick's place, hit a homer. The run, immediately cancelled by a Giants' appeal, created a putout and a time at bat charged to the proper batter—Medwick!

Wow, it's a good thing Allen was back up there, this time popping out, before Medwick could have swung something at him, a bat or a fist. By the Hungarian Rhapsody, Muscular Magyar or any other fancy sobriquet, Medwick was just about the most cantankerous member of Frisch's rowdy roughnecks, the Gas Housers. Therefore, the old Flash's favorite—Joey.

Medwick was one of the best hitters of his time, most certainly the best bad-ball hitter, hitching his left leg toward third base instead of back toward the mound, throwing his hips into the pitch. So the righthanded .324 career hitter was devastating to all fields, especially right-center.

Medwick, a great all-around athlete at Carteret, N.J., turned down a football scholarship from Notre Dame's Knute Rockne and, playing under a nickname he liked and seldom heard, "Mickey" used King briefly as a surname. He hit .419 in the old Mid-Atlantic League in 1930 and soon was beating down fences in the Texas League.

The olive-skinned, handsome Medwick had a duck-wobbling walk, and soon had inspired a short-lived candy bar. By the time he joined the Cardinals late in the 1932 season—no wonder they sold batting champion Chick Hafey that spring—the Ducky-Wucky had been shortened to Ducky or to a nickname he liked best: Muscles!

From that month-long .349 start, Medwick was as devastating as his line drives and his tendency to hit more doubles than homers. Over one three-year stretch, leading in two-bases hits, Muscles had 64, 56 and 47 doubles.

With Frisch applauding from the field or the bench, then putting Johnny Mize into the muscular middle of the batting order, Medwick rewarded the "Dutchman" with three successive seasons of .353, .351, and a Triple-Crown .374. That year, 1937, Medwick not only also led with homers, 31, and RBIs, 154, but base hits, 237, his 56 doubles and 111 runs scored.

Those were happy, yet frustrating seasons for Medwick, trying to get a salary that would keep a lovely socialite bride in the style to which she was accustomed. Always, Branch Rickey had a criticism of his fielding or whatever.

After that triple-dip dandy season, the player wondered triumphantly what the general manager would find wrong with that one. B.R. dutifully suggested he see "Mr. Breadon." By now, Joe was the sassy protege of a fellow adopted St. Louisan, Durocher, who had taught him the finest haberdashery and other touches. They were manifest one time in an argument with Breadon over $2000. Said the boss, "It's just a matter of principle, Joe. I'd just as soon throw the $2000 out the window."

"If you did, Mr. Breadon,"wisecracked Medwick, "your arm still would be holding it."

With Medwick not endearing himself with new manager Ray Blades, who used late-inning defensive replacements for him, the player also angered labor union members who needled him for riding with Durocher and Leo's dress-designing wife across garment factory picket lines. The excuse enabled Breadon to sell Medwick and pitcher Curt Davis to Brooklyn early in 1940 for $125,000 and four stiffs.

Quickly, Medwick's career took a downward turn after Joe and Durocher met former Redbird teammates in an unpleasant exchange in a New York hotel elevator. At one point in rejoinder, Redbird righthander Bob Bowman threatened to "stick one" in Medwick's ear. Accidentally or not, he did, leading to a fight at Ebbets Field and—worse—Medwick as a hitter who lost some of his savagery.

Muscles helped Durocher win the 1941 pennant with a .318 season of little power. By the time World War II ended, Joe had bounced from the Dodgers to the Giants to the Boston Braves, then had been cut loose by the Yankees before swinging a bat in 1947.

One early-season Sunday, signed that morning by the Cardinals, famed number "7" stepped up in a new number as a pinch-hitter. A surprise crowd gasped, then roared. And when he hit one off the right-center field wall for a double, he got a standing-room reception.

For the next season and a half, usually pinch-hitting, Muscles was again the bad-ball-batting terror who years earlier had bought his evening newspaper on a drive-by stop from an awed kid impressed with his hitting and his technique. Yogi Berra, the awed kid, didn't hit too many strikes, either.

JOHNNY MIZE

If Johnny Mize's nickname—the "Big Cat", hung on him derisively by teammate Buddy Blattner—had meant that the giant Georgian was a good fielder at first base, heck, the Hall of Fame's Veterans Committee wouldn't have had to tap him for Cooperstown.

After all, John Robert Mize, the slugging

The Other "M-Man": Johnny Mize played only the last month of the 1941 season with Stan Musial. The Man Stan, like Terry Moore, Enos Slaughter and Marty Marion, thought Mize could have helped win more pennants in St. Louis.

son of the South, was an outstanding hitter, better than a .312 career average. Of the mighty Mize, then playing with St. Louis in a career that featured two New York clubs, Casey Stengel put it best.

Then managing the lowly Boston Braves and regarded as a comic-opera character rather than a smart man, Stengel said admiringly in 1941, "Mize is a slugger who hits like a leadoff man."

Indeed, rarely striking out, a rarity for a power hitter, he could swish the long ball to right field with a sweet swing or reach out and stroke a base hit to left. His averages of .329, .364, .337, .349, .314, .317, .305, .337 and .302 for his first nine seasons speak for themselves. So does his power production.

A 6-2, 215-pound husky even before he ballooned, Mize came out of Demorest, Ga., his birth and burial place, as a good prospective college basketball player who preferred to swing at the ball. Yet only a physical mishap and a gifted surgeon's skill kept him for the Cardinals when Branch had him dealt to Cincinnati.

Before the caveat emptor approach by a commissioner would freeze damaged goods on a roster, the Reds appealed. Rickey took back the round-faced athlete bothered by a painful spur growth in his groin area. St. Louis' Dr. Robert F. Hyland, designated by Judge Landis in tribute as "the surgeon-general of baseball," repaired the problem.

A year later, 1936, as a rookie with the Redbirds, spelling ailing Ripper Collins at first base when neither could play the outfield, Mize broke in robustly with that .329 average and 19 homers in 126 games.

From then until Joe Medwick was dealt to Brooklyn a year before he was shipped to the Giants, Mize and Medwick teamed for a mid-lineup "M and M" combination, the kind New York would know later with Roger Maris and Mickey Mantle.

Mize's average went up and his homers, too, though Rickey grumbled after big Jawn's league-leading .349, 28 homers and 108 RBIs in 1939, that he ought to hit more dingers in a small ball park. "So I hit 43 the next year, but they (Rickey and Sam Breadon) said I'd let my average drop too far," Johnny groaned.

Mize's .314 with a still-standing St. Louis record of 43 homers, one more than Rogers Hornsby's output in 1922, won him second-place finish to Cincinnati first baseman Frank McCormick in the MVP race. Mize led in RBIs with 137.

With the swift team Rickey had built and Billy Southworth managed, the ponderous first baseman didn't quite fit in, creating some unhappiness in the front office and from the field foreman when he sat out often with a bad thumb in 1941, a year a ball club of major injuries lost the pennant in a courageous close race with the Dodgers.

So the dip to .317 with 16 homers in 126 games brought a deal with the Giants a week after Pearl Harbor, at a time higher salaries and service vulnerabilities became manifest. New York gave up three players and $50,000 for Mize, who was service bound a year later.

Over close-call pennant races lost in the post-war period, established St. Louis players would lament the loss of Mize's firepower and Walker Cooper's, also sold for delivery to the Polo Grounds. The Cardinals' first-base shortage ultimately required Stan Musial to move in from the outfield.

At New York, rooming with St. Louis infielder Blattner, later a topflight broadcaster, the Big Cat sweated off service suet by playing table tennis in a tent, swathed in a rubber sweat suit. Adjusting in the Polo Grounds, Mize emerged with 51 home runs in 1947, tying Pittsburgh's young Ralph Kiner. Amazingly, Johnny struck out only 42 times. A year later, hitting 40 homers, he whiffed just 37 times.

By August of 1949, the 35-year-old Mize had felt the brush of Leo Durocher, hired to replace Mel Ott. Obviously Mize didn't fit Leo's notion of nine nimble players. Typically in the Yankees' surge to pennants, encouraged by Casey Stengel, the American League club bought Mize for $40,000.

For Ol' Case, the Big Cat was one more arsenal, starting or pinch-hitting, finding Yankee Stadium's right-field Ruthville with a frequency that delighted the Babe's widow for whom Mize was a shirt-tail relative.

Although his average dipped, the firepower remained and he helped the Yankees to five straight pennants, including league-leading totals in pinch-hit appearances (61) and pinch hits (19) his last season, 1953, when he was 40. The peak production, though, occurred in '50 when Mize homered 25 times in just 90 games and 274 times up.

As late as 1952, retirement age for most players, Mize came alive in a Series win over the Dodgers, contributing three homers and a double in 15 trips over five games. Yes, if John Robert Mize had been the Big Cat in fact as well as fancy, he would have been an early baseball writers' Hall of Fame choice rather than a 1981 Veterans' nominee, 12 years before he died.

After all, the drawling chatterbox, who looked like Gen. Norman Schwartzkopf, is the only player to hit three homers in a game six times.

STAN MUSIAL

Once upon a time an angel in charge of taking care of nice guys answered an emergency call to help a handsome Slavic kid faced with a problem as a dead-armed baseball pitcher with a wife to feed and an infant son. The sentimental seraph swooped down with a miracle wand, touched the young man's bat and, lo, overnight Stan Musial became one of the best hitters ever and a great player.

Fact is, except for the left arm injured a year earlier in an outfield fall in Class "D", then baseball's lowest rung on the steep ladder to the majors, Musial would have wound up a perfect player, a star with no first-person temperament.

If this sounds syrupy, the authors of this encyclopedia of St. Louis's baseball past and present emphasize that they hoped to have both feet on the ground in assessment of talent as Musial did in displaying it. Truthfully, since the National League's first season in St. Louis, 1876, the old major Association's debut in 1882 and the return of the National as the turn-of-the-century Redbirds, no player has captivated so many constantly as Stan the Man.

He was, in short, the best player in a town that had so many as reflected by Hall of Fame individuals and by championship ball clubs. The first retired Redbird number—"6"—stands in bronze at the northeast corner of Busch Stadium.

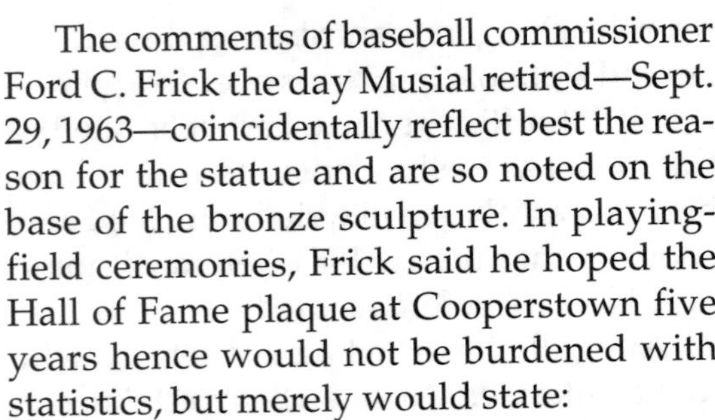

The comments of baseball commissioner Ford C. Frick the day Musial retired—Sept. 29, 1963—coincidentally reflect best the reason for the statue and are so noted on the base of the bronze sculpture. In playing-field ceremonies, Frick said he hoped the Hall of Fame plaque at Cooperstown five years hence would not be burdened with statistics, but merely would state:

"Here stands baseball's perfect warrior, here stands baseball's perfect knight."

Here, indeed, stands a fairy tale actually too sugary for a Walt Disney script. In the summer of 1940, sitting in a Florida rooming house, keeping score like any rabid baseball fan at the radio account of the All-Star game at Sportsman's Park, the 19-year-old kid almost helped the big club Cardinals win a National League pennant the next season on the same St. Louis field.

What's in a Number?: When Stan Musial came up late in the 1941 season, he was handed "19," shown here. Next spring, equipment manager Butch Yatkeman gave him the number he made famous – "6" – one last worn by former second basemen, Stu Martin and then Floyd (Pep) Young.

The surge from sore-armed Class "D" pitcher, spurned the spring of '41 by minor league managers in Class "A" and Class "B", was incredible. The angel found him as an outfielder accepted by Ollie Vanek, playing pilot at Springfield, Mo., and a man who had scouted him three years earlier.

Amazingly, the trim, fleet player could have won three batting championships that Cinderella season—Springfield in the Western Association, Rochester, N.Y., in the International League and St. Louis in the National—if he had stayed long enough.

If Rochester just had been eliminated earlier from the International League playoffs, maybe—just maybe No. "19"—"6" became his historic number when Floyd Young was dropped in 1942—just might have made a difference. He popped up on the first knuckler he ever saw, thrown by Boston's Jim Tobin, but he tattooed the right-field wall with the second for a double. In a dozen sizzling games he hit .426—20 for 47—as the crippled Cardinals hung tough in their season-long struggle with Brooklyn. They finished two and a half games out, just after Musial had thrilled himself and family and friends with his first homer off Rip Sewell at Pittsburgh.

By then, he had provided a laugh for the Cardinals as well as considerable help. The laugh came when he innocently mentioned to Terry Moore and Johnny Mize, he had seen them before. "You guys hit homers off me in Georgia when you were barnstorming north."

His greatest contributions came in the final home games with the race still on. Against the Cubs, playing left field in the first game, he made two diving catches and threw out a runner at the plate. Following his fourth hit and second double, he scored spectacularly from second with the winning run on a soft infield single toward third base. Second game, playing right, making it a six-hit day, he singled and beat out a bunt. Afield, he dived to his right for one liner, then charged and made a double-somersault grab of another dipping drive.

Cubs manager Jimmy Wilson was furious. "Nobody can be that good," he exploded, "nobody!"

No, but good enough to star on four pennant-winning ball clubs his first four full seasons in the majors, to win two of his seven batting championships, two of his Most Valuable Player awards and to become the highest-priced handyman of his day, en route to 3630 hits and innumerable records.

This was, to be sure, fairy-tale fast and a far cry from a suburban Pittsburgh scenario, Donora, Pa., where his wiry Polish immigrant father met Musial's mother, a sturdy second-generation Czech who as a hearty girl had rowed her father across the turgid Monongahela river to the mine fields.

Times were tough for a large family, but the boy's first gift from his mother was a ball. At 13, neighbor Joe Barboa, who had played minor-league ball, permitted the kid—to elder players' dissent—to participate with grown men in zinc-mill ball games. And he was so good in basketball that Lukasz Musial dreamed of Stanley Frank Musial—"Stashu" to him—taking the offered University of Pittsburgh scholarship.

If he had gone to college or, worse, if he had failed in baseball, Stan might have been down on his financial luck, as were so many of his boyhood buddies when the mines closed and the smoke stacks of the zinc mills went cold, but mother Mary stubbornly bulldozed Lukasz into appreciating, reluctantly, that this was a free country not to go to college if the boy didn't want to.

So for $65-a-month, scouted by Ollie Vanek and signed by the Monessen farm club for future delivery, Musial's name appeared on a professional contact when he was only a 17-year-old high-school junior. Married on his nineteenth birthday to lovely Lillian Labash, who said she fell in love with Stan's legs and Musial with her father's grocery-store lunch meat, the crisis came in his fragmentary fourth professional season.

Although he was strong-armed and wild, he still had won 18 games and lost only 5, batting .311 as a part-time outfielder at Daytona Beach, Fla., but he had fallen heavily on his pitching shoulder in an outfield mishap. Moved up more to protect him from loss in the draft rather than promise, he simply couldn't throw when he reported to Columbus, Ohio, at Hollywood, Fla., in 1941.

This was the burden when the $100-a-month 20-year-old with a wife and baby needed a friend who would take him as an outfielder because Branch Rickey had liked the sound of the ball off his bat. Stan found one, Vanek, and maybe that angel in the outfield because the magic wand—and his bat—created a bottom-to-top sensation.

That first full season, 1942, he became the swiftest of the St. Louis Swifties, as Billy Southworth's hare-and-hounds were labeled. They won a spectacular season, 106-48, by just two games, a result of a 42-of-52 surge. Musial batted .315, third high in the league. When the Cardinals upset the Yankees in a five-game World Series, he stood crying for joy in departure at New York's Penn Station and for good reason—his skimpy $4250 rookie salary just had been virtually doubled by a $6000 World Series check.

Dear Cardinal fan,

I hope that you like this autographed picture of your favorite Cardinal player. Best wishes.

AUGUST A. BUSCH, JR.

In 1943, en route to a .357 batting championship and also league-leading with 220 hits, 48 doubles and 20 triples, Musial experienced a battle with a "beanbag" ball, the balata, a sad war-time substitute for the rubber center. Run scoring and homer hitting dipped dramatically into the dead-ball era until permission was obtained to use Spalding's 1942 ball. The world champions didn't even score until Stan stole home in the third game. Southworth pleaded with players to choke batting grips.

Musial's power began to manifest itself after the war when, moving to first base to solve a problem, he hit .365 for the pennant-winning 1946 club and included 16 homers to go with first-place totals in hits, 226; doubles, 56; triples, 20; and runs scored, 124.

Even when sidelined briefly with strength-sapping appendicitis in 1947, playing five fewer games and hitting "only" .312, he hit 19 homers. Appendix out and infected tonsils, too, he came out smoking in 1948, winning his third MVP with a savage .376 season marked by 230 hits that missed by just one home run—rained out—of becoming the first batter ever to lead in average, runs scored, hits, doubles, triples, homers and RBIs. His 39-homer output, second to 40 by Ralph Kiner and Johnny Mize, produced the first .700 slugging season (.702) since Hack Wilson's 56-homer, 190 RBIs orgy with the Chicago Cubs in

1930, and Musial's 103 long hits were the most since Chuck Klein's record 107 in Philadelphia's bandbox Baker Bowl the same '30 season.

By then, the Donora Greyhound had become The Man, as nicknamed by admiring Brooklyn fans. (You didn't have to be a brain scientist to make it "Stan the Man".) Amazingly, the Flatbush faithful saluted Stan as "The Man"—even before he hit above .500 against the dimpled darling Dodgers two straight years!

Over a period of good—but not good-enough play—for the Cardinals, his boxoffice value and the far-flung radio network of the Redbirds made Musial worth his weight in gold as, first ever to play 1000 games each in the infield and outfield, he became the first salaried National Leaguer at $100,000.

The prestigious pay hike of hitting consistently close to .340 came just after a dip to .319 in 1955 and .310 in '56. A controversial trade of close friend and road roommate Red Schoendienst brought a new roommate and an inherited cigarette-smoking habit that, Musial conceded, wasn't healthy or helpful.

Nixing the nicotine habit for 1957, he also adjusted his crouched stance, even deeper in the box, to compensate for the slider, a pitch Musial and American League rival Ted Williams both respected. Revived, The Man picked up his pace for the seventh batting title, even though forced by a hairline shoulder fracture in August to punch at the ball down the stretch of a close race lost to Schoendienst's Milwaukee. His average was a like-old-times .351.

Still favoring a reduced swing, though he never had struck out often, the veteran headed toward 38, reached magical hit No. 3000 remarkably fast—43 hits in 22 games.

The six-figure super-star sagged, after the emotional lift and with an effort to produce more power. Musial's continued downward spiral in 1959 to .255 after 17 seasons above .300 seemed shocking and revealing. Sorry, wrong number. Convinced he had been held out of too many spring games and hadn't run enough, Stan junked his relaxed off-season life-style.

As a result, rebounding off the bench early in 1960, he hit productively in a drive that almost cost his home-town Pittsburgh fans a first pennant in 33 years. They weren't happy campers when the old Forbes Field favorite beat the Pirates three times with late-inning homers.

By 1962, nearly 42 and playing enough games to qualify as a batting-title contender, Musial batted .330, only a point lower than a career that ended in 1963, the day they unveiled artist Amadee's two-figured statue, The Boy and The Man, one more warmly accepted by the modest hero than the giant crouching bronzed singleton erected outside Busch Stadium five years later.

Significantly, finishing with 1815 hits home and away, Musial singled his last two times at bat, to the right and then to the left of a curious Cincinnati rookie second baseman who quickly became a durable, hit-hungry, record-conscious standout—Pete Rose.

Musial, involved in successful restaurant and hotel pursuits with colorful Julius (Biggie) Garagnani, took time off to general-manage the 1967 Cardinals to a world championship, then bowed out with the unexpected death of his partner and a desire to get away from the unlimited slavery of the GM to Alexander Graham Bell's invention.

The Man Stan soon would become The Harmonica Man, captivating young and old with the same loosey-goosey atmosphere consistent with Cardinal clubhouses the near quarter-century No. "6" sat in there as No. 1 in most hearts.

KID NICHOLS

By the time Kid Nichols pitched for the Cardinals he was an old man, by use of baseball standards even more than now, but, unusually, he came off the retired list to pitch and manage the Redbirds, too briefly in a career of 361 victories.

One-time pitching standout for the Boston Beaneaters when Frank Selee put together a ball club that won five pennants, Nichols was good—and independent enough—to quit in a huff when owner Arthur Soden pinched pennies and permitted prominent players to jump to the American League.

Nichols, 10 straight years a winner, broke in with the Beaneaters with a 27-game season in 1890, then went over 30 for eight straight seasons, three times leading in victories and also three times in shutouts.

A "Chicago," as a calcimine was called, was rare enough in those days that three, four and five could top a league. Unusually, too, Nichols achieved his stature even though he rarely threw a breaking ball.

Always "Kid" from his youthful days in Boston, Charles Augustus Nichols simply left after the 1901 season and bought an interest in the Western League franchise at his adopted home town, Kansas City. He pitched and managed there until the Robisons offered an obvious financial incentive to come to St. Louis in 1904 as pitcher and manager.

At 35, the Kid was good enough to post a 20-13 record with a 2.02 earned-run average, accounting for a sizable contribution to his fifth-place season, 75-79. In addition, the attendance of 386,750 was their largest of the century until1911.

Presumably many came to see the manager pitch—by the way, Kid only once took himself out of a game in 36 starts—but when Nichols started even more poorly than his ball club in '05, winning just one of six decisions as the Redbirds fluttered 5-and-9, the Robisons fired him as foreman and waived the pitcher to Philadelphia.

The Cards replaced Nichols with a home-town favorite, Sunset Jimmy Burke, a third baseman, but Burke had a bad year at the plate (.225) and the ball club a worse one in the standings, sixth with a 58-96 record.

The Kid, meanwhile, righted himself to .500 the rest of the season, then bowed out early in 1906, returning to KayCee and to Hall of Fame recognition in 1949, four years before he died.

BRANCH RICKEY

If the owner of the American League club had liked or listened to the man, St. Louis baseball would have had a brown taste to it, no pun intended, and if the bushy-browed mental giant had decided he'd rather be a lawyer or a politician or a preacher, chances are that Wesley Branch Rickey would have finished first in those fields other than rank as the brain of baseball.

The only reason Rickey couldn't be admitted to the baseball Hall of Fame earlier than 1967 was because Cooperstown rule prohibited its Committee on Veterans to be eligible for election. And Rickey obviously was as good evaluating past-tense players for induction as he did rookies for selection.

Mr. Rickey—dear wife Jane even called him formally in public—could emerge at times as a stuffed shirt or in the view of many as a man whose Christian conscience about the need for black players bothered him only when he had run out of virgin territory for talent. But those would be harsh evaluations.

Simply put, a fringe player and a manager whose blackboard ideas might have been too complex, Rickey well could have been the smartest executive in baseball history, and St. Louis benefited from his presence and wisdom for most of his half-century in the Grand Old Game.

Rickey, a farm kid with religious fervor from Sciota County, Ohio, was a pretty good athlete at Ohio Wesleyan in baseball and football. He even got to the bigs as a catcher with the Browns briefly in 1905 and for 64 games in '06 in which he batted .284, but, sorearmed, had the embarrassment of a record 13 bases stole off him one day. He caught briefly for the Yankees a year later, too, before his nimble cerebrum medulla told him he had a better chance in law if he could afford to go to presigious University of Michigan.

There, helping with football and coaching baseball as well as studying, Rickey discovered two things: a great baseball prospect, George Sisler, and the fact that through overwork he had become vulnerable to tuberculosis. So by direction he went out to Idaho, to hang his shingle and just maybe, as mentioned, perfect his skills in efforts where his oratory and polysyllabics could have been first rate, too.

B.R.: Catching for the Browns early in the century.

But Branch loved baseball, and the owner of the Browns, Robert Lee Hedges, knew and appreciated him enough to lure him back as business manager and assistant manager. Soon, Rickey was field foreman late in 1913 and through '14, a fifth-place finish and then sixth in 1915. By then, Phil Ball, who owned the Federal League competitor to the Browns and Cardinals, had taken over the American League club.

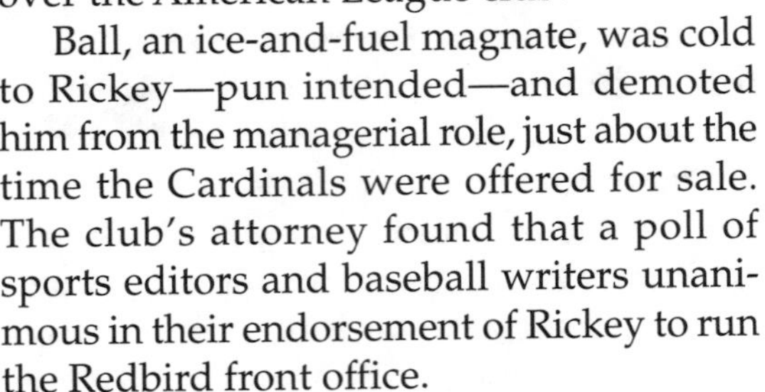

Ball, an ice-and-fuel magnate, was cold to Rickey—pun intended—and demoted him from the managerial role, just about the time the Cardinals were offered for sale. The club's attorney found that a poll of sports editors and baseball writers unanimous in their endorsement of Rickey to run the Redbird front office.

By then, Ball stubbornly rejected the idea of releasing Rickey, leading to a lawsuit, just as he earlier had rejected the suggestion that the one way to compete against wealthier clubs was to scout and develop your own. Too often independent clubs to which a player was sent for seasoning was sold to a higher bidder rather than returned to the club that originally signed him.

When Ball lost the suit and Rickey, he inadvertently lost the town because Rickey, taking over as business manager and manager of the Cardinals, soon persuaded new president Sam Breadon of the Cardinals to pony up the money necessary for his farm-system concept.

Within six years from 1920, Rickey's plan paid off. By then, he had been relieved as manager, angrily selling out his stock, though retaining the job Breadon thought correctly would make him famous—general manager.

From 1926 through the next 21 seasons, the Cardinals won nine pennants and six world championships, as Rickey built up the farm system to include 29 clubs, either owned or with a working agreement. In the process, B.R. angered commissioner K.M. Landis, the judge who had been brought into business shortly after Rickey won a dispute with Pittsburgh over the contract of Michigan super-star Sisler. A three-man commission of the two league presidents and one clubowner just didn't work.

Landis frowned on St. Louis's "chain-gang" system as it was called, notably the fact that the Cardinals often had two farm teams in the same league or, as in the case of one league, the Nebraska State, all teams.

When the commissioner freed 101 St. Louis minor-league players in 1938, Breadon was offended that his integrity had been questioned. Pridefully, he made a commitment not to renew Rickey's seven-year contract a third time. With war clouds forming, the clubowner also could have questioned Rickey's salary, a whopping $80,000 just after the Depression, a combination of guaranteed income and 20 percent of profits, one that encouraged player sales that helped off the field, not on it.

So Rickey's farewell was the famed 1942 St. Louis Swifties, a young, rapid-running team of strong pitching and good defense. With 43 victories in the last 52 games, the Cardinals won with a 106-48 record, two games better than the Brooklyn ball club Rickey took over in '43.

At Ebbets Field, at a time most clubs retrenched or even cut out scouting completely, Rickey pursued aggressively and, when possible, even signing younger players. Also, he gingerly suggested with no encounter that there might be an occasional black player.

So Jackie Robinson came in, a player of character and quality, fulfilling Rickey's hopes by keeping his competitive fire under control. Quickly, because he had deserved a considerable lead with his incentive, B.R. also had lined up two other players, Roy Campanella and Don Newcombe, who would form with Robinson a backbone trio of competence that would lead over 10 years to six pennants and a world championship.

By then, Rickey was out at Brooklyn, ousted in a power play by Walter F. O'Malley, who took the Dodgers to Los Angeles after the 1957 season. By then, Rickey was running Pittsburgh for an old Ohio friend, sportsman John Galbreath, putting in nine years of an expensive, painful five-year plan, as comedian catcher Joe Garagiola cracked. Rickey didn't win in that pitiful period for the Pirates, but they soon did for successor Joe L. Brown.

With his charm and guile, threatening establishment of a third major league, the Continental, Rickey pressured the National League to moving back into New York with the Mets in 1962, a year their expansion also included Houston.

At an advanced baseball age, Rickey became a senior consultant to August A. Busch Jr. and the brewery, creating considerable strain when he looked upon general manager Bing Devine as he first had known him, a glorified office boy just out of college 30 years earlier. Devine lost out, ultimately, but so did Rickey, dropped by Busch.

Dramatically, Wesley Branch Rickey, accepting induction in the Missouri State Sports Hall of Fame in late fall, 1965, collapsed fatally when speaking of spiritual courage at Columbia, Mo. He was 84.

Through his knowledge of the game, his overall ability to pick brains, to organize and to lead, Rickey probably had no equal. Most certainly he was even more colorful than the nicknames used for him. In New York, the "Mahatma," invented at a time Mohandas K. Gandhi of India was prominent, fit more than "El Cheapo" a deragatory dig used by one newspaper because of his tendency for tightfistedness at contract time.

Rickey's colorful legacy includes the language as well as his accomplishments. The wordmaster had a way with the King's English as, for example, explaining elimination of an unnecessary player or situation. "An addition by subtraction,"he called it.

Or an athlete just good enough to keep on a roster, yet one of limited contributions, he labeled "an anesthetic player". For pitchers, he referred to ability to change speeds as "variable velocities" and he best described the screwball, one in which the pitcher turns the wrist abnormally inward than outward, as "the reverse curve."

Rickey honored the "spirit of adventure," obviously in himself as well as others. He never drank, rarely swore, using "Judas Priest" as a helpful substitute for an expletive. He toyed lovingly with cigars until forced by doctors merely to suck on the nicotine. In an apparent youthful promise to his dear mother, he never attended a Sunday ball game as player, manager or executive, though he always managed to phone in to check the attendance.

He was, for a fact, a man of variable velocities himself, as variable as the time he was asked a tough question and answered, "possibly, probably and in a given sense, yes."

That would fit right in with the favorite word of unswerving syncophants of which he had many:

"Yes, Mr. Rickey!"

WILBERT ROBINSON

Wilbert Robinson was one of the nicest men in baseball. Too bad he me-tooed John McGraw and jumped the Cardinals after one season here, 1900.

"Uncle Robbie," as they knew him through years, spent 18 seasons at Brooklyn through 1931 managing just two pennant winners, 1916 and '20, yet achieving such affection that many sports writers and newpapers those years referred to the Dodgers as the "Robins".

A sturdy, chunky catcher for 17 years

beginning with Philadelphia of the old American Association in 1886, Robinson had his years with five seasons over .300 and a career .273. He caught his last games in 1902 as a player-coach for his long-time friend, John McGraw.

A playing highlight of Robinson's career was a 7-for-7 game, still the best for a big leaguer.

Robinson, coaching for McGraw with the Giants, moved across the Brooklyn bridge with the Dodgers in 1914. Suddenly his friendship with McGraw became as bitter enmity as the natural borough rivalry between the Giants and the Dodgers.

Somehow, endearing to many, including the writers, Uncle Robby lasted long at Ebbets Field even though his team became knows as the Daffiness Dodgers because of mishaps by which one time three Brooklyn players reached base at one time—the same base.

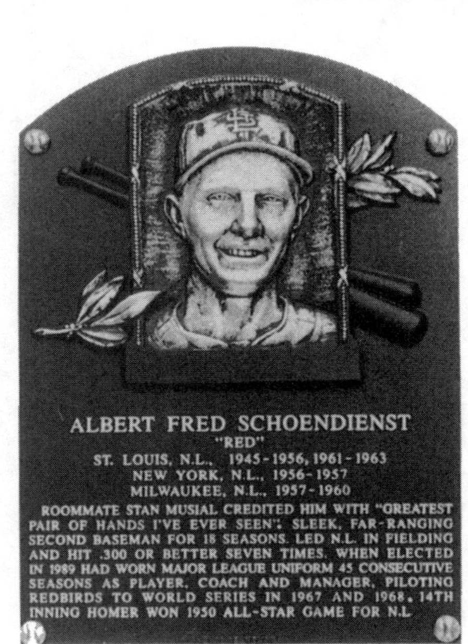

One time early in Robinson's life, which lasted until he was 68 years, the old catcher offered to catch a baseball dropped from an airplane. His comedic outfielder, Casey Stengel, substituted a grapefruit for the baseball. When Uncle Robby made the catch as the impact thundered his glove against his chest, he heard and felt the squish and thought he was bleeding.

For a brief time because he was that kind of guy, who liked to entertain folks at his winter hunting lodge in Gerogia, Wilbert Robinson was unforgiving. Truly he wasn't the brightest man. For instance, the time a young St. Louis outfielder named Oscar Roettger was trying to make a spring-training impression on the Dodger manager. A writer wanted to know the batting order. Uncle Robby got to the proper spot, then stalled.

"Uh," he said, "it's a—uh!—a funny name like Rott...er, hell, I can't spell or pronounce it. Put Babe Herman in right field."

RED SCHOENDIENST

If Red Schoendienst hadn't suffered an eye injury at 17 and come out of military service prematurely a few years later with suggestions of an enervating tuberculosis bug, this 7-come-11 natural undoubtedly would have been a rousing Hall of Fame selectee by baseball writers rather than a Cooperstown choice by the Veterans Committee.

Rarely—at least in prejudiced judgment of one who helped resurrect many rejects for the highest honors—has the distinction gone more justly than to the lanky, loosey-goosey second baseman. Despite his physical handicaps, Schoendienst hit .289 over a fragmentary 19 years in the majors. Six of the 17 full seasons he hit over .300.

Even though he didn't know how well he should have felt until after TB surgery—just after hitting .300 in the 1958 World Series, weak, wan and coughing—the gifted, willowy, freckled redhead fielded with a brilliant surehandedness. Relaxed, he adopted the maddening habit of Pepper Martin by removing his glove between pitches and holding it in his bare throwing hand until just before the next delivery.

Red might have run like the colorful Martin, for whom he played briefly in the minors, because, in truth, he broke in as a base stealer. But he was advised early that he had a shallow shoulder socket, one that tended to pop out in headfirst or excessive slides. So he ran well, fast, but prudently.

The physical malfunction took enough toll that it limited Schoendienst's place at his primary position—shortstop—where his heavier hitting for that key defensive position would have meant earlier and better Hall of Fame consideration.

Alfred Fred Schoendienst's boyhood at Germantown, Ill., near St. Louis, where he played, coached and managed most of his incredibly long uniformed career, was right out of Mark Twain's Huckleberry Finn. A member of a large small-farm family, whose father worked the mines and state highway jobs, Red played hooky to catfish on the Kaskaskia river, to hunt bobwhites for the dinner table and to play baseball and basketball.

In the Civil Conservation Corps, a national depression gimmick for out-of-work kids, Schoendienst suffered permanent damage to his left eye when it was struck by a ricocheting nail in a fence post mishap. At 19 in 1942, shooting pool with a boyhood buddy, Red and Joe Linneman decided to hitch-hike to St. Louis for a Cardinal tryout camp with a chance to see the Cardinals play bitter rival Brooklyn.

The night before, Red slept in a public park across from Union Station, but he never got to see the following evening's big-league ball game. At the morning tryout he was so outstanding that a Cardinal scout hustled across the river and got from Pa Schoendienst, necessary parental approval. By game time, Red was headed by bus to Union City, Tenn., where he got eight straight hits righthanded, then requested permission from manager Everett Johnson to switch to the left side.

The startling explanation was that because of the blurred effect, his nose kept him from picking up a righthanded pitcher's breaking ball. So doing what he'd been required to do by the kids back home, to balance the scales between his skills and theirs, Red batted both ways.

A year later, hitting .373 at Lynchburg, Va., he was assigned to Pepper Martin's 1943 Rochester clubhouse, where Pepper interrupted a clubhouse cussing to tell the kid knocking at the door that he didn't need a batboy. But, Mr. Martin, he'd been assigned to come there, and Pepper twanged "John Brown, you must be that "Shone" or something or other they're sending me. Criminy, war sure is hell. Now they're sending me babies."

But that boyish baby was only one short season and a brief career in the Army away from the Cardinals, whom he joined in 1945 after that quick medical washout. Schoendienst was so good chasing down fly balls that with master Marty Marion at shortstop, he played left field. He hit .278, stole a league-leading 28 bases and was so quick cutting down balls hit between him and the foul-line that coach Buzzy Wares reached back into antiquity to compare him

THE NATURAL: Plain ol' Red, gifted switch-hitting Red Schoendienst, played and managed with the instinct of a natural player who wore well in a record 12 seasons as manager even though the Cardinals won just two pennants.

with Pittsburgh's Fred Clarke 40 years earlier.

When the men came home from service in 1946, and new manager Eddie Dyer envisioned the 23-year-old war replacement as his "No. 1 utility man", Schoendienst had a throaty answer that rhymed with horsefeathers. By spring training's end, after filling in for late-reporting Stan Musial in left field and holdout Whitey Kurowski at third base, second base glared as a position where neither Lou Klein nor Emil Verban could compare with Red. Verban was dealt to Philadelphia and Klein soon joined pitchers Max Lanier and Fred Martin in a flight to Mexico for Pasquel pesos.

Schoendienst was more than adequate with a .281 average for a pennant-winning ball club, but when he tailed off in a heavy-duty 1947, Dyer rejected clubowner Sam Breadon's concern about "a .250 second baseman". Red, marrying lovely Mary O'Reilly late season, mollified her concern about his arm trouble and future.

"Don't worry," he said, "I'm working out throwing lefthanded. I can play first base."

Although 1948 wouldn't be significant in Red's comeback, he did put together one of the most remarkable weekends in a June extra-base batting spree. Using a choked grip, though he later moved up farther from the knob, Schoendienst tattooed the right-field screen and fence at St. Louis, setting two major-league records and tying four.

Against Brooklyn June 5, he hit three doubles and a single. Next day against Philadelphia in a doubleheader, he had three more two-base hits and a homer in the first game and added two more doubles in the second contest. The records broken were for eight doubles in three straight games and seven long hits in two successive contests.

By 1949, what might well have been a second pennant-winning season, the Cardinals folded late, in part because Schoendienst tailed off from a batting-title contention to a .297. Presumably aware that the 150-game player was weary, manager Dyer called up Solly Hemus from minor-league Houston to give Red a precious couple of days of rest the final week, but in fielding practice at Pittsburgh, Hemus suffered a broken nose. Playing, Red was so tired that on a routine skipping outfield throw-in the final series at Chicago, the adhesive-handed infielder suffered a broken thumb.

At the 1950 All-Star game at Chicago's Comiskey Park, where the summer attraction began 17 years earlier, Schoendienst pointed to the upper left-field stands and cracked, "I wish the old man (Burt Shotton) would give me a shot. I'd hit one up there."

Spotting Jackie Robinson in a 14-inning thriller, Schoenienst hit one "up there," a game-winning homer off Detroit lefthander Ted Gray. The game turned about the All-Star series from American to National.

Now, to the annoyance of new Redbird clubowner Fred Saigh, at a time of no sports agents, Mary O'Reilly Schoendienst could walk in and in a sweet voice suggest that her Red was half as good as his roommate and close friend Stan Musial, then making $80,000, so he should be worth—yeah, $40,000.

Hitting better each season, Huckleberry Finn grew up at 30 with his best season, hitting .342 and finishing second to Brooklyn's Carl Furillo. This time, an enforced illness produced the rest that might have been necessary other years. A bad infield throw at New York's Polo Grounds almost chewed off Schoendienst's left eyebrow as he turned when stepping on first base. With the player down, blood spurting, he was rushed to the Polo Grounds' first-aid room, where doctors mumbled, fearing for his sight, until informed he already had that scarred left eye.

Despite the dancing visual spots, Schoendienst was a fourth outfielder on pop flies—even without sun glasses—but the biggest problem was encroaching darkness he would recall years later. Past 75, the body fleshy after TB surgery at 36, he still was vigorous enough to set an unofficial record by wearing his number "2" in pregame practice.

That famed "2" was traded by Frank Lane to New York in a controversial deal in 1956, prompting club president Gussie Busch to clamp down on Lane. Schoendienst, rebounding, was dealt from the Giants to Milwaukee Braves in an early season deal that helped the Braves win the 1957 World Series and '58 pennant.

After acquiring Red, jubilant manager Fred Haney wanted to make him captain, but Schoendienst talked him out of the obvious intrusion the domicile of established stars, i.e., Hank Aaron, Warren Spahn, Eddie Mathews. Red assured the manager he would take charge.

With Haney advising his outfielders in vulgar terms to throw the blankety-blank ball regularly to Schoendienst at second base, rather than risk ridiculous long throw-ins, Red also helped at bat with 200 hits and a .309 average.

In the trained eye of a long-time Schoendienst observer and admirer, the offensive figures of the key man in the Braves' climb from close to top reflected what well might have been if he hadn't had the physical problems. The weakening began to manifest itself more in '58 despite the World Series specter of a sick man hitting .300.

Rest home confinement and surgery almost immediately followed his wife's delivery of their fourth child and only son immediately after the '58 Series.

Schoendienst missed all except five games in '59 and couldn't impress new Milwaukee skipper Charley Dressen in '60. Then 37, playing 68 games, Schoendienst was released.

Here came a pivotal point in the career of one of the Cardinals' longest-serving, most popular players. Haney, taking over as general manager of the new American league West Coast team, the Angels, wanted Schoendienst to play second base regularly. The Cardinals' Bing Devine could offer only a return role as utility player and a chance to coach.

Red stayed in St. Louis. Pinch-hitting, more than playing, Schoendienst had a remarkable second season coming off the bench, batting .301 in 1962 with a league-leading 22 pinch-hits in 72 attempts. Early in '63, at 40, Schoendienst moved off the playing list to coach full-time under Johnny Keane.

When Keane jumped to the New York Yankees in an ugly reaction for management after winning the 1964 season, there was only one 7-come-11 choice for replacement. That would be 7-come-11 coach named Red Schoendienst, pronounced Germanically "Shane-deenst" and, meaning happily and appropriately, "nice servant."

Indeed, the Old Redhead, as most could call him, recorded a record 12 seasons as manager of the Cardinals, a hard-to-satisfy ownership most of the years over championship success that began when Huckleberry Finn was a kid of three in 1926.

By the time he stepped into the shadows as a coach for another country kid from St. Louis's east side, Whitey Herzog of New Athens, Ill., Red Schoendienst was a likable legend. His "2" was retired late in 1996, his last in the bird-and-bat raiment of the Redbirds—except for pre-game practice!

ENOS SLAUGHTER

Although Enos Slaughter is best remembered by his romantic first-to-home dash, winning the seventh game of the 1946 World Series for St. Louis over Boston, that's really only a tip of the iceberg of a growling, gravel-voiced, no-nonsense baseball hustler.

Slaughter, stung by a managerial dig his second professional season in the minors at 20, used a rebuke—"I'll get some help for you kid if you're tired," Eddie Dyer said sarcastically—to never walk again on the field. He jogged briskly in and out always—even on bases on balls. He inspired a young Cincinnati fan who duplicated his style as "Charley Hustle": Pete Rose!

Slaughter, though he missed three salad season in military service, was a solid .300 hitter, though really better than that because of higher averages in 10 of his 19 years. Fact is, at age 42, a year before he retired in 1959, he hit .304 as a part-time player.

But Slaughter was more than just a hitter through 13 playing seasons with the Cardinals, typifying the dash and daring of the Gas House Gang, for which he really was only a token member. At 22 in 1938, Frank Frisch's last season as manager, the country kid called "Country" by minor-league manager Burt Shotton seemed awed by the old Flash.

Batting only .276 in comparison with .381 the previous season in Triple-A at Columbus Ohio, Slaughter also came off poorly in comparison with the rookie season of fellow Columbus outfielder, Johnny Rizzo, who had been sold to Pittsburgh. So Enos Bradsher Slaguhter, son of a tobacco farmer at Roxboro, N.C., faced an early career climax—and nearly death—after rabbit-hunting with father Zadok on New Year's Day, 1939. The haste was to get back to listen to nearby Duke seek an unscored-on season in a Rose Bowl game against Southern California.

Before USC upset the Blue Devils with a final-second pass,7-3, both Slaughters became critically ill. The rabbits they hunted and cleaned were infected. The illness took the father's life before nightfall. Enos barely made it.

BY ANY OTHER NAME: Enos Slaughter was ALWAYS a hustler.

Two months later, still experiencing dizzy spells, hot-and-cold chills and with boils under both arms, Slaughter reported to St. Petersburg, Fla., on time, seeking to impress new manager Ray Blades. He did. The stocky lefthanded hitter responded with one of the greatest seasons of his career, batting .320 with a league-leading 52 doubles.

Through his career as "Country", "Bosco" and the "Old War Horse," Slaughter drove in more than 100 runs three times, but was close six other seasons. He scored 100 runs three times, and led in triples twice and base hits once.

When the 1941 Cardinals made a gallant pennant bid in a tight season-long race with the Brooklyn Dodgers, a fractured skull suffered by Slaughter, diving into the right-field concrete to avoid collision with center fielder Terry Moore, was a critical loss. In only 113 games he had 76 RBIs.

Improving from .311 to .318 in 1942, a season of low scoring, Slaughter was second only to league-leading Ernie Lombardi in average. He also paced the National League with 188 hits, 17 triples, and followed the 43-of-52 surge to a pennant with a blue-ribbon play that typified his competitive clutch ability.

Scoring the leading run in the second game of the 1942 upset over the New York Yankees, Slaughter followed with quick fielding and a remarkably accurate throw that knocked off the potential tying run in New York's ninth. The play preserved a 4-3 victory, the first of four straight.

Another pivotal play came in the next game at Yankee Stadium, where the outfield of Stan Musial, especially Moore and Slaughter backed up Ernie White's remarkable pitching. With the Yankees trailing in the ninth, one on and two out, Charley Keller flied deep to right, where Slaughter made a leaping catch as, he recalled later, just as an orange thrown from the stands whizzed across his face and vision.

Slaughter, a shy guy as a kid taught to run better by future manager Billy Southworth at a 1935 tryout camp, still was introverted when he moped in from the outfield a year later at Columbus, Ga., earning manager Dyer's caustic comment that changed his life and career.

"Not hitting, I'd let it affect my play," recalled Slaughter, "but from my rooming-house bed that night, aware folks were paying two bits or a half buck at tough times, I vowed never to walk again."

But not to avoid expressing his opinion, as reflected when he returned from service with other big leaguers he had shown up by playing hard in games played to entertain troops. He acknowledged sliding on coral island sand in the Pacific had a razor effect on legs, but, as he put it, "The least I could do for guys who were saving my life was to play hard."

Slaughter, back at 30, hit his career even .300 with a league-leading 130 RBIs and the sweet-stroking batter's high for home runs, 18. He starred in the historic first pennant playoff with Brooklyn, then, as suggested, in the World Series—even before the most remarkable run since Paul Revere.

Himself a hard-sliding, aggressive baserunner, whose action caused him problems at times, Slaughter groused at one point to Dyer, the minor-league manager who had followed him to the majors, that coach Mike Gonzalez held him up at third base when he could have scored on an over-throw. Wearily, Dyer, chiding the right fielder about his youthful former speaking reticence, told the bitching ball player that if it happened again, to use his own judgment and go. The manager would take responsibility.

Hmmm, temptation. Slaughter played the last two games of the Series over doctor's objections, fearful a painful clot suffered when he had been hit with a pitch might dissolve to the heart. "It's my life, Doc, and I'll play," Enos rasped.

So Slaughter, off and running on a pitch to Harry Walker in the seventh game of the '46 Series, decided by the time he reached second base that he would score on the looping high fly to medium left center. For all his bravado, Slaughter was aware that injured defensive star Dom DiMaggio was out.

So, rounding third past a flapping-armed Gonzalez's attempted stop sign, Slaughter actually scored easily when shortstop Johnny Pesky, taking outfielder Leon Culberson's soft throw, turned in the early October shadow to find the aggressive athlete well on his way home. Pesky's off-balance throw, pulling up catcher Roy Partee to smother the ball, wasn't even close.

Scorers, not quite believing what they had seen, called the hit a double, but the bold venture lingers as exceptional, which scoring on a two-out, two-base hit would not necessarily connote. Final, 4-3, St. Louis.

Slaughter, a half-century later, still was annoyed at suggestion he "deliberately" spiked Jackie Robinson in the black player's rookie 1947 season. From boyhood to manhood, Slaughter has kneeled and worked with his black tobacco-farm tenants.

"I put Eddie Stanky in a hospital, cut Bill Rigney, because I asked no quarter and gave none," Slaughter would argue, "but I never 'deliberately' spiked anyone."

Right or wrong, fact is that Monte Irvin confirms that once when Slaughter almost cut him at first base, Enos scolded the black player new to the bag to watch his foot. "They're still on me about Robinson," Slaughter complained.

Actually, Bosco had more trouble keeping a wife—he struck out with five!—and, as a result, really had no bargaining leverage at contract time. So his highest salary was only $28,000, modest and surprising because he still had first-rate skills through the mid-1950s.

Back in 1949, nosing out defending champion teammate Stan Musial, Slaughter finished second only to Robinson with his highest average, .336. A year later, reluctantly moved to center field for the All-Star game because he was picked by public with two defensive clydesdales, Ralph Kiner and Hank Sauer, Slaughter made a spectacular leaping catch at Comiskey Park.

Three years later in All-Star play at Cincinnati, at 37, he got two hits, stole a base and made a patented seat-of-the-pants slide for a National League victory, impressing many, including Yankee manager Casey Stengel, who respected him from younger days when Stengel managed the Boston Braves.

1-2 PUNCH ON 1-2 TEAM: With Enos Slaughter (left) and Stan Musial as the heart of their batting order, the Cardinals were constant contenders, 1941-53. The two left-handed hitters faced so many southpaws that, Slaughter rasped, "We hit 'em as well as we did the right-handers."

So in a shock to many, including Slaughter and irate fans, Enos was dealt to the Yankees just before the 1954 season, causing the balding baseball old-timer to cry in the clubhouse. The embarrassed ball club and brewery ownership heard plenty about it because old E-n-o, as a leather-lunged fan would symbolize his following, was one of the most popular Cardinal players ever.

At one juncture when the Yankees still treated Kansas City like an old farm club, Slaughter was palmed off to the Blues...er, A's, and he brought back St. Louis memories with .322 games in 108 in 1955, but he was back in Yankee blue in time to help win the 1956 World Series.

Oh, sure, playing left field, which he never did like, he misplayed a line drive into a game-winning hit by Robinson in one Series game, but the old War Horse, then 40, hit .350 and won one game for Stengel with a three-run homer.

Slaughter was permitted to linger to the Veterans Committee of the Hall of Fame, perhaps because the big New York voting bloc of writers couldn't understand how a guy would cry when asked to leave a second-division St. Louis club in the National League for New York and the world champion Yankees.

But St. Louis understood, enough years after he won Hall of Fame election in 1985, to retire his number "9" in 1996. Even though he had hinted enough, the colorful character was happy, gravelly-voiced glad.

DAZZY VANCE

Maybe colorful Dazzy Vance's greatest contribution to the 1934 Cardinals Gas House Gang surge to a pennant—the only one the big 44-year-old battler ever enjoyed—would be the victory cocktail concoction he whipped up before the World Series upset over the Detroit Tigers.

At the Redbirds' private pennant-winning party, located at Jim Mertikas's famed Grecian Gardens near current Busch Stadium, Vance couldn't find a bartender who knew how to make a "Dazz-Marie". So the Dazzler stepped behind the bar and filled an oversized, ice-laden glass with rye, bourbon, scotch, gin, sloe gin, vermouth, brandy and benedictine. Next, he added powdered sugar, stirred, topped the witch's brew with a cherry—and then found no teammate willing to join him in drinking the alcoholic doozy.

The Dazzler was a doozy, himself, from the time Clarence Arthur Vance fell in love with a cowboy entertainer who pronounced "Daisy" as "Dazzy". That's how nicknames are born, at least in Orient, Ia.

Incredibly, nine years after the florid-faced giant joined Red Cloud in the Nebraska State League in 1912, he still was in the minors, but one spring exhibition with Brooklyn in '22, after he had posted a 21-game season for New Orleans in the Southern Association, he faced the pennant-contending Browns in an exhibition—and struck out master hitter George Sisler four straight times. Said The Sizzler to the old *St. Louis Globe-Democrat*'s Mike Haley, "He'll be great."

Vance was, even though at 31 he was two years older than Brooklyn thought. An immediate success with an 18-12 season, he followed with a Most Valuable Player award-winning 28-6 with a 2.14 earned-run average in a close-call 1924 loss to the rival Giants. A year later Dazzy led again with 22-7.

Tall, stocky and overpowering, Vance helped himself by pitching with a tattered shirt sleeve, until ultimately forced to forego the distraction for hitters, but, mainly, he had a high, leg-kicking hard one and a jagged, overhanded curve, a strikeout pitch.

By the time he had his last hurrah at Ebbets Field, a 17-15 record with a league-leading ERA in 1930, Dazzy was the highest-paid pitcher in the National League at $25,000. He threw one curveball too many, and the Cardinals' Handy Andy High belted it for a game-winning hit that enabled St. Louis to catch Brooklyn in September.

But Vance always had impressed

Frankie Frisch, the Cardinals' new player-manager, so he came aboard to help in 1934 with another 40-year-old gaffer, Jesse (Pop) Haines, a season of only eight Redbird pitchers.

The old Dazzler, a Hall of Famer with a 197-140 record despite his late big-league start, got into one game of the 1934 World Series after polishing off that "Dazz-Marie" pennant-celebrating potion. Vance had waited a long time for the spotlight. In a scoreless stretch of five batters in relief, he showed why he had been the highest-paid NL pitcher until Dizzy Dean. He struck out three.

BOBBY WALLACE

If there ever was a guy who worked both sides of the major-league baseball street in St. Louis, it would be Bobby Wallace, a Hall of Fame shortstop who spent 20 of his 25 years in St. Louis uniform, more of them with the Browns than the Cardinals.

Rhoderick James Wallace, the Pittsburgh product's proper handle, was a converted pitcher with the Cleveland Spiders of the National League, moved off the mound by the intensity of enemy bats in his third big-league season, 1897.

By the time the Robisons moved their Cleveland talent to St. Louis in that unique roster transfer of players in 1899, Wallace quickly became a St. Louis favorite at shortstop, hitting .295 with 108 RBIs. Two years later, Bobby had upped his average to .322.

So it was a blow to the red-uniformed side when he jumped to the American League with the Browns—a five-year deal averaging nearly $7500 when the Cards and NL had that chintzy $2400-a-player salary cap—but, curiously, Wallace never again hit so consistently.

Truth is, the Browns were as bad as the Cardinals most of the years except for a close-call fourth in 1908, a year eccentric Rube Waddell helped win games and fans. By the time Wallace became player-manager in 1911, dipping to .232 at the plate and plunging to a last-place 45-107 in the standing, his role as skipper in '12 was even shorter than years later (1937) when he was fill-in foreman at Cincinnati.

By the time owner Robert Lee Hedges asked him to step down with the St. Louis Americans in '12, the popular player had become a benchwarner, an ornament of the past. When World War I thinned ranks in 1917, the Browns released him so that he could return to the Cardinals.

Playing eight games for Miller Huggins in '17 and eight more in '18, Wallace hung it up at 45, still a ripe baseball age, and distinguished later as a baseball scout, living to another ripe age, 87, to enjoy Cooperstown designation seven years earlier, 1953.

He was the first Hall of Fame shortstop elected from the American League.

HOYT WILHELM

Hoyt Wilhelm, no spring chicken or Carolina gamecock when he joined the Giant in 1952 at nearly 29, had a career considerably more romantic—and longer—than the fact that he homered his first time up in the bigs and never hit another.

From that first-swing four-bagger at the Polo Grounds, Wilhelm flailed away another assorted 431 times up, batting just a miserable .088, but he was just as miserable on opposing teams with a knuckleball that did the hootchy-cootchy in its shimmering flight to the plate.

Standing out there at six feet, relaxed head cocked to one side as if he were waiting your next question, Wilhelm pitched until he was old enough for the pension—49—and became the first relief pitcher ever elected to the Hall of Fame in 1985.

Wilhelm's first season, 1952, was the Year of the Relief Pitcher, further glamoriz-

ing a situation that existed after the Yankees' Joe Page and Dodgers' Hugh Casey were out of the bullpen daily in the 1947 World Series. Topping Brooklyn's Joe Black and St. Louis's Al Brazle and Eddie Yuhas, Wilhelm led National League pitchers in relief victories and earned run average.

The finger-tip master of the knuckler was 15-3 and, at a time the ERA leader had to work at least an inning a game, 154, the reliever led with 2.43. Eight times later in his 21 seasons of a record 1070 appearances, his ERA was lower at a time the annual honor award was acknowledged differently.

Wilhelm's only appearance in a St. Louis uniform was in 1957, a result of a trade with New York that sent first baseman-outfielder Whitey Lockman back to the Giants. With the Redbirds, an undistinguished 1-and-4, Hoyt lasted only long enough for Frantic Frank Lane to sell him to Cleveland later that year.

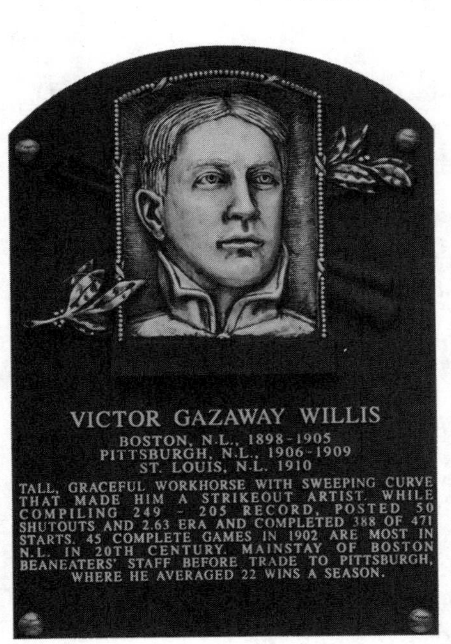

So it wasn't until 1958, six years and nearly 400 games after he first toed a big-league slab, that Wilhelm started a game in the majors. Baltimore manager Paul Richards, who had acquired Hoyt on waivers after Lane took his itchy roster movements to Cleveland, started the pitcher, but not before he provided his catchers with an oversized, pancake-looking glove to reduce passed balls. Hoyt pitched a no-hitter late that season against the Yankees.

After tying his personal high of 15 victories in 1959, Wilhelm gravitated back toward the bullpen and made his last start his first season with the Chicago White Sox, 1963. He was dealt to the Sox in a four-for-two trade that took Hall of Fame shortstop, Luis Aparicio to the Orioles.

Washed up at 40? Not phlegmatic, tobacco-chawing James Hoyt Wilhelm with the deadpanned humor. Wilhelm bounced around like his knuckler to California, Atlanta, the Cubs, Braves again, to Los Angeles—and then to Cooperstown.

VIC WILLIS

Appropriately named "Victor"—Victor Gazaway Willis—got to the Cardinals too late with too little, acquired from pennant-winning Pittsburgh for the 1910 season. The rag-tag Redbirds finished far back—seventh—and Vic Willis contributed only nine of his 249 career victories.

Troubled with an arm that wouldn't permit him to go beyond his thirteenth season, Willis quit at 34 and ultimately wound up with his own small hotel back home in Cecil County, Md.

Willis, tall, rangy and reliable, made it to Cooperstown the long, hard way, deceased 48 years earlier at Elkton. Fact is, when selected in 1995, he once before had enough votes from the Hall of Fame Veterans Committee, but was prevented from election because another had more votes.

Willis never led the National League with victories, though he won 20 or more games eight times, but three times he led in defeats with bad ball clubs, the Boston Beaneaters with whom he had been a rousing early success. He was 25-13 his rookie season, 1898, helping Frank Selee to his fifth and last pennant.

A year later Willis was even better, 27-8, but the early-day Braves finished second and began their descent when Vic had an off-season, 10-17.

Wheelhorse Willis was the work horse through subpar seasons after Selee was seduced by Chicago. Twice he won 20 more in the Hub, but he led in defeats with 20 in 1902, 25 in '04 and 29 in '05, yet was good enough that Pittsburgh's playing pilot, Fred Clarke wanted him.

With the Pirates from 1906, he put together four straight 20-plus seasons and had a 1.73 earned-run average in 1906. When the Bucs ended the world champion Cubs' string of pennants in '09, he was 22-11. Ineffective in the World Series, he was available for sale.

Barney Dreyfuss shrewdly sold him to the Cardinals, managed then by Roger Bresnahan who knew Willis from better days when Vic stood for victory. All he did was to achieve a milestone with the last of 50 shutouts.

St. Louis never knew, close up, wheelhouse Willis, who one year at Boston appeared in 51 games, completing all except one of 46 starts, worked 410 innings—and still lost 20.

CY YOUNG

One day late in Cy Young's life as the winningest baseball pitcher ever, a young reporter asked respectfully, "Did you ever pitch in the major leagues, Mr. Young?"

Old Tuscarawas, close to the end at 88 in 1955, removed a pipe from his mouth, smiled around watery blue eyes and said, "Sonny, I won more games than you'll ever see."

True—as undoubtedly True as Denton Young's middle name—because most folks don't see 511 games, the number Cy won over a 23-year period from 1890 to 1911, 12 years in the National League, 11 in the American.

Of Young's amazing winning total, only 46 were gained in the first bright red uniform of the Cardinals in two years, 1899-1900, but St. Louis is privileged to have had the strapping 6-2, 210-pound sodbuster super-star pitch for the home team.

St. Louis thought so then, too, because even though there was a streetcar strike at a time few owned the rare horseless carriage, 18,000 crammed old League Park to see Cy beat Cleveland 10-1 in the '99 opener. He went 26-15 that year and 20-18 in the new century, another fifth-place season.

For the Ohio farm boy, then 33 and baseball's big-name pitcher after a decade in Cleveland, the St. Louis climate was too hot, and the money not so warm as newspaperman Ban Johnson's $600 increase to leave the National League individual salary limit ($2400) for Boston.

With the Red Sox, Cy, short the "cyclone" nickname of his fireball, helped Boston to win the first official World Series over Pittsburgh in 1903, winning two games.

Boston was so happy with the rubber-armed workhouse that they passed the hat in a pre-planned ball-park party planned for him in 1908 and contributed $7500, a handsome amount larger than a season's salary.

Big, rugged, round-faced Young, keeping shipshape by working his Tuscarawas County hills, hunting and running, insisted that strong legs kept him pitching often enough to post 16 seasons with 20 or more victories, 14 in a row and five beyond 30.

St. Louis got to see him on the home side only because the Robison brothers, Frank and Stanley Matthew, were so displeased with attendance at Cleveland that they swiped the Spiders' stars from Lake Erie to the Mississippi.

Young pitched so long in both centuries that confused writers didn't elect him to the Hall of Fame until the second voting at Cooperstown in 1937, but he was there for the museum opener two years later. Old Tuscarawas still might have been pitching except that by the time he was 44 in 1911, he was so rotund that they bunted him into retirement.

They wouldn't have done that to him in the prime of a master for whom Hall of Fame creator Ford Frick recommended designation of the annual prestigious Cy Young pitching award.

Back in Cy's heyday, fancy-hitting Slidin' Billy Hamilton, a master of bunting, base-stealing and fouling off pitches, bragged how he had fouled off 29 straight pitches the day before. First time, facing Young, Hamilton fouled off three straight pitches.

Cy called time, walked part way to the plate and said, "Billy, I'm firing the next one right over the plate. If you foul it off, I'll stick the next one in your ear." Forewarned, Billy bounced out. He couldn't steal first.

St. Louis National Baseball Club

GROUNDS
Sportsman's Park
GRAND BLVD. & DODIER STS.

OFFICES
3623 DODIER ST.

Saint Louis, Mo. August 1, 1927.

Mr. J. B. Sheridan,
c/o Sporting News,
St. Louis, Mo.,

Dear Mr. Sheridan:

Just a disconnected note in reply to yours of July 5th.

A couple of trades helped the ball club but out of twenty-four men on the team, I believe sixteen of them came from replacement camps and at least four men who came to us in trades were secured in exchange for "farm" players. O'Farrell, Southworth and McGraw were direct results of exchanges for such products and that is the team, except Frisch. Alexander came by waiver price purchase.

And, if you do not believe in high prices for players, how can you help but subscribe to the replacement camp idea?

Not one Minor League club president out of a dozen pretends to know a ball player. It seems to me to be silly to wait, therefore, for those birds to find or develop players.

Yes, the Minor Leagues ought to go in for a liberal draft but they have not done it and they won't do it. Baseball isn't being run on the oughtness of things at all. We have got to deal with competition as we find it. Professional baseball in America is not being played in Utopia by any manner of means.

Now, just a word about an item you have often mentioned to me, my failure to find a catcher. Well, that is just it, I have not found one. I got O'Farrell and I consider him pretty good but I have never developed a great catcher and for the simple reason that I have never "found" one. Do you know of any that I have passed up? Ruel was my own boy for a year after you gave him to me and I thought well of him. I believed that he was going to be a great catcher and had the right to purchase him from Memphis for $1,000.00. I wanted to repurchase him the worst way, but Fielder Jones would have none of him, said he was too small and would not have him around. I think I did fairly good with such material as Clemons and Agnew - and Severeid had practically all of his early Major League work with me. I am not proud of what I have done with catchers. In fact, I mm not proud at all about anything.

I think you are probably right about what you could do at Springfield, and after all is said and done the success of all these undertakings depends upon the good fortune of getting the right personnel in charge of the club affairs.

Schuble is just so-so, unlimited nerve, good arm, pretty fast and not enough sense to be afraid. He was the best man available and if the Danville Club can stay in its race after losing Schuble, or perchance win the Three I League pennant, and if, at the same time, the Cardinals can keep in the race, - I'll take my hat off to the replacement camp idea whether anyone else does or not.

Sincerely yours,

Branch Rickey

BR:F Vice-President.

Yes, Mr. Rickey: Branch Rickey defends his baby – the farm system he calls "replacement camps" – in a letter to J.B. Sheridan. Mr. Rickey was right in everything except that Heinie Schultz, the fill-in for injured shortstop Tommy Thevenow, was not ready.

Coaches and Managers

Some of the Greats: Top row (from left to right): Clyde "Buzzy" Wares, Jack Crooks, Eddie Stanky, August A. Busch, Jr., Harry Walker. Middle row: Ken Boyer, Gussie Busch shaking Eddie Stanky's hand. Bottom row: Dave Duncan, Stan Musial and Billy Southworth.

CARDINAL COACHES

Auferio, Tony
In St. Louis: 1973
Number: 50

Baylor, Don
In St. Louis: 1992
Number: 24

Becker, Joe
In St. Louis: 1965-66
Number: 4

Benson, Vern
In St. Louis: 1961-64, 70-75
Number: 8, 7

Blades, Ray
In St. Louis: 1930-32, 1951
Number: 37, 33

Boyer, Ken
In St. Louis: 1971-72
Number: 14

Braun, Steve
In St. Louis: 1990
Number: 26

Cardenal, Jose
In St. Louis: 1994-95
Number: 7

Chambliss, Chris
In St. Louis: 1993-95
Number: 10

Coleman, Joe
In St. Louis: 1991-94
Number: 30

Collins, Dave
In St. Louis: 1991-92
Number: 15

Cooper, Walker
In St. Louis: 1957
Number: 30

Cunningham, Joe
In St. Louis: 1982
Number:

Dent, Bucky
In St. Louis: 1991-94
Number: 30

DeJohn, Mark
In St. Louis: 1996-97
Number: 34

Duncan, Dave
In St. Louis: 1996-97
Number: 18

Gibson, Bob
In St. Louis: 1995
Number: 45

Gomez, Preston
In St. Louis: 1976
Number: 18

Gonzalez, Mike
In St. Louis: 1934-46
Number: 25, 35

Hack, Stan
In St. Louis: 1957-58
Number: 35

Hacker, Rich
In St. Louis: 1986-90
Number: 7

Hassey, Ron
In St. Louis: 1996
Number: 28

Hendrick, George
In St. Louis: 1996-97
Number: 25

Hiller, Chuck
In St. Louis: 1981-83
Number: 4

Hollingsworth, Al
In St. Louis: 1957-58
Number: 33

Hopp, Johnny
In St. Louis: 1956
Number: 40

Hubbard, Jack
In St. Louis: 1993
Number: 7

Johnson, Darrell
In St. Louis: 1960-61
Number: 8

Kahn, Lou
In St. Louis: 1954-55
Number: 27

Katt, Ray
In St. Louis: 1959-61
Number: 9

Kaufmann, Tony
In St. Louis: 1947-50
Number: 25

Keane, Johnny
In St. Louis: 1959-61
Number: 5

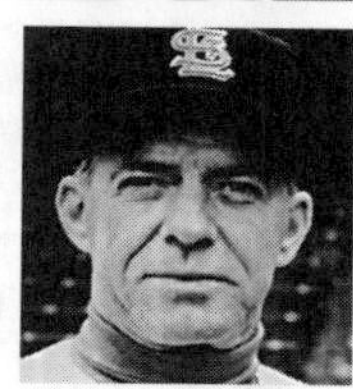

Killefer, Bill
In St. Louis: 1926

Kissell, George
In St. Louis: 1969-75
Number: 3

Kittle, Hub
In St. Louis: 1981-83
Number: 9

Knowles, Darold
In St. Louis: 1983
Number:23

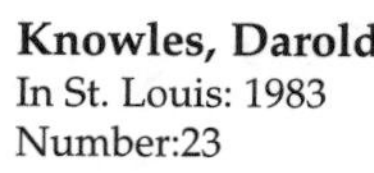

Koenig, Fred
In St. Louis: 1976
Number: 8

Krol, Jack
In St. Louis: 1977-80
Number: 8

Lachemann, Rene
In St. Louis: 1997
Number: 15

Lanier, Hal
In St. Louis: 1981-85
Number: 8

Lansford, Carney
In St. Louis: 1997
Number: 12

Lewis, Johnny
In St. Louis: 1973-75, 1984-89
Number: 30, 48, 8

Leyva, Nick
In St. Louis: 1984-88
Number: 16

Marion, Marty
In St. Louis: 1950
Number: 4

Maxvill, Dal
In St. Louis: 1979-80
Number: 27

McKay, Dave
In St. Louis: 1996-97
Number: 39

McKechnie, Bill
In St. Louis: 1927

Milliken, Bob
In St. Louis: 1965-70, 76
Number: 8, 33

Moore, Terry
In St. Louis: 1949-52, 56-58
Number: 8, 34

Mozzali, Mo
In St. Louis: 1977-78
Number: 4

Muffett, Billy
In St. Louis: 1967-70
Number: 4

Neale, Greasy
In St. Louis: 1929

O'Leary, Charley
In St. Louis: 1913-17

Onslow, Jack
In St. Louis: 1928

Osteen, Claude
In St. Louis: 1977-80
Number: 18

Peitz, Heine
In St. Louis: 1913

Pitts, Gaylen
In St. Louis: 1991-95
Number: 4

Pollet, Howie
In St. Louis: 1959-64
Number: 4, 26

Posedel, Bill
In St. Louis: 1954-57
Number: 33

Quirk, Jamie
In St. Louis: 1984
Number: 16

Reynolds, Tommy
In St. Louis: 1996
Number: 15

Ricketts, Dave
In St. Louis: 1974-75, 78-91
Number: 14, 15, 3

Riddle, John
In St. Louis: 1952-55
Number: 29

Riggins, Mark
In St. Louis: 1995
Number: 12

Riggleman, Jim
In St. Louis: 1989-90
Number: 5

Roarke, Mike
In St. Louis: 1984-90
Number: 4

Ruberto, Sonny
In St. Louis: 1977-78
Number: 3

Ryba, Mike
In St. Louis: 1951-54
Number: 35

Schoendienst, Red
In St. Louis: 1962-64, 1979-95
Number: 2

Schultz, Barney
In St. Louis: 1971-75
Number: 33

Schultz, Joe Jr.
In St. Louis: 1963-68
Number: 3

Shotton, Burt
In St. Louis: 1923-25

Sisler, Dick
In St. Louis: 1966-70
Number: 5

Smith, Hal
In St. Louis: 1962
Number: 18

Sothoron, Al
In St. Louis: 1927-28

Sugden, Joe
In St. Louis: 1921-25

Thomas, Lee
In St. Louis: 1972, 83
Number: 50

Thomas, Tom
In St. Louis: 1922

Thompson, Tim
In St. Louis: 1981
Number: 5

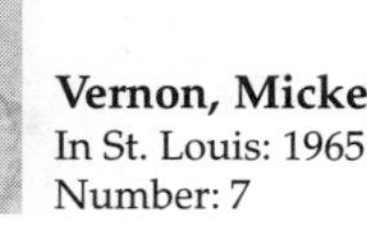
Turner, Tuck
In St. Louis: 1924

Vernon, Mickey
In St. Louis: 1965
Number: 7

Walker, Dixie
In St. Louis: 1953, 55
Number: 30

Wares, Buzzy
In St. Louis: 1930-51
Number: 26, 36

Zeller, Bart
In St. Louis: 1970
Number: 29

Walker, Harry
In St. Louis: 1959-62
Number: 3

Williams, Otto
In St. Louis: 1926

Zimmer, Tom
In St. Louis: 1976
Number: 50

The Last of the Four Time Winners!: 1888 Browns American Association Champions.
Top Row, Left to Right: Latham, Mascot Louis Comiskey, O'Neill
Middle Row, Left to Right: White, Devlin, Robinson, McCarthy, King, Herr
Front Row, Left to Right: Boyle, Hudson, Comiskey, Milligan, Dolan
Floor, Left to Right: Fly (greyhound), Chamberlain, Lyons, Prince (greyhound)

CARDINAL MANAGERS

Blades, Ray
In St. Louis: 1939-40
Number: 37

Boyer, Ken
In St. Louis:1978-80
Number: 14

Bresnahan, Roger
In St. Louis:1909-12

Buckenburger, Al
In St. Louis: 1895

Burke, Jimmy
In St. Louis: 1905

Campau, Count
In St. Louis: 1890

Caruthers, Bob
In St. Louis: 1892

Comiskey, Charlie
In St. Louis: 1883-89, 1891

Connor, Roger
In St. Louis: 1896

Crooks, Jack
In St. Louis: 1892

Cuthbert, Ned
In St. Louis: 1882

Diddlebock, Harry
In St. Louis: 1896

Donovan, Patsy
In St. Louis: 1901-03

Dowd, Tommy
In St. Louis: 1896-97

Dyer, Eddie
In St. Louis: 1946-50
Number: 30

Frisch, Frankie
In St. Louis: 1933-38
Number: 3

Gerhardt, Joe
In St. Louis: 1890

Glasscock, Jack
In St. Louis: 1892

Gonzalez, Mike
In St. Louis: 1938, 1940
Number: 35

Gore, George
In St. Louis: 1892

Hack, Stan
In St. Louis: 1958
Number: 35

Hallman, Bill
In St. Louis: 1897

Heilbroner, Louis
In St. Louis: 1900

Hemus, Solly
In St. Louis: 1959-61
Number: 7

Hendricks, Jack
In St. Louis: 1918

Herzog, Whitey
In St. Louis: 1980-90
Number: 3, 24

Hornsby, Rogers
In St. Louis: 1925-26

Huggins, Miller
In St. Louis: 1913-17

Marion, Marty
In St. Louis: 1951
Number: 4

Quinn, Joe
In St. Louis: 1895

Hurst, Tim
In St. Louis: 1898

McCarthy, Tommy
In St. Louis: 1890

Rapp, Vern
In St. Louis: 1977-78
Number: 9

Hutchinson, Fred
In St. Louis: 1956-58
Number: 29

McCloskey, John
In St. Louis: 1906-08

Rickey, Branch
In St. Louis: 1919-25

Jorgensen, Mike
In St. Louis: 1995
Number: 22

McKechnie, Bill
In St. Louis: 1928-29

Robison, Matthew
In St. Louis: 1905

Keane, Johnny
In St. Louis: 1961-64
Number: 5

Miller, George
In St. Louis: 1894

Roseman, Chief
In St. Louis: 1890

Kerins, John
In St. Louis: 1890

Nichols, Kid
In St. Louis: 1904-05

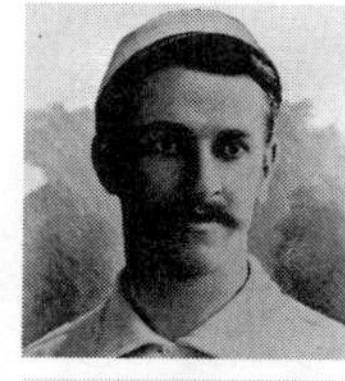

Schoendienst, Red
In St. Louis: 1965-76, 80, 90
Number: 2

Krol, Jack
In St. Louis: 1978, 1980
Number: 8

Nicol, Hugh
In St. Louis: 1897

Southworth, Billy
In St. Louis: 1929, 1940-45
Number: 30

LaRussa, Tony
In St. Louis: 1996-present
Number: 10

O'Farrell, Bob
In St. Louis: 1927

Stanky, Eddie
In St. Louis: 1952-55
Number: 12

Latham, Arlie
In St. Louis: 1896

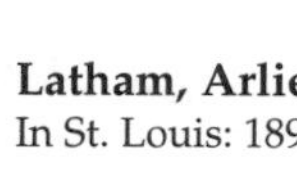

Phelan, Lew
In St. Louis: 1895

Street, Gabby
In St. Louis: 1929-33
Number: 25

Stricker, Cub
In St. Louis: 1892

Sullivan, Ted
In St. Louis: 1883

Tebeau, Patsy
In St. Louis: 1899-1900

Torre, Joe
In St. Louis: 1990-95
Number: 22, 9

Von der Ahe, Chris
In St. Louis: 1895-97

Walker, Harry
In St. Louis: 1955
Number: 5

Watkins, Bill
In St. Louis: 1893

Williams, Jimmy
In St. Louis: 1884

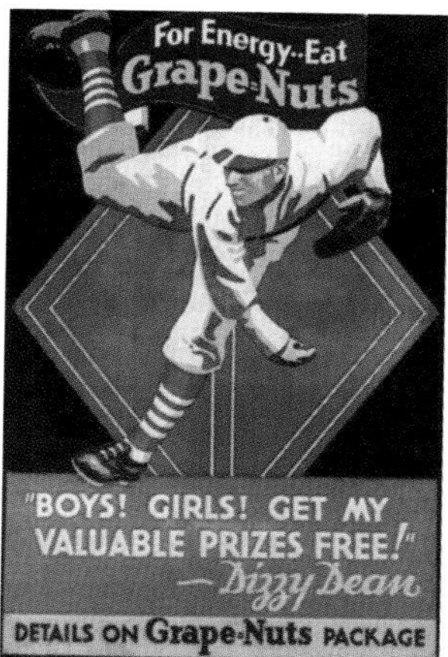
For Energy..Eat
Grape-Nuts
"BOYS! GIRLS! GET MY VALUABLE PRIZES FREE!"
—Dizzy Dean
DETAILS ON Grape-Nuts PACKAGE

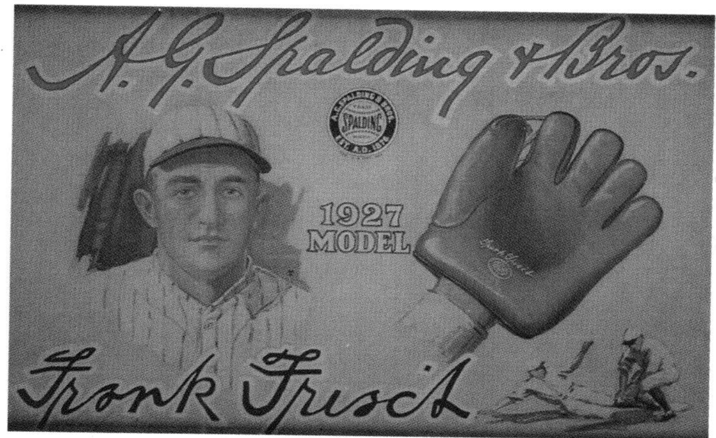
A. G. Spalding & Bros.
SPALDING
1927 MODEL
Frank Frisch

Pepper Martin

SUPER STAR II 1992 SUPER-ÉTOILE II
Post
OZZIE SMITH
ST. LOUIS CARDINALS DE ST. LOUIS

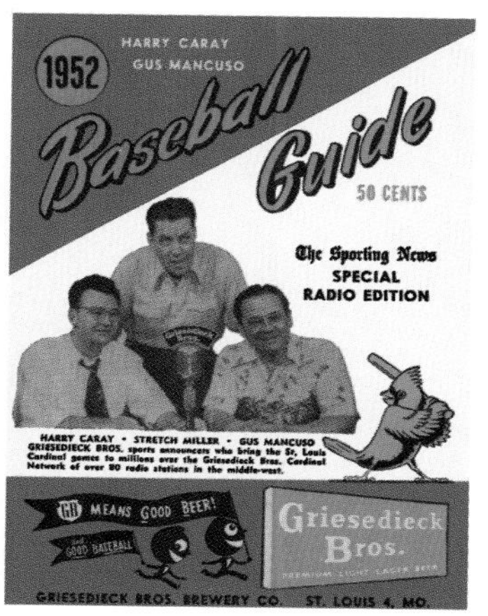
HARRY CARAY
GUS MANCUSO
1952
Baseball Guide
50 CENTS
The Sporting News SPECIAL RADIO EDITION
HARRY CARAY • STRETCH MILLER • GUS MANCUSO
GB MEANS GOOD BEER!
Griesedieck Bros.
GRIESEDIECK BROS. BREWERY CO. ST. LOUIS 4, MO.

fifty cents
1960 BASEBALL GUIDE
BUSCH BAVARIAN BEER
PUBLISHED BY The Sporting News

Rawlings
ATHLETIC EQUIPMENT 1957
spring and summer
Player of the Decade
Stan Musial

TED WILLIAMS OF

RED SOX

ROGERS HORNSBY 2B

Your 1977 Cardinal Pass
ST. LOUIS NATIONAL BASEBALL CLUB, INC.
1977

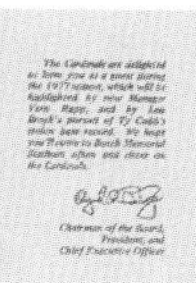

The SPORTING NEWS
Record Book for 1927
Published by
CHARLES C. SPINK & SON
ST. LOUIS, MO.
Price: Ten Cents the Copy

The SPORTING NEWS
Record Book for 1922
Published by
CHARLES C. SPINK & SON
ST. LOUIS, MO.
Price: Ten Cents the Copy

BAT
THE FOUNDATION OF BASEBALL

CURT FLOOD OF

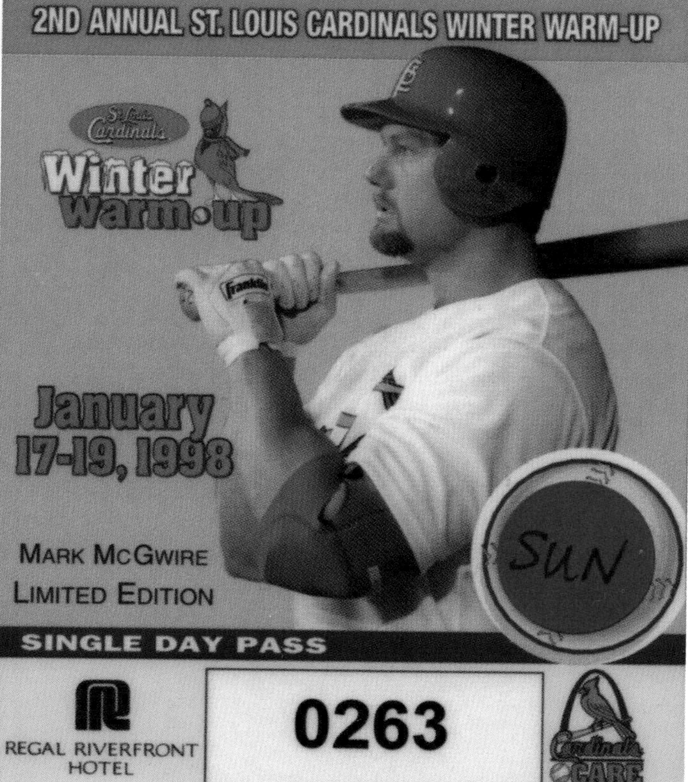
2ND ANNUAL ST. LOUIS CARDINALS WINTER WARM-UP
St. Louis Cardinals
Winter Warm-up
January 17-19, 1998
MARK MCGWIRE
LIMITED EDITION
SUN
SINGLE DAY PASS
REGAL RIVERFRONT HOTEL
0263
Cardinals CARE

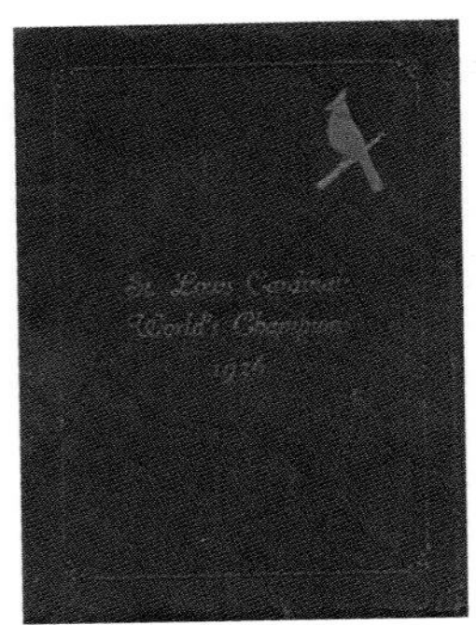

CARDINALS
50c
1 9 5 1

ST. LOUIS
Cardinals
1952
50¢

ST. LOUIS
Cardinals
1953
50¢

st. louis
Cardinals
50c
yearbook 1959

ST. LOUIS
Cardinals
50c
YEARBOOK

St. Louis
CARDINALS
50c
1961 Yearbook
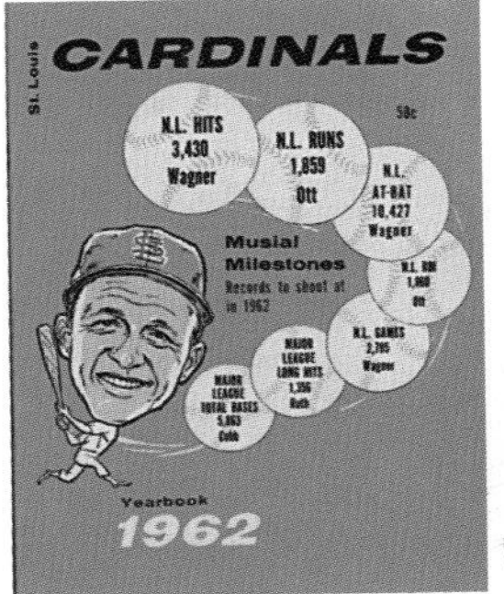
St. Louis
CARDINALS
50c
Musial Milestones
Yearbook
1962

St. Louis
CARDINALS
Yearbook/1963

St. Louis Cardinals
'67 World Champions
1968 SOUVENIR YEARBOOK
$1.00

St. Louis Cardinals
'68 National League Champions
1969 Souvenir Yearbook

St. Louis
Cardinals
1970 Souvenir Yearbook

St. Louis Cardinals 1971
souvenir yearbook

St. Louis Cardinals
OFFICIAL SOUVENIR YEARBOOK
1977

St. Louis Cardinals
1988

$5.00
"Thief" and "Fireman"
St. Louis Cardinals
1989 YEARBOOK

ST. LOUIS
Cardinals
YEAR-BOOK
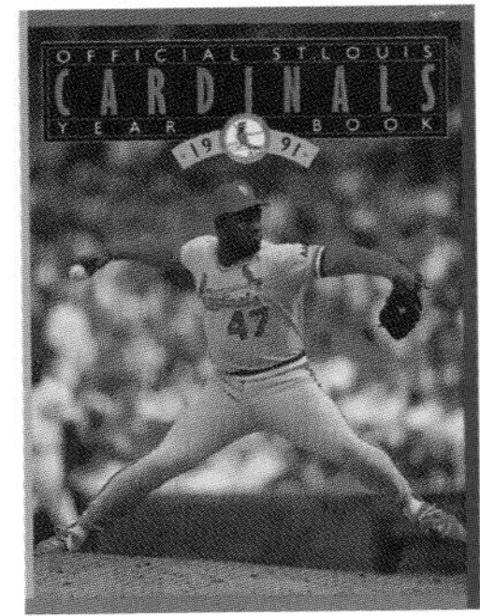
OFFICIAL ST. LOUIS
CARDINALS
YEAR BOOK
47

THE '78
WE CAN DO IT.
St. Louis Cardinals
$1.00

St. Louis Cardinals
1979
$1.00
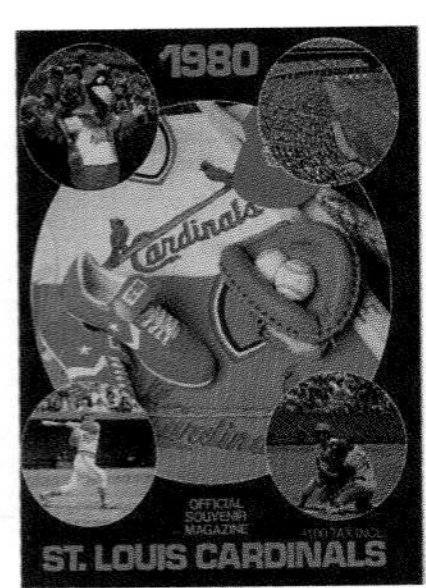
1980
Cardinals
ST. LOUIS CARDINALS

OFFICIAL SOUVENIR MAGAZINE
1981 ST. LOUIS
CARDINALS

$1.00
NOW INCLUDES SCORECARD
St. LOUIS
CARDINALS
1982 Official Scorebook

THE ST. LOUIS
CARDINALS
1982 WORLD CHAMPIONS
1983 OFFICIAL SCOREBOOK

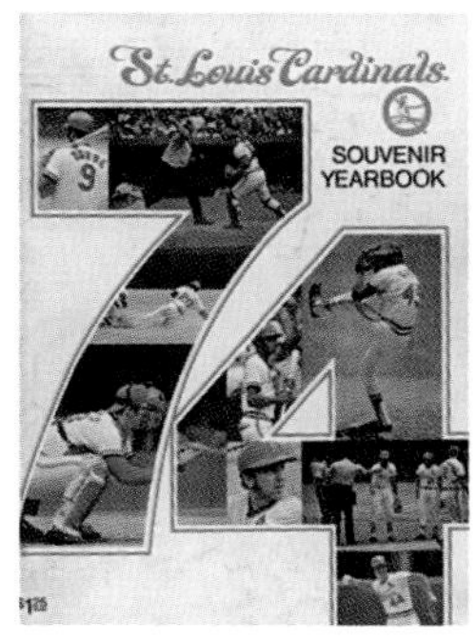

THROUGH THE YEARS: Above, a selection of Cardinal Yearbooks from 1926 (upper left-hand corner) to 1995. Left, Cardinals' Scorebooks from 1978-1986.

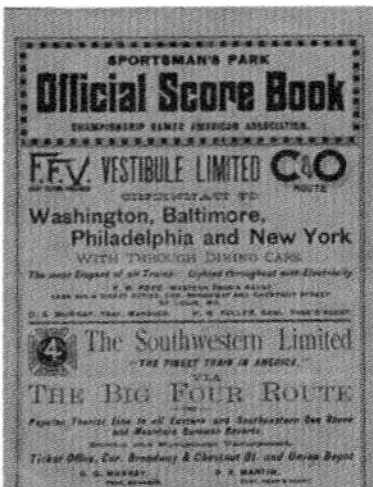

SPORTSMAN'S PARK
Official Score Book
Washington, Baltimore, Philadelphia and New York
The Southwestern Limited
The Big Four Route

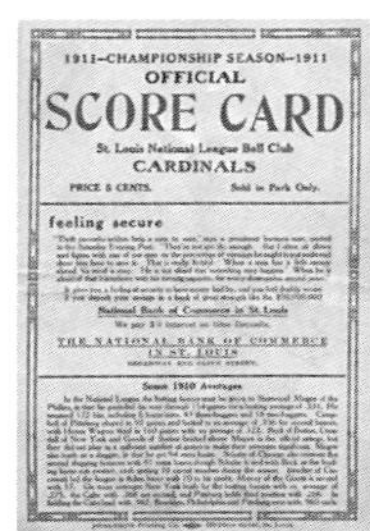

1911—CHAMPIONSHIP SEASON—1911
OFFICIAL
SCORE CARD
CARDINALS

BOATMEN'S NATIONAL BANK
Thirsty? Just—
A Home Run!

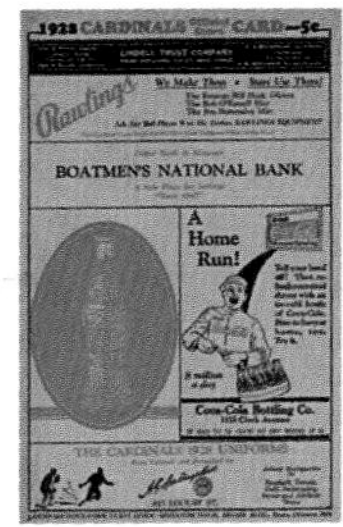

1928 CARDINALS
BOATMEN'S NATIONAL BANK
A Home Run!

1930 CARDINALS
EMANELO
BOATMEN'S NATIONAL BANK
That 7th Inning
KANSAS CITY

ST. LOUIS CARDINALS OFFICIAL SCORE CARD
THE DRINK EVERYBODY KNOWS
OLD GOLD

It's Chesterfield
"ICE-COLD COCA-COLA"
OLD GOLD

ST. LOUIS CARDINALS OFFICIAL SCORE CARD
It's Chesterfield
"ICE-COLD COCA-COLA"
OLD GOLD

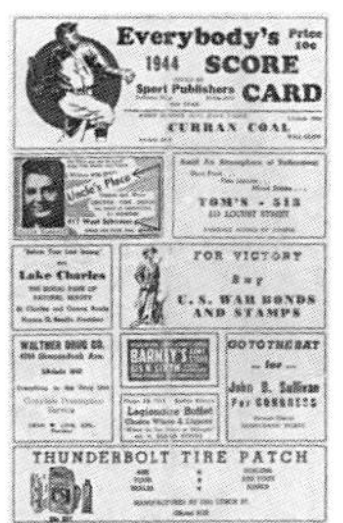

Everybody's
1944 SCORE
CARD
FOR VICTORY
U. S. WAR BONDS AND STAMPS
THUNDERBOLT TIRE PATCH

CAMELS
CHESTERFIELD
For refreshment ... Have a Coke
OLD GOLD

ST. LOUIS
Cardinals
1952
SOUVENIR PROGRAM
PRICE 10¢

ST. LOUIS
1953
Cardinals
souvenir program

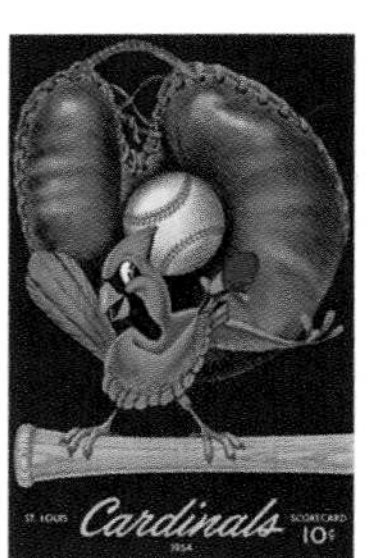

Cardinals
SCORECARD
10¢

ST. LOUIS
Cardinals
1955
BUSCH STADIUM
SCORECARD
10¢

ST. LOUIS
Cardinals
BUSCH STADIUM SCORECARD 10¢

St. Louis Cardinals
1967 SCORECARD
Kroger

SUN AIRLINES
St. Louis Cardinals
World Champions
1968 SCORECARD
Kroger

DX
Known by the customers we keep.
Drive in and see why.
St. Louis Cardinals
National League Champions
LIGHTNING LOW PRICES
Kroger

SUNOCO
The Sunoco Eight are here.
St. Louis Cardinals.
1970 Scorecard
LIGHTNING LOW DISCOUNT PRICES
Kroger

Get A Piece of the Action
SUNOCO
1971 scorecard 25¢

TURN TO THE LEADERS IN TOTAL SPORTS COVERAGE.
KTVI
St. Louis Cardinals 1977
25¢
STEAK n SHAKE
Famous For Steakburgers

ALL SPORTS FOLLOW THE LEADER
2
St. Louis Cardinals 1978

ALL SPORTS FOLLOW THE LEADER
2
KTVI
St. Louis Cardinals 1979
For the score and so much more
ST LOUIS POST-DISPATCH

NEWS WEATHER SPORTS
We get it all for you firsthand.
2
St. Louis Cardinals 1980
Fly Red Birds Fly
League Leader in Taste

CONNERS & KIDD
NEWS 2
1981 ST. LOUIS CARDINALS
League Leader in Taste

ST LOUIS
News at 9
SAVE 50¢

CARDINALS & 11
SCORECARD

St. Louis
Cardinals
Visit the New St. Louis Cardinals Hall of Fame Museum

Cardinals
1995
OFFICIAL
SCORECARD
TRIPLE PLAY!

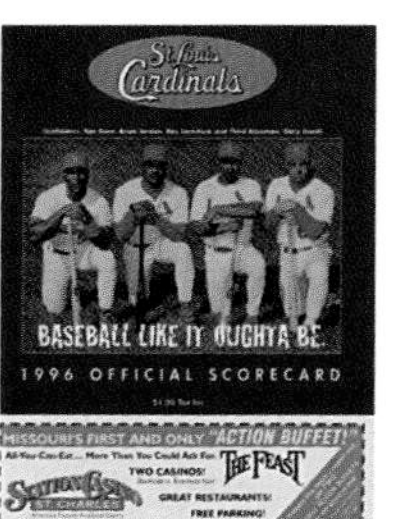

St. Louis
Cardinals
BASEBALL LIKE IT OUGHTA BE.
1996 OFFICIAL SCORECARD
THE FEAST

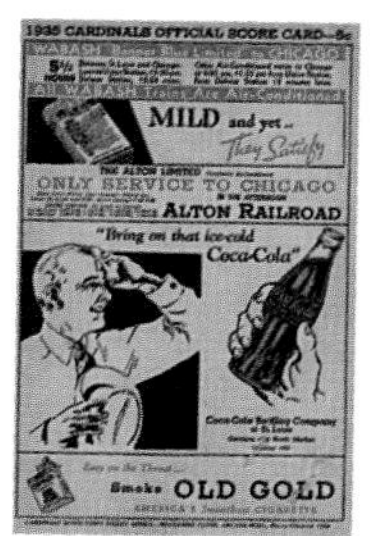

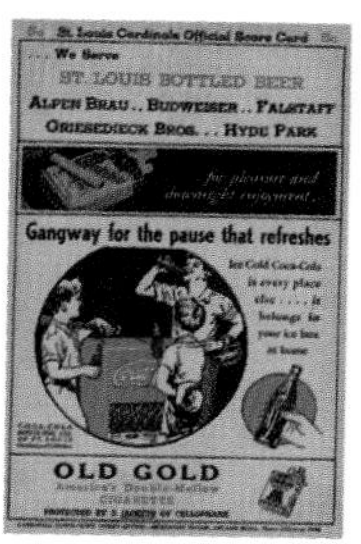

Know the Score: Official Scorecards dating all the way back to 1891(upper left-hand corner). However, please note that the only exception to this rule is "Everybody's Scorecard" from 1944 (second row, fourth from the left); that card was created by an outside source. At the end of the list, we find two anniversary programs, one from 1969 celebrating 100 years of professional baseball and another from '76 marking the 50th reunion of the 1926 World Championship Redbirds.

1957
ALL-STAR
GAME
BUSCH STADIUM • SAINT LOUIS
AMERICAN
NATIONAL
50¢
OFFICIAL SCORECARD PROGRAM

RAIN CHECK
• NATIONAL LEAGUE vs. AMERICAN LEAGUE •
ALL★STAR GAME
BUSCH MEMORIAL STADIUM
IN CASE OF POSTPONEMENT THIS TICKET WILL BE GOOD FOR PLAYOFF AT TIME ANNOUNCED
ADMIT ONE
NOT GOOD IF DETACHED
ALL★STAR GAME
BUSCH MEMORIAL STADIUM
ST. LOUIS NATIONAL BASEBALL CLUB, INC., Agent
ALL CLUB, INC. Agent
TUESDAY • JULY 12, 1966 • 1:00 P. M.
3
135 SEC.
9 ROW
6 SEAT
FIELD BOX $6.00
Taxes Incl.

BUSCH STADIUM
• NATIONAL LEAGUE vs. AMERICAN LEAGUE •
RETAIN THIS STUB
ALL★STAR GAME
RAIN CHECK
IN CASE OF POSTPONEMENT THIS TICKET WILL BE GOOD FOR PLAYOFF AT TIME ANNOUNCED
ADMIT ONE
NOT GOOD IF DETACHED
ALL★STAR GAME
BUSCH STADIUM
ST. LOUIS NATIONAL BASEBALL CLUB, INC., Agent
ALL CLUB, INC. Agent
TUESDAY • JULY 9 • 1957
Y SEC.
10 ROW
4 SEAT
UPPER DECK RESERVED SEAT $4.00

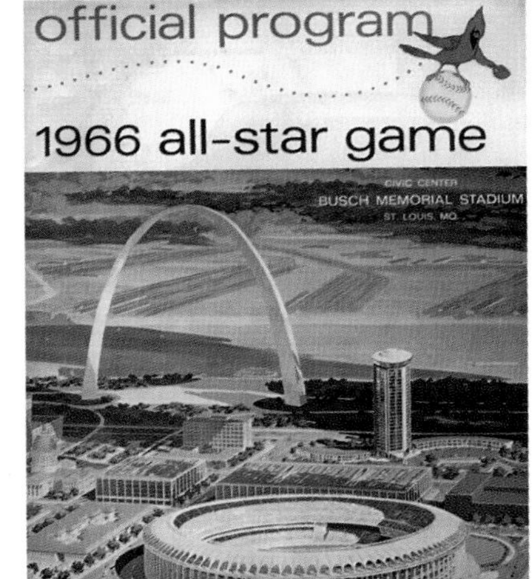
official program
1966 all-star game
CIVIC CENTER
BUSCH MEMORIAL STADIUM
ST. LOUIS, MO.
50¢

★ OFFICIAL PROGRAM ★
MAJOR LEAGUE
ALL STAR
GAME
SPORTSMANS PARK SAINT LOUIS
Price 25 Cents
TUESDAY JULY 9, 1940 1:30 P.M.

UPPER GRAND STAND
SEC. J
ROW 9
SEAT 2
All☆Star☆Game
TUESDAY, JULY 9 1940
SPORTSMEN'S PARK
St. Louis, Mo.
GAME STARTS AT 1:30 P. M.
IN CASE OF POSTPONEMENT, THIS COUPON WILL BE GOOD FOR PLAY OFF TO BE PLAYED AT
9 A. M. WEDNESDAY, JULY 10, 1940
Est. Price 1.228
Federal Tax .13
Sales Tax .025
License Fee .037
TOTAL $1.42
WELDON, WILLIAMS & LICK, FT. SMITH, ARK

1987 NATIONAL LEAGUE
CHAMPIONSHIP SERIES
$3.00
O. SMITH 1

100% Nylon Sewn
NATIONAL LEAGUE
Celebration
1982
PLAYOFFS
CHAMPIONSHIP
$2.00

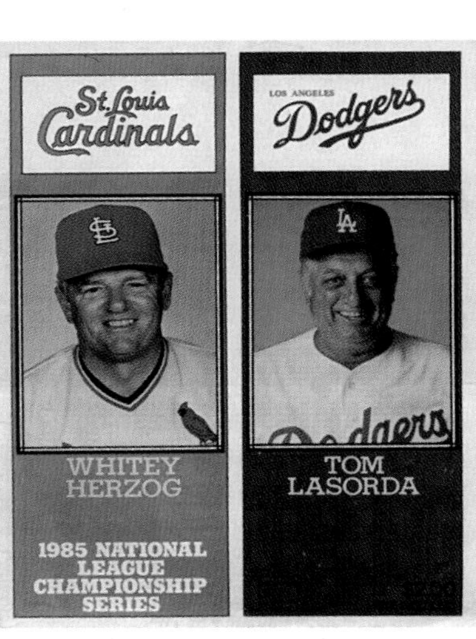
St. Louis Cardinals
LOS ANGELES Dodgers
WHITEY HERZOG
TOM LASORDA
1985 NATIONAL LEAGUE CHAMPIONSHIP SERIES

"C'mon, SPARK UP!"
Said Stan Musial,
of the St. Louis Cardinals
"I COULDN'T HIT WELL ENOUGH TO MAKE MY SCHOOL TEAM UNTIL STAN MUSIAL SHOWED ME HOW TO SPARK!"
Cut this photo out. Look for different champion pictures in other Dell Comics.
FOLLOWING THROUGH ON YOUR SWING LIKE THIS HELPS YOU GET MORE HITS. AND BE SURE YOU HAVE LOTS OF SPARK!
GET PLENTY OF PRACTICE, SLEEP AND EAT ENERGY FOODS LIKE WHEATIES! THAT'S HOW I SPARK UP!
MMMMMM! WHEATIES SURE TASTE GOOD!
THAT'S SPARKIN'!
ANOTHER HIT! THAT WHEATIES SPARK SURE HELPS!
WHEATIES
"Breakfast of Champions"
THERE'S A WHOLE KERNEL OF WHEAT IN EVERY WHEATIES FLAKE
WHOLE WHEAT FOR GROWTH
WHOLE WHEAT FOR STAMINA
WHOLE WHEAT FOR RED BLOOD
SPARK UP WITH WHEATIES!

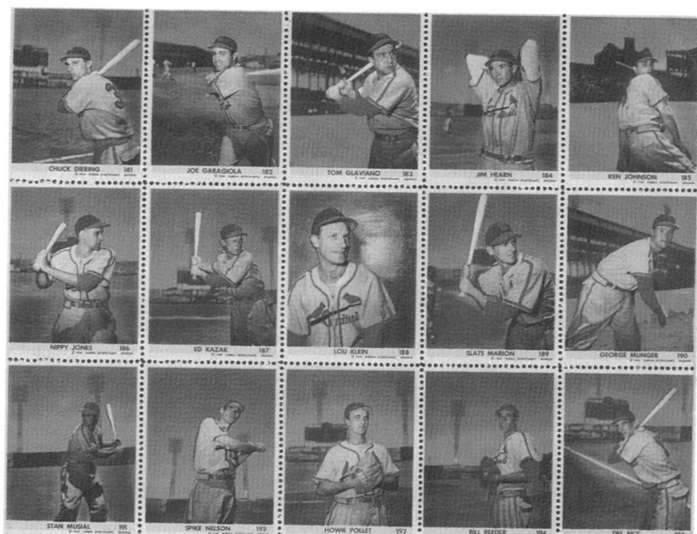
CHUCK DIERING 181
JOE GARAGIOLA 182
TOM GLAVIANO 183
JIM HEARN 184
KEN JOHNSON 185
NIPPY JONES 186
ED KAZAK 187
LOU KLEIN 188
SLATS MARION 189
GEORGE MUNGER 190
STAN MUSIAL 191
SPIKE NELSON 192
HOWIE POLLET 193
BILL REEDER 194
DEL RICE 195

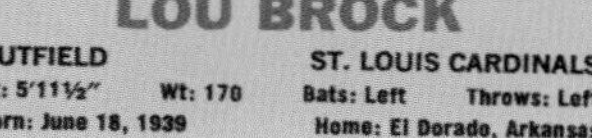
LOU BROCK
OUTFIELD
ST. LOUIS CARDINALS
Ht: 5'11½"
Wt: 170
Bats: Left
Throws: Left
Born: June 18, 1939
Home: El Dorado, Arkansas

ENOS SLAUGHTER
ST. LOUIS CARDINALS

ST. LOUIS
BRESNAHAN, ST. LOUIS NAT'L

A TRIBUTE TO GREATNESS
September 26, 1996
8 pm • The Fox Theatre
A Walk Down The Yellow Brick Road
with The Wizard of Oz and Friends
OZZIE 1978 OZ 1996 SMITH
ADMIT ONE
0875

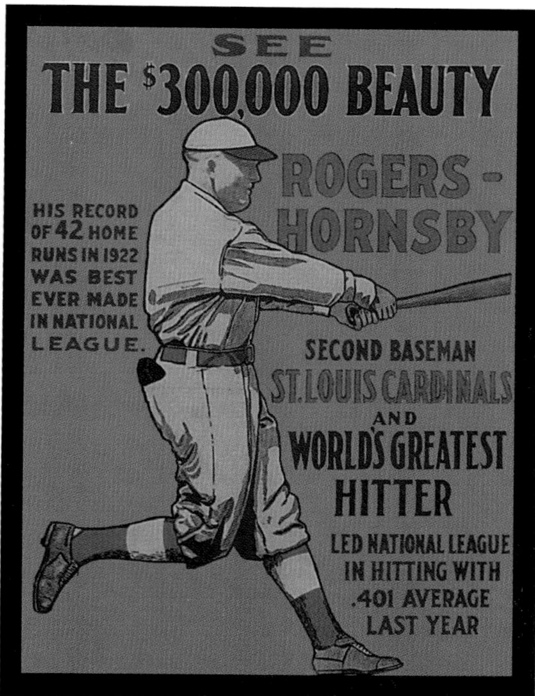
SEE
THE $300,000 BEAUTY
ROGERS - HORNSBY
HIS RECORD OF 42 HOME RUNS IN 1922 WAS BEST EVER MADE IN NATIONAL LEAGUE.
SECOND BASEMAN
ST. LOUIS CARDINALS
AND
WORLD'S GREATEST HITTER
LED NATIONAL LEAGUE IN HITTING WITH .401 AVERAGE LAST YEAR

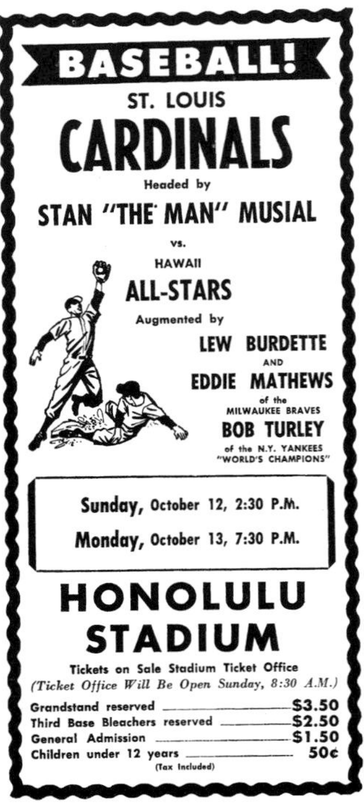

BASEBALL!

ST. LOUIS

CARDINALS

Headed by

STAN "THE MAN" MUSIAL

vs.

HAWAII

ALL-STARS

Augmented by

LEW BURDETTE

AND

EDDIE MATHEWS

of the MILWAUKEE BRAVES

BOB TURLEY

of the N.Y. YANKEES "WORLD'S CHAMPIONS"

Sunday, October 12, 2:30 P.M.

Monday, October 13, 7:30 P.M.

HONOLULU STADIUM

Tickets on Sale Stadium Ticket Office

(Ticket Office Will Be Open Sunday, 8:30 A.M.)

Grandstand reserved ________ $3.50
Third Base Bleachers reserved ________ $2.50
General Admission ________ $1.50
Children under 12 years ________ 50¢

(Tax Included)

Welcome Dinner

in honour of

The Members of the St. Louis Cardinals

given by under the joint auspices of

Mr. Bunzo Akama, Governor of Osaka Prefecture,

Mr. Mitsuji Nakai, Mayor of Osaka City

and

Mr. Michisuke Sugi, President,

Osaka Chamber of Commerce and Industry

at Hotel New Osaka

on October, 31st, 1958.

Menu

DÎNER

Consommé Bouquetière

Salmon-Trout Meunière

Broiled Ribs Steak Maître d'Hôtel Butter

Roast Chicken with Dressing

Season Salad

Vanilla Ice Cream Chocolate Sauce

Fruits

Coffee

FLANNELED DIPLOMACY: When the 1958 Cardinals made a flying trip to Japan, by way of Hawaii, they impressed veteran promoter Yetsuo Higa with their spirited off-the-field camaraderie and their spirited play on it. They were honored in many ways then and in a second trip to the Land of the Rising Sun ten years later. Musial is still *ichiban star* to the Japanese.

An Ownership Chronology

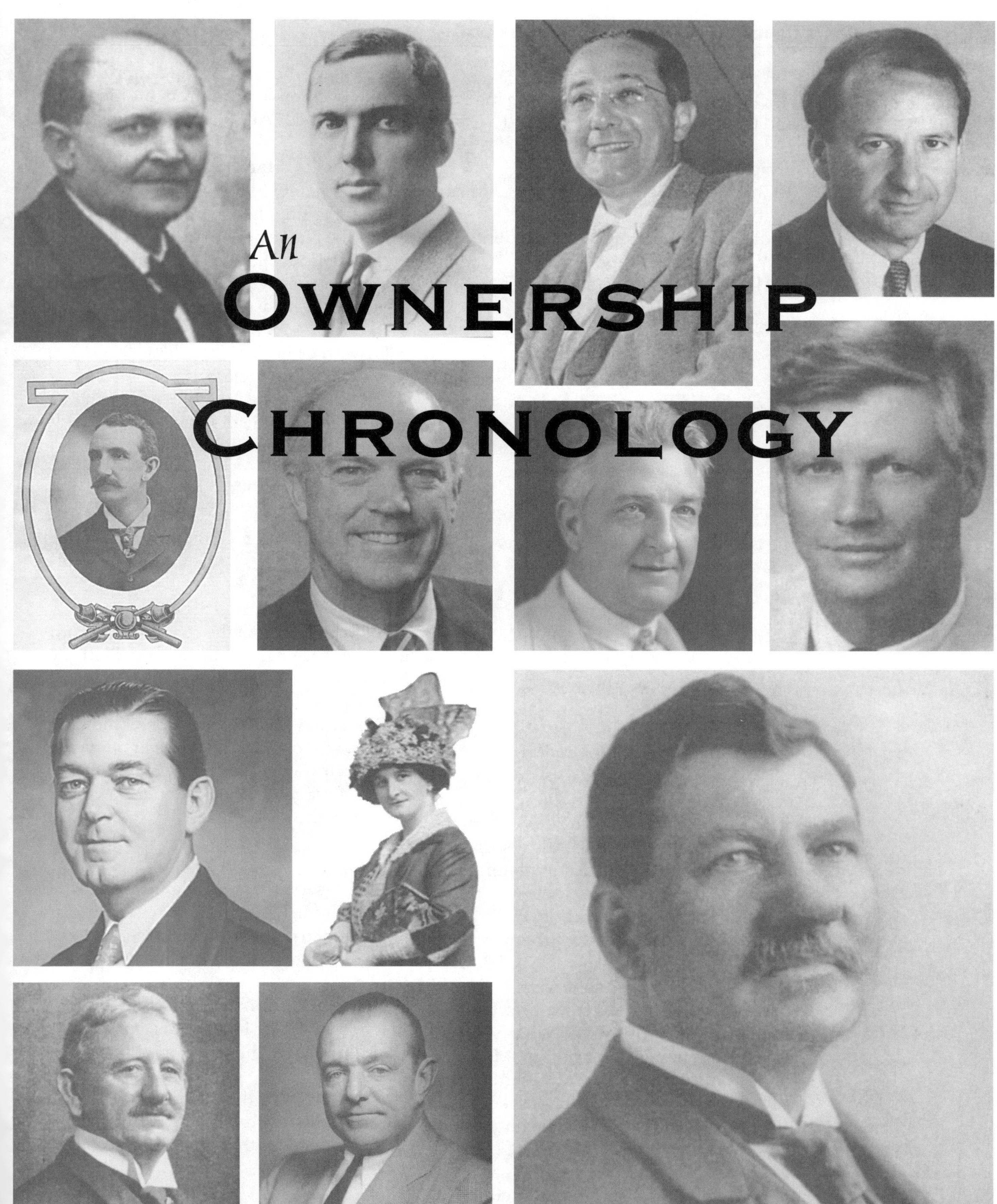

THE CARDINAL OWNERS: Top Row, Edward C. Becker, Sam Breadon, Fred M. Saigh and William O.DeWitt Jr.; Second Row, Stanley M. Robison, Frederick O. Hanser, James C. Jones and Andrew N. Baur; Third Row, Robert E. Hannegan and Helene Hathaway Robison Britton; Bottom Row, Frank D. Robison and August Busch, Jr.; Bottom Right Corner, Chris Von der Ahe.

Chris Von der Ahe

1880

On February 16, 1880 Sportsmans Park and Club Association is organized.

Principles include the following:

- Chris Von der Ahe, President and Majority Owner,
- John W. Peckington, Vice President,
- W.W. Judy, Treasurer,
- Al Spink, Secretary,
- J.T. Farrell, W. F. Noelker, and Ed Goodfellow.

Spring of 1881

St. Louis Browns organized, though considered professionals they were not affiliated with any professional league.

Fall of 1881

Chris Von der Ahe and D.S. Reid attend the first meeting of the American Association at Pittsburgh.

1882

St. Louis Browns Base Ball Club joins American Association of Base Ball Clubs with Chris Von der Ahe, Owner and President.

1898

Von der Ahe is majority owner and President to January 12, 1898 where he is removed as President by a vote of the club's board of directors. Club secretary Benjamin S. Muckenfuss is installed as President.

Frank Robison

After a series of events only Hollywood could have invisioned, the Browns are put into receivership on August 9th, 1898.

At public auction on the steps of the old courthouse March 14,1898 Chris Von der Ahe's Browns are sold to what was believed to be the highest bidder, Mr. G. A. Gruner, a local attorney representing the interest of nearly all of the secured creditors of Chris Von der Ahe. The only exclusion from the list was Edward C. Becker who was known as Von der Ahe's angel as he had helped Chris out financially on many occasions.

Edward C. Becker contested the sale and placed a bid for the team that would satisfy all of the existing creditors and put him in position to profit from his long support of Von der Ahe and the Browns.

March, 1899

Immediately following the awarding of the team to him, he incorporated the Team under the Name of The American Base Ball and Athletic Exhibition Company. Date of Incorporation was March 17, 1899. The principles were as follows:

- Edward C. Becker, President: 996 shares
- Guy T. Billon: 1 share
- Jonathan "Broker" H. Blessing: 1 share
- Samuel G. Payne: 1 share
- William G. Schoefield: 1 share

The name of the company would be changed March 18th to The American Base Ball and Exhibition Company of St. Louis Mo.

April 1899

Before the start of the 1899 season, brothers Frank DeHass Robison and Matthew Stanley Robison of Cleveland purchase a majority ownership of the franchise and take over day-to-day operation of the Club. Their first move was the transfer of players from their Cleveland club to St. Louis.

The first game played under new ownership, April 15, 1899.

1905

Frank served as president through the 1905 season with Stanley remaining in Cleveland to manage their business interest there including the National League Cleveland club.

The exception was Matthew's brief managerial career in St. Louis at the end of the 1905 season, mainly to avoid paying a new man to close out the season. It was similar to Frank's hiring of Louis Heilbroner the club's concessionaire, in 1900 to finish out the season.

1906

The 1906 season brought Matthew to St. Louis as President with Frank remaining in Cleveland.

1908

Frank DeHass Robison dies September 25th,1908 and Mathew Stanley Robison assumes complete control of the franchise.

1911

Matthew Stanley Robison dies March 24th ,1911 and the club passes to Mrs. Frank (Sarah) DeHass Robison and Frank's only daughter, Mrs. Helene Hathaway Robison Britton.

Cardinal Manager Roger Bresnahan organizes a group of investors that offers $500,000 for the club and grounds prior to Mrs. Helene Hathaway Robison Britton's petition to the courts. Their offer is refused.

E.A. Steininger, the Robison's legal advisor, is appointed President of the club and serves in that capacity.

1912

Through the 1912 season, due mainly to the lengthy processing of the estate and to the settlement of claims from Matthew's in-laws, the courts decide the ball club's new owner to be Mrs. Helene Hathaway Robison Britton with her mother Mrs. Sarah C. Hathaway Robison signing over her interest. Mid-way through the 1912 season, Helene's first action is to appoint her personal legal advisor St. Louis Attny. James C. Jones as president of the club.

The Brittons resided at the Jefferson Hotel while in St. Louis with their two children, Marie and DeHass.

1913

For the start of the 1913 season, Lady Bee, as she would come to be known, would install her husband Schyler P. Britton as president.

1916

Schyler would lose the jobs of president and husband mid-way through the 1916 season with Lady Bee taking over as president and head of household for the remainder of the season.

The battles with the St. Louis Federal League and American League teams, not to mention her own players and managers plus her own husband, proved to Lady Bee that baseball wasn't all it was cracked up to be. At the close of the 1916 season, she agreed to sell to a consortium, headed by her long-time advisor, James C. Jones.

1917

On May 2nd, 1917 the club is incorporated under the name of St. Louis National Baseball Club. The preferred shareholders were as follows:

- Fred M. Cheney of St. Louis: 2,450 shares
- John Q. Day of St. Louis: 10 shares
- Oliver Abel of St. Louis: 10 shares
- R.A. Hoffmann of St. Louis: 10 shares
- George E. Black of St. Louis: 10 shares
- Frank I. Walsh of St. Louis: 10 shares

Common shareholders were as follows:

- Branch Rickey of St. Louis: 200 shares
- Benjamin G. Brinkman of St. Louis: 200 shares
- Martin J. Collins of St. Louis: 40 shares
- John A. Leschen of St. Louis: 200 shares
- John C. Reid of St. Louis: 100 shares
- G. H. Williams of St. Louis: 200 shares
- C.E. Salisbury of St. Louis: 10 shares
- James C. Jones of St. Louis: 3,276 shares
- Lon O. Hocker of St. Louis: 40 shares
- George A. Meyer of St. Louis: 40 shares
- S. R. Ward of St. Louis: 280 shares
- W. E. Bilheimer of St. Louis: 10 shares
- R. A. Hoffmann of St. Louis: 26 shares
- Oliver Abel of St. Louis: 10 shares
- John Q. Day of St. Louis: 4 shares
- H. D. Seekamp of St. Louis: 284 shares
- V. L. Boisaubin of St. Louis: 10 shares
- James P. Newell of St. Louis: 40 shares
- Frank A. Mohr of St. Louis: 10 shares
- E. F. Shaw of St. Louis: 10 shares
- Allen McReynolds of St. Louis: 10 shares

Branch Rickey is installed as president of the club for the 1917 season and would serve in that capacity through the 1919 season.

1920

On May 20th, 1920 Samuel Breadon becomes a director of the club as the corporation is re-capitalized with the issue of additional stock.

New Shareholders were as follows:

LUCKY SAM:
The 27-year president, Sam Breadon, until too old, loved to play in his Cardinals' lunch-time spring break.

- O. T. Hodge of St. Louis: 14 shares
- Robert Hutcheson of St. Louis: 6 shares
- Phil Mohr of St. Louis: 5 shares
- Ernest Lucas of St. Louis: 4 shares
- L. W. Petty of St. Louis: 5 shares
- O. H. Leimbrock of St. Louis: 2 shares
- Charles W. Ermes of St. Louis: 1 share
- Thomas Foerstel of St. Louis: 11 shares
- S. B. Williams of St. Louis: 3 shares
- J. R. Cooke of St. Louis: 4 shares
- W. G. Schofield of St. Louis: 18 shares
- R. J. Guthrie of St. Louis: 2 shares
- G. W. Simmons of St. Louis: 10 shares
- W. C. Erman of St. Louis: 4 shares
- John C. Reid of St. Louis: 49 shares
- F. R. Pierce of St. Louis: 4 shares
- W. K. Stanard of St. Louis: 180 shares
- James R. Crawford of St. Louis: 1 share
- John Q. Day of St. Louis: 8 shares
- George Daurus Sr. of St. Louis: 1 share
- George Daurus Jr. of St. Louis: 1 share
- J. F. Hickey of St. Louis: 5 shares
- John A. Leschen of St. Louis: 360 shares
- Martin J. Collins of St. Louis: 296 shares
- Frank Z. Walsh of St. Louis: 10 shares
- R. A. Hoffmann of St. Louis: 26 shares
- L. F. Schultz of St. Louis: 3 shares
- John P. Woods of St. Louis: 2 shares
- John A. Bruner of St. Louis: 1 share
- Charles L. Niemeier of St. Louis: 4 shares
- M. E. Read of St. Louis: 1 share
- S. C. Sutherland of St. Louis: 27 shares
- F. O. Watts of St. Louis: 10 shares
- H. Vinsonhaler of St. Louis: 10 shares
- Adolph M.Diez of St. Louis: 429 shares
- James C. Jones of St. Louis: 319 shares
- Lon O. Hocker of St. Louis: 215 shares
- I. H. Cohn of St. Louis: 62 shares
- Phillip A. Riley of St. Louis: 2 shares
- George S. Levis of St. Louis: 3 shares
- R. Morton Moss of St. Louis: 4 shares
- F. D. Miller of St. Louis: 1 share
- J. C. Mitchell of St. Louis: 1 share
- William E. Bernthal of St. Louis: 2 shares
- W. L. Evans of St. Louis: 1 share
- Robert W. Hall of St. Louis: 1 share
- W. V. Eaton of St. Louis: 3 shares
- J. I. Epstein of St. Louis: 2 shares
- William Orthwein of St. Louis: 11 shares
- E. C. Dreyer of St. Louis: 6 shares
- Samuel Breadon of St. Louis: 1,173 shares
- G. A. Roth of St. Louis: 2 shares
- Charles F. Barrett of St. Louis: 6 shares
- I. W. Powell of St. Louis: 4 shares
- W. C. Anderson of St. Louis: 661 shares
- G. J. Tremayne of St. Louis: 3 shares
- Charles Stix of St. Louis: 1 share

GRANDSTAND BEST: Showman Gussie Busch his first spring as Cards' president, 1953, at St. Petersburg, Florida.

Samuel Breadon is installed as president for the 1920 season and would serve in that capacity through the 1947 season. Samuel Breadon would die May 10, 1949, shortly after selling the club.

1947

On November 25, 1947 St. Louis National Baseball Club was purchased by Robert Emmet Hannegan, Fred M. Sigh and a group of prominent St. Louisans. The group in addition to Hannegan and Sigh includes the following:

- David R. Calhoun Jr., President of the St. Louis Union Trust Co.
- William C. Connett, Vice President of the First National Bank of St. Louis
- Gwynne Evans, Former President of Evans Coffee Co.
- Sidney Solomon Jr., St. Louis Insurance man and former executive assistant to Hannegan in the Post Master General Office
- George W. Simpkins, St. Louis Attorney and Hannegan's chief council.

Robert E. Hannegan, Ex-PostMaster General and former Head of the Democratic National Committee, is installed as president of the club and would serve in that capacity until January 27th, 1949 when doctors advised he step down. At that time he sold his interests to Sigh. Hannegan died October 6, 1949.

Fred M. Saigh, listed as principle minority stockholder, installed as vice president and treasurer.

1949

On January 27, 1949 Fred M. Saigh purchased controling interest in The St. Louis National Baseball Club.

Saigh was installed as president of the club.

1953

On February 20,1953 Anheuser Busch Incorporated purchased the St. Louis National Baseball Club.

August A. Busch Jr. was installed as president of the club and would serve in that capacity through the 1973 season.

1973

January 1, 1973 Richard A. Meyer was installed as president only to be replaced by August A. Busch Jr. on February 28, 1974.

1974

August A. Busch Jr. resumed his duties as president for the 1974 season.

1989

October 30, 1989 August A. Busch Jr. stepped down as president and Fred L. Kuhlmann assumed the role of club president and would serve in that capacity through December 31, 1991.

August A. Busch Jr. died September 29th, 1989 at age 90.

1992

On January 1,1992 Stuart F. Meyer was installed as president of the club and would serve in that capacity through August 19, 1994.

1994

On September 1, 1994 Mark C. Lamping the current club president was installed.

1996

On March 21st, 1996 the St. Louis National Baseball Club was sold by Anheuser Busch Inc. Mark C. Lamping continues as club president.

PASSING THE BATON: August A. Busch Jr. to son August A. Busch III.

Labeled as the St. Louis Cardinals L.P., the new 18-membership group was formed as follows:

- William O. DeWitt Jr., Chairman of the Board and General Partner
- Frederick O. Hanser, Chairman
- Andrew N. Baur, Secretary-Treasurer
- Stephen F. Brauer
- Robert H. Castellini
- G. Watts Humphrey Jr.
- Nick D. Kladis
- Donna DeWitt Lambert
- Michael McDonnell
- David C. Pratt
- Michael E. Pulitzer
- Mercer Reynolds
- Richard H. Sutphin
- Dudley S. Taft
- John K. Wallace Jr.
- T.L. Williams
- W.J. Williams

MARK C. LAMPING

M-AND-M: Before the candy bar or Mantle and Maris, the Cardinals had their M-and-M men, muscular Joe Medwick (7) and Johnny Mize of the mid-to-late 1930s and early '40s. Here, at St. Petersburg, Fla., Medwick signs for that young kid in the foreground with Mize waiting to hit behind Medwick in the batting change as customarily in the line-up.

SPORTSMANS PARK AND CLUB
ST. LOUIS, MO.
ST LOUIS BROWNS

The BALLPARKS

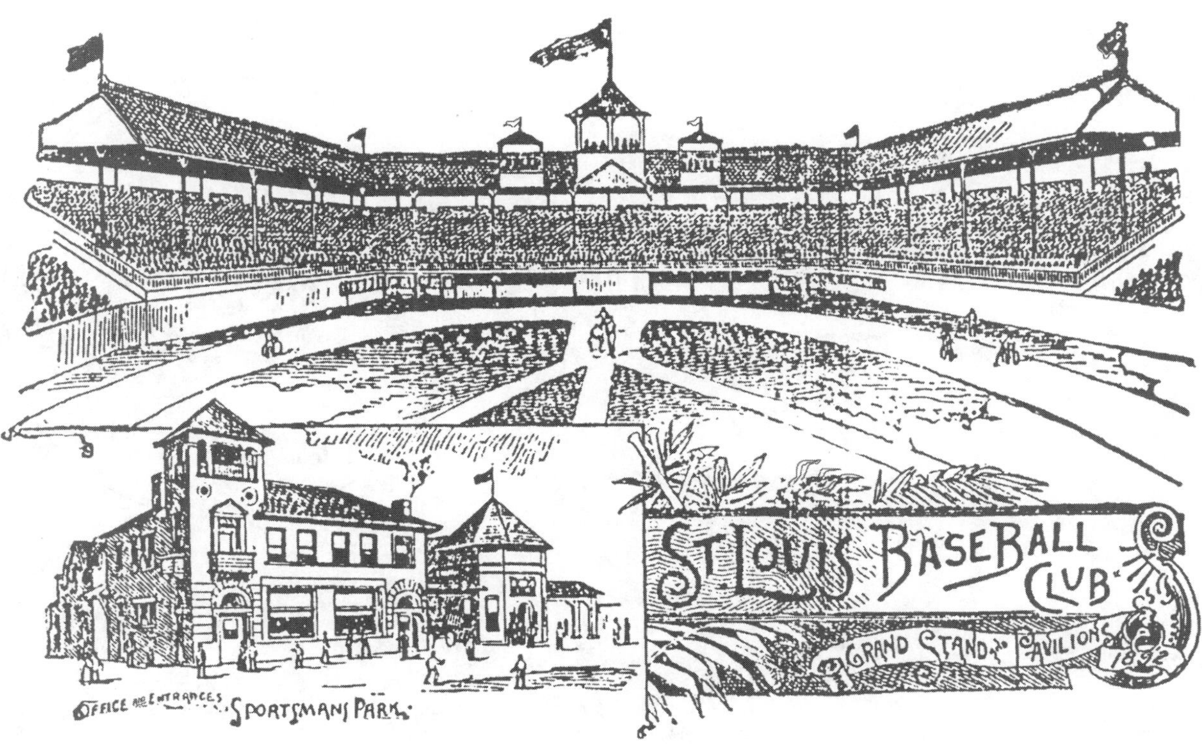

A GRAND TRADITION: Top, Logo for Sportsmans Park and Club pre-1900; Middle row, Sportsman's Park, 1866-1966, and Busch Stadium, 1966-present; Bottom, Sportsman's Park before Browns' Robert Lee Hedges rebuilt it in 1909, the first concrete stadium west of the Mississippi. Nifty offices on Grand Avenue, too.

Von For The Road: Colorful Chris Von der Ahe's last hurrah – a cardboard souvenir given out when he opened his own ball park in 1893, just before he went broke.

February 16, 1880

Sportsmans Park and Club Association organized for the purposes of outfitting the Grounds located on Grand Avenue between Dodier and Sullivan Streets on St. Louis' north side.

A grandstand and bleachers are constructed and the field is enclosed by a fence to accommodate only paying customers.

1881

Sportsmans Park is home of a semi-pro contingent called the Browns and games are scheduled with teams passing through and virtually anyone who would play them. Their first game is on March 22, 1881 against the Cincinnati Reds operated by O.P. Caylor.

1882

Sportsmans Park and Club Association secures a franchise in the newly formed American Association of Base Ball Clubs. The club is to be known as the Browns.

May 5th 1882 is the First game played by the American Association Browns at Sportsmans Park.

December 18, 1891

The American Association Browns join the National League of Professional Baseball Clubs. They play their first game at Sportsmans Park as members of the National League on April 12, 1892.

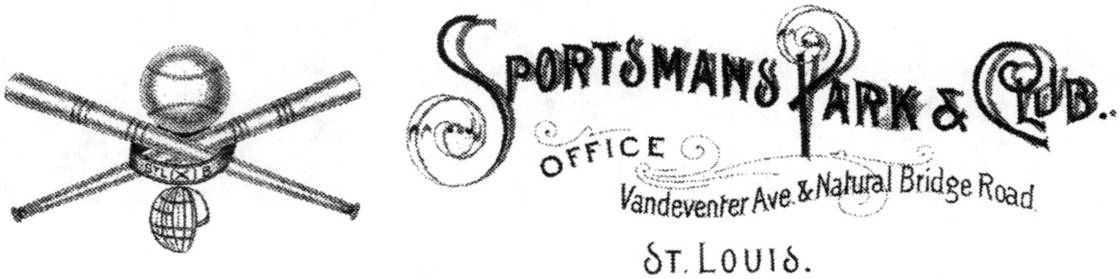

Sportsmans Park & Club.
Office
Vandeventer Ave. & Natural Bridge Road
St. Louis.

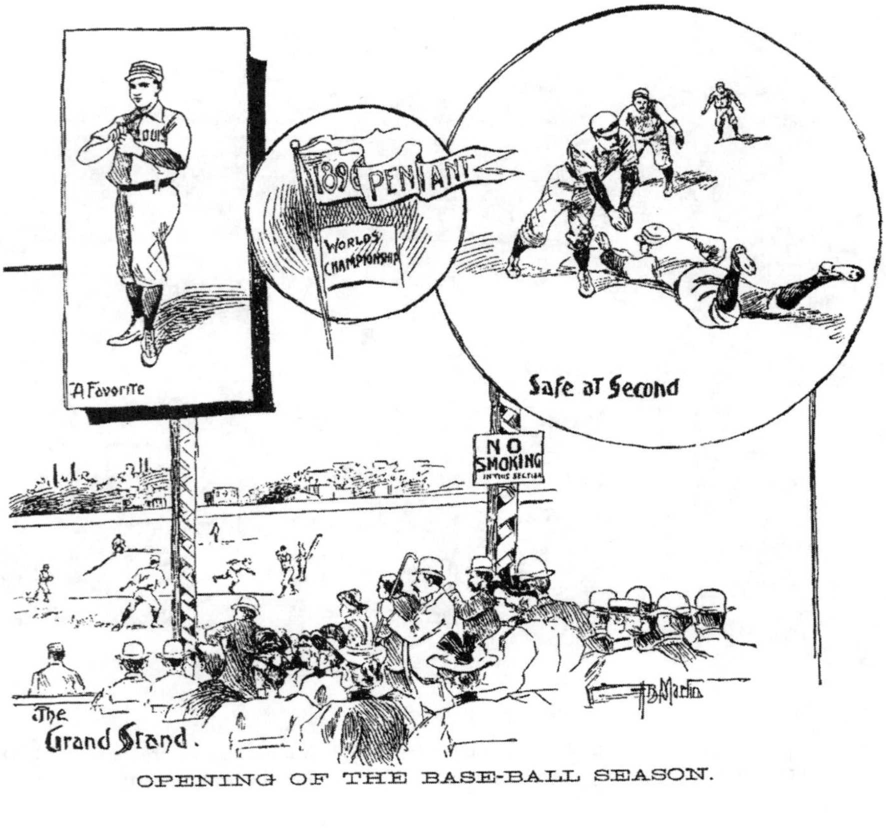

A Favorite
1896 Pennant
Worlds Championship
Safe at Second
No Smoking in this section
The Grand Stand.

OPENING OF THE BASE-BALL SEASON.

Beautiful Dreamer: Tra-la, even a newspaper cartoon hailed the 1896 team in an opening day montage, but Vondy's guys finished 11th in the 12-team NL. Note the "No-Smoking" section!

October 13, 1892

The St. Louis Browns of the National League play their last game at Sportsmans Park on Grand Avenue between Dodier and Sullivan Streets.

April 27, 1893

The St. Louis Browns of the National League play their first game at new Sportsmans Park located at the intersection of Vandeventer and Natural Bridge.

April 16, 1898

The first fire: the grandstand and offices are a total loss when a fire breaks out during a game with the Cubs. One man is killed, many are injured.

April 15, 1899

The St. Louis Browns of the National League become the St. Louis Perfectos of the National League and they play their first game at League Park, formally new Sportsmans Park, at the intersection of Vandeventer and Natural Bridge.

1900

With the team name Perfectos not widely accepted, the Cardinals are born.

1911

Upon the death of Matthew Stanley Robison in 1911, League Park, located at Vandeventer and Natural Bridge, is renamed Robison Field to honor Frank DeHass Robison and Matthew Stanley Robison.

1917

In the spring of 1917 the new ownership group renames Robison Field, located at Vandeventer and Natural Bridge, Cardinal Field. It would be Major League Baseball's last all wooden park.

1920

On June 6th, 1920 the Cardinals play their last game at Cardinal Field located at Vandeventer and Natural Bridge.

Ball Park confusion is nearly complete as the St. Louis Cardinals National League Club formally playing at Cardinal Field located at Vandeventer and Natural Bridge, A.K.A. the St. Louis Cardinals National League Club formally playing at Robison Field located at Vandeventer and Natural Bridge, A.K.A. the St. Louis Cardinals National League Club formally playing at League Park located at Vandeventer and Natural Bridge, A.K.A. the St. Louis Perfectos National League Club formally playing at League Park located at Vandeventer and Natural Bridge, A.K.A the St. Louis Browns National League Club formally playing at New Sportsmans Park located at Vandeventer and Natural Bridge, A.K.A. the St. Louis Browns National League Club formally playing at Sportsmans Park located at Grand Avenue between Dodier and Sullivan Streets, A.K.A. the St. Louis Browns American Association Club formally playing at Sportsmans Park located at Grand Avenue between Dodier and Sullivan Streets, plays its first game on July 1st, 1920 as tenants of the American League St. Louis Browns in their park which so happened to be located at Grand Avenue between Dodier and Sullivan Streets and coincidentally was still called Sportsmans Park.

What goes around comes around is not over yet.

A STREETCAR NAMED DISGUST: Fort Wayne transition men, Frank DeHaas Robison and brother Matthew Stanley, dedicated sportsmen, couldn't win even though they gave St. Louis their better Cleveland ball club in a 1899 roster shift that would be a no-no now.

THE SECOND FIRE: League Park (Robison Field), May 4, 1901: The grandstand and offices are damaged when fire breaks out during a game with the Reds. The team would play one home game at near-by athletic park at Grand Avenue and Sullivan Street.

Up and Up: About Chirs Von der Ahe's chute-the-chutes, they were located just in the vast outfield of the Vandeventer and Natural Bridge Park.

1953

On February 20,1953, Anheuser Busch buys Sportsmans Park located at Grand Avenue between Dodier and Sullivan Streets, and renames it Busch Stadium. The St. Louis Browns American League Club moves to Baltimore. Team name confusion can end. Sportsmans Park confusion can end. The St. Louis Cardinals National League Club plays its first game April 16,1953 at Busch Stadium located at Grand Avenue between Dodier and Sullivan Streets

1966

May 8th, 1966 the St. Louis National League Club plays its last game at Busch Stadium located at Grand Avenue between Dodier and Sullivan Streets. Mercifully the Stadium is torn down and in its place Herbert Hoover Boys Club is built with their baseball field in place of the legendary Diamond.

May 12th, 1966 the St. Louis Cardinals National League Club plays its first Game at New Busch Memorial Stadium located downtown near the Riverfront on Stadium Plaza. Through tender care, officially, Busch Stadium didn't show its age when past 30 years old.

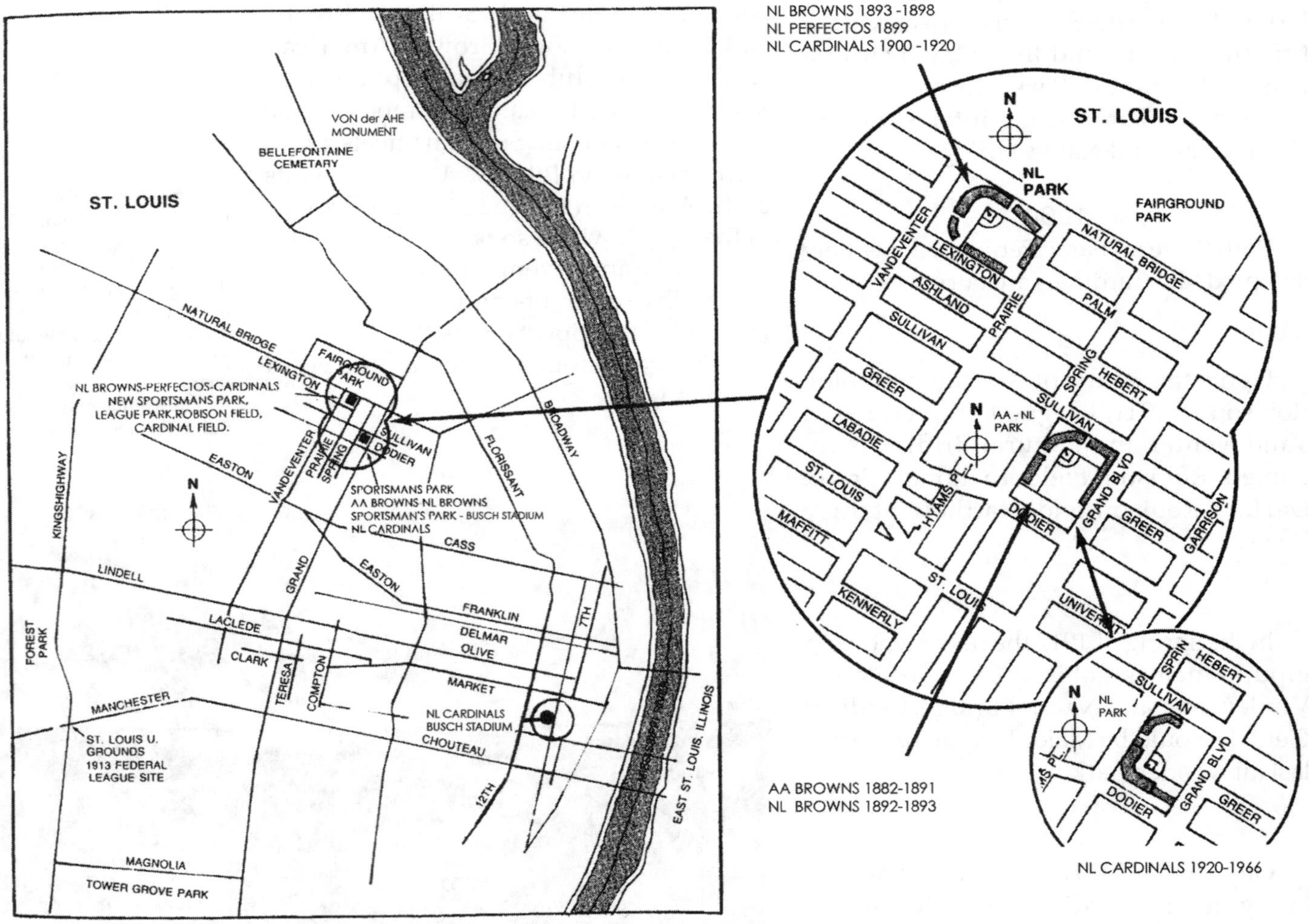

Lewis and Clark: You might have to be one of the great explorers to determine this map, but dotted spots in the first sketch show how close the parks were in North St. Louis. The second close-up proves it – three blocks from Grand and Dodier to Vandeventer and Natural Bridge.

The Numbers Through the Years

August 29, 1936 THE LITERARY DIGEST 3

DIZZY & DAFFY talk INGRAM'S Shaving Contest and its $2,500 FIRST PRIZE

ALSO 10 PRIZES OF $100 EACH AND 2,000 RUBBERSET SHAVING BRUSHES—2011 PRIZES IN ALL

Dizzy Dean says "COOLNESS"

"I LIKE HOT ARGUMENTS AND COOL SHAVES. THE BEST IS NONE TOO GOOD FOR A STAR LIKE I. SUPPOSE INGRAM'S DOES LAST LONGER—WHAT OF IT—I MAKE PLENTY OF JACK—SO I GO ALL OUT FOR LUXURY—LUXURY—LUXURY!"

"WHEN IT COMES TO INGRAM'S, LAY OFF THAT 'ME AND PAUL' GAG. THIS IS ONE SPOT WHERE THE DEAN BOYS DIFFER. I'M FOR INGRAM'S ECONOMY—HOOK, FAST BALL AND SINKER. SAVE ... MONEY ..."

... question in 50 words or less

Which is more important to You?

1. INGRAM'S FAMOUS COOLNESS
2. INGRAM'S CONCENTRATED ECONOMY

shaving brushes worth $2.00 each.

"What do men like best about Ingram's?" What wins them and *holds* them to this fast-selling cream—its *famous* "Coolness" or the *downright, rock-bottom* "Economy" of its concentrated form? And now we want this big question settled—and we're paying heavy money for the winning answers.

Try Ingram's today! You can win dollars—thousands of them! You can win a lifetime of comfortable shaves. For Ingram's is the Arctic and Antarctic of shaving creams—the chilliest, ... that ever made wire- ... "Uncle." It's a triple-play formula that ... you cream, lotion ... every cool brushful.

Before you vote "Coolness"—test its "Economy." A little Ingram's goes a longer way because it's concentrated—with a laboratory finding over other creams of 15% to 20% more lather and cool shaves from the same amount of cream.

TRY INGRAM'S AND THEN TELL US

But try Ingram's and give us your verdict. Your face can't lose. Read the rules in the box to the right. Then send us your entry. Remember, there are 3,500 Ingram cash dollars and 2,000 Rubberset brushes for winning answers.

READ THESE EASY RULES!

A LITTLE INGRAM'S GOES A LONGER WAY BECAUSE—*it's Concentrated*

RESERVED SEAT 5 SEAT 2 ROW C SEC.

St. Louis National Base Ball Club
NATIONAL LEAGUE SPORTSMAN'S PARK

Good This Date Only SEPT 12

ADMIT ONE

Subject to conditions set forth on the back hereof.

Cardinals

S. Breadon
President

Reserved Seat

Adm.	1.32
State Tax	.028
Fed. Tax	.26
Lic. Fee	.042
Total	$1.65

WELDON, WILLIAMS & LICK, FT. SMITH, ARK.

Through the Years: Topside, Ken Boyer and Tommy Herr fan buttons; "Me 'n Paul" Dean Brothers plug shaving cream. Below, Rip Collins boosts an open-faced match box and a ticket keepsake when Sam Breadon's Cardinals gave you a reserved-seat thrill for only $1.65.

1882

Finish: 5
Won: 37
Lost: 43
Winning Percentage: .463
Attendance: 155,000
Manager: Ned Cuthbert

1883

Finish: 2
Won: 65
Lost: 33
Winning Percentage: .663
Attendance: 260,000
Manager: T. Sullivan, Chas. Comiskey

1884

Finish: 4
Won: 67
Lost: 40
Winning Percentage: .625
Attendance: 220,000
Manager: Jimmy Williams, Chas. Comiskey

1885

Finish: 1
Won: 79
Lost: 33
Winning Percentage: .705
Attendance: 150,000
Manager: Chas. Comiskey

1886

Finish: 1
Won: 93
Lost: 46
Winning Percentage: .669
Attendance: 240,000
Manager: Chas. Comiskey

1887

Finish: 1
Won: 95
Lost: 40
Winning Percentage: .704
Attendance: *265,000
Manager: Chas. Comiskey

1888

Finish: 1
Won: 92
Lost: 43
Winning Percentage: .681
Attendance: 185,000
Manager: Chas. Comiskey

1889

Finish: 2
Won: 90
Lost: 45
Winning Percentage: .667
Attendance: 180,000
Manager: Chas. Comiskey

1890

Finish: 3
Won: 78
Lost: 58
Winning Percentage: .574
Attendance: 135,000
Manager: Tommy McCarthy (2) occ., John Kerins, Chief Roseman, Count Campau, Joe Gerhardt

1891

Finish: 2
Won: 86
Lost: 52
Winning Percentage: .623
Attendance: *245,000
Manager: Chas. Comiskey

1892

Finish: 11
Won: 56
Lost: 94
Winning Percentage: .373
Attendance: 192,422
Manager: Jack Glasscock, Cub Stricker, Jack Crooks, George Gore, Bob Caruthers

1893

Finish: 10
Won: 57
Lost: 75
Winning Percentage: .432
Attendance: 195,000
Manager: Bill Watkins

1894

Finish: 9
Won: 56
Lost: 76
Winning Percentage: .424
Attendance: 155,000
Manager: George Miller

1895

Finish: 11
Won: 39
Lost: 92
Winning Percentage: .298
Attendance: 170,000
Manager: Al Buckenberger, Joe Quinn, Lew Phelan, Chris Von der Ahe

1896

Finish: 11
Won: 40
Lost: 90
Winning Percentage: .308
Attendance: 184,000
Manager: Harry Diddlebock, Arlie Latham, Chris Von der Ahe, Roger Connor, Tommy Dowd

1897

Finish: 12
Won: 29
Lost: 102
Winning Percentage: .221
Attendance: 136,400
Manager: Tommy Dowd, Hugh Nicol, Bill Hallman, Chris Von der Ahe

1898

Finish: 12
Won: 39
Lost: 111
Winning Percentage: .260
Attendance: 151,700
Manager: Tim Hurst

1899

Finish: 5
Won: 84
Lost: 67
Winning Percentage: .556
Attendance: 373,909
Manager: Oliver Tebeau

1900

Finish: 5T
Won: 65
Lost: 75
Winning Percentage: .464
Attendance: 270,000
Manager: Oliver Tebeau, Louis Heilbroner

1901

Finish: 4
Won: 76
Lost: 64
Winning Percentage: .543
Attendance: *379,988
Manager: Patsy Donovan

1902

Finish: 6
Won: 56
Lost: 78
Winning Percentage: .418
Attendance: 226,417
Manager: Patsy Donovan

1903

Finish: 8
Won: 43
Lost: 94
Winning Percentage: .314
Attendance: 263,538
Manager: Patsy Donovan

1904

Finish: 5
Won: 75
Lost: 79
Winning Percentage: .487
Attendance: 386,750
Manager: Kid Nichols

1905

Finish: 6
Won: 58
Lost: 96
Winning Percentage: .377
Attendance: 292,800
Manager: Kid Nichols, Jimmy Burke, Matthew Robinson

1906

Finish: 7
Won: 52
Lost: 98
Winning Percentage: .347
Attendance: 283,770
Manager: John J. McCloskey

1907

Finish: 8
Won: 52
Lost: 101
Winning Percentage: .340
Attendance: 185,377
Manager: John J. McCloskey

1908

Finish: 8
Won: 49
Lost: 105
Winning Percentage: .318
Attendance: 205,129
Manager: John J. McCloskey

1909

Finish: 7
Won: 54
Lost: 98
Winning Percentage: .355
Attendance: 299,982
Manager: Roger Bresnahan

1910

Finish: 7
Won: 63
Lost: 90
Winning Percentage: .412
Attendance: 363,624
Manager: Roger Bresnahan

1911

Finish: 5
Won: 75
Lost: 74
Winning Percentage: .503
Attendance: 447,768
Manager: Roger Bresnahan

1912

Finish: 6
Won: 63
Lost: 90
Winning Percentage: .412
Attendance: 241,759
Manager: Roger Bresnahan

1913

Finish: 8
Won: 51
Lost: 99
Winning Percentage: .340
Attandance: 203,531
Manager: Miller Huggins
Coaches: Heinie Peitz, Charley O'Leary

1914

Finish: 3
Won: 81
Lost: 72
Winning Percentage: .529
Attendance: 346,025
Manager: Miller Huggins
Coach: Charley O'Leary

1915

Finish: 6
Won: 72
Lost: 81
Winning Percentage: .471
Attendance: 252,657
Manager: Miller Huggins
Coach: Charley O'Leary

1916

Finish: 7T
Won: 60
Lost: 93
Winning Percentage: .392
Attendance: 224,308
Manager: Miller Huggins
Coach: Charley O'Leary

1917

Finish: 3
Won: 82
Lost: 70
Winning Percentage: .539
Attendance: 301,948
Manager: Miller Huggins
Coach: Charley O'Leary

1918

Finish: 8
Won: 51
Lost: 78
Winning Percentage: .395
Attandance: 110,596
Manager: Jack Hendricks

1919

Finish: 7
Won: 54
Lost: 83
Winning Percentage: .394
Attendance: 173,604
Manager: Branch Rickey

1920

Finish: 5
Won: 75
Lost: 79
Winning Percentage: .487
Attendance: 325,845
Manager: Branch Rickey

1921

Finish: 3
Won: 87
Lost: 66
Winning Percentage: .569
Attendance: 384,790
Manager: Branch Rickey
Coach: Joe Sugden

1922

Finish: 3T
Won: 85
Lost: 69
Winning Percentage: .552
Attendance: 536,343
Manager: Branch Rickey
Coaches: Joe Sugden, Tom Thomas

1923

Finish: 5
Won: 79
Lost: 74
Winning Percentage: .561
Attendance: 338,548
Manager: Branch Rickey
Coaches: Burt Shotton, Joe Sugden

1924

Finish: 6
Won: 65
Lost: 89
Winning Percentage: .422
Attendance: 272,884
Manager: Branch Rickey
Coaches: Burt Shotton, Joe Sugden, Tuck Turner

1925

Finish: 4
Won: 77
Lost: 76
Winning Percentage: .503
Attendance: 405,297
Manager: Branch Rickey, Rogers Hornsby
Coaches: Burt Shotton, Joe Sugden

1926

Finish: 1
Won: 89
Lost: 65
Winning Percentage: .578
Attendance: 681,575
Manager: Rogers Hornsby
Coaches: Bill Killefer, Otto Williams

1927

Finish: 2
Won: 92
Lost: 61
Winning Percentage: .601
Attendance: 763,615
Manager: Bob O'Farrell
Coaches: Bill McKenchnie, Alan Sothoron

1928

Finish: 1
Won: 95
Lost: 59
Winning Percentage: .617
Attendance: 778,147
Manager: Bill McKechnie
Coaches: Jack Onslow, Alan Sothoron

1929

Finish: 4
Won: 78
Lost: 74
Winning Percentage: .513
Attendance: 410,921
Manager: Bill McKechnie, Billy Southworth
Coach: Greasy Neale

1930

Finish: 1
Won: 92
Lost: 62
Winning Percentage: .597
Attendance: 519,647
Manager: Gabby Street
Coaches: Buzzy Wares, Ray Blades

1931

Finish: 1
Won: 101
Lost: 53
Winning Percentage: .656
Attendance: 623,960
Manager: Gabby Street
Coaches: Buzzy Wares, Ray Blades

1932

Finish: 6T
Won: 72
Lost: 82
Winning Percentage: .468
Attendance: 290,370
Manager: Gabby Street
Coaches: Buzzy Wares, Ray Blades

1933

Finish: 5
Won: 82
Lost: 71
Winning Percentage:.536
Attendance: 268,404
Managers: Gabby Street, Frank Frisch
Coach: Buzzy Wares

1934

Finish: 1
Won: 95
Lost: 58
Winning Percentage: .621
Attendance: 334,863
Manager: Frank Frisch
Coaches: Buzzy Wares, Mike Gonzalez

1935

Finish: 2
Won: 96
Lost: 58
Winning Percentage: .623
Attendance: 517,805
Manager: Frank Frisch
Coaches: Buzzy Wares, Mike Gonzalez

1936

Finish: 2T
Won: 87
Lost: 67
Winning Percentage: .565
Attendance: 457,925
Manager: Frank Frisch
Coaches: Buzzy Wares, Mike Gonzalez

1937

Finish: 4
Won: 81
Lost: 73
Winning Percentage: .526
Attendance: 443,039
Manager: Frank Frisch
Coaches: Buzzy Wares, Mike Gonzalez

1938

Finish: 6
Won: 71
Lost: 80
Winning Percentage: .470
Attendance: 295,229
Manager: Frank Frisch, Mike Gonzalez
Coaches: Buzzy Wares, Mike Gonzalez

1939

Finish: 2
Won: 92
Lost: 61
Winning Percentage: .601
Attendance: 410,778
Manager: Ray Blades
Coaches: Buzzy Wares, Mike Gonzalez

1940

Finish: 3
Won: 84
Lost: 69
Winning Percentage: .549
Attendance: 331,899
Manager: Ray Blades, Mike Gonzalez, Billy Southworth
Coaches: Buzzy Wares, Mike Gonzalez

1941

Finish: 2
Won: 97
Lost: 56
Winning Percentage: .634
Attendance: 642,496
Manager: Billy Southworth
Coaches: Buzzy Wares, Mike Gonzalez

1942

Finish: 1
Won: 106
Lost: 48
Winning Percentage: .688
Attendance: 571,626
Manager: Billy Southworth
Coaches: Buzzy Wares, Mike Gonzalez

1943

Finish: 1
Won: 105
Lost: 49
Winning Percentage: .682
Attendance: 535,014
Manager: Billy Southworth
Coaches: Buzzy Wares, Mike Gonzales

1944

Finish: 1
Won: 105
Lost: 49
Winning Percentage: .682
Attendance: 486,751
Manager: Billy Southworth
Coaches: Buzzy Wares, Mike Gonzalez

1945

Finish: 2
Won: 95
Lost: 59
Winning Percentage: .617
Atttendance: 594,180
Manager: Billy Southworth
Coaches: Buzzy Wares, Mike Gonzalez

1946

Finish: 1
Won: 98
Lost: 58
Winning Percentage: .628
Attendance: 1,062,553
Manager: Eddie Dyer
Coaches: Buzzy Wares, Mike Gonzalez

1947

Finish: 2
Won: 89
Lost: 65
Winning Percentage: .578
Attendance: 1,248,013
Manager: Eddie Dyer
Coaches: Buzzy Wares, Tony Kaufman

1948

Finish: 2
Won: 85
Lost: 69
Winning Percentage: .552
Attendance: 1,111,454
Manager: Eddie Dyer
Coaches: Buzzy Wares, Tony Kaufmann

1949

Finish: 2
Won: 96
Lost: 58
Winning Percentage: .623
Attendance: 1,430,676
Manager: Eddie Dyer
Coaches: Buzzy Wares, Tony Kaufmann, Terry Morre

1950

Finish: 5
Won: 78
Lost: 75
Winning Percentage: .510
Attendance: 1,093,199
Manager: Eddie Dyer
Coaches: Buzzy Wares, Tony Kaufmann, Marty Marion, Terry Moore

1951

Finish: 3
Won: 81
Lost: 73
Winning Percentage: .526
Attendance: 1,013,429
Manager: Marty Marion
Coaches: Buzzy Wares, Ray Blades, Terry Moore, Mike Ryba

1952

Finish: 3
Won: 88
Lost: 66
Winning Percentage: .571
Attendance: 913,113
Manager: Eddie Stanky
Coaches: Terry Moore, John Riddle, Mike Ryba

1953

Finish: 3T
Won: 83
Lost: 71
Winning Percentage: .539
Attendance: 880,242
Manager: Eddie Stanky
Coaches: John Riddle, Mike Ryba, Dixie Walker

1954

Finish: 6
Won: 72
Lost: 82
Winning Percentage: .468
Attendance: 1,039,698
Manager: Eddie Stanky
Coaches: Lou Kahn, Bill Posedel, John Riddle, Mike Ryba

1955

Finish: 7
Won: 68
Lost: 86
Winning Percentage: .442
Attendance: 849,130
Manager: Eddie Stanky, Harry Walker
Coaches: Lou Kahn, Bill Posedel, John Riddle, Dixie Walker

1956

Finish: 4
Won: 76
Lost: 78
Winning Percentage: .494
Attendance: 1,029,773
Manager: Fred Hutchinson
Coaches: Johnny Hopp, Terry Moore, Bill Posedel

1957

Finish: 2
Won: 87
Lost: 67
Winning Percentage: .565
Attendance: 1,183,575
Manager: Fred Hutchinson
Coaches: Walker Cooper, Stan Hack, Al Hollingsworth, Terry Moore, Bill Posedel

1958

Finish: 5T
Won: 72
Lost: 82
Winning Percentage: .468
Attendance: 1,063,730
Manager: Fred Hutchinson, Stan Hack
Coaches: Stan Hack, Al Hollingsworth, Terry Moore

1959

Finish: 7
Won: 71
Lost: 83
Winning Percentage: .461
Attendance: 929,953
Manager: Solly Hemus
Coaches: Ray Katt, Johnny Keane, Howie Pollet, Harry Walker

1960

Finish: 3
Won: 86
Lost: 68
Winning Percentage: .558
Attendance: 1,096,632
Manager: Solly Hemus
Coaches: Darrell Johnson, Ray Katt, Johnny Keane, Howie Pollet, Harry Walker

1961

Finish: 5
Won: 80
Lost: 74
Winning Percentage: .519
Attendance: 855,305
Manager: Solly Hemus, Johnny Keane
Coaches: Vern Benson, Darrell Johnson, Ray Katt, Johnny Keane, Howie Pollet, Harry Walker

1962

Finish: 6
Won: 84
Lost: 78
Winning Percentage: .519
Attendance: 953,895
Manager: Johnny Keane
Coaches: Vern Benson, Howie Pollet, Red Schoen-dienst, Hal Smith, Harry Walker

1963

Finish: 2
Won: 93
Lost: 69
Winning Percentage: .574
Attendance: 1,170,546
Manager: Johnny Keane
Coaches: Vern Benson, Howie Pollet, Red Schoendienst, Joe Schultz, Jr.

1964

Finish: 1
Won: 93
Lost: 69
Winning Percentage: .574
Attendance: 1,143,294
Manager: Johnny Keane
Coaches: Vern Benson, Howie Pollet, Red Schoendienst, Joe Schultz, Jr.

1965

Finish: 7
Won: 80
Lost: 81
Winning Percentage: .497
Attendance: 1,241,195
Manager: Red Schoendienst
Coaches: Joe Becker, Bob Milliken, Joe Schultz, Jr., Mickey Vernon

1966

Finish: 6
Won: 83
Lost: 79
Winning Percentage: .512
Attendance: 1,712,980
Manager: Red Schoendienst
Coaches: Joe Becker, Bob Milliken, Joe Schultz, Jr. Dick Sisler

1967

Finish: 1
Won: 101
Lost: 60
Winning Percentage: .627
Attendance: *2,090,145
Manager: Red Schoendienst
Coaches: Bob Milliken, Billy Muffett, Joe Schultz, Jr., Dick Sisler

1968

Finish: 1
Won: 97
Lost: 65
Winning Percentage: .599
Attendance: 2,011,177
Manager: Red Schoendienst
Coaches: Bob Milliken, Billy Muffett, Joe Schultz, Jr., Dick Sisler

1969

Finish: 4
Won: 87
Lost: 75
Winning Percentage: .537
Attendance: 1,682,583
Manager: Red Schoendienst
Coaches: George Kissell, Bob Milliken, Billy Muffett, Dick Sisler

1970

Finish: 4
Won: 76
Lost: 86
Winning Percentage: .469
Attendance: 1,628,729
Manager: Red Schoendeinst
Coaches: Vern Benson, George Kissell, Bob Milliken, Billy Muffet, Dick Sisler, Bart Zeller

1971

Finish: 2
Won: 90
Lost: 71
Winning Percentage: .556
Attendance: 1,604,671
Manager: Red Schoendienst
Coaches: Vern Benson, Ken Boyer, George Kissell, Barney Schultz

1972

Finish: 4
Won: 75
Lost: 81
Winning Percentage: .481
Attendance: 1,196,894
Manager: Red Schoendienst
Coaches: Vern Benson, Ken Boyer, George Kissell, Barney Schultz, Lee Thomas

1973

Finish: 2
Won: 81
Lost: 81
Winning Percentage: .500
Attendance: 1,574,012
Manager: Red Schoendienst
Coaches: Tony Auferio, Vern Benson, George Kissell, Johnny Lewis, Barney Schultz

1974

Finish: 2
Won: 86
Lost: 75
Winning Percentage: .534
Attendance: 1,838,413
Manager: Red Schoendienst
Coaches: Vern Benson, George Kissell, Johnny Lewis, Dave Ricketts, Barney Schultz

1975

Finish: 3T
Won: 82
Lost: 80
Winning Percentage: .506
Attendance: 1,695,394
Manager: Red Schoendienst
Coaches: Vern Benson, George Kissell, Johnny Lewis, Dave Ricketts, Barney Schultz

1976

Finish: 5
Won: 72
Lost: 90
Winning Percentage: .444
Attendance: 1,207,036
Manager: Red Schoendienst
Coaches: Preston Gomez, Fred Koenig, Bob Milliken, Tom Zimmer

1977

Finish: 3
Won: 83
Lost: 79
Winning Percentage: .512
Attendance: 1,659,287
Manager: Vern Rapp
Coaches: Jack Krol, Mo Mozzali, Claude Osteen, Sonny Ruberto, Barney Schultz

1978

Finish: 5
Won: 69
Lost: 93
Winning Percentage: .426
Attendance: 1,278,215
Manager: Vern Rapp, Jack Krol, Ken Boyer
Coaches: Jack Krol, Mo Mozzali, Claude Osteen, Dave Ricketts, Sonny Ruberto

1979

Finish: 3
Won: 86
Lost: 76
Winning Percentage: .531
Attendance: 1,627,256
Manager: Ken Boyer
Coaches: Jack Krol, Dal Maxvill, Claude Osteen, Dave Ricketts, Red Schoendienst

1980

Finish: 4
Won: 74
Lost: 88
Winning Percentage: .457
Attendance: 1,385,147
Manager: Ken Boyer, Jack Krol, Whitey Herzog, Red Schoendienst
Coaches: Jack Krol, Dal Maxvill, Claude Osteen, Dave Ricketts, Red Schoendienst

1981

Finish: 1T
Won: 59
Lost: 43
Winning Percentage: .578
Attendance: 1,010,247
Manager: Whitey Herzog
Coaches: Chuck Hiller, Hub Kittle, Hal Lanier, Dave Ricketts, Red Schoendienst, Tim Thompson

1982

Finish: 1
Won: 92
Lost: 70
Winning Percentage: .568
Attendance: 2,111,906
Manager: Whitey Herzog
Coaches: Joe Cunningham, Chuck Hiller, Hub Kittle, Hall Lanier, Dave Ricketts, Red Schoendienst

1983

Finish: 4
Won: 79
Lost: 83
Winning Percentage: .488
Attendance: 2,317,914
Manager: Whitey Herzog
Coaches: Chuck Hiller, Hub Kittle, Darold Knowles, Hal Lanier, Dave Ricketts, Red Schoendienst, Lee Thomas

1984

Finish: 3
Won: 84
Lost: 78
Winning Percentage: .519
Attendance: 2,037,448
Manager: Whitey Herzog
Coaches: Hal Lanier, Johnny Lewis, Nick Leyva, Jamie Quirk, Dave Ricketts, Mike Roarke, Red Schoendienst

1985

Finish: 1
Won: 101
Lost: 61
Winning Percentage: .623
Attendance: 2,637,563
Manager: Whitey Herzog
Coaches: Hal Lanier, Johnny Lewis, Nick Leyva, Dave Ricketts, Mike Roarke, Red Schoendienst

1986

Finish: 3
Won: 79
Lost: 82
Winning Percentage: .491
Attendance: 2,471,817
Manager: Whitey Herzog
Coaches: Rich Hacker, Johnny Lewis, Nick Leyva, Dave Ricketts, Mike Roarke, Red Schoendienst

1987

Finish: 1
Won: 95
Lost: 67
Winning Percentage: .586
Attendance: *3,072,121
Manager: Whitney Herzog
Coaches: Rich Hacker, Johnny Lewis, Nick Leyva, Dave Ricketts, Mike Roarke, Red Schoendienst

1988

Finish: 5
Won: 76
Lost: 86
Winning Percentage: .469
Attendance: 2,892,629
Manager: Whitey Herzog
Coaches: Rich Hacker, Johnny Lewis, Nick Leyva, Dave Ricketts, Mike Roarke, Red Schoendienst

1989

Finish: 3
Won: 86
Lost: 76
Winning Percentage: .531
Attendance: 3,080,980
Manager: Whitey Herzog
Coaches: Rich Hacker, Johnny Lewis, Dave Ricketts, Jim Riggleman, Mike Roarke, Red Schoendienst

1990

Finish: 6
Won: 70
Lost: 92
Winning Percentage: .432
Attendance: 2,573,225
Manager: Whitey Herzog, Red Schoendienst, Joe Torre
Coaches: Steve Braun, Rich Hacker, Dave Ricketts, Jim Riggleman, Mike Roarke, Red Schoendienst

1991

Finish: 2
Won: 84
Lost: 78
Winning Percentage: .519
Attendance: 2,448,699
Manager: Joe Torre
Coaches: Joe Coleman, Dave Collins, Bucky Dent, Gaylen Pitts, Dave Ricketts, Red Schoendienst

1992

Finish: 3
Won: 83
Lost: 79
Winning Percentage: .512
Attendance: 2,418,483
Manager: Joe Torre
Coaches: Don Baylor, Joe Coleman, Dave Collins, Bucky Dent, Gaylen Pitts, Red Schoendienst

1993

Finish: 3
Won: 87
Lost: 75
Winning Percentage: .537
Attendance: 2,844,328
Manager: Joe Torre
Coaches: Chris Chambliss, Joe Coleman, Bucky Dent, Jack Hubbard, Gaylen Pitts, Red Schoendienst

1994

Finish: 3
Won: 53
Lost: 61
Winning Percentage: .465
Attendance: 1,866,544
Manager: Joe Torre
Coaches: Jose Cardenal, Chris Chambliss, Joe Coleman, Bucky Dent, Gaylen Pitts, Red Schoendienst

1995

Finish: 4
Won: 62
Lost: 81
Winning Percentage: .434
Attendance: 1,756,127
Manager: Joe Torre, Mike Jorgensen
Coaches: Jose Cardenal, Chris Chambliss, Bob Gibson, Gaylen Pitts, Mark Riggins, Red Schoendienst

1996

Final: 1
Won: 88
Lost: 74
Winning Percentage: .543
Attendance: 2,654,718
Manager: Tony LaRussa
Coaches: Mark DeJohn, Dave Duncan, Ron Hassey, George Hendrick, Dave McKay, Tom Reynolds

1997

Finish: 4
Won: 73
Lost: 89
Winning Percentage: .451
Attendance: 2,658,357
Manager: Tony LaRussa
Coaches: Mark DeJohn, Dave Duncan, George Hendrick, Rene Lachemann, Carney Lansford, Dave McKay

1998

Manager: Tony La Russa
Coaches: Mark DeJohn, Dave Duncan, Rene Lachemann, Carney Lansford, Dave McKay, Dave Parker

---

TOTALS

Games Won: 8950
Games Lost: 8472
Winning Percentage: .514
Attendance: 107,623,783

N.L. TOTALS

Games Won: 8168
Games Lost: 8039
Winning Percentage: .504
Attendance: 105,788,783

A.A. TOTALS

Games Won: 782
Games Lost: 433
Winning Percentage: .644
Attendance:2,035,000

Attendance figures courtesy of Bob Tieman

All-Time Records and Achievements

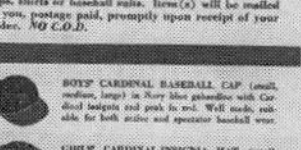

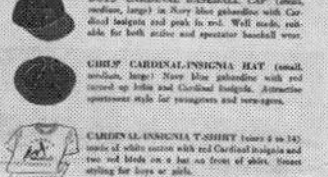

1942 ★ SPORTSMAN'S PARK

Souvenir Program
TWENTY-FIVE CENTS

WORLD SERIES

CARDINALS YANKEES

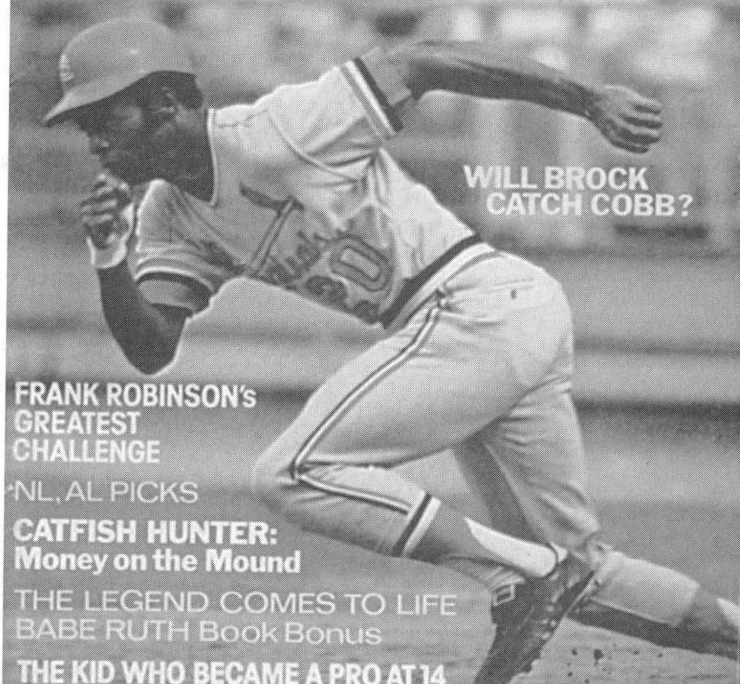

Played With Both American Association (Browns) and National League (Browns) Teams in Different Organization

Ned Cuthbert	1876 NL Browns	1882 AA Brown
Jack Gleason	1877 NL Browns	1882-83 AA Browns
Tom Loftus	1877 NL Browns	1883 AA Browns

Played With Both American Association Browns and National League (Browns, Perfectos, Cardinals) in Same Organization

Ted Breitenstein	1891 AA Browns	1892-96,01 NL Browns, Cardinals
Bob Caruthers	1884-87 AA Browns	1892 NL Browns
James Donnelly	1890 AA Browns	1898 NL Browns
John Easton	1891 AA Browns	1892 NL Browns
Arlie Latham	1883-89 AA Browns	1896 NL Browns
Dennis Lyons	1891 AA Browns	1895 NL Browns
Charles Miller	1890 AA Browns	1899 NL Perfectos
John Ricks	1891 AA Browns	1894 NL Browns

Slim Jim: Lanky lefty Grover Lowdermilk pitched for Cards (1909-1912) and for the Browns (1915, 1917-19)

Played With Both American Association (Browns) and Union Association (Maroons) Teams

Tom Dolan	1883-84, 88 AA Browns	1884 UA Maroons
Jack Gleason	1882-83 AA Browns	1884 UA Maroons
Charlie Hodnett	1883 AA Browns	1884 UA Maroons
Fred Lewis	1883-84 AA Browns	1884 UA Maroons
Sleeper Sullivan	1882-83 AA Browns	1884 UA Maroons

Played With Both American Association (Browns) and National League (Maroons) Teams

Tom Dolan	1883-84, 88 AA Browns	1885-86 NL Maroons
Jack Gleason	1882-83 AA Browns	1885 NL Maroons
Charlie Krehmeyer	1884 AA Browns	1885 NL Maroons
Fred Lewis	1883-84 AA Browns	1885 NL Maroons
Trick McSorley	1886 AA Browns	1885 NL Maroons
Joe Murphy	1886-87 AA Browns	1886 NL Maroons

Played With Both National League (Browns, Perfectos, Cardinals) and Union Association (Maroons) Teams

Joe Quinn	1893-96, 98 NL Browns, 1900 NL Cardinals	1884 UA Maroons
Perry Werdon	1892-93 NL Browns	1884 UA Maroons

Played With Both National League (Browns) and National League (Maroons) Teams

Jack Glasscock	1892-93 NL Browns	1885-86 NL Maroons
Joe Quinn	1893-96 NL Browns	1885-86 NL Maroons

Played With Both National League (Browns, Perfectos, Cardinals) and American League (Browns) Teams

Ethan Allen	1933 NL Cardinals	1937-38 AL Browns
Bill Bailey	1921-22 NL Cardinals	1907-12 AL Browns
Jim Bottomley	1922-32 NL Cardinals	1936-37 AL Browns
Harry Brecheen	1940-52 NL Cardinals	1953 AL Browns
Herman Bronkie	1918 NL Cardinals	1919, 22 AL Browns
Frank Buelow	1899-1901 NL Cardinals	1902-04 AL Browns
Jesse Burkett	1899-01 NL Cardinals	1902-04 AL Browns
Verne Clemons	1919-24 NL Cardinals	1916 AL Browns
Bill Cox	1936 NL Cardinals	1938-40 AL Browns
Doc Crandell	1913 NL Cardinals	1916 AL Browns
Lou Criger	1899-1900 NL Cardinals	1909, 12 AL Browns
Dizzy Dean	1930, 32-37 NL Cardinals	1947 AL Browns
Paul Dean	1934-39 NL Cardinals	1943 AL Browns
Frank Demaree	1943 NL Cardinals	1944 AL Browns
Red Donahue	1895-97 NL Cardinals	1902-03 AL Browns
Hal Epps	1938-40 NL Cardinals	1943-44 AL Browns
George Fisher	1930 NL Cardinals	1932 AL Browns
Debs Garms	1943-45 NL Cardinals	1932-35 AL Browns
Don Gutteridge	1936-40 NL Cardinals	1942-45 AL Browns
Bob Habenicht	1951 NL Cardinals	1953 AL Browns
Hal Haid	1928-30 NL Cardinals	1919 AL Browns
John Heidrick	1899-1901 NL Cardinals	1902-04, 08 AL Browns
Charlie Hemphill	1899 NL Perfectos	1902-04, 06-07 Browns
Rogers Hornsby	1915-26, 33 NL Cardinals	1933-37 AL Browns
Frank Huelsman	1897 NL Browns	1904 AL Browns
Pat Hynes	1903 NL Cardinals	1904 AL Browns
Darrell Johnson	1960 NL Cardinals	1952 AL Browns
Ellis Kinder	1956 NL Cardinals	1946-47 AL Browns
Clyde Kluttz	1946 NL Cardinals	1951 AL Browns
Max Lanier	1938-46, 49-51 NL Cardinals	1953 AL Browns
Lyn Lary	1939 NL Cardinals	1935-36, 40 AL Browns
Doc Lavan	1919-24 NL Cardinals	1913-17 AL Browns
Dick Littlefield	1956 NL Cardinals	1952-53 AL Browns
Grover Lowdermilk	1909,11 NL Cardinals	1915, 17-19 AL Browns
Marty Marion	1940-50 NL Cardinals	1952-53 AL Browns
Ed Mickelson	1950 NL Cardinals	1953 AL Browns
Buster Mills	1934 NL Cardinals	1938 AL Browns
Gene Moore	1933-35 NL Cardinals	1944-45 AL Browns
Heine Mueller	1920-26 NL Cardinals	1935 AL Browns
Bob Nieman	1960-61 NL Cardinals	1951-52 AL Browns
Jack O'Connor	1899-1900 NL Cardinals	1904-07, 10 AL Browns
Dick Padden	1901 NL Cardinals	1902-05 AL Browns
Al Papai	1948,50 NL Cardinals	1949 AL Browns
Gene Paulette	1917-19 NL Cardinals	1916-17 AL Browns
Ray Pepper	1932-33 NL Cardinals	1934-36 AL Browns
Jeff Pfeffer	1921-24 NL Cardinals	1911 AL Browns
J.W. Porter	1959 NL Cardinals	1952 AL Browns
Nelson Potter	1936 NL Cardinals	1943-48 AL Browns
Red Powell	1899-1901 NL Cardinals	1902-03, 05-19 AL Browns

Played With Both National League (Browns,Perfectos, Cardinals) and American League (Browns) Teams (cont.)

Irish-Born:
Ted Sullivan managed the old Browns (1883) and the Association Maroons (1884).

George Puccinelli	1930, 32 NL Cardinals	1934 AL Brown
Stan Rojek	1951 NL Cardinals	1952 AL Browns
John Schulte	1927 NL Cardinals	1923, 32 AL Browns
Charlie Shields	1907 NL Cardinals	1902 AL Browns
Burt Shotton	1919-23 NL Cardinals	1909-17 AL Browns
Allen Sothoron	1924-26 NL Cardinals	1914-15,17-21 AL Browns
John Sudhoff	1897-1901 NL Cardinals	1902-05 AL Browns
Joe Sugden	1898 NL Browns	1902-05 AL Browns
Bill Trotter	1944 NL Cardinals	1937-42 AL Browns
Bobby Wallace	1899-1901, 17-18 NL Cardinals	1902-16 AL Browns
Art Weaver	1902-03 NL Cardinals	1905 AL Browns
Bob Weiland	1937-40 NL Cardinals	1935 AL Browns
Hal White	1953-54 NL Cardinals	1953 AL Browns
Joe Willis	1911-13 NL Cardinals	1911 AL Browns
Bobby Young	1948 NL Cardinals	1951-53 AL Browns

Managed Both American Association (Browns) and Union Association (Maroons) Teams

Ted Sullivan	1883 AA Browns	1884 UA Maroons

Managed Both National League (Cardinals) and American League (Browns) Teams

Jimmy Burke	1905 NL Cardinals	1918-20 AL Browns
Rogers Hornsby	1925-26 NL Cardinals	1933-37,52 AL Browns
Marty Marion	1951 NL Cardinals	1952-53 AL Browns
Branch Rickey	1919-25 NL Cardinals	1913-15 AL Browns
Gabby Street	1929-33 NL Cardinals	1938 AL Browns

Mr. Blunt:
Rogers Hornsby led the Redbirds to their first title (1926) and the Browns to oblivion twice (1933-37 and 1952).

St. Louis Players Who Were Active in Four Major Leagues During Their Careers

Lave Cross	1887-1907	AA-PL-NL-AL	2275 Games
Edgar Cuthbert	1871-1884	NA-NL-AA-UA	451 Games
William Hallman	1888-1903	FL-PL-AA-AL	1503 Games
William E. Hoy	1888-1902	NL-PL-AA-AL	1798 Games
Morgan Murphy	1890-1901	PL-AA-NL-AL	566 Games
Joseph J. Quinn	1884-1901	UA-NL-PL-AL	1768 Games
William Robinson	1882-1892	NL-UA-AA-PL	978 Games
August Weyhing	1887-1901	AA-PL-NL-AL	538 Games

Most Years Regular Starter by Position

Position	*Player*	*Years*
C	Ted Simmons	11
1B (Tie)	Jim Bottomley	9
	Charles Comiskey	9
2B	Julian Javier	10
3B	Ken Boyer	10
SS	Ozzie Smith	15
LF	Lou Brock	15
CF	Curt Flood	11
RF	Enos Slaughter	11

Most Years With St. Louis (Browns, Perfectos, Cardinals) Teams

Stan Musial	22	1941-44, 46-63
Jesse Haines	18	1920-37
Bob Gibson	17	1959-75
Lou Brock	16	1964-79
Bob Forsch	15	1974-88
Red Schoendienst	15	1945-56, 61-63
Ozzie Smith	15	1982-96
Bill Sherdel	14	1918-30, 32

BROTHER THREESOME: Jose Cruz (center), a star, and younger brothers, Hector (right) and Tommy.

Brothers Who Played With St. Louis

Dick Allen	1970	Ron Allen	1972
Alan Benes	1995-Present	Andy Benes	1996-97
Cloyd Boyer	1949-52	Ken Boyer	1955-65
Joe Connor	1895	Roger Connor	1894-97
Mort Cooper	1938-45	Walker Cooper	1940-45, 56-57
Cirilio Cruz	1973	Hector Cruz	1973, 75-77
		Jose Cruz	1970-74
Dizzy Dean	1930, 32-37	Paul Dean	1934-39
Henry Fuller	1891	William Fuller	1889-91
Jack Gleason	1882-83	Will Gleason	1882-87
Grover Lowdermilk	1909-11	Lou Lowdermilk	1911-12
Lindy McDaniel	1955-62	Von McDaniel	1957-58
Jack O'Neill	1902-03	Mike O'Neill	1901-04
Heinie Peitz	1892-95, 1913	Joe Peitz	1892
Dick Ricketts	1959	Dave Ricketts	1963, 65, 67-69

Father and Son Who Played With St. Louis

(Father) Ed Olivares	1960-61	(Son) Omar Olivares	1990-94

St. Louis Players Who Served in the Military

World War I
Edward Ainsmith
G.C. Alexander
Doug Baird
Rube Bressler
Tony Brottem
Jimmy Cooney
Walton Cruise
Pickles Dillhoefer
Marv Goodwin
Andy High
Bruce Hitt
Hal Janvrin
Duster Mails
Rabbit Maranville
Jakie May
Bob McGraw
Dots Miller
Clarence Mitchell
Lou North
Jeff Pfeffer
Jack Smith
Frank Snyder
Frank Woodward

World War II
John Beazley
Al Brazle
Jimmy Brown
Walker Cooper
Frank Crespi
Jeff Cross
Murry Dickson
Erv Dusak
Bill Endicott
George Fallon
John Grodzicki
Harry Gumbert
Andy High
Ira Hutchinson
Nippy Jones
Lou Klein
Ernie Koy
Jim Konstanty
Howie Krist
Danny Litwhiler
Peanuts Lowrey
Fred Martin
Johnny Mize
Terry Moore
Whitey Moore
George Munger
Stan Musial
Sam Nahem
Ron Northey
Don Padgett
Howie Pollet
Hank Sauer
Fred Schmidt
Red Schoendienst
Walter Sessi
Clyde Shoun
Enos Slaughter
Max Surkont
Harry Walker
Lon Warneke
Ernie White
Burgess Whitehead

Korean War , Vietnam War , and All Other Military Service to Our Country
Ken Boyer
Tom Cheney
Al Hrabosky
Vinegar Bend Mizell
Tom Poholsky
Curt Simmons
Ted Simmons
Jimy Williams

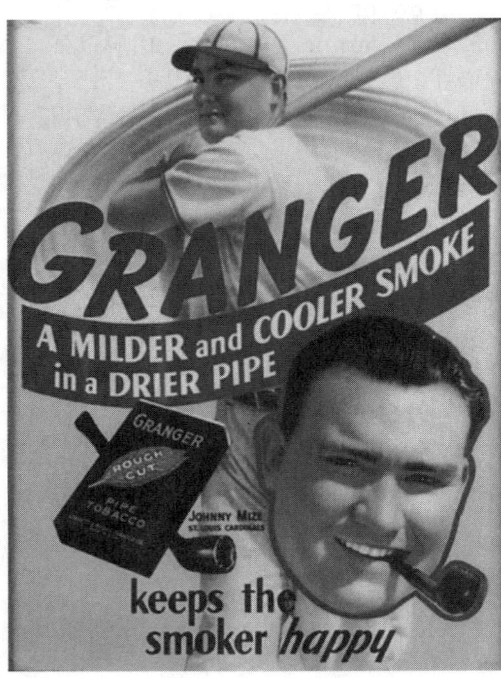

A Pipe Full: Before smoking became a no-no, Johnny Mize picked up an endorsement.

Longest Streaks

Hitting		
Rogers Hornsby	1922	33 Games
Stan Musial	1950	30 Games
Harry Walker	1943	29 Games
Ken Boyer	1959	29 Games
Joe Medwick	1935	28 Games
Red Schoendienst	1954	28 Games
Lou Brock	1971	26 Games

Pitching Wins		
RHP… Bob Gibson	1968	15 Games
LHP… John Tudor	1985	11 Games

What's This?: Rogers Hornsby recommending a bat not made by famed Louisville Slugger, i.e., Hillerich and Bradsby. Below, Stan the Man advertised in Hawaii on the Cardinals' trip to Japan, 1958.

Cardinals in Pro Basketball

Name	Position	Years With Cards
Bill Crouch	P	1941
George Crowe	1B	1959-61
Frank Frisch	2B	1927-37
Bob Gibson	P	1959-75
Grant Dunlap	OF	1953
Dick Groat	SS	1963-65
Irv Noren	OF	1957-59
Ron Reed	P	1975
Del Rice	C	1945-55, 60
Dick Ricketts	P	1959

Cardinals in Pro Football

Name	Position	Years With Cards
George Barclay	OF	1902-04
Matt Kinzer	P	1989
Brian Jordan	OF	1992-present
Charles Moran	1P	1903, 08
Ernie Vick	C	1922, 24-26

St. Louis Players With Shortest STL Careers

One Game	Date STL Appearance
Babe Adams	4-18-1906
Joe Adams	4-26-1902
Walt Alston	9-27-1936
Frank Barrett	10-01-1939
John Bellman	4-23-1889
Joe Bernard	9-23-1909
Hal Betts	9-22-1903

St. Louis Players With Shortest STL Careers (cont.)

ONE CUP OF COFFEE: Arthur (Bud) Teachant, 1932.

REDBIRD DEMI-TASSE: Walter Alston (left) played just one game, 1936, en route to Hall of Fame as Dodger manager.

Coonie Blank	8-15-1909
Bud Bloomfield	9-25-1963
Harvey Branch	9-18-1962
James Brown	9-13-1915
Cal Browning	6-12-1960
Ed Burns	6-25-1912
James Burns	7-06-1901
Al Cabrera	5-16-1913
Bill Chambers	1-11-1910
John Coleman	9-25-1895
Ed Conwell	9-22-1911
Mays Copeland	4-27-1935
Dave Dowling	10-03-1964
Bob Ewing	4-19-1902
Fred Fagin	6-25-1895
Chauncey Fisher	1901
Tom Flanigan	4-15 -1958
Hod Ford	1932
Julie Freeman	10-10-1888
Harry Fuller	4-08-1891
Chick Fulmer	1884
Fred Gaiser	9-03-1908
Joe Gannon	8-28-1898
Danny Gardella	1950
Jim Gill	6-27-1889
Mike Goodfellow	6-13-1887
Herb Gorman	4-19-1952
Jack Gorman	7-01-1883
Fred Hahn	4-19-1952
Lou Harding	10-05-1886
Clarence Heise	4-22-1934
Ed Hock	7-28-1920
Eddie Hogan	7-05-1882
Earl Howard	4-18-1918
Pat Hynes	9-27-1903
Mike Jackson	9-26-1971
Tony Jacobs	1955
Jack Knight	9-20-1922
Will Koenigsmark	9-10-1919
Lew Krausse	9-07-1973
Leonard	9-12-1892
Barry Lersch	9-21-1974
Larry Locke	4-22-1962
Memo Luna	4-20-1954
Ernie Lush	7-20-1910
Hersh Lyons	4-17-1941
Fred Marolewski	9-19-1953
Charlie Marshall	6-14-1941
Mark McGrillis	9-17-1892
Ted Menze	4-23-1918

St. Louis Players With Shortest STL Careers (cont.)

John Mercer	6-25-1912
Ed Mierkowicz	1950
Frank Millard	5-04-1890
Frank Miller	9-16-1892
Larry Milton	5-07-1903
Tim Murchison	6-21-1917
Mike Murphy	5-17-1912
Mike Naymick	1939
Mike Pasquella	7-09-1919
Harry Patton	8-22-1910
Gil Paulsen	10-03-1925
George Paynter	8-12-1894
Frank Pears	1893
Tim Plodinec	6-02-1972
Milt Reed	9-09-1911
Dennis Ribant	6-05-1969
Bob Sadows	9-16-1960
Bill Schindler	9-03-19201
John Schultz	8-07-1891
Harry Stanton	10-14-1900
Gabby Street	1931
Rube Taylor	8-8-1903
Bud Teachout	1932
John Vann	6-11-1913
Dick Ward	1935
James Webb	7-20-1932
Jim Whelan	4-24-1913
John Wood	5-09-1896
Red Worthington	1934
Joe Young	6-10-1892
Bart Zeller	5-21-1970

Silver King: By Charles Koeneg's anglicized version of his German surname, the King was a St. Louis favorite.

AGREEMENT OF MEMBERSHIP in the

CARDINAL KNOT HOLE GANG

In becoming a member of the Cardinal Knot Hole Gang, and in accepting tickets to the games of the Cardinals, I agree that—

1. I will not at any time skip school to attend a game.

2. I will attend no game against the wishes of my parents or employer.

3. I will uphold the principles of clean speech, clean sports and clean habits, and will stand with the rest of the Gang against cigarettes and profane language on the field.

I understand that a breaking of this agreement may cost me my membership in the Cardinal Knot Hole Gang.

Boy's Ticket...Season 1935

CARDINAL KNOT HOLE GANG

Nº 425

Is a regular member of the Cardinal Knot Hole Gang, and has subscribed to the agreement on the back of this card.

AGENCY

J. Hugo Grimm
Chairman
Executive Committee

S. Breadon
President

Not good Sundays or Holidays. This Card Good for Admission When Presented at the Gate.

Passport to Paradise: Left, the back-of-the-card promise by which kids achieved the annual Knot Hole Gang pass (right), good for FREE admission to Cardinal ballgames, 1917 to World War II.

League Leaders in Hitting

TIP OF THE HAT TO TIP: James (Tip) O'Neill, batting star who hit .435 in 1887.

Average

Year	Player	Average
1887	Tip O'Neill	.435
1888	Tip O'Neill	.335
1901	Jesse Burkett	.382
1920	Rogers Hornsby	.370
1921	Rogers Hornsby	.397
1922	Rogers Hornsby	.401
1923	Rogers Hornsby	.384
1924	Rogers Hornsby	.424
1925	Rogers Hornsby	.403
1931	Chick Hafey	.349
1937	Joe Medwick	.374
1939	John Mize	.349
1943	Stan Musial	.357
1946	Stan Musial	.365
1948	Stan Musial	.376
1950	Stan Musial	.346
1951	Stan Musial	.355
1952	Stan Musial	.336
1957	Stan Musial	.351
1971	Joe Torre	.363
1979	Keith Hernandez	.344
1985	Willie McGee	.353
1990	Willie McGee	.335

Runs

Year	Player	Runs
1886	Arlie Latham	152
1887	Tip O'Neill	167
1901	Jesse Burkett	139
1921	Rogers Hornsby	131
1922	Rogers Hornsby	141
1924	Rogers Hornsby	121
1925	Rogers Hornsby	133
1933	Pepper Martin	122
1937	Joe Medwick	111
1939	John Mize	104
1946	Stan Musial	124
1948	Stan Musial	135
1951	Stan Musial	124
1954	Stan Musial	120
1967	Lou Brock	113
1971	Lou Brock	126
1979	Keith Hernandez	116
1980	Keith Hernandez	111
1982	Lonnie Smith	120

INSURANCE POLICY: Chances are that Rogers Hornsby didn't offer it to opposing pitchers.

Hits

1887	Tip O'Neill	225
1888	Tip O'Neill	177
1901	Jesse Burkett	228
1920	Rogers Hornsby	218
1921	Rogers Hornsby	235
1922	Rogers Hornsby	250
1924	Rogers Hornsby	227
1925	Rogers Hornsby	227
1936	Joe Medwick	233
1937	Joe Medwick	237
1942	Enos Slaughter	188
1943	Stan Musial	220
1944	Stan Musial	197
1946	Stan Musial	228
1948	Stan Musial	230
1949	Stan Musial	207
1950	Stan Musial	192
1952	Stan Musial	194
1964	Curt Flood	211
1971	Joe Torre	230
1985	Willie McGee	216

Doubles

1887	Tip O'Neill	52
1911	Ed Konetchy	38
1920	Rogers Hornsby	44
1921	Rogers Hornsby	44
1922	Rogers Hornsby	46
1924	Rogers Hornsby	43
1925	Jim Bottomley	44
1926	Jim Bottomley	40
1931	Sparky Adams	46
1936	Joe Medwick	64
1937	Joe Medwick	56
1938	Joe Medwick	47
1939	Enos Slaughter	52
1941	John Mize	39
1942	Marty Marion	38
1943	Stan Musial	48
1944	Stan Musial	51
1946	Stan Musial	50
1948	Stan Musial	46
1949	Stan Musial	41
1950	Red Schoendienst	43
1952	Stan Musial	42
1953	Stan Musial	53
1954	Stan Musial	41
1963	Dick Groat	43
1968	Lou Brock	46
1979	Keith Hernandez	48
1989	Pedro Guerrero	42

MUSCLES: Joe Medwick, Triple-Crown star of 1937 and aggressive Gas Houser.

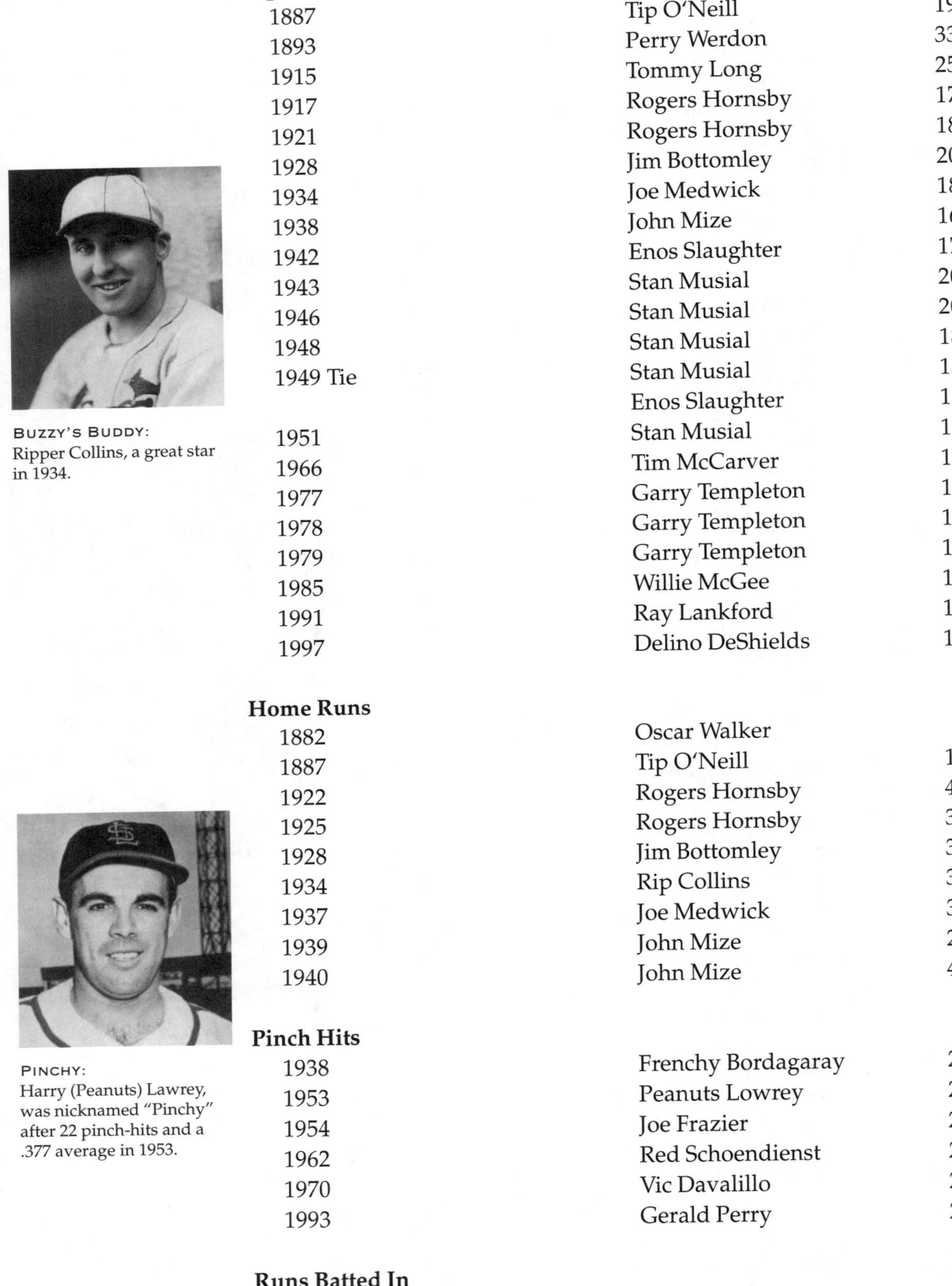

Buzzy's Buddy: Ripper Collins, a great star in 1934.

Pinchy: Harry (Peanuts) Lawrey, was nicknamed "Pinchy" after 22 pinch-hits and a .377 average in 1953.

Triples

Year	Player	Number
1887	Tip O'Neill	19
1893	Perry Werdon	33
1915	Tommy Long	25
1917	Rogers Hornsby	17
1921	Rogers Hornsby	18
1928	Jim Bottomley	20
1934	Joe Medwick	18
1938	John Mize	16
1942	Enos Slaughter	17
1943	Stan Musial	20
1946	Stan Musial	20
1948	Stan Musial	18
1949 Tie	Stan Musial	13
	Enos Slaughter	13
1951	Stan Musial	12
1966	Tim McCarver	13
1977	Garry Templeton	18
1978	Garry Templeton	13
1979	Garry Templeton	19
1985	Willie McGee	18
1991	Ray Lankford	15
1997	Delino DeShields	14

Home Runs

Year	Player	Number
1882	Oscar Walker	7
1887	Tip O'Neill	14
1922	Rogers Hornsby	42
1925	Rogers Hornsby	39
1928	Jim Bottomley	31
1934	Rip Collins	35
1937	Joe Medwick	31
1939	John Mize	28
1940	John Mize	43

Pinch Hits

Year	Player	Number
1938	Frenchy Bordagaray	20
1953	Peanuts Lowrey	22
1954	Joe Frazier	20
1962	Red Schoendienst	22
1970	Vic Davalillo	24
1993	Gerald Perry	24

Runs Batted In

Year	Player	Number
1886	Tip O'Neill	107
1887	Tip O'Neill	123
1920	Rogers Hornsby	94

1921	Rogers Hornsby	126
1922	Rogers Hornsby	152
1925	Rogers Hornsby	143
1926	Jim Bottomley	120
1928	Jim Bottomley	136
1936	Joe Medwick	138
1937	Joe Medwick	154
1938	Joe Medwick	122
1940	John Mize	137
1946	Enos Slaughter	130
1948	Stan Musial	131
1956	Stan Musial	109
1964	Ken Boyer	119
1971	Joe Torre	137

Stolen Bases

1888	Arlie Latham	109
1890	Tommy McCarthy	83
1927	Frank Frisch	48
1931	Frank Frisch	28
1933	Pepper Martin	26
1934	Pepper Martin	23
1936	Pepper Martin	23
1945	Red Schoendienst	26
1966	Lou Brock	74
1967	Lou Brock	52
1968	Lou Brock	62
1969	Lou Brock	53
1971	Lou Brock	64
1972	Lou Brock	63
1973	Lou Brock	70
1974	Lou Brock	118
1985	Vince Coleman	110
1986	Vince Coleman	107
1987	Vince Coleman	109
1988	Vince Coleman	81
1989	Vince Coleman	65
1990	Vince Coleman	77

STAN'S PAL:
Stan Musial strokes his bat with obvious affection. They call it "boning" the bat.

Total Bases

1887	Tip O'Neill	357
1901	Jesse Burkett	314
1917	Rogers Hornsby	253
1920	Rogers Hornsby	329
1921	Rogers Hornsby	378
1922	Rogers Hornsby	450
1924	Rogers Hornsby	373
1925	Rogers Hornsby	381

1926	Jim Bottomley	305
1928	Jim Bottomley	362
1934	Rip Collins	369
1935	Joe Medwick	365
1936	Joe Medwick	367
1937	Joe Medwick	406
1938	John Mize	326
1939	John Mize	353
1940	John Mize	368
1942	Enos Slaughter	292
1946	Stan Musial	366
1948	Stan Musial	429
1949	Stan Musial	382
1951	Stan Musial	355
1952	Stan Musial	311
1971	Joe Torre	352

Slugging Average

1886	Bob Caruthers	.527
1887	Tip O'Neill	.691
1917	Rogers Hornsby	.484
1920	Rogers Hornsby	.559
1921	Rogers Hornsby	.639
1922	Rogers Hornsby	.722
1923	Rogers Hornsby	.627
1924	Rogers Hornsby	.696
1925	Rogers Hornsby	.756
1927	Chick Hafey	.590
1934	Rip Collins	.615
1937	Joe Medwick	.641
1938	John Mize	.614
1939	John Mize	.626
1941	John Mize	.636
1943	Stan Musial	.562
1944	Stan Musial	.549
1946	Stan Musial	.587
1948	Stan Musial	.702
1950	Stan Musial	.596
1952	Stan Musial	.538
1987	Jack Clark	.597

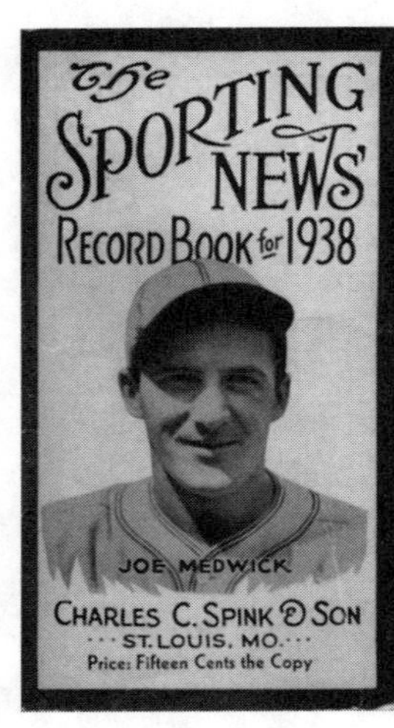

Cover Boy: The reward for Joe Medwick's Triple Crown season – his face on the cover of *The Sporting News' Record Book* in 1938.

Bases On Balls

1882	Jack Gleason	27
1888	Yank Robinson	116
1889	Yank Robinson	118
1891	Dummy Hoy	119
1910	Miller Huggins	116
1914	Miller Huggins	105
1924	Rogers Hornsby	89
1953	Stan Musial	105
1987	Jack Clark	136

All-Time St. Louis Leaders

Games Played

Stan Musial	3026
Lou Brock	2289
Ozzie Smith	1990
Enos Slaughter	1820
Red Schoendienst	1795
Curt Flood	1738
Ken Boyer	1667
Rogers Hornsby	1580
Julian Javier	1578
Ted Simmons	1564

At Bats

Stan Musial	10,972
Lou Brock	9125
Ozzie Smith	7160
Red Schoendienst	6841
Enos Slaughter	6775
Ken Boyer	6334
Curt Flood	6318
Rogers Hornsby	5881
Ted Simmons	5725
Julian Javier	5631

Hits

Stan Musial	3630
Lou Brock	2713
Rogers Hornsby	2110
Enos Slaughter	2064
Red Schoendienst	1980
Ozzie Smith	1944
Ken Boyer	1855
Curt Flood	1853
Jim Bottomley	1727
Ted Simmons	1704

Doubles

Stan Musial	725
Lou Brock	434
Joe Medwick	377
Rogers Hornsby	367
Enos Slaughter	366
Red Schoendienst	352
Jim Bottomley	344
Ozzie Smith	338
Ted Simmons	332
Frank Frisch	286

Triples

Stan Musial	177
Rogers Hornsby	143
Enos Slaughter	135
Lou Brock	121
Jim Bottomley	119
Ed Konetchy	93
Willie McGee	82
Joe Medwick	81
Pepper Martin	75
Tip O'Neill	70

Home Runs

Stan Musial	475
Ken Boyer	255
Rogers Hornsby	193
Jim Bottomley	181
Ted Simmons	172
John Mizek	158
Joe Medwick	152
Enos Slaughter	146
Bill White	140
Ray Lankford	135

Extra-Base Hits

Stan Musial	1377
Rogers Hornsby	703
Lou Brock	684
Enos Slaughter	647
Jim Bottomley	644
Joe Medwick	610
Ken Boyer	595
Ted Simmons	541
Red Schoendienst	484
John Mize	442

Total Bases

Stan Musial	6134
Lou Brock	3776
Rogers Hornsby	3342
Enos Slaughter	3138
Ken Boyer	3011
Jim Bottomley	2852
Red Schoendienst	2657
Ted Simmons	2626
Joe Medwick	2585
Curt Flood	2464

HANDICAPPED HERO: Williams (Dummy) Hoyt, a mute, played 14 years in the majors, 1331 games, with the old Association Browns.

Campaign Button:
Not really, but Ken Boyer was a good Hall of Fame candidate.

Runs

Stan Musial	1949
Lou Brock	1427
Rogers Hornsby	1089
Enos Slaughter	1071
Red Schoendienst	1025
Ozzie Smith	991
Ken Boyer	988
Jim Bottomley	921
Curt Flood	845
Frank Frisch	831

Runs Batted In

Stan Musial	1951
Enos Slaughter	1148
Jim Bottomley	1105
Rogers Hornsby	1072
Ken Boyer	1001
Ted Simmons	929
Joe Medwick	823
Lou Brock	814
Frank Frisch	720
Ozzie Smith	664

Batting Average (Min. 2,500 AB)

Rogers Hornsby	.359
Tip O'Neill	.343
Johnny Mize	.336
Joe Medwick	.335
Stan Musial	.331
Chick Hafey	.326
Jim Bottomley	.325
Frank Frisch	.312
George Watkins	.309
Joe Torre	.308

Slugging Percentage (Min. 2,500 AB)

Johnny Mize	.600
Rogers Hornsby	.568
Chick Hafey	.568
Stan Musial	.559
Joe Medwick	.545
Jim Bottomley	.537
Ripper Collins	.517
Jesse Burkett	.499
Ray Lankford	.498
Tip O'Neill	.489

Stolen Bases

Lou Brock	888
Vince Coleman	549
Ozzie Smith	433
Arlie Latham	369
Tommy McCarthy	323
Willie McGee	287
Yank Robinson	221
Jack Smith	203
Ray Lankford	199
Frank Frisch	195

Pinch Hits

Gerald Perry	70
Steve Braun	60
Red Schoendienst	53
Dane Iorg	47
Peanuts Lowery	47
Stan Musial	35
George Crowe	33
Vic Davalillo	33
Tito Landrum	32
Tim Mc Carver	31
Milt Thompson	31

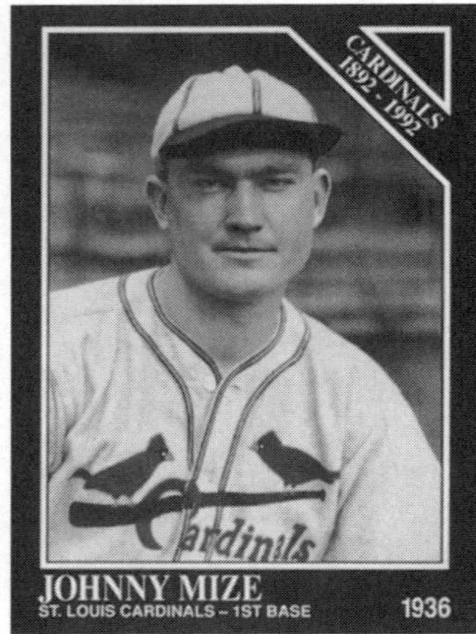

The Mighty Mize:
Record Cardinal home-run hitter, 43, in 1940.

The Wizard:
If there was someting Ozzie Smith could do, other than to hit and field, it was make Page One of magazines.

Club's Triple Crown Leaders

Player	Year	BA	HR	RBI
Charlie Comiskey	1883	.294	2	64*
Tip O'Neill	1887	.435**	14	123*
Lave Cross	1898	.317	3T	79
Homer Smoot	1905	.311	4T	58
Red Murray	1907	.262	7	46
Red Murray	1908	.282	7	62
Ed Konetchy	1909	.286	4	80
Ed Konetchy	1912	.314	8	82
Rogers Hornsby	1916	.313	6TT	65
Rogers Hornsby	1917	.327	8	66
Rogers Hornsby	1919	.318	8	71
Rogers Hornsby	1921	.397	21	126
Rogers Hornsby	1922	.401	42	152
Rogers Hornsby	1925	.403	39	143
Chick Hafey	1931	.349	16	95
Rip Collins	1934	.333	35	116
Joe Medwick	1935	.353	23 T	126
Joe Medwick	1937	.374	31	154
Johnny Mize	1940	.314	43	137
Johnny Mize	1941	.317	16	100
Enos Slaughter	1942	.318	13	98
Stan Musial	1943	.357	13 T	81
Stan Musial	1948	.376	39	131
Stan Musial	1949	.338	36	123
Stan Musial	1950	.346	28	109
Stan Musial	1951	.355	32	108
Stan Musial	1954	.330	35	126
Stan Musial	1956	.310	27	109
Ken Boyer	1960	.304	32	97
Ken Boyer	1961	.329	24	95
Joe Torre	1971	.363	24	137
Ted Simmons	1973	.310	31	91
Ray Lankford	1997	.295	31	98

* RBI totals as calculated by the Society for American Baseball Research (SABR).

** Batting average adjusted to .435, from all-time high .492 to reflect walks counting as hits during the 1887 season.

BIG ED:
Ed Konetchy – they called him "Koney" – was a popular first-base star for nine years in 1914.

St Louis Triple Crown Winners (League)

Player	Year	BA	HR	RBI
Tip O'Neill	1887	.435	14	123*
Rogers Hornsby	1922	.401	42	152
Rogers Hornsby	1925	.403	39	143
Joe Medwick	1937	.374	31	154

* RBI total as calculated by the Society for American Baseball Research (SABR).

Hitting for the Cycle

Cliff Heathcote	7-13-1918
Jim Bottomley	7-15-1927
Chick Hafey	8-21-1930
Pepper Martin	5-25-1933
Joe Medwick	6-29-1935
John Mize	7-13-1940 1st Game DH
Stan Musial	7-24-1949
Bill White	8-14-1960 1st Game DH
Ken Boyer	9-14-1961 1st Game DH
Ken Boyer	6-16-1964
Joe Torre	6-27-1973
Lou Brock	5-27-1975
Willie McGee	6-23-1984
Ray Lankford	9-15-1991
John Mabry	5-18-1996

Bright Idea: Cornflake king Kellogg offered a cut-away chance to carve out a sunvisor from the cardboard container.

Season Batting Leaders by Position

Average

Pos.	Player		Year
P	Curt Davis	.381	1939
C	Ted Simmons	.332	1975
1B	Jim Bottomley	.371	1923
2B	Rogers Hornsby	.424	1924
3B	Joe Torre	.363	1971
SS	Rogers Hornsby	.327	1917
LF	Tip O'Neill	.435	1887
CF	Willie McGee	.353	1985
RF	George Watkins	.373	1930

Home Runs

Pos.	Player		Year
P	Bob Gibson	5	1965, 1972
C	Ted Simmons	26	1979
1B	John Mize	24	1940
2B	Rogers Hornsby	42	1922
3B	Ken Boyer	32	1960
SS	Solly Hemus	15	1952
LF	Stan Musial	32	1951
CF	Ray Lankford	31	1997
RF	Stan Musial	39	1948

Runs Batted In

Pos.	Player		Year
P	Dizzy Dean	21	1935
C	Ted Simmons	96	1972
1B	Jim Bottomley	137	1929
	John Mize	137	1940
2B	Rogers Hornsby	152	1922
3B	Joe Torre	137	1971
SS	Doc Lavan	82	1921
LF	Joe Medwick	154	1937
CF	Willie McGee	104	1987
RF	Stan Musial	131	1948

Cardinals Pitching All-time Top 10

Games

Jesse Haines	554
Bob Gibson	528
Bill Sherdel	465
Bob Forsch	455
Al Brazle	441
Bill Doak	376
Lindy McDaniel	336
Larry Jackson	330
Al Hrabosky	329
Slim Sallee	316

Innings Pitched

Bob Gibson	3885
Jesse Haines	3204
Bob Forsch	2658
Bill Sherdel	2450
Bill Doak	2387
Slim Sallee	1902
Ted Breitenstein	1897
Harry Brecheen	1790
Dizzy Dean	1736
Larry Jackson	1672

Wins

Bob Gibson	251
Jesse Haines	210
Bob Forsch	163
Bill Sherdel	153
Bill Doak	145
Bob Caruthers	138
Dizzy Dean	134
Harry Brecheen	127
Dave Foutz	114
Silver King	112

Complete Games

Bob Gibson	255
Jesse Haines	209
Ted Breitenstein	196
Dave Foutz	156
Silver King	154
Bob Caruthers	151
Bill Sherdel	144
Bill Doak	144
Dizzy Dean	141
Slim Sallee	141

Shutouts

Bob Gibson	56
Bill Doak	32
Mort Cooper	28
Harry Brecheen	25
Jess Haines	24
Dizzy Dean	23
Max Lanier	20
Howie Pollet	20
Bob Forsch	19
Ernie Broglio	18

Earned Run Average

Bob Caruthers	2.50
John Tudor	2.52
Dave Foutz	2.67
Slim Sallee	2.67
Jack Taylor	2.67
Silver King	2.70
Johnny Lush	2.74
Red Ames	2.74
Mort Cooper	2.77
Fred Beebe	2.79

Winning Percentage

Bob Caruthers	.742
John Tudor	.705
Dave Foutz	.704
Silver King	.696
Mort Cooper	.677
Dizzy Dean	.641
Lon Warneke	.629
Grover Alexander	.618
Harry Brecheen	.617
Al Brazle	.602
George Munger	.602

Strikeouts

Bob Gibson	3117
Dizzy Dean	1087
Bob Forsch	1079
Jesse Haines	979
Steve Carlton	951
Bill Doak	938
Larry Jackson	899
Harry Brecheen	857
Vinegar Bend Mizell	789
Bill Hallahan	784

SEWED UP:
Dave (Scissors) Foutz was a slender star for the early Browns, 41-16 for their 1886 world championship.

FROM MAKING ADS:
Dizzy Dean as a cereal salesman pitching to...

Saves

Lee Smith	160
Todd Worrell	129
Bruce Sutter	127
Dennis Eckersley	66
Lindy McDaniel	64
Joe Hoerner	60
Al Brazle	60
Al Hrabosky	59
Ken Dayley	39
Tom Henke	36
Dizzy Dean	30

40 Game Winners

Silver King	45	1888
Dave Foutz	54	1886
Bob Caruthers	40	1885

30 Game Winners

Tony Mullane	35	1883
Silver King	34	1889
Dave Foutz	33	1885
Jack Stivetts	33	1891
Silver King	32	1887
Icebox Chamberlain	32	1889
Bob Caruthers	30	1886
Dizzy Dean	30	1934

20 Game Winners

Jumbo McGinnis	25	1882
Tony Mullane	35	1883
Jumbo McGinnis	28	1883
Jumbo McGinnis	24	1884
Bob Caruthers	40	1885
Dave Foutz	33	1885
Dave Foutz	41	1886
Bob Caruthers	30	1886
Silver King	32	1887
Bob Caruthers	29	1887
Dave Foutz	25	1887
Silver King	45	1888
Nat Hudson	25	1888
Silver King	32	1889
Icebox Chamberlain	32	1889
Jack Stivetts	27	1890
Toad Ramsey	23	1890
Jack Stivetts	33	1891
Kid Gleason	20	1892
Ted Breitenstein	27	1894
Ted Breitenstein	20	1895
Cy Young	26	1899
Jack Powell	23	1899

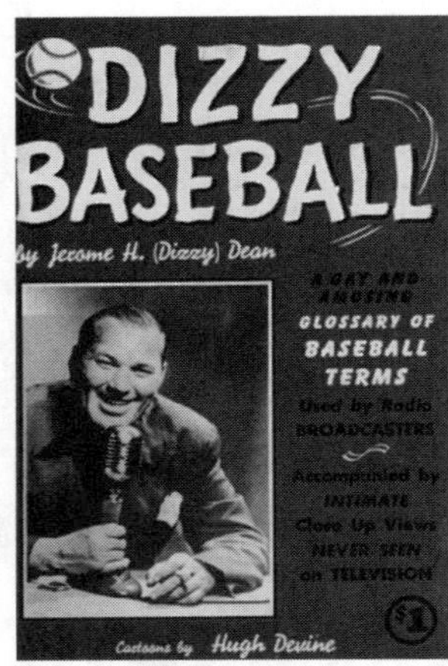

Dizzy (continued): To a beer salesman whose colorful comments came out in book form by the TV star.

20 Game Winners (cont.)

Cy Young	20	1900
Jack Harper	20	1901
Kid Nichols	21	1904
Jack Taylor	20	1904
Bob Harmon	23	1911
Bill Doak	20	1920
Jesse Haines	20	1923
Flint Rhem	20	1926
Jesse Haines	24	1927
Grover Alexander	21	1927
Bill Sherdel	21	1928
Jesse Haines	20	1928
Dizzy Dean	20	1933
Dizzy Dean	30	1934
Dizzy Dean	28	1935
Dizzy Dean	24	1936
Curt Davis	22	1939
Mort Cooper	22	1942
Johnny Beazley	21	1942
Mort Cooper	21	1943
Mort Cooper	22	1944
Red Barrett	23	1945
Howie Pollet	21	1946
Harry Brecheen	20	1948
Howie Pollet	20	1949
Harvey Haddix	20	1953
Ernie Broglio	21	1960
Ray Sadecki	20	1964
Bob Gibson	20	1965
Bob Gibson	21	1966
Bob Gibson	22	1968
Bob Gibson	20	1968
Bob Gibson	23	1970
Steve Carlton	20	1971
Bob Forsch	20	1977
Joaquin Andujar	20	1984
Joaquin Andujar	21	1985
John Tudor	21	1985

NL Strikeout Leaders

1891	Jack Stivetts	259
1906	Fred Beebe	171
1930	Bill Hallahan	177
1931	Bill Hallahan	159
1932	Dizzy Dean	191
1933	Dizzy Dean	199
1934	Dizzy Dean	195
1935	Dizzy Dean	182
1948	Harry Brecheen	149
1958	Sam Jones	225
1966	Bob Gibson	268
1989	Jose DeLeon	201

NL ERA Leaders

1885	Bob Caruthers	2.07	53 Games	482.1 IP
1886	Dave Foutz	2.11	59 Games	504 IP
1888	Silver King	1.64	66 Games	585.2 IP
1889	Jack Stivetts	2.25	26 Games	191.2 IP
1893	Ted Breitenstein	3.18	48 Games	382.2 IP
1914	Bill Doak	1.72	36 Games	256 IP
1921	Bill Doak	2.58	32 Games	209 IP
1942	Mort Cooper	1.77	37 Games	279 IP
1943	Howie Pollet	1.75	16 Games	118 IP
1946	Howie Pollet	2.10	40 Games	226 IP
1948	Harry Brecheen	2.24	33 Games	233 IP
1968	Bob Gibson	1.12	34 Games	305 IP
1976	John Denny	2.52	30 Games	207 IP
1988	Joe Magrane	2.18	24 Games	165 IP

Cardinals No-Hitters

9/23/1890	George Nicol	Philadelphia	AA	21-2 (7 in.)
10/4/1891	Ted Breitenstein	Louisville	AA	*8-0
9/24/1906	Stoney McGlynn	Brooklyn	NL	** 1-1 (7in.)
8/11/1907	Ed Karger	Boston	NL	4-0 (7 in.)
8/6/1908	Johnny Lush	Brooklyn	NL	2-0 (6 in.)
7/17/1924	Jesse Haines	Boston	NL	5-0
9/24/1934	Paul Dean	Brooklyn	NL	3-0
8/30/1941	Lon Warneke	Cincinnati	NL	2-0
9/18/1968	Ray Washburn	San Francisco	NL	2-0
8/14/1971	Bob Gibson	Pittsburgh	NL	11-0
4/16/1978	Bob Forsch	Philadelphia	NL	5-0
9/23/1983	Bob Forsch	Montreal	NL	3-0

* No-hitter came in first Major League start
** McGlynn pitched 7 perfect innings

PROMOTIONAL PROGRESS: It's a rare day when the Redbirds don't offer a box office goodie for their fans.

Most Valuable Player National League (BBWAA)

Rogers Hornsby	1925
Bob O'Farrell	1926
Jim Bottomley	1928
Frank Frisch	1931
Dizzy Dean	1934
Joe Medwick	1937
Mort Cooper	1942
Stan Musial	1943
Marty Marion	1944
Stan Musial	1946
Stan Musial	1948
Ken Boyer	1964
Orlando Cepeda	1967
Bob Gibson	1968
Joe Torre	1971
Keith Hernandez	*1979
Willie McGee	1985

*Co-recipient with Pittsburgh's Willie Stargell

The Sporting News Man of the Year

Lou Brock	1974
Whitey Herzog	1982
Mark McGwire	1997

Sports Illustrated Man of the Year

Stan Musial	1957

Most Valuable Player (The Sporting News, TSN)

Dizzy Dean	1934
Joe Medwick	1937
Mort Cooper	1942
Stan Musial	1943
Marty Marion	1944
Stan Musial, OF – 1B	*1948
Enos Slaughter, OF	1949
Howie Pollet, P	1949
Stan Musial, OF	1951
Stan Musial, 1B	1957
Ken Boyer, 3B	1964
Orlando Cepeda, 1B	1967
Bob Gibson, P	1968
Bob Gibson, P	1970
Joe Torre, 3B	1971
Lou Brock, OF	1974
Keith Hernandez	1979
Willie McGee	1985

* Beginning in 1948 *The Sporting News* selected a player , and pitcher in each league.

National League Rookie of the Year (BBWAA)

Wally Moon	1954
Bill Virdon	1955
Bake McBride	1974
Vince Coleman	1985
Todd Worrell	1986

Rookie of the Year (TSN)

Wally Moon	1954
Bill Virdon	1955
Dick Hughes	1967
Reggie Cleveland	1971
Vince Coleman	1985
Todd Worrell	1986
Alan Benes	1996
Matt Morris	1997

Player of the Year (TSN)

Marty Marion	1944
Stan Musial	1946
Stan Musial	1951
Ken Boyer	1964
Joe Torre	1971
Lou Brock	1974

Player of the Decade (TSN) 1946-55

Stan Musial

National League Cy Young Award (BBWAA)

Bob Gibson	1968
Bob Gibson	1970

Fireman of the Year (TSN)

Lindy McDaniel	1960
Al Hrabosky	1975
Bruce Sutter	1981
Bruce Sutter	1982
Bruce Sutter	1984
Todd Worrell	1986
Lee Smith	1991
Lee Smith	1992

Rolaids Relief Man Award

Bruce Sutter	1981
Bruce Sutter	1982
Bruce Sutter	1984
Todd Worrell	1986
Lee Smith	1991
Lee Smith	1992
Tom Henke	1995

Major League Manager of the Year (TSN)

Billy Southworth	1941
Billy Southworth	1942
Eddie Dyer	1946
Eddie Stanky	1952
Fred Hutchinson	1957
Johnny Keane	1964
Whitey Herzog	1982

Major League Executive of the Year (TSN)

Branch Rickey	1936
Branch Rickey	1942
Frank Lane	1957
Bing Devine	1963
Bing Devine	1964

Rawlings Gold Glove Award Winners

Ken Boyer, 3B	1958
Ken Boyer, 3B	1959
Bill White, 1B	1960
Ken Boyer, 3B	1960
Bill White, 1B	1961
Ken Boyer, 3B	1961
Bobby Shantz, P	1962
Bill White, 1B	1962
Bobby Shantz, P	1963
Bill White, 1B	1963
Ken Boyer, 3B	1963
Curt Flood, OF	1963
Bill White, 1B	1964
Curt Flood, OF	1965
Bob Gibson, P	1965
Bill White, 1B	1965
Curt Flood, OF	1965
Bob Gibson, P	1966
Curt Flood, OF	1966
Bob Gibson, P	1967
Curt Flood, OF	1967
Bob Gibson, P	1968
Dal Maxvill, SS	1968
Curt Flood, OF	1968
Bob Gibson, P	1969
Curt Flood, OF	1969
Bob Gibson, P	1970
Bob Gibson, P	1971
Bob Gibson, P	1972
Bob Gibson, P	1973
Ken Reitz, 3B	1975
Keith Hernandez, 1B	1978
Keith Hernandez, 1B	1979

Rawlings Gold Glove Award Winners (cont.)

Keith Hernandez, 1B	1980
Keith Hernandez, 1B	1981
Keith Hernandez, 1B	1982
Ozzie Smith, SS	1982
Ozzie Smith, SS	1983
Willie Mc Gee, OF	1983
Joaquin Andujar, P	1984
Ozzie Smith, SS	1984
Ozzie Smith, SS	1985
Willie McGee, OF	1985
Ozzie Smith, SS	1986
Willie McGee, OF	1986
Terry Pendleton, 3B	1987
Ozzie Smith, SS	1987
Ozzie Smith, SS	1988
Terry Pendleton, 3B	1989
Ozzie Smith, SS	1989
Ozzie Smith, SS	1990
Tom Pagnozzi, C	1991
Ozzie Smith, SS	1991
Tom Pagnozzi, C	1992
Ozzie Smith, SS	1992
Tom Pagnozzi, C	1994

SUNNY JIM
Pulling them down with his Rawlings-Bottomley Mitt

IT PAYS TO ADVERTISE: For a St. Louis institution using Jim Bottomley was a no-brainer.

Silver Slugger Team (TSN)

Keith Hernandez, 1B	1980
Garry Templeton, SS	1980
George Hendrick, OF	1980
Ted Simmons, C	1980
Bob Forsch, P	1980
George Hendrick, OF	1983
Jack Clark, 1B	1985
Willie McGee, OF	1985
Jack Clark, 1B	1987
Ozzie Smith, SS	1987
Bob Forsch, P	1987

The Sporting News' NL All-Star Teams

Jim Bottomley, 1B	1925
Rogers Hornsby, 2B	1925
Rogers Hornsby, 2B	1926
Bob O'Farrell, C	1926
Grover Alexander, P	1926
Frank Frisch, 2B	1930
Frank Frisch, 2B	1931
Dizzy Dean, P	1934
Joe Medwick, OF	1935
Pepper Martin, 3B	1935
Dizzy Dean, P	1935
Joe Medwick, OF	1936

A GOOD JOE: When Joe Torre won the 1971 batting title and MVP award , a souvenir button was a "must."

The Sporting News' NL All-Star Teams (cont.)

Dizzy Dean, P	1936
Joe Medwick, OF	1937
Joe Medwick, OF	1938
Joe Medwick, OF	1939
Enos Slaughter, OF	1942
Mort Cooper, P	1942
Stan Musial, OF	1943
Walker Cooper, C	1943
Mort Cooper, P	1943
Stan Musial, OF	1944
Ray Sanders, 1B	1944
Marty Marion, SS	1944
Walker Cooper, C	1944
Mort Cooper, P	1944
Marty Marion, SS	1945
Whitey Kurowski, 3B	1945
Stan Musial, 1B	1946
Enos Slaughter	1946
Stan Musial, OF	1948
Harry Brecheen, P	1948
Stan Musial, OF	1949
Stan Musial, OF	1950
Stan Musial, OF	1951
Stan Musial, OF	1952
Stan Musial, OF	1953
Red Schoendienst, 2B	1953
Stan Musial, OF	1954
Ken Boyer, 3B	1956
Stan Musial, 1B	1957
Stan Musial, 1B	1958
Ernie Broglio, P	1960
Ken Boyer, 3B	1961
Ken Boyer, 3B	1962
Bill White, 1B	1963
Ken Boyer, 3B	1963
Dick Groat, SS	1963
Bill White, 1B	1964
Ken Boyer, 3B	1964
Dick Groat, SS	1964
Orlando Cepeda, 1B	1967
Tim McCarver, C	1967
Curt Flood, OF	1968
Bob Gibson, P	1968
Steve Carlton, P	1969
Bob Gibson, P	1970
Steve Carlton, P	1971
Joe Torre, 3B	1971
Lou Brock, OF	1974
Garry Templeton, SS	1977
Ted Simmons, C	1977
Ted Simmons, C	1978
Keith Hernandez, 1B	1979
Ted Simmons, C	1979
Garry Templeton, SS	1979
George Hendrick, OF	1980
Keith Hernandez, 1B	1980
Garry Templeton, SS	1980
Ozzie Smith, SS	1982
Lonnie Smith, OF	1982
George Hendrick, 1B	1983
Ozzie Smith, SS	1984
Tom Herr, 2B	1985
Willie McGee, OF	1985
Ozzie Smith, SS	1985
John Tudor, P	1985
Ozzie Smith, SS	1986
Jack Clark, 1B	1987
Ozzie Smith, SS	1987
Lee Smith, P	1991

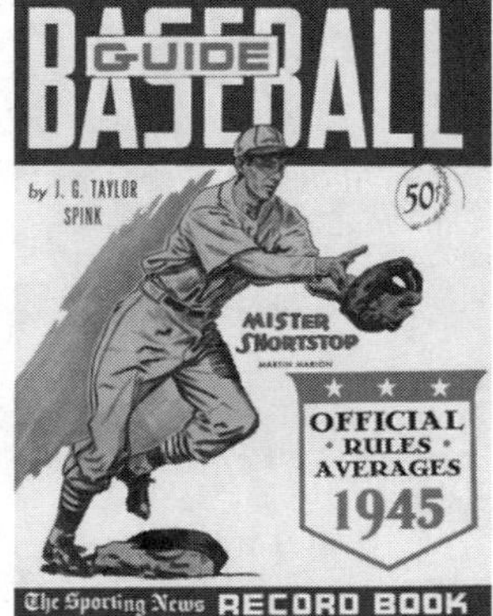

TAKE A BOW: Hailed as "Mr. Shortstop," Marty Marion, National League MVP, won the honor of appearing on the cover of the 1945 *Baseball Guide*. Below, Al Spink, founder of the Spink brother publication, wrote baseball's first history book in 1910 – *The National Game*.

Cardinals Selected for All-Star Game

1933
- Frank Frisch, 2B
- Bill Hallahan, P
- Pepper Martin, 3B
- Jimmy Wilson, C

1934
- Dizzy Dean, P
- Frank Frisch, 2B
- Pepper Martin, 3B
- Joe Medwick, OF

1935
- Frank Frisch, Mgr.& 2B
- Rip Collins, 1B
- Dizzy Dean, P
- Pepper Martin, 3B
- Joe Medwick, OF
- Burgess Whitehead, 2B

1936
- Rip Collins, 1B
- Dizzy Dean, P
- Leo Durocher, SS
- Stu Martin, 2B
- Joe Medwick, OF

1937
- Dizzy Dean, P
- Pepper Martin, OF
- Joe Medwick, OF
- Johnny Mize, 1B

1938
- Joe Medwick, OF
- Curt Davis, P
- Johnny Mize, 1B
- Terry Moore, OF
- Lon Warneke, P

1940
- Johnny Mize, 1B
- Terry Moore, OF

1941
- Johnny Mize, 1B
- Terry Moore, OF
- Enos Slaughter, OF
- Lon Warneke, P
- Jim Brown, 2B
- Mort Cooper, P
- Walker Cooper, C
- Terry Moore, OF
- Enos Slaughter, OF

1943
- Billy Southworth, Mgr.
- Mort Cooper, P
- Walker Cooper, C
- Whitey Kurowski, 3B
- Max Lanier, P
- Marty Marion, SS
- Stan Musial, OF
- Howie Pollet, P
- Harry Walker, OF

1944
- Billy Southworth, Mgr.
- Walker Cooper, C
- Whitey Kurowski, 3B
- Max Lanier, P
- Marty Marion, SS
- Red Munger, P
- Stan Musial, OF

1945
- No Game

1946
- Whitey Kurowski, 3B
- Marty Marion, SS
- Stan Musial, OF
- Howie Pollet, P
- Red Schoendienst, 2B
- Enos Slaughter, OF

1947
- Eddie Dyer, Mgr.
- Harry Brecheen, P
- Whitey Kurowski, 3B
- Marty Marion, SS
- Red Munger, P
- Stan Musial, 1B
- Enos Slaughter, OF

1948
- Harry Brecheen, P
- Marty Marion, SS
- Stan Musial, OF
- Red Schoendienst, 2B
- Enos Slaughter, OF

1949
- Eddie Kazak, 3B
- Marty Marion, SS
- Red Munger, P
- Stan Musial, OF
- Howie Pollet, P
- Red Schoendienst, 2B
- Enos Slaughter, OF

"JOHN BROWN": To use his favorite substitute for a profanity, it's Johny Leonard Roosevelt (Pepper) Martin. A colorful character who didn't answer to "John."

The Kitten:
Slick southpaw Harvey Haddix. Enos Slaughter thought he was even better than his predecessor Harry (The Cat) Brecheen.

1950
Marty Marion, SS
Red Schoendienst, 2B
Stan Musial, 1B
Enos Slaughter, OF

1951
Stan Musial, OF
Red Schoendienst, 2B
Enos Slaughter, OF
Wally Westlake, OF

1952
Stan Musial, OF
Red Schoendienst, 2B
Enos Slaughter, OF
Gerry Staley, P

1953
Harvey Haddix, P
Stan Musial, OF
Del Rice, C
Red Schoendienst, 2B
Enos Slaughter, OF

1954
Harvey Haddix, P
Ray Jablonski, 3B
Stan Musial, OF
Red Schoendienst, 2B

1955
Luis Arroyo, P
Harvey Haddix, P
Stan Musial, 1B
Red Schoendienst, 2B

1956
Ken Boyer, 3B
Stan Musial, OF
Rip Repulski, OF

1957
Larry Jackson, P
Wally Moon, OF
Stan Musial, 1B
Hal Smith, C

1958
Don Blasingame, 2B
Larry Jackson, P
Stan Musial, 1B

1959 – 1st Game
Ken Boyer, 3B
Joe Cunningham, OF
Wilmer Mizell, P
Stan Musial, 1B
Hal Smith, C
Bill White, OF

1959 – 2nd Game
Ken Boyer, 3B
Joe Cunningham, OF
Wilmer Mizell, P
Stan Musial, 1B
Hal Smith, C

1960 – 1st Game
Ken Boyer, 3B
Larry Jackson, P
Lindy McDaniel, P
Stan Musial, OF
Bill White, 1B

1960 – 2nd Game
Ken Boyer, 3B
Larry Jackson, P
Lindy McDaniel, P
Stan Musial, OF
Bill White, 1B

1961 – 1st Game
Ken Boyer, 3B
Stan Musial, OF
Bill White, 1B

1961 – 2nd Game
Ken Boyer, 3B
Stan Musial, OF
Bill White, 1B

1962 – 1st Game
Ken Boyer, 3B
Bob Gibson, P
Stan Musial, OF

1962 – 2nd Game
Ken Boyer, 3B
Bob Gibson, P
Stan Musial, OF

1963
Ken Boyer, 3B
Dick Groat, SS
Julian Javier, 2B
Stan Musial, OF
Bill White, 1B

1964
Ken Boyer, 3B
Curt Flood, OF
Dick Groat, SS
Bill White, 1B

1965
Bob Gibson, P
Curt Flood, OF
Bob Gibson, P
Tim McCarver, C

1967
Lou Brock, OF
Orlando Cepeda, 1B
Bob Gibson, P
Tim McCarver, C

1968
Red Schoendienst, Mgr.
Steve Carlton, P
Curt Flood, OF
Bob Gibson, P
Julian Javier, 2B

1969
Red Schoendienst, Mgr.
Lou Brock, OF
Steve Carlton, P

1970
Rich Allen, 1B
Bob Gibson, P
Joe Torre, C

1971
Lou Brock, OF
Steve Carlton, P
Joe Torre, 3B

1972
Lou Brock, OF
Bob Gibson, P
Ted Simmons, C
Joe Torre, 3B
Red Schoendienst, Coach

1973
Ted Simmons, C
Joe Torre, 3B
Rick Wise, P

1974
Lou Brock, OF
Lynn McGlothen, P
Ted Simmons, C
Reggie Smith, OF
Red Schoendienst, Coach

1975
Lou Brock, OF
Reggie Smith, OF
Red Schoendienst, Coach
Bake McBride, OF

1977
Ted Simmons, C
Garry Templeton, SS

1978
Ted Simmons, C

1979
Lou Brock, OF
Keith Hernandez, 1B
Ted Simmons, C
Garry Templeton, SS
Dave Ricketts, Coach

1980
George Hendrick, OF
Keith Hernandez, 1B
Ken Reitz, 3B

1981
Bruce Sutter, P

1982
Lonnie Smith, OF
Ozzie Smith, SS
Gene Gieselmann, Trainer

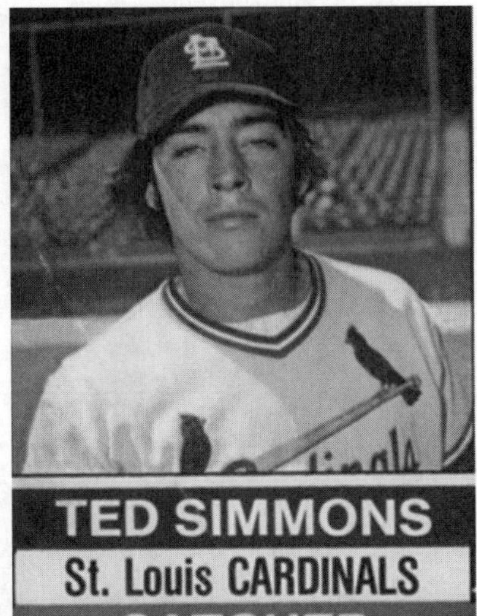

THE LION KING: Ted (Simba) Simmons, nicknamed for his flowing mane, was one of baseball's best hitting catchers ever. Below, Wally Moon, who filled in for Enos Slaughter at a tough start for a good career.

1983
Whitey Herzog, Mgr.
George Hendrick, OF
Willie McGee, OF
Ozzie Smith, SS
Chuck Hiller, Coach
Dave Ricketts, Coach

1984
Joaquin Andujar, P
Ozzie Smith, SS
Bruce Sutter, P

1985
Joaquin Andujar, P
Jack Clark, 1B
Tom Herr, 2B
Willie McGee, OF
Ozzie Smith, SS

1986
Whitey Herzog, Mgr.
Ozzie Smith, SS
Mike Roarke, Coach

Cooper's Corner: A Hall of Fame souvenir of the 1985 Hall of Fame weekend at Cooperstown. Left to right on a big day for the Redbirds: Lou Brock, Arky Vaughan, Hoyt Wilhelm and Enos Slaughter. All except Vaughan wore the St. Louis uniform.

1987
Jack Clark, 1B
Willie McGee, OF
Ozzie Smith, SS
Gene Gieselmann, Trainer

1988
Whitey Herzog, Mgr.
Vince Coleman, OF
Willie McGee, OF
Ozzie Smith, SS
Todd Worrell, P
Rich Hacker, Coach
Nick Leyva, Coach
Johnny Lewis, Coach

1989
Vince Coleman, OF
Pedro Guerrero, DH
Tony Pena, C
Ozzie Smith, SS

1990
Ozzie Smith, SS

1991
Felix Jose, OF
Lee Smith, P
Ozzie Smith, SS

1992
Tom Pagnozzi, C
Lee Smith, P
Ozzie Smith, SS
Bob Tewksbury, P
Joe Torre, Coach

1993
Gregg Jefferies, 1B
Lee Smith, P
Gene Gieselmann, Trainer

1994
Gregg Jefferies, 1B
Ozzie Smith, SS

1995
Tom Henke, P
Ozzie Smith, SS

1996
Ozzie Smith, SS

1997
Royce Clayton, SS
Ray Lankford, OF

Cardinal Players Who Earned Major Awards While Performing for Another Organization

MVP Award

Year	*Name*	*Organization*	*League*
1928	Dazzy Vance	Brooklyn	NL
1929	Rogers Hornsby	Chicago	NL
1950	Jim Konstanty	Philadelphia	NL
1952	Hank Sauer	Chicago	NL
1952	Bobby Shantz	Philadelphia	AL
1960	Dick Groat	Pittsburgh	NL
1960	Roger Maris	New York	AL
1961	Roger Maris	New York	AL
1972	Dick Allen	Chicago	AL
1991	Terry Pendleton	Atlanta	NL
1992	Dennis Eckersley	Oakland	AL

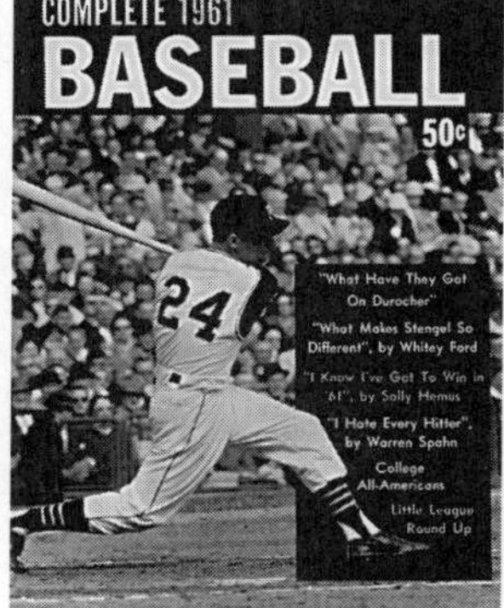

THINKING MAN:
Dick Groat, former Duke basketball All-American and Pittsburgh MVP, starred with the 1964 Cardinal champions. Below, Ted Sizemore, 1971-76 second baseman.

Cy Young Award

Year	*Name*	*Organization*	*League*
1969	Mike Cuellar	Baltimore	AL
1972	Steve Carlton	Philadelphia	NL
1977	Steve Carlton	Philadelphia	NL
1979	Bruce Sutter	Chicago	NL
1980	Steve Carlton	Philadelphia	NL
1981	Fernando Valenzuela	Los Angeles	NL
1982	Steve Carlton	Philadelphia	NL
1982	Pete Vuckovich	Milwaukee	AL
1983	John Denny	Philadelphia	NL
1984	Rick Sutcliffe	Chicago	NL
1992	Dennis Eckersley	Oakland	AL

Rookie Of The Year

Year	*Name*	*Organization*	*League*
1948	Alvin Dark	Boston	NL
1954	Bob Grim	New York	AL
1958	Orlando Cepeda	San Francisco	NL
1964	Dick Allen	Philadelphia	NL
1966	Tommie Agee	Chicago	AL
1969	Ted Sizemore	Los Angeles	NL
1976	Butch Metzger	San Diego	NL
1978	Bob Horner	Atlanta	NL
1979	Rick Sutcliffe	Los Angeles	NL
1981	Fernando Valenzuela	Los Angeles	NL
1987	Mark McGwire	Oakland	AL
1988	Chris Sabo	Cincinnati	NL

THE MONARCHS OF THE SPHERE